International LGBTQ+ Literature for Children and Young Adults

International LGBTQ+ Literature for Children and Young Adults

Edited by

B. J. Epstein and Elizabeth L. Chapman

ANTHEM PRESS

Anthem Press
An imprint of Wimbledon Publishing Company
www.anthempress.com

This edition first published in UK and USA 2021
by ANTHEM PRESS
75–76 Blackfriars Road, London SE1 8HA, UK
or PO Box 9779, London SW19 7ZG, UK
and
244 Madison Ave #116, New York, NY 10016, USA

British Library Cataloguing-in-Publication Data
A catalogue record for this book is available from the British Library.

Library of Congress Control Number: 2021942255

ISBN-13: 978-1-78527-984-3 (Hbk)
ISBN-10: 1-78527-984-X (Hbk)

Cover credit: Spacal, Alenka. 2013a. Mavrična maškarada
(Rainbow Masquerade). Ljubljana: Škuc (Lambda)

This title is also available as an e-book.

In memory of my mum, with love. ELC

To my loves – Fi, Esther and Tovah. BJE

We would also like to dedicate this book to the memory of Bernat Cormand, who sadly died before it was published.

CONTENTS

List of Illustrations		ix
Acknowledgements		xiii
Notes on contributors		xv
	Introduction *B. J. Epstein and Elizabeth L. Chapman*	1
Chapter One	– BRAZIL Self-Help and Coming Out: LGBTQ+ Themes in Contemporary Brazilian Young Adult Literature *Rosa Maria Hessel Silveira, Luiz Felipe Zago and Daniela Ripoll*	11
Chapter Two	– FRANCE We're Not Here and We're Not Queer: Bisexual Erasure and Stereotyping in French Young Adult Fiction *Elizabeth L. Chapman*	29
Chapter Three	– GERMANY/AUSTRIA Stuck in the Binary: Heteronormativity and the Binary Conception of Gender in German-Language Trans YA *Katrin Waldhart*	55
Chapter Four	– GREENLAND Homo Sapienne: A Mirror of Modern Greenlandic Life *Mette Laustsen*	73
Chapter Five	– INDIA Out of the Closet? Exploring the Infoscape of LGBTQ+ Fiction For/About Youth in India *Bharat Mehra and Chris Barrett*	93
Chapter Six	– INDIGENOUS WRITING Un-settling Gender and Sexuality: Indigenous LGBTQ+/ Two-Spirit Literature for Young People *Thaddeus Andracki*	117
Chapter Seven	– ITALY LGBTQ Families and Picturebooks: New Perspectives in Italian Children's Literature *Dalila Forni*	129

Chapter Eight	– MULTINATIONAL Heather Has a Donor: 30 Years of International Lesbian-Themed Children's Picture Books about Donor Insemination, 1989–2019 *Patricia Sarles*	147
Chapter Nine	– MULTINATIONAL Morals, Society and Distribution: LGBTQ+ Literature for Young Readers in the Arab World *Anonymous*	181
Chapter Ten	– MULTINATIONAL Sameness and Difference in Visual Representations of Same-Sex Couples in International Children's Picture Books *Jamie Campbell Naidoo and Mercedes Zabawa*	183
Chapter Eleven	– THE PHILIPPINES Of Fabulous Flowers and Powers: Queer Narratives of/for the Filipino Child in Philippine Contemporary Children's Literature *Cheeno Marlo M. Sayuno*	199
Chapter Twelve	– SLOVENIA Between Literature, Ideology and Pedagogy: LGBTQ+ Fiction for Children and Young Adults in Slovenia *Andrej Zavrl*	225
Chapter Thirteen	– SOUTH KOREA Boys Who Wear Dresses: Queer Narrative Strategies in Korean Children's Literature *Anton Hur*	251
Chapter Fourteen	– SPAIN Stories out of the Closet: LGBTQ+ Children's Picturebooks in Spain *Bernat Cormand*	257
Chapter Fifteen	– SWEDEN 'I'm Sure This Whole Boy Thing is Just a Phase': Transgender Narratives in Contemporary Swedish Children's and Young Adult Literature *Åsa Warnqvist*	275
Chapter Sixteen	– SWEDEN Becoming Versus Being: Nature, Nurture and Stereotypes in Swedish LGB Young Adult Novels *B. J. Epstein*	303
List of Primary Texts		319
Index		331

ILLUSTRATIONS

Figures

1	Barbero, Cinzia. 2011. *Più ricche di un re* (Richer Than a King). Milan: Lo Stampatello	136
2	Pardi, Francesca. 2012. *Perché hai due mamme?* (Why Have You Got Two Mummies?). Illustrated by Annalisa Sanmartino and Giulia Torelli. Milan: Lo Stampatello./Pardi, Francesca. 2014. *Perché hai due papà?* (Why Have You Got Two Daddies?). Illustrated by Annalisa Sanmartino and Giulia Torelli. Milan: Lo Stampatello	138
3	Pardi, Francesca. 2011. *Piccolo uovo* (Little Egg). Illustrated by Altan. Milan: Lo Stampatello	139
4	Coding Sheet for Sameness & Difference in Visual Representations of LGBTQ Characters in International Children's Picturebooks	186
5	Neri, Bernadette Villanueva. 2012. *Ang Ikaklit sa aming hardin. (Ikaklit in our Garden)*. Illustrated by CJ de Silva. Manila: Raintree Trading & Publishing, Inc./Publikasyong Twamkittens	206
6	Guzman, Michael de. 2018. *Dalawa ang daddy ni Billy. (Billy Has Two Daddies)*. Illustrated by Daniel Palma Tayona. Makati City: Tahanan Books for Young Readers	206
7	Evasco, Eugene Y. 2018. *Ang nanay ni Erwin/Ang tatay ni Klara. (Erwin's Mama/Klara's Papa)*. Illustrated by Tokwa Peñaflorida. Translated by Karen Ferry-Fernandez. Quezon City: Kahel Press	208
8	Garcia, Kata. 2018. *My Family*. Illustrated by Borg Sinaban. Quezon City: Adarna House	209
9	Ruedas, Mondi. 2018. *What's My Power Gear?* Illustrated by Ruthie Genuino. Quezon City: Center for Youth Advocacy and Networking, Inc	210
10	Alberto, Jesh. 2018. *Bukas na si Cajon* (Cajon is Now Open). Illustrated by Gabbi Ramirez. Quezon City: Center for Youth Advocacy and Networking, Inc	211
11	Dancel, Godfrey T. 2018. *Dumating na si Manang Elisa.* (Sister Elisa Finally Came). Illustrated by Gabbi Ramirez. Quezon City: Center for Youth Advocacy and Networking, Inc	212

12 Garlítos, Rhandee. 2013. *Ang bonggang-bonggang batang beki! (The Fierce and Fabulous Boy in Pink!)* Illustrated by Tokwa Salazar Peñaflorida. Quezon City: Chikiting Books 214

13 Benavidez, Angelo. 2018. *Si Chowchow*. Illustrated by Aiko Shimizu. Quezon City: Center for Youth Advocacy and Networking, Inc 215

14 Frany, Arkin. 2018. *One of the Boys (or How Kenny Saved the City of Toyland)*. Illustrated by Fides Balmaceda. Quezon City: Center for Youth Advocacy and Networking, Inc 217

15 Mozetič, Brane. 2014. *Prva ljubezen* (First Love). Illustrated by Maja Kastelic. Ljubljana: Škuc (Lambda) 229

16 Mozetič, Brane. 2020a. *Ahil in Patrokles* (Achilles and Patroclus). Illustrated by Ana Lucija Šarić. Ljubljana: Škuc (Lambda) 231

17 Spacal, Alenka. 2013a. *Mavrična maškarada* (Rainbow Masquerade). Ljubljana: Škuc (Lambda) 239

18 Cormand, Bernat. 2012. *El niño perfecto* (The Perfect Boy). Barcelona: Sd·edicions. [Spanish edition] 263

19 Cormand, Bernat. 2018a. *Els dies feliços* (Happy Days). Barcelona: A Buen Paso. [Catalan edition] 265

20 Quintiá, Xerardo. 2007. *Titiritesa (Titiritess)*. Illustrated by Maurizio. A. C. Quarello. Pontevedra: OQO Editora. [Galician edition] 267

21 Pita, Charo. 2009. *Velliñas* (Little Old Ladies). Illustrated by Fátima Afonso. Pontevedra: OQO Editora. [Galician edition] 268

22 Schimel, Lawrence. 2018. *No es hora de jugar (Bedtime, Not Playtime)*. Illustrated by Elina Braslina. Barcelona: Editorial Egales. [Spanish edition] 269

23 Dios, Olga de. 2013. *Monstruo rosa* (Pink Monster). Zaragoza: Apila Ediciones. [Spanish edition] 271

24 Moscada, Neus. 2009. *Dues rodones idèntiques?* (Two Identical Circles?). Barcelona: Sd·edicions. [Catalan edition] 272

25 Ericson, Elias S. 2013. *Åror* (Oars). Stockholm: Ordfront Galago, 12 288

26 Gustavsson, Hanna. 2015. *Iggy 4-ever*. Stockholm: Ordfront Galago, 198 296

27 Sandgren, Hilding. 2016a. *Vägarna är som tvättbrädor här* (The Roads Are Like Washboards Here). Stockholm: Galago, 94 296

Tables

1 Select publishers of books in India for young readers 108

2 Analysis of English-language fiction in 'best lists' aimed specifically at youth in India 109

3 Select examples of 'non-best list' general sources 110

4 Lesbian-themed children's books that discuss sperm donation 175

ACKNOWLEDGEMENTS

B. J. Epstein and Elizabeth L. Chapman

We would like to express our gratitude to a number of people who made this book possible. First of all, of course, we wish to thank all the contributors, whose passion for the subject of LGBTQ+ books for young readers has been so inspiring. We also are grateful to those who got in touch with us to share ideas, information and contacts, even though they felt unable to write chapters given the political or cultural situations in their countries.

We are also thankful for the support of Anthem Press, and especially to Megan Greiving, Jayashree from the Production team, and Tej P. S. Sood. We appreciate that they were willing to take a chance on a book with a topic that is important but less familiar in academia at the moment, and we hope this book brings greater awareness.

Thank you as well to the peer reviewers who gave us such positive and helpful feedback. We are so grateful that you took the time to read the manuscript and to share your thoughts with us. This book is stronger because of your insight.

B. J. wishes to acknowledge all of Liz's enthusiasm and hard work over the course of this book; Liz's knowledge, attention to detail, kindness and dedication made her a fantastic co-editor. B. J. also would like to thank her wife, Fi, and their daughters, Esther and Tovah, for sharing her passion for children's literature, and for their incredible amounts of love and support.

Liz would like to thank her marvellous co-editor, B. J., for her expertise and in-depth knowledge of the field; for proposing this collaboration in the first place; and for her patience, support and compassion during a very difficult period. She would also like to thank her Francophone Twitter contacts, most especially @MxCordelia, for assistance in locating French-language LGBTQ+ titles, and the Sheffield Hallam University library staff for their assistance in swiftly procuring electronic resources during lockdown. Last but not least, she would like to thank her dad and late mum, Ron and Margaret Chapman, for their love and their support of her work; all the friends who are such a significant part of her life; and her dear and wonderful partner Matt.

It is important to recognize all the writers of LGBTQ+ books for children and young adults and to thank them for all their hard work and their concern about raising awareness of queer issues for a wide variety of audiences, and we also want to thank all those who read these books, learning about themselves and others through them.

Finally, we want to say thank you to the readers of this book. We hope you enjoy and learn from the fascinating chapters here, and we hope the work inspires further activism, writing and research.

Thank you so much!

NOTES ON CONTRIBUTORS

Thaddeus Andracki is a white settler living and working on land stolen by the United States from the Council of Three Fires – the Potawatomi, Odawa and Ojibwe Nations. He is a middle-school librarian at the University of Chicago Laboratory Schools. His research focuses on theoretical and practical aspects of race, gender, sexuality and Indigeneity in children's and young adult literatures.

Chris Barrett conducted research on LGBTQ+ literature for young readers in an international context as a master's student in the School of Information Sciences at the University of Tennessee. Since graduation in December 2018, Chris has been Senior Assistant at Lawson McGhee Library located in Knoxville, Tennessee.

Elizabeth L. Chapman completed her PhD on the provision of LGBTQ+ fiction to children and young people in English public libraries. She now works for Sheffield Libraries and as a freelance French-to-English translator, interspersed with teaching in Education Studies at Sheffield Hallam University and Library & Information Studies at the University of Sheffield. Her teaching, research and professional work centres around issues of in/exclusion in libraries and educational contexts. She was a judge for the CILIP Carnegie & Kate Greenaway Children's Book Awards in 2019 and 2020, and has previously been an editor for *Public Library Journal* and *Journal of Radical Librarianship*. Her publications include papers in *Journal of Library and Information Science* and *Library Trends*.

Bernat Cormand is a philologist and illustrator. He has a bachelor's degree in Catalan Studies from Universitat de Barcelona and a master's degree in Comparative Literature from Universitat Autònoma de Barcelona Postgraduate School, where he wrote a thesis on 'The Lyrical Conception of Homosexual Feeling in the Poetry of C. P. Kavafis, Luis Cernuda and Jaime Gil de Biedma'. His artistic training includes sculpture, drawing and illustration, and he has worked in publishing as a desk editor, proofreader and editor. He is currently the chief editor of *Faristol*, a magazine specialized in literature for children and young people, and he is a part-time professor in the Faculty of Translation and Interpreting at Universitat Pompeu Fabra. His books include *El dibujante de osos* (The Bear Sketcher), *El niño perfecto* (The Perfect Boy) and and *Los días felices* (Happy Days).

B. J. Epstein is a senior lecturer in literature and translation at the University of East Anglia in England. She is also a writer, editor and Swedish-to-English translator. Her PhD, from Swansea University, was in translation studies, and she wrote her thesis on the translation of children's literature. She is the author of *Are the Kids All Right? The Representation of LGBTQ Characters in Children's and Young Adult Lit*, *Translating Expressive*

Language in Children's Literature, and *Ready, Set, Teach!*; the editor of two books on translation in the Nordic countries and the co-editor of *Queer in Translation*; and the translator, editor or writer of many other essays, articles, short stories and other texts. Her translation of the children's book *The Bird Within Me* by Sara Lundberg was published in 2020 and she is currently completing a book on the depiction of breastfeeding in literature for adults and children.

Dalila Forni, Ph.D., is a Research Fellow in Education at the University of Florence, where she is researching gender stereotypes in Italian picturebooks. She graduated in European and Extra-European Languages and Literature from the University of Milan. Her interests include children's literature, visual narratives for children and YA, and gender studies. Her publications include *Children's Literature across Media: Film and Theatre Adaptations of Roald Dahl's* Charlie and the Chocolate Factory (ETS, Italy, 2020).

Anton Hur is a literary translator. He earned his LLB from Korea University and an MA from Seoul National University. He divides his time between Seoul and Incheon.

Mette Laustsen is a Danish librarian who worked at Nunatta Atuagaateqarfia, the public library of Nuuk and central library of Greenland, from 2008 to 2019. While there, she was, among other things, the library's representative in the Allatta project, designed to find and foster new young Greenlandic authors. The project has so far put out three anthologies of literary works by and for Greenlandic young adults. Mette Laustsen is now a children's librarian at Dansk Centralbibliotek for Sydslesvig, a library for the Danish minority in the border-region of Schleswig, Germany.

Bharat Mehra, EBSCO Endowed Chair in Social Justice and Professor in the University of Alabama's School of Library and Information Studies, focuses his research on diversity and intercultural communication, social justice in library and information science, critical and cross-cultural studies, and community informatics or the use of information and communication technologies to empower minority and underserved populations to make meaningful changes in their everyday lives. He has conducted action research with racial/ethnic groups; international communities in the diaspora; lesbian, gay, bisexual and transgender populations; low-income families; rural librarians; and small businesses, amongst others, to shape the design and development of various community-based information systems and services.

Jamie Campbell Naidoo is the Foster-EBSCO Endowed Professor at the University of Alabama School of Library and Information Studies in the USA. A former elementary school librarian and public youth librarian, Naidoo's research interests include library services to diverse populations and diversity in children's print and digital media. He has authored numerous books, research articles, book chapters and professional publications related to library programmes and services for specific culturally diverse groups, including *Rainbow Family Collections: Selecting and Using Children's Books with Gay, Bisexual, Transgender, and Queer Content*. In 2016, he was awarded the Achievement in Library Diversity Research Award by the American Library Association and he served as 2018–2019 president of the ALA's Association for Library Services to Children.

Daniela Ripoll has a degree in biological sciences, a master's in education and a PhD in education, all from the Federal University of Rio Grande do Sul, Brazil. She is a Professor in the Postgraduate Programme in Education at the Lutheran University of Brazil, and she primarily works on cultural studies in education and also on education in science.

Patricia Sarles is the founder of the blogs *Gay-Themed Picture Books for Kids* and *Books for Donor Offspring*. She discovered an interest in children's books on these topics when she and her wife explored their family-building options via sperm donation and found that there were very few books for children on donor insemination in lesbian families. Being the gumshoe librarian she is, she discovered that the problem was not that these books did not exist, but that there were no Library of Congress subject headings for them. She has now found over 500 books written for donor offspring children from all around the world. Patricia has published in *Children & Libraries*, *Teacher Librarian* and *Voice of Youth Advocates*, as well as several other library publications. She holds master's degrees in both anthropology and library science.

Cheeno Marlo del Mundo Sayuno is an Assistant Professor of Communication, Research and Children's Literature at the University of the Philippines (UP) Los Baños and an Affiliate Assistant Professor of the MA in Language and Literacy Education at the UP Open University. He is also currently a PhD candidate in Communication at UP Diliman. He has received recognition from the prestigious Carlos Palanca Memorial Awards for Literature in 2013 and 2017, and the Philippine Board on Books for Young People's Salanga Prize (honourable mention) in 2015, for his stories for children. He has published storybooks with Adarna House, Lampara Books, Anvil Publishing and Chikiting Books in the Philippines, as well as various textbooks in communication, media and related fields. His research interests include children's literature, child studies, (trans) media studies, discourse analysis and qualitative communication research.

Rosa Maria Hessel Silveira has a master's degree in language arts (Portuguese and Greek) and a PhD in education, both from the Federal University of Rio Grande do Sul, Brazil. She also has postdoctoral degrees from the University of Lisbon and the Autonomous University of Barcelona. She is a Professor in the Postgraduate Programme in Education at the Federal University of Rio Grande do Sul. She is the author of the book *Differences in Children's Literature: Narratives and Readings*, selected by the National School Library Programme, which distributes books to school libraries throughout Brazil. For more than 10 years, she coordinated research projects on children's literature, as a research fellow at the Brazilian National Research Council.

Katrin Waldhart studied English and American Studies, German and Comparative Literature at the Universities of Vienna, Austria, and Maryland, USA, and obtained a teaching degree from the University of Vienna. She worked in publishing for several years. Currently, she teaches English as a Foreign Language and German in Vienna. Her research focuses on the representation and deconstruction of gender in children's and young adult literature. In her master's thesis, she examines possibilities of constructing non-binary or non-conforming gender identities in YA literature.

Åsa Warnqvist is now Docent and Research Manager and Director Research Manager and Director of the Swedish Institute for Children's Books. She is also affiliated with Linneaus University. Warnqvist's research has primarily been focused on the Canadian writer L. M. Montgomery, the Swedish children's book market, gender studies and normativity studies. Her ongoing research is on depictions of fat characters in children's and young adult literature, transgender narratives and the impact of L. M. Montgomery's writing on Swedish readers. Warnqvist is the editor of the Swedish academic journal *Barnboken: Journal of Children's Literature Research.* She is also a member of the International Research Society for Children's Literature (IRSCL) executive board and vice-president of IRSCL, and she was the primary organizer of the IRSCL Congress in 2019.

Mercedes Zabawa is a youth services librarian in Tuscaloosa, Alabama. She holds a BA in English from Earlham College in Indiana and a Master's of Library and Information Studies from the University of Alabama. She presented at the 36th International Board on Books for Young People World Congress in Athens, Greece (2018) and served on the 2020 Pura Belpré Award committee.

Luiz Felipe Zago holds a Master's and PhD in Education (emphasis in Sexuality and Gender Relations) and a Bachelor's degree in Social Communication (emphasis in Journalism) from Universidade Federal do Rio Grande do Sul. He has worked as coordinator of intervention projects in public health in the LGBT civil movement and at the Ministry of Health in Brazil. He also has experience in Communication, focusing on Communication and Health. He worked as a Professor at Universidade Luterana do Brasil (Professor in the Undergraduate Course of Journalism and in the Postgraduate Program of Education) from 2014 to 2020.

Andrej Zavrl has an MA in English and American Literature from Leiden University, in the Netherlands, and a PhD in literary studies from the University of Ljubljana, Slovenia. He is an independent teacher, translator and researcher. His research has primarily focused on the intersection of gender, sexuality and early modern literature. Zavrl has also contributed to research into Slovenian LGBTQ+ history. He has published a number of scholarly articles, introductions and reviews as well as an academic study of the constructions of Christopher Marlowe's dissidence in criticism, translation and performance. He has translated literary and academic texts from English into Slovenian, and vice versa, and co-authored a children's picture book.

INTRODUCTION

B. J. Epstein and Elizabeth L. Chapman

This book stems from what might seem like a simple question: What sort of LGBTQ+ books for young readers are being written around the world? To develop this initial query further, we wondered how different languages and different cultures approach LGBTQ+ topics, especially in works for children and young adults. We had seen little written about this in English, which is not a surprise given how myopic English-speaking cultures tend to be about literature from other countries (Post suggests that the number of translations to English is holding steady at 2 to 4 per cent (2019, n.p.)), and we felt it was time to rectify this gap in knowledge and to bring a comparative approach to a growing field of study, namely LGBTQ+ children's literature.

As the academic study of children's literature has developed over the past few decades (see, among many other examples, work such as Coats 2017; Hunt 1994, 2005; Lerer 2008; Lurie 1990; Maybin and Watson 2009; Nikolajeva 1996; Nikolajeva and Scott 2006; Nodelman and Reimer 2002; Reynolds 2005, 2007, 2011; Reynolds and Tucker 1998; Rose 1993; and Townsend 1990), more attention has been paid to topics such as the depiction of gender identity and sexuality (for example, Abate and Kidd 2011; Bruhm and Hurley 2004; Cart and Jenkins 2006; Epstein 2013; Flanagan 2008; Gillis and Simpson 2015; James 2009; Jenkins and Cart 2018; and Naidoo 2012). Furthermore, there has been an increased focus on diversity and multicultural literature more generally (Gopalakrishnan 2011; Nel 2017; O'Sullivan 2005; Ramdarshan Bold 2019; Sands-O'Connor 2017); the translation of children's books (Epstein 2012; Lathey 2006, 2010; Oittinen 2000); the roles of authors, illustrators, publishers, editors, translators, librarians, teachers and others in the production and usage of books for children (which is touched on in many of the works already cited here); and the interaction of words and images (Hamer et al. 2017; Kümmerling-Meibauer 2018; Nodelman 1988), among many other issues relevant to the discussions in this book. What texts are made available for children, and how, reflects the larger society and time period that the works are produced in; children's literature is especially prone to (ab)uses of power, given that in general, books for young readers are made for children but not by them, unlike in the case of adult literature, which is obviously produced by adults for adults. Furthermore, as queer rights have expanded to a certain extent around the world in recent decades, with marriage equality, access to fertility treatment and the right to adopt becoming legal in some (though far from all) countries, this has influenced children's literature in that adults in many countries now feel able to write about queerness, in its many forms, in texts read by children; we must add, of course, that not all discussions or representations of queerness are positive or accurate (see, for instance, Crisp 2011 or Epstein 2013). However, as noted, there has been little research into how literature written in different countries and different languages and aimed at young people has depicted LGBTQ+ people and issues. We therefore feel that the time is ripe for bringing together these various strands of research and political movement so that we can explore both individual cultural shifts as well as larger linguistic and global ones in the depiction of LGBTQ+ people and topics in writing for young readers. In short: to what extent is queer literature available to children and young people around the world, who is writing these works, what messages do they offer and how are the books received in the countries where they are published?

Before moving on to discuss this book and the specific chapters in more detail, it is necessary to pause over the problematic issue of terminology. As is well known, the letters in the queer acronym have proliferated over the years. In this book, we aim to be as inclusive as possible, though we know not everyone will agree with us regarding which words, concepts and letters are included. By LGBTQ+, we are referring to: lesbian, gay, bisexual, trans, queer, intersex, asexual, kink, non-monogamy and more, although it is worth noting that we did not receive any submissions relating to the latter three identity groups, and there is certainly scope for more scholarship in these areas. We are, of course, aware that not all people who consider themselves LGBTQ+ in some way would include all the other letters or experiences under the same umbrella, and that not all LGBTQ+ people would use any of those letters or words themselves or are comfortable with terms such as 'queer'. Furthermore, we have deliberately chosen to use the plus sign to show that much more can and does fit into the acronym; we have also seen people use an asterisk or an ampersand. Conversely, we use the term 'trans' without an asterisk; while this usage was briefly popular (although contested) as a signifier of inclusion (Tompkins 2014), our perception is that it is no longer the preferred term (Vincent 2017). As queer cis women, we believe it is important to take our lead from trans communities on such issues. We thus define 'trans' broadly as 'an overarching but open-ended means to describe bodies, identities and experiences that that defy normative notions of sexual possibility, encompassing (potentially) all individuals whose gender identity and/or physical body differs in any way from that they were assigned at birth' (Pearce et al. 2020, 2).

We are also aware, particularly in the context of this book, that terminology differs hugely by language and country. For this reason, we have encouraged each scholar or scholarly team who has contributed to this volume to use the terms that are most appropriate to or common in their area, and therefore the chapters define them as appropriate. We apologize in advance to anyone who is made uncomfortable by any of these words or who feels excluded by them, and we hope each chapter will clarify why particular words are employed. We also hope people will consider queering terminology in their own languages and cultures.

International LGBTQ+ Literature for Children and Young Adults brings together contributions from across the academic and activist spectrum to explore all the issues mentioned heretofore in this introduction, i.e. terminology, depiction, inclusion, messages, power, politics, culture and more. We have tried to balance contributions from a variety of countries and languages, and with different analytical styles and foci. For example, we look at picturebooks, middle-grade books and young adult novels, and for one country, we have separate LGB and trans chapters, in order to explore the literary and political situations in as detailed a way as possible; we also have several chapters that explore a particular topic across linguistic and political boundaries. We also tried to include a range of contributors, which means that some are academics, some are librarians, some are other kinds of practitioners, some write for children, some are activists, and some have a combination of these and other roles. Since not all the contributors are academics, this means that not all the chapters were written in a formal academic style, but we think that this enhances the book and its perspective on the subject. Likewise, each individual contributor has their own linguistic style and this was something we were keen to retain; indeed, we were grateful that so many people were willing to write about this topic even if English was not their first language, and we are aware that this required an extra level of effort.

In addition, we attempted to find contributors from most continents and as many countries as possible; in several cases, unfortunately, we were assured that such literature 'does not exist', as we will discuss further below. Our book looks both to the specific cultures and languages, but also makes connections between them, and ultimately, although the individual chapters can be read separately and are helpful for understanding particular parts of the world, as a whole, the book comments on what is at stake when and how we write (or do not write) about LGBTQ+ topics for young readers.

While English-language LGBTQ+ literature for young readers has been explored in some depth in the academy over the past decade or so, and continues to be, it is less common to analyse non-English-language works. *Queer in Translation*, edited by B. J. Epstein and Robert Gillett (2017), approaches the issue of the influence of language and culture on literature by discussing the translation of queer books, including for children, as do a number of individual journal articles, but there has not yet been a single book to compare LGBTQ+ children's literature from around the world and to connect the literature to greater societal, political, linguistic, historical and cultural concerns. The aim of this book, then, is to explore LGBTQ+ literature for young readers around the world, particularly beyond English-speaking countries/cultures.

As noted, our goal for this book was to be as comprehensive as possible, ideally covering every region in the world. Unfortunately, we rather quickly discovered to our disappointment that this was not going to happen. We received plenty of proposals in response to our call for papers from scholars in Europe and a range of English-speaking countries, but it was harder to find people elsewhere, particularly from majority world (Alam 2008) countries. We acknowledge that this is likely due in part to biases and limitations in our own networks, knowledge and linguistic competencies; to the Anglophone- and minority world-centric nature of major academic databases that might otherwise have helped us to locate scholars; and to the constraints of academic publishing that required contributors to this volume to write in English (see, for example, Lillis and Curry 2010 for more on these barriers). In an attempt to partially redress this, we contacted scholars and children's book experts, including members of national sections of the International Board on Books for Young People, around the world, only to find that in a number of countries/cultures, no one was able or willing to put their name to a text about

LGBTQ+ literature for younger readers. For some countries, although we are aware that LGBTQ+ literature exists, including some for younger readers, we nonetheless did not receive any submissions; examples include China, where queerness is beginning to be addressed in young adult novels (Shen 2020), and Japan, where same-sex relationships and gender non-conformity are well-established tropes in manga and light novels that are often read by (if not always published for) young people (Dahlberg-Dodd 2020; Madill 2017; Welker 2015). In other cases, someone agreed to contribute a chapter, only to pull out of the project with the explanation that it was too risky or challenging; examples here included scholars from Indonesia and Mongolia. In another case, a scholar from an Arabic-speaking country decided in the end that due to political pressures, they did not feel they could write the chapter under their own name, but they instead provided us with some notes so we could pull together a short analysis on their behalf. Finally, some scholars stated that they were sure such literature was not available in their country. Most markedly, we were unable to find any scholars who were in a position to produce a chapter on any country in Africa, and we acknowledge this as a limitation of the book.

In general, the reasons that scholars offered for declining to contribute to the present volume were that their specific culture/country did not publish such texts and/or did not have LGBTQ+ rights more generally; that is to say, they felt that if their country did not approve of same-sex relationships, among other queer issues, then that would mean that LGBTQ+ characters and topics were not deemed acceptable or appropriate for children and young adults in their nation or language, and that therefore there would be little that they could comfortably and safely write about. This was, obviously, upsetting to us as editors who wanted to provide a comprehensive look at the topic, but it was also an important reminder of how different the circumstances can be in regard to writing and publishing texts for young people, and also of how life for LGBTQ+ people themselves can be incredibly varied around the world. While we are often rightly critical of what gets published in English-speaking countries, we should not forget how lucky we are that such literature exists at all.

Rather than aiming to create thematic links in readers' minds by arranging the chapters by, say, subject or genre or continent or intended audience age or any other characteristic, we opted for the method of working alphabetically by country. This will allow readers to form their own opinions and to find their own associations and connections between the chapters. We hope that this will prove interesting and profitable. The chapters in this book are wide-ranging in terms of the countries, cultures and languages featured, and also in regard to the texts explored, and indeed even the style and substance of the chapters themselves; as already noted, in our editing, we aimed to keep the flavour of the contributors' writing styles instead of forcing a standard Western European approach on them, while also ensuring that there was a clarity, legibility and coherence to the chapters. Although academic evidence is used to support claims, we also wanted to be certain that the book would be accessible to readers of all backgrounds, as the topics discussed here are not purely academic ones.

Based on the individual chapters and the findings of the book as a whole, it is evident that the availability of different types of LGBTQ+ literature for young people varies substantially both within and between countries. While this volume provides only a snapshot of certain countries and languages, there does seem to be a tendency for publications to increase in line with improvements to the legal and social position of LGBTQ+ people, and with their greater visibility in society. However, a number of authors note that certain types of literature remain in shorter supply, such as books featuring bi and/or trans characters, depictions of characters facing intersecting oppressions, and topics considered to be 'niche', such as donor insemination (DI). Another interesting finding was that in some countries, many of the LGBTQ+ texts available are in fact translations and/or imports rather than works originally written in that language. This points to the importance of translation as a way of bringing in new ideas to the target countries, but also invites us to reflect critically on the hegemony of the English language and the ongoing impacts of colonialism.

It seems obvious from the research explored here that although there have been some developments to LGBTQ+ literature for children and young adults all around the world and although there is much to be proud of, there is still far to go in terms of ensuring that there is diverse, quality literature available for young readers. As will become apparent, an increase in the quantity of publications does not necessarily always equate to an improvement in quality. Many of the scholars featured in this volume acknowledge the good intentions on the part of authors and publishers in their country, but nonetheless also find much to critique.

The first chapter typifies this issue. Rosa Maria Hessel Silveira, Luiz Felipe Zago and Daniela Ripoll explore the situation in Brazil, finding, among other things, that there is an overarching pedagogical style to Brazilian LGBTQ+ books for young readers, as well as stereotyped depictions when it comes to portraying LGBTQ+ people. The scholars fear that, due to a shift to the right in the politics of the country, this will not improve in the future.

Elizabeth L. Chapman looks at bisexual young adult fiction from France and discovers negative tropes there too. Relatively few books with bisexual characters have been published, which contributes to societal bi erasure. Out of those books that do write about bisexual people, they tend to rely on stereotypes and tropes, such as greedy, cheating bisexuals, or bisexuality conceptualized as a problem.

We then move to France's near neighbours Germany and Austria. Katrin Waldhart explores how German-language young adult literature seems to reinforce the binary conception of gender and heteronormative standards, whereas literature translated to German currently seems somewhat more open about gender beyond the binary. As implied above, perhaps translations will help to create a change in society by importing new ideas.

Heading northwards, Mette Laustsen analyses the first Greenlandic YA novel about LGBTQ+ characters. This novel, which features an array of LGBTQ+ people but primarily does not focus on queerness as a problem, fills a number of gaps, as there is little young adult or new adult fiction written in Greenlandic, and LGBTQ+ literature – even for adults – is likewise in short supply. The novel has, interestingly, now been translated to English, something else that is rare for a Greenlandic novel.

Like Greenland, India has relatively little homegrown LGBTQ+ literature. Bharat Mehra and Chris Barrett provide an overview of the situation for English-language LGBTQ+ literature for young readers in India. They show that much of the work available is imported rather than produced in India, which means that it is in general not about Indian LGBTQ+ people or for a specifically Indian audience, and this makes it quite limited in interest and usefulness. There are, however, some works available written by authors from the South Asian diaspora, and/or based in diasporic settings.

The situation is rather different when it comes to Indigenous queer and Two-Spirit literature, as Thaddeus Andracki discusses in his chapter. He argues that works written by Indigenous authors can unsettle dominant Western and colonial conceptions of what 'queerness' is. In this way, these works can contribute towards liberation and reparation.

In the following chapter, Dalila Forni analyses Italian picturebooks and finds that one publisher in particular is doing a lot to provide LGBTQ+ narratives for children, although sometimes the approach is rather didactic. Italy is not the only example of a country where it is primarily one or a couple of smaller publishers who focus on LGBTQ+ topics or other aspects of diversity.

From Italy, we then move to three chapters that are all broadly multinational in their outlook, making connections across a range of countries and cultures. The first one, by Patricia Sarles, offers an extensive analysis of lesbian DI in picture books from around the world, covering many different languages and countries. She discovers that many of them are aimed at the children produced by DI rather than simply being books for anyone that happen to include DI. They are often written by lesbians who have experienced DI themselves and who may not be professional writers.

The next chapter in the book is also our shortest. Based on notes provided to us by a scholar who wishes to remain anonymous, it explores the Arab region. The chapter reminds us how many different countries and cultures make up this region, but despite this diversity, in general it appears that LGBTQ+ topics are not considered acceptable as a subject for young readers.

The third and final multinational chapter, by Jamie Naidoo and Mercedes Zabawa, discusses the depiction of same-sex couples in picturebooks from around the world. They analyse how lacking in diversity many of these representations continue to be, in terms of race/ethnicity, class, age and gender (non-)conformity. Sadly, this is a finding that other chapters note as well.

Moving back to explorations of single countries, Cheeno Marlo Sayuno writes about the Philippines and discusses how children's picturebooks and stories depict struggles in being LGBTQ+. This is a finding that, as has already been noted, appears in other chapters in this volume, as well as in extant research on LGBTQ+ works for younger readers. Such portrayals suggest to young people that living a queer life may be challenging or problematic in the future.

The theme of LGBTQ+ as a 'problem' recurs in the next chapter, on Slovenia, as well as elsewhere in this volume. Here, Andrej Zavrl looks at the situation for contemporary children's and young adult literature on LGBTQ+ themes, concluding that much of it, although well-intentioned, is issue-driven and presents LGBTQ+ lives as inevitably unhappy.

Moving around the world to South Korea, Anton Hur explores the queer narrative strategies used by authors there, with a focus on the trope of the 'boy in a dress'. Hur suggests that a move from fairy-tale settings and anthropomorphized animals to a more realistic setting may signal a greater openness to queerness in Korean children's literature.

We then return to Europe, and this chapter shares some themes with a number of the previous ones. Bernat Cormand looks at Spanish picturebooks and finds that there is much to praise, but that – once again – pedagogy is sometimes prioritized over the literary quality of the works. A question is whether LGBTQ+ books for young readers are meant to teach or to be pleasurable to read, or whether they can do both.

Finally, we end up in Scandinavia, with two chapters that explore different aspects of Swedish literature. In the first one, Åsa Warnqvist finds that trans literature was late to arrive in Sweden – or to be recognized as such – despite Sweden's relative openness. While progress is being made, much of the available literature continues to problematize trans experiences.

And in the last chapter, B. J. Epstein discusses Swedish LGB literature in particular and finds that it is not quite as progressive as one would imagine. On the contrary, Swedish YA books have a tendency to explain why characters have 'become' queer, and often show a reason, such as abuse or difficult relationships with parents, for why someone is LGBTQ+.

As the brief summaries here suggest, despite progress being made in politics and literature around the world, much of what is available for young readers is still problematic or lacking. There appears to be a real discomfort around the world with the idea of depicting LGBTQ+ characters and issues in an honest, open way in children's and YA literature, and also in such a way that it appeals to all readers, not just those who are themselves LGBTQ+ or the children of LGBTQ+ parents. In other words, many works are well-intentioned but pedagogical and explanatory, and they focus on queerness as a struggle, a problem or a topic that needs to be explained, instead of allowing characters to be LGBTQ+ and to live their lives as queer people.

Other commonalities across some of these chapters include the reliance on stereotyped ideas of LGBTQ+ people, the employment of animal versus human characters, the import of LGBTQ+ literature in translation instead of the production of original texts in the country or region's language, the actual or perceived risk of backlash from conservative institutions, and the important role self-publication plays when it comes to LGBTQ+ literature. All this, together with the previously mentioned finding that many of the works are rather didactic in nature, suggests that LGBTQ+ literature for young readers is still quite firmly in 'issue book' territory. Writing about and/or for LGBTQ+ people appears to be seen as a niche area in publishing, rather than simply being a reflection of the world we live in today. It is fascinating to see how much so many countries' literatures have in common, and how far we still have to go.

The book closes with a chapter listing all the primary texts found in all the regions discussed here. We hope this will provide a starting point for those who are interested in reading and analysing the works, and we also hope it encourages writers, translators and publishers to produce more LGBTQ+ work in as many languages and countries as possible.

In short, we believe that this volume can provide some essential information about LGBTQ+ people, rights and literature around the world. Far from being a niche subject, in this era of increasing LGBTQ+ rights in many countries and growing knowledge of LGBTQ+ issues, the study of LGBTQ+ literature is extremely important. What we tell children and young adults about what it means to be LGBTQ+ will form their beliefs about themselves and others as well as their behaviour, and in turn this will shape the world in the coming years. Children's literature reflects the society in which it is written, because the messages that adults want to offer young people will differ according to religion, culture, history and politics. What messages do we want to offer the next generations about being queer and how can we ensure the messages are positive, accurate and inclusive?

References

Abate, Michelle Ann, and Kenneth Kidd, eds. 2011. *Over the Rainbow: Queer Children's and Young Adult Literature.* Ann Arbor, MI: University of Michigan Press.

Alam, Shahidul. 2008. 'Majority World: Challenging the West's Rhetoric of Democracy'. *Amerasia Journal* 34, no. 1: 88–98. https://doi.org/10.17953/amer.34.1.l3176027k4q614v5

Bruhm, Steven, and Natasha Hurley, eds. 2004. *Curiouser: On the Queerness of Children.* Minneapolis, MN: University of Minnesota Press.

Cart, Michael, and Christine A. Jenkins. 2006. *The Heart Has Its Reasons.* London: Scarecrow Press.

Coats, Karen. 2017. *The Bloomsbury Introduction to Children's and Young Adult Literature.* London: Bloomsbury.

Crisp, Thomas. 2011. 'The Trouble with *Rainbow Boys*'. In *Over the Rainbow: Queer Children's and Young Adult Literature*, edited by Michelle Ann Abate and Kenneth Kidd, 215–54. Ann Arbor, MI: University of Michigan Press.

Dahlberg-Dodd, Hannah E. 2020. 'Script Variation as Audience Design: Imagining Readership and Community in Japanese *Yuri* Comics'. *Language in Society* 49, no. 3: 357–78. https://doi.org/10.1017/S0047404519000794

Epstein, B. J. 2012. *Translating Expressive Language in Children's Literature.* Oxford: Peter Lang.

———. 2013. *Are the Kids All Right? Representations of LGBTQ Characters in Children's and Young Adult Literature.* Bristol: HammerOn Press.

Epstein, B. J., and Robert Gillett, eds. 2017. *Queer in Translation.* London: Routledge.

Flanagan, Victoria. 2008. *Into the Closet.* New York: Routledge.

Gillis, Bryan, and Joanna Simpson. 2015. *Sexual Content in Young Adult Literature.* Lanham, MD: Rowan and Littlefield.

Gopalakrishnan, Ambika. 2011. *Multicultural Children's Literature: A Critical Issues Approach.* Thousand Oaks, CA: Sage Publications.

Hamer, Naomi, Perry Nodelman, and Mavis Reimer, eds. 2017. *More Words about Pictures: Current Research on Picture Books and Visual/Verbal Texts for Young People.* New York: Routledge.

Hunt, Peter. 1994 *An Introduction to Children's Literature.* Oxford: Oxford University Press.

———. 2005. *Understanding Children's Literature* London: Routledge.

James, Kathryn. 2009. *Death, Gender and Sexuality in Contemporary Adolescent Literature.* New York: Routledge.

Jenkins, Christine A., and Michael Cart. 2018. *Representing the Rainbow in Young Adult Literature: LGBTQ+ Content since 1969.* London: Rowman & Littlefield.

Kümmerling-Meibauer, Bettina, ed. 2018. *The Routledge Companion to Picturebooks.* London: Routledge.

Lathey, Gillian, ed. 2006. *The Translation of Children's Literature.* Clevedon: Multilingual Matters.

———. 2010. *The Role of Translators in Children's Literature: Invisible Storytellers.* New York: Routledge.

Lerer, Seth. 2008. *Children's Literature: A Reader's History from Aesop to Harry Potter.* Chicago, IL: University of Chicago Press.

Lillis, Theresa, and Mary Jane Curry. 2010. *Academic Writing in a Global Context: The Politics and Practices of Publishing in English*. Abingdon: Routledge.

Lurie, Alison. 1990. *Don't Tell the Grown-ups: Subversive Children's Literature*. Boston, MA: Little, Brown.

Madill, Anna. 2017. 'Erotic Manga: Boys' Love, *Shonen-ai, Yaoi* and (MxM) *Shotacon*'. In *The Routledge Companion to Media, Sex and Sexuality*, edited by Clarissa Smith, Feona Attwood and Brian McNair, 130–40. London: Routledge.

Maybin, Janet, and Nicola J. Watson, eds. 2009. *Children's Literature: Approaches and Territories*. Hampshire: Palgrave Macmillan.

Naidoo, Jamie Campbell. 2012. *Rainbow Family Collections: Selecting and Using Children's Books with Lesbian, Gay, Bisexual, Transgender and Queer Content*. Santa Barbara, CA: Libraries Unlimited.

Nel, Philip. 2017. *Was the Cat in the Hat Black? The Hidden Racism of Children's Literature, and the Need for Diverse Books*. New York: Oxford University Press.

Nikolajeva, Maria. 1996. *Children's Literature Comes of Age*. London: Routledge.

Nikolajeva, Maria, and Carole Scott. 2006. *How Picturebooks Work*. London: Routledge.

Nodelman, Perry. 1988. *Words about Pictures*. Athens, GA: University of Georgia Press.

Nodelman, Perry, and Mavis Reimer. 2002. *The Pleasures of Children's Literature*. Boston, MA: Allyn & Bacon.

Oittinen, Riitta. 2000. *Translating for Children*. New York: Garland, Inc.

O'Sullivan, Emer. 2005. *Comparative Children's Literature*. Translated by Anthea Bell. London: Routledge.

Pearce, Ruth, Kat Gupta, and Igi Moon. 2020. 'Introduction: The Many-Voiced Monster: Collective Determination and the Emergence of Trans'. In *The Emergence of Trans: Cultures, Politics and Everyday Lives*, edited by Ruth Pearce, Igi Moon, Kat Gupta, and Deborah Lynn Steinberg, 1–12. Abingdon: Routledge.

Post, Chad. 2019. 'Will Translated Fiction Ever *Really* Break Through?' *Vulture*, 7 May. https://www.vulture.com/2019/05/translated-fiction-has-been-growing-or-has-it.html

Ramdarshan Bold, Melanie. 2019. *Inclusive Young Adult Fiction: Authors of Colour in the United Kingdom*. Cham: Springer International Publishing.

Reynolds, Kimberley, ed. 2005. *Modern Children's Literature*. Houndsmills: Palgrave.

Reynolds, Kimberley. 2007. *Radical Children's Literature* London: Palgrave Macmillan.

———. 2011. *Children's Literature: A Very Short Introduction* Oxford: Oxford University Press.

Reynolds, Kimberley, and Nicholas Tucker, eds. 1998. *Children's Book Publishing in Britain Since 1945*. Aldershot: Scolar Press.

Rose, Jacqueline. 1993. *The Case of Peter Pan: Or the Impossibility of Children's Fiction*. Philadelphia, PA: University of Pennsylvania Press.

Sands-O'Connor, Karen. 2017. *Children's Publishing and Black Britain, 1965–2015*. New York: Palgrave Macmillan.

Shen, Lisa Chu. 2020. 'The Effeminate Boy and Queer Boyhood in Contemporary Chinese Adolescent Novels'. *Children's Literature in Education* 51, no. 1: 63–81. https://doi.org/10.1007/s10583-018-9357-7

Tompkins, Avery. 2014. 'Asterisk'. *Transgender Studies Quarterly* 1, no. 1–2: 26–27. https://doi.org/10.1215/23289252-2399497

Townsend, John R. 1990. *Written for Children*. London, England: The Bodley Head Children's Books.

Vincent, John. 2017. 'Trans – with or without an asterisk'. Post to the LGBT@JISCMAIL.AC.UK mailing list, 5 September 2017.

Welker, James. 2015. 'A Brief History of *Shōnen'ai, Yaoi,* and *Boys Love*'. *In Boys Love Manga and Beyond: History, Culture, and Community in Japan*, edited by Mark McLelland, Kazumi Nagaike, Katsuhiko Suganuma and James Welker, 42–75. Jackson, MS: University Press of Mississippi.

Chapter One

SELF-HELP AND COMING OUT: LGBTQ+ THEMES IN CONTEMPORARY BRAZILIAN YOUNG ADULT LITERATURE[1]

Rosa Maria Hessel Silveira, Luiz Felipe Zago and Daniela Ripoll

Introduction

In Brazil, the theme of differences has acquired great visibility in educational circles and in society in general over the last 20 years (Silveira et al. 2012). This is largely due to a series of cultural, political and legal changes (which are still ongoing, and which are briefly explained in the next section) promoted by various sectors, groups and social agents, similar to trends observed in other Western countries. Such changes can be identified in the criteria that have been established for selecting works in government programmes, such as the *Programa Nacional Biblioteca da Escola* (National School Library Programme), and *Programa Nacional Biblioteca da Escola – Temático* (National School Library Programme – Themes).[2] Hence, literary works for young people selected for these programmes were reviewed according to criteria relating not only to the aesthetic and literary quality of the works and their potential to stimulate reading practices, but also in regard to the absence of prejudicial and stereotypical representations (concerning what it is like to be black, indigenous, female, homosexual, fat, etc.). This allowed the promotion of (and respect for) differences concerning ethnicity, gender, sexuality, disability, bodily features, age groups, and so on. One of the results of such trends and measures has

1 Part of this work was produced in the context of the project 'Paths and Representations of Childhood in Children's Books – a study of works and readings' (sponsored by CNPq, carried out by NECCSO-UFRGS) and presented at the Fifth International Congress on Cultural Studies: Gender, Human Rights and Activism, University of Aveiro, Portugal, in 2016.

2 Both programmes were initiatives of the Brazilian federal government and existed between 1998 and 2014. The programmes aimed to establish and maintain school libraries through the selection and construction of literary collections with works distributed to all public schools in Brazil. When the impeachment of former President Dilma Rousseff (of the Workers' Party) occurred, there were profound changes to the orientation and political priorities of the interim government; among them was the suspension of several public policies of social inclusion, like the National School Library Programme and the National School Library Programme – Themes.

been the proliferation, especially in the last 15 years, of literary works for young adults, deliberately written to meet the need to discuss such differences. There was an increase in the number of books addressing differences as a whole (and the enrichment resulting from diversity), with stories about black people, disabled people, old people, and so on, and also addressing the prejudice against fat people, the questioning of gender roles and so on. However, in recent years, as we will discuss later, some of these approaches in Brazilian education have been questioned from a conservative point of view.

A significant number of the demands for incorporating themes about differences in multiple dimensions of Brazilian society, among them the National Education Programmes, emerge from the activities carried out by civil society movements. Therefore, we will start this chapter by discussing the organization of social movements committed to policies concerning sexual identity in the country, aiming at delimiting the past and current historical-political conditions in which homosexuality could and may be addressed, especially in the context of the YA literature analysed here.

Our analysis shows that the works discussed in this chapter seek, in different ways, to break the silence on LGBTQ+ topics in literature for young adults. The five Brazilian books covered here address the discovery and/or experience of the protagonists' homosexuality, presenting to their readers – with a greater or lesser degree of literary elaboration – a multiplicity of subjective feelings and dilemmas, as well as experiences and difficulties resulting from the reactions of those in their society.

Policies on Sexual Identity in Brazil

In Brazil, discussions about sexual rights gained greater visibility following the International Conference of Population and Development held in Cairo, Egypt, in 1994.[3] At this event, coordinated by the United Nations, the discussion of sexuality as a human right emerged for the first time (Vianna and Lacerda 2004). However, such discussion was marked by heteronormativity to the extent that it aimed at ensuring room for future debates on reproductive rights, whose prioritized political subject was women, and specifically pregnancy. At the World Conference on Women held in Beijing, China, in 1995, discussions about 'sexual orientation' were (in)tense, since people were starting to understand that the complexity of sexuality could not be limited only to the 'reproductive female'. The World Conference Against Racism held in Durban, South Africa, in 2001, was fundamental for public discussion of the expression 'sexual orientation' in a more comprehensive and intersectional way. However, the theme was strongly opposed by delegations from Islamic countries to the extent that such terminology was deleted from the documents produced at the conference (Correa 2003).

If, in the international context of the debates promoted by the United Nations, sexuality emerged as a theme linked to women in the mid-1990s, the social movements that

3 In 1994, Brazil was experiencing the consolidation of the feminist and LGBTQ+ movements, which were organized more consistently with the country's redemocratization from the beginning of the 1990s.

politicized sexual identities in the West had already been organized in the early 1970s, mainly in Europe and in the United States of America. At that time, inspiration came not just from the hippie and the peace movements (which might be considered more acceptable), but also from the academic consolidation of the second-wave feminist movement (more intellectualized), the punk movement, and the counterculture, linked to the May '68 Revolution in France. These last movements were more disruptive and hostile, and comprised a resistance strategy involving explicit confrontation (symbolic and physical), such as the Stonewall riots in New York in June 1969. As is well known, homosexuals who used to frequent the Stonewall Inn Pub resisted for three days against the frequent police raids on the site, which were always abusive. They engaged in a very violent, urban guerrilla war against the city police (Eribon 2008). The day the Stonewall riots began is now the day that is conventionally named Gay Pride Day in the US, the 27th June. It is worth mentioning, therefore, that the Stonewall riots are part of a broader context of social movements of resistance, in particular feminist movements, which emerged to oppose the concealment and silencing of the experiences of non-heterosexuality (Louro 2004).

In Brazil, records of the first organizations of what was then called the 'Brazilian homosexual movement' date back to the late 1970s, when Brazil was still ruled by the military regime (Green 2000). The group *Somos* (We Are), from São Paulo, with no funding of any kind, gathered gay men and lesbian women in order to discuss the homosexual situation – primarily, at the time, meaning the situation of the urban and white middle classes (Mantega 1979). When the HIV/AIDS epidemic emerged in Brazil, in 1981, there were already rudiments of social organizations that aimed at problematizing the status of homosexuality in order to politicize it. Therefore, while the HIV/AIDS epidemic in Brazil during the 1980s reinforced the stigma and discrimination against homosexuals (gay men in particular), it was also widely exploited in the following two decades as an opportunity for creating, developing and consolidating political movements focusing on sexual identity (Galvão 2000). In particular, due to funding from the World Bank (known as the 'AIDS I' project, in 1994, and 'AIDS II' project, in 1998), there were significant financial contributions that sustained prevention measures for the epidemic among gay men, and which directly maintained active non-governmental organizations that composed what was named the 'Brazilian response to AIDS' (Mattos et al. 2001; on the Brazilian response to AIDS, see also Paiva 2002).

Financial support from organized civil society institutions working towards AIDS prevention measures and which, therefore, explicitly addressed elements linked to the experiences of sexuality, meant that, for a certain time, discussions about sexual identity policies were limited to the sphere of health. As a result, important debates emerged within the 'Brazilian homosexual movement' that problematized both the link between sexual identities and illness, and the normative bias (in terms of gender, ethnicity and class) that was always present when the theme was non-heterosexual sexuality (Carrara 2010). Especially during the 1990s, the supposedly homogeneous 'Brazilian homosexual movement' multiplied the political subjects to which it referred: the LGBTQ+ acronym was introduced to give visibility to the different demands for citizenship of each of the several groups that make up the movement. It is worth noting that the inclusive status of the LGBTQ+ acronym in Brazil is still an unresolved political issue, and although there is no space to discuss this further here, it is an important topic for the future.

In the first half of the 2000s, connected in part to a newly elected left-wing government, the Brazilian LGBTQ+ movement was organized and consolidated, and even referenced more in the media, in both positive and negative ways (Carvalho 2012; Diniz 2014), particularly thanks to the attendance of millions of people at the Gay Pride Parades in large urban centres of Brazil. On the other hand, cases of violence against LGBTQ+ people were also noted, and the records of murders motivated by hatred against homosexuals increased in the country. It was in this context that, in 2004, the *Programa Brasil Sem Homofobia* (Brazil Without Homophobia Programme) was launched, which provided a comprehensive set of actions that were opposed to the various forms of discrimination and violence against LGBTQ+ people. Education, and teaching materials that supported inclusive pedagogical practices, played an eminent role in this programme (Vianna 2015). The Brazil Without Homophobia Programme proposed significant activities encompassing the field of education, with the main goal being to work to prevent violence against LGBTQ+ students in Brazilian public schools. Some activities included brief texts about sexuality and sexual discrimination to be read in class, from which debates amongst students were encouraged by the teachers. Throughout the first decade of the twenty-first century, there was increased awareness of the demand for preventative measures against AIDS and homophobia, as well as more work towards the political recognition of LGBTQ+ rights, such as different representations of LGBTQ+ people in the media, access to specialized healthcare services (including gender-confirmation surgical procedures), and the right to common-law marriage and same-sex marriage. Thus, the multiplication of political subjects of the LGBTQ+ movement was followed by a proportional increase in demands for rights.

Such visibility, however, has also provoked quite reactionary and conservative positions in recent years. These positions have support from large parts of the population, and also from political authorities themselves. For instance, the *Escola Sem Homofobia* (School Without Homophobia) initiative, based on the actions provided for in the Brazil Without Homophobia Programme, was rejected by then-President Dilma Rousseff. The veto occurred due to the controversy provoked by the representation of Evangelical Christians in the National Congress, who are against addressing any aspect of sexuality in schools. Several conservative groups concerned about the social role of the school in the country came together to form the *Escola Sem Partido* (School Without Parties) initiative. Among other things, it demands that there be no discussions on the school syllabus of gender construction and LGBTQ+ sexual identity among children and young students (Reis and Eggert 2017).

Addressing LGBTQ+ Themes in Young Adult Literature

Regardless of this path towards (and, more recently, contestation of) policies on sexual identity in Brazil, there are few LGBTQ+ themes or references in works of literature for young adults. A brief analysis of three studies (Ramos 2009; Sefton 2011; Silveira and Kaercher 2013) that sought to map and analyse some books for children and young people with such themes seems to confirm this first impression. Hence, focusing on the Portuguese context, Ramos states that 'sexuality, especially that which disagrees with the heteronormative paradigm, remains a universe perceived almost as untouchable, target of both sporadic and distant recreations, at least concerning the Portuguese literary production' (Ramos 2009, 296). The author points out that the 'literary transposition of a theme with deep sociological implications, in addition to the atavistic moral and religious constraints, will explain the relative silence surrounding it, which is symptomatic of a more general discomfort, especially when it comes to an axiological and unequal dialogue between adults and children' (ibid.).[4] Despite this, Ramos shows that there are some books published in Portugal that seek to approach the topic, especially those translated from other languages.

Sefton (2011), who is more interested in the Brazilian context, begins with a brief overview of the publications of children's books on the subject and their circulation in several countries (with far more works available in the United States of America, the United Kingdom, the Netherlands and Spain). She then focuses on four well-publicized books that address, in a more or less superficial way, the topic of sexuality. The author presents the well-known book by Babette Cole, *Mummy Never Told Me*, in which the writer includes a series of children's questions, introduced by the refrain 'Mummy never told me'. There is a lack of explanation on the part of the 'mummy' with regard to falling in love and to relationships between women and men (but remember: no questions are answered in the book). In addition to two books originally written in English, *And Tango Makes Three* and *The Sissy Duckling*, with no Portuguese translation or circulation in Brazil (though there are translations available in Portugal), Sefton suggests that arguably the first Brazilian children's book on the topic is *O menino que brincava de ser* (The Boy who Pretended to Be, 2000), by Georgina Martins, about a boy who adopts practices traditionally assigned to the female gender such as dressing up and wearing a dress.

In an article published in 2013, Silveira and Kaercher focus specifically on the representation of same-sex-parent families in seven books directed at child readers and published in Brazil (five of them) and Portugal (two of them) since 2007. The authors observed that, despite the remarkable differences between the works, concerning the balance or imbalance between literary quality and pedagogic intentions, the most frequently recurring trend among these books was to characterize the love between men or women in a similar way to how heterosexual relationships are traditionally represented, i.e. focusing on romantic love. Other themes of the books include family happiness and discussions about raising children and the division of home chores.

We therefore see a slow but consistent increase in fictional literary works for children and adolescents that incorporate LGBTQ+ topics, and where the LGBTQ+ theme generally constitutes the central conflict in the narrative. In our study, we have a different thematic focus: we address five literary works written for young adults, published since 1999 and written by Brazilian authors. The five works, in different ways and using different fictional elements, approach the 'discovery' of homosexuality in adolescence;

4 All translations our own unless otherwise stated.

they were the only works with literary content for young adults that addressed the theme and were in national circulation in the Brazilian market in 2016. The aforementioned books are: *Sempre por perto* (Always Around) by Anna Cláudia Ramos (1999); *Eu é um outro* (I'm Another One) by Hermes Bernardi Jr. (2014); *Do jeito que a gente é* (Just the Way We Are) by Márcia Leite (2009); *Sofia e Mônica* (Sofia and Mônica) by Leonardo Brasiliense (2014); and *Bem-te-vi* (Great Kiskadee) by Marli Porto (2014). Here, we analyse the texts and paratexts based on post-structuralist theoretical perspectives.

Presenting the Books

Eu é um outro (I'm Another One) (Bernardi Jr. 2014), written in first-person narrative, focuses on a teenage character named Edu, and on his thoughts, feelings, memories, actions and daydreams. We follow the character on his first trip to a therapy session; later, we see the internal dialogue of the boy in the waiting room of the psychology clinic. Edu likes another boy, Manon, but his father says there is treatment for 'loving differently' (Bernardi Jr. 2014, 19).[5][6] In this dialogue, in which it is not clear whether Eduardo is talking to his therapist or to himself, he tries to establish boundaries between what is 'normal' and what is 'strange' about his loving and there is also some consideration of some stereotypical representations[7] of gender and sexuality:

> I'm feeling strange things for another boy. I mean, I do not think they're weird. I think it's normal. I like to like it that way. The others think it's strange. The others make me think it's strange what I do not even think is strange. The few who now know, of course. Those who don't know it, just imagine it. I don't know if it's my way of speaking, my sensitive way of saying thanks, please, excuse me. What I know is I'm so happy when I talk with him, when I'm around this boy, you know? I like riding a bike with him, walking with him, chatting about football. About poetry … (Bernardi Jr. 2014, 18)[8]

Throughout the narrative, flashbacks from various moments of Edu's life must be solved like a puzzle by the reader, and we find out that Manon has a girlfriend and that Edu had suffered violence (including sexual violence) in the bathroom of a football stadium. The protagonist spends two months in the hospital, but the violence is not much discussed or focused on (and, at times, it seems to have no importance); what matters to the character

5 All excerpts from the analysed books were translated/paraphrased by the authors of this study, unless otherwise noted.

6 In Portuguese: 'gostar diferente'.

7 The concept of 'stereotype' used in this article is based on Hall (1997).

8 'Estou sentindo coisas estranhas por outro garoto. Quer dizer, não acho que sejam estranhas. Acho normal. Gosto de gostar assim. Os outros é que acham estranho. Os outros me fazem pensar que é estranho o que eu nem acho estranho sentir. Os poucos que agora sabem, claro. Os que não sabem, imaginam. Não sei se pelo meu jeito de falar, meu jeito sensível de dizer obrigado, por favor, com licença. O que eu sei é que fico feliz quando converso, quando estou perto desse garoto, sabe? Gosto de andar de *bike* com ele, de caminhar com ele, de falar de futebol. E de poesia' (Bernardi Jr. 2014, 18).

is the fact that his friend went away over the course of his recovery, and had plans to travel and live with Clara, his girlfriend, in another country. In the end, Manon gives up on the trip, acknowledges the feelings he has for Edu, and goes to meet him when he is discharged from the hospital. They exchange hugs and looks in front of Edu's family and leave together, to discover the world, sharing the same bike.

Sofia e Mônica was written and illustrated by Leonardo Brasiliense, a writer who won a *Prêmio Açorianos* award (a regional Brazilian literature award) and a *Prêmio Jabuti* award (the most traditional and prestigious award for Brazilian literature) for a previous book and who, in an interview about writing this specific book, stated that he spent 'months reading magazines, such as *Capricho*,[9] to incorporate the language of teenagers. I guess it worked. On the magazine website, readers say they relate to the stories' (*Diário de Santa Maria* 2014, n.p.). The work has a particularly ingenious compositional organization, in the way that the text and the graphic design are laid out. It is composed by intercalating diary pages and inner monologues of both protagonists, who often have different point of views on the same event, in addition to flashbacks and reflections.

The plot can be summarized as follows: two girls, Sofia and Mônica, who are very close friends (and have been since they were 10 and 11 years old, respectively), decide to do a ritual, in the bathroom of Mônica's room, using a needle to turn them into 'blood sisters' (Brasiliense 2014, 7).[10] According to Sofia, the friendship between them is 'something else': 'Since I met Mônica, it has been like this for me: like a mirror. If I had a twin sister, I think I'd hate it. I'm sure of it. But with Mônica I'm talking about something else. I can't tell. But it's something else' (Brasiliense 2014, 9).[11] The narrative is developed around the everyday life of the (until then) inseparable 14-year-old protagonists (at school, in Mônica's room, in the kitchen of Mônica's place), until Pedro emerges on the scene; he is a young delivery boy (who first delivered gas, and then started delivering pizza). Sofia is enchanted with the boy and Mônica is clearly upset and jealous: 'Sofia's crossed the line. What a foolish girl. Player. Ridiculous [...]. Women don't make the first move. Women play hard to get. Our affection must be won. What am I talking about? She's 14. Why did the damn gas company not send the usual old, bald and big-bellied guy?' (Brasiliense 2014, 19).[12] Both girls end up liking Pedro, which results in multiple disagreements and new encounters. An additional character, Amanda, gets Sofia's attention, making Mônica jealous, but by the end Amanda is dating Pedro. The two protagonists eventually grow apart. Unlike Bernardi Jr.'s book, as discussed above, in which the issue of homosexuality,

---

9 *Capricho* magazine was founded in 1952 by Editora Abril and is currently an exclusively online publication. Its target audience is mostly teenage girls.

10 In Portuguese: 'irmãs de sangue'.

11 'Desde que nos encontramos a Mônica foi isto para mim: um espelho. Se eu tivesse uma irmã gêmea, acho que ia odiar. Tenho certeza. Mas com a Mônica estou falando de outra coisa. Nem sei dizer. É outra coisa' (Brasiliense 2014, 9).

12 'Sofia abusou. Guria mais sem noção. Oferecida. Ridícula. [...] Mulher não se atira assim. Mulher é difícil. Tem que ser conquistada. O que é que eu estou falando? Ela tem 14 anos. Por que será que a maldita empresa do gás não mandou o velho careca e barrigudo de sempre?' (Brasiliense 2014, 19).

in its subjective and social dimensions, is openly addressed, *Sofia e Mônica* only leaves traces, allusions and mentions of small details that invite readers to make a reading that suggests a homosexual or homosocial friendship between the teenagers – without, however, unequivocally narrowing down to such a reading.

Do jeito que a gente é (Just the Way We Are) by Márcia Leite (2009) alternates the points of view of two main characters, Beá and Chico, whose lives intersect when their parents get married after ending other relationships. Maria Beatriz, called Beá, 14 years old, characterizes herself as a 'scared scarecrow'[13]: blonde, green eyes, tall and thin, 'highly valued ingredients on the female market',[14] but with very curly hair, 'a minor manufacturing defect',[15] clumsy, ugly, awkward, 'with no breasts or butt',[16] shy, insecure, with low self-esteem, who suffers a series of humiliations in school and at home. Her mother comments on her skinny figure, saying that 'bad things do not get fat' (Leite 2009, 16),[17] while at school she is called a series of names relating to her curly hair and facial appearance: 'hang-glider, airplane, parachute, parasol, Dumbo's ear, and "the most feminine nicknames", so to speak, were lampshade and fern' (Leite 2009, 14, quotation marks in the original).[18] Meanwhile, 17-year-old Chico faces problems when coming out to his friend, Johnny, who rejects him, and leaves Chico feeling betrayed. He is then unable to find the courage to come out to his father. The two step-siblings, Beá and Chico, start living together and, after five months in the same home, Beá falls in love with Chico, who is then forced to tell her he is gay in order not to hurt her. Beá accepts him: 'I love you, Chico. I like you just the way you are. And you are who you are, that's it' (Leite 2009, 144),[19] after which the two get closer and end up becoming inseparable. In the epilogue we read how, one year later, their lives are completely transformed: Maria Beatriz 'changed school, hair, glasses, clothing, style, and classmates. She got her braces off and got rid of self-pity' (Leite 2009, 174)[20] and Chico Dornelles 'had finally managed to come out of the closet and open up to his father [...]. The conversation was less difficult than Chico thought, but it was not easy. Marcelo said that he already suspected and guaranteed that the son's sexual orientation would never interfere with his love for him or contaminate the relationship between the two. But just so he could get his head round the idea, he asked to be warned in advance before introducing him to a boyfriend'

13 In Portuguese, 'espantalho assustado' (Leite 2009, 12).

14 'ingredientes muito valorizados no mercado feminino' (Leite 2009, 14).

15 'esse pequeno "defeito" de fabricação' (Leite 2009, 14, quotation marks in the original).

16 'sem peito e sem bunda' (Leite 2009, 16).

17 'Minha mãe gosta de dizer que coisa ruim não engorda. A coisa ruim sou eu' (Leite 2009, 16).

18 'Por causa dos meus cabelos já fui chamada de asa-delta. De aeroplano. De paraquedas. De guarda-sol. De orelha de Dumbo. Os mais femininos, digamos assim, foram abajur e samambaia' (Leite 2009, 14).

19 'Eu adoro você, Chico. Gosto de você pelo que você é. E você é o que é, pronto' (Leite 2009, 144).

20 'Maria Beatriz Rinaldi Lobato mudou de colégio, de penteado, de óculos, de roupas, de estilo e de colegas. Tirou o aparelho dos dentes e se livrou da autopiedade' (Leite 2009, 174).

(Leite 2009, 174–75).[21] As in the book by Brasiliense (2014), the issue of homosexuality and of its acceptance and disclosure by teenagers is the core of Leite's novel.

In *Sempre por perto* (Always Around), a novel by Anna Claudia Ramos (1999), the author narrates Clara's story through an omniscient narrator. In it, Clara, now an adult, visits the home of her grandmother, who recently died, and remembers several episodes from her childhood and adolescence (in addition to the many feelings involved in such moments): the cold and distant relationship she had with her father; the jokes she shared and the genuine love she had for her brother, Beto; and the apparent disconnection between the behaviours socially accepted as girly, and her wishes and desires. Clara remembers, in particular, a conversation with her brother Beto, when she was 10 and he was 13 years old:

> – Beto, why wasn't I born as a boy like you and dad?
> – Stop talking nonsense, Clara. You're a pretty girl.
> – Oh! Being a girl is not fun at all. Grandma keeps saying that I have to be *well-behaved*, to always be *dressed up*, to sit like a *lady*. You can go out alone, I can't. It's dangerous for a girl to walk alone on the street. Mom keeps saying that. (Ramos 1999, 11, emphasis in the original)[22]

Clara remembers the demands of her family regarding her legs (which were always bruised and bandaged), the fact she used to play football so well, and how she thought it ridiculous to see 'those little girls in starched dresses, like a wedding cake' (Ramos 1999, 13).[23] Adult Clara remembers herself as a girl with a lot of energy, and these memories appear in the words of the omniscient narrator:

> [Clara] had to exercise a lot. But not all adults understood that. [...]. There was energy coming out of her pores, and at the same time she was the most tender and sweet of the girls. Always so divided between two worlds. The male, the father and the brother, and the female, the mother. Clara was a woman like her mother, but she wanted to be a man like her father. The masculine world was much more interesting in that girl's imagination. (Ramos 1999, 12)[24]

---

21 'Chico Dornelles finalmente conseguiu chutar a porta do armário e se abriu para o pai [...]. A conversa foi menos difícil do que Chico pensava, mas nem por isso foi fácil. Marcelo disse que já desconfiava e garantiu que a orientação sexual do filho jamais iria interferir no amor que sentia por ele ou contaminar a relação entre os dois. Mas, apenas para que pudesse incorporar bem a ideia, pediu que o avisasse com antecedência antes de lhe apresentar um namorado' (Leite 2009, 174–75).

22 '– Beto, por que eu não nasci menino igual a você e ao papai?
– Deixa de falar besteira, Clara. Você é uma menina linda.
– Ah! Ser menina não tem graça nenhuma. A vovó fica dizendo que eu tenho de ser *comportadinha*, andar *arrumadinha*, sentar feito *mocinha*. Você pode sair sozinho e eu não. É perigoso uma menina andar sozinha na rua. A mãe vive falando isso' (Ramos 1999, 11).

23 'aquelas garotinhas de vestidinho engomado, como um bolo de casamento' (Ramos 1999, 13).

24 'Precisava se exercitar muito. Mas nem todos os adultos entendiam isso. [...]. Tinha energia saindo pelos poros e, ao mesmo tempo, era a mais sensível e doce das meninas. Sempre tão dividida entre dois mundos. O masculino, do pai e do irmão, e o feminino, da mãe. Clara era

The character also remembers her parents' divorce and the changes that occurred in her and her brother's lives; her teenage adventures at the Carnival ball; her early homosexual experiences; her forbidden love for Luna (the discovery of desire, heartbreak, and the subsequent rediscovery of love with another girl). The pace of the narrative is fast and somewhat shallow – mimicking the flow of the protagonist's memories. And after evoking these memories, Clara awakens with the arrival of her father and there is a moment of reconciliation between them – though Clara, now age 35, still hides her homosexual experiences from her father. In this work, we observe the use of several gender stereotypes, as well as their questioning by the narrator; the book is rather didactic, which weakens the literary project as a whole.

Finally, *Bem-te-vi* (Great Kiskadee), by Marli Porto (2014), was published thanks to the Government of the State of São Paulo, by the State Department of Culture and the Programme for Cultural Action, through a contest for supporting projects that promote LGBTQ+-themed cultural manifestations. The title of the work comes from the name of a bird that symbolizes, to the teenage protagonist, the freedom to be and to fly. The third-person narrative allows us to follow Daniel, a boy who feels different and recognizes himself as gay. The plot combines Daniel's family – father, mother, older brother – and their difficulty in accepting his identity, with episodes that occur at school, while at the same time a football championship takes place. At school, Daniel has a confidante, Bianca; he faces many instances of bullying; and gets closer to Matheus, an excellent football player and well-known high school bully, who defends him from the threats of other bullies. For him, two animals – his dog, Duke, and the Great Kiskadee, whose singing the protagonist often listens to – represent freedom and the lack of demands. It is through dialogues with his friend that readers begin to understand Daniel's feelings and thoughts, although the dialogues sometimes comprise a pedagogical intent, as in this example: 'You know, Bianca, all places seem to be difficult for a gay boy at my age. And now that I'm in love, being accepted as a normal person seems to be the most important thing in the world. But I know I won't be normal. So, I've been thinking of hiding, 'cause I might have a happier life, with more friends, you know?' (Porto 2014, 50).[25]

Following Bianca's advice, Daniel socializes with a football team, which includes Matheus, and the relationship between them gets stronger. On the other hand, in the family sphere, Daniel's parents continue to be worried and to suspect the possible homosexual orientation of their son, a suspicion which is confirmed on the day his mother finds an envelope where the teenager keeps his diary and other memories of his love for his friend. His mother, predictably, is revolted and upset, and Daniel feels very sad and cries a lot. But the story ends with the revelation of Matheus's secret: he declares he is

mulher como a mãe, mas queria ser homem feito o pai. O mundo masculino era muito mais interessante na imaginação daquela menina' (Ramos 1999, 12).

25 'Sabe, Bianca, todos os lugares parecem ser difíceis para um menino *gay* na minha idade. E agora que me vejo apaixonado, ser aceito como uma pessoa normal parece ser a coisa mais importante do mundo. No entanto, sei que não serei. Então, estou pensando em me esconder, porque talvez eu tenha uma vida mais feliz, com mais amigos, entende?' (Porto 2014, 50, italics original).

in love with Daniel and they kiss. Once again, the discovery of the homosexual affection between two teenagers and the incomprehension and intolerance on the part of the family and their social group are the core of the narrative.

Analysis

The theme of looking for answers (or for a definition concerning sexuality) is recurrent in four of the five books in the corpus. The main characters in these works look for answers (rational justifications or explanations for what they feel) that, supposedly, exist within themselves. Such a pursuit, always conflicted and tortuous, is carried out by the characters in different ways: sometimes autonomously (for example, the character of Clara, in Ramos 1999); with the complicity of the mother (which is the case with Chico (Leite 2009) and Clara (Ramos 1999)); with the support of a friend (in the case of Daniel, in Porto 2014); and sometimes with the aid of professionals (which is the case with Edu and the therapist in Bernardi Jr. 2014). In fact, the presence of therapists in both Bernardi Jr. (2014) and Ramos (1999) helps reinforce the contemporary representation of adolescence as a period of doubts and conflicts, as well as the idea that sexuality is a problem – and which, therefore, requires resolutions. On the back cover of Bernardi Jr. (2014), the publishers claim that the protagonist Edu, in the psychology clinic, 'let go of his thoughts in profusion, in a disconnected manner, a whirlwind, which is very common in this stage of life, when we seek answers for our questions, and some natural questions aim to take shape and personality' (Bernardi Jr. 2014, back cover).[26] But, interestingly, the therapist in Ramos (1999) (remembered in a flashback) says to young Clara that she does not have 'to live all that makes up her fantasy' (Ramos 1999, 20)[27] and that the desire for her friend is not real, so the therapist is then labelled as 'prejudiced' by the teenager.[28] When the therapist states that she needs to understand, Clara snaps back: 'Understand? I don't want to understand. I'm sick of understanding, I need to live. [...] I've just decided to never come back here. I don't wanna hear you speaking of my fantasies anymore. I wanna be happy' (Ramos 1999, 21).[29]

In at least three books, the process of looking for answers is considered to be exposing the truth about yourself and necessarily includes the act of confessing.[30] Fischer (1996, 134), in analysing media productions of the 1990s targeted at a teenage audience, shows

26 [...] 'Eduardo solta seus pensamentos em profusão, em ordem desconexa, um turbilhão, muito comum nesta fase da vida, quando perguntas buscam respostas e algumas dúvidas naturais desejam ganhar forma de personalidade' (Bernardi Jr. 2014, back cover).

27 'Você não precisa viver tudo o que sua fantasia apresenta' (Ramos 1999, 20).

28 'Preconceituoso' (Ramos 1999, 20).

29 'Entender? Eu não quero entender. Chega de entender, eu preciso viver. [...] acabei de resolver que não volto mais aqui. Não quero mais ouvir você falar das minhas fantasias. Eu quero ser feliz' (Ramos 1999, 21).

30 See, especially, Jorge Larrosa (2010), who discusses this contemporary imperative of self-confession which, obviously, affects not only teenagers, but all humans, through psychological and psychoanalytic discourses.

that such an exposure of intimacy, of what is private, and of the 'most hidden truths about love and sexual experience' has been taught through the media, recurrently, as necessary and vital. Similarly, we perceive this need for exposure in the analysed books. On the back cover of *Do jeito que a gente é* (Leite 2009), for instance, there is a review whose author seeks, in a direct and honest way, to delineate the core facts of the plot, making an appeal to teenage readers, addressing one of the dimensions that most often draws their attention – 'truth' and 'authenticity':

> Exposing the truth about yourself requires a courage that few people have. Often, lying seems more comfortable than *facing who we are*. Chico wants to change this reality. To do so, he is going to come out of the closet to the people closest to him. And this *gets harder* after the reaction of his best friend, who immediately stays away from him after discovering it. Beá also wants *to be braver*. She wants to know how to improve her relationship with her mother, who just blames her; she doesn't want to accept the insults of her school friends anymore; she wants to like herself better. *And have no worries*. The stories of Chico and Beá intersect. Together, they will help each other live their lives to the fullest *and be less afraid* of being themselves. Entirely. (Leite 2009, back cover, emphasis in the original)[31]

A key moment in four of the five analysed books is, undoubtedly, coming out – except for in *Sofia e Mônica*, whose protagonists are only children, have no other friends, and seem to share the domesticity of everyday life in a relatively distant way from adults. In addition, the main characters write their questions and deepest desires (Sofia on a laptop computer, Mônica in a notebook), and thus the confessions are made very differently: Sofia is writing on the computer and suddenly she sees that Mônica added Pedro on Facebook. Her doubts (and, also, her certainty about what she feels for her friend) echo in her words: 'Why did that S.O.B. find Mônica before me?' (Brasiliense 2014, 27).[32]

In *Eu é um outro* (Bernardi Jr. 2014), Edu tells Márcia, his best friend, that he is gay. When he realizes she does not care that much (and suggests she already knew it), Edu gets pretty hurt by Márcia's apparent indifference. She says, 'You seem more sensitive, affectionate, but it isn't too obvious, if that's what is bugging you. And if it were, what would it matter?' (Bernardi Jr. 2014, 41).[33] On the other hand, when he wants to tell Manon that he is physically attracted to boys, he steps back and feels weak, cowardly and sorry: 'But I was hurting for not saying to anyone that I liked boys, that in school I felt attracted to

31 'Expor a verdade sobre si mesmo exige uma coragem que poucas pessoas têm. Muitas vezes, mentir parece mais confortável do que *encarar aquilo que a gente é*. Chico quer mudar esse quadro. Para isso, vai ter que assumir sua homossexualidade para as pessoas mais próximas. O que fica *mais difícil* depois da reação de seu melhor amigo que, quando soube, se afastou imediatamente. Beá também quer *ter mais coragem*. Quer saber melhorar o relacionamento com a mãe, que só a detona; não quer mais engolir desaforos dos colegas da escola; quer gostar mais do seu jeito. *Sem encanações*. As histórias de Chico e Beá se cruzam. Juntos, eles vão se ajudar a viver com mais verdade e *menos medo* de se mostrar. Por inteiro' (Leite 2009, back cover).

32 'Por que o fdp achou a Mônica antes de mim?' (Brasiliense 2014, 27).

33 'Você parece mais sensível, carinhoso, mas não dá pinta não, se essa é a sua preocupação. E se desse?' (Brasiliense 2014, 41).

them during P.E. That's what I wanted to say, doc, but I didn't. I wasn't brave enough. I lack this warrior side in me, in this other self who lives in a kingdom of cowardice and of conditional conjunctions. If, if, if' (Bernardi Jr. 2014, 40).[34] On the other hand, in *Bem-te-vi* (Porto 2014), the protagonist Daniel tries to tell his mother, but she does not want to hear him.

> – So, you want me to have a son like me?
> His mother was completely embarrassed.
> – Like what?
> – You know what!
> – No, I don't. – that was the answer of Ms Silvia, even though her eyes could not hide how much she knew.
> – But, Mom… […]
> – Look, Daniel, please don't even dream about discussing this matter with your father.
> – What matter, Mom?
> Daniel wanted his mother to speak the right word. But she only said:
> – That you want to be different. (Porto 2014, 28–29)[35]

Actually, it is only in his friend Bianca that the character Daniel finds enough affection to say who he truly is.

In the works discussed here, the bodies of the teenage characters are depicted from a psychological and biological perspective – thus, we see bodies and minds frequently depicted as divided, unsure, in transformation, or undergoing changes. In *Eu é um outro* (Bernardi Jr. 2014), for example, Edu's desire for Manon is explicit – 'I already masturbate thinking of boys, Dad' (Bernardi Jr. 2014, 35)[36] – and this is naturally represented from the biological point of view: thus, there are many references to bodily changes

---

34 'Mas estava doendo não conseguir dizer pra alguém que eu gostava dos caras, que no colégio eu me sentia atraído por eles quando treinavam na educação física. Era isso que eu queria dizer, doutor, mas não disse. Faltou coragem. Falta um pouco de guerreiro nesse outro eu que vive num reino de covardia e de conjunções condicionais. Se, se, se' (Bernardi Jr. 2014, 40).

35 '– Então, você deseja que eu tenha um filho assim como eu?
A mãe ficou completamente sem graça.
– Assim como?
– A senhora sabe!
– Não, eu não sei. – foi a resposta de dona Sílvia, mesmo estando claro nos olhos dela o quanto sabia.
– Mas mãe....
[...]
– Olha, Daniel, por favor, nem sonhe em falar desse assunto com o seu pai.
– Que assunto, mãe?
Daniel queria que a mãe falasse a palavra certa. Mas ela apenas respondeu:
– Que você quer ser diferente' (Porto 2014, 28–29).

36 'Eu já me masturbo pensando em garotos, pai' (Bernardi Jr. 2014, 35).

characteristic of adolescence ('facial hair, pubic hair [...] waking up with a hard penis, or all wet and sticky')[37] caused – and explained – by 'hormones' and the action of 'testosterone' in the body. Furthermore, we note that the pedagogical intent throughout the narrative of *Bem-te-vi* (Porto 2014) is emphasized when the narrator devotes a whole chapter to a science class (see the Conclusion below for more on the didactic nature of these works). The teacher, presented as a friend of the teenagers, discusses several topics deemed important to them: drugs, sexuality, diversity, homophobia. Following the description of the class, Daniel reaffirms his identity: 'Homosexual, that's who I am' (Porto 2014, 83).[38]

Another interesting aspect is the fact that the young protagonists in four of the five books under consideration are characterized as intelligent regarding conflicts and sexual and affective relationships, as well as the social implications of diverging from stereotypes and heteronormativity. This is similar to what was identified by Silveira et al. (2013) when they analysed 10 children's books whose plots focused mainly on the diseased bodies of old people. In this study, the authors argued that several young characters are represented as excessively rational and incredibly mature when acknowledging the physical and mental decay in their grandparents due to illness. In this sense, the character Beá (Leite 2009), for instance, seems largely resigned to her terrible relationship with her mother. Edu (Bernardi Jr. 2014), when talking to himself, seems to know perfectly how to distinguish desire from love. Clara (Ramos 1999, 26) knows that her love for Luna is 'forbidden'[39] – in her own words – but ends up confessing it to her mother as follows: 'Oh, Mama! I don't know where to start. But if you wanna know it, here we go. [...] I'm in love with Luna, Mom. We kissed the other day and it was very intense' (Ramos 1999, 26).[40] Or, moreover, when Daniel (Porto 2014) says to a friend: 'But I'd like to be born in a different era, in which human diversity was accepted with ease. [...] Does being the way I am disqualify me as a person?' (Porto 2014, 64).[41] In addition to the apparent self-awareness, some characters demonstrate much maturity and wisdom. Edu, for example, reads both Caio Fernando Abreu (a well-known Brazilian author who publicly came out of the closet in the 1980s) and Plato.

We note that two of the analysed books – *Eu é um outro* (Bernardi Jr. 2014) and *Sofia e Mônica* (Brasiliense 2014) – feature a compositional sophistication and use literary elements that make them far from trivial within the literary universe of works written for teenagers, as can be seen by the non-linear narrative time, the combination of inner monologues and dialogues, and the use of several narrative voices, which assumes a careful and sensitive teenage reader. In the case of *Sofia e Mônica*, the topic of homosexuality is not addressed in a direct and problematized way, but emerges as one possible

---

37 'pelos na cara, no pinto [...] acordar de pinto duro, ou todo melecado' (Bernardi Jr. 2014, 35).

38 'Homossexual, é o que sou, pensava Daniel' (Porto 2014, 83).

39 'Proibido' (Ramos 1999, 26).

40 'Ah, mãezinha! É tão difícil começar. Mas se você quer saber, vamos lá. [...]. Eu tô apaixonada pela Luna, mãe. A gente se beijou outro dia e foi muito forte' (Ramos 1999, 26).

41 '[...] gostaria de nascer em outra época, em que a diversidade humana fosse aceita com naturalidade. [...]. Ser como sou me desqualifica enquanto pessoa?' (Porto 2014, 64).

reading, from clues in the text itself: would the relationship between the teenagers be just a typical friendship in this age group or would it have a homoerotic nature? Meanwhile, *Eu é um outro*, by specifically focusing on the issue of 'discovering yourself', although employing some stereotypes, uses metaphors (including the drawing of the wing, already printed on the cover) and the deliberate dive into the complexity of feelings, indecisions and doubts of the protagonist, Edu, in an non-linear narrative to allow teenage readers to get involved in an intricate game of representations and meanings. In the paratext on the back cover only one paragraph of the book is quoted, and it deals, metaphorically, with 'internal tattoos', or the way experiences leave a trace on someone.[42] In the case of these two works, in addition to the bold innovation in approaching – in an open or implicit way – the theme of homosexuality among teenagers, we should highlight the quality of the writing and the editing, which allows teenage readers a rich and complex reading, and which is different from books that try to help readers with the hard truths of life. Regardless of their theme, Brazilian books written for young adults can simply reproduce stereotypes and present a formative, pedagogical approach, or they can be innovative and creative, enabling fruitful readings.

Reception

Although there is a lack of comprehensive data on the reception of these five books, it can be pointed out that some of them received positive responses and criticism. Thus, *Sempre por perto* (Ramos 1999) was nominated as part of the 1999 Basic Book Collection by the *Fundação Nacional do Livro Infantil e Juvenil* (National Foundation for Children's and Young People's Books), the Brazilian section of the International Board on Books for Young People (IBBY), a Brazilian private non-profit institution, whose objective is to promote reading. Moreover, the book *Eu é um outro* (Bernardi Jr. 2014) won the 22nd Prêmio Açorianos de Literatura (Azorean Literature Prize) in the Children and Young Adults category.[43] However, some authors have reported difficulties in publishing LGBTQ+ books. For example, Anna Cláudia Ramos, Márcia Leite and Hermes Bernardi Jr. participated in a Roundtable Discussion at the Porto Alegre Book Fair in Brazil on 6 November 2014, where they spoke about the difficulty encountered in regard to publishing companies being willing to publish works addressing this theme. Márcia Leite reported that, in the case of *Do jeito que a gente é*, the acceptance of the novel for publication, after five years of conversations with the publishing company, came with the condition that the homosexual character would not be the protagonist. The authors have stated that, although they are invited to go to schools and discuss their books with the students, they have never been asked to talk about these specific books.

---

42 'tatuagens internas' (Bernardi Jr. 2014, back cover).

43 It is a regional award, distributed annually by the Porto Alegre City Hall, which aims to recognize, promote and stimulate the production of authors, graphic artists and publishers of the state of Rio Grande do Sul (RS, Brazil).

Conclusion

To conclude this brief journey through five Brazilian books that address the issue of homosexuality in childhood and adolescence, we can summarize our findings as follows: first, we want to draw attention, once again, to the effectively pedagogical nature of two of the five literary productions (Leite 2009 and Ramos 1999), which suggest that it is necessary to disclose yourself, discover yourself, confess, decide, expose yourself entirely, and have courage to face who you are (as if sexuality were a defining – and definitive – part of who you are). While it is positive that such books increase the visibility of the homosexuality theme, it is also negative in that some of these books have a self-help tone (and intent), and focus on sexuality as being definitive.

We can observe that most of these books focus on coming out, and feature a rather stereotypical representation of adolescence as a time of confusion and looking for answers – an aspect that is also frequent in books with other subjects and young adult protagonists. On the other hand, in some of them, the protagonists tend to be almost unrealistically mature and perceptive.

As noted above, the books vary in literary quality. Three of them (*Do jeito que a gente é*, *Bem-te-vi* and *Sempre por perto*) are particularly overly didactic, while the other two (*Eu é um outro* and *Sofia e Mônica*) are complex and nuanced. It should be noted, finally, that one of the books, *Sofia e Mônica*, because of its polyphonic narrative construction and because of the fact that it does not directly address the issue of LGBTQ+ affection, implies that its narrative is focused on the identification of the rivalry of two teenage friends over a boy.

While the emergence of these titles points to a greater openness in recent years to the LGBTQ+ theme in books for young adults in Brazil, the future prospects for this area do not look promising. With the rise and strengthening of extreme right-wing political parties in Brazil – especially between the impeachment of Dilma Rousseff in 2016 and the elections of October 2018 – as well as the strengthening of politicians aligned with religious conservatism, the future does not look bright for the LGBTQ+ literature scene. The topic of the discovery of homosexuality was already treated in a timid, sometimes clichéd way, and circumscribed to a small niche of authors and publishers; in the coming years, it may be relegated to total invisibility outside the LGBTQ+ cultural circuit. But only time will tell.

References

Bernardi Jr., Hermes. 2014. *Eu é um outro* (I'm Another One). Porto Alegre: Edelbra.

Brasiliense, Leonardo. 2014. *Sofia e Mônica* (Sofia and Mônica). Porto Alegre: Edelbra.

Carrara, Sérgio. 2010. 'Políticas e direitos sexuais no Brasil contemporâneo' (Sexual Policies and Rights in Contemporary Brazil). *Revista Bagoas* 4, no. 5: 131–47. https://periodicos.ufrn.br/bagoas/issue/view/191

Carvalho, Carlos Alberto. 2012. *Jornalismo, homofobia e relações de gênero* (Journalism, Homophobia and Gender Relations). Curitiba: Editora Appris.

Correa, Sonia. 2003. 'Direitos sexuais numa perspectiva nacional e histórica' (Sexual Rights from a National and Historical Perspective). In *Direitos Sexuais e Reprodutivos como Direitos Humanos* (Reproductive and Sexual Rights as Human Rights), edited by Veriano Terto Jr., Ceres Gomes Victora and Daniela Riva Knauth, 7–16. Porto Alegre: NUPACS.

Diário de Santa Maria. 2014. 'Leonardo Brasiliense lançará *Sofia e Mônica* na Feira do Livro' (Leonardo Brasiliense to Launch *Sofia and Mônica* at the Book Fair). https://diariosm.com.br/cultura/leonardo-brasiliense-lan%C3%A7ar%C3%A1-sofia-e-m%C3%B4nica-na-feira-do-livro-1.2021813

Diniz, Debora. 2014. 'O escândalo da homofobia – imagens de vítimas e sobreviventes' (The Scandal of Homophobia – Images of Victims and Survivors). *Revista ECOPÓS* 17, no. 1, 1–19. https://revistas.ufrj.br/index.php/eco_pos/article/view/1285/pdf_15

Eribon, Didier. 2008. *Reflexões sobre a questão gay* (Réflexions sur la question gay). Translated by Procópio Abreu. Rio de Janeiro: Companhia de Freud.

Fischer, Rosa Maria Bueno. 1996. *Adolescência em discurso. Mídia e produção de subjetividades.* (Adolescence in Discourse. Media and Production of Subjectivities). Porto Alegre: FACED/UFRGS.

Galvão, Jane. 2000. *AIDS no Brasil: agenda de construção de uma epidemia* (AIDS in Brazil: An Agenda for the Construction of an Epidemic). São Paulo: Editora 34.

Green, James. 2000. *Além do carnaval: A homossexualidade masculina no Brasil do século XX* (*Beyond Carnival: Male homosexuality in Twentieth-Century Brazil*). Translated by Cristina Fino and Cássio Arantes Leite. São Paulo: UNESP.

Hall, Stuart. 1997. *Representation: Cultural Representations and Signifying Practices.* London/Thousand Oaks/New Delhi: Sage/Open University.

Larrosa, Jorge. 2010. 'Tecnologias do eu e educação'. (Technologies of the Self and Education). In *O sujeito da educação: Estudos foucaultianos* (The Subject of Education: Foucauldian Studies), edited by Tomaz Tadeu da Silva, 35–86. Rio de Janeiro: Vozes.

Leite, Márcia. 2009. *Do jeito que a gente é* (Just the Way We Are). São Paulo: Ed. Ática.

Louro, Guacira. 2004. *Um corpo estranho – ensaios sobre sexualidade e teoria queer* (A Strange Body – Essays on Sexuality and Queer Theory). Belo Horizonte: Autêntica.

Mantega, Guido. 1979. *Sexo e poder* (Sex and Power). Rio de Janeiro: Círculo do Livro.

Martins, Georgina. 2000. *O menino que brincava de ser* (The Boy who Pretended to Be). São Paulo: Difusão Cultural do Livro.

Mattos, Ruben Araújo, Veriano Terto Jr., and Richard Parker. 2001. *As estratégias do Banco Mundial e a resposta à AIDS no Brasil* (The World Bank Strategies and the AIDS Response in Brazil). Rio de Janeiro: ABIA. http://www.abiaids.org.br/_img/media/colecao%20politicas%20publicas%20N1.pdf

Paiva, Vera. 2002. 'Sem mágicas soluções: a prevenção e o cuidado em HIV/ AIDS e o processo de emancipação psicossocial' (Beyond Magical Solutions: Prevention of HIV and AIDS and the Process of 'Psychosocial Emancipation'). *Interface – Comunicação, Saúde, Educação* 6, no. 11: 25–38. http://www.scielo.br/pdf/icse/v6n11/02.pdf

Porto, Marli. 2014. *Bem-te-vi* (Great Kiskadee). São Paulo: Editora Orgástica.

Ramos, Ana Margarida. 2009. 'Saindo do armário – Literatura para a Infância e a reescrita da homossexualidade'. (Out of the Closet: Literature for Infancy and the Rewriting of Homosexuality). *Forma Breve*, no. 7. http://revistas.ua.pt/index.php/formabreve/article/view/2298/2158

Ramos, Anna Cláudia. 1999. *Sempre por perto* (Always Around). Rio de Janeiro: Ao Livro Técnico.

Reis, Tony, and Edla Eggert. 2017. 'Ideologia de gênero: uma falácia construída sobre os planos de educação brasileiros' (Gender Ideology: A Fallacy Built around the Brazilian Education Plans). *Educação e Sociedade* 38, no. 138: 9–26. http://www.scielo.br/pdf/es/v38n138/1678-4626-es-38-138-00009.pdf

Sefton, Ana Paula. 2011. 'Sexualidade para além da heterossexualidade: representações de homossexualidade na literatura infanto-juvenil'. (Sexuality Beyond Heterosexuality: Representations of Homosexuality in Children's and Young Adults' Literature). *Textura Canoas*, no. 24: 52–74. http://www.periodicos.ulbra.br/index.php/txra/article/viewFile/878/653

Silveira, Rosa Maria Hessel, Edgar Roberto Kirchof, Gladis Kaercher, Iara Tatiana Bonin Liebgott, Maria Isabel Dalla Zen, Carolina Hessel Silveira, Daniela Ripoll, and Carolina Fonseca

Richthoffen De Freitas. 2012. *A diferença na literatura infantil: narrativas e leituras.* (Difference in Children's Literature: Narratives and Readings). São Paulo: Moderna.

Silveira, Rosa Maria Hessel and Gladis E. da Silva Kaercher. 2013. 'Dois papais, duas mamães: novas famílias na literatura infantil' (Two Daddies, Two Mommies: New Families in Literature for Children). *Educação & Realidade* 38, no. 4: 1191–206. http://seer.ufrgs.br/index.php/educacaoerealidade/article/view/38164/27755

Silveira, Rosa Maria Hessel, Iara Tatiana Bonin, and Daniela Ripoll. 2013. 'Corpos velhos e doentes para crianças: uma análise de livros de literatura infantil'. (Old and Ill Bodies for Children: Analysing Children's Literature). *Nonada – Letras em Revista* 2, no. 21. http://seer.uniritter.edu.br/index.php/nonada/article/view/791/517

Vianna, Adriana, and Paula Lacerda. 2004. *Direitos e políticas sexuais no Brasil – o panorama atual* (Sexual Policies and Rights in Brazil – The Contemporary Overview). Rio de Janeiro: CEPESC.

Vianna, Cláudia Pereira. 2015. 'O movimento LGBT e as polÍticas de educação de gênero e diversidade sexual: perdas, ganhos e desafios' (The LGBT Movement and Gender and Sexual Diversity Education Policies: Losses, Gains and Challenges). *Educação e Pesquisa* 41, no. 3: 791–806. http://www.scielo.br/pdf/ep/v41n3/1517-9702-ep-1517-97022015031914.pdf

Chapter Two

WE'RE NOT HERE AND WE'RE NOT QUEER: BISEXUAL ERASURE AND STEREOTYPING IN FRENCH YOUNG ADULT FICTION

Elizabeth L. Chapman

Introduction

In this chapter, I discuss seven works of French young adult (YA) fiction featuring bisexual characters: five stand-alone novels, and two books from a series. Bisexuality is a topic that has not been addressed in extant literature on queer YA fiction written in French, and one in which, as a bi woman myself, I have a personal interest. In my analysis, I explore the epistemic construction of bisexuality within these novels; that is, the ways in which the depiction (or non-depiction) of bisexuality and bisexual characters contributes to a supposed body of 'knowledge' about bisexuality, both within and beyond the novels. I identify a number of themes in the corpus, namely: bisexuality as a 'problem'; bisexual erasure; stereotypes and the 'bisexual plot'; and bisexual people as 'normal' and straight-passing.

When I began conducting preliminary research for this chapter, it quickly became apparent that very few French-language YA novels with bisexual characters were available. Many of the limited number of titles included in bibliographies and booklists were translations from English,[1] and one blogger noted that bisexuality is still 'appallingly neglected'[2] in YA literature (Gabriel 2018, n.p.). The advantage, from a research perspective, of this otherwise disappointing situation was that it gave me a defined corpus to work with.[3] For this chapter, I have chosen to focus on YA novels originally written in

---

1 Bisexual characters have until recently been conspicuous by their absence in English-language YA fiction as well (Epstein 2013, 2014; Kneen 2015). However, Jenkins and Cart (2018) note a recent increase in novels with bisexual content, although the number is still very small in absolute terms.

2 'désespérément oubliée'. All translations are my own unless otherwise noted.

3 I cannot claim that my search and resultant list were exhaustive; for example, I did not contact French publishers to ask whether their lists included any YA novels with bisexual characters. However, I hope that I have included the majority of the novels that fit my criteria. A full list of sources consulted is available in Appendix 2.

French and published in France during the second decade of the twenty-first century. Epstein (2013, 238) suggests that LGBTQ+ books for children and young people tend to reflect the legal and social realities of the countries they are written in, and I was thus interested in looking at more recently published books, as France has seen substantive legal changes affecting LGBTQ+ people over the past two decades (discussed further below). Picture books, middle-grade works or graphic novels might well portray bisexuality differently from YA novels, while texts written and published in other Francophone countries (such as Canada) would have a different social, cultural and legal context. Thus, my corpus comprises the following works, in chronological order: *Un garçon comme une autre* (A Boy Like Any Other Girl) by Joël Breurec (2013); *Dysfonctionnelle* (Dysfunctional) by Axl Cendres (2015); *À ma source gardée* (At My Secret Spring) by Madeline Roth (2015); *Sauveur & fils: Saisons 1 & 2* (Saviour & Son: Seasons 1 & 2) by Marie-Aude Murail (both originally published 2016);[4] *J'ai avalé un arc-en-ciel* (I Swallowed a Rainbow) by Erwan Ji (2017); and *Georges, le monde et moi* (Georges, the World and Me) by Illana Cantin (2018).

In this chapter, I follow the definition of bisexuality used by Robyn Ochs and other bi activists and academics. Ochs writes, 'I call myself bisexual because I acknowledge that I have in myself the potential to be attracted – romantically and/or sexually – to people of more than one gender, not necessarily at the same time, in the same way, or to the same degree' (2016, n.p.). In other words, bisexuality does not presuppose a binary definition of gender. Where I use phrases such as 'both genders' or 'the opposite gender', this is in order to reflect the language used in the text under discussion.

Bisexuality, like other queer sexualities, has been theorized in terms of a number of different dimensions: identity, behaviour and attractions (Meyer and Wilson 2009). While I believe it is important to respect the ways in which people self-identify, this can be limiting for research on bisexuality, as many people experience attraction to more than one gender, or engage in sexual or romantic relationships with people of more than one gender, without necessarily choosing to identify using the term 'bisexual' (Barker et al. 2012; OECD 2019). For the purposes of this chapter, I consider bisexuality in terms of attractions and behaviour as well as identity. I also use the term in an inclusive sense, as an umbrella term that brings together other non-monosexual identities (Eisner 2013). However, in practice there is little mention of other non-monosexual identities in the corpus.

In the sections that follow, I begin by giving an overview of the legal and social context for bisexual people in France, followed by a brief summary of extant scholarly work on queer YA literature in France. I then explore the four main themes identified above, concluding that bisexuality is simultaneously erased and reified as problematic within the corpus.

4 It was difficult to find information online as to which volumes in the series included bisexual characters. I have subsequently discovered that volume 3 also includes a bisexual character, but it was not published in the affordable *livre de poche* format (broadly equivalent to paperback) until July 2020, too late to be included in this chapter.

The Social and Legislative Context in France

Accurate statistics on the number of LGBTQ+ people in general are notoriously difficult to come by (Chapman 2015), and Trachman and Lejbowicz observe that bisexuality is particularly difficult to capture in surveys due to its relative invisibility (2018). A large French survey, carried out in 2015, found that 0.8 per cent of respondents self-defined as bisexual, but a higher proportion reported sexual practices with 'both' sexes (1.9 per cent) and even more reported attraction to 'both' sexes (2.7 per cent) (Trachman and Lejbowicz 2018). Meanwhile, an online survey by the French opinion poll company IFOP found that 9.3 per cent of respondents reported some degree of attraction to 'both' sexes, with 4.8 per cent actually identifying as bisexual (IFOP 2019b). Writing in the UK context, Barker et al. suggest that the number of people who have ever had an attraction to one more than one gender 'may be a significant minority, or even majority, of the population' (2012, 13).

Attitudes towards LGBTQ+ people in France are generally positive, with 85 per cent of heterosexual cisgender respondents to a 2019 IFOP survey agreeing that homosexuality is as valid a sexual orientation as any other.[5] A somewhat lower proportion (72 per cent) said they would accept their own child being gay. Meanwhile, 85 per cent of LGBTQ+ respondents said they felt very or fairly well integrated into French society (IFOP 2019b).

Despite this, in another survey also by IFOP, 55 per cent of LGBTQ+ people said they had experienced LGBT-phobic harassment during their lifetime, 31 per cent over the past 10 years, and 17 per cent during the past year. Bisexual people appeared to be experiencing rising levels of LGBTphobia, with particularly high levels of harassment reported by both lesbian and bisexual women over the previous year (IFOP 2019a). A recent report by SOS Homophobie, an LGBTQ+ organization, observed an alarming increase in the number of hate crimes reported to the organization in 2019 (up 26 per cent to 2,396), although it notes that this may be in part because more people feel able to report such incidents. Four hundred and eighty-five cases were reported by bisexual people, of whom under-18s constituted the largest age group (23 per cent). In a section focusing specifically on biphobia, the report notes the lack of visibility of bisexual identities, and the persistence of stereotypes such as the unfaithful, over-sexed bisexual (SOS Homophobie 2020, 41).

The legislative environment in France has become steadily more supportive of LGBTQ+ people over the first two decades of the twentieth century. Article 225-1 of the French Criminal Code was amended in 2001 to prohibit discrimination on grounds of sexual orientation,[6] and additional legislation prohibiting homophobic insults, defamation

---

5 'une manière comme une autre de vivre sa sexualité'.

6 Code pénal – Article 225-1. Version en vigueur du 17 novembre 2001 au 5 mars 2002. Modifié par Loi n° 2001-1066 du 16 novembre 2001 - art. 1 JORF 17 novembre 2001. Accessed 2 July 2020. https://www.legifrance.gouv.fr/affichCodeArticle.do;jsessionid=44BFA4C641830EE6CA52FAC2AC808990.tplgfr23s_1?idArticle=LEGIARTI000006417829&cidTexte=LEGITEXT000006070719&categorieLien=id&dateTexte=20020304.

and violence was passed in December 2004.[7] Transgender identity was added to the Criminal Code as a protected characteristic in 2012 (Chopin et al. 2018, 37), and a bill permitting trans people to legally change their gender without requiring surgery or sterilization was passed in November 2016.[8] However, rather than being able to self-identify, trans people must still demonstrate to a judge that they have met certain criteria in order to legally change to their true gender (Inter-LGBT 2016).

The PACS (*pacte civil de solidarité*, broadly equivalent to a civil partnership) was introduced in France in 1999 (INSEE 2019); however, same-sex couples did not have marriage or adoption rights until 2013.[9] At the time of writing in July 2020, same-sex female couples do not yet have access to assisted reproductive technology (ART), although a draft law opening up ART to same-sex female couples and single women has been approved by both the National Assembly and the Senate, and only remains to be signed into law by the President.[10] However, surrogacy will continue to be prohibited under the new law (Vie Publique 2020).

In regard to literature specifically, the French publishing world is governed by the 1949 *Loi sur les publications destinée à la jeunesse* (Law on Publications Aimed at Young People). Until 2011, the law prohibited the publication of any content in works for young people that promoted any of a list of supposed moral failings, including 'debauchery or any act classified as a crime or misdemeanour or of such nature as to negatively impact the morals of children or young people'.[11] In the 1980s and 1990s, the law was used by 'family values' organizations and the *Front National* in support of censorship campaigns targeting books with gay content (deliberately conflated with paedophilia) as well as an eye-opening range of other materials, including books relating to Jewish culture or featuring black children (Lominé 2006; Soulé 1999). In 2011 (two years prior to the publication of the oldest book in my corpus), the law was modified, and now prohibits, among other things:

> any content that is dangerous to young people due to its pornographic nature or because it is likely to encourage discrimination or hatred towards a specific person or a group of people [...] or any act classified as a crime or misdemeanour or of such nature as to harm the physical, mental or moral development of children or young people.[12]

---

7 Loi n° 2004-1486 du 30 décembre 2004. Accessed 2 July 2020. https://www.legifrance.gouv.fr/eli/loi/2004/12/30/SOCX0400130L/jo/texte.

8 Loi n° 2016-1547 du 18 novembre 2016. Accessed 20 May 2020. https://www.legifrance.gouv.fr/affichTexte.do?cidTexte=JORFTEXT000033418805&categorieLien=id.

9 Loi n° 2013-404 du 17 mai 2013. Accessed 20 May 2020. https://www.legifrance.gouv.fr/affichTexte.do?cidTexte=JORFTEXT000027414540&dateTexte=&categorieLien=id.

10 Projet de loi n° 2187 relatif à la bioéthique. Accessed 2 July 2020. http://www.assemblee-nationale.fr/dyn/15/textes/l15b2187_projet-loi#.

11 'la débauche ou tous actes qualifiés crimes ou délits ou de nature à démoraliser l'enfance ou la jeunesse'. Loi n° 49-956 du 16 juillet 1949. Version initiale. Accessed 15 July 2020. https://www.legifrance.gouv.fr/affichTexte.do?cidTexte=JORFTEXT000000878175&categorieLien=id

12 'aucun contenu présentant un danger pour la jeunesse en raison de son caractère pornographique ou lorsqu'il est susceptible d'inciter à la discrimination ou à la haine contre

This still seems rather broad and subjective, and thus open to misuse for purposes of censorship.

Queer YA Fiction in France

Although there is no space in this chapter for a long discussion of extant literature on this topic, a few points merit a mention. The first relates to the dearth, until relatively recently, of YA literature with any LGBTQ+ content, never mind bisexuality specifically. Lagabrielle (2007, 16) states that the first French novel for young people with homosexuality as a central theme was published in 1989, with a further 11 published over the next decade, and 18 between 2000 and 2003 (a sharp uptick, but still a very low number in absolute terms). He relates the late appearance of the first novel on the topic, and the continued lack of publications, to the impact of the 1949 *Loi sur les publications destinée à la jeunesse*, discussed above (Lagabrielle 2007, 19). Publishers have acknowledged that they have been cautious (or, in other words, have self-censored) due to this law, and to the fear of a backlash from parents, who are potential buyers (Chaimbault 2002; Soulé 1999).

The dearth of primary texts is mirrored by a lack of scholarly literature on the topic.[13] Small bodies of work on French-language LGBTQ+ YA fiction exist in the European context (Behoteguy 2013; Butstraen 2019; Chaimbault 2002; Clermont 2011; Lagabrielle 2007; Lominé 2006) and the Québécois context (Champagne 2012, 2018; Dénommé-Baudoin 2003; Dufresne 2011; Esposito 1996; Noël-Gaudreault and de Launay 2013). However, as reflected in the use of the term 'homosexualité(s)' in the titles of the vast majority of these works, bisexuality is conspicuous by its absence. Even in the rare cases where bisexual characters are mentioned, they are conflated with gay characters in the analysis (for example, Dénommé-Baudoin subsumes the three bisexual characters in the corpus under the category of 'boys or men who are "obviously" homosexual' (2003, 55)).[14]

'All These Situations in a Single Story': The 'Problem Novel'

LGBTQ+ YA fiction written in English has historically often taken the form of the 'problem novel', with sexuality or gender identity forming the central issue with which the protagonist must struggle throughout the book. In the early days, gay characters (there were fewer lesbian characters, and bi and trans characters were conspicuous by their absence at this stage) led tragic lives, facing isolation and abuse, and frequently

---

une personne déterminée ou un groupe de personnes [...] ou à tous actes qualifiés de crimes ou de délits ou de nature à nuire à l'épanouissement physique, mental ou moral de l'enfance ou la jeunesse'. Loi n° 49-956 du 16 juillet 1949. Accessed 15 July 2020. https://www.legifrance.gouv.fr/affichTexte.do?cidTexte=JORFTEXT000000878175&dateTexte=20200715

13 I acknowledge that it is possible there may be other publications that I have missed, not least due to the English-language bias of the main databases and search engines available to me in the UK.

14 'des garçons ou des hommes « clairement » homosexuels'.

dying at the end of the novel (Bosman and Bradford 2008; Cart and Jenkins 2006). Even as storylines shifted away from tragedy, and from the idea of homosexuality as inherently problematic in itself, novels still tended to focus on a young person's struggle to come out, with Cart and Jenkins commenting as recently as 2006 that coming-out books continued to account for the lion's share of the literature. Epstein, examining books published up to 2009, found that bisexual characters in particular were 'not always described positively, nor are they shown living happy bisexual lives' (2014, 119). However, over the second decade of the twentieth century, there has been a notable increase in the number of titles in which a queer character's sexuality or gender identity – while still important – does not form the central issue of the novel. For example, there has been an increase in queer YA genre fiction, in which the story tends to focus on something other than the sexuality or gender identity of the character (Jenkins and Cart 2018; Lo 2019).

Scholars of French-language queer YA fiction note a similar pattern, with a shift from novels that depict homosexuality as tragic, to those that offer the possibility of happy endings for gay characters (Chaimbault 2002).[15] Nonetheless, even more recent publications note a continued heavy focus on the trials and tribulations faced by gay characters in everyday life before they reach their happy ending. The majority of the novels discussed by all the scholars focus on a character's realization that they are gay, and their (usually long and painful) journey towards acceptance of this fact, sometimes including coming out to others (Behoteguy 2013; Butstraen 2019; Chaimbault 2002; Champagne 2012, 2018; Dénommé-Baudoin 2003; Lagabrielle 2007; Lominé 2006). Dufresne notes that, whatever a character's background or personal situation, they generally experience 'intimidation, rejection, vilification, isolation and homophobic violence, both verbal and physical' and sometimes 'all these situations in a single story' (2011, 18).[16] Interestingly, nearly all of the authors cited above seem to accept or even welcome the depiction of all these internal and external troubles as a realistic depiction of what a gay life is inevitably like.

I was interested to investigate whether these trends held true for bisexual characters, particularly in view of the fact that the novels in my corpus were all written in the second decade of the twenty-first century, at a time when English-language LGBTQ+ YA fiction has (to some extent) branched out into more varied storylines and the legal situation in France has become more supportive of LGBTQ+ people. In fact, two of the novels have very traditional coming-out storylines. Both *Georges, le monde et moi* and *J'ai avalé un arc-en-ciel* focus primarily on the main character's gradual, long-drawn-out realization that they are attracted to someone of the same sex, and the struggle to process what this means for their sexual identity. Both protagonists remain in a state of denial for a large portion of the book, continuing to resist the possibility even after a kiss with their same-sex crush

15 Chaimbault's corpus includes novels translated into French from other languages, including several originally published in English. It is thus perhaps unsurprising that he has observed the same trend as in the US and UK.

16 'l'intimidation, du rejet, du dénigrement, de l'isolement et de la violence homophobe, tant verbale que physique [...] toutes ces situations dans une même histoire'.

has evoked unexpected feelings (Cantin 2018, 92; Ji 2017, 193). Priam, the protagonist of *Georges*, eventually acknowledges his attraction to Georges on page 129 (of 314) but the problems are far from being over: he continues to be afraid of other people finding out for another 50+ pages, with some justification, as his supposed best friend Eliott reacts to the news with active homophobia (Cantin 2018, 180–82). He struggles with the physical side of his relationship with Georges; he suffers from panic attacks; he continues to face homophobic abuse; and in a rather out-of-character development, Georges runs away, having concluded that 'you'd be better off without me in your life' (238).[17] However, the novel does have a happy ending: Georges and Priam get back together and make love for the first time, with Priam's enthusiastic consent; Eliott is convinced of the error of his ways; and with the help of a therapist, Priam learns to manage his anxiety. However, despite this happy outcome, the book certainly merits the descriptor 'problem novel', with the lion's share of the text devoted to a series of problems, many of them relating to Priam's sexuality. Towards the end of the novel, Priam observes, 'I had about five low points during the year and about eight hundred high points' (297).[18] Unfortunately, the structure and content of the novel do not reflect this.

Arc-en-ciel (Ji 2017) follows a similar structure, with protagonist Capucine not acknowledging her same-sex attraction until page 215 (of 384). As in *Georges*, the problems are only just beginning, with Capucine's lesbian love interest Aiden initially treating her declaration of love as a straight girl's curiosity (e.g. 237). Just as they finally start dating, Capucine's ex unexpectedly returns to the city and she finds herself torn between the two of them (discussed further in the 'Stereotypes' section, below). Like Priam, Capucine is afraid of other people finding out, and also like Priam, she has some cause for this: her sexuality opens her up to blackmail (313) and her best friend is, again, actively homophobic (337). As in *Georges*, the ending is happy, with Aiden and Capucine planning a future together, but once again, so little space is devoted to this that the overriding impression is one of a long struggle.

A ma source gardée is a problem novel of a different type. It is told from the point of view of Jeanne, a straight girl who falls in love with a bisexual boy, Lucas, while on holiday in her grandma's village. They become friends and then lovers, having sex on repeated occasions, apparently tenderly and lovingly – although we have only Jeanne's word for this – but always in secret. Jeanne becomes pregnant with his baby (Roth 2015, 45). However, on returning to the village unexpectedly at the end of one summer, Jeanne sees Lucas kissing another boy, Tom, and becomes distraught: she cuts her wrist (28), seemingly with the deliberate intention of making him feel guilty (31), and subsequently aborts the foetus (56). The book dwells emotively and at length on the terrible emotional impact that this betrayal has had on Jeanne, even a year later, and, she hints darkly, potentially for the rest of her life. The reader is left with the impression that falling in love with a bisexual person is a dreadful mistake that will potentially ruin one's life.

17 'si je sortais de ta vie, tu irais mieux'.

18 'Approximativement, j'avais eu cinq bas dans l'année contre environ huit cent hauts'.

The *Sauveur et fils* series does not follow the traditional 'problem novel' format: the main character is a psychotherapist, and the novel is structured around his recurring weekly appointments with certain regular clients, with an ongoing overarching story arc dealing with his family life. Two of the clients are (arguably) bisexual: Blandine, whose possible bisexuality is touched on only very briefly in passing, and Alex, who attends with her new girlfriend Charlie, her male ex-partner and her children from that previous relationship, to discuss the issues raised by her leaving her partner for a woman. As the novel is about a psychotherapist, it follows that Sauveur's clients are attending the sessions due to some (perceived) problem, regardless of whether they are straight, gay or bisexual.[19] However, in the case of Alex, her bisexuality does seem to be positioned as the 'cause' of the problem, breaking up the family and leading to disagreements with her two elder daughters, who are actively homophobic towards Charlie (Murail 2018, 163, 310).

Un garçon comme une autre (Breurec 2013) is the only novel in the corpus that moves away from portraying bisexuality through a 'problem' lens. It is true that Ewen and his main love interest, Mathis, do face some challenges in the course of the novel, primarily as a result of other people's bigotry. Mathis' parents are very angry when they learn that his sister has seen him kissing Ewen; he is banned from seeing Ewen (36) and his father threatens Ewen with physical violence (31). Later in the book, Yves (Mathis' grandfather and the caretaker of Ewen's family's holiday home) sees Ewen engaged in a fondling session with a girl and hurls abuse at him:

> 'I'll tell your mother! Boys aren't enough for you, eh? [...] You're sex-mad, aren't you? Little slut! [...] You're a proper little pervert ... You molested my grandson! Faggot!' (53)[20]

Despite this, Ewen and Mathis both remain clear throughout that their relationship was unequivocally a good thing. Although the anger they face from others is upsetting (and a practical annoyance, in that it prevents them from seeing one another), neither boy gives any indication that it has affected their own sense of self. Mathis writes Ewen a love letter in which he expresses his disdain for the judgements of others, and his gratitude to Ewen for their experiences together:

> We had a great time on holiday, and everything we did was good. I think of you often. [...] These holidays were the best. It sucked that it ended badly. Luckily we had the nights. [...] [My parents] had a proper go at me, so did my sister, so did my granddad. I don't care. And I want to say thank you, thank you, thank you, thank you ...

---

19 Sauveur also has a client who appears to be a trans boy, although this subplot is unfortunately not handled well. Elliot is deadnamed and referred to by female pronouns throughout by the narrative voice, and in book 2, Sauveur himself returns to addressing him by his female name, as he feels it is counter-productive to enter into Elliot's 'fantasy' (fantasme; 157, 200). Elliot's identity is also pathologized through a suggestion that it may be 'caused' by his parents' previous loss of a son, who was to have been called Elliot (book 1, 143, 208).

20 '– Toi, je vais le dire à ta mère! Les garçons, ça te suffit pas… […] Tu as ça dans la peau, hein? Petite salope! […] Toi, tu es un drôle de vicieux … Tu t'en es pris à mon petit-fils! Pédale!'

> I miss you
> Mathis
> I <3 U (Breurec 2013, 57)[21]

Mathis' own perspective on the situation thus sheds a very different light from that of his grandfather. The language used by the first-person narrative voice to describe the boys' relationship similarly forms a stark contrast to the vulgar abuse hurled by Yves, being often rather poetic:

> In fact, we had both been led on by a golden current, a breath of light, such that he had never known. (Breurec 2013, 54)[22]

The novel thus underlines, through its form as well as its content, that the boys' relationship is something beautiful, rather than something disgusting or illicit. Ewen himself does not see his sexuality as a problem: this novel contains none of the endless soul-searching that characterizes *Georges* or *Arc-en-ciel*. He is open about his sexuality with himself and the reader from the start, and although he is wary about telling some people (e.g. 23–25, 41, 43), the response from those close to him is, in the event, almost entirely positive. His mother is supportive (32); his sister and best friend each experience a brief moment of confusion, but are then accepting, reaffirming how important Ewen is to them (29, 45–46). The novel is a coming-out story in that it is a journey of self-discovery, but it is not an anguished process.

'The Elephant in the Room': Bisexual Erasure

Much has been written about bisexual invisibility and bisexual erasure, with the latter term referring to the processes by which bisexuality is made invisible within society (see *inter alia* Barker et al. 2012; MacDowall 2009; McLean 2018; Yoshino 2000). This is reflected in the small number of French-language YA novels that contain bisexual characters (cf. the discussion of the corpus, above). While all the novels discussed in this chapter contain characters who are attracted to more than one gender, they differ in the extent to which bisexuality is recognized as a valid orientation, and indeed in whether the word 'bisexual' is even used.

21 'On a passé de bonnes vacances, tout ce qu'on a fait, c'était bien. Je pense à toi souvent. […] Ces vacances, c'était les meilleures. Ça s'est mal terminé, c'est trop con. Heureusement il y avait le soir. […] [Mes parents] m'ont vraiment cassé, et ma sœur, et mon grand-père. Je m'en fous. Et je te dis merci, merci, merci, merci …

> Tu me manques
> Mathis
> Je t'm!'

22 'Alors que nous avons été entraînés tous les deux par un courant d'or, un souffle de lumière que lui n'a jamais connu.'

Priam in *Georges* is repeatedly faced with incorrect assumptions on the part of various people – including his close friends – who leap to the conclusion that because he is attracted to Georges, he must be gay (Cantin 2018, 157, 180, 225). This is a realistic representation that reflects the real-life experiences of many bisexual people (see, for example, Eisner 2013, 68). However, Priam's older sister explicitly tells him – and thus the reader – that other labels are available:

> 'God, Priam. I'm not asking you whether you're gay, I'm asking whether you think you might be attracted to boys. [...] "Gay" isn't the only other option apart from straight,' replied my sister with a huge sigh, speaking very slowly and clearly, as if I were a bit soft in the head. 'Priam, you might be bi, you might be pansexual. Maybe you like girls as well as Georges. All of those things are possible.' (Cantin 2018, 110–11)[23]

This is the only one of the books to even mention the word pansexual.[24] Meanwhile, two other books use the term bisexual, but in contexts that undermine the concept of bisexuality as a valid sexual identity. In *Dysfonctionnelle*, a friend of the lesbian protagonist Fifi evokes the idea of bisexuality as a trend (cf. Feinstein et al. 2019):

> 'Haven't you seen how the girls look at you? Wake up, bisexuality is trendy, all the girls are "bi" at the moment! Make the most of it: who knows, in ten years' time everyone will be into dwarfs!' (Cendres 2015, 245)[25]

The character who is speaking here is portrayed quite clearly as a negative influence on Fifi, as can be inferred from his ableist and fetishizing reference to dwarfs. Thus, his opinions are not necessarily representative of the authorial voice or the book as a whole. However, the term 'bisexual' occurs only in this quotation, and is never used of Fifi's long-term partner Sarah, despite the fact that Sarah is portrayed throughout the book as attracted to (and involved with) people of different genders. The closest we get to an acknowledgement of her bisexuality is when she says to Fifi: 'I don't think one falls in love with a boy or a girl, but with a person.' (139)[26]

A similar pattern recurs in *Sauveur*. The term 'bisexual' is used once, when one of Sauveur's patients says rather dismissively of her younger sister, the 11-year-old Blandine, that '[she] thinks she is bisexual since she started reading manga' (Murail 2018, 19).[27]

23 'Bordel, Priam. Je ne te demande pas si tu es gay, je te demande si tu penses pouvoir être attiré par des gars. [...] « Gay » n'est pas la seule sexualité qui existe à côté d'hétéro, m'a répondu ma sœur avec un gros soupir, en articulant bien les mots, comme si j'étais un peu ramolli du bulbe. Priam, tu es peut-être bi, peut-être pansexuel. Peut-être que tu aimes les filles, mais aussi Georges. Tout ça, c'est possible.'

24 People who are attracted to people of all genders, or to multiple genders (Eisner 2013).

25 'T'as pas vu comment les filles te regardent?! Réveille-toi, c'est la mode des bisexuelles, elles sont toutes "bi" en ce moment! Faut que t'en profites: si ça se trouve, dans dix ans ce s'ra la mode des nains!'

26 'Je pense qu'on ne tombe pas amoureux d'un garçon ou d'une fille, mais d'une personne.'

27 '[elle] se croit bisexuelle depuis qu'elle lit des mangas'.

Blandine later explains to Sauveur that she and her friends plan to marry each other in later life as they dislike boys; however, Sauveur suggests that Blandine may well change her mind (117), evoking the common stereotype of bisexuality as just a phase (Bostwick and Hequembourg 2014; Callis 2013; Feinstein et al. 2019). Blandine's character is not really developed until book 2 in the series, and her bisexuality is never[28] confirmed (or denied). Meanwhile, the character Alex, who could easily be read as bisexual, is never described as such. She spent 18 years with a male partner, has three children with him, and 'thought' she was in love with him, before leaving him because she fell in love with a woman (Murail 2018, 63–64, 269). She also notes that she was previously always attracted to men (272). Despite this, the word 'bisexual' is never used of her, and in book 2 she is explicitly described as 'a homosexual parent' (Murail 2019, 63) and a 'lesbian' (183).[29] She also appears less in book 2, with her lesbian partner often attending sessions without her and discussing her in her absence; her voice is thus silenced, as well as her bisexuality being erased.

Neither Ewen in *Un garçon* nor Lucas in *Source* is described as bisexual; however, labels are not used for any of the other characters either. Instead, they are described in terms of who they are attracted to. However, the two books differ significantly in the extent to which bisexuality and other queer sexualities are made visible. Lucas in *Source* appears to be behaviourally bisexual: he has sex with Jeanne, the straight female narrator, several times prior to his public kiss with Tom, but we learn virtually nothing about his feelings towards either of them. Near the end of the novella, he attempts to defend himself, explaining – in his only instance of direct speech – that it is difficult for him too, but this is rubbished by Jeanne:

> 'It's not just you that it's difficult for, I can tell you.'
>
> I yelled, 'Don't you give a fuck about me? No, but seriously, Lucas, don't you? No, tell me, I don't know, because it didn't look like you were finding it particularly difficult kissing Tom last night, were you? How long have you been kissing him for? Tell me.' 'Jeanne. Stop. Let me speak. I haven't had chance to say anything yet. Sit down.' (Roth 2015, 50–51)[30]

We then skip forward eight months to the following April and the reader never learns what Lucas may or may not have had to say. Quite apart from the common stereotypes of bisexual infidelity, and being torn between a man and a woman – which are discussed further below – this book has little to offer queer readers who wish to see themselves in literature. Lucas is less a fully-fledged character than a beautiful, unfaithful enigma.

---

28 Thus far in the series.

29 'un parent homosexuel' / 'lesbienne'.

30 '« Y a pas que pour toi que c'est difficile, je te le promets. »

J'ai crié:

> « Tu te fous de moi? Non mais Lucas, vraiment, tu te fous de moi? Non, dis-moi, je sais pas, parce que ça m'a pas paru particulièrement difficile, pour toi, hier soir, d'embrasser Tom, non, c'était difficile? Depuis quand, tu l'embrasses? Dis-moi. – Jeanne. Arrête. Laisse-moi parler. J'ai rien eu le temps de dire encore. Assieds-toi. »'

The secondary characters in this novella are little more than wallpaper for the personal tragedy of the straight female narrator who is betrayed by her (presumably) bisexual lover. However, we are given a brief potted history of the straight characters' love lives, but learn little about Tom:

> Baptiste went out for two years with a little bitch, as Chloé described her, and the girls went out with a series of boys while they waited for their princes to come. Tom didn't have a lot going on [in his love life]. (25)[31]

A queer reading of this may infer that Tom is gay and not interested in girls, but we learn no more about his orientation beyond the fact that he kisses Lucas. The erasure of bisexuality in this book thus extends to all non-straight sexualities.

In contrast, bisexuality and other queer sexualities in *Un garçon* are discussed explicitly and openly, even though labels such as 'gay' or 'bisexual' are not used. Ewen's attraction to both boys and girls is placed front and centre and is impossible to overlook.[32] Near the start of the book, he observes, 'I realised that I was attracted to boys just as much as to girls, or even more' (Breurec 2013, 6).[33] This reflects the argument, frequently made by bisexual activists, that one does not need to have 50:50 attraction to men and women in order to 'qualify' as 'bisexual enough' (Ochs 2016). He is very clear and untroubled about the fact that it is perfectly possible to like both boys and girls (Breurec 2013, 26)[34] and his actions and remarks throughout the course of the novel testify to the fact that he has a high level of sexual interest in both. In addition to his sexual relationship with Mathis, which begins when they lose their virginity to one another on page 23, he has a couple of sexual interactions with the beautiful, large-breasted Raphaëlle, stopping short of penetrative sex only because they do not have a condom (34–35, 67). Both boys and girls form the subject of his masturbatory fantasies (11, 25–26, 48, 70, 103) and he constantly comments on the physical attractions of both boys and girls:

> On the main beach, I noticed several other attractive specimens, both boys and girls. Particularly a short dark-haired boy in turquoise bathing trunks. And a blonde girl with curves … to die for. (Breurec 2013, 12)[35]

Thus, although the term 'bisexual' is not used, this novel foregrounds bisexuality more than any other in the corpus, through what Kneen refers to as 'a recognition of the embodied plural sexual desires of bisexual characters' (2015, 361).

---

31 'Baptiste était sorti pendant presque deux ans avec une petite connasse, comme disait Chloé, et les filles enchaînaient un peu les mecs en attendant leur prince. Tom pas grand-chose.'

32 Ewen's love interest Mathis is similarly described in terms of who he is attracted to, rather than using a label. 'I'm just not interested in girls.' ('Les filles, ça ne m'intéresse pas.') (33)

33 'J'ai eu la confirmation que les garçons m'attiraient autant que les filles, et même plus.'

34 'Aimer les garçons et les filles, ça se peut.'

35 'Sur la grande plage, j'ai remarqué d'autres jolis spécimens, filles et garçons. Notamment un petit brun avec un slip bleu turquoise. Et une blonde aux courbes … d'enfer.'

In contrast, the most egregious example of bisexual erasure is Capucine in *Arc-en-ciel*. Like Sarah in *Dysfonctionnelle*, Capucine has historically been interested in boys, has had sex with a boy (Ji 2017, 163) and continues to be attracted to boys despite her growing attraction to Aiden, who is female. Throughout the novel, she appears to be baffled by this, and the implications for whether she is gay or straight – the only options considered.

> I wonder if I'm gay. The idea terrifies me. But I don't think I'd be having erotic dreams about JM if I were gay. [...] It would be simpler if you could diagnose it with a test. You go to the pharmacy, you say you want to know if you're gay, and they give you a thing to wee on. If it's blue you like boys, if it's rainbow you like girls. (Ji 2017, 214)[36]

On more than one occasion she explains that she is not gay, she is simply in love with one girl, Aiden. 'I'm neither heterosexual nor homosexual, I'm Aidensexual.'[37] (361; see also p. 313). At one point, one of Capucine's friends describes the rumour that she is a lesbian as 'the elephant in the room' (311, in English in original). However, bisexuality is the real elephant in the room here, and it continues to be stubbornly ignored throughout the entirety of the novel.

Thus, bisexuality is erased within the corpus through the small number of bisexual characters, the failure to use the word 'bisexual' to identify them, and the reluctance on the part of the characters themselves (including behaviourally bisexual characters) to recognize bisexuality as a valid identity. This mirrors the situation in much English-language queer YA fiction, where there are still relatively few YA novels featuring major bisexual characters (Epstein 2014; Kneen 2015; Jenkins and Cart 2018). Epstein (2014), Coletta (2018) and Jenkins and Cart (2018) all identify a number of books in which the word 'bisexuality' seems to be studiously avoided; Epstein notes that euphemisms such as 'maybes' or 'both' are sometimes used instead (2014: 120–21). Moreover, she concludes that in many cases, 'bisexuality is not portrayed as an acceptable identity' even in the eyes of the characters themselves (121).

In real life, I believe it is very important to respect each individual's right to self-identify using whatever label (or lack thereof) they feel is most appropriate. It is also well documented that some people experience their sexuality as fluid, and may as a result change the way they self-describe throughout their lives (Fahs and Koerth 2018). Nonetheless, in a fictional context, in which characters' identities are the result of authorial choices, it remains significant if the word 'bisexual' is not used for characters whose behaviours and attractions would appear to merit it. Coletta (2018) argues that clearly identifying characters as bisexual is key to effective bisexual representation, and draws on social media posts to illustrate that there is a high demand among young

36 'Je me demande si je suis *gay*. Ça me fait super peur. Mais je ne crois pas que si j'étais *gay*, je ferais des rêves érotiques sur JM. [...] Ce serait plus pratique s'il y avait un test de dépistage. Vous allez à la pharmacie, vous dites que vous voulez savoir si vous êtes *gay*, et ils vous donnent un truc où il faut faire pipi dessus. Bleu vous aimez les garçons, arc-en-ciel vous aimez les filles.' (italics in original)

37 'Je ne suis ni hétérosexuelle ni homosexuelle, je suis Aidensexuelle.'

readers for books that explicitly name bisexuality. By omitting and/or diminishing the term 'bisexual', the texts in the corpus erase bisexual identity, rendering it less available to young people who might otherwise recognize themselves in it.

'She Was Afraid I Would Flake Out On Her': Stereotypes and the 'Bisexual Plot'

There has been substantial research on stereotypes of bisexual people (see Dyar and Feinstein 2018 for an overview). Garber (1995) identifies four characteristics of what she terms the 'bisexual plot' in film and literature: the idea that it is just a 'phase'; the trope of 'confusion'; rivalry between a man and a woman for the affection of a third party, who is interested in both; and a relationship with a couple ('having it all'). Bringing these four themes together, she concludes that, 'The bisexual plot, as I conceive it, is a mode of erotic triangulation in which one person is torn between life with a man and life with a woman' (456). As bisexual people thus supposedly cannot be satisfied with a monogamous relationship, another common stereotype is the idea that they (we) are inherently untrustworthy and likely to be sexually unfaithful (Dyar and Feinstein 2018; Eisner 2013).

Despite the fact that around two decades have passed between the publication of Garber's research and that of the majority of books studied here, these stereotypes persist. Two inter-related stereotypes were especially prevalent in the corpus: the trope of 'confusion' (Dyar and Feinstein 2018; Feinstein et al. 2019), and the theme of bisexual promiscuity and infidelity – particularly with someone of the 'opposite' gender to the bisexual character's primary partner.

As discussed above, in the 'Problem Novel' section, two characters in particular take a very long time to come to terms with their bisexuality: Priam in *Georges*, and Capucine in *Arc-en-ciel*. The situation is depicted as baffling, distressing and confusing to them, as well as frustrating to their gay/lesbian love interests, who are strung along for quite some time while they make their minds up. However, a key difference between Priam and Capucine is that the former does not give any indication that he is tempted by the prospect of a sexual or romantic relationship with a girl, instead of or as well as with Georges. At the start of the book he is attracted to his friend Gabrielle, but as she is not interested in him, this possibility is rapidly closed down.[38]

Capucine, in contrast, has a very predictable 'bisexual plot'. When she finally confesses that she thinks she is in love with Aiden, Aiden initially reacts by treating her as if she is a curious straight girl who wants to experiment (Ji 2017, 237).[39] Even after they have resolved their argument and Aiden has apologized, she remains wary of embarking on a relationship with Capucine, because, 'she was afraid I would flake out on her' (250).[40]

---

38 However, *Georges* does include a brief mention of a potentially bisexual character who does indeed fit the 'untrustworthy' stereotype. The two boys initially meet when Georges climbs through Priam's bedroom window to escape from an angry girl whose boyfriend cheated on her with Georges (14). Neither the girl nor the boyfriend is mentioned again.

39 '« Tu es curieuse. Je comprends que tu aies envie d'essayer des trucs. »'

40 'Elle avait juste peur que je me dégonfle'.

While this is unfortunately an accurate representation of biphobia that exists in some parts of the gay community (Bostwick and Hequembourg 2014; Callis 2013; Doan Van et al. 2019), Capucine immediately proceeds to live up (or down) to the stereotype. She cancels their first date by text at the last minute because her once-beloved ex-boyfriend has returned unexpectedly from the other side of the country, throwing her once again into confusion and resulting in a moment of semi-infidelity, described in a way that evokes the idea of being on the fence:

> Just as I thought I finally knew what I wanted, Ben came back and ruined everything. […] He kissed me. I didn't really kiss him back, but I didn't push him away either.' (Ji 2017, 257)[41]

The bisexual subplot in *Sauveur* does not give any indication of infidelity, but nonetheless hints at unreliability and reiterates stereotypical ideas that bisexual people will inevitably leave their partner for someone of the 'opposite' gender (Yoshino 2000, 421). Alex has, in fact, left her long-term male partner for a female partner and, as discussed above, this is the 'problem' at the root of the extended family's decision to visit a psychotherapist. In book 2, it becomes apparent that there are tensions in Alex's new relationship with Charlie, and, although it is Charlie who eventually leaves Alex and moves on at the end, there are indications throughout that the lesbian partner Charlie is more committed to the relationship than the bisexual partner Alex (notably, being far keener to get married and have a child together; see for example Murail 2019, 62). At one point, Alex states openly to the therapist, in Charlie's presence, that she fantasizes about being back in her old life with her male partner, which was in some ways easier: 'I wasn't happy, but … it was less complicated' (65).[42] This reflects stereotypical assumptions faced by bisexual people in real life, where same-sex partners express fears they will choose the 'easier' straight path (Doan Van et al. 2019; Eisner 2013; Ochs 1996).

Thus far, we have not seen significant evidence of actual infidelity beyond Capucine's failure to resist kisses instigated by someone else (in *Arc-en-ciel*). However, some bisexual characters within the corpus are less restrained. As we have seen in the 'Problem Novel' section above, Lucas in *Source* occasions the main drama of the novella by kissing a boy, Tom, despite having an ongoing sexual relationship with the female protagonist. The entire novel revolves around this supposedly horrific betrayal, and the consequences include self-harm and the termination of a (previously wanted) pregnancy. The novella never explores the reasons why Lucas felt the need to keep his relationship with Jeanne secret, but we can infer that he may have been hiding it from Tom, thus betraying everybody. Although we learn little about Lucas' feelings on the matter, his comment that it is 'difficult' for him too (Roth 2015, 50) potentially suggests that he has feelings for both Tom and Jeanne and is torn between them.

41 'Au moment où j'avais l'impression d'avoir enfin quelques certitudes, Ben revenait et fichait tout par terre. […] Il m'a embrassée. Je ne l'ai pas vraiment embrassé en retour, mais je ne l'ai pas repoussé non plus.'

42 'Je n'étais pas heureuse, mais … c'était moins compliqué.'

Sarah's plotline in *Dysfonctionnelle* forms yet another iteration of Garber's 'bisexual plot' (1995, 456). From the start of this subplot, the lesbian protagonist Fifi feels threatened by the existence of Sarah's ex-boyfriend (Cendres 2015, 113, 152). Sarah had sex with this young man before meeting Fifi and is depicted throughout as more obviously interested in sex than Fifi. Fifi is a virgin and is reluctant to change this state of affairs – in part because she lacks confidence in her ability to live up to the standard of Sarah's ex-boyfriend, and in part because she is ashamed of the large scar on her back, dating from an incident of childhood abuse (141). Sarah persistently pressures her and, when Fifi says she is not ready, Sarah eventually has sex with her ex-boyfriend – on multiple occasions – during her summer holiday in Nice. She attempts to justify this by reproaching Fifi for not fulfilling her sexual needs: 'Women have needs! And you turned me down!' (167).[43] This feeds into another bisexual stereotype: that bisexual people are hypersexual and highly promiscuous (Bostwick and Hequembourg 2014; Callis 2013; Dyar and Feinstein 2018; Yoshino 2000).

Following an interim period of happiness together, Fifi and Sarah's relationship faces further challenges towards the end of the novel; they split up and get back together again twice. The first break-up is not due to issues around sexuality, but stems from an argument around jobs, career success and, more broadly, class – another key issue of the novel (Cendres 2015, 235). Five years later, they get back together, but this time the relationship lasts only just over a year – summarized in a single chapter using the metaphor of a single long, glorious day on which the sun eventually goes down.[44] This time, the cause of the break-up is quite explicitly the lure of life with a man, and the access to 'normal' societal institutions that this supposedly offers:

> 'I love you, but I want to be able to get married with all my family around me, to have children …' (278)[45]

Sarah wants to 'have it all' and proposes that they should continue their relationship in secret, behind the back of her (at this point entirely hypothetical) future husband, but Fifi refuses. A little over two years later, Sarah contacts Fifi to tell her that she is getting married to a man; the wedding is planned for later that year (287). However, fate intervenes when, a month before the wedding, Fifi is knocked down by a scooter and breaks her hip. Notified of this event by one of Fifi's siblings, Sarah finally realizes what is really important to her, calling off the wedding and indeed the relationship with her male partner (290). We learn virtually nothing about this man, other than that he is a surgeon from New York, but can hypothesize that he might reasonably be expected to be upset about this. Although this permits Sarah and Fifi to have a happy ending, Sarah's frequent

---

43 'J'ai des besoins de femme! Et toi, tu t'es refusée à moi!'

44 The chapter heading for chapter 41 is 'Une belle et longue journée' (A long, glorious day) and that for chapter 42 is 'Quand le soleil se couche' (When the sun goes down). See also page 269 for a further instance of this imagery.

45 '« Je t'aime, mais j'ai envie de me marier avec toute ma famille autour, d'avoir des enfants … »'

changes of mind further underline the trope of the untrustworthy bisexual who struggles to choose, and who is likely to abandon a relationship at the slightest provocation.

As discussed in the 'Bisexual Erasure' section, Ewen in *Un garçon* has sexual interactions with both male and female characters in the course of the novel; indeed, it is strongly hinted that he would be open to further sexual exploits with other characters (such as his friend Theo,[46] who, unfortunately for Ewen, is straight) if only the opportunity were to present itself. Interestingly, Ewen and Mathis do discuss the issues of relationship boundaries and jealousy:

> I tell him about Raphaëlle and I feeling each other up. It amuses him. I ask him, 'You're not jealous, are you?'
>
> 'No. If it had been with a boy, I might be.' (Breurec 2013, 38)[47]

However, it is important to note that Ewen does not clarify the situation until *after* his first sexual encounter with Raphaëlle. It is also significant that Mathis gives Ewen a free pass for girls only, perhaps playing into a stereotyped assumption that bisexual people need to have sexual interactions with 'both' sexes (Callis 2013; Yoshino 2000, 421–22).

Subsequent events in *Un garçon* raise further questions about Ewen's sexual (and general) morality. He persistently makes advances to his father's much younger[48] girlfriend; this seems to be only partly due to her physical attractions, and partly an attempt to challenge, prove himself to, and/or get revenge on his father, with whom he is angry for introducing this young woman into the household. Although at times she appears to be attracted to him (although we have only his word for this), at other points his actions are clearly non-consensual. He begins by groping her under the water (Breurec 2013, 79), pesters her until she agrees to kiss him on the mouth (81), and subsequently uses this kiss to blackmail her when she threatens to tell Ewen's father that he has been asking to see her pubic hair (90). Eventually he goes too far – stroking her breast and embracing her tightly – and she slaps him (95). In short, the depiction of Ewen reiterates the stereotype of the untrustworthy, over-sexed, promiscuous bisexual.

Thus, the corpus presents multiple iterations of Garber's 'bisexual plot'. The novels draw heavily on established stereotypes, portraying bisexual characters as confused, unreliable and/or hypersexual. This parallels the situation in English-language YA fiction, where, despite an increase in the number of novels with bisexual characters, common tropes persist (Epstein 2014; Jenkins and Cart 2018).

---

46 See for example pages 40, 42, 65.

47 Je lui raconte mon pelotage avec Raphaëlle. Ça l'amuse. Je lui demande:
  – T'es pas jaloux?
  – Non. Si c'était avec un garçon, je le serais peut-être.

48 The girlfriend is 24 (page 81) and Ewen's father is in his late 40s (page 71). Ewen himself is 14 (page 15). If this were a real-life situation, it would of course be necessary to consider the power relations inherent in the fact that Ewen is a child. However, I am here concerned more with the authorial choices that contribute to the epistemic construction of bisexuality within and beyond the novel.

'Just a Regular Guy': The 'Normal' Bisexual

Despite the reliance on stereotypes of bisexual behaviour, the large majority of the bisexual characters depicted in the corpus are depicted as extremely 'normal' in terms of their appearance and cultural interests, with more in common with mainstream straight culture than with queer visual stereotypes. In the case of Priam from *Georges*, this is such a key character trait that it is flagged up in the blurb on the back of the book: 'Before, I'd have described myself as just a regular guy: average grades, a loving family, a small group of friends. Before, I was the stereotypical geek who gets the pretty girl at the end of the film. Basically, I had an ordinary life' (Cantin 2018).[49] Although Priam has an unusual name and is, as the preceding quotation notes, a little geeky, he is indeed very ordinary, as typified by his love of Coldplay (115): a mainstream band often considered to be somewhat anodyne, and rarely associated with queer culture.

Capucine in *Arc-en-ciel* is similarly middle-of-the-road, although this is not self-consciously flagged up in the same way as in *Georges*. The story is set in an American high school and the usual cliques exist, e.g. 'les Populaires' (the Popular Kids) and 'les Nerds' (the Nerds). Capucine does not fall within either group, but most of the time is able to get along with both. Whenever there is a special fancy-dress event, Capucine dresses up in the same style as the other girls (e.g. Ji 2017, 115), although it should also be noted that she does not generally wear make-up and finds high heels too uncomfortable and impractical (59–60). On several occasions she makes remarks about how baffling boys are and how oddly their minds work; this *Men Are From Mars, Women Are From Venus*-style thinking owes much more to mainstream heterosexual culture than to queer culture, which might well question such gender stereotypes and divisions:

> I spoke to James about it, to test out how he felt. He shrugged his shoulders. If I ruled the world, all boys would be required to wear bracelets that changed colour depending on their mood. That way we would know what was going on, however much they shrugged. (317–18)[50]

The majority of the bisexual characters[51] have a primary same-sex love interest or partner. In all of these cases, the love interest or partner is gay or lesbian rather than bi, and in all cases but one, the gay or lesbian characters are closer to gay stereotypes than their bisexual counterparts. The eponymous Georges is more outgoing and flamboyant than Priam, and is also described as less stereotypically 'masculine':

---

49 'Avant, je me serais décrit comme le mec de base: des notes dans la moyenne, une famille aimante, un petit groupe d'amis. Avant, j'étais l'archétype du geek qui termine avec la jolie fille à la fin d'un film. Bref, j'avais une vie banale.'

50 'J'en ai parlé à James, pour le tester. Il a haussé les épaules. Si j'étais présidente du monde, tous les garçons devraient porter des bracelets qui changent de couleur selon leurs sentiments. Comme ça, ils pourraient hausser les épaules tant qu'ils veulent, on saurait à quoi s'en tenir.'

51 The exceptions to this are Lucas from *Source* and Blandine from *Sauveur*. As *Source* is narrated by Lucas's straight female love interest, this is the relationship that is the focal point of the novel, while Blandine is only 11 and there is no mention of any specific crush or love interest.

> He was smaller than me, less stocky, beardless [...] In fact, now he was relaxed and illuminated by the light of the screen, his features looked softer. His jawline was less prominent than mine, his eyebrows were slightly curved. He had a little beauty spot on his left cheekbone, just below his eye. (Cantin 2018, 13, 15)[52]

In the case of the female couples, this fits with the butch/femme stereotype for female same-sex couples (cf. Epstein 2013, 98). In all three of the couples (Aiden and Capucine, Fifi and Sarah, Charlie and Alex), the lesbian partner is more butch, while the bi partner is more femme and could 'pass' for a straight girl. This is particularly marked in the case of Charlie and Alex:

> She cultivated the bad-boy look, with piercings, tattoos and cowboy boots, while Alexandra, a little too heavily made up, waxed and tanned, was like an advert for her own beauty salon. (Murail 2019, 62)[53]

The three lesbians all have a more 'alternative' style: Aiden has facial piercings like Charlie, and also wears her hair in dreadlocks (Ji 2017, 80), while Fifi has habitually worn a leather jacket since age five (Cendres 2015, 56) and, as with Charlie and Alex, her rocker look is explicitly contrasted with that of her high femme girlfriend (131). The lesbian characters are also more politically aware, and 'educate' their bisexual girlfriends, thus fitting the feminist intellectual lesbian stereotype identified by Epstein (2013, 118). In *Sauveur* this is made very explicit:

> I was always attracted to boys. I thought girls were jealous and gossipy. Charlie says that these are just sexist ideas that are put into our heads, we are taught to see each other as rivals instead of learning female solidarity ... (Murail 2018, 272)[54]

Aiden in *Arc-en-ciel* attends the LGBT Club (Ji 2017, 120) and introduces Capucine to queer culture and community (274, 345); even before they are together, she inspires Capucine to become vegetarian (151). Similarly, Fifi introduces Sarah to the world of the squat where her sister lives, which is focused on political activism and demonstrations (211–17), as well as generally broadening Sarah's horizons in terms of class. Despite this, as we saw in the previous section, Sarah is sufficiently tempted by the lure of a 'normal

52 'Il était plus petit que moi, moins trapu, imberbe. [...] En vérité, une fois détendus et éclairés par la lumière de l'écran, ses traits paraissaient plus doux. Sa mâchoire n'était pas aussi dessinée que la mienne, ses sourcils se courbaient en un arc peu prononcé. Il avait un petit grain de beauté sur la pommette gauche, juste en-dessous de l'œil.' The word 'imberbe' (beardless) has connotations in French of a beautiful and perhaps rather gender-ambiguous youth.

53 'Elle cultivait le look bad boy, piercings, tatouages, santiags, tandis qu'Alexandra, un peu trop maquillée, épilée et bronzée, était une publicité pour son cabinet d'esthéticienne.'

54 'J'ai toujours été attirée par des garçons. Les filles, je les trouvais jalouses, cancanières. Charlie dit que c'est des idées sexistes qu'on nous met dans la tête, qu'on nous dresse les une contre les autres au lieu de nous apprendre la solidarité féminine ...'

life' (277)[55] – by which she seems to mean heteronormative institutions such as marriage and children – that she leaves Fifi at one point and becomes engaged to a man.

The only couple who do not fit the pattern of a visibly queer gay/lesbian partner and a straight-passing bisexual partner are Mathis and Ewen from *Un garçon*. Ewen states very specifically that neither of them is a gay stereotype: 'He wasn't the gay "type", nor was I. We still looked just like any other boys' (Breurec 2013, 23).[56] Thus, although Mathis differs from other gay characters in the corpus, Ewen conforms to the trend within the corpus of bisexual characters as 'just like anyone else'.

This pattern of bisexual characters as 'normal' and gay characters as more visibly 'queer' is one that I have not encountered previously in any scholarly work on either French- or English-language queer YA literature. Instead, the trend in French-language literature, according to other scholars, seems to be for the majority of gay characters to be depicted as very ordinary, unlike the visible queers of stereotype, as if to reassure the reader that it is possible to be gay and 'normal' (Chaimbault 2002; Champagne 2012; Lominé 2006). Champagne suggests that this is to facilitate the reader's identification with the character (2012, 132–33); however, this does not seem to allow for the possibility that the reader *is* visibly queer (cf. Chaimbault 2002, 33). In any case, this does not seem to be what is happening in my corpus, where visible queers do exist. Perhaps the epistemic construction of bisexuals as 'normal' and straight-passing in fact points back to another stereotype: the idea that bisexuals (and bisexual women in particular) are 'really' just straight after all (Hayfield et al. 2014; Yost and Thomas 2012).

Conclusion

In this chapter, I have examined seven French-language YA novels featuring characters who can be identified as bisexual based on self-definition, attraction and/or behaviour. My analysis has identified a number of themes, namely: bisexual erasure; bisexuality as a 'problem'; stereotypes and the 'bisexual plot'; and bisexual people as 'normal' and straight-passing. The first three themes mirror Epstein's observation that bisexual characters in English-language YA fiction were either 'invisible or negatively portrayed [...] missing or stereotyped' (2014, 110–12).

The small number of French-language novels featuring bisexual characters is itself an example of the erasure of bisexuality. This is compounded by the fact that terms such as 'bisexual' or 'bisexuality' are rarely used in the corpus: they appear in just three of the seven novels, while the term 'pansexual' is used once. Moreover, in two of these three novels, the term is used only to be instantly invalidated through the implication that it is 'trendy' or 'just a phase'. Behaviourally bisexual characters in these same novels are not described as such.

55 'vie normale'.

56 'Il n'avait pas le « genre » gay, moi non plus. Nous semblions encore des garçons comme les autres.'

At the same time, bisexuality is construed as a 'problem' within the corpus, both for the bisexual characters themselves and for their gay, lesbian or straight love interests, who have to put up with their vacillation, confusion and sometimes infidelity. Of the novels with bisexual protagonists, only one (*Un garçon*) has a protagonist who embraces his sexuality throughout; the other two (*Georges* and *Arc-en-ciel*) follow a traditional 'problem novel' format. Although both end happily, the overriding impression is that being bisexual is difficult and confusing, and coming out (to oneself and to others) is a long and wearing struggle.

Moreover, all but one of the novels draw to a greater or lesser extent on Garber's 'bisexual plot' (1995, 456) – the trope of being torn between a man and a woman. This reinforces the stereotypes that bisexual people are confused, and that there is a constant risk they will fall for someone of a different gender. Four of the novels contain instances of actual infidelity (or at least, sexual interactions with someone other than the character's primary partner), ranging from kissing to repeated sexual intercourse. In two of these novels, the bisexual character is depicted as hypersexual, another common stereotype. It is important to note here that there is nothing inherently wrong with being hypersexual or non-monogamous, and it would be problematic on a number of levels to attempt to restrict the sphere of bisexuality to only what is deemed to be 'safe' and 'appropriate' by mainstream society (Eisner 2013). Nonetheless, it is disappointing that the corpus continues to draw on the same set of ideas about bisexuality, rather than expanding the range of depictions available to young people.

Despite the extent to which the corpus draws on ingrained stereotypes of bisexual people, it also constructs an image of bi people as extremely 'normal' – particularly in terms of their visual appearance and, to some extent, their cultural interests and reference points. All but two of the bisexual characters in the corpus have a partner or primary love interest who is gay or lesbian (rather than bisexual), and in the majority of cases, the partner is more visibly queer. Notably, the same-sex female couples all fit the stereotypical butch/femme dyad, and the lesbians are also more politically aware and connected to queer culture. I suggest that this may be a way of further invisibilizing a distinct bisexual identity.

Obradors-Campos uses Iris Marion Young's (1990) concept of 'cultural imperialism' to illustrate how the existence of bisexuality is denied at the very same time as stereotypes are used to create a clear, though biased, image of bisexual people:

> … those people who believe that bisexuality does not exist […] also tend to believe that bisexual persons are promiscuous, unreliable, voluble and sources of transmission of pandemics (Ochs & Rowley, 2009). Yes, we are perceived through those stereotypes even though we are also perceived as nonexisting. (2011, 218)

This is a remarkably accurate description of bisexuality as portrayed in my corpus. Within the novels, bisexuality is simultaneously erased and reified as a 'problem', with tired tropes and stereotypes reiterated. The epistemic construction of bisexuality in the corpus contributes to maintaining an existing body of supposed 'knowledge' about bisexuality and bisexual people, which is in fact limited to a narrow range of stereotypes and identity positions. There thus appears to be substantial room for improvement in the depiction of bisexuality in French young adult literature.

Bibliography

Barker, Meg-John, Christina Richards, Rebecca Jones, Helen Bowes-Catton, Tracey Plowman, Jen Yockney and Marcus Morgan. 2012. *The Bisexuality Report: Bisexual Inclusion in LGBT Equality and Diversity.* Milton Keynes: The Open University. http://www.open.ac.uk/ccig/sites/www.open.ac.uk.ccig/files/The%20BisexualityReport%20Feb.2012_0.pdf

Behoteguy, Gilles. 2013. 'Etre gay dans le roman contemporain pour la jeunesse'. In *Esthétiques de la distinction: «gender» et mauvais genres en littérature de jeunesse*, edited by Philippe Clermont, Laurent Bazin and Danièle Henky, 145–60. Frankfurt am Main: Peter Lang.

Bosman, Ellen, and John P. Bradford. 2008. *Gay, Lesbian, Bisexual, and Transgendered Literature: A Genre Guide.* Westport, CT: Libraries Unlimited.

Bostwick, Wendy, and Amy Hequembourg. 2014. '"Just a Little Hint": Bisexual-Specific Microaggressions and their Connections to Epistemic Injustices'. *Culture, Health & Sexuality* 16, no. 5: 488–503. https://doi.org/10.1080/13691058.2014.889754

Breurec, Joël. 2013. *Un garçon comme une autre* (A Boy Like Any Other Girl). Paris: Oskar.

Butstraen, Marie. 2019. 'L'homosexualité dans la littérature jeunesse francophone du XXIe siècle: une représentation arc-en-ciel dans un ciel qui s'ouvre'. Master's dissertation, Université catholique de Louvain. http://hdl.handle.net/2078.1/thesis:21397

Callis, April Scarlette. 2013. 'The Black Sheep of the Pink Flock: Labels, Stigma and Bisexual Identity'. *Journal of Bisexuality* 13, no. 1: 82–105. https://doi.org/10.1080/15299716.2013.755730

Cantin, Illana. 2018. *Georges, le monde et moi* (Georges, the World and Me). Vanves: Hachette Livre.

Cart, Michael, and Christine A. Jenkins. 2006. *The Heart Has Its Reasons: Young Adult Literature With Gay/Lesbian/Queer Content, 1969–2004.* Lanham, MD: Scarecrow Press.

Cendres, Axl. 2015. *Dysfonctionnelle* (Dysfunctional). Paris: Éditions Sarbacane.

Chaimbault, Thomas. 2002. 'L'homosexualité dans la littérature de jeunesse'. Master's dissertation, Université de Lille. http://www.vagabondages.org/public/Documents%20à%20joindre%20aux%20billets/Memoire2.pdf

Champagne, Samuel. 2012. 'Double échappée, suivi de Se dire, se comprendre: L'homosexualité adolescente dans les romans québécois pour la jeunesse'. Master's dissertation, Université de Montréal. http://hdl.handle.net/1866/8963

———. 2018. 'Laisse-moi parler! Homosexualités en littérature destinée aux adolescents'. *Postures* 28. http://revuepostures.com/fr/articles/champagne-28

Chapman, Elizabeth L. 2015. 'Provision of LGBT-Related Fiction to Children and Young People in English Public Libraries: A Mixed-Methods Study'. PhD thesis, University of Sheffield. http://etheses.whiterose.ac.uk/11802/

Chopin, Isabelle, Carmine Conte and Edith Chambrier. 2018. *A Comparative Analysis of Non-Discrimination Law in Europe 2018.* Brussels: European Commission. https://op.europa.eu/en/publication-detail/-/publication/5637af4b-1234-11e9-81b4-01aa75ed71a1/language-en/format-PDF

Clermont, Philippe. 2011. 'Identité de sexe, identité de genre: le roman pour adolescent-e-s est-il engagé?' In *Contre l'innocence: esthétique de l'engagement en littérature de jeunesse*, edited by Britta Benert and Philippe Clermont, 229–48. Frankfurt am Main: Peter Lang.

Coletta, Jennifer. 2018. 'The Missing B Word: Compulsory Binarization and Bisexual Representation in Children's Literature'. *Jeunesse: Young People, Texts, Cultures* 10, no. 1: 85–108. https://doi.org/10.1353/jeu.2018.0004

Dénommé-Baudoin, Maude. 2003. 'L'homosexualité dans la littérature jeunesse québécoise (1988–2003): du paratexte au personnage'. Master's dissertation, Université de Sherbrooke. http://savoirs.usherbrooke.ca/handle/11143/2356

Doan Van, Emilie E., Ethan H. Mereish, Julie M. Woulfe, and Sabra L. Katz-Wise. 2019. 'Perceived Discrimination, Coping Mechanisms, and Effects on Health in Bisexual and Other Non-Monosexual Adults'. *Archives of Sexual Behavior* 48, no. 1: 159–74. https://doi.org/10.1007/s10508-018-1254-z

Dufresne, Rhéa. 2011. 'L'homosexualité dans la littérature pour la jeunesse'. *Lurelu* 33, no. 3: 17–19. https://id.erudit.org/iderudit/60943ac

Dyar, Christina, and Brian A. Feinstein. 2018. 'Binegativity: Attitudes Toward and Stereotypes About Bisexual Individuals'. In *Bisexuality: Theories, Research, and Recommendations for the Invisible Sexuality*, edited by D. Joye Swan and Shani Habibi, 95–111. Cham, Switzerland: Springer.

Eisner, Shiri. 2013. *Bi: Notes for a Bisexual Revolution*. Berkeley, CA: Seal Press.

Epstein, B. J. 2013. *Are the Kids All Right? The Representation of LGBTQ Characters in Children's and Young Adult Literature*. Bristol: HammerOn Press.

———. 2014. '"The Case of the Missing Bisexuals": Bisexuality in Books for Young Readers'. *Journal of Bisexuality* 14, no. 1: 110–25. https://doi.org/10.1080/15299716.2014.872483

Esposito, Tony. 1996. 'Présence de l'absence: L'homosexualité dans le roman jeunesse québécois'. *Lurelu* 18, no. 3: 53–54. https://id.erudit.org/iderudit/13471ac

Fahs, Breanne, and Kimberly M. Koerth. 2018. 'Female Bisexuality: Identity, Fluidity, and Cultural Expectations'. In *Bisexuality: Theories, Research, and Recommendations for the Invisible Sexuality*, edited by D. Joye Swan and Shani Habibi, 113–26. Cham, Switzerland: Springer.

Feinstein, Brian, Marisa Franco, Regine Henderson, Laniqua Kemecee Collins and Jaleh Davarib. 2019. 'A Qualitative Examination of Bi+ Identity Invalidation and Its Consequences for Wellbeing, Identity, and Relationships'. *Journal of Bisexuality* 19, no. 4: 461–82. https://doi.org/10.1080/15299716.2019.1671295

Gabriel. 2018. 'Des livres jeunesse LGBTQ+'. *La mare aux mots*, 29 June. https://lamareauxmots.com/des-livres-jeunesse-lgbtq/

Garber, Marjorie. 1995. *Vice Versa: Bisexuality and the Eroticism of Everyday Life*. London: Hamish Hamilton.

Hayfield, Nikki, Victoria Clarke and Emma Halliwell. 2014. 'Bisexual Women's Understandings of Social Marginalisation: "The Heterosexuals Don't Understand Us But Nor Do the Lesbians"'. *Feminism & Psychology* 24, no. 3: 352–72. https://doi.org/10.1177/0959353514539651

IFOP. 2019a. *Observatoire des LGBTphobies: État des lieux 2019*. Paris: Institut Français d'Opinion Publique. https://www.ifop.com/wp-content/uploads/2019/05/116079_Ifop_FJR_Observatoire_2019.05.16.pdf

———. 2019b. *Observatoire des LGBTphobies: Le regard des Français sur l'homosexualité et la place des LGBT dans la société*. Paris: Institut Français d'Opinion Publique. https://www.ifop.com/wp-content/uploads/2019/06/116079_Ifop_FJR_2019.06.24.pdf

INSEE. 2019. 'Pacte civil de de solidarité / PACS'. Montrouge: INSEE. Accessed 2 July 2020. https://www.insee.fr/fr/metadonnees/definition/c1281

Inter-LGBT. 2016. 'Changement d'état civil: un grand pas pour les transidentités'. Paris: Inter-LGBT. http://www.inter-lgbt.org/changement-detat-civil-un-grand-pas-pour-les-transidentites/

Jenkins, Christine A., and Michael Cart. 2018. *Representing the Rainbow in Young Adult Literature: LGBTQ+ Content since 1969*. London: Rowman & Littlefield.

Ji, Erwan. 2017. *J'ai avalé un arc en ciel* (I Swallowed a Rainbow). Paris: Éditions Nathan.

Kneen, Bonnie. 2015. 'Neither Very Bi Nor Particularly Sexual: The Essence of the Bisexual in Young Adult Literature'. *Children's Literature in Education* 46, no. 4: 359–77. https://doi.org/10.1007/s10583-014-9237-8

Lagabrielle, Renaud. 2007. *Représentations des homosexualités dans le roman français pour la jeunesse*. Paris: L'Harmattan.

Lo, Malinda. 2019. 'A Decade of LGBTQ YA Since Ash'. *MalindaLo.com*. https://www.malindalo.com/blog/2019/3/18/a-decade-of-lgbtq-ya-since-ash

Lominé, Loykie L. 2006. 'The "Coming-Out" of French Youth Literature in the 1990s'. *Modern & Contemporary France* 14, no. 2: 221–34. https://doi.org/10.1080/09639480600667756

MacDowall, Lachlan. 2009. 'Historicising Contemporary Bisexuality'. *Journal of Bisexuality* 9, no. 1: 3–15. https://doi.org/10.1080/15299710802659989

McLean, Kirsten. 2018. 'Bisexuality in Society'. In *Bisexuality: Theories, Research, and Recommendations for the Invisible Sexuality*, edited by D. Joye Swan and Shani Habibi, 77–93. Cham, Switzerland: Springer.

Meyer, Ilan H., and Patrick A. Wilson. 2009. 'Sampling Lesbian, Gay, and Bisexual Populations'. *Journal of Counseling Psychology* 56, no. 1: 23–31. https://doi.org/10.1037/a0014587

Murail, Marie-Aude. (2016) 2018. *Sauveur & fils: Saison 1* (Saviour & Son: Season 1), 2nd ed. Paris: L'École des Loisirs.

———. (2016) 2019. *Sauveur & fils: Saison 2* (Saviour & Son: Season 2), 2nd ed. Paris: L'École des Loisirs.

Noël-Gaudreault, Monique, and Caroline de Launay. 2013. 'Représentation de l'homosexualité chez les garçons en littérature jeunesse québécoise'. In *Esthétiques de la distinction: « gender » et mauvais genres en littérature de jeunesse*, edited by Philippe Clermont, Laurent Bazin and Danièle Henky, 161–75. Frankfurt am Main: Peter Lang.

Obradors-Campos, Miguel. 2011. 'Deconstructing Biphobia'. *Journal of Bisexuality* 11, no. 2–3: 207–26. https://doi.org/10.1080/15299716.2011.571986

Ochs, Robyn. 1996. 'Biphobia: It Goes More Than Two Ways'. Originally published in *Bisexuality: The Psychology and Politics of an Invisible Minority*, edited by Beth A. Firestein, 217–39. Thousand Oaks, CA, London and New Delhi: SAGE. Accessed online: https://robynochs.com/biphobia-it-goes-more-than-two-ways/

———. 2016. 'Selected Quotes by Robyn Ochs'. Accessed 25 June 2020. https://robynochs.com/quotes/

OECD. 2019. *Society at a Glance 2019: OECD Social Indicators*. Paris: OECD Publishing. https://read.oecd.org/10.1787/soc_glance-2019-en?format=pdf

Roth, Madeline. 2015. *À ma source gardée* (At My Secret Spring). Paris: Éditions Thierry Magnier.

SOS Homophobie. 2020. *Rapport sur les LGBTIphobies 2020*. Paris: SOS Homophobie. https://www.sos-homophobie.org/sites/default/files/rapport_homophobie_2020_interactif.pdf

Soulé, Véronique. 1999 'Censures et autocensures: Autour du livre de jeunesse'. *Bulletin des bibliothèques de France* 44, no. 3: 44–48. https://bbf.enssib.fr/consulter/bbf-1999-03-0044-005

Trachman, Mathieu, and Tania Lejbowicz. 2018. 'People Who Identify as Bisexual in France'. *Population and Societies* 561, December 2018. https://www.ined.fr/fichier/s_rubrique/28720/population.societies.561.december.2018.bisexual.en.pdf

Vie Publique. 2020. *Projet de loi relatif à la bioéthique*. Paris: Direction de l'information légale et administrative. Accessed 2 July 2020. https://www.vie-publique.fr/loi/268659-projet-de-loi-bioethique-pma

Yoshino, Kenji. 2000. 'The Epistemic Contract of Bisexual Erasure'. *Stanford Law Review* 52, no. 2: 353–461. http://www.jstor.com/stable/1229482

Yost, Megan R., and Genéa D. Thomas. 2012. 'Gender and Binegativity: Men's and Women's Attitudes Toward Male and Female Bisexuals'. *Archives of Sexual Behavior* 41, no. 3: 691–702. https://doi.org/10.1007/s10508-011-9767-8

Young, Iris Marion. 1990. *Justice and the Politics of Difference*. Princeton, NJ: Princeton University Press.

Appendix 1: The Corpus

Breurec, Joël. 2013. *Un garçon comme une autre* (A Boy Like Any Other Girl). Paris: Oskar.

Cantin, Illana. 2018. *Georges, le monde et moi* (Georges, the World and Me). Vanves: Hachette Livre.

Cendres, Axl. 2015. *Dysfonctionnelle* (Dysfunctional). Paris: Éditions Sarbacane.
Ji, Erwan. 2017. *J'ai avalé un arc-en-ciel* (I Swallowed a Rainbow). Paris: Éditions Nathan.
Murail, Marie-Aude. (2016) 2018. *Sauveur & fils: Saison 1* (Saviour & Son: Season 1), 2nd ed. Paris: L'École des Loisirs.
———. (2016) 2019. *Sauveur & fils: Saison 2* (Saviour & Son: Season 2), 2nd ed. Paris: L'École des Loisirs.
Roth, Madeline. 2015. *À ma source gardée* (At My Secret Spring). Paris: Éditions Thierry Magnier.

Appendix 2: Sources Consulted

Arnoi, Joannic. n.d. 'Livres pour ados ayant une thématique LGBT'. *Le blog de Joannic Arnoi.* Accessed 26 June 2020. http://joannic-arnoi.over-blog.fr/article-10112949.html
Cat_deer. 2019. 'Ces romans jeunesse qui abordent les thèmes LGBT'. *Sens critique.* Accessed 26 June 2020. https://www.senscritique.com/liste/Ces_romans_jeunesse_qui_abordent_les_themes_LGBT/391767
Chaimbault, Thomas. 2002. 'L'homosexualité dans la littérature de jeunesse'. Master's dissertation, Université de Lille. http://www.vagabondages.org/public/Documents%20à%20joindre%20aux%20billets/Memoire2.pdf
Cordélia. n.d. 'Cordélia > Books: lgbt'. *Goodreads.* Accessed 26 June 2020. https://www.goodreads.com/review/list/33828542-cord-lia-cord-lia?shelf=lgbt
Gabriel. 2018. 'Des livres jeunesse LGBTQ+'. *La mare aux mots*, 29 June. https://lamareauxmots.com/des-livres-jeunesse-lgbtq/
Labosse, Lionel. 2020. 'La sélection altersexualité.com et les « Isidor » '. *Altersexualité.* Accessed 26 June 2020. http://www.altersexualite.com/spip.php?article100
Lagabrielle, Renaud. 2007. *Représentations des homosexualités dans le roman français pour la jeunesse.* Paris: L'Harmattan.
Le Point G. n.d. *Bibliographies jeunesse.* Lyon: Bibliothèque Municipale de Lyon. Accessed 26 June 2020. https://www.bm-lyon.fr/nos-blogs/le-centre-de-ressources-sur-le-genre-le-point-g/bibliographies/article/bibliographies-jeunesse
La Rainbowthèque. n.d. *La Rainbowthèque.* Accessed 26 June 2020. https://rainbowtheque.tumblr.com/tagged/littérature-jeunesse
SOS Homophobie. n.d. 'Liste générale des romans ado LGBT'. *C'est comme ça.* Accessed 3 March 2019. http://www.cestcommeca.net/livres-jeunesse-home.php [Site now no longer available. The list can still be accessed using the Wayback Machine: https://web.archive.org/web/2019*/http://www.cestcommeca.net/livres-jeunesse-home.php]

Chapter Three

STUCK IN THE BINARY: HETERONORMATIVITY AND THE BINARY CONCEPTION OF GENDER IN GERMAN-LANGUAGE TRANS YA

Katrin Waldhart

Introduction

With the publication of Julie Anne Peters's *Luna* in 2004, the existence of trans[1] young adults was acknowledged in young adult (YA) literature in the English-speaking world. Despite reports saying that the number of YA books featuring trans characters is still rather low and that many titles are published by small presses that have little or no marketing, the presence of trans teenagers in English-language YA has been growing ever since (Bittner et al. 2016, 948; Sokoll 2013, 23).[2] In German-language YA, the idea of the trans teenage protagonist does not seem to have caught on to the same extent. While several novels, such as *Luna* or Alex Gino's *George* (2015), have been translated into German, original German-language trans YA is rare. Noteworthy titles include Karen-Susan Fessel's YA novel *Jenny mit O* (Jenny with an O, 2005), a novel about a trans boy, assigned female at birth, who runs away from home; Lilly Axster's *Atalanta Läufer_in*[3] (Atalanta Runner, 2014) about a teenage runner who questions and transcends traditional gender classification; and Christine Fehér's *Weil ich so bin* (Because That's the Way I Am, 2016), a story about an intersex teenager struggling with their ambiguous gender expression.

---

1 Throughout this chapter, the term trans is used as an umbrella term to describe people whose (sense of) gender identity is different from the gender they were assigned at birth (either male or female in Germany and Austria). Among these trans persons, those who additionally evade a binary classification are specifically referred to as genderqueer (in accordance with, for instance, Kuklin 2016, 175).

2 For a list of trans and genderqueer English-language YA see, for instance, GayYA 2016, n.p.

3 The German suffix *_in* can be used to render a word gender-neutral. Thus, the word *Läufer_in* can refer to a male as well as a female runner. The suffix is seldom used and not as common as the *Binnen-I* that is often applied in order to create a gender-neutral plural noun (*LäuferInnen* are male and female runners). Recently, the asterisk has been used frequently for the same purpose (*Läufer*in, Läufer*innen*). It is important to note, however, that none of these options is considered to be orthographically correct.

The reason for the lack of attention to the topic of trans teenagers in German-language YA is difficult to pin down, but may be attributed to the fact that awareness of the existence and needs of trans people in Germany and Austria, where the aforementioned novels were published , has only been raised in recent years in these countries. It is still a challenge to find reliable figures regarding the number of trans people in Germany or Austria, but what can be evaluated is the current legal and policy situation. In its 2018 Rainbow Europe Map and Index, the NGO ILGA-Europe (the European Region of the International Lesbian, Gay, Bisexual, Trans and Intersex Association) lists Germany with a score of 59 per cent and Austria with a score of 56 per cent when assessing the LGBTI equality laws and policies of 49 European countries (100 per cent meaning full equality). These figures take into consideration matters of gender identity pertaining to the constitution, employment, goods and services, education, health, and laws for intersex people (only in Germany). Moreover, the Rainbow Europe Index shows that in both countries name change is possible and there is no compulsory requirement of medical or surgical intervention for legal gender recognition (ILGA-Europe 2018, n.p.). With regard to young adults, recent studies acknowledge the existence of gender dysphoria in adolescence and strive to suggest ways of achieving the well-being of trans adolescents (see Becker et al. 2017 (Germany) and Riedl 2018 (Austria)). The studies report an approximate estimation of transgender prevalence among adolescents of only 1 per cent[4] (Becker et al. 2017, 88; Riedl 2018, 60), but, nonetheless, take the issue seriously and discuss treatment options such as hormone therapy (Riedl 2018, 61–62).

While Germany and Austria rank among the top ten of ILGA-Europe's list and there seems to have been a tremendous development in recognition of trans and intersex persons as well as relevant laws and policies since 2010 (compare to ILGA-Europe 2011, n.p.), the two countries lag far behind the top three: Malta (91 per cent), Belgium (79 per cent) and Norway (78 per cent). According to the Rainbow Europe Index, some laws and policies that the two countries lack are those managing conversion therapy, gender expression, hate crime and hate speech, and prohibition of medical intervention without informed consent (affecting intersex people).[5] In summary, we might surmise that the

4 Note that Becker et al. only state results from a regional study in Hamburg and align their result of 0.9 per cent with the results of international studies to give an approximate estimation of transgender prevalence among adolescents of 1 per cent. Riedl exclusively refers to data from international studies; Austrian data does not seem to be available.

5 At the time of writing in summer 2018, one currently ongoing legal debate in Germany and Austria concerns the option of a gender marker in identity documents that is neither male nor female, which is something ('a third gender option') recommended by the EU parliament (Parliamentary Assembly 2015, 2). The Commissioner of Human Rights of the European Union recommends the complete omission of gender markers in official documents (referring to intersex persons) (Commissioner of Human Rights 2015, 9). No laws have been passed yet, but individuals are claiming their right to a third gender marker. A recent successful outcome was achieved in the case of Austrian Alex Jürgen, an intersex person who won the right to a third gender marker in the Austrian constitutional court in 2018. See news stories about the issue, for instance, Gaigg 2018, n.p.

reason why *Jenny mit O* is the only German-language trans YA novel with a publication date as early as 2005 is because the existence and the needs of trans people were at this time not acknowledged to the extent seen after 2011 in the German-speaking world. Likewise, the continuing dearth of German-language YA may be related to the fact that the recognition of trans people, let alone trans adolescents, in Germany and Austria still lags far behind that in the countries seen as forerunners in trans and intersex recognition, laws and policies.

Despite the fact that the topic of trans teenagers has rarely been addressed by German-speaking authors of YA fiction (whatever the reason may be, as this chapter cannot offer anything but assumptions), German-language and English-language trans YA seem to have something in common: what appears to remain intact in most novels are the binary conceptions of gender and sexuality, and the dominant notion of heteronormativity, i.e. a person is either male or female and desires the opposite gender. In *Luna* and in Meredith Russo's *If I Was Your Girl* (2016), the trans character transitions from male to female, and in *Jenny mit O* and Ellen Wittlinger's *Parrotfish* (2007) a transition from female to male takes place, and the protagonists feel attracted to the respectively 'opposite' gender. This is not to claim that the aforementioned books do not challenge traditional ideas of gender identity and sexuality – indeed, this is exactly what they do. Nonetheless, by establishing gender and sexuality as dichotomies, these novels affirm the gender binary as 'a pivotal structural principle of societies' (Frevert 1995, 10). The representation and the underlying conception of gender and sexuality do not function independently of the male/female binary.

This chapter examines the protagonists' non-conforming gender identities in the three German-language trans YA novels mentioned above (*Jenny mit O*, *Weil ich so bin* and *Atalanta Läufer_in*) and attempts to answer the following question: to what extent can they provide a critical challenge to the conventional (i.e. binary) conception of gender identity and the dominance of heteronormativity in Western societies despite their apparent adherence to these concepts? The idea that literature or, to put it more generally, stories are capable of influencing one's conceptions of reality at all is based on Mark Turner's argument that '[s]tory is a basic principle of mind', by which he means that '[m]ost of our experience, our knowledge, and our thinking is organized as stories' (1996, v). We use one story to make sense of another, i.e. we interpret our impressions and experiences by means of parable, '[t]he projection of one story onto another', which is a basic cognitive principle (Turner 1996, v). Consequently, literature and other storytelling media create models for the perception of reality and the reconstruction of experience, but equally they constitute a space in which complex models of agency as well as models of societal coexistence and social organization are not only depicted but can also be anticipated (Turner 1996, v). Hence, literature, to focus on the medium relevant for the present article, prefigures our expectations (Gellhaus 2011, 80), meaning that, in particular, literature for young readers has high potential: readers can 'gain additional tools for enacting acceptance and negotiating change in the far more complex and emotionally charged real world' after '[h]aving "acted out" situations with a literary character' (McNeil 2008, 91). Notwithstanding the fact that the protagonists of all three YA books pose challenges to a conventional understanding of gender and sexuality, the novels still reinforce the binary conception of gender and heteronormative standards, which may impede the admittance of gender complexity into the young readers' minds.

The Role of the Gender Binary in the Construction of Gender Identity

'Right now, lying here quietly and staring into the twilit night, I begin to realize that the best moments in my life have indeed been those in which I became a boy. And this is no coincidence. No temporary fad. And no hobby. This is me. Really me'[6] (Fessel 2005, 189). Jenny or, later in the book, Jonny, Fessel's protagonist in *Jenny with an O*, desperately wants to be a boy. Born with a girl's body, Jenny detests everything about their appearance or bodily functions that marks them as a girl, such as their breasts or having their period (see Fessel 2005, 58, 67 and 189). Over the course of the story, Jenny's gender identity is male, while their body is female. Even though this state of being does not conform to traditional ideas of gender (identity) and thus creates a condition of feeling and living 'between the genders'[7] (Fessel 2005, 197), it is exactly this condition of existing between male and female that nonetheless refers back to the binary conception of gender. Neither the author nor, in consequence, the protagonist of the novel seem to think of gender beyond the binary. To be fair, there are instances in which Jenny is confronted with the notion that trans means to feel neither male nor female, but completely different or both at the same time 'and so much more'[8] (Fessel 2005, 193). Towards the end of the novel, Jenny still hopes to one day be a man in a man's body, but for a brief moment they do not even mind whether they are called Jenny (a female name) or Jonny (a male name), because they just are what they are. However, only a few sentences later, the binary reemerges and Jenny again stresses that they are a young man in a young woman's body (Fessel 2015, 305–6).

It is repeatedly mentioned and once even illustrated with the idiom '[caught] between two stools'[9] (Fessel 2005, 240) that there are only two alternatives for Jenny: to be male or to be female. In consideration of the separation of sex and gender, Jenny's body and gender identity are not yet congruent: 'My body simply doesn't match my feelings. Or, in other words: my sex doesn't match my gender'[10] (Fessel 2005, 269). Nonetheless, neither category supplies them with any other option than to be either male or female. The novel's idea of sex and gender is strongly rooted in the dichotomous quality of these two categories. Raia Prokhovnik refers to this understanding of a category by the term 'hard-shelled holism' (1999, 36): When reality is understood as being constituted

---

6 'Jetzt, während ich still da liege und in die dämmrige Nacht hinaussehe, wird mir klar, dass tatsächlich genau das immer die allerbesten Momente in meinem Leben gewesen sind: wenn ich mich in einen Jungen verwandelt habe. Und das ist kein Zufall. Keine Marotte. Und auch kein Hobby. Das bin ich. Wirklich ich.'

7 'zwischen den Geschlechtern'.

8 '[u]nd noch viel mehr'.

9 'zwischen den Stühlen'.

10 'Mein Körper passt bloß nicht zu meinen Gefühlen. Oder, anders gesagt: Mein Geschlecht passt nicht zu meinem Gender.'

of wholes that can only be subdivided into two parts, no other possibilities of thinking and being can exist. The range of possibilities is summed up by the two opposed entities of a dichotomy, which means that heterogeneity is therefore denied. When, in the dominant view, someone's gender must be either male or female, it is hard, and for some even impossible, to think beyond the binary, i.e. to imagine and furthermore accept non-binary gender identities.

The perception of sex and gender as hard-shelled holisms further forms the basis for the social construction of gender that limits the environment's perception of the protagonist as well as Jenny's own constitution of their gender identity. What constitutes a person's gender and subsequently their gender identity is not generated or performed entirely by this person, but also outside of them where the terms that make up one's gender are situated (Butler 2004, 1). This 'outside' is society (primarily those societies based on Western philosophy), a realm in which the gender binary is firmly established. Thus, for individuals to be recognized and accepted by society, they need to assume a gender identity oriented towards the gender binary: A person 'only become[s] intelligible through becoming gendered in conformity with recognizable standards of gender intelligibility' (Butler 2007, 22). The consequence for Fessel's protagonist is that society offers them only two options: Jenny is, for instance, constantly asked about their gender ('"What are you anyway?" he asked furtively. "Boy or girl?"'[11] (Fessel 2005, 167)); they have to decide whether to use the men's or the women's toilet; and even though a person's gender can be changed in official registers, the registers do not offer an alternative to male or female (Fessel 2005, 284).[12] Even intersex people (referred to as 'hermaphrodites' in the novel, a term that might have been common in Germany in 2005 to denote intersex people) are regarded by Jenny not as a gender beyond the binary but as 'people with two genders'[13] (Fessel 2005, 172), because male and female seem to be the only available options. Only the two people closest to Jenny, Moni and Bifi, encourage them to be the way they are regardless of their gender: '"So what?" he asked. "Jonny just is what he is. Or she. That's right, isn't it?"'[14] (Fessel 2005, 187). Since Jenny's reaction to such comments is either non-existent or not indicative of their thoughts on the topic, and as these comments are above all rare, it is the socially omnipresent gender binary that seems to dictate the constitution of Jenny's gender identity: they feel they are a young man in a young woman's body.

What complicates the constitution and representation of a non-binary gender identity in German-language YA in general even further is the heavily gendered German language. German has a grammatical gender system in which articles and the inflection

11 '„Was bist du denn überhaupt?", fragte er lauernd. „Junge oder Mädchen?"'

12 As the brief discussion in the Introduction to this chapter illustrates, the legal situation concerning an alternative, i.e. non-binary, gender marker in official registers has not changed since 2005 in Germany. However, ongoing and recently intensifying legal debates suggest that this policy may be subject to change in the near future.

13 'Leute mit zwei Geschlechtern'.

14 '„Na und?", fragte er. „Ist doch egal, oder nicht? Jonny ist halt, was er ist. Oder sie. Stimmt doch, oder?"'

of adjectives and nouns disclose a person's gender, or force an author to choose their character's gender.[15] In all three novels – *Jenny mit O*, *Weil ich so bin* and *Atalanta Läufer_in* – the authors appear to try to minimize the effect gendered language has on the perception of their protagonists by using a first-person perspective. They allow their protagonists to tell their stories themselves, to talk rather than just be talked about, thereby leaving it to them to introduce their gender identity to the readers in the first place. Nevertheless, whenever the outside world refers to them, a gendered address or reference is inevitable. Personal pronouns or names have to be used, both of which are gendered according to binary standards. While Jenny changes her female name into its male counterpart (Jonny), Jona in *Weil ich so bin* is actually given a gender-neutral name by (too-good-to-be-true) unconditionally loving parents who spontaneously make up a name when they learn that their new-born can neither be called Jonas (a boy's name) nor Joana (a girl's name) (Fehér 2016, 12). However, Jona is referred to as *er* (he) (Fehér 2016, 21) or *ihm* (him) (Fehér 2016, 22) by their friends as an adolescent, and when the author describes an episode from Jona's childhood, the female article *die* in 'die fünfjährige Jona' ('the five-year-old Jona') (Fehér 2016, 30) creates a distinctly gendered character in the readers' minds. Even Jona once uses the introduction 'Reporterin Joana' ('reporter Joana') (Fehér 2016, 68) applying both the suffix *in* to form the female version of 'reporter' and a female name. Hence the image of a genderqueer or gender-neutral child or adolescent cannot be maintained.

The Performing of Gender along Binary Lines and Its Apparent Inevitability

Whereas in Christine Fehér's *Weil ich so bin* the outset is entirely different from *Jenny mit O*, as the protagonist Jona is born as an intersex person, the gender binary is still reinforced – only here by means of the performativity of gender. However, before amplifying Judith Butler's idea of performing gender and linking it to *Weil ich so bin*, Jona's gender identity and environment need to be briefly outlined. Indeed, the circumstances of Jona's life seem to be ideal to form a gender identity beyond the binary: Jona is born as an intersex person and is immediately accepted by their parents as such. They base their perception of Jona on what is biologically given and do not force them to adopt either a male or a female gender identity until puberty. However, as open-minded as Jona's parents may seem to be, their attitude still suggests an essentialist viewpoint. It is implied that only male sexual characteristics can result in a male gender (identity), and only female sexual characteristics can result in a female gender (identity). Consequently, having 'something of everything'[16] (Fehér 2016, 60) means that one's gender identity has to be both male and female. That the parents' ideas of gender, furthermore, adhere to binary standards shows when Jona reaches puberty: their parents want them to choose

---

15 Although a gender-neutral pronoun (*es*; it) exists in German, it is exclusively used for animals and objects. When used to refer to a person, the pronoun has a pejorative meaning.

16 '[v]on allem etwas'.

one of the two options based on whether they feel more like a boy or a girl (Fehér 2016, 25). Jona refuses and thereby discards traditional ideas of gender identity; nonetheless, their thinking is still strongly anchored in the gender binary, as they do not consider their gender to be beyond the binary, but rather use the binary as a basis for arguing that they are both: '"But I still feel like both. Sometimes more like a boy, sometimes more like a girl. Joana instead of Jona, Jona instead of Joana. That's just the way I am. Why should I pretend?"'[17] (Fehér 2016, 25). Just like *Jenny mit O, Weil ich so bin* features passages in which there is a hint at a gender identity beyond the binary: 'There is Jona and there is Joana and also something in-between'[18] (Fehér 2016, 47). However, this idea is never fully considered or implemented. Eventually, Jona concludes that, 'I just carry both sides inside of me. And I don't want to suppress either of them'[19] (Fehér 2016, 82). Thus, even though Jona's character bears the potential of a gender identity beyond the binary, Fehér complies with binary standards regarding her protagonist's gender identity. This becomes even more evident when the concept of the performativity of gender is taken into consideration.

The basic idea of Judith Butler's concept is that 'gender [is] a kind of doing, an activity incessantly performed' (2004, 1). However, there are limitations to a human being's performance of gender: society is just as much the author of one's gender as one is oneself, as, for instance, how one feels about one's gender is influenced by the options for gender expression one comes to know during the process of socialization in a society that knows primarily binary gender expressions, i.e. expressions that are either male or female. As a specific gendered meaning is assigned to every performance within a society, 'the terms that make up one's own gender are, from the start, outside oneself', and there is 'no single author' of gender (Butler 2004, 1). One further important aspect regarding the performance of gendered acts is repetition: the constitution of gender requires a repeated performance of the stylized acts. Butler claims that '[t]his repetition is at once a reenactment and reexperiencing of a set of meanings already socially established' (2007, 191), which means that society provides us with conventional gestures, movements or styles that produce us as gendered through their continued performance. Hence, the options in a society that regards gender as a dichotomy are limited: gendered acts are predominantly subdivided into male and female, as they are the results of social scripts that most members of a society actively perform and conform to (Pilcher and Whelehan 2005, 130).

In *Weil ich so bin*, Jona applies conventional gendered gestures, movements and styles according to their needs. Their friend Mia once remarks: '"You can run around as a boy or as a girl, just as you like"'[20] (Fehér 2016, 16). When Jona wants to be seen as a boy, they choose to wear loose jeans and hoodies (Fehér 2016, 17); by contrast, when they

17 '„Aber ich fühle mich eben immer noch als beides. Mal mehr wie ein Junge, mal mehr wie ein Mädchen. Joana statt Jona, Jona statt Joana. So bin ich eben. Warum sollte ich mich verstellen?"'

18 'Es gibt Jona und es gibt Joana und auch irgendwas dazwischen.'

19 'Ich trage nun mal beide Seiten in mir. Und ich will keine unterdrücken.'

20 '„Kannst als Junge oder Mädchen herumlaufen, je nachdem, wonach dir ist."'

want to be seen as a girl, they wear pink clothes and eyeliner (Fehér 2016, 22), earrings and lipstick (Fehér 2016, 29), or feminine clothes such as cardigans, ballerina shoes (Fehér 2016, 67) or skirts (Fehér 2016, 72). Notwithstanding the fact that Jona seems to choose their gender expression freely and apparently matches it with whatever gender (role) they want to be identified with, they are limited in their performance: '"Can you also do my hair? Tonight I'm Joana, not Jona. I will decide tomorrow what I will be then"'[21] (Fehér 2016, 18). Even though Jona is under the impression that they are able to choose their gender expression without constraint, they can only be either Joana or Jona. Society provides only those acts for re-enactment that are already gendered along binary lines. Jona's choice to alternate between male and female gender expressions may be novel as such and undoubtedly defies traditional gender roles, but it is still based on a binary conception of gender and thereby evokes the understanding of gender as binary in the readers' minds.

In view of the defining story element that Jenny in *Jenny mit O* strives to be perceived as a boy, it is no wonder that they too incorporate the binary conception of gender in their gender expression. Gendered styles, acts and movements that signal 'boy/male' are consciously as well as naturally employed at different instances in the novel. Throughout the book it is repeatedly stressed that Jenny dresses like a boy by, for instance, wearing boxer shorts (Fessel 2005, 19) or loose T-shirts (Fessel 2005, 58) – primarily to hide their female body features, which they detest: 'And this is exactly what I want: to look not in the least girly'[22] (Fessel 2005, 58). Moreover, Jenny trains their arm muscles (Fessel 2005, 11), observes men's postures and ways of walking only to imitate them (Fessel 2005, 66), adopts a male vernacular (Fessel 2005, 142), wears their hair short (Fessel 2005, 169), sometimes pees standing up (Fessel 2005, 188) and occasionally wears a jockstrap (Fessel 2005, 287). Primarily, Jenny's behaviour emphasizes the artificiality and arbitrariness of gendered acts and styles, as they are indeed perceived as a boy, even though they have the body of a girl. Traditional and essentialist ideas of gender identity are undone by Jenny's behaviour, since they highlight the missing link between biological features and gender expression. Nonetheless, the gender binary is still reinforced, since Jenny utilizes stereotypical ways of expression ascribed to the male gender to distance themselves from the other side of the dichotomy, the female gender.

Heteronormativity in German-Language YA: Affirmation and Challenge

Heteronormativity is a concept firmly established in Western societies, since heterosexuality has for a long time been at the core of social institutions such as the family or marriage, and even though some countries (among them Germany and Austria) now allow gay people to marry and have children, normative heterosexuality still defines these

21 '„Machst du mir noch die Haare? Heute Abend bin ich Joana, nicht Jona. Was morgen ist, entscheide ich."'

22 'Und genau das will ich ja auch: kein Stück mädchenhaft aussehen.'

social institutions: heterosexuality 'is constructed as a coherent, natural, fixed and stable category; as universal and monolithic' (Richardson 2000, 20). The prevalent idea is that two people from 'opposite sexes' desire each other, because difference is not only assumed to be indispensable for reproduction, but also for sexual arousal (Richardson 2000, 25). This suggests a widely accepted coherence of sex, gender and sexuality: '[F]or bodies to cohere and make sense there must be a stable sex expressed through a stable gender (masculine expresses male, feminine expresses female) that is [...] defined through the compulsory practice of heterosexuality' (Butler 2007, 208). Butler calls this the heterosexual matrix, which is used as a 'grid of cultural intelligibility through which bodies, genders, and desires are naturalized' (2007, 208). Considering the fact that all three German-language YA novels examined in this chapter feature an adolescent trans protagonist who gradually learns about their desires and own sexuality as well as further negotiates them with society, one would assume that they all critically question and challenge the idea of heteronormativity. To a certain degree, all three YA novels do indeed defy the idea of heterosexuality as 'normal'. However, it is exactly this degree in which they strongly differ.

In *Jenny mit O*, the young adult reader is confronted with both a challenge to and an affirmation of heteronormativity. To begin with, there is no doubt that the character of Jenny as such questions common and essentialist standards of heterosexuality as normative; Jenny was born with distinctly female biological characteristics and nonetheless identifies as a boy. The heterosexual matrix does not apply, as Jenny's sex and gender do not match, which, following the usual categorization, renders it impossible to clearly denominate them as heterosexual (or homosexual for that matter). In general, Jenny feels sexually attracted to girls (Fessel 2005, 25, 37) and has already had sex with female friends several times (ibid.), but refuses to identify as homosexual, since it does not feel right: 'The whole thing is headed in the right direction, but things don't add up. I just don't know how exactly'[23] (Fessel 2005, 38). They frequently ask themselves whether they are a lesbian, because they have a female body and prefer to sleep with girls (Fessel 2005, 108), although, on the other hand, they are convinced that they are not at all homosexual (Fessel 2005, 109, 196 and 280). Only when they are on a date with a homosexual woman do they recognize and label their sexuality for the first time: they think of themselves as heterosexual (Fessel 2005, 192 and 281). They tell Carolin, the heterosexual girl they are in love with, that they do not only want to be a boy, but that they are a boy – they have just got the wrong body (Fessel 2005, 262). The fact that Jenny refers to themselves as heterosexual is the reason why heteronormativity is partly affirmed in *Jenny mit O*: regardless of numerous homosexual secondary characters, the protagonist, whose perspective the reader shares, ends up in a heterosexual relationship between a (self-defined but nonetheless) boy and a girl. Being anything else but either heterosexual or homosexual is not even taken into consideration.

23 'Das läuft schon in die richtige Richtung, das Ganze, aber irgendwas stimmt daran nicht. Ich weiß bloß nicht, was.'

Just like Jenny in *Jenny mit O*, Jona in *Weil ich so bin* finds out which of the 'two' genders exactly they desire towards the end of the story: they are into boys, and into one in particular (Leon) (Fehér 2016, 103). Notwithstanding the observation that people's desirability apparently depends on their belonging to one specific gender, whereby gender is perceived as binary, in *Weil ich so bin* Fehér offers a greater challenge to heteronormativity than Fessel does in *Jenny mit O*. Firstly, Jona resembles Jenny since their gender and sexuality do not comply with the heterosexual matrix. Jona's gender identity is not 'stable' (i.e. in accordance with the binary conception of gender), it is not either male or female, and hence cannot 'naturally' result in a desire for the opposite gender. Secondly, the story's representation of desire and sexuality does not only question heteronormativity, but also undoes the dichotomy of heterosexual and homosexual by abstaining from applying labels. Jona's remarkably understanding father states the following: '"It is the person who matters, not whether you fall in love with a boy or with a girl. It has to be someone by whom you feel accepted. Who you can tell what's going on with you, and who stands by you no matter who you are"'[24] (Fehér 2016, 27). When it comes to falling in love, Jona's father is the only adult (and thus the only authority figure) in the story with an opinion on the subject. Therefore, his opinion strikes the reader as rather significant. Jona's parent's statement combined with the fact that no attempt is made at labelling Jona's sexuality suggest an understanding of desire and sexuality beyond the confines of the heterosexual/homosexual dichotomy, detached from heteronormativity.

Atalanta Läufer_in: A Journey beyond the Binary

While Lilly Axster's *Atalanta Läufer_in* does not completely dispense with the binary conception of gender, in which approach it resembles *Jenny mit O* and *Weil ich so bin*, it nonetheless dares to take a few more steps beyond the binary, which is the reason for its discussion in a separate section. The protagonist Atalanta's world is a speculative space; it does not actually exist and consists of imagined countries such as Festland (which means 'mainland' in English) or Eiland (reminiscent of the English word 'island'). The constant intertextual references to the mythological story of Atalanta and the fact that many characters bear adapted mythological names or the names of writers of myths (for instance, Ovid) alone give the story an air of the mythical. It could be argued that it is this fictitious space that allows Axster to play with non-conforming possibilities of gender identity. However, these countries' immigration policies and the questions directed at Atalanta about what they are (Axster 2014, 127) suggest a society not unlike ours in the Western world. Society's expectations of sex and gender hardly seem to differ: '[…] Ilia and Ovid imagined how their child had survived school without having been crushed

24 '„Es kommt auf den Menschen an, nicht darauf, ob du dich in einen Jungen oder ein Mädchen verknallst. Es muss jemand sein, von dem du dich angezogen fühlst. Dem du erzählen kannst, was mit dir los ist, und der zu dir hält, so wie du bist."'

by a taken-for-granted binary gender order and its body norms'[25] (Axster 2014, 142). Apparently, the binary gender order and its body norms exist just as well in the fictional world. What differentiates Atalanta's environment from Jenny's or Jona's is that there are some people who refrain from asking whether they are a boy or a girl. While Atalanta's trainer regards them as a 'child between girl and boy'[26] (Axster 2014, 117), which refers back to the gender binary, others seem to already have a concept of gender beyond those binary definitions: 'Apart from all that, they could not agree on what Lan [Atalanta] eventually was, a young woman, a young man, trans, intersex or none of all those options'[27] (Axster 2014, 127). The significant part of this sentence is the phrase 'none of all those options': it seems to be imaginable that a person is not either male or female but something completely else. Ovid, one of Atalanta's foster-fathers, even uses the English word 'queer'[28] (Axster 2014, 139) when referring to the mythological Atalanta.

First and foremost, it is Axster's well-thought-out and playful handling of language that creates room for non-conforming possibilities of gender. People, for instance, claim to have always known that Atalanta was 'neither boy nor girl'[29] (Axster 2014, 67), which can only mean that they are something else altogether. Furthermore, even though Axster cannot shed a constant evocation of the binary conception of gender by using personal pronouns or gendered articles and nouns (der Läufer, die Läuferin[30]) for Atalanta either in another character's reference to them, or in chapters in which a third-person narrator tells about Atalanta's childhood, she plays with these gendered elements of language. When Atalanta and her friends in the container town[31] dress up as beings that are male, female and unisex all at once, they decide to call themselves neither '*Er*' (he) nor '*Sie*' (she) but '*SEHR*' (the German word for 'very') (Axster 2014, 81). *SEHR* sounds like a mixture of *sie* and *er*, but is indeed situated beyond this binary classification, as it uses a different spelling. It is not a 'both', but rather something else entirely. What is more, while Atalanta may be a female name, for the larger part of the story, Atalanta uses the

---

25 '[...] malten Ilia und Ovid sich aus, wie ihr Kind die Schulzeit überstanden hatte, ohne von einer als selbstverständlich angenommenen Zweigeschlechterordnung und deren Körpernormen plattgemacht worden zu sein.'

26 'Kind zwischen Mädchen und Junge'.

27 'Über alldem konnten sie sich nicht einigen, was Lan jetzt war, eine junge Frau, ein junger Mann, transident, intersexuell oder nichts von allem.' Note: Atalanta sometimes uses the name Lan.

28 The author uses the English word *queer* in the original German text. Even though *queer* is listed in the Duden, a dictionary of the German language, the word is not frequently used by German speakers. What is more, the Duden gives only one explanation of the word, which is non-heterosexual. However, in this passage, German readers may still understand the term as referring to not only sexuality but also to gender identity, especially because of the context at hand.

29 'weder Junge noch Mädchen'.

30 *der Läufer* is a male runner; *die Läuferin* is a female runner.

31 The *Containerstadt* (container town) (Axster 2014, 59) is a small town in Festland consisting entirely of shipping containers. Presumably, it was erected to temporarily house illegal immigrants or refugees. The child Atalanta lives there for a while after having left the freight ship on which she fled her home country.

names Lan or Ata, which may be gendered in other languages, but in the story are only parts of Atalanta's whole name; their whole being therefore consists of male, female and ungendered parts.

In accordance with Axster's language, which appears to strive to create a character beyond the gender binary, Atalanta's gender identity and expression try to elude binary categorization. In some chapters Atalanta is Ata, a female child, in some they are Mr. Lan (Axster 2014, 32), a male runner, but predominantly the first-person narrator is not concerned about matters of gender identity. When Miles gropes them to reveal their secret and when they lose a tampon (Axster 2014, 6), their biological features point to a female Atalanta, but this binary categorization seems all too limiting for the protagonist. They may pose as a male person as a young adult by wearing a mock penis (Axster 2014, 8), by peeing standing up (Axster 2014, 24), by binding their chest (Axster 2014, 28), and by wearing male clothes, which all imply an identification along binary lines. Nevertheless, there is hardly any mention of Atalanta's motivation for their 'performance'. They do not desire to be a man like Jenny or consciously act in a masculine or feminine way to be perceived as a specific gender like Jona. When they disguise their identity, they have to wear lipstick, make-up and feminine clothes, and feel no discomfort either (Axster 2014, 40). As a child they wear girl's and boy's clothes at the same time to create a 'unisex' (Axster 2014, 44) look (the English word is used, although this is acceptable in German), and during the child's play in the container town, breasts, penises, vaginas and testicles are created out of pieces of cloth and put on randomly (Axster 2014, 81).

All in all, they want to be flat-chested like a boy, but want likewise to be a girl, which is why they are glad there is no penis to help with unambiguous identification: 'For this reason, I placed a bandage around my chest to guarantee my staying flat-chested like a boy. However, I still wanted to be a girl too and so I didn't mind the fact that I didn't have a penis'[32] (Axster 2014, 62). Once Atalanta even wonders why they are addressed as he when 'I could have been everything'[33] – with 'everything' here pointing to something beyond the binary options. Atalanta has always been a child 'that defied classification'[34] (Axster 2014, 92). They are not only both 'a female runner and a male runner'[35] (Axster 2014, 23), as Miles once remarks, since they just try on gender like clothes: '[…] Lan comes to terms with a new life and tries on the HE like the underpants or the new tracksuit top […]'[36] (Axster 2014, 110). It does not seem to matter at all that, when Lan arrives at Eiland, people suddenly see them as a boy. The key to Lan's attitude towards their gender identity is the following sentence: 'The HE that everyone in boarding school automatically uses to address him is okay too. Lan doesn't think about the reason. It is

32 'Damit legte ich einen Stützverband um meinen Brustkorb, um zu garantieren, dass ich flachbrüstig wie ein Junge bliebe. Trotzdem wollte ich auch ein Mädchen sein und so kam mir der Umstand, dass ich kein Glied hatte, sehr entgegen.'

33 'ich doch alles hätte sein können'.

34 'das sich nicht einordnen ließ'.

35 'eine Läuferin und ein Läufer'.

36 '[…] findet Lan in ein neues Leben hinein und probiert das ER an wie die Unterhosen und wie die neue Trainingsjacke […].'

what it is, it is new, everything is new, what once was is in the past'[37] (Axster 2014, 111). In other words, Atalanta is simply not bothered at all about traditional concepts or, in general, matters of gender identity. On the whole, there are instances in *Atalanta Läufer_in* in which the gender binary is certainly evoked. Yet, Axster's story and language lean far more obviously and strongly towards a representation of gender identity beyond a binary order than the other two YA novels discussed.

As far as *Atalanta Läufer_in*'s critique of heteronormativity is concerned, it is rather subtle, as desire and sexuality are not as present as they are in *Jenny mit O* or *Weil ich so bin*. The message is clear nonetheless: in the minds of the protagonists, labelling a person's sexuality seems to be just as insignificant as defining their gender identity along binary lines. Ovid and Ilia, who are in a relationship, can be Atalanta's foster-fathers, which is a state that is never questioned by anyone, and Atalanta could fall in love with 'either a male or a female person'[38] (Axster 2014, 37). Despite their biological features, Atalanta feels themselves to be not only female, which is why they are confused about the question whether to call sex between them and a woman lesbian sex: 'What would we be, our bodies, would that be called lesbian sex. But I was Lan after all … LAN. I didn't know anything'[39] (Axster 2014, 120). The labels of a heteronormative society simply do not apply, which is also illustrated in the following quote: 'A man who was a woman, and a hetero who was a homo. And what if I'm not gay, Miles thought, if I want her. Because Lan is a runner. Am I neutral then. He ran out of terms and with that of further images of himself'[40] (Axster 2014, 123). When Miles ponders over his sexuality after having realized that he feels attracted to Atalanta, he notices that hetero and homo do not apply, as he might just desire Atalanta because they are a runner and not on account of their gender. He considers himself neutral, but then runs out of appropriate terms. The last sentence may be understood as a hint at a language's duty to provide its speakers with enough material to form and express whatever they imagine. In Miles's case, language failed him: drawing on the dichotomy of homosexual/heterosexual, language shaped for and by a heteronormative society does not yet provide terms to denominate sexualities or desires beyond this limitation, which then again is not such a subtle critique of heteronormativity after all.

Conclusion

All things considered, *Jenny mit O*, *Weil ich so bin* and *Atalanta Läufer_in*, to a certain degree, reinforce the binary conception of gender and heteronormative standards, even though

37 'Das ER, mit dem ihn alle im Internat automatisch adressieren, passt auch. Lan denkt nicht darüber nach, wieso das so ist. Es ist so, es ist neu, alles ist neu, was war, das war.'

38 'die eine oder den anderen'.

39 'Was wären wir, unsere Körper, hieße das lesbischer Sex. Aber ich war doch Lan, … LAN. Ich wusste nichts.'

40 'Ein Mann, der eine Frau war, und ein Hetero, der ein Homo war. Und wenn ich aber nicht schwul bin, dachte Miles, wenn ich sie will. Weil Lan eine Läuferin ist. Bin ich dann neutral. Ihm gingen die Begriffe aus und damit weitere Vorstellungen von sich selbst.'

they depict protagonists whose gender identity and expression do not exactly conform to binary standards and the norms of a heteronormative society. On the one hand, the YA novels can, of course, be given credit for questioning and challenging a heterosexual matrix, essentialist ideas about the correlation between sex and gender, and the formation of one's gender identity along binary lines. After all, the protagonists are a boy inside a girl's body, an intersex adolescent who poses both as a boy and a girl, and a biological girl who wants to be both male and female, but in the end, simply does not care and adopts whichever gender is assigned by their environment. On the other hand, the protagonists and their environment predominantly rely on the gender binary for matters of classification: one can either be born a girl or a boy, identify as either male or female (or both alternately), gendered styles and acts are either masculine or feminine, and a person's sexuality is predominantly believed to be either heterosexual or homosexual.[41] This representation evokes the notion of a heterosexual norm (homosexuality is the only other option in this dichotomy, and as a dichotomy is essentially asymmetrical, homosexuality is 'the other'), and impedes the admittance of gender complexity into the young readers' minds. However, Axster's *Atalanta Läufer_in* stands out as a YA novel that manages to create a narrative space somewhat further beyond the gender binary, which is primarily achieved through the author's well-thought-out as well as playful and experimental handling of language.

All the previous considerations are not to say that the existence of the gender identities male and female as such is problematic, but that these two identities are dichotomized, which leads to an exclusion of other possible gender identities. The solution may not be a neutralization of gender and a complete annihilation of gender differences (in life as well as in literature), but an undoing of the male/female binary and a recognition of diverse gender identities beyond it. Genderqueer characters in YA, a genre which is usually read at an age at which young people's view of the world is still open and malleable, can show adolescents that the norms that govern our notions of reality are not written in stone, but are feeble constructions, which are only upheld because we act and write in accord with them (Butler 2004, 29). Provided that such characters' representations are not based on the gender binary, and their desire is in no way evocative of heteronormative standards, they could indeed cause young readers to question and challenge prevailing ideas of gender identity and sexuality, and create acceptance and recognition of people with a non-binary gender identity.

41 All of these points are a very true-to-life depiction of the current prevalent thinking in Germany and Austria. In particular, the heterosexual/homosexual dichotomy is firmly established. There is no doubt that some people may identify as bisexual or pansexual, but such identities are hardly taken seriously, which is not surprising given the fact that both countries have only in recent years conceded to same-sex unions the same rights that heterosexual couples have. (For instance, the Austrian Constitutional Court has only announced in December 2017 that same-sex couples are no longer limited to registered partnerships, but are going to be allowed to marry as of 31 December 2018 (see Verfassungsgerichtshof Österreich 2017, n.p.).) In the light of these developments, any official acknowledgement of bisexual or pansexual identities seems to be far off.

Only in recent years have books for young adults been published in the English-speaking world that are willing to focus on clearly non-binary gender identities and their expression. Adolescent protagonists beyond the gender binary, or, in other words, genderqueer characters can be found in, for instance, Steve Brezenoff's *Brooklyn, Burning* (2011), David Levithan's *Every Day* (2012), Pat Schmatz's *Lizard Radio* (2015) or Jeff Garvin's *Symptoms of Being Human* (2016), of which only Levithan's book has been translated into German. This is not to say that these novels entirely succeed in refraining from any evocation of the gender binary or of heteronormative standards. Nevertheless, the engagement with gender possibilities detached from a binary conception seems more frequent and committed in English-language YA, whereas it is already a big step in German-language YA to write about trans and intersex adolescents at all. The reason for German-language YA's being behind with respect to the representation of non-binary gender identities in comparison to the English-speaking world may well be found in the German language, which is heavily gendered along binary lines, and in the fact that public and legal recognition of non-conforming gender identities has only come into being quite recently, as was outlined in the introduction. Lately, in Germany and Austria, the public's attention may have been drawn to non-binary gender identities more frequently by events such as Conchita Wurst's (a woman with a beard impersonated by Austrian drag artist Tom Neuwirth) Eurovision Song Contest victory (Baier 2017, 11), but changes in language, laws and policies are slow to come. While, for instance, certain US states already legally recognize a third gender option regardless of physical characteristics (see, for example, California's Gender Recognition Act (California Legislative Information 2017, n.p.)), Austrian courts have just started to consider such an option for intersex people (see the Introduction to this chapter).

Consequently, just like the German language, and the German and Austrian legislation, German-language YA still has a long way to go – in the direction that *Jenny mit O*, *Weil ich so bin* and especially *Atalanta Läufer_in* begin to head in. However, the engagement with gender possibilities beyond the binary is intensifying, as can already be observed when comparing *Jenny mit O* from 2005, in which the gender binary is firmly established, and *Atalanta Läufer_in* from 2014, in which the conception of gender is situated somewhat further beyond the binary. The reception of *Atalanta Läufer_in*, including, for instance, the facts that it was turned into and performed as a play (Studio Theater Akzent in Vienna, 2016), and that it received an honorary prize from the city of Vienna in 2015, shows that the YA novel has struck a chord and may have brought non-conforming gender identities to public attention in Austria. Nonetheless, the discourse about trans, or, to use a more encompassing term, genderqueer individuals needs to be more open and to include male-to-female or female-to-male transitions as well as genderqueer characters in order to question and challenge the usefulness of a binary conception and classification of gender in the quest to admit gender complexity into the terms that govern reality (Butler 2004, 31).

Bibliography

Axster, Lilly. (2014) 2016. *Atalanta Läufer_in* (Atalanta Runner). Wien: Zaglossus.

Baier, Angelika. 2017. *Inter_Körper_Text: Erzählweisen von Intergeschlechtlichkeit in deutschsprachiger Literatur*. Wien: Zaglossus.

Becker, Inge, Ulrike Ravens-Sieberer, Veronika Ottová-Jordan, and Michael Schulte-Markwort. 2017. 'Prevalence of Adolescent Gender Experiences and Gender Expression in Germany'. *Journal of Adolescent Health* 61, no. 1: 83–90.

Bittner, Robert, Jennifer Ingrey, and Christine Stamper. 2016. 'Queer and Trans-Themed Books for Young Readers: A Critical Review'. *Discourse: Studies in the Cultural Politics of Education* 37, no. 6: 948–64.

Brezenoff, Steve. 2011. *Brooklyn, Burning.* Minneapolis: Carolrhoda Lab.

Butler, Judith. (1990) 2007. *Gender Trouble.* New York: Routledge.

———. 2004. *Undoing Gender.* New York: Routledge.

California Legislative Information. 2017. *Senate Bill No. 179.* https://leginfo.legislature.ca.gov/faces/billNavClient.xhtml?bill_id=201720180SB179

Commissioner of Human Rights. 2015. *Human Rights and Intersex People: Issue Paper.* Strasbourg: Éditions du Conseil de l'Europe. https://book.coe.int/eur/en/commissioner-for-human-rights/6683-pdf-human-rights-and-intersex-people.html

Fehér, Christine. 2016. *Weil ich so bin* (Because That's the Way I Am). Hamburg: Carlsen.

Fessel, Karen-Susan. 2005. *Jenny mit O* (Jenny with an O). Berlin: Querverlag.[42]

Frevert, Ute. 1995. *"Mann und Weib, und Weib und Mann": Geschlechter-Differenzen in der Moderne.* München: Beck.

Gaigg, Vanessa. 2018. 'Was die Option des dritten Geschlechts bedeutet'. *derStandard.at.* 3 July. https://derstandard.at/2000082685118/Was-die-Option-des-dritten-Geschlechts-bedeutet

Garvin, Jeff. 2016. *Symptoms of Being Human.* New York: Balzer + Bray.

GayYA. 2016. 'Masterlist: Transgender'. *GayYA.* Accessed 27 August 2018. http://www.gayya.org/masterlist-transgender

Gellhaus, Axel. 2011. 'Kognitive Aspekte der Literatur'. In *Neuroästhetik: Perspektiven auf ein interdisziplinäres Forschungsgebiet,* edited by Karin Herrmann, 77–86. Kassel: kassel university press.

ILGA-Europe. 2011. *ILGA-Europe Annual Review 2011.* Brussels: ILGA-Europe. https://www.ilga-europe.org/resources/rainbow-europe/ilga-europe-annual-review-2011

———. 2018. *Rainbow Europe 2018.* Brussels: ILGA-Europe. https://www.ilga-europe.org/resources/rainbow-europe/rainbow-europe-2018

Kuklin, Susan. (2014) 2016. *Beyond Magenta: Transgender Teens Speak Out.* London: Walker.

Levithan, David. 2012. *Every Day.* New York: Alfred A. Knopf.

McNeil, Elizabeth. 2008. 'Ellen Wittlinger's *Parrotfish*: Normalizing Transgender in Young Adult Literature'. *ALAN Review* 36, no. 1: 89–92.

Parliamentary Assembly. 2015. *Resolution 2048 (2015): Discrimination Against Transgender People in Europe.* Accessed 14 August 2018. http://semantic-pace.net

Pilcher, Jane, and Imelda Whelehan. 2005. *Fifty Key Concepts in Gender Studies.* London: SAGE.

Prokhovnik, Raia. 1999. *Rational Woman: A Feminist Critique of Dichotomy*. London: Routledge.

'queer'. *Duden.de.* Accessed 17 May 2020. https://www.duden.de/rechtschreibung/queer

Richardson, Diane. 2000. *Rethinking Sexuality.* London: SAGE.

Riedl, Stefan. 2018. 'Management von Jugendlichen mit Transidentität'. *Pädiatrie und Pädologie* 53, no. 2: 58–63.

Schmatz, Pat. 2015. *Lizard Radio.* Somerville: Candlewick Press.

Sokoll, Talya. 2013. 'Representations of Trans* Youth in Young Adult Literature: A Report and a Suggestion'. *Young Adult Library Services* 11, no. 4: 23–26.

42 Querverlag is a German publishing house specializing in queer texts. They call themselves 'Deutschlands erster lesbisch-schwuler Verlag' (Germany's first lesbian-gay publishing house) on their homepage.

Turner, Mark. 1996. *The Literary Mind: The Origins of Thought and Language*. New York: Oxford University Press..

Verfassungsgerichtshof Österreich. 2017. 'Unterscheidung zwischen Ehe und eingetragener Partnerschaft verletzt Diskriminierungsverbot'. Wien: Verfassungsgerichtshof Österreich https://www.vfgh.gv.at/medien/Ehe_fuer_gleichgeschlechtliche_Paare.de.php

Chapter Four

HOMO SAPIENNE: A MIRROR OF MODERN GREENLANDIC LIFE

Mette Laustsen

Introduction

Homo Sapienne was the debut novel by Niviaq Korneliussen, a young Greenlandic woman, and was published in 2014. *Homo Sapienne* is an anomaly in Greenlandic literature, which hardly ever gets translated into other languages, because it has in fact been translated quite widely.[1] So far it has been published in German,[2] French (Canada and France), Swedish, and English[3] in the United Kingdom. As I write this, it is due to be published in English in the USA, Norwegian, Finnish, Icelandic and Czech, and publishing houses in Spain, Italy and South Korea are interested. That amount of interest, translation and publication never happens for a Greenlandic book; nor are Greenlandic books generally covered in foreign media. So what makes *Homo Sapienne* special? To answer that question, it is necessary to first look at the history of Greenlandic literature and LGBTQ+ issues in Greenland. In this chapter, I will discuss what makes this book unique: not only the LGBTQ+ subject matter, but also the style in which it is written and the gap it filled in Greenland.

Some Background on Greenland and the Greenlandic Literary Tradition

Greenland is a former colony of Denmark. In 1979, Greenland received home rule and in 2009 self-government, but Greenland is not totally independent of Denmark. Denmark still rules over foreign affairs and the military, and Greenlandic and Danish are both recognized as official languages.

There are about 56,000 people in Greenland. In the capital and the biggest city, Nuuk, there are about 17,000 people. With so few Greenlanders, there is a need for a foreign workforce, since there are not enough Greenlanders with the right education to

1 Fairly often, a Greenlandic book will be simultaneously be published in Greenlandic and Danish, but that has to do with Greenland being bilingual and because Greenland is not fully independent of Denmark.

2 The German title is *Nuuk #ohneFilter* (Nuuk #nofilter).

3 The English title is *Crimson.*

fill all the different jobs. As a result, there are a lot of Danes working in Greenland, especially in Nuuk.

For the purposes of this chapter, I differentiate between 'books in Greenlandic' and 'Greenlandic books'. Books in Greenlandic are defined here as translations into Greenlandic, not originally written in Greenlandic, while Greenlandic books I see as books originally written in Greenlandic.

Reading and writing traditions in Greenland were established relatively recently compared to other countries. As with most other indigenous populations, the Greenlandic people had an oral culture, until the Europeans introduced writing as a medium for a new and different culture and outlook.

In 1721, the Norwegian missionary Hans Egede arrived in Greenland and started converting the Greenlanders to Christianity. One of the ways to introduce Christianity to the Greenlanders was by translating parts of the Bible and other Christian texts into Greenlandic, so they could hear the Christian texts in their own language. Greenlandic was not a written language until the missionaries came and made it so. In 1739, the first four chapters of the New Testament were published in Greenlandic. By 1799, a total of 20 books in Greenlandic had been published, and all were about religion. In the 1800s, 115 religious or non-fiction books in Greenlandic were published.

The first Greenlandic novel *Sinnattugaq* (The Dream)[4] by Mathias Storch was published in 1914 and was about social conditions and the future; these were the topics for most poetry of that time period as well. From the 1920s, authors such as Frederik Nielsen, Pavia Petersen and Hans Lynge looked to the past for inspiration to produce poetry and prose. At the time, Greenland was still a traditional hunter society, in which most Greenlanders lived much as they had for centuries. Until 1940, Greenland was a protected and fairly isolated country, and the outside world had minimal influence on everyday Greenlandic life.

In 1950, the Danish government started a project that they called the 'reorganization'. The idea was that Greenland should be transformed into a modern European country. Education and modernization were the keys, so the Danish language was to be introduced to children from the first grade. Danish teachers were brought in and as the demands on the schools increased, the shortage of Greenlandic teachers became more noticeable and so even more Danish teachers came to the Greenlandic schools. That had an impact on the schools and on education, which became very Danish and marked by the Danish language. There was also some oppression of traditional spiritual and cultural activities. The process could be called a 'Danification' of Greenland. In that process, some Greenlanders growing up in the '50s and '60s lost their language and in some cases their Greenlandic identity.

Some literary progress happened in the '50s. In 1959, the first Greenlandic children's novel was published: *Kâle: atuagaK mêrarsiut* (Karl, the Book for Children) by Jørgen Fleischer. From the end of the 1960s onwards, social conditions were again taken up as subject matter, in some cases in a very satirical and/or polemical style. Among the

4 All translations are my own, unless otherwise noted.

authors were names like Moses Olsen, Aqqaluk Lynge and Ole Korneliussen. Political and cultural works started to make Greenland Greenlandic again. People began to want to reclaim their identity. After home rule in 1979, the focus was put back on the Greenlandic language. For the schools, that meant that Greenlandic officially became the language that the schools should teach in and Danish became the pupils' first foreign language. A Greenlandification was started, which is still in progress today.

Compared to some other indigenous cultures, the Greenlandic language and culture is not in such a dire situation. Greenlanders have comparatively many books in their own language and their cultural heritage is still largely intact. They have not fully lost their identity in spite of the issues of the '50s and '60s, and they have their own country, though not full independence.

The Greenlandic language is not just one language. Due to the huge distances between different areas of the country and the isolation of some parts of Greenland, there are four different versions or dialects of Greenlandic: North Greenlandic, East Greenlandic, South Greenlandic and West Greenlandic. People from the different parts of Greenland can have trouble understanding each other. West Greenlandic is the standard language and the language used in school books, among other texts.

In 1974, a new Greenlandic orthography was introduced, which is significantly different from the old one. Greenlanders who grew up reading the old way find reading books with the new orthography challenging and some do not read new books, so they have even fewer books to read in their own language. The converse applies to the younger Greenlanders: the older books may not be accessible to them, because it is a written Greenlandic that they do not easily understand.

Greenlandic Young Adult Books

Some years ago, I came across an article by Rudine Sims Bishop called 'Mirrors, Windows, and Sliding Glass Doors' (1990). It is an article I often use when talking and writing about Greenlandic literature, because it clearly and understandably states the issues Greenlandic literature faces. In the article, the author talks about children's literature and compares it to windows, sliding doors and mirrors. She explains that windows offer views of worlds real or imagined, familiar or strange. These windows can become sliding doors, if the readers via their imagination walk through to become part of the author's world. If the book transforms human experience and reflects it back to the reader, and the reader can see their own lives and experiences as part of the larger human experience in that reflection, then the window becomes a mirror. Readers often search for the mirrors in their books. Though the author talks about children's literature specifically, the same principles can certainly be applied to materials for young adults.

In the Danish books available in Greenland, there are plenty of windows and sliding doors for Greenlandic youth. It is not hard for them to get a view of a different world or culture. But what is lacking are the mirrors. It is not often that Danish books, or foreign books translated into Greenlandic, mirror Greenlandic life. There are some books written by Danish authors that take place in Greenland, but a lot of them describe Greenlandic life through Danish eyes and they often focus on history or the parts of

Greenlandic life that are foreign to non-Greenlandic readers. They do not really give a real picture of modern Greenlandic life. For example, *Et halvt hjerte* (Half a Heart)[5] by Lene Fauerby and *Slædehundene hyler* (The Sleighdogs' Howls)[6] by Charlotte Blay are both by Danes about Greenland, and it is not fair to expect Danish books about Greenland to be more than a Dane's version of windows and sliding doors regarding Greenlandic life. But it is acceptable to expect Greenlandic books to be mirrors, at least to a certain extent. Unfortunately, the low number of Greenlandic books makes those expectations hard to fulfil. There simply are not enough books to provide mirrors for all the different aspects of the Greenlandic culture and ways of life.

Young adults as a separate reader group are not a major target audience for publishers in Greenland. Books are mostly either children's books or adult books, with very few written especially for young adults currently. But there are of course books that are suitable and might be interesting for the young Greenlander. Looking at just the books classified in libraries as young adult books, there are in total only about 100[7] fiction and non-fiction titles suitable and potentially interesting for young adults originally written in Greenlandic or translated into Greenlandic. Of the 100, about 50 are fiction. Of the 50 fiction books, about 30 were written by Greenlanders (referred to in this chapter as 'Greenlandic books'). The rest have been translated into Greenlandic. Of the 50 titles, half are more than 20 years old. Twelve of the titles are less than 10 years old, of which 11 were written by Greenlanders. Five of the 12 titles are less than five years old and all five were written by Greenlanders. This means that only 5 per cent of the books available for young adults are recent fiction titles written by Greenlanders.

With the continuing focus being on supporting Greenlandic culture and language, hardly any books published in Greenlandic are translations now. The money being spent on publishing books is spent on books written by Greenlanders. The small quantity does not say anything about the quality of the books; of course there are some good books in the collection. But the data I presented show clearly that many of them are unfortunately quite old and therefore may have cover art or subject matter that does not appeal to the modern Greenlandic child or young adult. In general, it could be argued that the content in most of the Greenlandic literature available is not written with young adults in mind.

Many of the 100 books mentioned above are what we could call 'kayak literature', meaning books that take place in the good old days, where the men went out hunting in their kayaks, or else they are works that describe the political development in Greenland. These are two different and interesting subjects but they are not always appealing to most modern young Greenlanders. In school, children and young adults have to read about those subjects, which can make them feel boring and too much like school assignments

5 This is a story about a girl grieving the death of her mother and sister. In the mountains, she finds a mystical comfort and she is transported into the imagined life of the Qilakitsoq mummies. Past and present are bound together.

6 A story about 14-year-old Nannavina set in the small Greenlandic village where she grew up. Her brother has disappeared and she does not know who she can trust. She goes on a dogsled ride, but things go wrong.

7 The numbers are as of June 2018 and are my own calculations, as checked by colleagues.

and not leisure reading. Speaking with the Greenlandic youth in my role as a librarian, a lot of them told me that for them, Greenlandic literature has the reputation of being boring and uninteresting. It does not mirror modern Greenlandic young adult life. The young Greenlander cannot recognize their voice or their life in them. Thus, there is clearly a gap in the market for modern Greenlandic young adult books, and efforts have been made to address this recently.

In 2012 NAPA (Nunani Avannarlerni Piorsarsimassutsikkut Attaveqaat, or the Nordic Institute in Greenland), Nunatta Atuagaateqarfia (Central Library of Greenland), NUIF (Nuuk Ungdom I Fremdrift, the youth club in Nuuk) and milik publishing launched a short story competition. The name Allatta was chosen. Translated to English, 'allatta' means 'let's write'. The name was chosen for the simple reason that it was what needed to be done: let's write the stories that are missing. So far the Allatta project has resulted in three anthologies: *Inuusuttut – nunatsinni nunarsuarmilu / Ung i Grønland – Ung i verden* (Young in Greenland – And in the World) (Vahl and Therkildsen 2013), *2040* (Kleist et al. 2015) and *Paasininneq / Rum* (Room)[8] (Didriksen et al. 2018). Several of the winners from the two first anthologies have been, or are currently, working on new literary projects and three of the winners from the first anthology have since had their own books published. One of these was *Homo Sapienne,* which became a milestone in Greenlandic young adult literature and Greenlandic LGBTQ+ literature.

LGBTQ+ History in Greenland

Homosexuality is not an unknown subject in Greenlandic culture. In the traditional myths, which stem from before Christianity was introduced into Greenland, there are some featuring LGBTQ+ persons and subjects. The traditional myths are not generally judgemental. The LGBTQ+ persons are not necessarily the bad characters or depicted as wrong in the myths. The myths are the historic sources we have to tell us about the older history of Greenlandic LGBTQ+, which means we do not have much to go by. I will discuss them further below.

Written sources only became available after the Christian missionaries arrived, and Christianity certainly did not bring acceptance of LGBTQ+ people or issues. After Christianity, the stance was to ignore the subject. Leise Johnsen, director of Kalaallit Illuutaat – Det Grønlandske Hus, the Greenland Institute in Copenhagen, sums it up precisely, when she writes, 'Det, man ikke taler om, findes ikke', or 'That which you don't speak about, does not exist' (Johnsen 2012, 280). Homosexuality became taboo for a very long time. It was not really spoken about and mostly just ignored. Many homosexuals moved to Denmark if they wanted to live their life out in the open.

Luckily, attitudes started to change, and there have been a lot of new developments, especially in the last 20 years. Registered partnership became a possibility for Greenlanders in 1996 by law. In 2002, Qaamaneq, which means light, was founded as

8 The title has a double meaning, and also means broadminded.

an interest group for Greenlandic LGBTQ+ people. It ran until 2007 and was restarted again around 2014.

In 2005, *Qattuneq issiavilik* (Bench with a View), the first Greenlandic LGBTQ+ novel, was published. On 5 May 2010, the first Gay Pride was held in Greenland, in Nuuk. In 2011, there were Gay Pride events in both Nuuk and Sisimiut (the second largest town in Greenland). Since then, there have been several more Prides.

At the Nuuk Gay Prides in 2011 and 2012, 'non-heterosexuals' were invited to have their portrait taken and to offer a quote about their sexuality. The portraits and quotes were turned into the exhibition Gay Greenland, which was shown in Nuuk and Sisimiut, and parts of it have been shown in most of the municipality offices in Greenland. It was the first time faces and words had been put to a Greenlandic minority that traditionally had been silent and largely hidden. By touring Greenland, the exhibition introduced people in the small towns to a minority that they might not know much about and therefore might have prejudices against. By making them visible, the exhibition showed that LGBTQ+ people looked just like everyone else and were not so different after all. The exhibition has also been shown in Reykjavik, Thorshavn and Copenhagen. In 2015, it won the culture prize at Axgil, which is the Danish LGBTQ+ community's prize ceremony (Kruse 2015).

Most recently, from 1 April 2016, by law, same-sex couples could be married in church. So a lot of positive change has happened in the last 23 years concerning LGBTQ+ visibility and rights.

LGBTQ+ Literature in Greenland

When *Homo Sapienne* was published it became one out of only seven Greenlandic LGBTQ+ books. The seven are:

Aamma illit inuuneraat… HIV AIDS-ilu pillugit oqaluttuat / Livet er også dit… Historier om HIV og AIDS (Life is Also Yours… Stories about HIV and AIDS) from 2004, edited by Káte Hansen. A non-fiction book about Greenlanders who have HIV or AIDS. The book is bilingual in Greenlandic and Danish.

Qattuneq issiavilik (Bench with a View) by Jørgen Petersen from 2005, which was the first Greenlandic fiction LGBTQ+ book. It is about a young man's realization and acceptance of his sexuality. The book is only available in Greenlandic.

Kakiorneqaqatigiit[9] from 2010 and *Alumiguulik*[10] from 2013 by Kristian Olsen Aaju. Two crime fiction stories, where a lesbian couple are the main characters. The books have been published both in Greenlandic and Danish. They do not take place in Greenland and they do not provide much insight into Greenlandic life or being Greenlandic and LGBTQ+.

---

9 The Danish title is *Det tatoverede budskab*. Translated to English it would be The Tattooed Message. I read the Danish version.

10 The Danish title is *Den tatoverede strandvasker*. Translated to English it would be The Tattooed Body Washed Ashore. I read the Danish version.

Gay Greenland is the catalogue for the photographic exhibition with portraits of Greenlandic LGBTQ+ people from 2012.

...*Inuugatta: Nunatsinni angutit anguteqatiminnik arnallu arnaqatiminnik aappaqartartut pillugit* (...Because We Are Alive: About Gays and Lesbians in Greenland) from 2014, written by Hjalmer Dahl. A non-fiction book about being gay in Greenland.

Homo Sapienne from 2014 written by Niviaq Korneliussen. A young adult/adult fiction book initially published in both Greenlandic and Danish. More on this below.

Besides those seven, there are a few more Greenlandic LGBTQ+ stories:

'Svigermoderen, som giftede sig med sin svigerdatter (The Mother-in-Law Who Married Her Daughter-in-Law)',[11] and 'Arnaussâq'[12]. Two examples of traditional Greenlandic myths with LGBTQ+ elements.

'San Francisco' written by Niviaq Korneliussen. One of the winning short stories in *Inuusuttut – nunatsinni nunarsuarmilu / Ung i Grønland – Ung i verden* from 2013. Again, I will return to this below.

All of the above-mentioned titles are written and published for adults except 'San Francisco', which is part of a young adult short story anthology, and *Homo Sapienne*. As is clear from the dates mentioned above, *Homo Sapienne* was published nine years after the first Greenlandic LGBTQ+ novel. But one could say that the Greenlandic LGBTQ+ story tradition is a lot older than the 13 years the books have been around, because of the traditional myths.

'The Mother-in-Law Who Married Her Daughter-in-Law'

In this section, I will analyse a version of the traditional myth that was collected near the beginning of the 1900s by Knud Rasmussen and was first published at the beginning of the 1920s (Taateraaq 2000).[13] Written down in Danish, 'Svigermoderen, som giftede sig med sin svigerdatter (The Mother-in-Law Who Married her Daughter-in-Law)' is over 100 years old, but in the oral storytelling tradition it is many years older, although exactly how old is not known.

The myth is very short, only about 19 lines, but much happens in those lines. Ukuamaaq,[14] a man, mistreats his wife, so she runs away from him. Her mother-in-law finds her, and they make a life together. The mother-in-law is described as behaving like a man and as using a reindeer penis. She goes hunting and brings home many reindeer. However, Ukuamaaq finds them and he shames his mother by laughing at her when she drops the reindeer penis. He chases her, but she commits suicide from shame by jumping into a big waterfall. Ukuamaaq takes his wife back home with him and the

11 There are several different versions of this myth. More about this below.

12 It is a name, so no translation is needed.

13 This version can be read in *Myter og sagn fra Grønland*. Collected by Knud Rasmussen. Forlaget Sesam.

14 In the version that was my main focus, Ukuamaaq is the name of the son. In other versions, it is the name of the daughter-in-law. Language-wise it is probably more correct that it is the name of the daughter-in-law.

story ends. It is, obviously, not a happy story. The bad man gets what he wants and the lesbian relationship (or, perhaps to be more precise, the females living as a man and woman) ends with a suicide and the woman back in a difficult heterosexual relationship. However, it is important to note that the relationship between the mother-in-law and the daughter-in-law is not described as a bad thing or deemed to be reprehensible. The mother-in-law commits suicide because Ukuamaaq laughs at her reindeer penis and through his laughter he shames her. Being a laughing-stock and having to cope with the loss of honour was (and perhaps still is) a very serious matter. When such a loss of honour happened, Greenlanders could be so ashamed that they would go out into the mountains and become *qivittoq*, or a hermit who in time would take on animal-like abilities, such as heightened senses and supernatural abilities (Kreutzmann 2018). When a *qivittoq* died, he/she was believed to become a ghost. I would argue that it is not the act of their relationship in itself that results in the suicide, but the shaming done by a bad man. Ukuamaaq is not the hero of the story. He might be the winner, but it is the mother-in-law (his mother) who is the hero. She took good care of her daughter-in-law and treated her well. In the story, a female living as a man is shown to be capable of providing for a wife; the problems stem from a third party. This might be a lot to read into 19 lines, but short myths and tales are meant to be read into.

There are different versions of the myth from around Greenland. In some, the mother-in-law is said to force her daughter-in-law to go with her, and in others, the man kills his mother and his wife. A version written down and first published in 1875 is somewhat different. In this version, the mother-in-law is killed and called despicable (Rink 1974). I cannot help but wonder if the description of the mother-in-law as despicable is the original storyteller's description or if the word and the judgement come from the man who wrote the myth down and published it in 1875. It is also in this version that the mother-in-law is most clearly described to be forcing her daughter-in-law, and nothing is said about her hunting abilities. The already short myth is more than halved in the judgemental 1875 version, which I read as a religious damnation of an unnatural woman. In all the other versions of the myth I have read, the mother-in-law is not despised as such, and is shown to be very capable of providing for her daughter-in-law.

'Arnaussâq'

'Arnaussâq' is a myth about a man, Arnaussâq, who acted like a woman. The translation of the name would be 'Looks like a woman'. If the women in the village needed help with sewing they asked Arnaussâq and he could always help. When sleeping next to the young women he never touched them, but when sleeping next to the young men he touched them. After Arnaussâq's death, it became a tradition for the young hunters when going out to hunt to make sexual movements towards Arnaussâq's grave and yell: Arnaussâq, we are coming to have sex with you. That brought good luck for their hunting trips.

The myth/story is believed to be based on an historical event from the 1800s. It was a common belief that women and dead people could attract animals and ensure a good hunt, whereas in this story it is a dead homosexual man bringing good luck to the hunters. Arnaussâq is accepted and treated as they would treat a woman or dead member of their village. There is no judgement. Arnaussâq is liked and his abilities in regard to the traditionally female tasks are respected and sought out.

Qattuneq Issiavilik

Many years went by before *Qattuneq issiavilik* (Bench with a View) by Jørgen Petersen was published in 2005. *Qattuneq issiavilik* is a traditional LGBTQ+ novel in the sense that it tells the story of a young man, Kari, on his journey of discovery and his acceptance of his sexuality. While on holiday, Kari wakes up after a night on the town, and realizes that he has been with a man. That leads to some soul-searching and the realization that even though he has been with women, he has always done so without feelings. These relationships were a means of suppressing his homosexuality. He accepts his true feelings and attractions. Kari is very afraid of his family's reaction, especially since he knows someone who lost their family after coming out. After some time, Kari finally comes out to his mother and twin brother. Luckily, their reaction is very positive and they accept him as he is. His mother promises to help him tell his father and persuade him to accept the situation as well. The book is written for adults, but can certainly be read by young adults also.

Qattuneq issiavilik has only been published in Greenlandic, which is a shame, because that means that the book and the story are only available for the relatively few that can read Greenlandic well enough, so it really is just for Greenlandic-speaking Greenlanders. It would be beneficial if it were available for more interested readers. If the first Greenlandic LGBTQ+ book could be read by more LGBTQ+ people and indeed more people generally outside Greenland, readers would have a window that opens onto Greenlandic LGBTQ+ life.

'San Francisco'

Of the ten winning short stories in the first Allatta competition, one was an LGBTQ+ story: 'San Francisco' by Niviaq Korneliussen, a young Greenlandic lesbian born in 1990. When the anthology was published in 2013, it was the first time that a young Greenlandic LGBTQ+ woman had written for her peers and had her writing published. When I interviewed Niviaq some years ago about her participation in the Allatta project, she told me that she mostly only reads Danish books, and that as a writer she can only get inspiration from other countries. There are too few books in her own language that she can be inspired by. She writes about what she feels is missing in Greenlandic literature; in other words, she writes her own mirrors.

'San Francisco' is a road story. Fia is travelling across the USA, having run away to the States from Nuuk. She is grieving and losing herself completely in her grief, and has flashbacks to her life with Sara in Nuuk. Back in Nuuk, Fia had felt watched and judged and that had caused problems in her relationship with Sara. After a big fight about Fia's discomfort with people seeing them as a couple, Sara left their home and was hit by a car and died. But 'San Francisco' is not a short story where being homosexual is the main issue; rather, it is mainly a story about grief and finding light again after a great loss. The fact that Fia's love is a woman is not the main issue. It does, however, feature death, as is common in many LGBTQ+ works from around the world.

Homo Sapienne

One year after 'San Francisco', Niviaq Korneliussen had her first novel published by the same publisher who published the first Allatta anthology. *Homo Sapienne* was and still is something new and different in both Greenlandic young adult and Greenlandic LGBTQ+ literature. In *Homo Sapienne*, the author writes with a clear young Greenlandic voice, using text messages, Facebook, loan words, music and other intertextual references to give the reader a direct insight into the lives and culture of young Greenlanders. This is how the author and her peers speak and act. Niviaq Korneliussen also plays with Greenlandic words and names and lets them play a part in the stories. The names of three of the five main characters all have an additional meaning; they become metaphors of a sort, as will be discussed below.

In a lot of literature set in Greenland, there are long passages devoted to the beautiful natural wilderness. But life in Greenland is about so much more, especially for young Greenlanders. *Homo Sapienne* is about modern Greenlandic city life as seen through the eyes of five different but intertwined Greenlanders, each of whom has their own chapter. Each chapter has a song title as the heading.

Fia (song: Crimson & Clover by Joan Jett and the Blackhearts)

The first chapter is Fia's story. She is unhappy with her boyfriend of three years, Peter. They live together. The chapter begins with several of Fia's long trains of thought:

> Peter. One man. Three years. Thousands of plans. Millions of dinner invitations. Vacuuming, dishwashing and cleaning. Rushing on forever towards infinity. False smiles turning uglier. Dry kisses stiffening like desiccated fish. Bad sex should be avoided at all costs. My fake orgasms get harder to believe as time goes by. But we're still making plans. (Korneliussen 2018, 5)[15]

The reader can feel her unhappiness and her inner turmoil. She only expresses her true feelings about her life with Peter in her head. Outwardly, she plays the role of the girlfriend planning on a lifetime together. But on the inside she is dying:

> Death has begun to appear in my dreams and I am petrified. Murder. Death of the soul. A shrivelled corpse. Suicide. Death has begun to visit me, and I am petrified. Mass murder. A failed suicide attempt. Envious of the dead. I've begun to walk hand in hand with it, and I'm petrified. I make up my mind because death won't leave my mind. There has always been something missing here. (Korneliussen 2018, 10)

---

15 All of the quotations from *Homo Sapienne* are taken from the UK translation by Anna Halager, published in 2018.

The dark thoughts scare her enough to change her situation. After Fia breaks up with Peter, her friend and new roommate, Arnaq, takes her to a party to try to find her a new man. At the party, Fia meets Sara and falls for her instantly, but Sara has a girlfriend. Fia tries to forget Sara and forget that she felt attracted to another woman. She takes another man home with her, but she does not really feel like sleeping with him.

The next time Arnaq and Fia go to a bar, they meet Sara and her girlfriend. Fia can no longer ignore that she is attracted to women. She tries out her attractions with Arnaq by having sex with her. Arnaq is a Greenlandic name, but it is also the Greenlandic word for woman. So Fia replaces Sara with Arnaq, another *arnaq* (woman). The experience with Arnaq gives Fia her answer: she is a lesbian. After sex, Fia goes into her own room to think. She calls her brother to talk and he invites her to an afterparty. At the party Fia meets Sara again, and Sara kisses her. The readers can see how Fia begins to accept her feelings and who she is. She is no longer indifferent or depressed. She is free and in love:

> She walks over to me, and my world is totally silent. I only look at her, and the sensation within me is infinite. She takes hold of me and escorts me out of the door, and I don't resist. The spring night is invigorating. Nature has quietly come to life again, and that's all I hear. There's something beautiful in front of me. From Greenland to infinity, and back again … What a day to be alive. She reads the note I have been carrying around for two weeks. The spring night gives me life, and Sara kisses me. What a day to realise I'm not dead. Love has rescued me. (Korneliussen 2018, 33)

Inuk (Song: Home by Foo Fighters)

Over the course of three months, we follow Inuk's life as he runs away from Greenland due to a possible scandal. He experiences blame, self-hatred, the 'killing' of the old, rebirth and finally acceptance. He had told his best friend Arnaq, in confidence, that a male politician had made a pass at him, and Arnaq told the story at a party to get attention from the rest of the partygoers. The chapter consists of diary entries and letters to and from his sister Fia and former friend Arnaq. Most of the entries and letters are signed differently, depending on how he feels about himself at that moment. He calls himself, for example, a runaway, a survivor, a refugee, a liar, a claustrophobic homophobe, a man who wishes he was not a Greenlander, a Greenlander by force, silent, lost, unemployed, not angry, dead, loved, devoted, brother, home, and homo sapiens. Inuk writes:

> I wouldn't have survived if I hadn't escaped. But here they can't touch me. Never again will I return to Greenland. Never again will I be holed up in prison again. Never again will I be walled up behind tall mountains. Never again will I call a Greenlander my fellow countryman. Never will I go back to live among the prison inmates. Because I'm ashamed to call myself a Greenlander. Refugee. (Korneliussen 2018, 43–44)

He runs away from Greenland, which he sees as a prison of eyes that stare, judge and condemn. He writes:

> Dear Fia
>
> Do you remember when I first discovered that you had started drinking and smoking? Do you remember how sad I was when I found out? I often wonder whether your bad friends influenced you or whether this was something you decided on your own. [...] You are not into women. I know that. You're ok. You're not evil. Arnaq has just dragged you down with her. You're so much better than that. I'm asking you to drop Arnaq and never go back. I don't want to lose you.
>
> Inuk (Korneliussen 2018, 47–49)

He cannot accept homosexual feelings in himself and therefore he cannot accept those feelings in his sister. He blames Arnaq for everything: she is the evil that ruined his life and now he feels she is doing the same to Fia. He sends her a letter with a questionnaire for her to fill out, in which all the questions are essentially a way for him to tell her how much he hates her. In return, he receives this letter:

> My dearest Inuk
> I've filled these out:
> Do you think I'll forgive you? x No
> Are you a heartless bitch? x Yes
> Forgive me.
> Arnaq. (Korneliussen 2018, 57)

Slowly, over the course of more letters and diary entries, Inuk changes. He forgives and accepts:

> Dear Fia
> I'm into men.
> Inuk. (Korneliussen 2018, 73)

A subsequent letter reads:

> Dear Inuk
> I know. You're not alone. You'll never be alone
> Fia (Korneliussen 2018, 74)

And at last:

> The last day
> Finally, I am home.
> Homo. Sapiens. Inuk (Korneliussen 2018, 75)

Inuk's chapter is comprised of 32 letters and diary entries made at different points in Inuk's internal journey during the course of three months. We do not get the whole story, all the whys and hows. But through the 32 letters and diary entries, we follow his journey towards self-acceptance. Inuk is the Greenlandic word for human, and his chapter is about finding home in the acceptance of oneself. He is human, he is a man and he is a man who loves men.

Arnaq (Song: Walk of Shame by P!nk)

The title of the song the author chose for this chapter is significant. Arnaq's chapter is full of shame hidden under a brave, always-partying, always-happy face. It is a shame that she numbs with alcohol. Arnaq lives for Fridays when it is time to party. Every Friday, she is on the lookout for parties to go to and people to end the night with; it does not really matter where or who. She wants to lose herself in partying and sex. She drinks to forget. The morning after is always the worst, trying to remember what she did the night before. How much money has she spent? Did she do something bad? This time she has. She has spent all her money, so she cannot afford to buy food and, even worse, Arnaq betrayed her best friend's trust to try to score the one person she is in love with. She wants to forget what she did and the relationships she ruined. The only way she knows to forget is to party, but she has no money. In desperation, she calls her father, who sexually abused her when she was a child:

> 'Sweetheart? My sweet daughter, my darling, my love!'
> That motherfucker. His voice makes me want to throw up.
> 'I'm out of money. Can you send me some?'
> 'My sweet daughter, my darling. I miss you. Do you miss me?'
> His voice changes. I recognise this voice. It's terrifying.
> It's a trick, you know. I give. He gives. I give, he gives. I give, he gives. A trick.
> Always have been, always will be. I give, he gives. I give, he gives.
> 'Yeah,' I say, almost inaudibly.
> 'Yeah what? Answer me properly.'
> Just you wait. When I get my hooks into you one day…
> 'Yeah. I miss you.'
> Just you wait. I'll stab you both.
> 'Do you miss me a lot?'
> 'Yeah, I miss you.'
> Just you wait, I'll murder you.
> 'A lot?'
> 'Yeah.'
> Just you wait.
> 'I'll put some money in your account.' That's the trick. I give, he gives. The trick.
> (Korneliussen 2018, 104–5)

She is trapped in a spiral of shame. She parties to forget her shame about what her father did to her. But in partying she spends all her money and in desperation she turns to her father to be able to continue to party. She gives, he gives. Her feelings and her free will are still being abused, so the shame continues. After that, she finds someone to party with, a man who will provide alcohol so she can party again and bury her shame again in alcohol. Her weekend shame circle continues.

Ivik (Song: Stay by Rihanna)

Ivinnguaq has always felt different. She preferred to play with the boys and was not interested in getting a boyfriend. All through her childhood, she was asked why she was the way she was. She never had an answer and therefore hated the question. When she moved to a bigger town at 18 to study, she got her confirmation. She liked girls.

Now she lives with her girlfriend Sara, whom she loves and wants very much. But she has an issue that is becoming a big problem in her relationship: she cannot stand for Sara to touch her sexually. Ivinnguaq is very afraid of losing Sara. She does not understand why she does not like to be touched during sex, so readers might wonder if she is a stone butch or if she is uncomfortable with her body or ashamed of her sexuality. Ivinnguaq and Sara fight because Sara feels pushed away. Ivinnguaq ends up having a one-night stand with Arnaq, during which Arnaq is so drunk that she does not try to touch Ivinnguaq. Sara finds out about the infidelity and dumps Ivinnguaq, who tries without success to gain her forgiveness. Finally, after two weeks, Sara asks if they can talk. The following conversation takes place, with Sara explaining Ivinnguaq to herself:

> 'Ivik, I'm gay.'
> 'I know…'
> 'Please listen to me,' she says. 'I'm into women. I'm not into men.'
> I can't admit what she's trying to tell me.
> 'Because I like women, I can't be with a man,' she repeats.
> 'What do you mean by that?' I ask.
> 'I can't be with you.'
> I stare at her.
> 'I can't be with you because you are a man.' (Korneliussen 2018, 143)

Sara has figured out the answer to Ivinnguaq's and everybody else's question: 'My soul finds solace in my body. Now that my body has finally found the answer, my soul is no longer in doubt. I was born again when I was twenty-three years old. I was born as Ivik' (Korneliussen 2018, 144).

Ivinnguaq, which means dear little Ivik, is a commonly used name for women, while Ivik is a name commonly used for men. So Ivik can now start a new life as a man, finally feeling right.

Sara (Song: What a Day by Greg Laswell)

Sara's chapter starts with the birth of her niece. Sara wants it to be a good experience, with nothing to ruin the happiness of her niece's birth. But she cannot help but think about Ivinnguaq. Did she do the right thing? Why did Ivinnguaq, or Ivik as she prefers to be called, cheat? Why does she not like to be touched? All becomes clear during a text message conversation with her sister, who says that she is planning to call her daughter Ivinnguaq, but that the daughter can call herself Ivik, if she feels like a boy. Suddenly Sara understands what was wrong with her relationship with Ivinnguaq: Ivinnguaq is not Ivinnguaq, but rather Ivik. Sara meets with Ivik and has the conversation discussed above. After that conversation, Sara uses male pronouns for Ivik when she thinks and talks about him. It is an accepting goodbye, but despite this, Sara cannot seem to get out of her negative thought spiral. She feels as if everything she touches goes bad, a mindset with which many readers will surely be able to empathize (and thus another mirror). For Sara, it takes holding her niece to free her from her negativity: a kind of rebirth. She goes to a party, where she meets Fia again (the same party as at the end of Fia's chapter). They kiss. They begin.

The book is full of metaphors of life and death. Fia chooses to change her situation and start living. Inuk has to go through 'death' to accept and also start living his true life. Ivinnguaq is reborn as Ivik and also starts a new life in acceptance. And Sara welcomes a new life, accepts the 'new' Ivik and her own life, and starts something new. Fia, Inuk, Ivik and Sara all start over and are reborn into new and truer lives. Their chapters all end with them looking optimistically towards a new future. Arnaq's story is the opposite. She is heading straight to the bottom. Shame and the need to lose herself is stronger than anything else in her life. The other chapters may offer hope, though; perhaps Arnaq, too, will one day be reborn.

Blomsterdalen

Niviaq Korneliussen's second book, *Blomsterdalen*,[16] was published in August 2020 and has already been sold to France and Canada. Niviaq Korneliussen is not specifically a young adult writer, but rather a young writer writing about and for other people her age. Similarly, she is not marketed within a particular market segment (young adult or adult), but *Homo Sapienne* can be seen as fitting within both categories, whereas *Blomsterdalen* is more of a book for adults. For example, the sex scenes in *Blomsterdalen* are quite direct and graphic; nonetheless, it would also be suited to the mature young adult.

Blomsterdalen is a book about friendship and love, but mostly it is a book about suicide. In interviews, the author refers to a suicide culture in Greenland that is not being talked about (Ravn Nielsen 2020). Suicide is unfortunately a big problem in Greenland, with a suicide rate among the highest in the world. It is not an LGBTQ+ problem specifically, but across the population as a whole. Niviaq Korneliussen hopes that her book can help start conversations about a topic that needs to be talked about, so something can be done.

Blomsterdalen is about a young lesbian girl who is moving to Denmark to study. In the plane travelling to Denmark, she gets talking with the woman sitting next to her. She says,

16 In contrast to *Homo Sapienne*, this novel was originally written in Danish and then translated into Greenlandic by the author as *Naasuliardarpi*. Both the Greenlandic and the Danish titles translate as Valley of Flowers, a location in East Greenland. Due to the publication schedule of the present volume, I am only able to provide a brief discussion here.

'My family is afraid I will get lost. I do that often'[17] (Korneliussen 2020a, 31). This sums up both the character and the book rather well. It is about a girl who was lost, then found, but continues to get lost again and again in her actions, her memories and her thoughts. She gets more and more lost until she loses herself completely and commits suicide in the end. She has a girlfriend and is accepted by her family, so it is not her sexuality that makes her lost and makes her feels like she is wrong, like she doesn't fit in. Instead, it is about how she looks, acts, is, and so on. She is a girl with very low self-esteem and a drive to self-sabotage. It is as if she is lost even before the book starts.

Conclusion

In Greenland, *Homo Sapienne* (and subsequently *Blomsterdalen*) filled a gap. Before *Homo Sapienne*, there were no novels depicting modern LGBTQ+ life for young Greenlanders or even many books depicting modern young adult lives in general. When finding one's identity, it is important to have books and stories that describe one's history and the traditions that form where one comes from. But the past is not enough. Now is equally important. Greenlandic young adults have plenty of the past, but the now was missing. Young Greenlanders could not find books and stories describing their now. They could not be inspired or feel themselves reflected in the books made available to them. But *Homo Sapienne* changed that. Every young Greenlander can recognize the struggles or at least part of the struggles that Fia, Inuk, Arnaq, Ivik and Sara have, even if they themselves are not LGBTQ+, because identity and finding yourself are common themes for all people at some points in their lives. It is that recognition, the mirror, that attracts the reader. Young Greenlanders (and young people from other countries) can recognize themselves in the platforms of communication, the forms of expression, the feelings, the struggles, the searching and the way of life. With *Homo Sapienne*, young Greenlanders could read about lives like their own, written in a voice like their own. Older people can also recognize some of the same feelings and experiences from when they were younger.

Homo Sapienne and *Blomsterdalen* have certainly also filled another gap in Greenlandic literature, that of LGBTQ+ literature. As mentioned previously in this chapter, when *Homo Sapienne* was published, it became one out of only seven Greenlandic books with LGBTQ+ themes, three of which were non-fiction. *Homo Sapienne*, and now *Blomsterdalen*, are the only ones both written by a young Greenlander and that depict young Greenlandic LGBTQ+ lives. LGBTQ+ Greenlanders are now, for the first time, properly represented in Greenlandic fiction literature. Furthermore, *Homo Sapienne* contains many different stories, since there are five characters on the LGBTQ+ spectrum. It could be argued that the author wants to cram too much into a relatively short book by covering many different sexualities and gender identities. However, although the main characters each have their struggles to deal with and overcome, in the majority of cases (with the exception of Inuk), the fact that they are LGBTQ+ is not the main topic or problem. Like the

17 My translation from the original Danish: 'Min familie er bange for, at jeg farer vild. Det gør jeg tit.'

mother-in-law and Arnaussâq in the myths, they are judged on their actions and their personalities and not on their sexuality or gender identity. *Homo Sapienne* is a novel about five young Greenlandic people with relationship problems, emotional problems, identity problems and so on, the same problems that people not on the LGBTQ+ spectrum struggle with. Being LGBTQ+ is not the main focus of *Homo Sapienne*. Being young and finding one's way in life is the main focus.

Moreover, it is understandable that people on the LGBTQ+ spectrum might choose to move away from the smaller towns to the capital, Nuuk. As in many other countries, the capital and bigger cities are often more accepting of LGBTQ+ people. In Greenland the towns and cities are comparatively small compared to other countries. Nuuk, the capital, is by far the largest Greenlandic city, but it is still a relatively small city of only about 17,000 people. So the pool of LGBTQ+ people is small and it is therefore natural that many of them know each other and that their lives are very intertwined. The structure and content of the book reflect this.

In this chapter, I have explored some of the reasons why *Homo Sapienne* became and continues to be such a success. You do not have to be on the LGBTQ+ spectrum or have a specific interest in LGBTQ+ subjects to read and enjoy *Homo Sapienne*; you just have to want to read and experience the life of five young Greenlanders, who happen to be LGBTQ+. As mentioned before, the book filled some gaps in Greenlandic literature: young adult literature, new adult literature and LGBTQ+ literature. However, I would argue that this is not the only reason for its popularity: another likely factor is the book's stylistic innovation. The play with formats, timelines and the disregard of traditions of how to write came as a breath of fresh air to modern young reading audiences. The author's voice comes over very strongly, and has a sense of authenticity: she writes just as young people think, act and talk about subjects that are important to them.

But why the unprecedented level of international success?[18] Lene Therkildsen, the publisher of the book, has said that she does not really do any special PR for the books she publishes, other than sending the book out widely to the media. But milik publishing and Niviaq Korneliussen did attend Bogforum, which is a big book fair in Denmark. There, Niviaq and the book caught the eye of Jes Stein Pedersen, a literary critic for the Danish newspaper Politiken. He wrote a glowing review, concluding with: 'Homo Sapienne er, bogen man kan bede sine forældre, venner og klassekammerater om at læse, hvis man synes, de trænger til at ankomme til the real world …' (Homo Sapienne is the book you can ask your parents, friends and classmates to read, if you think that they need to arrive in the real world) (Pedersen 2014, 16). *Homo Sapienne* can be a mirror of this real world for young Greenlanders, and part mirror and part window or sliding door for the rest of us.

I would like to thank Henriette Christensen, the team leader at Groenlandica (Greenland's national library), for her help with finding the older literature and myths, and with fact-checking.

18 Measured in translations and media coverage.

Bibliography

'Arnaussâq'. n.d. https://arktiskinstitut.dk/vidensdatabaserne/groenlandske-sagn-myter-sonnes-base/soeg-i-sagn-myter/

Bishop, Rudine Sims. 1990. 'Mirrors, Windows, and Sliding Glass Doors'. *Perspectives* 6, no. 3: ix–xi.

Dahl, Hjalmar. 2014. *…Inuugatta: Nunatsinni angutit anguteqatiminnik arnallu arnaqatiminnik aappaqartartut pillugit* (…Because We Are Alive. About Gays and Lesbians in Greenland). Nuuk: milik publishing.

Didriksen, Onu, Malik Sophus Schøller Jørgensen, Kaaleeraq Møller Andersen, Navarana Lennert, Erninnguaq Reimer, Tukumminnguaq Nykjær Olsen, Najannguaq Berthelsen, Stine Buur Hvistendahl, Paninnguaq Møller, and Katrine Poulsen. *Paasininneq / Rum* (Room). 2018. Nuuk: milik publishing.

Gay Greenland. 2012. Nuuk: NAPA.

Hansen, Káte, ed. 2004. *Aamma illit inuuneraat… HIV AIDS-ilu pillugit oqaluttuat / Livet er også dit… Historier om HIV og AIDS* (Life is Also Yours… Stories about HIV and AIDS). Nuuk: Paarisa.

Johnsen, Leise. 2012: Gay pride i Grønland og historien om Ukuamaaq (Gay Pride in Greenland and the Story about Ukuamaaq). *Tidskriftet Grønland*, 13 December. https://issuu.com/greenland/docs/tg_04_dec_2012

Kleist, Debora Hansen, Kenny J. Fisker, Nukappi Boassen Wille, Karoline Lennert Sørensen, Sandra Matiasen, Maasi Brøns Chemnitz et al. 2015. *2040.* Nuuk: milik publishing.

Korneliussen, Niviaq. 2013. 'San Francisco'. In *Inuusuttut – nunatsinni nunarsuarmilu / Ung i Grønland – Ung i verden* (Young in Greenland – And in the World), 64–82 (Greenlandic edition) / 86–106 (Danish edition), edited by Katja Vahl and Lene Therkildsen. Nuuk: Atuakkiortut, NAPA and milik publishing.

———. 2014. *Homo Sapienne.* Nuuk: milik publishing.

———. 2018. *Crimson.* Translated by Anna Halager. London: Virago Press.

———. 2020a. *Blomsterdalen* (Valley of Flowers). Copenhagen: Gyldendal. [Danish version]

———. 2020b. *Naasuliardarpi* (Valley of Flowers). Nuuk: milik publishing. [Greenlandic version]

Kreutzmann, Maria Bach. 2018. *Bestiarium Groenlandica: An Illustrated Guide to the Mythical Creatures, Spirits and Animals of Greenland.* Translated by Charlotte Barslund. Nuuk: milik publishing.

Kruse, Kathrine. 2015. '"Gay Greenland" vinder dansk kulturpris' ("Gay Greenland" Wins Danish Cultural Prize'). *Sermitsiaq*, 5 February. https://sermitsiaq.ag/node/176038

Marteeraq (Martêraq). 1967. 'Arnaussâq'. In *Inugpât*, collected by Hans Lynge, 91. Kalâtdlitnunãne naKiterisitsissarfik.

Olsen Aaju, Kristian. 2010. *Kakiorneqaqatigiit* (The Tattooed Message).[19] Nuuk: Forlaget Atuagkat.

———. 2013. *Alumiguulik* (The Tattooed Body Washed Ashore).[20] Nuuk: Forlaget Atuagkat.

Pedersen, Jes Stein. 2014. 'Romandebutant fortæller modigt om at finde sig selv seksuelt i Nuuk'. *Politiken*, 20 November. https://politiken.dk/kultur/boger/boganmeldelser/skonlitteratur_boger/art5553459/Romandebutant-fort%C3%A6ller-modigt-om-at-finde-sig-selv-seksuelt-i-Nuuk

Petersen, Jørgen. 2005. *Qattuneq issiavilik* (Bench with a View). Nuuk: Atuakkiorfik.

Ravn Nielsen, Marie. 2020. 'Ung forfatter vil bryde tabu med ny bog: Stop selvmordskulturen'. *DR*, 24 August. https://www.dr.dk/nyheder/kultur/boeger/ung-forfatter-vil-bryde-tabu-med-ny-bog-stop-selvmordskulturen?cid=newsletter_nb_boger_20200829075828

Rink, Henrik. (1875) 1974. 'The Woman Who Wanted to Be a Man'. In *Tales and Traditions of the Eskimo*, 442–43. London: C. Hurst & Co.

Taateraaq. (1921) 2000. 'Svigermoderen, som giftede sig med sin svigerdatter' (The Mother-in-Law Who Married her Daughter-in-Law). In *Myter og sagn fra Grønland* (Myths and Legends from Greenland), collected by Knud Rasmussen, 223. Copenhagen: Forlaget Sesam.

19 My translation of the Danish title: *Det tatoverede budskab.*

20 My translation of the Danish title: *Den tatoverede strandvasker.*

'Ukuamaaq'. n.d. https://arktiskinstitut.dk/en/knowledge-database/greenlandic-stories/search-in-greenlandic-myths-stories/

Vahl, Katja, and Lene Therkildsen, eds. 2013. *Inuusuttut – nunatsinni nunarsuarmilu / Ung i Grønland – Ung i verden* (Young in Greenland – And in the World). Nuuk: Atuakkiortut, NAPA and milik publishing.

Chapter Five

OUT OF THE CLOSET? EXPLORING THE INFOSCAPE OF LGBTQ+ FICTION FOR/ ABOUT YOUTH IN INDIA

Bharat Mehra and Chris Barrett

Introduction

This chapter provides a glimpse into contemporary English-language lesbian, gay, bisexual, transgender and other queer, including questioning, (LGBTQ+)[1] fiction for/ about youth in India. The study of LGBTQ+ representatives in 'best' book lists for/ about youth in India and other sources analysed in this chapter presented a dismally limited collection containing very few works on LGBTQ+ and other non-conforming gender representations. Walter Dean Myers' (2014) powerful opinion piece in response to a study by the Cooperative Children's Book Center at the University of Wisconsin finding merely 93 children's books about black people out of 3,200 published, primarily in the U.S., in 2013 reflects similar poignancy.

The dataset for the present study included titles that were retrieved by focusing specifically on young readers in India, such as by looking for Best Young Adult Fiction in India from the search engine available on goodreads.com (2018); reading articles such as 'Food for Thought: What's Young India Reading, And Why?' (Hazra 2013) in the *Hindustan Times*, the third most widely read daily English-language newspaper in India with a circulation of 993,645 copies January–July 2017 (Audit Bureau of Circulations 2017); and exploring 'must' reads for an average Indian teenager from Quora.com (Agarwal 2017); amongst others. A similar trend of limited inclusion of pertinent content was documented in works available on websites of Indian publishers such as Children's Book Trust (pioneer publisher of children's books in India) (2017), Amar Chitra Katha (one of India's largest selling comic book series) (2018), and others. Websites of some

1 The plus sign '+' is included in the acronym LGBTQ+ to represent all the diversities associated in the intersections of non-heterosexual orientations and gender identities. The '+' also symbolizes the authors' understanding of the ambiguous and fluid nature of sexuality and gender identity in its plural sense going beyond the limited constructions presented in the 'nature-nurture' debate (Ceci and Williams 2000; Goldhaber 2012; Katyal 2017). Further, it signifies a resistance to meanings developed around notions of heterosexuality that are culturally imposed in a hegemonic sense all around the world (Mehra 2019a).

select Indian publishers studied in this research project are listed in Table 1. This chapter focuses on fiction works available in English for/about LGBTQ+ youth in India and it showcases select examples, though implications are also relevant for non-English literature in the other 22 official languages listed in the Eighth Schedule of the Constitution of India (Pandharipande 1997; Sarangi 2010). Based on analysis conducted for this chapter, it turns out that sadly none of these select books written originally in English were translated to and available in other non-English Indian languages (see more commentary in the Findings and Discussion sections).

Non-fiction writings 'about' LGBTQ+ literature for youth (and others) in India are also selectively analysed to provide useful background and identify the cultural constraints tying down the growth and development of the genre. Select fiction works provide a glimpse of positive examples for/about a minority voice that has been long ignored. The negative connotations of so few works, which are limited in scope, content and coverage, reflecting authentic LGBTQ+ experiences and accurate cultural portrayals in the Indian context, is a tragic reflection of the publishing industry and others (Rao 2017). It also calls into question a need for a serious critical evaluation of the reasons behind such limited availability and the politics of decision making that should be representative of more diverse content in the twenty-first century (Joseph 2018). Proactive strategies are urgently required for libraries, booksellers, publishers and other stakeholders in the industry to adopt in order to circumvent the challenges presented in the context of a politically charged milieu of limitations thanks to an archaic law that until recently still considered homosexuality a crime.

The Indian Context

On 6 September 2018, the Supreme Court of India unanimously declared unconstitutional Section 377 of the Indian Penal Code, a colonial inheritance of one of humankind's hoariest injunctions on consensual gay sex, and also ruled all the protections of the Constitution applicable to LGBTQ+ people (Kidangoor 2018; United Nations 2018). The Chief Justice of India, Dipak Misra, reported from the relevant section of the court's verdict that 'Social morality cannot be used to violate the fundamental rights of even a single individual … Constitutional morality cannot be martyred at the altar of social morality' (Sinha 2018, n.p.). Is it not astounding that the Indian Supreme Court in the world's second most populated country, with its long history of culture and civilization and 'self-proclaimed, righteous spiritual and religious tolerance', has awakened from its slumber towards this realization only now in the second decade of the twenty-first century after more than 70 years of independence from the British? (Mehra 2019b, 3). Probably not, if one considers this in the recent tragic context of the Supreme Court of India's 'pendulum swings', moving from one extreme to the other, after it reinstated a ban on gay sex in the world's largest democracy on 11 December 2013, following a four-year decriminalization period that had helped bring homosexuality out of the closet in the culturally and socially conservative country (Mehra and Hernandez 2016). The reasoning behind the reinstatement of the 153-year-old legislation conceded under British rule in 2013 was that 'carnal intercourse' between consenting adults of the same sex was once again defined as 'unnatural', punishable by up to 10 years in jail, based on the sixteenth-century English law (Burke 2013).

A globally widespread phenomenon has been how these political and legal sanctions and denial of human rights of LGBTQ+ people have continued to marginalize a historically disenfranchised population that existed on the fringes of society all around the world (Mehra et al. 2019). Even though today the situation varies from country to country, the progress towards LGBTQ+ equality that we take for granted in the western world is far from the harsh stigmatized reality experienced in most of Africa, Latin America, the Middle East and South Asia (Mehra et al. 2018). Such laws have perpetuated cultural ostracism, abuse, violence and hate based on socially imposed values of heterosexism, patriarchal taboos, male chauvinism and homophobia/biphobia/transphobia in many parts of the world, including India (Mehra et al. 2015; Vanita 2001). Based on his childhood experiences as a closeted person in India and on his work conducting formal research since 1994 on LGBTQ+ and other social justice issues in the United States, the first author's assessment is that the social and cultural heterosexist and patriarchal conservatism and heteronormative mores underlying India's protracted overdue legal protection are long and deep (Pandey 2018). The damaging implications for conceptualizations and constructions of sexuality and gender, child development, identity formation, and gender understanding and roles in India – amongst other aspects of human growth and social interactions – are unquestionable (Mehra 2016). Moreover, we must consider the extremely problematic impact of heterosexism and biased and prejudiced cultural beliefs on an understanding of LGBTQ+ identities and issues. We must consider, and challenge, how they are internalized and negatively expressed in people's psychological and emotional well-being and how they shape harsh human behaviours towards each other and towards those who are perceived as LGBTQ+ (Mogul et al. 2012). This is unfortunate in terms of the actual and potential damage it is causing in India where, of its 1.3+ billion people in 2017, which formed nearly a fifth of the world population (United Nations Department of Economic and Social Affairs 2017), more than 50 per cent were estimated to be below the age of 25 years, and it is expected that, in 2020, the average age of an Indian will be 29 years, compared to 37 for China and 48 for Japan (Basu 2007). In 2018, Ian Jack reported for *The Guardian* that there were about 600 million young people in India, surpassing the youth population in every country of the world. While there are no official demographics for the Indian LGBTQ+ population, the government of India's submitted conservative estimated figure of 2.5 million gay people in 2012 (0.20 per cent of total population) is based on self-declared numbers provided to the Ministry of Health with the expectation of much higher numbers to account for the individuals who concealed their identity owing to fear of discrimination (BBC News 2012). Thus, the demographic evidence reflects the existence of large numbers of youth in India and a potentially sizeable LGBTQ+ population.

The repressive cultural climate for LGBTQ+ people is also coupled with a limited availability of accurate and authoritative information on related topics and subjects (United Kingdom: Home Office 2017). Even after the landmark Supreme Court ruling in September 2018, LGBTQ+ activists continue 'preparing for resistance to the decision' with pressing unresolved legal questions including those, for example, regarding past criminal cases filed under the Victorian-era law, future practical gains in cases of harassment based on sexual orientation and same-sex marriage rights, implementation of the law in the context of other progressive rulings by the Supreme Court that have been often ignored in many parts of the country, such as the one in 2014 that recognized a third gender category (i.e. the *hijras*) (Varma and Najar 2014), and a lack of willingness of political leaders to comment on and respond to the gay rights debate (Gettleman and Schultz 2018). These broader political, legal and cultural challenges are indicative of a very slow and tortuous journey, and the potential for publishers, educators and librarians, amongst others, to play an important role in challenging centuries of dogma, patriarchy, stigma and cultural brainwashing of youth and young people in the traditionalist country (Mehra and Hernandez 2016). No wonder, some years back, Navi Pillay, the United Nations High Commissioner for Human Rights, challenged heterosexist and patriarchal beliefs and called 'on countries to repeal laws that criminalize homosexuality, abolish the death penalty for offences involving consensual sexual relations, harmonize the age of consent for heterosexual and homosexual conduct, and enact comprehensive anti-discrimination laws' (United Nations News Center 2011, n.p.). In addition, India is notorious for its child abuse, domestic violence, and mistreatment of children and youth that are treated as property of the parents and guardians (Deb 2018; Halder 2018; Kacker 2015). Legal bureaucracy and corruption are rampant and provide little hope (Carson and Foster 2015).

Perspectives from information and educational research are also potentially transferable to the Indian context. A few criticisms are presented here regarding the limited applications of select key constructs (e.g. multicultural literature, counter-storytelling) from these domains of study that have historically focused only on contexts related to western/white/heterosexual youth. For example, multicultural fiction that truly reflects young people's lives has promoted greater engagement and directly tackled the achievement gaps experienced by students of colour (Lafferty 2014; Sampson and Garrison-Wade 2011). The issue of concern has been that traditionally this notion of 'multicultural' has been applied in regard to only ethnicity and income or associated variables of demography, often overlooking the diverse cultural experiences and context of reality related to LGBTQ+ young people (Flores 2012, 2014, 2016; Smolkin and Young 2011). Some few works over the past two decades have sporadically filled these gaps and provided select theoretical frameworks and illustrative case studies that draw upon multicultural literature to identify strategies in the K–12 classroom that enhance the lives of LGBTQ+ students (e.g. Blackburn and Clark 2011; Ouellett 1996; Sokoll 2013). Taking this further, where is the application of multicultural literature on LGBTQ+ students in non-western international environments or relating to the experiences of LGBTQ+ students of colour? Again, these have been left out. Too few scholarly contributions from our white librarian colleagues and/or heterosexual youth researchers have provided a narrow conceptualization of the field in their self-absorbed vision of relevant concerns to only those like themselves (Dedeoglu et al. 2012; Kim and Tinajero 2016; Shelton and Winkelstein 2014).

Similarly, counter-storytelling as a topic was not initially inclusive of LGBTQ+ people in identifying opportunities to confront the mainstream stereotypes often held by the majority, giving representations of silenced voices including those of disenfranchised youth, and articulating the complexities associated with minority identity development (Hughes-Hassell 2013). In this way, LGBTQ+ experiences were not directly represented head-on in a culturally responsive classroom where urban fiction reflecting the cultural experience of the readers was getting effectively utilized in literacy instruction, including for at-risk and incarcerated youths (Guerra 2012). Nor did we often see novel thoughts, or attempts to shape the beliefs of adolescent males, or improvements to readability of and relatability to new LGBTQ+ related content (Escalas 2007; Fredrick 2006). This has resulted in most scholarship and research on counter-storytelling experiences being devoid of LGBTQ+ youth, and within the marginalized subset the counter-narratives of non-white and/or international LGBTQ+ young people have been totally missing from these initial discussions (Wargo 2017a, 2017b, 2017c). LGBTQ+ youth experiences in the international context and/or LGBTQ+ young people of colour have always been one of the last groups to get attention in public discourse, academic scholarship, public policy, education and legal representation, amongst other areas impacting everyday life (Coon 2018). Is this ever going to change? Probably not, perhaps due to intersections in colonialist/imperialist legacy and/or heteronormative mores, which have hegemonically shaped human history and evolution, though still it is important to point out this lapse (Mehra et al. 2019).

Relating to the context of India, exposure to LGBTQ+ content for youth and others is so important for its educational power in creating awareness and understanding of a subject that is culturally, politically and legally still considered taboo, in spite of the recent legislation (Dave 2012). It is also intimately tied to the development of psychological and mental health, emotional well-being and physical safety from harm and violence for not only LGBTQ+ youth, but all youth and adults in a heterocentric cultural environment (Chakraborty 2011; Roy 2015; Vanita 2005). This is particularly the case in a culture and environment where sex education is completely absent, discussion of sexualities is outside the realms of everyday discourse and conversation, and ignorance, superstitions and blind religious faith determine a majority of the population's understanding of matters related to reproductive health, sexual orientation and nearly every other related topic (Dasgupta and Dasgupta 2018). The high rate of suicide amongst LGBTQ+ youth in India is attributed to factors including: a high prevalence of bullying and ridicule by classmates in school and college; familial and social pressure to enter 'normal' heterosexual relationships and get married; lack of emotional support and counselling when things go wrong in relationships; internalized homophobic beliefs; physical and emotional violence within the relationship; the fear of a same-sex partner bowing to family pressure and getting married to an opposite-sex partner; isolation and fear of not finding love again, given the smaller number of out LGBTQ+ people in society; and the pressure of always keeping the relationship incognito (Gwalani 2015). These are reasons enough for an urgent imperative to authors and writers, book publishers, librarians, governments, human rights agencies, intellectuals and educators, and others associated with the publishing industry, to find ways to fill gaps associated with intellectual and physical access in this very important knowledge domain in India.

Research Methods

The following intertwined strategies of information collection and analysis identified themes that formed the basis of the discussion in this chapter:

- Assessment of 'best' book lists focused specifically on youth in India, such as Best Young Adults Fiction in India retrieved from the goodreads.com search engine (2018); 'Food for Thought: What's Young India Reading, And Why?' (Hazra 2013); 'must' reads for an average Indian teenager from Quora.com (Agarwal 2017); and others. See Table 2 for the select English-language fiction 'best lists' aimed specifically at youth in India that were included in this research.
- Browsing of English-language book lists recommended for the general Indian population such as summer book reads (Hasan 2018) from midday.com, amongst others (i.e. searching for young adult works not included in the 'best lists'). This also included conducting an 'all'-function broader search on goodreads.com and browsing English-language book lists recommended for the general Indian population. It also involved searching more than 500 Wikipedia pages related to 'LGBT India', as well as the websites of Indian LGBTQ+ organizations and advocacy groups (e.g. Nazariya, a non-profit queer feminist resource group; Humsafar Trust, a non-governmental organization in Mumbai, India, which promotes LGBT rights; Chennai Dost, a group whose mission is to create a safe social space for LGBT people in South India; and many more). Some additional works were located through popular search engines and online bookstores such as Amazon.com. See Table 3 for select examples of broader and general sources that were examined (i.e. not specific to LGBTQ+ youth in India) to explore if any pertinent materials got excluded in the 'best lists'.
- Content analysis of websites of Indian publishers, such as Children's Book Trust, Amar Chitra Katha, and others listed in Table 1 (where such search functionality was available). A search on the websites involved using a range of LGBTQ+-related vocabularies included the following key terms: bisexual, gay, hijra, intersexual, lesbian, LGBT, LGBTQ+, MSM ('men who have sex with men'), queer, questioning and trans. Search using a name of an Indian language (e.g. 'Hindi') with these vocabularies was used in many of the strategies.

The selection of resources studied in this research project was based on extensive searches on the Internet and exploration of relevant databases available on the topics. Content analysis of materials familiar to the first author owing to his Indian ethnic origins, gay identity and experience as a participant researcher in India was also useful (Mehra 2011). Descriptions of the works in the lists and information presented about each work on the appropriate website helped identify positive (and not so positive) examples and, where necessary, the texts themselves were studied to determine whether they merited inclusion. Analysis of relevant fields (e.g. subject headings, descriptors, abstracts, etc. where available) in the records of the works located via WorldCat identified themes in how select authors were providing stories that were meaningful for/about this underserved population. This chapter provides a glimpse of research during a select window of time. The study was conducted in October 2018–January 2019 and there might be newer materials on the subject that have emerged since.

Findings

For purposes of clarity and to ensure easier readability and flow, the structure of the findings is presented in separate sections. We focus initially on books that are actually relevant to the Indian context, whether directly inclusive of LGBTQ+ youth in India or in the Indian diaspora. We then go on to discuss works that were selected by source creators of Indian LGBTQ+ youth-related resources, which reflect universal themes relevant to LGBTQ+ youth but do not relate to Indian LGBTQ+ youth specifically. Findings from various research methods identified earlier are woven together to illustrate examples of fiction for/about LGBTQ+ youth in India or in the Indian diaspora and related materials.

Fiction for/about LGBTQ+ youth in India or in the Indian diaspora

Despite the wide range of research methods used and sources searched, it became apparent that very few young adult novels with LGBTQ+ content were published in India. Searching on the websites of the Indian publishers[2] (where such search functionality was available), using a range of LGBTQ+ vocabularies, retrieved no relevant results for/about Indian youth in the fiction category, although some non-fiction titles related to the topic were identified (and are discussed further below). Conducting an 'all' search on goodreads.com, of the 4,342,323 works related to India, 49 results were retrieved by adding the word 'youth'. Adding the word 'gay' or 'lesbian' to this search yielded no results. Twenty-four results all for adults were retrieved by searching 'India and gay' and five works by searching for 'India and lesbian'.

However, we were able to locate one relevant fiction title through reading articles and reviews: *Talking of Muskaan* by Hemanjali Sankar (published in 2017). This work was not included in any of the 'best books' lists studied, and may thus be more difficult for young people, librarians, educators, and so on to find.

- *Talking of Muskaan*, a novel that is funny yet poignant by turns, is narrated by three of a girl's classmates and is about her unsuccessful effort to commit suicide. Sayoni Basu, the publisher at Duckbill Books in Chennai who released this LGBTQ+ title, explains, 'There are kids who are aware of their sexual orientation early on, and who have difficulty fitting into conventional notions of gender behaviour. For this handful, it is important to know that there are other kids facing the same dilemma' (Singh 2014, n.p.). The focus on suicide is noteworthy. The emphasis on the topic seems to correspond with a much-criticized pattern in LGBTQ+ book publishing in the United States and other Anglophone countries where it emerged predominantly during the first

2 See Table 1 for the publisher list.

'wave' reflecting 'homosexual visibility' in the 'general types of stories with gay/lesbian characters published for a young adult audience from 1969 through 2016' (Jenkins and Cart 2018, xiv). Reflective of the medical and psychological misperceptions of homosexuality as a 'disorder' or 'deviance' during the early years, this trend has been identified as extremely problematic and outdated (Alexander and Miselis 2007; Stebbins 2015; Town 2017). The research also identified four LGBTQ+ young adult novels and one picture book that were published in North America but that feature characters who are Indian or from the Indian diaspora, or in one case from Sri Lanka, included here owing to its related geographical context.

- *The Boy & the Bindi* by Vivek Shraya and illustrated by Rajni Perera (2016) is the only picture book with relevant LGBTQ+ content located in the course of this research. As a transgender female Indian-Canadian musician/filmmaker/writer, Shraya presents a multicultural, intergenerational story in her children's picture book debut about a five-year-old South Asian boy who is intrigued by his mother's bindi, the red dot commonly worn by Hindu women as a symbol of marriage and the moment of creation. The boy wishes to have one of his own. With Perera's illustrations, the work skilfully explores aspects of difference and self-acceptance and the subversion of gender expectations, and it imparts an important lesson on inclusivity and individuality for young readers.
- *Blue Boy* by Rakesh Satyal (2009) was one of only two works featured on any of the 'best books' lists that had content of direct relevance to young LGBTQ+ people from India or the Indian diaspora (the other being *Shikhandi and Other Tales They Don't Tell You*, discussed further below). Set in early 1990s Cincinnati, Ohio, *Blue Boy* tells the story of an immigrant, social outcast, 12-year-old gay boy from India who does not fit in with other Indian kids or his public schoolmates until he realizes he is a god. The novel balances sexuality and ethnicity while also exploring the idea of staying true to oneself.
- *Babyji* by Abha Dawesar (2005) is an irresistible story of a spirited young student growing up in the Indian capital of New Delhi as she navigates her life journey, exploring sexuality, caste politics and Indian society. The sexually precocious heroine presents a delightful central character as she pursues three simultaneous same-sex affairs while studying chaos theory in physics and dealing with issues that would make adults 'even those twice her age falter at' (Yasmin 2017, n.p.).
- In *A Secret Edge*, author Robin Reardon (2007) tells the story of Jason, a senior athlete in high school, who is attracted to and ultimately falls in love with another male student, Raj, also an athlete from a different ethnic background (namely, a transplant from India in the United States).
- Finally, *Swimming in the Monsoon Sea* by Shyam Selvadurai (2005) is set in 1980s Sri Lanka, a country that shares some history and culture with India. In the novel, 14-year-old Amrith, an orphan on a holiday with his dead mother's friends, falls in love with his cousin, Niresh, visiting from Canada.

A valuable point of difference between the latter two works is that in *A Secret Edge*, the Indian male youth serves as a secondary character to a white male protagonist in a story told from the main character's point of view. Raj's ethnicity of 'difference' is highlighted in its contrast (and in its place) within the context and in the 'gaze' of the white character.

Further, the story is set in the United States with the 'Indian-ness' inserted as an identity marker flavoured within a diasporic context. On the other hand, in *Swimming in the Monsoon Sea*, the focus of the story is on a Sri Lankan character. Here, the narrative is embedded in the South Asian cultural setting. The story is part-and-parcel of the lived experience in the geographic setting and the culture that serves to shape and drive the narrative in a deeper and more integral manner. Also, the former work with the Indian boy as the secondary character was written by a white author while the latter work set in the Sri Lankan context was authored by a Canadian-born author with parents from the South Asian environment. Surely this authenticity in writing for/about LGBTQ+ youth in the region emerges thanks to the roots (and experiences) of authors from the region. This limited evidence suggests that books on LGBTQ+ youth in India should be written by Indian (or South Asian) authors and set in India (or South Asia) resisting the temptation, of 'armchair writers' (similar to nineteenth-century 'armchair anthropologists'), who author works about places (and experiences) that are foreign to them. #ownvoices is a hashtag movement that Corinne Duyvis, a bisexual and disabled young adult author, started in 2015 on Twitter as a result of her discontent with the contemporary focus on diverse books, instead of work by diverse authors (Vanderhage 2019). Readers and authors might find the resource of value on materials for/about Indian LGBTQ+ youth.

As so little relevant material seemed to be published for young adults, we felt it would also be pertinent to include books that were published for adults but that were recommended for young people or otherwise deemed to be relevant to young people's interests (e.g. coming-of-age novels featuring young adult characters).

- *Shikhandi and Other Tales They Don't Tell You* by Pattanaik Devdutt (2015) was featured on a 'best list' for young adults despite the fact that it is published for adults and its content, based on Indian mythology, is not necessarily directly related to young adults. The only work published in India found in the 'best list' sources, the publishers consider it a must read for LGBTQ+ readers in India because of the concept in this collection of Hindu stories that queer differences are not only modern, western or sexual, and that they are very much acceptable. This collection of mythological stories helps LGBTQ+ and non-LGBTQ+ readers to understand more about Hindu mythology in shaping the ways people look at their Indian-ness. It challenges all people (including LGBTQ+ youth) in their perceptions of faith and love and creates awareness that even if people deviate from the norm it does not mean that they do not have a place in their own religion or country.
- *No Other World: A Novel* by Indian author Rahul Mehta (2017) is a coming-of-age story set in rural America and India about a gay Indian American immigrant boy's saga and family struggles. The novel weaves a narrative of love, belonging and forgiveness as it traces the journey of an Indian American gay man torn between two cultures in a homophobic society (Krishna 2017).
- *Selection Day: A Novel* (Adiga 2017) was reviewed by Marcel Theroux (2017) in the *New York Times* under the title 'Aravind Adiga's Novel Is About the Game of Cricket – and Sexual Awakening'. This dark novel is about two brothers, one of whom may or may not be gay, raised in a Mumbai slum by their obsessive father to be star cricketers,

weaving together issues of class, religion and awakening sexuality. Though the novel is not marketed for young adults, it is about two male teenagers and the author traces the brave and important subject of homosexuality within the sport and the 'adolescent confusion over acknowledging one's sexual orientation and the responses – condemnation, abuse, patronizing sympathy – it elicits' (ibid., n.p.).

- *She of the Mountains* by Vivek Shraya (2014) is a beautifully illustrated novel that tells us the coming-out story of a gay Hindu boy growing up in Canada, discussing bisexuality and interweaving a re-imagining of the Hindu mythologies of Parvati, Vishnu and Ganesha. The intersecting threads in the narrative examine the wounding of the human heart in the policing of gender and sexuality and the complexities of embodiment. A picture book by the same author has been discussed above.
- *Me Hijra, Me Laxmi* by Raj Rao Laxmi and P. G. Joshi (2015) presents a semi-autobiographical account of the extraordinary, courageous journey of a hijra (India's transsexual/transgender community legally recognized in 2014 as the third gender category) who fought against tremendous odds and mental and physical abuse for the recognition of hijras and their rights. The work is not specifically identified as 'for' LGBTQ+ youth. Yet, it is very much 'about' the hijra child/youth's coming of age story in India, battling emotional turmoil, and growing up as a boy in a high-caste Brahmin household, but never identifying as one. Integrating the lead author's experiences as the first Indian hijra to attend the World AIDS Conference in Toronto, the work threads her struggles of feeling 'queer', experiencing attraction to boys, having feminine mannerisms and physical behaviours, cross-dressing, asserting her real sexual identity, and being taunted as 'queer'.
- Lastly, *Funny Boy* by Shyam Selvadurai (1994) is a coming-of-age novel that won the Lambda Literary Award for gay male fiction and the Books in Canada First Novel Award. The author, who also wrote the young adult novel *Swimming in the Monsoon Sea* (discussed above), is a Sri Lankan Canadian novelist, born to a Sinhalese mother and a Tamil father – members of conflicting ethnic groups. Important to note here is that that the Tamils are an ethnic group from India who have migrated for centuries to the island of Sri Lanka, where the novel's story is set. It is narrated in the form of six affecting interlocking experiences about a boy's coming-of-age in a wealthy Tamil family in Colombo, the country's cosmopolitan capital city. The novel weaves the boy's explorations of his sexual identity between the ages of seven and 14 as he is immersed in, and confronts, the Sinhala–Tamil tensions leading up to the 1983 riots.

Fiction with content for LGBTQ+ youth in the 'best lists' for/about youth in India

Table 2 summarizes the number of titles with LGBTQ+ content included in English-language 'best lists' of fiction targeted specifically at young readers in India. It was valuable to examine the extent of LGBTQ+ content coverage in these general resources for/about Indian youth since this information would have a substantial impact on awareness among librarians, educators, young people themselves, and so on. However, only seven out of 329 (2.13 per cent) unique works on these lists had LGBTQ+ content related to youth. There were no overlaps in the works located across the lists. Further, only two (0.61 per cent) had references for/about LGBTQ+ youth in India: namely *Blue Boy* (Satyal 2009) and *Shikhandi and Other Tales They Don't Tell You* (Pattanaik 2015). Both of these titles have been discussed above, in the section '*Fiction for/about LGBTQ+ youth in India or in the Indian diaspora*'. The remaining five retrieved from the 'best lists' search for/ about youth in India included content for/about LGBTQ+ youth but did not have any references to Indian settings or characters. They are briefly presented here (alphabetical list based on last name of author):

- Albertalli, Becky. 2016. *Simon vs. the Homo Sapiens Agenda*. New York: Balzer + Bray. This novel tells a twenty-first century coming-out story and is a geek romance set in a high school in Atlanta, Georgia. Its inclusion in the list for/about LGBTQ+ Indian youth might be owing to its topic of gay youth romance, completely missing the point that the Indian cultural and social environment is very different from that in the United States in its response towards matters associated with sexual orientation/sexual identity, coming out and so on.
- LaCour, Nina. 2017. *We Are OK*. New York: Dutton Books. This book tells the story of a girl, a bisexual college student in New York who moved from California after the death of her grandfather. Through flashbacks and conversations with a high school friend/possible former sweetheart, the novel explores the impact of grief, complicated by the silence and secrets and the discovery of the complicated person her grandfather was.
- Nelson, Jandy. 2015. *I'll Give You the Sun*. New York: Dial Books. This novel is told from the perspectives of teenage fraternal twins, a boy and girl, each of them recounting an accident that forever changed their lives. Some intersecting themes in the story are related to sexuality, identity, family, change and art, though not in an Indian context.
- Sáenz, Benjamin Alire. 2012. *Aristotle and Dante Discover the Secrets of the Universe*. New York: Simon & Schuster. This coming-of-age young adult novel set in El Paso, Texas, in 1987, follows the lives of two Mexican American boys, their friendship, and their struggles with racial and ethnic identity, sexuality and family relationships. No Indian connection here, though its inclusion on lists for/about LGBTQ+ youth in India might be related to intersections of content in ethnic identity and sexuality even when the story context is in a very different place, namely the United States.
- Wilde, Jen. 2017. *Queens of Geek*. New York: Swoon Reads. About three friends, two love stories and one convention, this novel is set at a 'SupaCon' in San Diego, California and it brings together sexuality, fun, geek culture and feminism.

Of the seven identified in the 'best list' search for/about LGBTQ+ youth in India, it is disheartening (and unfortunate) to find that not even one novel in the recommended lists all specifically for/about an audience of young readers in India is set in modern-day India for LGBTQ+ young people to identify with a setting that they are familiar with. One story tells the experience of an Indian boy in the diaspora, one captures elements from Indian mythology including LGBTQ-related threads, another is the young adult

Mexican American story, while there are four narratives about white LGBTQ+ young adults in the United States. One of the books in the selection was by an Indian author (Devdutt Pattanaik) and another by an American novelist of Indian origins (Rakesh Satyal); only one book was published in India and that was not intended for a young adult audience. In comparison, for non-LGBTQ+ books in the 'best lists' for/about youth in India that were analysed in this research, the Indian (or South Asian) versus non-Indian setting/publication of the books varied across the individual lists. For example, of the '8 Great YA Novels Featuring South Asian Protagonists' (Enjeti 2014) the settings of the story for all except two were in the diaspora and included Cincinnati (1) Melbourne (1), New Jersey (1), New York (2) and Wisconsin (1). One South Asian setting included Burma and another Madras (new name Chennai), India. All were published in the United States. Thus, this problem is not limited to books with LGBTQ+ content but could be said to be particularly acute in this context.

This evidence reveals a major lapse that might come as a huge shock to some western readers who take for granted social justice principles (i.e. fairness, equality/equity, justice) in collection development, expecting that the privilege of equitable/fair coverage of content they are used to in their European/American settings are reflective of similar trends all around the globe (Mehra 2015). Even though there has been a similar failure to centralize gay ethnic minority themes for/about youth in Europe/America with very recent and small improvements, the conditions in an international context (such as in India) are urgent owing to the harsh social and culture climate of homophobia and the pervasive unacceptance in these parts of the world. In the context of this limited availability of fiction for/about LGBTQ+ youth in India (or their exclusion from 'best lists'), inclusion of works reflecting universal themes and cross-cultural experiences provides some value to young LGBTQ+ readers in India. Better something than none at all. Nonetheless, there have to be more works for/about LGBTQ+ youth written by Indian authors and set in India to provide authentic representations and accurate portrayals and address this jarring shortcoming. Publishers should play a more active role in creating pressures and incentives as well appropriate calls for proposals of new literature to motivate and encourage creative writers and authors to traverse this uncharted intellectual territory. There are some niche publishers for LGBTQ+ content in India (e.g. Queer Ink, Yoda Press) who might expand their product lines to include materials for/about LGBTQ+ youth in the subcontinent. Additionally, there are also not-for-profit booksellers in India some of which focus on diverse materials (e.g. Pratham Books). They should make it their responsibility to find resources and publish LGBTQ+ fiction content for youth in India since there are so few materials available on the subject and the needs of this population are staying unmet and ignored.

Discussion

The marginal status and coverage of LGBTQ+ content for/about youth in a culturally relevant context across the various searches is obviously a big issue of concern (Dasgupta 2017). The evidence in this research reveals a similar problem to that noted by Epstein (2013) regarding the lack of diversity in young adult literature published in the United States/United Kingdom. With a huge gap in the availability of relevant

LGBTQ+ materials specifically for/about Indian young people, the social justice and ethical imperative emerges in problematizing the needs of a significant population niche that are not getting met. In the context of economic concerns in a neoliberal capitalist society, it also potentially represents a large market for publishers and distributers to tap into to further their profit-making agendas and keep pace with global advances around the world (Vachani 2012). This is important in the context of the following quote from Nielsen-Bookscan India's report (2015):

> India is the sixth-largest book market in the world, and currently the second largest for books in English, behind the United States ... Nielsen's survey among urban consumers shows that they buy more educational books than trade books. The educational books sector, which forms 70 percent of the book market in India, is the bulwark for the publishing industry ... Out of the 9,037 publishers identified in the Nielsen report, 8,107 publish books for schools, colleges and higher educational institutions. Only 930 are trade publishers ... the schoolbooks market in 2013–14 was worth Rs. 18,600 crore, and the market for books for higher education was valued at Rs. 5,600 crore in the same period. The trade books market was valued at Rs. 1,860 crore, a figure which would no doubt be higher if publishers not covered by BookScan, especially those who publish books in Indian languages, were added to the count. (n.p.)

In this recent study of the Indian book market, conducted on behalf of the Association of Publishers in India and the Federation of Indian Publishers, Nielsen BookScan India (2015) claims that the country ranks in second place among all nations as an English-language print book publisher, currently worth Rs. 261 million (approximately £2.7 million), making it the sixth largest in the world. It was predicted to reach Rs. 739 billion (approximately £7.7 billion) by 2020 (Press Trust of India 2015). With such a huge actual and potential publishing infrastructure and a niche in the market that has not been tapped in terms of LGBTQ+ content for/about youth, here are some suggested strategies for different stakeholders moving forward.

For authors and writers: This group should take the initiative and write about a diversity of experiences in their works for youth in India, and this means the inclusion of LGBTQ+ content. Not only is this important for educating youth and adults in India with accurate and authoritative information that reflects the humanity of LGBTQ+ people and challenges their demonization by politicians, conservatives and others with vested interests, but it is also important for LGBTQ+ youth to encounter representations and experiences of themselves in genre fiction because these materials have great appeal to them and it is what they tend to read (Agosto et al. 2003). Finding accurate and representative narratives that marginalized people, including LGBTQ+ youth, can relate to in genre fiction helps them develop positive identities, challenge prejudice, deal with trauma and abuse, and expose unacknowledged bias and intolerance (Landt 2011; Pullen 2014).

For reviewers and journalists: Reviewers and journalists should be careful in avoiding the use of stereotyping language, intentionally avoiding or ignoring same-sex couples/relationships in their writings and imposing their own biased value judgements. For instance, in Nilima Sinha's (2012) review, when she writes of the contemporary female teenager in India: 'She is prepared to deal with serious issues, is curious about and interested in the other sex and mature enough to read about broader social, national and international subjects' (n.p.).

This is an example of a negative assumption presented here by the reviewer, i.e. that all female teenagers will be interested in 'the other' sex. This chapter is not about the analysis of reviewers' biases expressed in their reviews of LGBTQ+ works (in India or elsewhere). Future research will focus on this topic since it is beyond the scope of this chapter, though the example presented here illustrates the problem.

For educators and librarians: On this group lies the burden of taking the lead in confronting social, cultural and political prejudice and ignorance. Raising LGBTQ+ topics, sexuality, sexual orientation and related issues via exposure to fiction and non-fiction works in the classroom is a strategy to equip young people (LGBTQ+ or otherwise) with tools to shape societal reform and mobilize youth activist forces (Sengupta 2017).

For booksellers and publishers: As in the west and everywhere else in the world, this constituency exists to generate income as a business enterprise. Booksellers, publishers and vendors need to sustain their existence by generating income and profit by packaging and disseminating information in products that the public can consume. That requires creative and strategic thinking and the ability to take calculated risks based on an analysis of potential demand and cost-benefit ratios. They have to look at LGBTQ+ content in this manner and recognize the potentialities to assist them in their business-oriented missions. Along the way, if they are able re-shape cultural values and achieve social justice for a marginalized population, all the better as a bonus to achieve their capitalist agendas. Some leading businesses are recognizing the need for diversity and inclusion initiatives, particularly for LGBTQ+ inclusion in varied work environments, as a smart business strategy to make themselves more attractive to employees and retain a happy, talented and productive staff that stays committed and inventive. For example, on 19 May 2017, RELX Group, the parent company of Elsevier, sponsored a symposium in Chennai, titled 'LGBT Workplace – Expanding the Dialogue in India', a landmark event never previously organized at this scale to address the challenges faced by the LGBTQ+ workforce in India (Kolman 2017). Niche publishers for LGBTQ+ content and not-for-profit booksellers in India can assist in collaborative alliances with big corporations and government agencies in resource sharing and knowledge management to publish LGBTQ+ fiction content for/about youth in India since this population continues to have a very limited selection of materials meaningful to them.

For activists and advocates: Some activists work to demand changes to content when certain materials are not available. Activists and advocates on behalf of LGBTQ+ issues have also played a significant role in India in challenging human rights denial and abuse at the hands of politicians, law enforcement, religious fanatics and others.

The search for relevant sources in this study was quite intensive based on information available on the Internet. However, many small and medium-sized Indian publishers and distributors of materials in English and non-English Indian languages who do not have a presence on the world wide web were excluded from this research (Mallya 2012). Google India has recognized this problem in its recent statement posted on Twitter: 'When you search in Indian languages, the content available is just 1 percent of what's available in English' (2018, n.p.). The vast digital divides related to a lack of online visibility of Indian publishers is itself quite a problem in the twenty-first century where in the western hemisphere the ubiquitous use and impact of the Internet and mobile technologies is almost undebatable (Armentano et al. 2017; Bechmann and Lomborg 2014). In 2013, Mark Monfasani of the Publishers Communication Group identified the need for rapid transformation of India's 'publishing industry and academic libraries in a relatively short span of time' and 'their strong commitments and progress toward digital conversion' (2013, n.p.) in response to an overall increase in the country's web users that had outpaced other countries (including Japan), with a 31 per cent annual growth rate over the previous year, to 73.9 million, making it the world's third-largest internet population (Gulati 2013). Recognizing the difficult and expensive process that English- and regional-language publishers in India go through to make their content available on the Internet, Google's Project Navlekha claims that its simple application will now be able to 'make offline content fully editable and publish online without the need of experts' and 'create a webpage out of scanned copies of pages' (Chakraborty 2018, n.p.).

In addition, there is a need to identify possible best practices related to building alliances and partnerships amongst these stakeholders and others (e.g. with government representatives, celebrities, businesses, etc.) to further the availability and publication of LGBTQ+ content for/about youth in India. Such bridges can continue to help in developing voices of resistance within a culturally homophobic environment steeped in challenges emerging from hegemonies associated with heterosexual norms, as well as patriarchal and chauvinistic values and practices that present insurmountable barriers to LGBTQ+ youth in their coming-out process.

Stakeholders outside India too have an important role. Indians in the diaspora and others should continue to write of Indian experiences that are meaningful to LGBTQ+ youth in India. LGBTQ+ writers and advocates in the western world should also highlight the experiences of non-white sexual minorities, instead of holding on to an outdated homogenized picture of 'global gay' (Martel and Baudoin 2018) and/or considering people of colour 'invisible' (Ocampo and Soodjinda 2016). A challenge for western librarians is to identify publishers from other parts of the world (including India) and use their books to diversify their collections. Such efforts will assist them to meet the needs of the Indian diaspora, but more importantly, could provide exposure to the public (especially youth and children) regarding the real diversity of the LGBTQ+ experience in other parts of the world and in their own countries via content delivered in a variety of formats and genres including non-print materials and picture books (Naidoo 2012). Another strategy is to establish book awards and other forms of recognition of work related to LGBTQ+ youth in India and other marginalized populations around the world; this should become a responsibility and mission of professional organizations and associations in more privileged countries where homosexuality is more accepted.

Conclusion

This chapter briefly highlighted trends and themes related to fiction works for/about LGBTQ+ youth in India. Supported by select evidence, the narrative informed readers of the major gaps in availability, access and representations of this population. Within a hegemonic homophobic and patriarchal society, this is not surprising. The restricted

Table 1: Select publishers of books in India for young readers.

Alphabetical List	URL
Amar Chitra Katha	http://amarchitrakatha.com/
Art Factory	https://www.facebook.com/shop.artfactory/
Children's Book Trust (CBT)	http://www.childrensbooktrust.com/
DC Books	http://www.deeceegroup.com/
Dey's Publishing	http://www.deyspublishing.com/
Dial Books for Young Readers	http://www.penguin.com/publishers/dialbooksforyoungreaders/
Duckbill	http://www.duckbill.in/
Eklavya	http://www.eklavya.org/publications.html
Holiday House	http://www.holidayhouse.com/
India Book House	http://www.ibhworld.com/
Inked	http://www.inkedpublisher.com/
Jaico Publishing House	http://www.jaicobooks.com/
Kalpavriksh	http://www.kalpavriksh.org/
Karadi Tales	https://www.karaditales.com/
Katha Books	https://books.katha.org/
Little Latitude	http://littlelatitude.com/
Mango Books	http://www.mangobooks.co.uk/about/
National Book Trust	http://www.nbtindia.gov.in/
Penguin India	https://penguin.co.in/
Pickle Yolk Books	http://pickleyolkbooks.com/
Pilgrims Book House	https://www.pilgrimsonlineshop.com/
Pratham Books	http://prathambooks.org/
Red Turtle	http://rupapublications.co.in/book_category/red-turtle/
Rupa Publications	http://rupapublications.co.in/
Seagull Books	https://www.seagullbook.com/
Tara Books	https://tarabooks.com/
Tulika Publishers	http://www.tulikabooks.com/
Undercover Books	https://undercoverbooks.org/
Utopia	https://d.facebook.com/utopiapublishing/?__tn__=%2AsH-R
Vishv Books	https://www.vishvbook.com/
Young Zubaan	http://zubaanbooks.com/product-category/books/yz/

nature of the cultural environment and the stifling impact it has had – resulting in a very limited selection of LGBTQ+ content *for* and *about* young people that is focused on their life experiences and understanding of the topic in India – has provided grounds for the emergence of a few themes that are very queerly reflective of the South Asian context. The role of the diaspora and writings by diasporic authors of Indian origins writing fiction with LGBTQ+ content for/about youth in India is one. At least it brings some level of authenticity and accuracy reflective of and relating to the Indian LGBTQ+ youth experience and context. Obviously, this is not a substitute for Indian authors living in India who should also be writing for/about LGBTQ+ youth in India. Since there is a very limited selection of materials that are directly and specifically for and about them, LGBTQ+

Table 2: Analysis of English-language fiction in 'best lists' aimed specifically at youth in India.

Title of list	Source	Type	Count	Number and % related to LGBTQ+
Best Young Adults Fiction in India [Praveen, (12/09/2011), searched October 2018]	goodreads.com	social media	186	0
10 Young Adult Fiction authors from India	blog.indiareads.com	blog	42	0
India: What Fiction Book Would You Recommend As a Must Read for a Young Indian Adult?	Quora.com	social media	30	0
15+ Books By Indian Authors All Kids And Young Adults Must Pick Up This Summer Break! (01/04/2016)	polkacafe.com	blog for teachers	15	0
15 Young Adult Books That'll Make Your 20s Just A Little Bit Easier [Farishte Irani (04/15/2018)]	filtercopy.com	online magazine	15	0
14 Young Adult Books For Every Indian Who Felt Too Much But Didn't Know How To Say It	filtercopy.com	online magazine	14	5 (36%)
8 Great YA Novels Featuring South Asian Protagonists [Anjali Enjeti (04/04/2014)]	pastemagazine.com	online magazine	8	1 (12.5%)
8 YA Books With Powerful Stories About Being South Asian [Pooja Makhijani (04/27/2017)]	teenvogue.com	online magazine	8	0
Food for thought: What's young India reading, and why? [Indrajit Hazra (08/04/2013)]	hindustantimes.com	online newspaper	6	0
IndiYA: Young Adult/ Crossover Titles from India [Yash Kesanakurthy (03-23-2017)]	bookriot.com	online magazine	5	1 (20%)
TOTAL			329	7 (2.13%)

youth in India might be seeking any LGBTQ+ content available to them, no matter how relevant or irrelevant it might be to their cultural contexts of experience, knowledge and understanding. The inclusion of some LGBTQ+ selections about youth experiences from around the world on the 'best lists' for youth in India might be reflective of this reality. Hence, in this chapter those reflecting universal themes, cross-cultural contexts, South Asian diasporic settings and Indian cultural environments are all included. Also, LGBTQ+ youth readers in India might be finding fiction materials more for adults and/or non-fiction readings, anything that they can get their hands on (or find available on the Internet) since more appropriate and pertinent materials are just not there for them

Table 3: Select examples of 'non-best list' general sources.

Alphabetical List	URL
'15 Books You Must Read To Understand Same-Sex Sexuality in India'. *Intersectional Feminism – Desi Style* [FII Team (07/22/2015)].	https://feminisminindia.com/2015/07/22/15-books-you-must-read-to-understand-same-sex-sexuality-in-india/
'10 Books By Indian Authors To Look Out For In 2017'. *Bustle* [Swapna Krishna (01/11/2017)].	https://www.bustle.com/p/10-books-by-indian-authors-to-look-out-for-in-2017-29680
'Are India's Young Adults Ready for LGBT Literature?' *midday.com: Culture News* [Preeti Singh (12/03/2014)].	https://www.mid-day.com/articles/are-india-s-young-adults-ready-for-lgbt-literature/15810191
'Books for Young Adults in India'– Review, The Book Review Literacy Trust [Nilima Sinha (2012)].	https://www.goodbooks.in/version2/2010/08/29/contemporary-childrens-literature-in-india/
Broad search on goodreads.com etc.	Goodreads.com
'Popular Writers Recommend Books To Read During Summer Holidays'. *midday.com: Culture News* [Snigdha Hasan (04/14/2018)].	https://www.mid-day.com/articles/popular-writers-recommend-books-to-read-during-summer-holidays/19318179
Popular search engines and online stores (LGBTQ+-related and India and/or youth)	amazon.com; barnesandnoble.com; google.com; yahoo.com; etc.
Wikipedia search (LGBTQ+-related and India)	wikipedia.com

(Cooper 2009). Our inclusion of materials that are *about* LGBTQ+ youth in India with mature content and themes for adults (not necessarily *for* LGBTQ+ youth) is reflective of this, and such materials might be getting read by Indian LGBTQ+ youth owing to poor relevant availability of contextually situated works for/about them.

So, the mainstream powerbrokers and vested constituencies in the publishing industry are not going to go out of their way to make content available to their children and young people, especially if that content provides a counter-narrative to the rigidity and misinformation of gender and sexuality-related understanding that is pervasive in the culture. Drawing attention to these matters in this chapter might serve as a wake-up call to the leaders, thinkers, creative writers and publishers in the country to do something positive in this regard. Otherwise, the future for LGBTQ+ youth in India does not look very bright, irrespective of the change in legal status of homosexuality recently made. Unless there are changes in the hearts and minds of people and more acceptance and better understanding towards sexuality and gender intersections, the cultural reality will not improve. More content for/about LGBTQ+ youth (and broader LGBTQ+ representations) in fiction, non-fiction and other media coverage will surely make a difference in dispelling ignorance and hate to further social justice advocacy beyond only its legal dimension.

References

Adiga, Aravind. 2017. *Selection Day: A Novel.* New York: Scribner.

Agarwal, Anirudh. 2017. 'Which are the Best Young Adult Fiction Books by Indian Authors?' *Quora.com,* 17 October. https://www.quora.com/Which-are-the-best-young-adult-fiction-books-by-Indian-authors

Agosto, Denise E., Sandra Hughes-Hassell, and Catherine Gilmore-Clough. 2003. 'The All-White World of Middle-School Genre Fiction: Surveying the Field for Multicultural Protagonists'. *Children's Literature in Education* 34, no. 4: 257–75.

Alexander, Linda B., and Sarah D. Miselis. 2007. 'Barriers to GLBTQ Collection Development and Strategies for Overcoming Them'. *Young Adult Library Services* 5, no. 3: 43–49.

Amar Chitra Katha. 2018. *Home.* Accessed 28 December 2018. http://amarchitrakatha.com

Armentano, Ricardo, Robin Singh Bhadoria, Parag Chatterjee, and Ganesh Chandra Deka. 2017. *The Internet of Things: Foundations for Smart Cities, eHealth, and Ubiquitous Computing.* Boca Raton, FL: Chapman and Hall.

Audit Bureau of Circulations. 2017. *Highest Circulated Amongst ABC Member Publications (Across Languages).* Mumbai: Audit Bureau of Circulations. http://www.auditbureau.org/files/JJ2017%20Highest%20Circulated%20amongst%20ABC%20Member%20Publications%20(across%20languages).pdf

Basu, Kaushik. 2007. 'India's Demographic Dividend'. *BBC News,* 25 July. http://news.bbc.co.uk/2/hi/south_asia/6911544.stm

BBC News. 2012. 'India has 2.5m Gays, Government Tells Supreme Court'. 14 March. https://www.bbc.com/news/world-asia-india-17363200

Bechmann, Anja, and Stine Lomborg. 2014. *The Ubiquitous Internet: User and Industry Perspectives* (Routledge Studies in New Media and Cyberculture). Abingdon, United Kingdom: Routledge.

Blackburn, Mollie, V., and Caroline T. Clark. 2011. 'Becoming Readers of Literature with LGBT Themes: In and Out of Classrooms'. In *Handbook of Research on Children's and Young Adult Literature,* edited by Shelby A. Wolf, Karen Coats, Patricia Enciso and Christine A. Jenkins, 148–63. New York: Routledge.

Burke, Jason. 2013. 'Indian LGBT Activists Outraged as Supreme Court Reinstates Gay Sex Ban'. *The Guardian,* 11 December. https://www.theguardian.com/world/2013/dec/11/india-supreme-court-reinstates-gay-sex-ban

Carson, David K., and Jennifer M. Foster. 2015. *Child Sexual Abuse in India: Understanding and Impacting Individuals, Families, and Socio-Cultural Systems.* Riga, Latvia: Lambert Academic Publishing.

Ceci, Stephen J., and Wendy M. Williams. 2000. *The Nature-Nurture Debate: The Essential Readings.* Oxford, United Kingdom: Wiley-Blackwell Publishers Ltd.

Chakraborty, Monotosh. 2011. 'Lesbian Couple Commits Suicide'. *The Times of India,* 24 January. https://timesofindia.indiatimes.com/city/kolkata-/Lesbian-couple-commits-suicide/articleshow/7351197.cms?referral=PM

Chakraborty, Sumit. 2018. 'Google's Project Navlekha to Help Indian Publishers Take Their Content Online'. *Gadgets 360: An NDTV venture,* 28 August. https://gadgets.ndtv.com/internet/news/google-for-india-project-navlekha-offline-publishers-online-adsense-1907390

Children's Book Trust. 2017. *Welcome to the Children's Book Trust.* Accessed 28 December 2018. http://www.childrensbooktrust.com/

Coon, David R. 2018. 'Mythgarden: Collaborative Authorship and Counter-Storytelling in Queer Independent Film'. *Journal of Film and Video* 70, no. 3–4: 44–62.

Cooper, Al. 2009. 'Sexuality and the Internet: Surfing into the New Millennium'. *CyberPsychology & Behavior* 1, no. 2: 187–93.

Cooperative Children's Book Center, School of Education, University of Wisconsin-Madison. Last updated 2018. *Publishing Statistics on Children's Books about People of Color and First/Native Nations and by People of Color and First/Native Nations Authors and Illustrators.* Accessed 31 December 2018. http://ccbc.education.wisc.edu/books/pcstats.asp

Dasgupta, Rohit K. (2017). *Digital Queer Cultures in India: Politics, Intimacies and Belonging.* New York: Routledge: Taylor & Francis Group.

Dasgupta, Rohit K., and Debanuj Dasgupta. 2018. *Queering Digital India: Activisms, Identities, Subjectivities* (Technicities). Edinburgh, Scotland: Edinburgh University Press.

Dave, Naisargi N. 2012. *Queer Activism in India: A Story in the Anthropology of Ethics.* Durham, NC: Duke University Press.

Dawesar, Abha. 2005. *Babyji.* Toronto: Anchor Books.

Deb, Sibnath. 2018. *An Empirical Investigation into Child Abuse and Neglect in India: Burden, Impact, and Protective Measures* (Springer Briefs in Well-Being and Quality of Life Research). Singapore: Springer Nature Singapore Pvt. Ltd.

Dedeoglu, Hakan, Mustafa Ulusoy and Linda L. Lamme. 2012. 'Turkish Preservice Teachers' Perceptions of Children's Picture Books Reflecting LGBT-Related Issues'. *The Journal of Educational Research* 105, no. 4: 256–63.

Enjeti, Anjali. 2014. '8 Great YA Novels Featuring South Asian Protagonists'. *Paste,* 4 April. https://www.pastemagazine.com/books/8-great-ya-novels-featuring-south-asian-protagonists/

Epstein, B. J. 2013. *Are the Kids All Right? Representations of LGBTQ Characters in Children's and Young Adult Literature.* Bristol, United Kingdom: HammerOn Press.

Escalas, Jennifer Edson. 2007. 'Self-Referencing and Persuasion: Narrative Transportation versus Analytical Elaboration'. *The Journal of Consumer Research* 33, no. 4: 421–29.

FII Team. 2015. '15 Books You Must Read to Understand Same-Sex Sexuality In India'. *Intersectional Feminism – Desi Style,* 22 July. https://feminisminindia.com/2015/07/22/15-books-you-must-read-to-understand-same-sex-sexuality-in-india/

Flores, Gabriel. 2012. 'Toward a More Inclusive Multicultural Education: Methods for Including LGBT Themes in K-12 Classrooms'. *American Journal of Sexuality Education* 7, no. 3: 187–97.

———. 2014. 'Teachers Working Cooperatively with Parents and Caregivers when Implementing LGBT Themes in the Elementary Classroom'. *American Journal of Sexuality Education* 9, no. 1: 114–20.

———. 2016. 'Best Not Forget Lesbian, Gay, Bisexual, and Transgender Themed Children's Literature: A Teacher's Reflections of a More Inclusive Multicultural Education and Literature Program'. *American Journal of Sexuality Education* 11, no. 1: 1–17.

Fredrick, Tim. 2006. 'Choosing to Belong: Increasing Male Engagement in the ELA Classroom'. *Changing English* 13, no. 1: 151–59. https://doi.org/l0.1080/13586840500523596

Gettleman, Jeffrey, and Kai Schultz. 2018. 'For Gay Indians, Landmark Ruling Is the Just the Beginning'. *The New York Times,* 7 September. https://www.nytimes.com/2018/09/07/world/asia/india-gay-rights-ruling.html

Goldhaber, Dale. 2012. *The Nature-Nurture Debates: Bridging the Gap.* New York: Cambridge University Press.

goodreads.com. 2018. *Best Young Adults Fiction in India.* Accessed 28 December 2018. https://www.goodreads.com/list/show/15102.Best_Young_Adults_Fiction_in_India

Google India. 2018. 'When you search in Indian languages, the content available is just 1% of what's available in English'. *Twitter.com,* 27 August. https://twitter.com/GoogleIndia/status/1034328109678510081

Guerra, Stephanie F. 2012. 'Using Urban Fiction to Engage At-Risk and Incarcerated Youths in Literacy Instruction'. *Journal of Adolescent and Adult Literacy* 55, no. 5: 385–94.

Gulati, Sonam. 2013. 'India Added 17.6M Internet Users Last Year, Becomes World's Third Largest Internet Population'. *TECHCIRCLE,* 26 August. https://techcircle.vccircle.com/2013/08/26/india-added-17-6m-internet-users-last-year-becomes-worlds-third-largest-internet-population

Gwalani, Payal. 2015. 'High Rate of Suicides Haunts LGBT Youth'. *The Times of India,* 17 November. https://timesofindia.indiatimes.com/city/nagpur/High-rate-of-suicides-haunts-LGBT-youths/articleshow/49808926.cms

Halder, Debarati. 2018. *Child Sexual Abuse and Protection Laws in India* (SAGE LAW). New Delhi, India: Sage.

Hasan, Snigdha. 2018. 'Popular Writers Recommend Books To Read During Summer Holidays'. *midday.com: Culture News,* 14 April. https://www.mid-day.com/articles/popular-writers-recommend-books-to-read-during-summer-holidays/19318179

Hazra, Indrajit. 2013. 'Food for Thought: What's Young India Reading, And Why?' *Hindustan Times,* 4 August. https://www.hindustantimes.com/books/food-for-thought-what-s-young-india-reading-and-why/story-MNfDT6Etby1tbFqrIsKLLK.html

Hughes-Hassell, Sandra. 2013. 'Multicultural Young Adult Literature as a Form of Counter-Storytelling'. *The Library Quarterly* 83, no. 3: 212–28.

Jack, Ian. 2018. 'India Has 600 Million Young People – And They're Set to Change Our World'. *The Guardian: Opinion India.* 13 January. https://www.theguardian.com/commentisfree/2018/jan/13/india-600-million-young-people-world-cities-internet

Jenkins, Christine A., and Michael Cart. 2018. *Representing the Rainbow in Young Adult Literature: LGBTQ+ Content Since 1969.* New York: Roman & Littlefield.

Joseph, Sherry. 2018. *Social Work Practice and Men Who Have Sex With Men* (First edition). New Delhi, India: Sage Publications Pvt. Ltd.

Kacker, Loveleen. 2015. *Childhood Betrayed: Child Abuse and Neglect in India.* Noida, India: HarperCollins Publishers India.

Katyal, Akhil. 2017. *The Doubleness of Sexuality: Idioms of Same-Sex Desire in Modern India.* India: New Text.

Kidangoor, Abhishyant. 2018. 'India's Supreme Court Decriminalizes Homosexuality in a Historic Ruling for the LGBTQ Community'. *Time,* 6 September 6. http://time.com/5388231/india-decriminalizes-homosexuality-section-377/

Kim, So Jung, and Josephia Tinajero. 2016. 'Teaching Diversity to Bilingual Children: Mexican-Origin Kindergarteners' Discussions about Children's Literature Depicting Non-traditional Gender Roles'. *Linguistics and Literature Studies* 4, no. 3: 171–80.

Kolman, Michael. 2017. 'Symposium Spotlights LGBT Workplace Inclusion in India'. *Elsevier: Symposium Spotlight,* 13 June. https://www.elsevier.com/connect/symposium-spotlights-lgbt-workplace-inclusion-in-india

Krishna, Swapna. 2017. '10 Books By Indian Authors To Look Out For In 2017'. *Bustle,* 11 January. https://www.bustle.com/p/10-books-by-indian-authors-to-look-out-for-in-2017-29680

Lafferty, Karen Elizabeth. 2014. ' "What Are You Reading?": How School Libraries Can Promote Racial Diversity in Multicultural Literature'. *Multicultural Perspectives* 16, no. 4: 203–9.

Landt, Susan M. 2011. 'Multicultural Literature and Young Adolescents: A Kaleidoscope of Opportunity'. *Journal of Adolescent & Adult Literacy* 49, no. 8: 690–97. https://doi.org/10.1598/JAAL.49.8.5

Laxmi, Raj Rao, and P. G. Joshi. 2015. *Me Hijra, Me Laxmi.* Oxford: Oxford University Press.

Mallya, Vinutha. 2012. 'Confronting the Big Issues in Indian Publishing'. *Publishing Perspectives: In Growth Markets,* 24 October. https://publishingperspectives.com/2012/10/confronting-the-big-issues-in-indian-publishing/

Martel, Frédéric, and Patsy Baudoin. 2018. *Global Gay: How Gay Culture Is Changing the World.* Cambridge, MA: MIT Press.

Mehra, Bharat. 2011. 'Use of Mixed Methods to Meet the Needs of Underserved Populations: A Reflective Analysis of My Research Efforts in the United States'. *Proceedings of the Qualitative and Quantitative Methods in Libraries International Conference (QQML 2011), Athens, Greece, 24–27 May 2011.*

———. 2015. 'Introduction'. *Library Trends: Social Justice in Library and Information Science & Services* 64, no. 2: 179–97.

———. 2016. 'Cultural Re-Interpretation of Race/Ethnicity and Sexuality: A Gay South Asian "Voice" From Between a Rock and a Hard Place'. In *Celebrating the James Partridge Award: Essays Toward the Development of a More Diverse, Inclusive, and Equitable Field of Library and Information Science*, edited by Diane L. Barlow and Paul T. Jaeger, 169–93. Bingley, United Kingdom: Emerald Group Publishing.

———. 2019a. 'Deconstructing "Boxes & Walls" in a Fluid Non-Binary Gendered Society: Gender Inclusivity and Equity in North American Academic Libraries [Section in 'Gender Inclusivity and Equity in Academic Libraries: Insights from Around the Globe' by Buhle Mbambo-Thata, Jia Tina Du, Ulrike Lang, Jesús Lau, Amal W. Mostafa, Bharat Mehra, Clara M. Chu, and Jaya Raju] 'International Insights' Column, *College & Research Libraries News (C&RL News)* 80, no. 8: 438–42. https://crln.acrl.org/index.php/crlnews/article/view/23546/30867

———. 2019b. 'Introduction'. In *LGBTQ+ Librarianship in the 21st Century: Emerging Directions of Advocacy and Community Engagement in Diverse Information Environments*, edited by Bharat Mehra, 3–14. Bingley, United Kingdom: Emerald Group Publishing.

Mehra, Bharat, Eric Haley, and Dylan Lane. 2015. 'Culturally Appropriate Information Support Services for Lesbian, Gay, Bisexual, and Transgender (LGBT) South Asians: Representing Multiple Shades of Identity Based on Sexual Orientation and Ethnicity'. In *Expanding the Circle: Creating an Inclusive Environment in Higher Education for LGBT Students and Studies*, edited by John C. Hawley, 317–39. New York: SUNY Press.

Mehra, Bharat, and Lisette Hernandez. 2016. 'Libraries as Agents of Human Rights Protection and Social Justice on Behalf of Sexual Minorities in India: An Action-Based Manifesto for Progressive Change'. In *Perspectives on Libraries as Institutions of Human Rights and Social Justice*, edited by Ursula Gorham, Natalie Greene Taylor and Paul T. Jaeger, 147–82. Bingley, United Kingdom: Emerald Group Publishing.

Mehra, Bharat, Paul A. Lemieux III, and Keri Stophel. 2019. 'An Exploratory Journey of Cultural Visual Literacy of "Non-Conforming" Gender Representations from Pre-Colonial Sub-Saharan Africa'. *Open Information Science* (Special Issue: Gender Issues in Library and Information Science: Focusing on Visual Aspects, edited by Lesley S. J. Farmer) 3, no. 1: 1–21. https://www.degruyter.com/view/j/opis.2019.3.issue-1/opis-2019-0001/opis-2019-0001.xml

Mehra, Bharat, Paul A. Lemieux III, Christie Burwell, Taylor Hixson, Robert P. Partee II, Keri Stophel, and Nicole E. Wood. (2018). 'Expanding LIS Education in the U.S. Department of State's Diplomacy Lab Program: GIS and LGBTI Advocacy in Africa and Latin America'. *Journal of Education for Library and Information Science* 59, no. 3: 4–16.

Mehta, Rahul. 2017. *No Other World: A Novel*. New York: HarperCollins.

Mogul, Joey L., Andrea J. Ritchie, and Kay Whitlock. 2012. *Queer (In) Justice: The Criminalization of LGBT People in the United States* (Queer Ideas/Queer Action). Boston, MA: Beacon Press.

Monfasani, Mark. 2013. 'India's Transition from Print to Digital'. *PCG Vantage*, Fall 2013. http://www.pcgplus.com/indias-transition-from-print-to-digital/

Myers, Walter Dean. 2014. 'Where Are the People of Color in Children's Books?' *New York Times*, 15 March. https://nyti.ms/1d03H2A

Naidoo, Jamie Campbell. 2012. *Rainbow Family Collections: Selecting and Using Children's Books with Lesbian, Gay, Bisexual, Transgender, and Queer Content* (Children's and Young Adult Literature Reference). Santa Barbara, CA: Libraries Unlimited.

Nielsen BookScan India. 2015. *The Nielsen India Book Market Report 2015: Understanding the India Book Market*. https://www.nielsen.com/us/en/press-room/2015/the-nielsen-india-book-market-report-2015-understanding-the-indian-book-market.html

Ocampo, Anthony C., and Daniel Soodjinda. 2016. 'Invisible Asian Americans: The Intersection of Sexuality, Race, and Education among Gay Asian Americans'. *Race Ethnicity and Education* 19, no. 3: 480–99.

Ouellett, Mathew L. 1996. 'Systemic Pathways for Social Transformation: School Change, Multicultural Organization Development, Multicultural Education, and LGBT Youth'. *Journal of Gay, Lesbian, and Bisexual Identity* 1, no. 4: 273–94.

Pandey, Rajesh Kumar. 2018. 'Gay Couple Seeks Security, Allahabad High Court Says No'. *The Times of India,* 28 September. https://timesofindia.indiatimes.com/city/allahabad/gay-couple-seeks-security-hc-says-no/articleshow/65988045.cms

Pandharipande, Rajeshwari. 1997. *Marathi* (Descriptive Grammars). Abingdon, United Kingdom: Routledge.

Pattanaik, Devdutt. 2015. *Shikhandi and Other Tales They Don't Tell You.* New Delhi: Zubaan and Penguin Books India.

Press Trust of India. 2015. 'Indian Book Market to Touch 739 Billion by 2020: Survey'. *Business Standard,* 1 December. https://www.business-standard.com/article/pti-stories/indian-book-market-to-touch-739-billion-by-2020-survey-115120100634_1.html

Pullen, Christopher. 2014. *Queer Youth and Media Cultures.* London, United Kingdom: Palgrave Macmillan.

Rao, R. Raj. 2017. *Criminal Love? Queer Theory, Culture, and Politics in India.* New Delhi, India: Sage Publications Pvt. Ltd.

Reardon, Robin. 2007. *A Secret Edge.* New York: Kensington.

Roy, Himadri. 2015. 'Claustrophobic Existence: Subjection of Personal Space of Lesbians in the Contemporary India'. In *Decoding the Silence: Reading John Stuart Mill's The Subjection of Women,* edited by Sarbojit Biswas and Saptarshi Mallick, 104–14. Indore, India: Aadi Publications.

Sampson, Darlene, and Dorothy F. Garrison-Wade. 2011. 'Cultural Vibrancy: Exploring the Preferences of African American Children Toward Culturally Relevant and Non-Culturally Relevant Lessons'. *The Urban Review* 43, no. 2: 279–309.

Sankar, Hemanjali. 2017. *Talking of Muskaan.* Chennai: Duckbill Books & Publications Pvt. Ltd.

Sarangi, Asha. 2010. *Language and Politics in India* (Themes in Politics). Oxford: Oxford University Press.

Satyal, Rakesh. *Blue Boy.* 2009. New York: Kensington Books.

Selvadurai, Shyam. 1994. *Funny Boy.* Toronto: McClelland and Stewart.

———. 2005. *Swimming in the Monsoon Sea.* New York: Tundra Books.

Sengupta, Somini. 2017. *The End of Karma: Hope and Fury Among India's Young.* New York: W. W. Norton & Company, Inc.

Shelton, Jama, and Julie Winkelstein. 2014. 'Librarians and Social Workers: Working Together for Homeless LGBTQ Youth'. *Young Adult Library Services* 13, no. 1: 20–24. http://www.ala.org/yalsa/sites/ala.org.yalsa/files/content/yalsarchives/YAL_Fall%202014-Combined_R06_FINAL.pdf

Shraya, Vivek. 2014. *She of the Mountains.* Vancouver, Canada. Arsenal Pulp Press.

———. 2016. *The Boy & the Bindi.* Illustrated by Rajni Perera. Vancouver: Arsenal Pulp Press.

Singh, Preeti. 2014. 'Are India's Young Adults Ready for LGBT Literature?' *midday.com: Culture News,* 3 December. https://www.mid-day.com/articles/are-india-s-young-adults-ready-for-lgbt-literature/15810191

Sinha, Bhadra. 2018. 'Gay Sex No Longer a Crime in India, Rules Supreme Court on Section 377 in Historic Judgment'. *Hindustan Times,* 6 September. https://www.hindustantimes.com/india-news/on-section-377-supreme-court-rules-gay-sex-no-longer-a-crime-in-india/story-CExF0q4BEQXRXWJIrfZY9K.html

Sinha, Nilima. 2012. 'For Teachers and Librarians: Books for Young Adults in India' (Review). *goodbooks.* New Delhi: The Book Review Literary Trust (The Goodbooks Trust). Accessed 10 May 2018. from http://www.thebookreviewindia.org

Smolkin, Laura B., and Craig A. Young. 2011. 'Missing Mirrors, Missing Windows: Children's Literature Textbooks and LGBT Topics'. *Language Arts* 88, no. 3: 217–25.

Sokoll, Talya. 2013. 'Representations of Trans* Youth in Young Adult Literature: A Report and a Suggestion'. *Young Adult Library Services* 11, no. 4: 23–26.

Stebbins, Anne E. 2015. 'Unproud Feelings; Negative Affects and their Unruly Pedagogies in 1960s to 1980s LGBT YA Novels'. PhD thesis, York University, Toronto. https://yorkspace.library.yorku.ca/xmlui/bitstream/handle/10315/30017/Stebbins_Anne_E_2015_PhD.pdf?sequence=2&isAllowed=y

Theroux, Marcel. 2017. 'Aravind Adiga's Novel Is About the Game of Cricket – and Sexual Awakening'. *The New York Times: Fiction,* 27 January. https://www.nytimes.com/2017/01/27/books/review/selection-day-aravind-adiga.html

Town, Caren J. *LGBTQ Young Adult Fiction: A Critical Survey, 1970s–2010s.* Jefferson, NC: McFarland & Company, Inc.

United Kingdom: Home Office. 2017. *Country Policy and Information Note – India: Sexual Orientation and Gender Identity*, v. 2.0, 21 February. http://www.refworld.org/docid/58aefa5e4.html

United Nations. (2018). 'UN Hails "Ground-Breaking" Supreme Court Ruling to Decriminalize Gay Sex in India.' *UN News,* 6 September. https://news.un.org/en/story/2018/09/1018531

United Nations Department of Economic and Social Affairs, Population Division. 2017. *World Population Prospects: The 2017 Revision.* Custom data accessed 31 May 2018. https://esa.un.org/unpd/wpp/DataQuery/

United Nations News Center. 2011. 'UN Issues First Report on Human Rights of Gay and Lesbian People'. 15 December. http://www.un.org/apps/news/story.asp?NewsID=40743#.Up4eNye0adx

Vachani, Shweta. 2012. 'Digital Rights Management: Which Way is India Headed?' In *PUBLICON 2012: Digital Publishing, Select Papers,* 3–4 September. http://ficci.in/spdocument/20177/Selected%20Papers%20for%20PubliCon%202012.pdf#page=8

Vanderhage, Gwen. 2019. 'What is #ownvoices?' *Brodart: Books & Library Services,* 21 August. https://www.brodartbooks.com/newsletter/posts-in-2019/what-is-ownvoices

Vanita, Ruth. 2001. *Queering India: Same-Sex Love and Eroticism in Indian Culture and Society.* Abingdon, United Kingdom: Routledge.

———. 2005. *Gandhi's Tiger and Sita's Smile: Essays on Gender, Sexuality and Culture.* New Delhi: Yoda Press.

Varma, Vishnu, and Nida Najar. 2014. 'India's Supreme Court Recognizes 3rd Gender'. *The New York Times,* 15 April. https://india.blogs.nytimes.com/2014/04/15/indias-supreme-court-recognizes-3rd-gender/

Wargo, Jon M. (2017a). 'Designing More Just Social Futures or Remixing the Radical Present? Queer Rhetorics, Multimodal (Counter)Storytelling, and the Politics of LGBTQ Youth Activism.' *English Teaching* 16, no. 2: 145–60.

———. (2017b). '#donttagyourhate: Reading, Collecting and Curating as Genres of Participation in LGBT Youth Activism on Tumblr'. *Digital Culture & Education* 9, no. 1: 14–31.

———. (2017c). 'Every Selfie Tells a Story: LGBTQ Youth Lifestreams and New Media Narratives as Connective Identity Texts'. *New Media & Society* 19, no. 4: 560–78.

Yasmin, Shahana. 2017. '6 Indian LGBT-Themed Books That Should Be Essential Reading for Everyone'. *Vagabomb: Art, Film & Culture,* 1 May. https://www.vagabomb.com/6-Indian-Books-about-Queer-Fiction-That-Should-Be-Essential-Reading-for-Everyone/.

Chapter Six

UN-SETTLING GENDER AND SEXUALITY: INDIGENOUS LGBTQ+/TWO-SPIRIT LITERATURE FOR YOUNG PEOPLE

Thaddeus Andracki

Strange Boy and Shadow Boy realized at last that they had never been alone. They were just the first to free their hearts and fly in their own beauty.

'The Boys Who Became the Hummingbirds' (Justice 2016, 57)

Context

It is impossible to understand the construction of LGBTQ+ Indigenous and Two-Spirit identities without understanding settler colonialism.[1] Colonialism wreaked havoc upon all aspects of Indigenous lives, and these included Indigenous perspectives and practices relating to gender and sexuality. However, until recently, much of the understanding of these perspectives outside of Indigenous communities was developed through non-Indigenous anthropological approaches to queer Indigenous lives, leading to further colonization of queer Indigeneity. These knowledges served not only the project of othering Indigenous peoples to settlers through the development of concepts like 'berdache' (discussed further below) but, as non-Native scholar Scott Lauria Morgensen has pointed out, also as stories that let 'non-Native and presumably white gays and lesbians … imagine that minoritized sexuality made them more like Native people than the settler society in which they lived' (Morgensen 2011, 63). This approach to understanding queer Indigeneity has often resulted in misinformation and appropriation.

It is critical to note that Indigenous nations have different traditions, histories and language surrounding variance in gender and sexuality within their communities: fa'afafine in Samoa, māhū among the Kanaka Maoli in Hawai'i, wíŋtke among the Lakota, nádleehi in the Diné Nation, among many others. Reading any of these as 'lesbian, gay,

1 I will take this opportunity to make note of the language I use in this chapter, noting that language used to describe Indigenous peoples is always political, and is often fluid, complex and contingent. These complexities are compounded by my position as a non-Indigenous interlocutor. I will use the term 'Indigenous' to refer to autochthonous peoples within a global context or to emphasize commonalities within experiences of colonization. 'First/Native Nations' refers to people and peoples indigenous to North America, noting that 'First Nations'

bisexual, transgender or queer' risks misunderstanding their unique situatedness within the cultures from which they arise, and it would, in fact, be an act of colonization to act as though they map neatly onto Western conceptions of gender or sexuality variance. Indigenous understandings of gender and sexuality arise from within specific nations, and it is not possible to separate these understandings from the traditions and spiritual practices of those communities. While Indigenous peoples share some experiences of colonization and resistance, these specificities inform much of how LGBTQ+ Indigenous, Two-Spirit, or takatāpui people understand their identities.

Within the United States, the term Two-Spirit rose to widespread usage after the Third Annual Native American Gay and Lesbian Gathering, which took place in Winnipeg, Manitoba in 1990, where resistance to continued use of the term 'berdache' to describe Native/First Nations genders and sexualities came out of the recognition of the term as both offensive and arising out of colonial, anthropological misperceptions of Native/First Nations traditions regarding gender and/or sexuality. The community, following the guidance of Native/First Nations groups across North America, decided to rename future meetings the International Two-Spirit Gathering (Thomas and Jacobs 1999). It is thus important to note that 'Two-Spirit' rose to prominence as a term for describing genders and sexualities from within First/Native Nations communities. While there remains some tension about the exact definition of 'Two-Spirit', it is commonly understood to encompass not only a definition of one's gender or sexuality but also of culture, Indigeneity and political orientation.[2] Two-Spirit, then, becomes an identity category in which Indigenous peoples are able to reclaim ownership of defining their own genders and sexualities. Though used across First/Native Nations, it does not intend to erase tribal or national specificity in each person's spiritual understanding of their gender or sexuality. Some Two-Spirit people consider themselves both Two-Spirit and gay, lesbian, bisexual, trans and/or queer members of their Indigenous nations, while others resist the use of those terms. Cherokee Two-Spirit (asegi) artist and scholar Qwo-Li Driskill notes the difficulty of pinning 'Two-Spirit' to a definition that is neatly understandable

---

is preferred within Canada and 'Native' is in common usage within the context of the United States. 'Aboriginal and Torres Strait Islander' is preferred for peoples indigenous to the land now known as Australia. I use names of specific nations when referring to individuals to acknowledge the sovereignties of the nations to which they belong. Furthermore, because this book as whole begins from a starting point to understand LGBTQ+ literatures for young people globally, this acronym will be used in addition to Two-Spirit, explained within the text, to describe Indigenous people who understand themselves, their genders and their sexualities outside dominant, colonial, heteropatriarchical systems. An additional term that has gained some traction within North America is the portmanteau 'Indigiqueer', highlighting the mutually constitutive nature of the identities of Indigenous LGBTQ+ people. Some Indigenous people disidentify with all of these terms and may instead describe their identities using Indigenous languages. To them, I apologize for the limitations of my language.

2 Indeed, by insisting on the linkages between gender, sexuality and traditional ways of life among Native/First Nations people, 'Two-Spirit' helps show how the categories of gay, lesbian, bisexual and transgender are also co-constructed with a predominantly white, Eurocentric perspective.

by non-Indigenous people – or indeed the imprecision it presents to First/Native Nations people: 'It is a sovereign term in the invaders' tongue' (Driskill 2004, 62).

Two-Spirit is often cited to come from an Anishinaabemowin phrase with spiritual significance. Yup'ik activist Anguksuar states regarding the choice of this label, 'What we who chose this designation understood is that *niizh manitoag* (two-spirits) indicates the presence of both a feminine and a masculine spirit in one person' (Anguksuar 1997, 221, italics in original). This statement has come to be misunderstood by outsiders that Two-Spirit can only refer to Indigenous people who somehow identify in a way that might be understood as outsiders as androgynous or non-binary. Oji-Cree author Joshua Whitehead, whose work is discussed later in this chapter, notably declined a nomination for a 2018 Lambda Literary Award in the trans poetry category on this basis: 'I note that it may be easy from an outside vantage point to read Two-Spirit as a conflation of feminine and masculine spirits and to easily, although wrongfully, categorize it as trans; I also note the appropriation of Two-Spirit genealogies by settler queerness to mark it as a reminder that Western conceptions of "queerness" have always lived due in part to the stealing of third, fourth, fifth, and fluid genders from many, although not all, Indigenous worldviews' (Whitehead 2018b, n.p.). While Two-Spirit understandings centre gender at the core of understanding queerness within Indigenous communities, they do not necessary dovetail neatly into Eurocentric understandings of non-binary identity, either.

The insistence of the centrality of spirituality in Two-Spirit identity is another aspect that separates it from categories of LGBTQ+. Two-Spirit also 'asserts ceremonial and spiritual communities and traditions and relationships with medicine as central in constituting various identities' (Driskill 2010, 73). The interbeing of gender, sexuality and traditional Native/First Nations religions, practices and worldviews is encompassed by definitions of Two-Spirit identity. That said, it is important to note, 'this is not because Two-Spirit people are somehow more spiritual than non-Two-Spirit people, as the appropriation of the term by New Agers might suggest. Rather, spiritual and ceremonial traditions are part of a continuance of cultural memory that Two-Spirit people, like other members of Native communities, are often a part of' (Driskill 2010, 88).

It is also worth noting that the use of Two-Spirit was and remains a term primarily of Turtle Island (that is, what is now known as North America). The political work of Indigenous self-definition for gender and sexual identities has worked in other ways in other settler societies. For example, among the Māori of Aotearoa New Zealand, takatāpui – first defined during early colonization as 'an intimate companion of the same sex' – has been used since the 1980s as a term that likewise insists on the centrality of Māori identity to takatāpui people's understanding of their gender or sexuality, naming their gender diversity or non-heterosexual relationships within their own language and from their own knowledge positions (Rainbow Youth and Tīwhanawhana Trust 2017).

Within Australia, Two-Spirit has gained some traction as a pan-Indigenous term among some Aboriginal and Torres Strait Islanders, although it is more common to see simply Queer Aboriginal as a descriptor of LGBTQ+ Aboriginal and Torres Strait Islander peoples. However, many Aboriginal people who might be considered 'transgender' from a settler perspective have begun to use the terms 'brotherboy' and 'sistergirl' to identify themselves and their understandings of their genders as separate from

Western conceptions of transness (Clark 2015, 244). Organizing around sistergirl and brotherboy identity has become an important part of Aboriginal Australian and Torres Strait Islander LGBTQ+ activism and healing (Burin 2016, n.p.).

Despite these efforts to recognize and name sovereign queer Indigeneity, homo-antagonism and trans-antagonism do exist within Indigenous communities, although this is recognized by many Indigenous people as an effect of colonization. As settlers invaded Indigenous lands, the projects of genocide and assimilation led, in many cases, to the introduction of European Christian-based values, including viewing gender or sexual variance as immoral. Some Indigenous activists view this as the primary mechanism by which homo- and trans-antagonism was introduced to Indigenous societies: by insisting that colonial anthropological knowledges are the only true knowledges about Indigenous peoples, and then by emptying those records of gender and sexual variance, colonialism was able to insist that these variances are at once a European 'perversion' of 'authentic' Indigeneity but also, from a European standpoint, unacceptable. Troy-Anthony Bayliss, an artist and scholar of Jawoyn descent, observes that, 'In Australia, that enactment has been so pervasive that Aboriginal people participate in the colonizer's work, refuting the possibility that non-heterosexuality is culturally authentic' (Bayliss 2014, n.p.).

As one example, Indigenous responses to the efforts to recognize same-sex marriage rights within settler states have been complicated. For example, in 2004 and 2005, the Cherokee Nation of Oklahoma and the Navajo Nation, respectively, passed laws that mirrored the United States' Defense of Marriage Act (DOMA) and defined marriage as between one man and one woman. This flashpoint brought forward questions of what would be 'authentically' Native. As Lenape scholar Joanne Barker points out, this quest for the 'authentic' Native tradition – whether one that is radically accepting or 'traditionally' Christian – binds Native peoples into a fixed, settler perception of what it means to be Native (Barker 2011, 197). On the other hand, before the *Obergefell v. Hodges* case that legalized same-sex marriage throughout the United States, several tribes had passed laws that allowed such marriages within their jurisdictions, including, for example, three located in what is now called Michigan (Little Traverse Band of Odawa Indians, Pokagon Band of Potawatomi Indians and Keweenaw Bay Indian Community), where they were otherwise not granted (NCAI Policy Research Center 2015, 2). Indeed, there has been discussion within queer Indigenous studies about the role that national marriage equality plays in furthering the control of the settler nation-state – a role that is antithetical to decolonization efforts (Driskill et al. 2011, 213; see also Byrd 2017, 208 and Kauanui 2017, 59).

There is no doubt, however, that queer antagonism, trans antagonism and anti-Two-Spirit bias have material effects on the lives of Indigenous LGBTQ+ and Two-Spirit peoples. Within the United States, according to a 2011 survey, 36 per cent of Native transgender people had reported losing a job because of their gender identity, and 56 per cent of Native transgender people had attempted suicide during their life (Grant et al. 2011, 4, 82). An earlier study had also found that 29.3 per cent of LGBTQ+ Native people had experienced hate violence, a rate higher than any other LGBTQ+ group within the United States (Frazer and Pruden 2010, 10). Similar research in what is now called Canada has found that Two-Spirit and LGBTQ+ Indigenous people experience devastatingly high levels of assault, abuse and poverty. In one study, 43 per cent of trans-identified Indigenous people living in Ontario reported having experienced transphobic violence (Laing 2016, 2–3). Even with this information, it is difficult to find further details about how Two-Spirit or LGBTQ+ Indigenous people's lives are affected by discrimination. Similar phenomena are discussed by Unangax̂ scholar Eve Tuck and non-Indigenous arrivant K. Wayne Yang in their research on Indigenous education, in which they show that studies that influence the material well-being of Indigenous people often relegate data regarding them to an asterisk due to small population sizes. The creation of 'asterisk peoples', as they write, assists in the trivialization of Indigenous people's concerns and subsumes the diversity of Indigenous peoples into a singular star (Tuck and Yang 2012, 22). Unfortunately, Two-Spirit and LGBTQ+ Indigenous peoples are all too often relegated to an asterisk in studies both among LGBTQ+ communities as well as within Indigenous communities as a whole.

Literature

Although there has been an invigorated conversation about Indigenous queer and Two-Spirit literatures in the academy with the publication of works such as Mark Rifkin's *The Erotics of Sovereignty* (2012); *Sovereign Erotics*, edited by Qwo-Li Driskill, Daniel Heath Justice, Deborah Miranda and Lisa Tatonetti (2011); and Lisa Tatonetti's *The Queerness of Native American Literature* (2014), much less attention has specifically attended to these concerns in literature for young people. The only scholarly study identified by this author that has addressed Two-Spirit children's and YA texts is Robert Bittner's 'Hey, I Still Can't See Myself'. Bittner limits his discussion to only two texts within this study, in part spurred by his focus on identifying texts that either explicitly identify characters as 'two souls' or that show characteristics of both masculine and feminine genders (Bittner 2014, 16). Furthermore, one of the books that Bittner discusses, *The Miseducation of Cameron Post*, is written by a non-Native white author, and has been critiqued by Nambé Pueblo scholar Debbie Reese as approaching Two-Spirit or wíŋtke identity from a colonial, anthropological point of view (Reese 2015, n.p.). The other does not explicitly engage in a discussion of Indigiqueer or Two-Spirit identity, but Bittner chooses to read a character with deep spiritual powers and who is identified as male but engages in some feminine behaviours as potentially Two-Spirit. While I deeply respect Bittner's careful approach to Two-Spirit identity in this study, I do worry that it participates in the misunderstandings that Whitehead (2018b) and Driskill (2010) identify in conflating masculine and feminine spirits or seeing Two-Spirit people as somehow excessively spiritual. With the limitations that Bittner has set, I worry that his approach offers a limited vision for how Two-Spirit and LGBTQ+ Indigenous young people may be able to find literature that represents them – as well as limiting the radical decolonial vision that children's and young adult Two-Spirit literature may provide. It is my hope that by attending to the literature for young people that comes from within Indigenous traditions (that is, primarily by Indigenous writers), this chapter will offer a glimpse of the richness of Two-Spirit and queer Indigenous lives, activism and visions for the future.

One of the earliest works for young people to couple Indigenous and queer concerns arises in the Aboriginal Australian and Torres Strait Islander context in the 1998 YA novel *Killing Darcy* by Melissa Lucashenko, a writer of Goorie heritage. In this complex novel, Cam and Fil – brother and sister in a white settler family that is comfortable trading in slurs and stereotypes and living in an imagined geographical location of bush near the border of Queensland and New South Wales – discover an abandoned house and, in it, a camera that takes photographs of the past. At the same time, a young gay Koori man, Darcy, comes to work for their father to take care of horses, and Darcy's friendship with Cam and Fil catches all three of them up in a mystery of past murders and the violent, ongoing nature of colonialism. Along the way, the novel tackles issues such as HIV, masculinity and the overlapping discriminations Darcy faces. *Killing Darcy* is not only one of the earliest YA books to address LGBTQ+ concerns in Australia at all, but it remains one of only a handful of books that represent Aboriginal LGBTQ+ young people.

Will's Garden by Stó:lō author Lee Maracle is the earliest contemporary Indigenous work for children to deal with LGBTQ+ concerns in the North American context that I have been able to find. Published by Theytus, a longstanding First Nations publisher, the book focuses on Will, a young Stó:lō man, who is about to embark on his Coming of Age Ceremony and who is figuring out the boundaries of his relationships with others in his family and community, defining what kind of man he will be. One of the ways he does this is by introducing his family to Wit, a gay classmate whom Will identifies as white (Wit is actually of mixed European and Squamish descent) and with whom Will has recently developed a friendship. While some family members initially react negatively to Wit, Maracle clearly shows that this rejection of homosexuality comes not from Stó:lō beliefs – Will reminds everyone that 'There is no word for devil or evil in the Sto: loh language and neither you nor I is in a position to determine what is natural or unnatural about love and sex' – but from the Catholicism brought by colonizing forces to Stó:lō communities (Maracle, 2002, 70). Will, in his quest to define himself as a contemporary Stó:lō man, explores what it would mean for him to identify as gay within his community (though he does not) and seeks to define himself and his own masculinity, particularly in relationship to the women around him. Wit, on the other hand, is shown as a good friend, secure in his identity as a gay man, and aware of both the social dynamics of his mixed community and the Squamish teachings of his grandmother. *Will's Garden*, then, makes a statement by displaying how colonialism affects the ways in which First Nations communities see not only LGBTQ+ people but also gender relationships as a whole.

Small presses both initiated and remain the vanguard of publishing queer Indigenous work. Magabala Press, like many of the other publishers of the works in this chapter, is a small press that focuses mostly on Indigenous – in this case, Aboriginal Australian and Torres Strait Islander – works. They published Nukunu author Jared Thomas's novel *Songs that Sound Like Blood* in 2006, marking one of the only examples of queer Indigenous work with a female protagonist. Roxy, also Nukunu, leaves her small town to go to Adelaide to study music at university. Much of the book focuses on Roxy's difficulties with adjusting to university life: her ties to community and country interrupt her ability to focus on her studies and musical aspirations, and her economic situation means that she is often financially at a loss compared to her peers. Roxy's biggest concern, however, is that she has fallen in love with Ana, a Māori music journalist in Adelaide. As Roxy comes out to her family, her Nanna draws parallels between the ways that judgement affected Aboriginal Australian and Torres Strait Islander communities, and Roxy's same-sex attraction: 'you know where that judgment got our people? It got your old people in mission, your great-grandmother charged with murder when her first child died in childbirth … Who are we to judge?' (Thomas 2016, 222). In this way, *Songs that Sound Like Blood* is notable not only for introducing a young Indigenous lesbian character but also in its forthrightness in addressing issues of discrimination, economic insecurity and mental health within Aboriginal Australian communities in the context of LGBTQ+ Aboriginal life.

Non-fiction work for young people that addresses the realities of queer Indigenous or Two-Spirit lives is sparse. One of the few titles that does is a comic written by Tłı̨chǫ author and storyteller Richard Van Camp called *Kiss Me Deadly*, which features a small group of First Nations teenagers talking about sexual health. One of the characters, Vern, is at a clinic getting tested for STIs to ensure his and his new boyfriend's safety in their burgeoning relationship. Later, the straight couple that Vern ran into in the clinic discuss definitions of Two-Spirit identity and the traditional love and respect that should be shown to Two-Spirit people.

More recently, Indigenous authors have been offering transformative visions of how LGBTQ+ Indigenous or Two-Spirit are key parts of Indigenous futurities through speculative fiction. For example, *The Way of Thorn and Thunder* by Daniel Heath Justice, a Cherokee author and scholar, provides a decidedly Indigenous vision of the fantasy genre. Originally published by Kegedonce Press, a small press that publishes in both the adult and children's markets, the three novels that make up the series (*Kynship*, *Wyrwood* and *Dreyd*) have been reissued in an omnibus edition published by the University of New Mexico Press. Although perhaps not strictly a 'YA' novel, Justice works in a similar vein as established fantasy authors C. S. Lewis, J. R. R. Tolkien and Ursula K. LeGuin, writing for an audience that reaches down into the teenage years. In his sweeping, epic fantasy, Justice develops an allegory of the colonization of Cherokee lands by overlaying this story in the fantasy world of Everland. The indigenous inhabitants of Everland, the Kyn, have been forcibly relocated by the human-dominated territory of Eromar in an event known as the Expulsion. Their traditions are thrown into disarray as many Kyn are drawn toward the human religion of the Celestials. Tarsa, the heroine of the trilogy, must draw strength from her motherhood and both he-Kyn and she-Kyn romantic partners, as she learns to become a healer based on the Kyn's connection to the 'Wyr', the life-force tied to the land and living things. In doing so, she and her allies hope to combat the colonial encroachment of Eromar. Furthermore, the Kyn recognize more than two genders: in addition to she-Kyn and he-Kyn, multiple zhe-Kyn – who 'straddled the male and female world in all things' – make significant appearances in the epic, showing how traditional understandings of gender resist colonizing, binary forces (Justice 2011, 10). Justice turns many of the conventions of the fantasy genre on its head: by focusing on telling the story from the perspective of those whose lands are being colonized, he is able to present a decolonizing view of the genre and show how Indigenous nationhood and knowledges provide ways of building a world differently. By centring women and queer Indigenous concerns, the book offers a radical approach to nationhood, gender and relationships.

The Marrow Thieves (2017) is a dystopian YA novel written by Cherie Dimaline, a member of the Georgian Bay Métis Nation. In this work, an imagined future has unfurled, in which climate change and industrialization have wreaked havoc on Earth and its resources. Most people have gone through health crises that have caused them to lose the ability to dream; it is implied that this eventually leads them to psychotic episodes and other mental health disasters. The only people who retain the ability to dream are Indigenous people, whose relationships to their ancestral teachings have caused dreams to find refuge in their bone marrow. In a parallel to the initial invasion of what is now known as North America and the subsequent establishment of residential schools, settlers have begun to capture Native/First Nations people and take them to 'schools', where their marrow is extracted for 'donation'. Frenchie, the narrator of the text, is a teenage boy on the run from school 'Recruiters' and finds himself in a makeshift family of other Native/First Nations teens on the run, led by two Elders: Minerva, a woman with 'old-timey' ways and knowledge of the Cree language, and Miigwans, a man whose loss of his husband at the hands of the schools motivates him to care for the young people he encounters and share Story with them. At the close of the novel, Miigwans and his husband Isaac are reunited as Isaac's ability to dream in Cree is shown to have the potential to undo the work of the dream-stealers. Queer First Nations people are not only written into this future imagined by Dimaline, but their love is shown to be central to saving the world.

Another example of work that imagines queer Indigenous futurities is *Love Beyond Body, Space, and Time* (2016), edited by non-Native Canadian Hope Nicholson. Each of the stories in this science fiction short story collection – again, published by a press that primarily focuses on adult readership but a collection that reaches a teen audience – explores how Two-Spirit or LGBTQ+ Indigenous people participate in speculative worlds. From a lesbian love story on a long journey to Mars to a trans woman participating in a study for experimental transition medications, each of the stories here shows how vital queer Indigeneity is to imagining revolutionary futures. The story from which this chapter takes its epigraph is one example: in 'The Boys Who Became the Hummingbirds' (Justice 2016), the love between Strange Boy and Shadow Boy becomes the first glimpse of hope that humanity has after having fallen under grim, post-apocalyptic conditions. Queer Indigeneity, in this story and throughout the collection, is the mechanism by which humanity is able to imagine an emancipatory future.

A newer addition to the collection of Indigenous LGBTQ+/Two-Spirit literature is *Fire Song* (2018), written by Cree author and filmmaker Adam Garnett Jones. The book is an adaptation of Jones's film by the same name, and features Anishinaabe teenager Shane, who is reeling from the suicide of his younger sister Destiny. He is also hiding the fact from everyone else on the reserve that he has been hooking up with best friend David. Shane wrestles with the possibility of leaving the reserve for university against remaining with David, who wishes to continue learning traditional ways from his grandmother. As funding for university falls through and Shane decides to sell drugs to try to make up the money, he must deal with the brutality of what coming out in his community would look like. David and Shane face homophobia on the reserve when their relationship is exposed, and the complexities of David's and Shane's situation are realistically portrayed as the two boys are left with few options but the hand they have been dealt. A story that not only lays bare the realities of gay life on a reserve in Canada, it is also a remarkable tale of LGBTQ+ Indigenous survivance – a term coined by White Earth Band of Ojibwe scholar Gerald Vizenor (1994) to describe 'new stories of tribal courage' that constitute an active, continual presence in the face of such hardships (4).

Joshua Whitehead, an Oji-Cree member of the Peguis First Nation (Treaty 1), is another Two-Spirit/Indigiqueer writer whose work is expanding the possibilities for Two-Spirit and Indigiqueer literatures for young people. Although his first novel, *Jonny Appleseed* (2018a), was primarily marketed by its publisher for an adult market and deals with explicit sexual content, it is in fact about a young adult and is intended to recognize the lives of the too-often unrecognized Two-Spirit and Indigiqueer young adults – a prime example of what might be characterized as the growing field of 'new adult' literature (Naughton 2014, n.p.). In the book, Jonny is scraping by in Winnipeg by selling cybersex when he receives a call that his stepfather, Roger, has passed. He has seven days to prepare and make it back to the reserve where he grew up before the funeral. While Roger made Jonny's childhood hellish by trying to force Jonny to perform a specific kind of straight masculinity – which Jonny resisted every chance he got – he recognizes that his ties to the land he grew up on and his love for his mother are greater than any spite he might feel toward Roger. In those seven days, Jonny reflects on his sexual and sometimes romantic relationship on the rez with his childhood friend Tias and his memories of his kokum (grandmother) who helped him come to terms with who he is, all while wrestling with sex, alcohol and identity within the confines of the life that he has been dealt. Jonny identifies the racism of the white settlers for whom he is expected to perform a stereotypical First Nations masculinity for him to be a desirable partner, while yearning for sexual companionship where he is understood. *Jonny Appleseed* is a reminder that the escape to the city that Shane of *Fire Song* hopes for is not the utopia he might envision. However, through his pain, the book is shot through with love, reminding readers that 'an NDN[3] "love you" sounds more like, "I'm in pain with you"' (Whitehead 2018a, 88).

New directions for Indigenous LGBTQ+ literature remain to be seen. The lack of picture books – or even middle-grade books – in this study is one conspicuous gap in the field. One picture book that makes small strides in approaching Indigenous LGBTQ+ or Two-Spirit identities is *Awâsis and the World-Famous Bannock* (2018), written by Dallas Hunt, a Cree member of Wapisewsipi (Swan River First Nation, Treaty 8) and illustrated by Michif artist Amanda Strong. In the story, Awâsis is a young girl who is charged with delivering her kôkhum's bannock to a relative, but who loses it over a bridge along the way. She reaches out to animal friends as she is on her journey, including Ôho, an owl identified using the gender-neutral, singular 'they'. Although a simple gesture, the use of

3 NDN is a shorthand term for 'Indian' commonly used by Native/First Nations communities in the United States and Canada.

a gender-neutral pronoun – one of the earliest in a picture book – within a First Nations context provides a powerful glimpse into what a Two-Spirit vision that includes young children might look like.

Conclusion

Much scholarship in children's and young adult literature in the United States attends to Rudine Sims Bishop's conceptions of 'mirrors and windows': the idea that good literature can act both as a mirror that affirms a young person's experience as part of 'the larger human experience' or a window into the experiences of others (Bishop 1990, ix). Bittner's article in search of Two-Spirit literature for young people speaks to this impulse to wish to help reflect Two-Spirit experiences and to explain what 'Two-Spirit' means to non-Indigenous audiences. However, I wish to take one step beyond this metaphor and insist that Two-Spirit and Indigiqueer literature is central to the acts of decolonization and queer liberation. Rather than describing how Two-Spirit people might live, I insist on paying attention to 'how queer literary texts do the work of caring for and attending to the wounds inflicted on queer subjects by homo-antagonism, trans-antagonism, racism, ableism, and patriarchy' (Fawaz and Smalls 2018,178). This is not to say that reflection and the opening of minds are not important – they are crucial – but I think this metaphor can obscure the work that the reading and writing of young Two-Spirit or Indigiqueer lives can actually do as a political act in and of itself. By writing and reading Two-Spirit and Indigenous LGBTQ+ lives, this literature can help provide maps toward a decolonial future.

What Indigenous queer and Two-Spirit literature has the potential to do is not only the work of reparation, of ensuring that young people are able to bind their wounds inflicted by queer-antagonism and colonialism, but also to participate in the project of decolonization itself. By unsettling colonial understandings of what queerness is, it offers a challenge to understanding the state of modern sexualities and genders of all kinds: 'The queer in Indigenous studies, then, challenges the queer of queer studies by offering not an identity or a figure necessarily, but rather an analytic that helps us relocate subjectivity and its refusals back into the vectors of on-going settler colonialism' (Byrd 2017, 226). The refusal of Indigenous queer and Two-Spirit literatures to be understood and settled within colonial frameworks provides methods of moving forward into indigenized literature.

That said, Unangax̂ scholar Eve Tuck and non-Indigenous arrivant K. Wayne Yang write, 'decolonization is not a metaphor' (Tuck and Yang 2012). There is a danger in assuming that writing and reading by themselves are all that is necessary for decolonization, but 'decolonization is accountable to Indigenous sovereignty and futurity … [it] is not an "and". It is an elsewhere' (Tuck and Yang 2012, 35–36). By writing maps for young people that show how sovereignty plays a part in identity and what Indigenous futurities may look like, Indigenous LGBTQ+ and Two-Spirit literatures for young people can help get us to that elsewhere.

Bibliography

Anguksuar (LaFortune, Richard). 1997. 'A Postcolonial Perspective on Western [Mis]Conceptions of the Cosmos and the Restoration of Indigenous Taxonomies'. In *Two-Spirit People: Native American Gender Identity, Sexuality, and Spirituality*, edited by Sue-Ellen Jacobs, Wesley Thomas, and Sabine Lang, 217–22. Urbana: University of Illinois Press.

Barker, Joanne. 2011. *Native Acts: Law, Recognition, and Cultural Authenticity*. Durham: Duke University Press.

Bayliss, Troy-Anthony. 2014. 'The Art of Seeing Aboriginal Australia's Queer Potential'. *The Conversation*, 15 April. https://theconversation.com/the-art-of-seeing-aboriginal-australias-queer-potential-25588

Bishop, Rudine Sims. 1990. 'Mirrors, Windows, and Sliding Glass Doors'. *Perspectives* 1, no. 3: ix–xi.

Bittner, Robert. 2014. 'Hey, I Still Can't See Myself!: The Difficult Positioning of Two-Spirit Identities in YA Literature'. *Bookbird: An International Journal of Children's Literature* 52, no.1 (January): 11–22. https://doi.org/10.1353/bkb.2014.0040

Burin, Margaret. 2016. 'Sistergirls and Brotherboys Unite to Strengthen Spirits'. *ABC News*, 20 November. https://www.abc.net.au/news/2016-11-21/sistergirls-and-brotherboys-unite-to-strengthen-spirits/8040928

Byrd, Jodi A. 2017. '*Loving* Unbecoming: The Queer Politics of the Transitive Native'. In *Critically Sovereign: Indigenous Gender, Sexuality, and Feminist Studies*, edited by Joanne Barker, 207–27. Durham: Duke University Press.

Center for American Progress and Movement Advancement Project. 2015. 'Paying an Unfair Price: The Financial Penalty for LGBT People of Color in America'. *Movement Advancement Project*. April 2015. http://www.lgbtmap.org/file/paying-an-unfair-price-lgbt-people-of-color.pdf

Clark, Maddee. 2015. 'Are We Queer?: Reflections from 'Peopling the Empty Mirror' Twenty Years On'. In *Colouring the Rainbow: Blak Queer and Trans Perspectives: Life Stories and Essays by First Nations People of Australia*, edited by Dino Hodge, 238–52. Mile End: Wakefield Press.

Dimaline, Cherie. 2017. *The Marrow Thieves*. Toronto: Dancing Cat.

Driskill, Qwo-Li. 2004. 'Stolen from Our Bodies: First Nations Two-Spirits/Queers and the Journey to a Sovereign Erotic'. *Studies in American Indian Literatures* 16, no. 2: 50–64. http://doi.org/10.1353/ail.2004.0020

———. 2010. 'Doubleweaving Two-Spirit Critiques: Building Alliances between Native and Queer Studies'. *GLQ: A Journal of Gay and Lesbian Studies* 16, nos. 1–2: 69–92. https://doi.org/10.1215/10642684-2009-013

Driskill, Qwo-Li, Chris Finley, Brian Joseph Gilley, and Scott Lauria Morgensen. 2011. 'The Revolution is for Everyone: Imagining an Emancipatory Future through Queer Indigenous Critical Theories'. In *Queer Indigenous Studies: Critical Interventions in Theory, Politics, and Literature*, edited by Qwo-Li Driskill, Chris Finley, Brian Joseph Gilley, and Scott Lauria Morgensen, 211–21. Tucson: University of Arizona Press.

Driskill, Qwo-Li, Daniel Heath Justice, Deborah Miranda, and Lisa Tatonetti, eds. 2011. *Sovereign Erotics: A Collection of Two-Spirit Literature*. Tucson: University of Arizona Press.

Fawaz, Ramzi and Shanté Paradigm Smalls. 2018. 'Queers Read This!: LGBTQ Literature Now'. *GLQ: A Journal of Gay and Lesbian Studies* 24, nos. 2–3: 169–85. https://doi.org/10.1215/10642684-4324765

Frazer, M. Somjen and Harlan Pruden. 2010. 'Reclaiming Our Voice: Two Spirit Health and Human Service Needs in New York State'. *New York State Department of Health*. https://www.health.ny.gov/diseases/aids/providers/reports/native_people/docs/reclaiming_our_voices.pdf

Grant, Jaime M., Lisa A. Mottet, Justin Tanis, Jack Harrison, Jody L. Herman, and Mara Keisling. 2011. *Injustice at Every Turn: A Report of the National Transgender Discrimination Survey*. Washington: National Center for Transgender Equality.

Hunt, Dallas. 2018. *Awâsis and the World-Famous Bannock*. Illustrated by Amanda Strong. Winnipeg: Highwater Press.

Jones, Adam Garnet. 2018. *Fire Song*. Toronto: Annick Press.

Justice, Daniel Heath. 2011. *The Way of Thorn and Thunder: The Kynship Chronicles*. Albuquerque: University of New Mexico Press.

———. 2016. 'The Boys Who Became the Hummingbirds'. In *Love Beyond Body, Space, and Time: An Indigenous LGBT Sci-Fi Anthology*, edited by Hope Nicholson, 54–59. Winnipeg: Bedside Press.

Kauanui, J. Kēhaulani. 2017. 'Indigenous Hawaiian Sexuality and the Politics of Nationalist Decolonization'. In *Critically Sovereign: Indigenous Gender, Sexuality, and Feminist Studies*, edited by Joanne Barker, 45–68. Durham: Duke University Press.

Laing, Marie. 2016. 'Two-Spirit and LGBTQ Indigenous Health'. *Rainbow Health Ontario*. https://www.rainbowhealthontario.ca/wp-content/uploads/2016/07/2SLGBTQINDIGENOUSHEALTHFactHeet.pdf

Lucashenko, Melissa. 1998. *Killing Darcy*. St. Lucia: University of Queensland Press.

Maracle, Lee. 2002. *Will's Garden*. Penticton: Theytus.

Morgensen, Scott Lauria. 2011. *Spaces Between Us: Queer Settler Colonialism and Indigenous Decolonization*. Minneapolis: University of Minnesota Press.

Naughton, Julie. 2014. 'New Adult: A Book Category for Twentysomethings by Twentysomethings'. *Publisher's Weekly*, 11 July. https://www.publishersweekly.com/pw/by-topic/industry-news/publisher-news/article/63285-new-adult-matures.html

NCAI Policy Research Center. 2015. 'A Spotlight on Two Spirit (Native LGBT) Communities'. *National Congress of American Indians*. http://www.ncai.org/policy-research-center/research-data/prc-publications/A_Spotlight_on_Native_LGBT.pdf.

Nicholson, Hope, ed. 2016. *Love Beyond Body, Space and Time: An Indigenous LGBT Sci-Fi Anthology*. Winnipeg: Bedside Press.

Rainbow Youth and Tīwhanawhana Trust. 2017. 'Definition of Takatāpui'. *Takatāpui: A Resource Hub*. https://takatapui.nz/definition-of-takatapui

Reese, Debbie. 2015. 'emily m. danforth's *The Miseducation of Cameron Post*'. *American Indians in Children's Literature*, 29 April. https://americanindiansinchildrensliterature.blogspot.com/2015/04/emily-m-danforths-miseducation-of.html

Rifkin, Mark. 2012. *The Erotics of Sovereignty: Queer Native Writing in the Era of Self-Determination*. Minneapolis: University of Minnesota.

Tatonetti, Lisa. 2014. *The Queerness of Native American Literature*. Minneapolis: University of Minnesota Press.

Thomas, Jared. 2016. *Songs that Sound Like Blood*. Broome: Magabala Books.

Thomas, Wesley, and Sue-Ellen Jacobs. 1999. '"...And We Are Still Here": From *Berdache* to Two-Spirit People.' *American Indian Culture and Research Journal* 23, no. 2: 91–107, https://doi.org/10.17953/aicr.23.2.k5255571240t5650

Tuck, Eve, and K. Wayne Yang. 2012. 'Decolonization is Not a Metaphor'. *Decolonization: Indigeneity, Education & Society* 1, no. 1: 1–40.

Van Camp, Richard. 2011. *Kiss Me Deadly*. Illustrated by C. Auchter. Courtenay: Healthy Aboriginal Network.

Vizenor, Gerald. 1994. *Manifest Manners: Postindian Warriors of Survivance*. Hanover: Wesleyan University Press.

Whitehead, Joshua. 2018a. *Jonny Appleseed: A Novel*. Vancouver: Arsenal Pulp Press.

———. 2018b. 'Joshua Whitehead: Why I'm Withdrawing From My Lambda Literary Award Nomination'. *The Insurgent Architects' House for Creative Writing*, 14 March. https://www.tiahouse.ca/joshua-whitehead-why-im-withdrawing-from-my-lambda-literary-award-nomination/

Chapter Seven

LGBTQ FAMILIES AND PICTUREBOOKS: NEW PERSPECTIVES IN ITALIAN CHILDREN'S LITERATURE

Dalila Forni

Introduction

LGBTQ[1] families and civil rights is a current hot topic in Italy. In June 2016, the Italian government approved a law that recognizes same-sex unions. The subject is still quite delicate and much discussed, but the country is slowly opening up to new realities. In particular, children's picturebooks presenting non-traditional families are becoming more and more popular. Among the Italian publishers whose aim is to promote diversity in children's literature, Lo Stampatello is one of the most active and innovative. The publishing house was created by Maria Silvia Fiengo and Francesca Pardi, a couple interested in queer families and gender identity. After a brief introduction to the Italian social and cultural context concerning LGBTQ identities, this chapter will present picturebooks written, illustrated and translated by Italian writers and artists. In particular, the chapter will focus on Lo Stampatello's works, considering both their merits and weaknesses. On the one hand, its picturebooks are opening the way to 'taboo topics' in children's literature; on the other, much has to be done to provide children with books of greater quality and depth.

Civil Rights in Italy: A Brief Historical Background

The topic of LGBTQ rights is usually perceived as extremely delicate and controversial by the Italian population. On the one hand, Italians are slowly opening up to new realities and accepting differences in sexual orientation; on the other, the country is still conservative and suspicious about LGBTQ lives, which are usually imagined in a highly stereotypical way in popular media (Malafreca 2007; Malici 2012).

1 In this chapter, LGBTQ is used as an umbrella term to encompass non-heteronormative identities. However, the chapter generally focuses on lesbian and gay identities since picturebooks addressing the topic of bisexuality, trans or other orientations or identities could not be found in Italian.

First of all, same-sex encounters have been considered legal since 1887, when the Zanardelli Code[2] was promulgated. In spite of this, during Mussolini's reign homosexuals were regularly persecuted or exiled since they were thought to act against moral and religious beliefs. As a matter of fact, the first draft of Codice Rocco (1930) included an article that limited LGBTQ rights; however, the article was rejected since homosexuality was considered a minor problem in fascist Italy (Rossi Barilli 1999, 20). The government simply preferred to keep silent on the subject instead of persecuting non-heteronormative Italians; indeed, in Italy, repression against the LGBTQ community has always been social rather than penal (Malici 2012, 116). There was an absence of rules concerning queer issues. From the Zanardelli Code on, civil rights for the Italian LGBTQ population have scarcely evolved.

A first step was made in 2003, when discrimination based on sexual orientation was banned, but a more recent law on this topic is still needed. For instance, in Italy there are no specific anti-discrimination laws concerning gender identity. Nowadays, activities, meetings and debates on LGBTQ topics are generally more and more common both in newspapers and on television, but part of the population still does not feel comfortable with such themes: a minority – often connected to the church – still believes homosexuality and LGBTQ families could undermine the institution of marriage and the traditional family's stability. A report conducted in 2009 by the European Union Agency for Fundamental Rights suggested that Italy has 'high rates of social and institutional homophobia' (Zappettini 2010, 117). In Zappettini's opinion, this is mainly due to Italy's religious values and its masculine index: as a 'masculine oriented country', homosexuality is perceived as a threat both to masculine norms and to religious views (Zappettini 2010, 120). Although numerous bills on civil unions were regularly introduced into the Parliament, the topic had never been considered a priority for the country. Finally, in June 2016, Italy became the 27th nation in Europe to recognize same-sex couples with a law on civil unions (Legge Cirinnà[3]). Same-sex couples were provided with rights generally comparable to marriage, such as pension rights and inheritance rights. In some cases, civil unions appear to be even more modern than marriage: for example, no banns have to be published before the ceremony and divorce is more immediate. However, an important part of the law – stepchild adoption[4] – was not approved and is still a current debate. The bill proposed by Monica Cirinnà initially wanted LGBTQ people to have rights fully comparable to marriage, but the bill was modified because of numerous amendments by right-wing parties. In particular, many politicians argued that civil unions were unjustly compared to traditional marriage; in their opinion, units composed of two people of the same sex could not be considered a real family (*Il Post* 2016). For this reason, stepchild adoption was eliminated, along with the duty of faithfulness. Unfortunately, the

2 The Zanardelli Code was the first Italian Penal Code, in force from 1890 to 1930, when Codice Rocco was passed.

3 Monica Cirinnà is a senator of the Italian Democratic Party. She is the author of the bill on civil unions.

4 Stepchild adoption is the right to adopt the partner's biological child.

first line of the law clearly demonstrates that civil unions are not comparable to heterosexual marriage: a unit composed of two same-sex partners is coldly defined a 'specifica formazione sociale' (specific social formation). Consequently, even though significant progress has been achieved, LGBTQ Italians still do not feel completely represented by this law, which, to some extent, is still discriminatory.

Thus, even though Italy is slowly increasing civil rights for LGBTQ people, gay marriage and adoption for same-sex couples are still forbidden. In particular, adoption is only allowed for married couples of opposite sexes, but there are no specific restrictions regarding foster care. In a few particular cases (Prati 2018), LGBTQ parents were given the opportunity to adopt their partner's children, but a law on this topic still has to be discussed and approved.

Even if the Italian government considers LGBTQ rights a secondary matter, LGBTQ couples and families are nowadays a reality. In the 2011 ISTAT[5] Census, 7,513 people were declared to be in a same-sex stable relationship, and 529 of them to have children. However, it was estimated that gay couples actually reach a higher number, about 200,000 (Gigli 2011), and that at least 100,000 children live with a homosexual parent. As a matter of fact, children raised by LGBTQ couples or by at least one non-heterosexual parent are a small but significant minority in the country, which has a population of around 60 million.

Despite this, in Italy, homosexuality – and male homosexuality in particular – seems to be the greatest offence of all and it is considered socially undesirable by a large part of the population (Malici 2012, 114). Over the last decade, many conservative groups have inveighed against homosexual unions; conservative parties or groups were mainly worried about the (potential) end of the Italian traditional family, undermined by LGBTQ families, and often demonstrated against 'gender ideology' (*Il Timone* 2014). The concept of 'gender ideology' is the result of a general lack of information on topics such as gender identity and sexual orientation. In the misleading view promoted by conservative organizations, gender ideology is a sort of LGBTQ propaganda encouraged in schools in order to foster homosexuality, sexual encounters at an early age, paedophilia and the open discussion of the supposedly fixed notion of being a girl or a boy (Marzano 2015). Gender ideology is thought to refuse moral and natural boundaries, aiming to create 'empty' families where gender roles are unclear and not fixed. This general fear started when the bill *La buona scuola* (Good School), among other things, suggested that schools pay more attention to gender identity and discrimination based on sexual orientation (Marzano 2015). It is important to notice that the English word 'gender' has always been used, rather than an Italian term, which promotes a misleading view that this ideology is a foreign import and which thus increases anxiety on the issue (Trisciuzzi 2017).

5 Italian National Institute of Statistics.

How Should We Talk About *That*?

Although Italian laws and cultural perceptions are now changing, LGBTQ families are still not visible from a legal, educational and cultural point of view. First of all, as stated previously, LGBTQ families have no legal rights concerning their children and LGBTQ people are not even allowed to adopt their partner's child. Secondly, schools too are usually not ready to deal with this subject. Gigli (2011) studied gay families' experiences in Italian primary schools through qualitative methods such as interviews. Her research demonstrates that educators, teachers and parents are often embarrassed and perplexed when asked questions about homosexual families and homosexuality or LGBTQ identities in general. These professional figures are not usually ready to answer the children's questions since the topic is typically unknown or considered a distant reality. This is not necessarily due to homophobia or closed-mindedness, but to the topic being unfamiliar and not well understood and, consequently, it is often uncomfortable for both parents and educators. As a matter of fact, LGBTQ families are a minority that is seldom represented in books, films, magazines and popular culture (Malici 2012, 114). For example, Malici argues that '[…] depictions of dissident sexualities and identities on the Italian small screen are still negotiated as highly problematic and based on compromises to accommodate a putatively heteronormative audience' (2012, 113–14).[6]

In addition, homosexuality is culturally considered to be a topic unsuitable for young children, both by parents and educators; therefore, it is not presented to them in schools or at home if not needed. However, since LGBTQ families are becoming an important part of our reality, this theme ought to be addressed in works for young audiences: the aim should be to provide children with a wide spectrum of identities and families, to foster diversity and to promote inclusion (Biemmi 2017; Fornara 2016).

One of the most important tools that may be used to present the topic of LGBTQ families to young schoolers is literature. Nevertheless, children's literature is still governed by extremely traditional standards concerning gender identity, sexuality and family dynamics. If this is true for European and American literature in general, Italy is particularly devoted to traditional families and traditional gender roles in books for young audiences. Probably this is due to the lack of knowledge on new families and gender dynamics, which are seldom portrayed in Italian media. Despite this, some small publishers are now trying to deal with this debated issue in the most simple and direct way possible.

Italy and LGBTQ Families in Picturebooks

Italian books for children often lack family diversity since they focus on a traditional kind of family composed of a mother, a father, a boy and a girl (Biemmi 2017). Non-traditional families (divorced parents, single parents, LGBTQ families, and so on) are

6 Malici focuses on queerness in Italian television, but this phenomenon concerns literature and popular culture as well.

hard to find in libraries and bookstores and are seldom considered either in books for pre-schoolers or in books for older audiences. Fortunately, a new trend is now growing, and other types of families have been slowly portrayed in picturebooks, but this process is still developing.

Nevertheless, talking about different realities in books for younger readers is not an easy task. Italian publishers usually prefer to invest money in stereotypical books in order to reach a wider audience and satisfy a larger number of readers, forgetting all kinds of minorities. In addition, people are still doubtful about these disruptive books that challenge long-lasting ideals. Authors and illustrators who decide to promote diversity in books on new issues are often attacked and banned. For example, in 2015 the mayor of Venice decided to ban more than forty books from school libraries since they were considered gay propaganda for children (De Luca 2015b).

Thus, despite the importance of LGBTQ books for children, they are not so common in the Italian publishing industry. Many publishing houses try to challenge gender stereotypes and to promote new ideas about gender and identity in books for younger readers. For example, some publishing houses – such as EDT's Giralangolo imprint or Settenove – offer stories about brave girls and sensitive boys, non-traditional families or new gender dynamics. The books have been well received, but they are not among the major best-selling products. Moreover, non-standard identities are often considered a dangerous topic (Fornara 2016). Therefore, Italian publishers show a general lack both of original Italian-language books about the LGBTQ community, and of translations on the same topic.

Considering picturebooks, the first work for children on LGBTQ families translated into Italian was *And Tango Makes Three* by Justin Richardson and Peter Parnell. The book was published in the US in 2005, but was translated into Italian five years later, in 2010. Although the book was welcomed in many bookstores, public libraries and school libraries, some teachers, parents and politicians protested in order to ban the picturebook, which was not considered suitable for young readers because of the gay penguin couple presented. The book, which was criticized in the US, also had a negative reception in Italy. Many politicians, journalists, teachers, parents and activists attacked the picturebook because it portrays a non-traditional family with two penguin dads. For example, the mayor of Verona, Federico Sboarina, wanted to 'banish from libraries and schools some books and publications since they promote equality of natural families and same sex unions' (Sorio 2017).[7] Likewise, the mayor of Venice, who decided to ban the book from school libraries, argued that:

> It is the parents that have to educate their children on these topics, not school. We do not wish to discriminate against children, parents may be called Dad 1 and Dad 2 at home, but I must take care of the majority of the families composed of a father and a mother. (Furlan 2015)[8]

7 Translated by the author: Italian version: 'ritirare dalle biblioteche e dalle scuole [...] libri e pubblicazioni che promuovono l'equiparazione della famiglia naturale alle unioni di persone dello stesso sesso'.

8 Translated by the author. Italian version: '[sono] i genitori a doversi occupare di educare i figli su queste cose, non la scuola. Noi non vogliamo discriminare i bambini, a casa i genitori

At the same time, many people counter-attacked and defended the book from the accusation of being gay propaganda. For instance, a newspaper article published in *Repubblica* argued that:

> What can you really find in these books? [...] Just our real world. Through stories of animals, princesses, heroes or real characters [...] these works represent a society where children are raised by a father and a mother, but also by two mothers. (De Luca 2015a)[9]

Similarly, an article published by *Internazionale* pointed out that: 'These books simply represent a reality that is far less rigid and suffocating than the (unreal) idea of a single kind of family, of culture, religion and thought' (Lalli 2015).[10]

In 2013, Todd Parr's *The Family Book* (2003) was translated into Italian, while in 2015, another famous book on same-sex parenting was translated and published in Italy: *Stella Brings the Family* (2015) by Miriam B. Schiffer, translated by E. Battista. However, key works on the topic are still unknown to Italian publishers; books such as *Heather Has Two Mommies* (Lesléa Newman, 1989) and *Daddy's Roommate* (Michael Willhoite, 1990) have never been translated into Italian. This is not surprising since the Italian publishing industry has always been particularly late in translating works that challenge family structures and gender identity; for example, the well-known picturebook *William's Doll* (1972) by Charlotte Zolotow was first published in Italy a few years ago, in 2014, translated by Isabella Maria. The book was perceived as unsuitable for children since it tells the story of a young boy who wishes to play with a doll. Another interesting element that should be highlighted is that most of the books translated into Italian present a family with two dads, while internationally picturebooks featuring two mums are more common. In their study, Sunderland and McGlashan (2011) estimate that a great majority of the books with same-sex families feature female relationships (19 out of 29); however, Italian publishers surprisingly prefer to translate picturebooks with two-dad families. Probably male parenting is perceived as more problematic and it is consequently considered an issue that should be addressed, while female parenthood is usually invisible or supposed to be a 'natural', innate desire for women, so two-mum families are less challenging.

Italian picturebooks featuring LGBTQ families were created in a cultural and literary context that had no knowledge of the subject. When Maria Silvia Fiengo and Francesca Pardi founded Lo Stampatello[11] – the first and only publishing house strongly involved

possono farsi chiamare papà 1 e papà 2 ma io devo pensare a quella maggioranza di famiglie dove ci sono una mamma e un papà.'

9 Translated by the author. Italian version: 'Ma cosa c'è davvero in questi libri [...]? Né più né meno che il mondo reale. Attraverso storie di animali umanizzati, principesse, eroi furbi o eroi sognatori, personaggi in carne ed ossa [...] ciò che si narra è una società dove si nasce da una mamma e da un papà, ma anche da due mamme.'

10 Translated by the author. Italian version: 'Questi libri non fanno altro che raccontare una realtà meno rigida e soffocante di quella – mai esistita – fatta da un solo modello di famiglia, di cultura, di religione e di pensiero.'

11 Capital letter, in Italian.

in promoting LGBTQ topics to children – just one book on the same subject had been translated into Italian, *And Tango Makes Three*. Consequently, there were no precise models to look at, even though Italian books present many similarities with foreign picturebooks on the same subject. After Lo Stampatello's books were printed, other publishers decided to address the topic too: an example is Terra Nuova Edizioni, which, in 2014, published two picturebooks called *Ho 2 papà* (I Have 2 Dads) and *Ho 2 mamme* (I Have 2 Mums) by Fabri Kramer and Luca Panzini. These works follow the same scheme presented by Lo Stampatello: the reader has the opportunity to spend a day in a family that is different. These books also address topics such as IVF. They will be analysed further below.

Lo Stampatello: Subverting the Italian Publishing Industry

Lo Stampatello was founded in 2011 by Francesca Pardi and Maria Silvia Fiengo. The two women were looking for gay-themed books for children since they wanted to explain to their little daughter how their family was born (Anonymous 2013). As there were no Italian picturebooks on the topic, they decided to write and publish some. However, Francesca and Maria Silvia discovered that the Italian publishing market is generally hostile to books for young readers concerning this specific topic: their books were rejected by numerous publishers because they were thought to be too risky and prickly (Illuminati 2017). Consequently, they chose to create their own publishing house to pursue this innovative project, i.e. to publish works on themes that are usually considered taboo in Italian children's literature. Francesca and Maria Silvia decided to broach a thorny and disruptive subject in an innovative way and became the first Italian publishing house directly addressing pre-schoolers about homosexuality. In order to do this, Lo Stampatello's books privilege simple and direct language that can easily make complex themes accessible to particularly young readers (or listeners). *Parlami in stampatello* (literally: speak to me in capital letters; metaphorically: speak to me in the clearest way possible) was immediately selected as the publishing house's motto.

Some of the texts chosen and printed by Lo Stampatello are translated works from different cultural backgrounds, while many others are written and illustrated by contemporary Italian artists and authors. Their works are mainly non-fiction: books with a strong didactic purpose and usually little narrative framing. Through a basic narrative of everyday activities, the picturebooks generally highlight the importance of love, trust and happiness as main values that bind a family, even if the family is composed of 'different' members, such as two dads and some children or two mums and some children. Shape, size, number and age are not key elements in defining what a family should or should not be, according to these books.

The first two books published by Lo Stampatello were *Perché hai due mamme?* (Why Have You Got Two Mummies?) (2011) by Francesca Pardi and *Più ricche di un re* (Richer Than a King) (2011), written by Cinzia Barbero and illustrated by Annalisa Sanmartino and Giulia Torelli. The main difficulty for the publisher with the two picturebooks was to advertise them outside the couple's small circle of supporters. The process was particularly hard since the two books are niche works that would not appeal to major distributors (Lo Stampatello 2014).

Figure 1: Barbero, Cinzia. 2011. *Più ricche di un re* (Richer Than a King). Milan: Lo Stampatello.

In both *Più ricche di un re* and *Perché hai due mamme?* (followed some years later by *Perché hai due papa?* (Why Have You Got Two Daddies?)), same-sex families are clearly portrayed engaging in everyday activities, such as having breakfast together, going to school, cleaning the house, and so on. The main aim of the books is apparently to show that LGBTQ families and traditional families share most of their habits and therefore should be considered equal from a legal and cultural point of view too. The books are characterized by colourful, simple and cartoon-like illustrations that increase the sense of ordinary life. Readers who are children born in a same-sex family will easily identify with the stories offered by Lo Stampatello; meanwhile, children in a family with heterosexual parents will understand clearly that many different families are now possible in our society. The characters presented in the picturebooks are extremely simple and, therefore, easy to understand and to identify with (Illuminati 2017, 9). As a consequence, the book may attract a wide, multifaceted audience.

Furthermore, *Perché hai due mamme?* and *Perché hai due papà?* are unusual works of art because they address a subject that is usually hidden in picturebooks: they do not simply deal with same-sex families, but also with how same-sex families can be created. In vitro fertilization (IVF) and surrogacy are explained to younger readers in a clear but non-technical way. For example, in *Perché hai due mamme?* Pardi writes:

> You need a man and a woman to make a baby: the woman has an egg in her tummy and the man puts his little seed … Meri and Franci were two women, they only had eggs. The seed was missing! In the Netherlands there's a clinic where some kind men donate their seed to those who don't have any or to those who have seeds that do not work properly (sometimes some dads need it). Franci got a seed in the Dutch clinic and … she put it in Meri's tummy, where it met an egg: Margherita started growing! (Pardi 2011, n.p.)[12]

Interestingly, the books also focus on love and physical contact between parents (both male and female), which is not common in Italian children's literature with heterosexual or cisgender parents. As highlighted by Sunderland and McGlashan:

> A challenge for the writers and illustrators of these books is to represent the gay parents as partners, not just friends or co-carers, and one way to do this is to index physical contact – visually or textually. But not only is publically visible physical contact between gay people marked in social practice to the extent of often being seen as transgressive and deviant, it is additionally marked representationally for the wider picturebook genre in that *heterosexual* parents are rarely shown in physical contact. (2013, 4)

In an earlier publication, Sunderland and McGlashan (2011) argue that physical contact is necessary to make it clear that the two parents are not simply friends. They also notice that contact is more frequent in two-dad texts and argue that women are represented as less physical and 'sexual' than men, following a common gender-based stereotype. In Lo Stampatello's books, the tendency is contrasting: the mothers tend to show a more intimate and passionate relationship. For example, in *Perché hai due mamme?* the two mothers kiss each other with their lips and the scene is presented directly in an illustration. The picture is free of overtly sexual overtones and focuses on the tenderness of the moment. In the male counterpart, *Perché hai due papà?*, the couple simply holds hands, a choice probably due to the common male-homosexuality taboo. Generally, the two adults, both males and females, are not merely portrayed as parents – as is common in standard picturebooks – but as a loving couple. Adults are depicted not just through their parental function, but as human beings with strong feelings.

Furthermore, in these books parental responsibilities are often interchangeable: mums and dads usually have the same tasks to do, and they are usually mixed. While in heterosexual couples depicted in picturebooks, mums and dads have precise roles in the house dictated by their sex, as some studies have demonstrated (Biemmi 2017), in same-sex families in these books, the roles are not so strict and are often transposable. Both parents bring the children to school and, similarly, both parents do the household chores. Consequently, there is no male-female division of the tasks, and gender roles are

12 Translation by the author. Original text: 'Ma per fare un bimbo ci vogliono un uomo e una donna: la donna ha l'ovino nella pancia e l'uomo mette il semino … Meri e Franci erano due donne, avevano solo ovini. Mancava il semino! In Olanda c'è una clinica dove dei signori gentili donano i loro semini per chi non ne ha, o per chi ne ha che non funzionano (a volte certi papà ne hanno bisogno). Franci si è fatta dare un semino nella clinica olandese e … l'ha messo nella pancia di Meri, dove ha incontrato l'ovino: Margherita ha cominciato a crescere!'

Figure 2: Pardi, Francesca. 2012. *Perché hai due mamme?* (Why Have You Got Two Mummies?). Illustrated by Annalisa Sanmartino and Giulia Torelli. Milan: Lo Stampatello./ Pardi, Francesca. 2014. *Perché hai due papà?* (Why Have You Got Two Daddies?). Illustrated by Annalisa Sanmartino and Giulia Torelli. Milan: Lo Stampatello.

challenged in books with gay parents and lesbian parents. As a matter of fact, in these books, the representation of two-mum families does not differ from that of two-dad families in their daily activities.

Although the project started by Francesca and Maria Silvia was extremely stimulating and modern, the limited public they addressed was a problem. As reported in the blog dedicated to their experience, Altan's contribution was crucial to reach a wider audience (Lo Stampatello 2014). Altan is a renowned Italian artist who created a cartoon called *Pimpa,* known and appreciated by many Italian children. With his collaboration, a good product addressed to an extremely specific audience could turn into an even better product directed to a larger number of readers. Thus, the picturebook *Piccolo uovo* (Little Egg) (2011) was published with Francesca Pardi's text and Altan's illustrations, and was immediately appreciated – but also criticized – by the Italian public.

Piccolo uovo deals with the topic of non-traditional families and addresses children from four onwards. Little Egg is a little, scared egg that does not know what family will welcome it when it[13] hatches. In order to discover what a family is, Little Egg decides to meet some families of the animal world. During its journey, the protagonist finds out that families can be composed of a single mum, a single dad, two dads, two mums, multiethnic couples or adoptive parents. By the completion of its journey, Little Egg realizes

13 The pronoun *it* is chosen since Piccolo Uovo is represented as a genderless character.

Figure 3: Pardi, Francesca. 2011. *Piccolo uovo* (Little Egg). Illustrated by Altan. Milan: Lo Stampatello.

that all families share a crucial element: love. At the end of the book, the reader is asked to choose their own family. As noted by Illuminati, this is one of the few books published by Lo Stampatello where animals represent the human world (2017, 8). The publishing house usually prefers human characters to explain in the most direct way possible everyday facts about non-traditional families. In *Piccolo uovo*, the readers addressed are so young that colourful images about animals could be seen as necessary to catch their attention, as the illustrator suggested to the authors (Lo Stampatello 2014). Despite many criticisms from parents and teachers who were worried about the influence of the book on young readers, in 2012, *Piccolo uovo* won the Italian Andersen Prize, which every year selects the best books for children published both in Italy and in foreign countries.

Considering the translated books published by Lo Stampatello, they include Mary Hoffman's *The Great Big Book of Families* (2010) (in Italian: *Il grande grosso libro delle famiglie*, 2012) and *Welcome to the Family* (2014b) (*Benvenuti in famiglia*, 2014a), both illustrated by Ros Asquith and translated by Nicoletta Pardi. Both works deal with the definition of family; families can be different in shape, size, habits, gender, religion, sexuality, and so on, but all families are equal as long as their members love each other. The style of the two books is simple, colourful and immediate, as usually preferred by Lo Stampatello. The books were well received and are usually found both in bookstores and libraries. The fact that the books address the topic of family in general, with no specific reference to LGBTQ families in the title or on the cover, probably made them more appealing to a wider audience.

Nevertheless, Trisciuzzi (2017) catalogues Hoffman's books as hyper-realistic works that are often oversimplified and stereotyped, with plain characters immediately recognizable and an extremely positive and softened plot. In her opinion, these books are adult-oriented: they fulfil the adult need to explain what a family is and to see themselves represented in literature, rather than presenting a complex subject to younger readers. Trisciuzzi applies this classification to Hoffman's books only, but her definition could partially apply to Lo Stampatello's works as well; its books are slightly didactic and, in some cases, naïve in their softened approach to the topic. The main aim of the works seems to be explaining how a same-sex family can deal with everyday life. However, a book offering fascinating adventures with a non-traditional family in the background could be a more effective tool in presenting family diversity in a more exciting way.

Thus, Lo Stampatello's books – and literature on LGBTQ families in general – should be carefully considered. To begin with, the books, even if different in style, usually present the same (poor, in my opinion) plot: a day spent in a 'different' family. There is a lack of variation in structures, feelings and problematics, which are usually limited to: 'how should I tell my classmates that I have two mums?', or 'how can you live in a family composed of two dads/mums?', and so on. Diversity is often restricted to an unvaried representation of family dynamics and structures. The books usually focus on white, middle-class characters, while different intersectional identities are forgotten. This feature is particularly common in Italian picturebooks – and literature for children – in general: gender roles regarding both children and adults are usually stereotyped and fixed. Mothers and fathers, girls and boys, women and men usually meet precise gender standards (Biemmi 2017). Besides, the activities performed by the characters, both males and females, are usually extremely similar and predictable. Moreover, the 'always-happy' representation of non-traditional families gives a false image of people that usually face the same problems and fears as traditional families. Lesbian mothers and gay fathers reprimand their children and get angry or scared just as heterosexual parents do, but these elements are usually ignored in picturebooks about gay parents, where the only issue is to explain how a gay family works. In same-sex families in these works, everything is always fine and all problems – usually linked to the external world – can be solved immediately and easily.

In addition, the books are extremely simple – in some cases even simplistic – and openly didactic and overly explanatory. The works do not recount the adventures of a child who just happens to have a 'special' family, but rather they clearly focus on homosexuality as the main topic and, consequently, they make homosexuality the overarching issue that needs to be discussed and may be potentially problematic. As a consequence, most of the books look more like a catalogue of different families that should be accepted in our society rather than 'real' literature on 'real' adventures that children may face in real or unreal worlds. In these books, it is not uncommon to find what Epstein calls 'mini-lectures', where a character educates another one about what it means to live in an LGBTQ family or being LGBTQ, and this process usually takes place in a holistic and unnatural way. Quoting her volume *Are the Kids All Right?*:

> In such works, the issue of whether queer families are different is dealt with by attempting to confirm that they are not. This is what we might term a normalising approach, assuring readers that queer families are just as valid, just as loving, just as good, just as normal, as non-queer families. […] [in these books] there is a regular theme that can be called confirmation of normality, where in LGBTQ people or children of LGBTQ parents are told that they are just as okay, just as 'normal', as the majority […] they end up actually encouraging the idea that being LGBTQ means being different, and that is an issue that must be dealt with. (2013, 40)

Considering these works from a literary and artistic point of view, again they appear particularly poor: most of the images are simple and lack imagination or creativity, while the style of the text is usually plain, with elementary, transparent words that do not try to offer a poetic text, but just to present a specific message to young readers. These books only aim to explain the numerous, different families in our society, but forget to do it with an involving and creative style. Therefore, the reader – and the parent/buyer – does not necessarily feel particularly captivated by the plot; consequently, these books might easily appeal to same-sex families, but may not attract traditional families' attention. On the contrary, complex works of art, with stimulating images and texts, would appeal to a wider audience and promote these books outside the LGBTQ community as well.

The general lack of variation in these works may be due to different factors. First of all, the Italian contemporary publishing market is one factor. Books on non-traditional families – and LGBTQ families in particular – are usually perceived as problematic and risky from both an economic and a cultural point of view (Chick 2008, 16). In publishing houses' opinions, these works would appeal to a small number of readers and would be attacked and considered inappropriate by a numerous group of conservative teachers, parents, activists, librarians and so on. This belief is common both in Italy and in foreign countries, where publishers are not interested in books that will not be readily purchased (Taxel 2002). As publishers are reluctant, authors or illustrators who wish to create books on this subject are not supported. Secondly, people interested in this topic are usually part of the LGBTQ community as well: as a result, books on same-sex families are addressed to and produced by an extremely small part of the Italian population, and the authors and illustrators are not necessarily professional artists.

However, Lo Stampatello was the first publishing house to offer books on taboo subjects in the clearest way possible and in this hostile cultural context, and thus Lo Stampatello is effectively opening the way to new books about non-traditional families, where the families will be backgrounded and not just foregrounded, and where the books will be for different audiences and will have plots that are not simply explanatory. Lo Stampatello is surely an admirable example of a new kind of literature that considers invisible topics and should be applauded for its courage. Building on Lo Stampatello's works, it is now time to work hard on the quality of these texts in order to reach wider audiences and offer a better selection from an artistic and literary point of view.

Contrasting Reactions to LGBTQ Picturebooks

Books concerning non-traditional families have mixed reviews in Italy: on the one hand, many parents and teachers are demonstrating that they are open to new perspectives of children's literature; on the other, some authorities consider such works a scandal. For example, in 2015, as mentioned above, Luigi Brugnaro, the mayor of Venice, banned from school libraries those books that presented new gender roles and non-traditional families (Fornara 2016). *Piccolo uovo* and *And Tango Makes Three* were among these books. However, many artists and authors disagreed with Brugnaro's choice: more than two hundred writers signed a letter where they asked to be banned too in order to show their solidarity with authors who were considered unsuitable for children. They asked: 'kindly ban our books as well, we don't want to stay in a city where the books of others are banned' (Flood 2015, n.p.). This situation aroused public interest and these texts were not only attacked and eliminated from school libraries, but also discussed and reconsidered by a larger audience. Critiques aroused interest and made Lo Stampatello a more popular publisher.

A similar case took place in Verona, where, in 2017, the new mayor Federico Sboarina decided to ban 'gender' books from public libraries and schools. This case aroused public interest as well and two opposing factions were featured in the Italian media to defend their ideas. On the one hand, the mayor and some conservative citizens wanted to protect children from 'gender ideology' in a supposedly delicate phase of their life; on the other, LGBTQ individuals and groups fought to see their families represented in public spaces too (De Luca 2015a).

Despite these varied reactions, picturebooks with LGBTQ families are now easy to find in the public libraries of major cities, in bookstores and – sometimes – in school libraries. Although we could argue about the location of these books in bookstores and libraries – they are usually kept in a particular section about 'challenging' topics, suggesting the idea that LGBTQ families are something troubling[14] – these books are now a reality in the country.

Conclusion

The Italian cultural context is slowly opening up to LGBTQ topics, but much has to be done to guarantee civil rights and equality. Books that deconstruct gender stereotypes and family dynamics could be an effective tool in explaining different families, sexual orientations and identities. For this reason, regardless of the lack of variation and of the simplistic approach to same-sex families, picturebooks on the topic – and in particular the books published by Lo Stampatello – are vital for the cultural growth of Italian society. These books prevent homophobia, foster inclusion and diversity and are pleasant – albeit highly didactic – narratives to read aloud in schools or at

14 Epstein (2013) describes this phenomenon in the UK, but her chapter on this issue could be applied to Italian libraries and bookstores too.

home. These works enforce the concept that there is no fixed idea of family, but that our social context is composed of different realities that should be acknowledged and respected. Writing can help people to challenge their ideas of sexuality and gender and can 'contest people's ideas and potentially even change their lives' (Epstein 2013, 1). Moreover, as argued by Chick (2008), these books may be an interesting and useful tool for teachers or parents who do not feel yet comfortable talking about LGBTQ realities.

Moving on from the work produced by Lo Stampatello, Italian authors, illustrators and publishers should take further steps to enhance these books. Firstly, creators ought to focus on the topic from an artistic and literary perspective too, which means creating works of art that will be considered not simply 'useful' for a minority, but masterpieces able to captivate children living in all kinds of families. Secondly, a further step would be including homosexual characters in the background in order not to focus on queer topics as an issue. Consequently, some stories should not just deal with ordinary life – which may appear boring to young audiences – but also add fantasy and adventure in LGBTQ-oriented books.

Bibliography

Anonymous. 2013. 'Il libro numero uno'. *Lo Stampatello*, 29 November. http://lostampatello.blogspot.com/2013/11/il-libro-numero-uno.html

Barbero, Cinzia. 2011. *Più ricche di un re* (Richer Than a King). Milan: Lo Stampatello.

Biemmi, Irene. 2017. *Educazione sessista. Stereotipi di genere nei libri delle elementari* (Sexist Education. Gender Stereotypes in Primary School Texts). Turin: Rosenberg & Sellier.

Chick, Kay. 2008. 'Fostering an Appreciation for All Kinds of Families: Picturebooks with Gay and Lesbian Families'. *Bookbird: A Journal of International Children's Literature* 46, no 1: 15–22.

De Luca, Maria Novella. 2015a. 'Figli di due mamme e lotta ai pregiudizi: ecco cosa c'è davvero nei libri "gender"'. *Repubblica*, 26 June. http://www.repubblica.it/cronaca/2015/06/26/news/figli_di_due_mamme_e_lotta_ai_pregiudizi_ecco_cosa_c_e_davvero_nei_libri_gender_-117762548/

———. 2015b. 'Venezia, nei libri all'Indice per il gender anche i capolavori per l'infanzia'. *Repubblica*, 4 July. https://www.repubblica.it/cronaca/2015/07/04/news/venezia_nei_libri_all_indice_per_il_gender_anche_i_capolavori_dell_infanzia-118306936/

Epstein, B. J. 2013. *Are the Kids All Right?: The Representation of LGBTQ Characters in Children's and Young Adult Literature*. Bristol: HammerOn Press.

Flood, Alison. 2015. 'Italian authors ask Venice to ban their books after gay children's stories pulled'. *The Guardian*, 16 July. https://www.theguardian.com/books/2015/jul/16/italian-authors-venice-mayor-ban-books-children-same-sex-family

Fornara, Simone. 2016. 'Nessuno tocchi Guizzino. Gli albi illustrati in Italia tra "teoria gender," false interpretazioni e censura' (Don't Touch Guizzino. Italian Picturebooks, Gender Theory and Censorship). *gender/sexuality/italy* 3. https://www.gendersexualityitaly.com/12-nessuno-tocchi-guizzino-gli-albi-illustrati-in-italia-tra-teoria-gender-false-interpretazioni-e-censura/

Furlan, Francesco. 2015. 'Il neo sindaco: "Via i libri gender dalle aule di Venezia"'. *Repubblica*, 25 June. http://www.repubblica.it/cronaca/2015/06/25/news/il_neosindaco_via_i_libri_gender_dalle_aule_di_venezia_ed_e_polemica-117663659/

Gigli, Alessandra. 2011. *Maestra, ma Sara ha due mamme? Le famiglie omogenitoriali nella scuola e nei servizi educativi* (Teacher, Has Sara Got Two Mommies? Same-Sex Families in Schools and Educational Services). Milan: Guerini Scientifica.

Hoffman, Mary. 2010. *The Great Big Book of Families*. Illustrated by Ros Asquith. London: Frances Lincoln.

———. 2012. *Il grande grosso libro delle famiglie*. Illustrated by Ros Asquith. Translated by Nicoletta Pardi. Milan: Lo Stampatello.

———. 2014a. *Benvenuti in famiglia*. Illustrated by Ros Asquith. Translated by Nicoletta Pardi. Milan: Lo Stampatello.

———. 2014b. *Welcome to the Family*. Illustrated by Ros Asquith. London: Frances Lincoln.

Illuminati, Valeria. 2017. '"Speak to Me in Capital Letters!" Same-sex Parenting, New Families and Homosexuality in Picturebooks Published by Lo Stampatello'. In *Fractures and Disruptions in Children's Literature*, edited by Ana Margarida Ramos, Sandie Mourão and Maria Teresa Cortez, 228–43. Newcastle-Upon-Tyne: Cambridge Scholars Publishing.

Il Post. 2016. 'Cosa c'è negli emendamenti al ddl Cirinnà' (What's Involved in the Amendments to the Draft Cirinnà Bill). 17 February. https://www.ilpost.it/2016/02/17/emendamenti-ddl-cirinna/

Il Timone. 2014. 'Contro la dittatura del gender, le Sentinelle in Piedi arrivano a Roma'. 3 April. http://www.iltimone.org/news-timone/contro-la-dittatura-del-gender-le-sentinelle-in-pi/

Kramer, Fabri, and Luca Panzini. 2014a. *Ho 2 mamme* (I Have 2 Mums). Illustrated by Luca Panzini. Florence: Terra Nuova Edizioni.

———. 2014b. *Ho 2 papà* (I Have 2 Dads) Illustrated by Luca Panzini. Florence: Terra Nuova Edizioni.

Lalli, Chiara. 2015. 'Il sindaco che a scuola grida al lupo contro il gender'. *Internazionale*, 25 June. https://www.internazionale.it/opinione/chiara-lalli/2015/06/26/gender-libri-scuola

Lo Stampatello. 2014. 'Piccolo uovo: la seconda volta che ho visto Babbo Natale. ("Little egg": The Second Time I Saw Santa Claus.)' *Lo Stampatello*, 11 February. http://lostampatello.blogspot.it/2014/02/piccolo-uovo-la-seconda-volta-che-ho.html

Malafreca, Miguel Andrés. 2007. *Queer Italy: Contexts, Antecedents and Representation*. New York: Peter Lang Publishing.

Malici, Luca. 2012. 'Queer in Italy: Italian Televisibility and the "Queerable" Audience'. In *Queer in Europe: Contemporary Case Studies*, edited by Lisa Downing and Robert Gillett, 113–28. Farnham: Ashgate Publishing.

Marzano, Michela. 2015. *Papà, mamma e gender* (Dad, Mum and Gender). Turin: UTET.

Newman, Lesléa. 1989. *Heather Has Two Mommies*. New York: Alyson Books.

Pardi, Francesca. 2011. *Piccolo uovo* (Little Egg). Illustrated by Altan. Milan: Lo Stampatello.

———. 2012. *Perché hai due mamme?* (Why Have You Got Two Mummies?). Illustrated by Annalisa Sanmartino and Giulia Torelli. Milan: Lo Stampatello.

———. 2014. *Perché hai due papà?* (Why Have You Got Two Daddies?). Illustrated by Annalisa Sanmartino and Giulia Torelli. Milan: Lo Stampatello.

Parr, Todd. 2003. *The Family Book*. New York: Little, Brown.

Prati, Andrea. 2018. 'Stepchild adoption, servono i giudici per portare l'Italia al livello europeo' (Stepchild Adoption: Judges Help to Bring Italy Into Line With the Rest of Europe). *Repubblica*, 31 July. https://www.repubblica.it/economia/diritti-e-consumi/famiglia/2018/07/31/news/stepchild_adoption_servono_i_giudici_per_portare_l_italia_al_livello_europeo-202530750/

Richardson, Justin, and Peter Parnell. 2005. *And Tango Makes Three*. Illustrated by Henry Cole. New York: Simon & Schuster.

Rossi Barilli, Gianni. 1999. *Il movimento gay in Italia* (Gay Movements in Italy). Milan: Feltrinelli.

Schiffer, Miriam B. 2015. *Stella Brings the Family*. San Francisco: Chronicle Books.

Sorio, Matteo. 2017. 'Sboarina e i libri "gender" a Verona, i titoli che rischiano la proibizione'. *Corriere del Veneto*, 7 July. http://corrieredelveneto.corriere.it/veneto/notizie/politica/2017/7-luglio-2017/sboarina-libri-gender-verona-titoli-che-rischiano-proibizione-2401770148818.shtml.

Sunderland, Jane, and Mark McGlashan. 2011. 'Stories Featuring Two-Mum and Two-Dad Families'. In *Language, Gender and Children's Fiction*, by Jane Sunderland, 142–72. London: Continuum.

———. 2013. 'Looking at Picturebook Covers Multimodally: The Case of Two-Mum and Two-Dad Stories'. *Visual Communication* 12, no. 4: 473–96.

Taxel, Joel. 2002. 'Children's Literature at the Turn of the Century: Toward a Political Economy of the Publishing Industry'. *Research in the Teaching of English* 37, no. 2: 145–97.

Trisciuzzi, Maria Teresa. 2017. 'Questioni di genere. Riflessioni sul tema tra letteratura per l'infanzia e albi illustrati' (Gender Issues. Reflections on the Topic in Picturebooks and Children's Literature). In *Decostruire l'immaginario femminile. Percorsi educativi per vecchie e nuove forme di condizionamento culturale*, edited by Anna Grazia Lopez, 71–92. Pisa: Edizioni ETS.

Willhoite, Michael. 1990. *Daddy's Roommate*. Los Angeles: Alyson Books.

Zappettini, Franco. 2010. 'Negotiating LGBTQ Identities in Italy: An Intercultural Perspective'. *Cultus: the Journal of Intercultural Mediation and Communication* 3: 115–35.

Zolotow, Charlotte. 1972. *William's Doll*. New York: Harper & Row.

Chapter Eight

HEATHER HAS A DONOR: 30 YEARS OF INTERNATIONAL LESBIAN-THEMED CHILDREN'S PICTURE BOOKS ABOUT DONOR INSEMINATION, 1989–2019

Patricia Sarles

Introduction

While children's literature with LGBTQ themes has been explored in the last three decades (see Abate and Kidd 2011; Cart and Jenkins 2006; Day 2000; DePalma 2016; Dorr and Deskins 2018; Epstein 2012a, 2012b, 2013, 2014; Jenkins and Cart 2018; Jiménez 2015; Lester 2014; McGlashan and Sunderland 2010; Miller 2019; Naidoo 2012; Sciurba 2017; Sunderland and McGlashan 2012, 2013; Taylor 2012, among others), a small but growing body of literature has remained uninvestigated: children's books about assisted reproductive technology and in particular, books about donor insemination used by lesbian mothers to build their families. While picture books for young children lack portrayals of lesbians in general (Cummins 2015; Jiménez 2015), they also lack representation of children who are donor-conceived in any type of family, straight or LGBTQ. Of the approximately 576 books extant on the subject of assisted reproductive technology for children in the world (Sarles 2019a), 241 of them, or approximately 42 per cent of them are about sperm donation. Of those, 47 (19 per cent) have been written specifically for the children of lesbians who were created via sperm donation.[1] That is, approximately one-fifth of all children's books written on sperm donation are written by or for lesbians.

In the context of global publishing, then, such books are noticeably rare, and are seldom found in the average public library (only 29 of them are found on library shelves somewhere around the world, according to WorldCat; see also Mendell and Sarles 2010b). This is remarkable given the fact that there has been a lesbian baby boom taking place around the world for the last 40 years (Agigian 2004; Patterson 1995). Nevertheless,

1 Artificial insemination, donor insemination and sperm donation are used interchangeably in this chapter. The reader should be aware though that artificial insemination does not always mean that a donor was used; rather it means that conception happened *artificially*, as in some cases when IVF, IUI and ICSI are employed. Artificial insemination *by donor*, sometimes referred to as AID, is the more specific term and is what is intended in this chapter.

the mere existence of these books is evidence of the increasing presence of lesbians with children conceived via sperm donation.

For this chapter, only those books written by lesbian mothers are examined; however, an exhaustive list is available on pages 321–23, of this book and on this author's blog (Sarles 2019a). Amongst other things, these books were analysed for how lesbian families are portrayed, how donors are depicted, and whether the children were conceived via known or unknown donor. In light of the literature on disclosure, I examined how the books measured up against what is known about information-sharing in known and unknown donor conception in lesbian families and how this is portrayed in children's books.

Demographic Data on Donor-Conceived Children in Lesbian Families

Charlotte Patterson, who helmed the first studies of children in LGBTQ households, wrote in 1995 that 'the frequency of lesbian childbearing ... has been growing in recent years to such an extent that many researchers have referred to a "lesbian baby boom"' (Patterson 1995, 115). This baby boom, also known as a 'gay-by boom' (Brower 2009, 1; Rivers 2013, 173), began in the United States in the 1980s, about a decade after the first commercial sperm banks appeared (Moore 2007; Swanson 2012). The timing was similar in the United Kingdom. In a short piece in a 1979 article in *Lesbian Tide* entitled *British Doctors OK A.I.* (1979, 18), it was reported that the Central Ethical Committee of the British Medical Association had made an official statement about the practice of artificial insemination on lesbians, determining that it was not 'unethical' to help lesbians to have babies.

However, hard data is lacking on how many children have been conceived through the sperm banking industry (Agigian 2004). In the United States, sperm donor recipients are not required to report back to the sperm bank whether they have had a live birth, thus no statistics are kept compared with some other countries, which regulate the use of assisted reproductive technology. Nevertheless, one estimate often cited is that there are over one million children conceived via donor insemination in the United States alone (Becker 2002; Ravitsky 2012).

Of these, it is even more difficult to determine how many of them are the children of lesbian mothers, although Gates, analysing multiple data sources, has concluded that 'as many as six million American children and adults have an LGBT parent' (2013 n.p.). Whether those children are adopted or conceived in opposite-sex relationships, via assisted reproductive technology, or at home via self-insemination, is unknown.

Books for Children Created by Alternative Means: Some Background

Unlike fertile heterosexual couples, women in lesbian relationships who want to start a family together invariably need help. In the case of artificial insemination, the sperm can be from either a known donor or an unknown donor. So how, then, is sperm donation addressed in books for children in lesbian families? What happens in a lesbian family when a child begins to ask the question, 'Where did I come from?' Is it different for these children than it is for the children in heterosexual households? To date, there has been no exploration into these books even though the first book broaching this topic was published over 30 years ago.

The groundbreaking *Heather Has Two Mommies* (1989) by Lesléa Newman was the first picture book to refer to the use of artificial insemination in lesbian families. Newman writes:

> Kate and Jane went to see a special doctor together. After the doctor examined Jane to make sure she was healthy, she put some sperm into Jane's vagina. The sperm swam up into Jane's womb. If there was an egg waiting there, the sperm and egg would meet, and the baby would start to grow. (1989, 7)

Newman was told to add this explanation to the book by an editor when she was looking for a publisher. 'Children know that two women can't make a baby,' she was told (Newman, personal communication, 3 July 2014).

Though *Heather* did not focus specifically on artificial insemination, it was an important publication in that it introduced children to the concept of donor insemination in lesbian families. It was published through a letter-writing campaign (Newman 1997), whereas thirty years later, nearly all of the obscure, little-known titles from all corners of the world are mostly self-published (see Table 4). Ironically, the tenth, twentieth and twenty-fifth anniversary editions of *Heather* have all removed the artificial insemination pages from the book even though more children in lesbian families are conceived via sperm donation today. When I asked Newman if she ever planned to reinstate the artificial insemination pages given that the times have changed, Newman responded in the negative, adding that the story flows better without those pages (Newman, personal communication, 3 July 2014).[2]

It took 10 years before the second book ever was published about lesbians who used artificial insemination to have their children. That book was published in Sweden in 1999. *Malins mamma gifter sig med Lisa* (Malin's Mother Marries Lisa), by Annette Lundborg, was one of the first lesbian-themed, not to mention LGBTQ-themed in general, children's books published in Sweden.[3] In a subplot, the main character learns that she is about to become a big sister when one night, her mother's new wife, Lisa, tells Malin that she is pregnant. Unlike three-year-old Heather who never asks questions about pregnancy in the book, five-year-old Malin does ask. Whereas Heather's parents go to a doctor for help with a (presumably) unknown donor, Malin and her soon-to-be new sibling were conceived with a known donor. In this case it is Malin's father, who Malin has

2 According to Newman, the story flows better because children are more interested in a story that 'moves forward, not backwards' and because Heather's conception is not pertinent to the overall point of the story. Newman tells me she also heard from several lesbian parents who wanted to bring the book to their children's school but felt they couldn't because the artificial insemination scenes were not suitable for the classroom. She also wanted to make the book shorter in later versions (Newman, personal communication, 3 July 2014; Newman, personal communication, 14 June 2020).

3 Published the same year was *Trollen på regnbågsbacken (The Trolls of Rainbow Hill)* about two female characters who are married (Epstein 2012a).

a relationship with. He is the gay male friend of her mother and she calls him 'Pappa' (1999, 3). Malin's new sibling-to-be was conceived with Pappa's partner, Niklas, for he 'wanted to become a father too' (1999, 21), Pappa tells her. In the book, Malin asks her mother how 'babies get in the stomach' (1999, 17). Malin's mother then goes on to describe how Malin got here:

> 'In the beginning there are small seeds that swim into the stomach where there is a tiny egg waiting,' answers her mother.
> 'Flower seeds?' wonders Malin.
> 'No, not flower seeds,' her mother laughs. 'There are special little seeds found in the father.'
> Malin thinks for a while. 'Did you get those seeds from Dad?'
> 'Yes,' answers her mother, 'a whole jar full of small, swimming seeds.'
> 'Was I one of those little seeds?' wonders Malin curiously.
> 'Yes, you could say. Lisa helped put the seeds into my stomach so they could swim around in there. Suddenly there was a seed that collided with the little egg and it was then that you became you.' (1999, 17)[4]

This is also the very first depiction that I have found in children's literature of a home insemination , a method used by lesbians for many years before it became either legal or more acceptable for doctors to treat lesbians with artificial insemination.[5] As Agigian writes in *Baby Steps: How Lesbian Alternative Insemination is Changing the World*, 'early in the lesbian baby boom, it was understood that AI was a simple, low-tech process that could be performed at home with materials you have around the house (e.g. a turkey baster and a mason jar)' (2004, x). In *Malin*, the text is accompanied by a picture of a mason jar with sperm floating around in it and a tag on it that says 'Malin-Frön' ('Malin-seeds'). As we will see, the term 'seeds' is commonly used in these books in place of 'sperm'.

Neither *Heather* nor *Malin* was specifically about artificial insemination: in both books the topic takes up a single page, and the words 'artificial insemination' are never used. However, it is revealing that between 1989 and 1999, no other children's books addressed the topic of artificial insemination.

Donor conception, the means by which a child is conceived with either the sperm or egg (or both) of a third party, is not a commonly encountered topic of inquiry in children's literature research. There has to date only been one published article in English[6] (Mendell and Sarles 2010b), one thesis in Dutch (Wauters 2014), one thesis in Swedish (Ernemar 2017) and one other article written in a Swedish journal (Andersson 2015). The latter two scrutinize how Swedish children's literature about human reproduction,

---

4 Quotations in languages other than English are my own translations unless otherwise noted.

5 Malin was published six years prior to the legalization of sperm donation for lesbians in Sweden ('Sweden to Allow IVF for Lesbians' 2005).

6 For articles on donor conception in young adult literature, there have been two. See Mendell and Sarles (2010a) and Nelson (2020).

including assisted reproductive technologies, has evolved. This chapter aims to fill the void in English by looking at the same topics, but specifically at those children's books from around the world about lesbians who built their families with the use of donor insemination.

Despite the lack of research, some scholars do entertain the prospect that such books could or should exist. In one article on how non-heterosexualities are portrayed in LGBTQ children's literature in both the Swedish- and English-language cultures, Epstein (2012b, 296) writes,

> … since there are many picture books teaching children about sex and how they were 'created,' there is an argument to be made that there could be such books teaching children about nonheterosexual sex and the 'creation' of babies in nontraditional stories.

Epstein provides the example of *Malin*, discussed above. In a second article, this one about the representation of sperm in 18 English-language children's books about human reproduction, Moore (2003, 282) writes that the 'origin story is not always true, and children who do not enter the world this way [through heterosexual sex] could be confused or shamed by reading it'. She continues, 'When I began my research, I was interested to see if the pace of technological innovation and changing methods of conception had amended children's books' contents' (ibid.). Although Moore did not discover any amended contents of children's books in her research, such books do exist, as I will establish in this chapter.

One more mention of such books is in an article from Sweden. The author writes that 'the new … stories are usually justified on the basis of the argument that it is important for children's security and identity development to know how they came to be and to see that reality embodied in the literature' (Andersson 2015, 22). Thus, in the words of Rudine Sims Bishop (1990, 3), these are the 'mirrors' that children need to see in the books they read. Because it is recommended that children be informed early about their donor origins (American Society for Reproductive Medicine 2004), this chapter focuses on literature designed for mostly preschool-aged children, as this is when children begin asking questions about where babies come from (Goldman and Goldman 1982; Richardson and Schuster 2004).[7]

Children's Books as a Means of Disclosure of Donor Conception

The first picture book specifically about sperm donation, and expressly written for children, was published in Australia in 1988. It was called *How I Began: The Story of Donor Insemination* (N. S. W. Infertility Social Workers Group 1988). While written for the children of heterosexual couples, its publication was significant in that it tackled a topic that, for the first time, gave parents a 'script' to work with in helping them explain

7 For an extensive list of young adult novels about teenagers who were conceived via sperm donation, see Sarles (2019b).

donor insemination to their children. It was also significant in that, at that time, medical professionals and mental health practitioners in the field of assisted reproductive technology were not necessarily recommending disclosure to children – a practice by which parents are encouraged to share information with their children about how they were conceived, especially if conceived with the use of a third party (Beeson et al. 2011). Up until the 1990s and the early 2000s, it was common practice in heterosexual families to *not* tell children about their donor conception for fear that children would reject their 'social father' (non-biological father) who raised them (Blyth 1999). However, writing in 1993, Daniels and Taylor believed that one of the reasons that parents might not have told their children was simply because they did not know *how* to tell their children that they were donor-conceived, and there were no children's books written prior to 1988 to provide 'scripts' for parents on how to tell their children. *How I Began,* therefore, was the first such resource for parents to begin to build upon the story of how their children began with the help of sperm donation. As of the 1990s, however, medical and social work literature began to recommend that children be told early and often of their donor origins, especially when they start to ask where they come from, as children inevitably do (see, for example, Blyth 1998; Cooke 1993; Daniels and Taylor 1993; Rumball and Adair 1999; Turner 1993).

In studies of parents who have disclosed to their children how they were conceived, some parents express a desire for their children to know about their donor origins to the point where there was never a time that they did not know (e.g. Blake et al. 2010; Hargreaves and Daniels 2007). A study of 181 heterosexual couples, asking them if they intended to tell their children about their donor origins, found that:

> … young children may be introduced to the story at an appropriate level and, as they grow up, the story grows with them. … In this way, the parents believe their children grow up knowing of their donor circumstances, and perceive it to be 'no big deal'. (Rumball and Adair 1999, 1397)

This can only be achieved by beginning disclosure early, and reading books as 'scripts' to children is one way that parents found to facilitate this disclosure (Blake et al. 2010). Kirkman (2003) also discusses the use of books as tools for disclosure. She explored some of the reasons that parents give for *not* telling their children they were donor-conceived and came to the same conclusions as Daniels and Taylor (1993); that is, parents simply did not know *how* to begin. She writes:

> A book may serve several purposes: it allows parents to work on an acceptable story at their own pace, which may in turn play a role in clarifying their own narrative identities; it encourages children to take the initiative in talking about their own stories and to indulge in the repetition that children enjoy; it is a fixed point to which they can refer when matters become confused; … and it has a status or legitimacy, like other books, that oral accounts may lack. (2003, 2237)

It may thus be easier for an adult to broach the topic of donor conception when it is in a children's book because the book provides the script.

Disclosure in Lesbian Families

Though disclosure is an issue in heterosexual families where the presence of a father lacking genetic ties to the child/ren can impact the family,[8] disclosure is a different matter in lesbian families where there is no father (Hunter et al. 2000; Vanfraussen et al. 2001; Van Parys et al. 2015). Ehrensaft (2011) writes that waiting to disclose donor conception in lesbian families is 'usually not possible' (Ehrensaft 2011, 186) with children because 'by the time they have finished preschool, they get it that most children have mothers and fathers and that not having a mother and father calls for some explanation' (Ehrensaft 2011, 186). In a study of 26 lesbian mothers by Mitchell (1998), the mothers were asked how they explained their child's origin to them. A composite story went something like this:

> So we went to the sperm bank to get some sperm. Some men know that women like your moms want to have babies, so they give some sperm to the sperm bank for us to use. When we were ready to make a baby, we went to the sperm bank and got some, and the sperm cell joined together with Mom's egg cell in a special part of Mom's tummy where you started to grow into a baby. (Mitchell 1998, 403)

One of the most interesting conclusions from Mitchell's study is that children are not asking about sex when they first ask where babies come from. What they do ask is where babies come from, why they do not have a dad and how they got here. In a 1990 article by Amy Blumenthal called *Scrambled Eggs and Seed Daddies: Conversations with My Son*, Blumenthal, a single lesbian mother who chose to have her child via anonymous sperm donation in the 1980s, writes about the questions her son started to ask at the age of two and a half, continuing over the next three years.

Blumenthal's journal account begins with her son's first question about why he does not have a daddy, to which his mother begins to explain that there are all different sorts of families. She records the next question as happening almost a year later when her son asked for the first time where babies come from. 'I told him that women have eggs inside them ("scrambled eggs?" he asked amazed) and men have sperm and when the two get mixed together a baby can start growing' (Blumenthal 1990, 173). A few months later, Jonathon asked if it was true that he didn't have a daddy after he was teased by his friend so his mother introduced the concept of the 'seed daddy – a man who is not really a parent, but one who helps a woman get a baby started' (Blumenthal 1990, 173). It was not for another year that her son 'finally asked how the sperm and egg get together' (Blumenthal 1990, 174) when he learned that his friend's mother was going to have a baby. She explains to him:

> I went to a doctor who had sperm from the seed daddy in a little straw, and she put it in my vagina to start him growing. He nodded a lot, looking serious and pleased. But when I told

8 This also happens in the case of the disclosure of the use of a donor egg in the instance of a mother who lacks genetic ties to her child.

> him about John's penis and Susan's vagina, he gasped and said, "But why didn't she just go to the doctor like you, Mama?" Oh the look of horror and confusion on that boy's face. (Blumenthal 1990, 174)

Blumenthal's pioneering account rings very similar to the very first children's story about artificial insemination specifically published for the children of lesbian mothers, a full 12 years after she wrote her narrative. It was published in 2002 as part of a series on assisted reproductive technology for children by Nicola Baxter and commissioned by the Donor Conception Network, a support group for gamete recipients and their offspring in the United Kingdom.

Called *Our Story*, it was written specifically as an instructional tool with which lesbian mothers could begin to explain to their children how they were conceived, and is remarkably similar to Blumenthal's account in terms of both the child's questions and the mothers' answers. The little boy in the story one day asks his mums, 'Do I have a dad?' (2002, 4) to which his mums begin to tell him that there are all different kinds of families and in his family 'there are two mums and you' (2002, 6). After an explanation about how you need 'sperm from a man and an egg from a woman' (2002, 12) to make a baby, they tell him that 'some very kind men' (2002, 13) give their sperm 'so that women like us could have babies' (2002, 13). In the end, the little boy asks, 'Do we know anything about the man who helped you to make me?' (2002, 19) and 'Will I ever meet him?' (2002, 21), to which his mums respond, 'He isn't going to be a part of our lives, but it is good to know how kind and generous he was' (2002, 22). It is notable to point out here that *Our Story* constructs the anonymous donor as a real person.

In the United States, the first book published specifically about donor insemination for the children of lesbian mothers was not published until 2004. Called *Before You Were Born: Our Wish for a Baby* (Grimes 2004), it too was part of a series with different versions for different donor and family scenarios. Written by fertility nurse Janice Grimes, it is also the story of a little boy whose mothers conceived him with the help of 'a nice man called a *donor*' (2004, 9, italics original). Grimes writes:

> So the doctor gave Mommy some medicine. When the time was right, the doctor took the donor cells and placed them inside Mommy. The tiny cells combined and a baby began to grow. That baby was you! (2004, 9)

Thus, by 2004, there were two books available that dealt briefly with artificial insemination in the context of broader fictional narratives about two-mum families (*Heather* and *Malin*, published in 1989 and 1999 respectively) and two non-fiction 'instructional' books written or commissioned by fertility professionals (*Our Story* and *Before You Were Born*, published in 2002 and 2004). What follows is a discussion of children's books on sperm donation in lesbian families published in Australia, France, Germany, Israel, Italy, Norway, Spain, the United Kingdom and the United States from 2008 onwards. Of the 47 children's books from around the world written on this topic, 22 of them, or nearly 48 per cent, have been written by lesbian mothers themselves, and due to space constraints, those are the books on which I focus here. How do these books support the disclosure process for children in lesbian families? What is the information that lesbian mothers want to convey to their children about how their family came to be? What are the common themes, and the specifics of each individual story?

Spain

Y nosotros—¿de dónde venimos? (And Us – Where Do We Come From?), by Isabel Carmen Rodríguez García, was the very first book written by a lesbian mother for her children about sperm donation. It was published in 2008 in Spain, a country that has always permitted sperm donation to lesbians (Jociles Rubio, personal communication, 15 May 2018). On the publisher's website, Rodríguez García writes that she wanted something to explain to her children about how they were conceived and thought that by publishing a story it might help other parents who conceived their children in the same way (Rodríguez García n.d.).

The story begins:

> One night like many others, I was in my children's room talking about how the day had gone. It was the prelude to the story that I would tell them each night leading them into a peaceful sleep. At one point in the conversation, one of my children asked me:
> 'Mum, can we have two mothers?'
> 'You know so,' was my answer.
> 'So where did we come from?'
> That was the question I had been waiting years for.
> My response was:

> 'Children, tonight I will not tell you the story of *Little Red Riding Hood, Sleeping Beauty,* or *The Three Little Pigs,* today I will tell you the story of your life.' And that was how my story began to take shape. (2008, 1)

In the story, there are two women who love each other very much and want to start a family:

> There was a time, very close to our city, that two people were in love. Their names were Elisa and Isabella. They loved each other very much and had spent years living together. They were happy, they had a house and a job. (2008, 3)

After a while the two women go to the doctor to learn what they need to do. One of them would get 'injections that do not hurt' (2008, 7) so that a baby could grow. When the story is over, the little boy asks, 'Mum, why didn't you tell us this story before?' And the mother responds, 'The truth is I did not know if you were ready to hear it'. 'But Mum, it is beautiful!' the little boy says (2008, 21). And the story ends when he tells his mum that he is going to draw a picture of the story and bring it to school.

The next book to be published in Spain, *Tenemos dos mamás* (We Have Two Mothers), was written and self-published by Violeta Morales Luelmo in 2013 (Flórez 2013). In contrast to *Y nosotros*, Morales Luelmo's book goes into specifics about how babies are made when there are two mothers involved. It is narrated by a child, who is a twin. The child feels pressured to explain to her classmates how two women can have children as she is called a 'liar' 'because you cannot have two mums' (2013, 8). The child narrator then goes on to explain to her classmates how her two mums had a baby. The mothers of this story have clearly informed their children, in much detail, how they were conceived through home insemination. After the requisite discussion of the need for sperm and eggs and the fact that women do not have sperm and need it from men in order to make a baby, the narrator informs the reader that her mums had to go to a clinic for help. 'There they keep sperm that some men have donated' (2013, 14). Although Spain has very lenient laws around the use of assisted reproduction, it used to be that only married, heterosexual couples did not have to pay for treatment. But according to new laws, enforceable in 2019, treatment costs for single women and lesbians are now reimbursable (Dunham 2018). However, at the time *Tenemos* was written in 2013, lesbians still had to pay out of pocket for the costs of fertility treatment. Morales Luelmo writes, 'My mums saved a lot of money because they had to do a lot of testing and all those tests are very expensive' (2013, 15). She continues, 'And when they finally had all the money and finished doing all the tests, Mummy carefully put sperm inside her body. And so she became pregnant with us!' (2013, 16). Of the four books all self-published in Spain, this is the only one that describes a home insemination.

The next book to be published in Spain was *¿Cómo es posible que tengan dos mamás?* (How is it Possible for Them to Have Two Mums?) by Paula López Navarro in 2017. As in *Tenemos*, the children in this story are also twins, Nela and Tina, who feel compelled to explain to their inquiring cousin how it is possible to have two mums. One day, the girls are playing with their cousins, Belinda and Carmen, when Belinda asks how it is possible to have two mothers. She tells the twins it is 'nonsense' (2017, 11) and that children must have a mum and a dad. At first not knowing what to say, Nela remembers the story her mums had told her about how they fell in love:

> Our mums were very good friends but one day they realized they felt more than just a friendship, that they were very much more than friends and wanted to form a Family together and continue on the Path of Life to Marriage. (2017, 12)

She then goes on to discuss the clinic where women get help making babies: 'Mum told me that when they were sure they wanted to have a child and expand the family, they went to a clinic where they helped them to be mothers' (2017, 14). And then the requisite discussion of sperm and eggs ensues when her twin, Tina adds:

> Women have eggs called ovules in the bellies and men have worms called sperm cells. When they give them to women who want to become mothers, they go to the clinic and they put some worms in the belly that together with the ovules form the babies. (2017, 14)

As in *Tenemos*, these mums explained to their daughters, very specifically, how they were made with sperm and egg and the help of a clinic.

The final book from Spain is a true story, according to an interview with the author in *El País* (Ferrero 2017). It is *Dos mamás: un cuento para todas las familias (Two Mums: A Story for All Families)* by Débora Alfonso. Self-published in 2018 through a crowdfunding campaign, it is a dual-language Spanish and English book, which tells the story of Debo and Carol's love for one another and how they wanted to get married and start a family together. The author wanted to fill a void in children's literature by writing about a same-sex family in order to 'normalize' it for children (Ferrero 2017). The day finally arrives when the couple 'decided they wanted to become mommies' (2018, 16). 'There were several options', which they do not particularize, 'but the one they liked best was to see Doctor Family, who would happily explain everything they needed to do' (2018, 18). So they go to the doctor and have some tests 'to make sure they are both healthy and strong' (2018, 20). Why both women needed to be healthy and strong is not clear, as only one of them can carry the baby. Four pages later, Alfonso writes, '... and finally, they needed to go back to see Doctor Family, who had selected the best sperm from the Sperm Bank to fertilize Carol and Debo's ova' (2018, 24). Why both of their ova? Was one going to donate her egg to the one who would give birth so that both women could have a biological connection to the child?[9] It is not clarified.

Germany

Access to reproductive medicine for lesbians in Germany is complicated. It is not outright illegal, but the country's laws do not make it easy for lesbians to start families. According to a paper deposited at the Official Website of the European Union (Pinter et al. n.d.), the use of artificial insemination for lesbian couples is not clearly specified by law in Germany. Each doctor reserves the right to inseminate or not inseminate as outlined in each state's professional medical guidelines (Calhaz-Jorge et al. 2020; Green 2006). 'While these guidelines are not legally binding, it is a gray area and some practitioners still fear they might lose their license' according to an article in *Exberliner* (Helms 2018).

The very first children's book to be published in Germany about sperm donation in a lesbian family was published by FamART and authored by Petra Thorn and Lisa Green. *Die Geschichte unserer Familie: ein Buch für lesbische Familien mit Wunschkindern durch Samenspende (The Story of Our Family: A Book for Lesbian Families with Children Conceived by Donor Insemination)* was published in 2009. FamART was established by Petra Thorn when she could not find a publisher in Germany for her children's books on assisted reproductive technology (FamART n.d.). She has also published books on sperm donation in heterosexual families and in single-mother families, as well as books on egg donation, embryo donation and IVF, all through FamART. *Die Geschichte unserer Familie* was also translated into English in 2013. Thorn is heterosexual and works in the fertility field, counselling couples and singles who need to build their families with assisted reproductive

9 This process is called reciprocal IVF or ROPA (Reception of Oocytes from Partner).

technology. Her co-author Green is a lesbian mother herself and had her own three children via donor insemination. In the back of the book, Green writes that she wishes she had had a book for her children, which would have helped her to educate her children and facilitate discussions with others about their use of donor conception in their family formation. She writes:

> Responding to inquiries of our child's peers was a bit trickier as these began when our daughter entered preschool at age two and a half. To answer these questions, it would have been easiest to discuss DI. How do you explain DI to children that young? I often wished a book such as this one had existed which I could just give the teacher to read to the children. (Thorn and Green 2013, 17)

Story is intended for children aged three to six years old and, like two of the books from Spain, is narrated by a child. It begins with two women who love each other very much and wanted to have a baby. It then goes on to discuss egg and sperm as necessary to make a baby. 'Babies grow when the egg from a woman and a sperm from a man come together' (2013, 4). But where to get sperm when neither of the couple has it? They needed sperm from a man to have a baby. Here the book is unique in that it has two different successive pages 7 and 8 so that it can be tailored to the specifics of the family. On the first page 7 and 8, Thorn and Green write: 'They went to see a doctor who helps couples to have a baby. The doctor put the sperm from a nice man into Mommy's tummy.' And on the second set of pages 7 and 8, they describe a home insemination: 'They knew a man who was happy to give them sperm. Mommy and Mamma put the sperm into Mommy's tummy.'

The only other children's book to be published in Germany was 2015's self-published *Maxime will ein Geschwister* (Maxime Wants a Sibling) by Cai Schmitz-Weicht and illustrated by her partner, Ka Schmitz. Like Thorn, Schmitz-Weicht and her partner started their own publishing company, Atelier 9¾, in order to publish books on LGBTQ topics that they had not seen published by traditional publishers in Germany (Atelier 9¾ 2020). The book begins with the main character, Maxime, the daughter of Melanie and Louise, who asks her mums if she can have a sibling. The book then goes into an account of how babies are made with sperm and egg.

> With people, a baby grows in the belly. There is a cosy baby cave called a uterus. Or womb. When an egg and a sperm cell are found in the uterus, a baby can grow there. (2015, 6)
>
> … Usually, women have a baby cave in their tummy. Most men have sperm cells. Maxime's mothers both have a baby cave with eggs. For a baby to grow, they need a sperm cell. (2015, 8)

In this particular story, Melanie and Louise use a midwife in order to get inseminated and in the end, Maxime asks her mothers if they know who this man is. Her mothers tell her that they do not but that they were happy for his help.

France

Unlike in Germany, where laws surrounding the use of sperm donation for lesbians are indeterminate, the laws in France are clear. Lesbians do not have access to artificial insemination or in vitro fertilization (IVF). At the time of this writing, however, a bill to allow artificial insemination to lesbians and single women has reached the French senate and a decision will be finalized soon (Kaplan 2019). It is no wonder, then, that the very first books for children to be published by lesbian mothers in France were not published until 2017 and 2018. The first was the dual-language French and English book, *Pourquoi tu as 2 mamans? (Why Do You Have 2 Mums?)* by Nathalie Sizaret. The author presents three options for lesbians to have a baby. On page 8, she writes:

> My mums chose to:
> Ask a male friend to donate one of his seeds …
> Ask 2 men in love with each other if they wanted to become fathers …
> Find one man who would donate one of his seeds (2017, 8)

Although we do not know which method the author eventually chose, in the end Sizaret writes that 'each day they thanked to the bottom of their heart the man who enabled them to live this happiness!' (2017, 18). Because access to reproductive medicine is currently not allowed, French lesbians can go abroad, or else the options Sizaret offers in her book are the only possibilities French lesbians have available.

Only one other book on sperm donation from France exists and it similarly places an emphasis on the sperm used to create the author's baby. It is written by Céline Lhuillier who herself is a partnered lesbian mother (Jannic-Cherbonnel 2018). It is called *Les graines magiques* (The Magic Seeds), published in 2018, and it has no plot. Rather, it is a tribute to the 'seeds' which helped her to create her baby. According to the author's website for her book, she consulted child educators for help in telling her story (Les Graines Magiques n.d.). She also writes that when she wanted to tell the story of her child's birth to her child, there was nothing out there to help her. This is often the reason these authors use for the impetus in writing their children's books – that there has been nothing published yet that has been helpful to them, although, as amassed here, that is not the case. What is the case is that each lesbian mother wants to tell the story in her own distinct way.

Lhuillier's book is written entirely about the sperm used to conceive her baby. She begins, 'This story is a great love story' (2018, 2) 'and it is about magic seeds' (2018, 4), or sperm. She does not tell the reader how she obtained the seeds, whether abroad or through the three possible channels described by Sizaret in *Pourquoi*. However, the seeds are of paramount importance in this story. She writes towards the end, 'And one day, from this little seed, a baby is born (2018, 24). 'This baby is you, my precious treasure' (2018, 28) 'born from a crazy love, and a little magic seed' (2018, 30). Although Lhuillier consulted with educators, as she states on her website, there is no real storyline to the book.

Italy

To date, 18 European countries allow lesbians access to sperm donation in order to build their families. Italy is not one of them. In what is the first and only Italian book, *Perché hai due mamme?* (Why Do You Have Two Mummies?) by Francesca Pardi,[10] published in 2012, the author and her partner go abroad in order to start their family (Pardi, personal communication, 2 December 2014). In this autobiographical account, she writes, 'Meri and Franci loved each other and wanted to start a family' (2012, 2). Then she discusses the egg and sperm required to make children and tells her children in the story that their mothers only had eggs. She does not tell her children that, in Italy, lesbians cannot make babies but she tells her children how both mothers went abroad in order to get pregnant. 'In the Netherlands, there is a clinic, where kind men donate their seeds for those who do not have seeds' (2012, 5). Pardi underscores the importance of both mothers in making their first of four children when she writes, 'Margaret has two mothers: she was only carried in one mother's belly, but both brought her into the world' (2012, 7).

Like Thorn and Schmitz-Weicht in Germany, Pardi self-published this book because she could not find a publisher in Italy (Anonymous 2013). Her publishing company, Lo Stampatello, has grown to publish multiple books for children and many of them are books for children with LGBTQ parents; according to her website, there are approximately 100,000 such families in Italy (Lo Stampatello n.d.).

Israel

The importance of the other mother, the one who does not carry the child, is emphasized in the Hebrew-language book בל אמא ,ןטב אמא (*Ima beten, ima lev*, or in English, Belly Mommy, Heart Mommy) by Lee Reuveny Bar David. The author's aim is to share with her son the concept that he is related to both of his parents since both of them brought him into the world through an act of wanting and love. Although lesbians have long been allowed access to sperm donation in Israel according to Israeli medical sociologist Daphna Birenbaum-Carmeli (personal communication, 13 August 2019), 2015 was the first year that a book for children on the topic had ever been published in that country. Narrated by the author's five-year-old protagonist, he recounts the story his parents told him of their meeting and falling in love and of how they decided to move in together and eventually start a family. Finally, on page 19, the narrator tells his readers:

> And here starts my favorite part of the story because it involves me. My mommies wanted a baby but to make a baby they needed a sperm and an egg. It happens easily with a mom and a dad but it is a bit more challenging with two moms. (Reuveny Bar David 2015, 19)

Like many of the other couples in the books discussed in this chapter, they visit a doctor who refers them to a sperm bank. 'They chose a donor and the doctor assisted them by inserting the sperm gently into her belly and I was made in her womb' (2015, 21). And, in

10 This book was first published as *Piccola storia di una famiglia* (Little Story of a Family) in 2011.

the end, even though only his 'belly mommy' carried him, he knows that both mommies are his mommies because 'One mommy grew me in her belly and the other one in her heart and after nine months I was a beautiful baby (2015, 23).[11] This book, like most of the books discussed here, was self-published and funded through a crowdfunding campaign (Shaked 2015).

Norway

Aside from *Malins mamma gifter sig med Lisa*, the only other children's book to come out of a Scandinavian country written by a lesbian mother was *Wilma har to mammaer* (Wilma Has Two Mothers), written by Lone Halvorsen and Maria Therese Olsen, and not published until 2015 in Norway (Erichsen 2015). Sperm donation did not become legal in Norway until 2009, when same-sex marriage also became legal (Hollekim et al. 2012). Unlike most of the children's books discussed here, Wilma was not self-published but rather published by a small publishing company in Norway (Bjerkli, personal communication, 10 July 2020)[12] and of all of the children's books discussed in this chapter, this is the only one that was written by both mothers.

Like five-year-old Malin in Lundborg's book, four-year-old Wilma learns in the story that she is about to become a big sister and she is just as excited as Malin is in her story. She then asks her mums to tell her 'the story of how you got me' (Halvorsen and Olsen 2015, 12), a story she has heard many times according to the narrator, 'but Wilma wants to hear it again' (2015, 12). The authors recount:

> Your moms had been girlfriends for a long time.
> We really wanted a baby.
> We didn't want any baby.
> We just wanted you.
> To make a baby, you need a woman's egg cell and a man's sperm.
> Inside Mamma Lone's stomach lay the egg cell.
> All we needed was a sperm. (2015, 13)

How they got the sperm is continued on the next page, which describes the clinical assistance they received as well as the kindness of the donor:

> In the hospital you can get sperm.
>
> A kind man had given away some sperm so that those who have only one egg cell can get what it takes to make a baby.
>
> The sperm was allowed to swim into the stomach until it hit the egg cell.
>
> The two became really good friends and decided to merge to become a baby. (2015, 14)

11 The author, Lee Reuveny Bar David, graciously translated this book from Hebrew for me.
12 Myriam H. Bjerkli is the owner of the publishing house LIV Forlag, *Wilma's* publisher.

A few pages later, the authors make sure to tell Wilma and the readers that 'the kind man' is not Wilma's father but rather a donor. They write:

> When you give something inside the body that someone else needs, it is called a donor. Wilma knows she can meet the donor when she grows up, but she can't think of that yet. Now she thinks of the little sister to come and the new princess dress she wants. (2015, 17)

United Kingdom

The United Kingdom has seen the publication of two books by lesbian mothers. Although sperm donation for lesbians has always been legal (Montuschi, personal communication, 12 August 2018), it would take a full 15 years after the publication of *Our Story*, published by the Donor Conception Network in 2002, for the United Kingdom to produce the first book written by an actual lesbian mother. It is called *Blib, Blob and Blub*, self-published in 2017 by Bianca Neumann-May (Mantell 2017). As in Reuveny Bar David's book (Belly Mommy, Heart Mommy), *Blib* also aims to emphasize the contributions of both mothers in the creation of their child. The story begins as many of them do, with two women who love each other very much and enjoy each other's company. In sometimes confusing language clearly meant for Neumann-May's child specifically, this is how she chose to tell the story to her child: 'Mamablib and Mummyblob were happy. But something was missing' (Neumann-May 2017, 7). She continues on the next page, 'They wanted a Babyblub. At night they dreamt how happy they'd be with a Babyblub' (2017, 8). So they go to a doctor who prescribes some medicine and then:

> … one day, Mamablib and Mummyblob had to go to the blubbahospital. There a very clever doctor said he was going to give Mamablib a very very important piece of jigsaw. It had parts of a Babyblub. The medicine had helped to make Mamablib's piece of the jigsaw get stronger. Mummyblob gave a piece of her jigsaw too so the doctor had to take Mamablib's piece and the very important other piece of the jigsaw and then work out how to put it together and add Mummyblob's piece. In a laboratory under a microscope he tried all sorts of ways until … it finally fitted. Then the doctor had to put the jigsaw into Mamablib's tummy so that the Babyblub could grow. (2017, 13–15)

This book at first read seems to be describing reciprocal IVF, in which one mother gives her egg to the other mother who will carry the child so that both women can have a biological connection to their child, but it is not. When the author writes, 'Mummyblob gave a piece of her jigsaw too' (2017, 14), it is her love, and not her egg that the author is writing about (Neumann-May, personal communication, 20 November 2019). The language the author chose to use to talk about her family, for example *Mummyblob* and *Mamablib*, is disorienting and not always clear. The accompanying illustrations are of blobs and do not delineate human forms so it is possible that it was the illustrations which dictated the use of blibs, blobs and blubs for the characters in the book.

The following year, another lesbian mother, Emma Wallis, self-published *How Mummy and Mama Made You: Conceived at Home* (Wallis 2018a). In a much more deliberate and straightforward way, Wallis describes the process of how she and her partner inseminated at home. In the beginning of the book is a description of how the two women love each other and all the fun things they like to do together until they finally decide they want to get married and be a family. Later in the book, after some discussion about sperm from a man and an egg from a woman, she explains that because they are two women, they did not have the sperm, 'but we can do things a bit differently' (2018a, 24). She continues, 'A man called a Sperm Donor gave us some sperm' (2018a, 26). There is an accompanying illustration of a box wrapped with rope and a tag spelling out 'sperm' attached to the rope. On the following page, the illustration shows Mummy lying on the sofa with her robe and slippers and Mama walking up to the couch in order to inseminate Mummy. Then, 'Mama spilt some of the sperm' (2018a, 28). Although the illustrations do not show the sperm being spilled, they include two pages of actual microscopic images of sperm under a blue light as they swim on a slide with the related text, 'But don't worry, there was still plenty left!' (2018a, 29). On the following page, she writes, 'Mama used a syringe to put the sperm inside Mummy's vagina' (2018a, 30), and the illustration on the following page shows a photograph of the syringe.

The detail in which the author describes how she accidentally spilled some of the sperm leads readers to believe that the account described in her children's book is autobiographical, which it is, according to the author (Wallis, personal communication, 4 February 2020). In her other book, *How Mummy and Mama Made a Baby: IVF*, Wallis discusses the fertility clinic that helped them to make a baby and describes exactly how babies are made with the help of a sperm donor (Wallis 2018b). She writes, 'A fertility clinic helps people have babies' (2018b, 27) and she includes a corresponding photograph of a lab technician doing something underneath a microscope. 'A man called a sperm donor donated some of his sperm to the sperm bank' (2018b, 28). 'The fertility doctor collected some eggs from Mummy' (2018b, 29). There is also an image of eggs being sucked out of an ovary. 'The fertility doctor introduced the sperm to the egg. This is called fertilization' (2018b, 30). On this page, the image shows a photograph again taken from under a microscope, of a needle inseminating an egg. 'The fertilized egg is called an embryo. The doctor put the embryo back into Mummy's tummy' (2018b, 31). Here there is a picture of a blastocyst showing that the cells have divided. 'The embryo started to form a baby … and the baby grew!' (2018b: 32–33).

After nine months, the baby is born and there is an illustration of the couple smiling and happy with their infant. All of these children's books have the same happy ending, with the birth of a healthy addition to their family.

Australia

As in Germany, lesbians' access to donor insemination in Australia varies by state (Sifris 2014), which means that some lesbians have to travel to other parts of the country in order to receive treatment (Wood 2006). As mentioned earlier, Australia was the very first country to produce a children's book on donor insemination, aimed at the children of heterosexual parents and published in 1988. It would take until 2012 for an Australian lesbian to write the very first children's book on sperm donation and lesbian families.

That book was called *Under a Rainbow*, self-published by Zera Walpole (2012). The story, told in rhyme, tells the story of two women who loved each other and wanted to start a family with a known donor:

> Mummy and Mum lived together at home
> Where they loved and they laughed and they sang and they hoped
> That one day their small family could be
> A family that had a small baby… or three!
> But a baby is made by a sperm and an egg
> And Mummy and Mum had no sperm it was said.
> So they searched for that special man who
> Could offer them sperm and be a great Daddy too!
> They looked near and far. They searched high and low
> For that one special man who their baby would know
> And just when they thought it couldn't be done
> our Daddy said, 'Hey, I think I'm the one!' (2012, 2–7)

According to Walpole (Walpole, personal communication, 8 December 2019), this is indeed an autobiographical account of her and her partner's journey to parenthood with a known donor.

The final book from Australia written by a lesbian mother was also self-published and came out in 2018. Called *One in Many Millions*, written by Rebecca J. Miles, it is the first to describe the process of IVF for lesbians in Australia. The author uses straightforward language to explain the process of artificial insemination, conception and IVF to her son, and to support other 'rainbow families' in having these conversations (Miles 2018, 1). The book is narrated by a child who begins the book with the question of where he came from. It then goes on to discuss the requisite sperm and eggs necessary for baby-making. When his mums explain to him that sperm come from men, the little boy is well aware that there are no men in his family. He tells his mums, 'We have a problem … Well, we don't exactly have a man in this family' (2018, 11–12). Then his mums go on to explain to him about fertility doctors and donors. Although the text does not use the word donor, there is an illustration on the next page of a man holding a jar of sperm with the word 'donor' labelled on the jar. His mums then describe the process of IVF in simple language with an accompanying illustration of sperm and eggs lounging in a petri dish as if in a jacuzzi. On the second to last page, the little boy asks, 'Where did I grow?' (2018, 21) to which his mothers tell him, 'You grew in Mama's uterus' (2018, 22). And, acknowledging the other mother's role in bringing him into the world, she continues, 'And Mum took excellent care of both of us while you were growing' (2018, 22).

United States

Sperm donation for lesbian women has always been legal in the United States, although early on, there were few American doctors who were willing to give lesbians access to clinical medical assistance (Esterberg 2010). However, lesbians resorted to their own methods of insemination with fresh sperm from both known and unknown donors (Agigian 2004; Esterberg 2010). In 1982, the Sperm Bank of Northern California became the first committed to specifically offering donor insemination services to lesbians and single women, and since that year, lesbians have had full access to clinical medical assistance with donor sperm in the United States (Esterberg 2010; Mundy 2008). Although the *Before You Were Born* series, as mentioned already, was published in 2004, it was not until 2012 that the first book appeared in the United States written by a lesbian mother on sperm donation for her children – *Special Man*. This self-published title, by Yevgeniya Kanterezhi, is dedicated to her sperm donor. She writes on the Acknowledgements page, 'I dedicate this book to a very special man, our sperm donor. He gave my wife and I the most precious gift of life. That gift provided us the opportunity to have our children' (Kanterezhi 2012, n.p.). Kanterezhi tells the autobiographical story of how her family came to be. It begins, like many of the books, by introducing two women who loved each other very much and wanted a baby. It then continues:

> So, one day they went to a doctor and asked for his help. The doctor gave them a special seed and planted it in Jeannie's belly. The seed was given to the doctor by a very special man. This man wanted to give women a chance to have their own babies. (2012, 1–5)

The concept of a 'nice', 'kind', 'generous', or in this case 'special' man is found in nearly all of the books. This is notable in that it dovetails with studies of how lesbians relate to their donor, especially their anonymous donors (Malmquist 2016; Vanfraussen et al. 2001; Wyverkens et al. 2014). In one study, Vanfraussen et al. found, out of 45 lesbian mothers, that two of them 'regretted not being able to thank the donor for his help' (2001, 2022). Kanterezhi found one way to do it – by writing a book for her children and letting them know that it was due to the 'special man' that she and her wife were able to have their children.

The next two books to be published in the United States by lesbian mothers came in 2014. The first one, *Zak's Safari: A Story about Donor-Conceived Kids of Two-Mom Families* by Christy Tyner, received quite a bit of attention on the Internet while still a crowdfunding campaign on Kickstarter. It also ended up winning the attention of the American Library Association by way of the Rainbow Project Booklist, quite an achievement for a self-published book (GLBTRT 2016). *Zak* is narrated by the child, Zak, who shares his depth of knowledge about how he was conceived. Following the common theme of two women who love each other very much, Zak tells his readers, 'Once upon a time my parents met, fell in love, and wanted *more than anything* to have a baby. So they decided to make one' (Tyner 2014, 10–11, italics original). Zak, who is taking his readers on a 'safari', then goes on to discuss the mechanics of baby-making:

> Now, as you super smart tourists may already know, there are two things you need to make a baby. Can anyone tell me what these are? That's right: an egg and a sperm! Most women's bodies make eggs and most men's bodies make sperm. (2014, 12–13)

He goes on to talk about the different kinds of families that there are, as well as where the sperm comes from when there are no men in the house.

> My moms got their sperm from a **sperm bank**. A sperm bank keeps the sperm until a family is ready to make a baby. There are a lot of really wonderful men who give their sperm to the sperm bank to help families make babies. We call these men donors. I have a donor! (2014, 16, emphasis original)

Zak then tells his readers how his parents used a catalogue in order to pick out the sperm they would use in order to have their baby:

> There were lots of donors for my parents to choose from. (2014, 17)
>
> I know my parents chose an awesome donor, 'cause I'm pretty sure I got some of his awesome genes. (2014, 20)

Before the book ends with Zak's birth, he describes what life is like with his two moms. 'My parents tell me that when I was born the adventure truly began. And it hasn't stopped since' (2014, 30).

The second book was *It Takes Love (And Some Other Stuff) to Make a Baby* by L. L. Bird, a lesbian mother and family physician. Although *Zak* received quite a bit of attention by way of multiple articles (for example, Leventry 2015; Rudolph 2014), *It Takes Love* shared a very similar storyline but did not receive the same publicity. Unlike *Zak*, which is narrated by the donor-conceived child, *It Takes Love* is narrated by one of the moms, who provides a gentle but detailed explanation to their child of how they came to be:

> Your mommies wanted to be parents, but they had one big problem: Their bodies only make eggs. To make a baby, they had to get sperm. They had to find a sperm donor. A donor is a person who likes to help other people by giving things they need. A sperm donor is a man who helps parents make their baby when they only have eggs. Sometimes parents know the sperm donor. He might be a friend or an uncle who gives them some of his sperm. Sometimes parents get sperm from a sperm bank. Now, this is not a bank where you take money out. It's a place that keeps donors' sperm until parents need it to have children. First, your mommies picked the sperm that was right for your family. Then, they decided who would grow you. The sperm was put inside her body so that it could join with the egg. Sometimes a doctor will help the parents with this part, and sometimes parents do it on their own. (Bird 2014, 11–16)

Another book by a lesbian mother on sperm donation in lesbian families had recently been published at the time of writing in 2019. That book is *The Little Embryo That Could: An Introduction to IVF for Children* by Megan Pounders. Pounders' book is a thorough and detailed description of what she and her wife went through in order to have their son via in vitro fertilization (IVF), and was written expressly to explain this process to him.

The author introduces the concept of the baby doctor who was needed in order to help them make a baby:

> You see, we knew we would need help to get you into Mama's tummy. So we found the best baby doctor in our town and went to see him. (Pounders 2019, 6)

She then goes on to describe all the testing done and medicines used in order to prepare the body for IVF:

> Mama had to have a lot of tests done to see if her body was in the right shape to have a baby.
>
> This meant a lot of shots and medicine for Mama but this was okay because you were worth it. (2019, 8)

As in the other books in this chapter, the author tells her son that they needed a donor as well to help them have a baby. However, she does not initially introduce the word 'sperm', instead calling it a 'part':

> The first thing we had to do was find a donor to help us. You see, to have a baby you need parts from a man and a woman.
>
> The doctor told us where to start, so we started looking through pictures and profiles to find the perfect fit for our family.
>
> After looking for a while, we found your donor. (2019, 10)

Four pages later, she introduces the words 'sperm' and 'eggs', though without explaining them:

> Inside the lab, the eggs were put with the donor's sperm.
>
> Next, we waited 5 days to see if the egg and the sperm would come together. (2019, 14)

After the embryo developed and was placed inside Mama's tummy, Pounders describes the need for both mommies to stay busy during the two-week wait to see if she would become pregnant. After that, she describes the regular ultrasounds and the nine months of anticipation to finally meet their son. Pounders' story is different from *Special Man*, *Zak* and *It Takes Love*, in that it is the only one from the United States that describes the IVF process, the five-day wait for the embryo to develop in the lab, the two-week wait to find out if they have become pregnant, the shots, the medicines, the laboratory and the blood work. However, except for the title, the word 'IVF' is never once used in the text although several big words are introduced, such as 'donor', 'sperm', 'eggs', 'pregnant', 'ultrasound' and 'embryo'. In contrast to the other books discussed, it focuses less on the concept of sperm donation and more on the process of IVF. It also differs from many of the others in that it does not begin with the theme of two women falling in love; rather, it focuses entirely on the baby-making process.

Conclusion

In a study of interview data of 37 lesbian couples who had formed or were forming their families with sperm donation, Ripper (2009) found that lesbian mothers, in having to disclose donor conception to their children, thought it to be a 'benefit because it meant that heterosexual reproduction and families were not taken for granted as normal or inevitable' (2009, 90). They also emphasized 'that their children would always have the benefit of knowing that they were really wanted and loved' (2009, 90), as has been portrayed in the books discussed here.

In a study of donor-conceived children with lesbian parents, 41 children aged between seven and 17 were asked about their concept of the donor. They found:

> All the children (n = 41; 100%) told a story in line with their age that made clear that they were well informed. They all mentioned the intervention of a hospital or a sperm bank and the fact that seeds were brought into the biological mother's belly. With respect to their donor concept, the majority of children (n = 26; 63%) only talked about 'seeds.' Eight children (20%) used the term 'unknown father' in their account. Of the latter group, the majority explained that he was only their father in a biological sense since he had never taken care of them. The remaining seven children (17%) talked about 'a donor' or an 'unknown man'. When we asked these children some questions about the structure of their family unit, all the children (n = 41; 100%) said they had two mothers. None of the children mentioned the donor as a family member. Many children also reported that their social mother and not the donor had taken care of them since birth. The donor had only fulfilled a biological task, not a nurturing one. (Vanfraussen et al. 2001, 2021)

Unquestionably, this is the case in the majority of the children's books examined in this chapter. The donor is generally depicted as a 'nice' or 'kind' man, but not as part of the families' lives. *Malin* and *Under a Rainbow* are exceptions to this, in that a known donor is used with whom the child then has an ongoing relationship.

The books vary slightly in the specifics, but many share the themes of: two women in love who want to start a family and need a sperm donor; sperm being 'seeds'; and feeling grateful towards the donor. The lesbian mothers did not have a guidebook to help them share their child's donor conception origins with them so they have had to produce their own. Although arguably there are as many donor origin stories in lesbian families as there are lesbian families with children conceived this way, the currently available books are very similar, which suggests a need for more works.

Children's books designed to help children understand their sperm donor origins were for all intents and purposes not commonplace before 2008, when only four books existed. After 2008, there was an explosion, relatively speaking, of stories published for children in lesbian families who were donor-conceived. In fact, every year from 2008 on, a book or books were published about lesbian mothers who built their families via sperm donation (Sarles 2019a).

The creators of these books, lesbian mothers who were looking for ways to share their children's birth stories, have several things in common. Clearly not prominent writers of children's literature, they nonetheless were compelled to write for their children. The books presented here all provide 'scripts' for lesbian mothers to use with their donor-conceived children, something that is otherwise largely lacking in the current societal context (Van Parys et al. 2015). Whether or not they provide varied or the *right* scripts is another area for investigation. Indeed, there is far more to explore about this topic in future research: for example, a comparative discourse analysis of books created by lesbian mothers versus books on the same topic by mental health professionals in the field of reproductive medicine, as well as how the discourse changes when the story is about a known versus an unknown donor. The steady pace of publication since 2008 holds a promise of even more books to explore in the future.

Acknowledgements

I am grateful to several people who provided additional resources for me to probe that in the end made this chapter more comprehensive. Dr Martha E. Thompson sent me the Amy Blumenthal article. Thanks also go to Dr B. J. Epstein for photocopying and mailing to me *Malins mamma gifter sig med Lisa* all the way from England, to Tin Eriksson from Sweden who found for me a copy of the long out-of-print *Malins mamma gifter sig med Lisa*, my friend, Luz García Goberna, who sent me books from Spain, and my friend Joan Lagache in France for help with French translations. Lastly, if it were not for social worker Patricia Mendell introducing me to children's books on this topic back in 2003, I would not have discovered such a rich niche area to explore.

Bibliography

Abate, Michelle Ann, and Kenneth B. Kidd. 2011. *Over the Rainbow: Queer Children's and Young Adult Literature*. Ann Arbor: University of Michigan Press.

Agigian, Amy. 2004. *Baby Steps: How Lesbian Alternative Insemination is Changing the World*. Middletown, CT: Wesleyan University Press.

Alfonso, Débora. 2018. *Dos mamás: un cuento para todas las familias (Two Mums: A Story for All Families)*. Madrid: Libros.com.

American Society for Reproductive Medicine. 2004. 'Informing Offspring Of Their Conception By Gamete Donation'. *Fertility and Sterility* 82, Suppl. 1: 212–16.

Andersson, Maria. 2015. 'Från stork till spermabank. Sexualupplysningslitteratur för barn 1965–2014'. *Samlaren: tidskrift för svensk litteraturvetenskaplig forskning* 136, pp. 5–37.

Anonymous. 2013. 'Il libro numero uno'. *Lo Stampatello*, 29 November. http://lostampatello.blogspot.com/2013/11/il-libro-numero-uno.html

Atelier 9 ¾. 2020. 'Über uns'. Darmstadt: Atelier 9 ¾. Accessed 1 August 2020. https://atelier-neundreiviertel.de/ka-schmitz-cai-schmitz-weicht/

Barnsley, Nina, and Stephanie Clarkson. 2018. *Our Story: How We Became a Family*. Nottingham: Donor Conception Network.

Baxter, Nicola, and Donor Conception Network. 2002. *Our Story (Sperm Donation for Lesbian Couples)*. Nottingham: Donor Conception Network.

Becker, Gay. 2002. 'Deciding Whether to Tell Children About Donor Insemination: An Unresolved Question in the United States'. *Infertility Around the Globe: New Thinking on Childlessness, Gender, and Reproductive Technologies*, edited by Marcia C. Inhorn and Frank van Balen, 119–33. Berkeley: University of California Press.

Beeson, Diane R., Patricia K. Jennings, and Wendy Kramer. 2011. 'Offspring Searching for their Sperm Donors: How Family Type Shapes the Process'. *Human Reproduction* 26, no. 9: 2415–24.

Bird, L. L. 2014. *It Takes Love (And Some Other Stuff) To Make a Baby*. Illustrated by Patrick Girouard. Richmond, CA: Catadon Press.

Birenbaum-Carmeli, Daphna. 2019. Personal communication.

Bishop, Rudine Sims. 1990. 'Mirrors, Windows, and Sliding Glass Doors'. *Perspectives* 6, no. 3: ix-xi.

Bjerkli, Myriam H. 2020. Personal communication.

Blake, Lucy, Polly Casey, Jennifer Readings, Vasanti Jadva, and Susan Golombok. 2010. '"Daddy Ran Out Of Tadpoles": How Parents Tell Their Children That They Are Donor Conceived, And What Their 7-Year-Olds Understand'. *Human Reproduction* 25, no. 10: 2527–34.

Blumenthal, Amy. 1990. 'Scrambled Eggs and Seed Daddies: Conversations with My Son'. *EMPATHY: Gay and Lesbian Advocacy Research Project* 2, no. 2: 173–76.

Blyth, Eric. 1998. 'Donor Assisted Conception and Donor Offspring Rights to Genetic Origins Information'. *International Journal of Children's Rights* 6, no. 3: 237–53.

———. 1999. 'Secrets and Lies: Barriers to the Exchange of Genetic Origins Information Following Donor Assisted Conception'. *Adoption & Fostering* 23, no. 1: 49–58.

'British Doctors OK A.I.' 1979. *Lesbian Tide* 9, no. 1: 18.

Brower, Todd. 2009. "'It's Not Just Shopping, Urban Lofts, and the Lesbian Gay-by Boom: How Sexual Orientation Demographics Can Inform Family Courts'. *Journal of Gender, Social Policy, and the Law* 17, no. 1: 1–38.

Calhaz-Jorge, C., C. De Geyter, M. S. Kupka, C. Wyns, E. Mocanu, T. Motrenko, G. Scaravelli, J. Smeenk, S. Vidakovic, and V. Goossens. 2020. 'Survey on ART and IUI: Legislation, Regulation, Funding and Registries in European Countries: The European IVF-Monitoring Consortium (EIM) for the European Society of Human Reproduction and Embryology (ESHRE)'. *Human Reproduction Open* 2020, no. 1: 1–15.

Cart, Michael, and Christine A. Jenkins. 2006. *The Heart Has Its Reasons: Young Adult Literature with Gay/Lesbian/Queer Content, 1969–2004.* Lanham, MD: Scarecrow Press.

Cooke, Ian D. 1993. 'Secrecy, Openness, and DI in the UK'. *Politics and the Life Sciences: The Journal of the Association for Politics and the Life Sciences* 12, no. 2: 176–77.

Cummins, June. 2015. From Overlooked to Looking Over: Lesbians in Children's and Young Adult Literature. *Journal of Lesbian Studies* 19, no. 4: 401–5.

Daniels, Kenneth R., and Taylor, Karyn. 1993. 'Secrecy and Openness in Donor Insemination'. *Politics and the Life Sciences* 12, no. 2: 155–70.

Day, Francis Ann. 2000. *Lesbian and Gay Voices: An Annotated Bibliography and Guide to Literature for Children and Young Adults.* Westport, CT: Greenwood Press.

DePalma, Renée. 2016. 'Gay Penguins, Sissy Ducklings … and Beyond? Exploring Gender and Sexuality Diversity Through Children's Literature'. *Discourse: Studies in the Cultural Politics of Education* 37, no. 6: 828–45.

Dorr, Christina H., and Liz Deskins. 2018. *LGBTQAI+ Books for Children and Teens.* Chicago: ALA Editions.

Dunham, Alex. 2018. 'Spain's Lesbians and Single Women Get Free Fertility Treatment Back'. *The Local,* 9 July. https://www.thelocal.es/20180709/lesbians-and-single-women-in-spain-get-free-fertility-treatment-back

Ehrensaft, Diane. 2011. *Mommies, Daddies, Donors, Surrogates: Answering Tough Questions and Building Strong Families.* New York: Guilford Press.

Epstein, B. J. 2012a. 'The Nuclear Gay Family: Same-Sex Marriage in Children's Books'. *Gay & Lesbian Issues & Psychology Review* 8, no. 3: 142–52.

———. 2012b. 'We're Here, We're (Not?) Queer: GLBTQ Characters in Children's Books'. *Journal of GLBT Family Studies* 8, no. 3: 287–300.

———. 2013. *Are the Kids All Right? Representations of LGBTQ Characters in Children's and Young Adult Literature.* Bristol: HammerOn Press.

———. 2014. '"The Case of the Missing Bisexuals": Bisexuality in Books for Young Readers'. *Journal of Bisexuality* 14, no. 1: 110–25.

Erichsen, Vilde Mebust. 2015. 'Historien gjorde Wilma (5) trygg på hvem hun var'. *Moss Avis,* 22 February. https://www.moss-avis.no/kultur/moss/historien-gjorde-wilma-5-trygg-pa-hvem-hun-var/s/5-67-44141

Ernemar, Lisa. 2017. 'Låt oss tala om Storken!: En komparativ studie av gestaltandet av icke-normativ reproduktion i 10 queera bilderböcker utgivna i Sverige 1999-2015'. Undergraduate dissertation, Uppsala University. https://www.diva-portal.org/smash/get/diva2:1106648/FULLTEXT01.pdf

Esterberg, Kristin G. 2010. 'Artificial Insemination'. In *Encyclopedia of Motherhood*, edited by Andrea O'Reilly, 82–85. Thousand Oaks, CA: Sage Publications.

FamART. n.d. 'Who is FamART?' Mörfelden: FamART. Accessed 9 August 2020. https://www.famart.de/en/who-is-famart/

Ferrero, Clara. 2017. 'Dos mamás', el cuento que explica a los niños por qué es normal tener padres del mismo sexo'. *El País*, 2 November. https://smoda.elpais.com/placeres/dos-mamas-cuento-nuevos-modelos-familia-homoparental/

Flórez, Antonio. 2013. 'Una nueva editorial en Rivas propone los cuentos como "herramientas para abordar situaciones complejas"'. *Rivas Actual*, 30 March. https://www.rivasactual.com/una-nueva-editorial-en-rivas-propone-los-cuentos-como-herramientas-para-abordar-situaciones-complejas/

Gates, Larry J. 2013. 'LGBT Parenting in the United States'. Los Angeles: The Williams Institute. https://williamsinstitute.law.ucla.edu/publications/lgbt-parenting-us/

GLBTRT. 2016. '2016 Rainbow Book List'. https://glbtrt.ala.org/rainbowbooks/archives/1207

Goldman, Ronald, and Juliette D. G. Goldman. 1982. 'How Children Perceive the Origin of Babies and the Roles of Mothers and Fathers in Procreation: A Cross-National Study'. Child Development 53, no. 2: 491–504.

Green, Lisa Katherine. 2006. 'Unconventional Conceptions: Family Planning in Lesbian-Headed Families Created by Donor Insemination'. PhD thesis, Universität Basel. https://kops.uni-konstanz.de/bitstream/handle/123456789/11856/Green_Lisa_diss.pdf

Grimes, Janice. 2004. *Before You Were Born: Our Wish for a Baby*. Illustrated by Mary Moye-Rowley. Webster, Iowa: X, Y, and Me.

Halvorsen, Lone, and Maria Therese Olsen. 2015. *Wilma har to mammaer* (Wilma Has Two Mothers). Larvik, Norway: LIV Forlag.

Hargreaves, Katrina, and Ken Daniels, Ken. 2007. 'Parents' Dilemmas in Sharing Donor Insemination Conception Stories with their Children'. *Children & Society* 21, no. 6: 420–31.

Helms, Franziska. 2018. 'Making Babies Without Blokes: How Berlin Women Are Doing It'. *Exberliner*, 28 March. https://www.exberliner.com/features/zeitgeist/making-babies-without-blokes-how-berlin-women-are-doing-it/

Hollekim, Ragnhild, Hilde Slaatten, and Norman Anderssen. 2012. 'A Nationwide Study of Norwegian Beliefs About Same-Sex Marriage and Lesbian and Gay Parenthood'. *Sexuality Research and Social Policy* 9, no. 1: 15–30.

Hunter, Myra, Salter-Ling, Natasha and Glover, Lesley. 2000. 'Donor Insemination: Telling Children about Their Origins'. *Child Psychology and Psychiatry Review 5*, no. 4: 157–163.

Jannic-Cherbonnel, Fabien. 2018. '3 questions à Céline Lhuillier, auteure d'un livre qui raconte la PMA aux enfants'. *Komitid*, 1 October. https://www.komitid.fr/2018/10/01/3-questions-a-celine-lhuillier-auteure-dun-livre-qui-raconte-la-pma-aux-enfants/

Jenkins, Christine A. and Michael Cart. 2018. *Representing the Rainbow in Young Adult Literature: LGBTQ+ Content Since 1969*. Lanham, MD: Rowman & Littlefield.

Jiménez, Laura M. 2015. 'Representations in Award-Winning LGBTQ Young Adult Literature from 2000–2013'. *Journal of Lesbian Studies* 19, no. 4: 406–22.

Jociles Rubio, Maria Isabel. 2018. Personal communication.

Kanterezhi, Yevgeniya. 2012. *Special Man*. Toms River, NJ: CreateSpace Independent Publishing Platform.

Kaplan, Isabel. *2019*. 'France Debates Single Women's and Lesbians' Access to IVF'. *The Nation*, 28 November. https://www.thenation.com/article/archive/france-ivf/

Kirkman, Maggie. 2003. 'Parents' Contributions to the Narrative Identity of Offspring of Donor-Assisted Conception'. *Social Science & Medicine* 57, no. 11: 2229–42.

Les Graines Magiques. n.d. 'Pourquoi ce livre?' Accessed 1 August 2020. http://lesgrainesmagiques.fr/about-us/

Lester, Jasmine Z. 2014. 'Homonormativity in Children's Literature: An Intersectional Analysis of Queer-Themed Picture Books'. *Journal of LGBT Youth* 11, no. 3: 244–75.

Leventry, Amber. 2015. 'Zak's Safari: A Children's Book About Donor-Conceived Kids and Two-Mom Families'. *The Next Family*, 12 January. https://thenextfamily.com/2015/01/a-review-on-a-book-for-lesbian-mom-families-with-donor-conceived-children/

Lhuillier, Céline. 2018. *Les graines magiques* (The Magic Seeds). Nancy, France: Independently published.

López Navarro, Paula. 2017. *¿Cómo es posible que tengan dos mamás?* (How is it Possible for Them to Have Two Mums?) Spain: Independently published.

Lo Stampatello. n.d. 'Chi siamo'. Milano: Lo Stampatello. Accessed 1 August 2020. http://lostampatello.it/chi/

Luelmo, Violeta Morales. 2013. *Tenemos dos mamás* (We Have Two Mothers). Madrid: Editorial Crececuentos.

Lundborg, Annette, and Mimmi Tollerup-Grkovic. 1999. *Malins mamma gifter sig med Lisa* (Malin's Mother Marries Lisa). Illustrated by Mimmi Tollerup-Grkovic. Stockholm, Sweden: Eriksson & Lindgren.

Malmquist, Anna, Anna Polski, and Karin Zetterqvist Nelson. 2016. 'No One of Importance: Lesbian Mothers' Constructions of Permanently Anonymous Sperm Donors'. In *Doing Good Parenthood: Ideals and Practices of Parental Involvement*, edited by Anna Sparrman, Allan Westerling, Judith Lind, and Karen Ida Dannesboe, 29–40. Cham: Springer International Publishing.

Mantell, Rowan. 2017. 'Made With Love, Our IVF Baby'. *Ipswich Star*, 23 March. https://www.ipswichstar.co.uk/news/made-with-love-our-ivf-baby-1-4944104

McGlashan, Mark, and Jane Sunderland. 2010. 'The Language of Children's Stories Featuring Two-Mum and Two-Dad Families'. In *Proceedings of the 6th Biennial International Gender and Language Association Conference: IGALA 6, Tokyo, 18–20 September 2010*, 225–49. Tokyo: Tsuda College.

Mendell, Patricia, and Patricia Sarles. 2010a 'Who Am I Really? Donor Offspring Characters in Young Adult Fiction'. *Voice of Youth Advocates* 32, no. 6: 460–61.

———. 2010b. '"Where Did I Really Come From?" Assisted Reproductive Technology in Self-Published Children's Picture Books'. *Children & Libraries: The Journal of the Association for Library Service to Children* 8, no. 2: 18–29.

Miles, Rebecca-Jayne. 2018. *One in Many Millions*. Illustrated by Anil Tortop. Boondall: Tadaa Book.

Miller, Jennifer. 2019. 'For the Little Queers: Imagining Queerness in "New" Queer Children's Literature'. *Journal of Homosexuality* 66, no. 12: 1645–70.

Mitchell, Valory. 1998. 'The Birds, the Bees… and the Sperm Banks: How Lesbian Mothers Talk With Their Children About Sex and Reproduction'. *American Journal of Orthopsychiatry* 68, no. 3: 400–409.

Montuschi, Olivia. 2018. Personal communication.

Moore, Lisa Jean. 2003. 'Billy, the Sad Sperm with No Tail: Representations of Sperm in Children's Books'. *Sexualities* 6, no. 3–4: 277–300.

———. 2007. *Sperm Counts: Overcome by Man's Most Precious Fluid*. New York: New York University Press.

Mundy, Liza. 2008. *Everything Conceivable: How the Science of Assisted Reproduction is Changing Our World*. New York: Anchor.

Naidoo, Jamie Campbell. 2012. *Rainbow Family Collections: Selecting and Using Children's Books with Lesbian, Gay, Bisexual, Transgender, and Queer Content*. Santa Barbara, CA: Libraries Unlimited.

Nelson, Margaret K. 2020. 'The Presentation of Donor Conception in Young Adult Fiction'. *Journal of Family Issues* 41, no. 1: 33–61.

Neumann-May, Bianca. 2017. *Blib, Blob, and Blub*. Harleston, UK: Independently published.
———. 2019. Personal communication.

Newman, Lesléa. 1989. *Heather Has Two Mommies*. Illustrated by Diana Souza. Boston, MA: Alyson Publications.
———. 1997. 'Heather and Her Critics'. *The Horn Book Magazine* 73, no. 2: 149–54.
———. 2014. Personal communication.
———. 2020. Personal communication.

N. S. W. Infertility Social Workers Group. 1988. *How I Began: The Story of Donor Insemination*. Carlton, Vic: Fertility Society of Australia.

Pardi, Francesca. 2012. *Perché hai due mamme?* (Why Do You Have Two Mummies?) Milano: Lo Stampatello.
———. 2014. Personal communication.

Patterson, Charlotte J. 1995. 'Families of the Lesbian Baby Boom: Parents' Division of Labor and Children's Adjustment'. *Developmental Psychology* 31, no. 1: 115–23.

Pinter, Bojana, Miguel Oliveira da Silva, Kitty Bloemenkamp, Inês Fronteira, and Helle Karro. n.d. *Assisted Reproductive Technologies in European Union: Findings of the Reproductive Health Report*. https://webgate.ec.europa.eu/chafea_pdb/assets/files/pdb/2007110/2007110_d12-01_en_ps.pdf

Pounders, Megan. 2019. *The Little Embryo That Could: An Introduction to IVF for Children*. Lexington, KY: Independently published.

Ravitsky, Vardit. 2012. 'Conceived and Deceived: The Medical Interests of Donor-Conceived Individuals'. *Hastings Center Report* 42, no. 1: 17–22.

Reuveny Bar David, Lee. 2015. לב אמא, בטן אמא (*Ima beten, ima lev* / Belly Mommy, Heart Mommy). Tel Aviv: Yuval Publishing.

Richardson, Justin, and Mark A. Schuster. 2004. *Everything You Never Wanted Your Kids to Know About Sex (But Were Afraid They'd Ask): The Secrets to Surviving Your Child's Sexual Development from Birth to the Teens*. New York: Random House Inc.

Ripper, Margie. 2009. 'Lesbian Parenting Through Donor Insemination: Implications for the Hetero-Normative Family'. *Gay & Lesbian Issues & Psychology Review* 5, no. 2: 81–95.

Rivers, Daniel Winunwe. 2013. *Radical Relations: Lesbian Mothers, Gay Fathers, and Their Children in the United States since World War II*. Chapel Hill: University of North Carolina Press.

Rodríguez García, Isabel Carmen. 2008. *Y nosotros—¿de dónde venimos?* (And Us – Where Do We Come From?) Illustrated by M. Luisa Guerrero. Alicante: ONG por la No Discriminación.
———. n.d. *No title*. http://www.trabajemosporelmundo.org/ong-nd/isabel_rodriguez.html

Rudolph, Dana B. 2014. 'New Picture Book for Donor-Conceived Kids of Two Moms'. *Mombian*, 5 November. https://www.mombian.com/2014/11/05/new-picture-book-donor-conceived-kids-two-moms/

Rumball, Anna, and Vivienne Adair. 1999. 'Telling the Story: Parents' Scripts for Donor Offspring'. *Human Reproduction* 14, no. 5: 1392–99.

Sarles, Patricia Ann. 2019a. *Assisted Reproductive Technology: Books for Children*. Accessed 24 August 2019. http://booksfordonoroffspring.blogspot.com
———. 2019b. *Donor Offspring: Books for Teenagers*. Accessed 24 August 2019. http://yabooksfordonoroffspring.blogspot.com

Schmitz-Weicht, Cai. 2015. *Maxime will ein Geschwister* (Maxime Wants a Sibling). Illustrated by Ka Schmitz. Darmstadt: Atelier 9¾.

Sciurba, Katie. 2017. 'Flowers, Dancing, Dresses, and Dolls: Picture Book Representations of Gender-Variant Males'. *Children's Literature in Education* 48, no. 3: 276–93.

Shaked, Merav. 2015. 'קמפיין עובשה: "לב אמא, בטן אמא"'. *Taasiya*, 2 August. https://www.taasiya.co.il/magazine/718.htm

Sifris, Adiva. 2014. 'Gay and Lesbian Parenting: The Legislative Response'. In *Families, Policy and the Law: Selected Essays on Contemporary Issues for Australia*, edited by Alan Hayes and Daryl

Higgins, 89–99. Melbourne: Australian Institute of Family Studies. https://aifs.gov.au/sites/default/files/publication-documents/fpl.pdf

Sizaret, Nathalie. 2017. *Pourquois tu as 2 mamans? (Why Do You Have 2 Mums?)* Illustrated by Daphné Dejay. Charenton-le-Pont: Le monde de Gritie.

Sjöström, Bodil. 1999. *Trollen på regnbågsbacken* (The Trolls of Rainbow Hill). Illustrated by Åsa Öhrn. Stockholm: Atlas.

Sunderland, Jane, and Mark McGlashan. 2012. 'The Linguistic, Visual and Multimodal Representation of Two-Mum and Two-Dad Families in Children's Picturebooks'. *Language and Literature* 21, no. 2: 189–210.

———. 2013. 'Looking at Picturebook Covers Multimodally: The Case of Two-Mum and Two-Dad Picturebooks'. *Visual Communication* 12, no. 4: 473–96.

Swanson, Kara W. 2012. 'The Birth of the Sperm Bank'. *Annals of Iowa* 71, no. 3: 241–76.

'Sweden to allow IVF for Lesbians'. 2005. *BBC News*, 3 March. http://news.bbc.co.uk/2/hi/europe/4315145.stm

Taylor, Nathan. 2012, 'U.S. Children's Picture Books and the Homonormative Subject'. *Journal of LGBT Youth* 9, no. 2: 136–52.

Thorn, Petra, and Lisa Green. 2009. *Die Geschichte unserer Familie: ein Buch für lesbische Familien mit Wunschkindern durch Samenspende (The Story of Our Family: A Book for Lesbian Families with Children Conceived by Donor Insemination)*. Illustrated by Tiziana Rinaldi. Mörfelden: FamART-Verlag.

———. 2013. *The Story of Our Family: A Book for Lesbian Families with Children Conceived by Donor Insemination.* Illustrated by Tiziana Rinaldi. Mörfelden, FamART.

Turner, Candace. 1993. 'A Call for Openness in Donor Insemination'. *Politics and the Life Sciences* 12, no. 2: 197–99.

Tyner, Christy. 2014. *Zak's Safari: A Story About Donor-Conceived Kids of Two-Mom Families.* Illustrated by Ciaee. New York: CreateSpace.

Van Parys, Hanna, V. Provoost, E. Wyverkens, P. De Sutter, G. Pennings, and A. Buysse. 2015. 'Family Communication About the Donor Conception: A Multi-Perspective Qualitative Study with Lesbian Parents and Their Children'. *Qualitative Health Research* 26, no. 14: 1998–2008.

Vanfraussen, Katrien, Ingrid Ponjaert-Kristoffersen, and Anne Brewaeys. 2001. 'An Attempt to Reconstruct Children's Donor Concept: a Comparison between Children's and Lesbian Parents' Attitudes Towards Donor Anonymity'. *Human Reproduction* 16, no. 9: 2019–25.

Wallis, Emma. 2018a. *How Mummy and Mama Made You: Conceived at Home.* Bognor Regis: Independently published.

———. 2018b. *How Mummy and Mama Made a Baby: IVF.* Bognor Regis: Independently published.

———. 2020. Personal communication.

Walpole, Zera. 2012. *Under a Rainbow.* Perth: Blurb.

———. 2019. Personal communication.

Wauters, Annelies. 2014. 'Een ethische analyse van kinderliteratuur over donorconceptie'. Master's dissertation, Ghent University, Belgium.

Wood, Miranda. 2006. 'Lesbians Flock North in Last Bid to Make Babies'. *The Sydney Morning Herald*, 28 May. https://www.smh.com.au/national/lesbians-flock-north-in-last-bid-to-make-babies-20060528-gdnmuz.html

Wyverkens, Elia, V. Provoost, A. Ravelingien, P. De Sutter, G. Pennings, and A. Buysse. 2014. 'Beyond Sperm Cells: A Qualitative Study on Constructed Meanings of the Sperm Donor in Lesbian Families'. *Human Reproduction* 29, no. 6: 1248–54.

Table 4: Lesbian-themed children's books that discuss sperm donation.

Year	Title	Author(s)	Country	Publisher	DI Allowed	Written by a lesbian mother	# of Libraries Owning it
1989	*Heather Has Two Mommies*	Lesléa Newman	USA	In Other Words Publishing (later purchased by Alyson Wonderland)	Yes	No	0
1999	*Malins mamma gifter sig med Lisa* (Malin's Mother Marries Lisa)	Annette Lundborg	Sweden	Eriksson & Lindgren	Yes (2005)	Yes	2
2002	*Our Story*	Nicola Baxter	UK	DC Network	Yes	No	10
2004	*Before You Were Born: Our Wish for a Baby: A Baby Conceived for Female Partners*	Janice Grimes	USA	X, Y, and Me	Yes	No	0
2008	*Y nosotros—¿de dónde venimos?* (And Us - Where Do We Come From?)	Isabel Carmen Rodríguez García	Spain	ONG por la No Discriminación	Yes	Yes	3
2009	*Die Geschichte unserer Familie: ein Buch für lesbische Familien mit Wunschkindern durch Samenspende (The Story of Our Family: A Book for Lesbian Families with Children Conceived by Donor Insemination)*	Petra Thorn; Lisa Green	Germany	FamART	Yes	Yes (Green)	4
2010	*Mom, Mama, and Me… and How I Came to Be!*	Tina Rella	USA	self-published	Yes	No	1
2010	*A Little Miracle*	Mireille van Seggelen	Netherlands	MVS Creations	Yes	No	1
2010	*A Very Special Baby (for Donor-conceived Children)*	Amanda MacLeod	New Zealand	self-published	Yes	No	5
2011	*Perchè hai due mamme?* (Why Do You Have Two Mummies?)	Francesca Pardi	Italy	Lo Stampatello	No	Yes	3

(continued)

Table 4: *(cont.)*

Year	Title	Author(s)	Country	Publisher	DI Allowed	Written by a lesbian mother	# of Libraries Owning it
2012	*Under a Rainbow*	Zera Walpole	Australia	self-published	Yes	Yes	0
2012	*Special Man*	Yevgeniya Kanterezhi	USA	self-published	Yes	Yes	1
2013	*Tenemos dos mamás* (We Have Two Mothers)	Violeta Morales Luelmo	Spain	Crececuentos (self-published)	Yes	Yes	2
2013	*Minhas mães e eu: a história Regina e Vanessa* (My Mothers and Me: Regina and Vanessa's Story)	Helena Prado Lopes	Brazil	self-published	Yes	No	0
2013	*The Story of Our Family: A Book for Lesbian Families with Children Conceived by Donor Insemination*	Petra Thorn; Lisa Green	Germany	FamART (self-published)		Yes (co-author, Green)	3
2013	*The Child in the Mamas' Hearts: A Story of Assisted Reproductive Technology Births for Families with Two Mothers*	Paul Janson	USA	self-published	Yes	No	1
2013	*Some People Have Two Mums*	Fabri Kramer; Luca Panzini	UK	self-published	Yes	No	2
2014	*Zak's Safari: A Story About Donor-Conceived Kids of Two-Mom Families*	Christy Tyner	USA	self-published	Yes	Yes	62
2014	*It Takes Love (And Some Other Stuff) To Make a Baby*	L. L. Bird	USA	Catadon Press (self-published)	Yes	Yes	3
2014	*The Pea That Was Me: A Two Moms' Sperm Donation Story*	Kimberly Kluger-Bell	USA	self-published	Yes	No	2
2014	*Nora y Zoe: dos mamás para un bebé* (Nora and Zoe: Two Mothers for a Baby)	Rosa Maestro	Spain	Masola.org (self-published)	Yes	No	2

2015	בל אמא ,וטב אמא (*Ima beten, ima lev* / Belly Mommy, Heart Mommy)	Lee Reuveny Bar David	Israel	Yuval Publishing	Yes	Yes	1
2015	*Mamá y mami sueñan con un bichito de luz (Mum and Mummy Dream About a Little Lightning Bug)*	Judit Franch	Spain	LiberumVox Books (self-published)	Yes	No	1
2015	*Maxime will ein Geschwister* (Maxime Wants a Sibling)	Cai Schmitz-Weicht	Germany	Atelier 9¾ (self-published)	No	Yes	5
2015	*Wilma har to mammaer* (Wilma Has Two Mothers)	Lone Halvorsen; Maria Therese Olsen	Norway	LIV Forlag	Yes (2009)	Yes	3
2016	*Family Stew: Two Moms Use a Sperm Donor to Build Their Family!*	Linda Stamm	USA	self-published	Yes	No	0
2016	*Mum and Mummy Dream About a Little Lightning Bug*	Judit Franch	Spain	Liberum Vox Bocks (self-published)	Yes	No	0
2017	*Pourquoi tu as 2 mamans? (Why Do You Have 2 Mums?)*	Nathalie Sizaret	France	Le Monde de Gritie (self-published)	Currently under review by the French senate	Yes	0
2017	*Blib, Blob, and Blub*	Bianca Neumann-May	UK	self-published	Yes	Yes	0
2017	*¿Cómo es Posible Que Tengan Dos Mamás?* (How is it Possible for Them to Have Two Mums?)	Paula López Navarro	Spain	self-published	Yes	Yes	0
2017	*Recettes de famille: ou comment Marou est né sans papa* (Family Recipes: Or How Marou Was Born Without a Daddy)	Aurélie Frisina	France	self-published	Currently under review by the French senate	No	1

(continued)

Table 4: *(cont.)*

Year	Title	Author(s)	Country	Publisher	DI Allowed	Written by a lesbian mother	# of Libraries Owning it
2018	*Tenemos 2 mamás: ¿de dónde venimos?* (We Have Two Mothers: Where Do We Come From?)	Olga Ibarra	Spain	La Locomotora Editorial	Yes	No	2
2018	*Mama + Mamusch: "Ich bin ein Herzenswunsch-Kind"* (Mum + Mummy: 'I Am a Longed-For Child')	Helene Düperthal; Lisa Hänsch	Germany	Lebensweichen-Verlag	Yes	No	7
2018	*How Mummy and Mama Made a Baby: IVF*	Emma Wallis	UK	self-published	Yes	Yes	0
2018	*How Mummy and Mama Made You: Conceived at Home*	Emma Wallis	UK	self-published	Yes	Yes	0
2018	*One in Many Millions*	Rebecca Jayne Miles	Australia	self-published	Yes	Yes	1
2018	*Zwei Mamas für Oscar: Wie aus einem Wunsch ein Wunder wird (The Yearnling: From Wish to Miracle)*	Susanne Scheerer	Germany	Ellermann	Yes	No	9
2018	*Our Story: How We Became a Family*	Nina Barnsley; Stephanie Clarkson	UK	DC Network	Yes	No	1
2018	*Les Graines Magiques* (The Magic Seeds)	Céline Lhuillier	France	self-published	Currently under review by the French senate	Yes	0
2018	*Dos Mamás: un cuento para todas las familias (Two Mums: A Story for All Families)*	Débora Alfonso	Spain	Libros.com (self-published)	Yes	Yes	0

2018	*Different Just Like Us*	Lexi Layton	USA	self-published	Yes	No (written from the donor child's perspective)	0
2019	*Hope & Rosie Have a Baby: The Gift of Family*	Iréné Celcer	USA	Graphite Press	Yes	No	0
2019	*Mummy and Mummy Want a Family*	Sandra Bateman	UK	National Fertility Society	Yes	No	0
2019	*The Yearnling: From Wish to Miracle*	Susanne Scheerer	Germany	Ellermann	Yes	No	0
2019	*Happy Together: A Two-Mom Sperm Donation Story*	Julie Marie	USA	self-published	Yes	No	0
2019	*You Were Made for Me: Mom Mom*	Sheri Sturniolo	USA	self-published	Yes	No	0
2019	*The Little Embryo That Could: An Introduction to IVF for Children*	Megan Pounders	USA	self-published	Yes	Yes	0

Chapter Nine

MORALS, SOCIETY AND DISTRIBUTION: LGBTQ+ LITERATURE FOR YOUNG READERS IN THE ARAB WORLD

Anonymous*

Introduction

As noted in the introduction to this book, we were disappointed but not surprised to discover that there were some countries or regions where we struggled to find scholars who were willing to write about LGBTQ+ literature for young readers. The Arab world, which of course is a large and very diverse area and cannot accurately be characterized or described as just one thing, is a region where we were unable to connect with an appropriate scholar who was willing and able to write a piece for us. Multiple academics who work on Arabic literature told us that there was no LGBTQ+ literature for children there, or that there only existed literature that could be read queerly by a knowing reader. Unfortunately, no one agreed to explore that perspective and write that analysis for us.

We did, however, find a scholar of Arabic-language children's literature who kindly provided us with some comments on the situation in their region, which we have lightly paraphrased and edited and are publishing anonymously here, at their request. We feel that it is helpful to try to understand why such literature apparently does not yet exist there, in order to consider whether this might change in the near future. This brief introduction to LGBTQ+ issues and books for children and young adults in the Arab world is a useful overview, and we can only hope that scholars, authors and publishers in the Arabic-speaking countries will feel able to produce, and eventually critique, more work for young readers in the very near future. Here is their paraphrased commentary, which we thank them for, even if we cannot give them credit as we would have liked, because they feel it is safer to remain anonymous.

Commentary

The Arab world is comprised of 22 countries with a population of more than 350 million people. The main language is Arabic and the main religion is Islam; culture and community

---

* The name of the author has been withheld by mutual agreement between the volume editors and the author.

play a major role in the region. The importance of being part of the community, following traditions and cherishing family bonds are some of the main traits that define Arabic society.

Lifestyles differ between countries; in some countries, society enforces more conservative roles and rules, such as that women are supposed to cover up, whereas in others, there are very few constraints that are enforced by the government. This reflects the diversity of the Arab world and the differences between countries depending on the government, religions, culture and location. Still, this diversity is less apparent when it comes to LGBTQ+ topics, which continue to be mostly considered to be inappropriate in Arabic-language books.

To analyse children's books, it is very important to look at the publishing industry, which plays a major role in providing printed material to the public. Publishers in the Arab states are mainly located in Lebanon and Egypt. Recently, the publishing industry has started to blossom in the United Arab Emirates and the Kingdom of Saudi Arabia too. Publishing is therefore influenced by the culture in the specific country where a given author and/or publisher is located.

One of the main problems that publishers in the Arab world face is distribution. There are very few channels through which to sell the books, and the publishers must ship their books to book fairs to sell directly to the public in the different countries. Lebanon, for example, is a very small market for Lebanese publishers, so they work on reaching other markets in the Arab world; many Lebanese publishers sell the majority of their books outside Lebanon, and thus must consider different cultures and conventions beyond their own country.

In the Arab states, many topics are still not discussed openly even though they might exist to a certain extent in a given society. Same-sex marriage, for example, is not legal, and many people do not approve of it (see, for example, Chalhoub 2018). Homosexuality is not accepted by most religions or societies in the region, even if some people do experience LGBTQ+ relationships, whether more or less secretly. This in turn means that it would not be seen as an appropriate topic for literature, especially literature for young readers.

I read about something that happened in 2017 at a school book fair in Beirut, when a girl in elementary school bought a children's book about a princess who decides to marry another princess. The mother of the child got furious and said that schools must filter (in other words, censor) the children's books that children buy.

In conclusion, children's books tend to reflect the lifestyles in the societies in which they are written, edited and published, and as long as these topics are not discussed, especially with children, they will not be included in children's books. The situation for Arabic-language literature is that homosexuality is not accepted in most parts of the region and is generally viewed as being against the primary religion of the Arab world, and therefore publishers would not take a chance on producing a book featuring it, given that they would need to distribute and sell the book in multiple countries and need to take consideration of a wide range of perspectives and morals.

Reference

Chalhoub, Samir. 2018. '#LoveWins, But Human Rights Are Under Attack in Lebanon'. *MiddleEastSight*, 11 October. https://www.middleeastsight.org/single-post/2018/10/11/Gay-marriage-in-Switzerland-causes-online-outrage-in-Lebanon

Chapter Ten

SAMENESS AND DIFFERENCE IN VISUAL REPRESENTATIONS OF SAME-SEX COUPLES IN INTERNATIONAL CHILDREN'S PICTURE BOOKS

Jamie Campbell Naidoo and Mercedes Zabawa

Introduction

Research indicates that it is important for all children to see representations of themselves and their families, as well as others from diverse cultures, in the books they encounter to better understand their sociocultural world and function successfully within a culturally pluralistic society (Botelho and Rudman 2009; Johnson et al. 2017). One way this occurs is through the illustrations in children's picture books. International picture books hold great potential to cross borders and reinforce the universality of experiences. Activist, scholar and librarian Jella Lepman (1969) advocated that international children's books could build bridges of understanding and break down psychosocial barriers created by larger politicized environments.

Unfortunately, children's literature around the globe has the propensity to highlight certain cultural groups over others, often depicting families and characters as heterosexual, ignoring lesbian, gay, bisexual, trans and queer (LGBTQ+) families and children. Within the growing body of queer-themed children's picture books, some titles are more successful than others at conveying a loving relationship between LGBTQ+ individuals and creating a safe space to explore queer themes (Epstein 2013; Naidoo 2012; Sunderland and McGlashan 2012).

Using semiotics and visual content analyses, this chapter critically examines illustrations within a selection of foreign-language children's picture books with queer themes to determine how LGBTQ+ families and characters are visually represented. Specifically, we focus on how same-sex couples (male-male or female-female)[1] are illustrated and note

1 All of the titles in our study were identified as having gay or lesbian couples using various publisher or recommended lists from around the world. However, since the focus of our research is on illustrations and not text within our picture book sample, we do not make assumptions as to the sexual orientation of characters. A character that appears gay or lesbian might also be bisexual or pansexual. At the same time, a character might present as male or female in an illustration, yet it is difficult to make assumptions about whether or not their gender identity aligns

any discernible differences or similarities across books from different countries. We also examine the overarching messages that children receive from the images in these books. The study provides insight into how books from specific countries depict physical contact between same-sex individuals and couples. While our sample of titles provides an opportunity to comparatively examine queer international children's books, it should be expressly understood that the low number of books prevents the study from being statistically generalizable to the larger body of this literature.

Previous Research

In 2011 and later in 2012, Jane Sunderland and Mark McGlashan published one of the first research studies in English critically examining how same-sex mums and same-sex dads were represented in the illustrations of English-language children's picture books. The researchers were interested in how gendered depictions of these couples compared to depictions of heterosexual couples in children's books. As part of the study of 24 English-language books, Sunderland and McGlashan focused on physical contact in linguistic descriptions in the text as well as visual depictions in the illustrations. As they point out, physical contact was selected as an identifier to study as a way to differentiate characters of the same sex that were friends from those in some type of romantic or sexual relationship (Sunderland and McGlashan 2012). In the follow-up study, which included an additional title as well as focusing on the multimodality of picture books, Sunderland and McGlashan noted that same-sex couples identified as male engaged in statistically more instances of romantic/sexual physical contact than same-sex female couples. At the time, they related this to the undersexualizing of lesbians versus gay men within general society. As we will discuss later, our research indicates the opposite, with more depictions of same-sex females engaged in romantic physical contact as compared to same-sex male couples.

In addition to Sunderland and McGlashan's research, a few other studies in English have critically examined a smaller subset of picture books, around 5–10 titles, with a focus on messages conveyed via both text and illustrations (Esposito 2009; Threlkeld 2014). Jamie Campbell Naidoo (2012), B. J. Epstein (2013) and Jasmine Lester (2014) all include a much larger examination of same-sex picture books within broader studies of LGBTQ+ children's books or young adult books with LGBTQ+ characters and themes. Both Naidoo and Epstein include titles from other countries and in other languages than English, but neither study expressly compares and contrasts only the visual aspects of

---

with their (apparent) sex. For the sake of discussing how children might infer a character's sex based upon their presentation, we will posit that if a character appears to have a male appearance then their sex is male and if a character has a female appearance then their sex is female. As such, we use the term *same-sex* to refer to these couples in general or *male-male* or *female-female* to capture specific representations in a particular title. No inferences will be made about sexual orientation (bisexual vs. pansexual vs. gay/lesbian).

same-sex picture books from different countries. This current study builds upon previous research in that it examines children's picture books published in multiple languages, rather than just English, and focuses exclusively on visual imagery in lieu of including linguistic elements from the narratives.

Book Sample

A total of 30 books comprised our study sample (see the booklist on pp. 323–25 of this volume for a list of these titles). Convenience sampling was used to identify representative titles, from a range of countries, that were part of a collection of over 300 international children's picture books acquired by the researchers for a concurrent project on LGBTQ+ foreign-language picture books. From this convenience sample of available picture books, two books were randomly selected from each country, when available. Some countries, such as Israel and the Philippines, are only represented by one title each. It was decided to keep books from these countries in our sample as we wanted to have as wide a range of countries represented as possible. Selected titles from the following countries were examined in this study: Argentina, Austria, Belgium, Brazil, Canada, the Czech Republic, Finland, France, Germany, Israel, Italy, the Netherlands, Peru, Philippines, Spain, Sweden, Switzerland, the United Kingdom and the United States.

A global phenomenon of LGBTQ+ children's books is the inclusion of queer penguins as the main characters. In these books, same-sex penguins, usually male, become gay icons and stand in for LGBTQ+ human characters in an attempt to make queer topics more palatable to educators, caregivers and other adults (DePalma 2016). For our sample, in instances where there was a title with a penguin character, that book was chosen in addition to other titles from a country to allow us to compare and contrast same-sex penguin depictions across countries. This resulted in a sample of five penguin books published in Austria, Germany, Spain, Sweden and the United States.

Methodology

Based on a coding sheet previously created by Jamie Naidoo (2012) and general questions about physical contact in children's same-sex picture books from Sunderland's study, we developed the 'Coding Sheet for Sameness & Difference in Visual Representations of LGBTQ Characters in International Children's Picture Books'. This tool (Figure 4) allowed us to conduct a visual content analysis of the illustrations in the books in our sample. When conducting a visual content analysis, the researcher identifies how many times something occurs in the illustrations throughout a book. The more often something occurs, the more salient it is to the theme of the book. By only focusing on the visual elements of the books, we were free to examine the depictions of physical contact among same-sex caregivers and children, nudity, racial diversity, and the presence of additional same-sex characters.

Figure 4: Coding Sheet for Sameness & Difference in Visual Representations of LGBTQ Characters in International Children's Picturebooks.

Title of Book:	**Publication Date:**	**Publisher:**			
Self Published: Yes No	**Country of Origin:**				
Book Characteristics: Please Circle ONE Answer					
1.	Are the main characters human or animals?	Human	Animal		
2.	If the characters are animals, are they penguins?	Yes	No	N/A	
3.	What is the language of the book?	Single Language What language:	Bilingual What languages:		

Characterization in Illustrations: Please Circle ONE Answer				
1. Is the main couple depicted two men or two women?	Two men	Two women		
2. Is another couple depicted? If yes, are they a straight couple or a LGBTQ couple?	Yes, straight	Yes, LGBTQ	No other couple	
3. Are any other LGBTQ characters depicted?	Yes	No	Unable to determine	
4. Does the main couple have a child or children together?	Yes, child	Yes, children	No child or children	
5. If the couple has a child or children, what is the child's/children's gender? (Circle all that apply)	Female	Male	Unable to determine/ Gender Fluid	No child
6. What is the race of the couple?	Both White	Both Non-white List if known:	Interracial List if known:	N/A (animal)
7. If the couple has a child or children, what is the race of the child or children?	White	Non-white List if known:	No child	N/A (animal)

8. Physical contact between partners:

a) How many pages with illustrations are in the story? *Note: Count illustrations spread over two pages as one page.*

b) In how many illustrations are the couple pictured together?

c) Of those illustrations, how many include physical contact between the couple?	Describe physical contact (tick number of times each occurs): Kissing Holding Hands Arms Around Hugging In Bed Sitting Together Other (list):

d) How many illustrations include both members of the couple and the child (if present in story)?	No child in story	
e) Of those illustrations, how many include physical contact between the couple with the child present?	No child in story	
9. If secondary couple is present, how many illustrations include physical contact?	Describe physical contact (tick number of times each occurs): Kissing Holding Hands Arms Around Hugging In Bed Sitting Together Other (list):	No other couple
10. Is there any nudity depicted in the illustrations?	Yes	No
11. Are there any LGBTQ symbols (i.e.: rainbow, pink triangle, equality sign) depicted in the illustrations?	Yes What symbol(s):	No

Concurrently, we employed semiotics to examine specific colour choices, placement of images and the use of internationally recognized LGBTQ+ symbols, such as rainbow flags or pink triangles. Semiotic analysis addresses the issue of how images create meaning (Leeuwen 2001; Stokes 2012). Specifically, 'how the producer of an image makes it *mean* something and how we, as readers get *meaning out*' (Stokes 2012, 71, emphasis in original). Within a book's illustration, there are two layers of meaning to be scrutinized: *denotation* – the characters or concept being depicted, and *connotation* – the ideals expressed in the visual representation (Leeuwen 2001). In our study, the first layer of meaning was the depiction of same-sex couples and their physical contact with each other, and the second layer of meaning consisted of what this representation of the physical contact (or lack thereof) symbolized. Analysing these two layers of meaning in the illustrations provided insight into the representational and symbolic messages associated with the physical contact between same-sex couples, and demonstrated the types of messages that children encounter from the books in our study. Semiotics is a much deeper method for examining an image than visual content analysis as it ascribes meaning to the way images are placed on the page such as the proximity between same-sex couples and the ways they touch (sexualized as in a kiss vs. non-sexualized such as sitting next to someone on a sofa).

After we conducted our visual content and semiotic analyses, we took the information from our coding sheets and entered them into a spreadsheet to identify trends, similarities and differences. We then used descriptive statistics to illustrate the most noteworthy findings, which we will discuss in the subsequent paragraphs.

General Similarities

While the books represented 19 different countries, some general similarities were observed in relation to character demographics, physical affection between characters and the presence of other couples or families.

Character demographics

Children's publishing in the Western world has been criticized for decades for its lack of racial diversity among characters depicted (see Centre for Literacy in Primary Education 2018; Horning 2014 for examples in the United Kingdom and United States, respectively). Based upon one of the authors' own study of children's picture books from around the world at the International Youth Library in Munich, Germany as well as examination of picture books at international book fairs, it seems the children's picture books in other countries also predominantly feature white characters in their illustrations (Naidoo, in press). Consistent with other studies of LGBTQ+ children's books (Epstein 2013; Lester 2014; Naidoo 2012; Sunderland 2011; Sunderland and McGlashan 2012; Threlkeld, 2014), most of the same-sex human couples in our sample were Caucasian and all appeared to be from at least middle-class homes. In 16 titles out of 24, or 66.7 per cent, both same-sex human characters presented as white. Of the remaining books, five titles featured interracial couples with one partner being white: the English-language UK book *Dad David, Baba Chris and Me* (Merchant 2010), the French title *Drôles de familles* (Funny Families) (Valente and Delrieu 2013), the Spanish-language Argentinian title *Anita y sus dos mamas* (Anita and her Two Moms) (Fernández 2013), the Belgian Dutch-language book *De mama's van Sterre* (The Mommies of Sterre) (Beuningen 2011) and the Portuguese-language Brazilian title *Meus dois pais* (My Two Fathers) (Carrasco 2010). Three books depicted non-white, same-race couples, specifically one African American couple in the English-language American book *Keesha's South African Adventure* (Clark, Bey-Clarke and Selyutina 2016), one Filipino couple in the Tagalog-language Filipino book *Ang Ikaklit sa aming hardin (Ikaklit in our Garden)* (Neri 2012), and one Latin American couple in the Spanish-language Peruvian book *Camila tiene dos mamas?* (Camila Has Two Moms?) (Ferrari and Avila 2015). For all children to see representations of their families in literature, greater intersectionality between race, class and sexual orientation is needed.[2]

In the United States, rainbow families (families with LGBTQ+ children and/or caregivers) are noticeably racially and ethnically diverse, with nearly 40 per cent of the caregivers and 50 per cent of the children identifying as non-white (Gates 2013). Although information is not readily available for other countries about the race or ethnicity of adults and children in rainbow families, considering that the majority of people in the world are not white[3] (United Nations 2016) and, as such, non-white caregivers presumably comprise many of the rainbow families in the world, it is appalling that global LGBTQ+ children's picture books do not capture this diversity.

---

2 The topic of intersectionality in LGBTQ+ children's picture books is explored at length by B. J. Epstein (2013) and by Jasmine Lester (2014).

3 This assertion is based on the United Nations Demographic and Social Statistics. In the 2016 Demographic Yearbook (United Nations 2016), the UN found that the majority of the world's population resides in Asia (60 per cent or 4.4 billion) and Africa (16 per cent or 1.2 billion). Based on the predominant racial and ethnic makeup of these continents, one can conclude that the majority of the world is non-white.

Another interesting characteristic of these books is that they did not feature any radical depictions of LGBTQ individuals. All same-sex characters were 'non-threatening' in their dress, overall appearance and mannerisms. In other words, the same-sex couples displayed characteristics that the heteronormative world deems acceptable. The one glaring exception to this is the Spanish children's book *Las bodas reales: Cuento para colorear* (The Royal Weddings: A Story to Colour) (Rossetti and Artajo 2005) where almost all characters were nude in most of the illustrations. We will discuss this book later in this chapter.

For the rest of the sample, male characters' physical appearances fell into socially prescribed heteronormative, hegemonic notions of how a male should dress and none appeared overtly effeminate. This is an important point to note as multiple studies demonstrate that when male characters in children's picture books are depicted in clothing that does not align with hegemonic views of masculinity there is the potential for controversy or, at the very least, avoidance on the part of educators and other 'caring' adults (Flanagan 2008; Herzog 2009; Naidoo 2012; Sciurba 2017). All books with female characters illustrated these individuals with at least one traditional depiction of femininity: long hair, feminine dress and/or makeup. The one book, *De mama's van Sterre* (The Mommies of Sterre) (Beuningen 2011) from Belgium, written in Dutch, that did depict a female-presenting character with a buzzed 'masculine style' hair cut still also showed her with lipstick and earrings. This depiction of non-threatening characters in same-sex relationships is consistent with other studies of homonormative behaviours in children's picture books (Bronski 1993; Epstein 2013; Esposito 2009; Lester 2014; Naidoo 2012).

Another noteworthy finding was the lack of senior LGBTQ+ individuals. Senior same-sex couples were only present in two titles: *Allan och Udo* (Allan and Udo) (Lindeberg and Bondestam 2001) from Finland, written in Swedish, and *Ils sont...* (They Are...) (Thériault and Ben 2017) from Canada, written in French. In both of the books, the older male-male couple does not have children. Of particular note in these titles is the physical contact between same-sex male characters (a topic we explore at length with relation to the overall sample in the next section). While both of these titles illustrated physical contact between the male-male couple, *Allan och Udo* (Allan and Udo) was the only book in our entire sample to feature a same-sex couple in bed together or with a hand on the other's bottom. The distinct sexualization of male characters in this book, which does not include child characters, flaunts gay behaviour in a way that is generally not permissible in children's books; we will explore this further later in this chapter (DePalma 2016; Epstein 2013; Esposito 2009; Lester 2014; Naidoo 2012). Arguably, most young readers will likely relate better to depictions of same-sex couples that have children. Yet it is certainly within the realm of possibility for children to have grandparents in same-sex relationships or to know elderly LGBTQ+ individuals, and books such as these two titles can provide potential windows into the lives of characters that might remind them of a friend or relative, while also reinforcing the longevity of same-sex relationships.

Physical affection

Displays of physical contact and affection are one of the predominant ways that an illustrator can depict that a same-sex couple in a children's book is romantically or sexually involved or, at the very least, shares more than a platonic friendship. In 14 out of 30 books (46.7 per cent), physical affection was shown between couples of the same sex. The most common types of visually depicted physical affection between the same-sex couples were holding hands and arms around each other. Only one book, *Wie heiraten eigentlich Trockennasenaffen* (How Do Dry-Nosed Monkeys Marry?) (Viogt and Gleich 2015) from Switzerland, written in German, depicted the main same-sex, in this case female, couple kissing. The amount of physical contact between same-sex couples without children present was also fairly consistent between depictions of male-male couples and female-female couples. Female-female couples were shown engaging in physical contact in 47.7 per cent of the illustrations of the couple whereas 36.1 per cent of the male-male couples were shown engaging in physical contact in illustrations of the couple. This is in direct contrast to previous research examining physical interactions between same-sex couples in children's picture books, which suggested that male same-sex couples engage in more visual displays of affection than female same-sex couples (Sunderland and McGlashan 2012). The depiction of physical affection did not vary significantly from one country to another. We also did not observe that physical contact was considerably less in one particular continent over the others: North America versus South America or Europe. Again, this might change through examination of additional titles from each country to create a statistically representative sample.

Illustrations of physical contact between the same-sex couples when children were present demonstrated interesting results. Twenty-eight books in the sample featured a couple with children; the three exceptions were the Finland-Swedish title *Allan och Udo* (Allan and Udo) (Lindeberg 2001), the French Canadian title *Ils sont…* (They Are…) (Thériault and Ben 2017), and the Spanish title *Las bodas reales: Cuento para colorear* (The Royal Weddings: A Story to Colour) (Rossetti and Artajo 2005). All 28 titles included illustrations of the same-sex couples with the children and 64.2 per cent of the books had visual representations of the couple with the children in at least 50 per cent of the illustrations. Yet the majority of the titles (17 of 28 titles or 60 per cent) depicted physical contact between the same-sex couples in less than 30 per cent of the illustrations when children were present. These findings suggest that while it is acceptable to have a male-male or female-female couple in the same illustration or two-page spread as children, it is not acceptable for them to demonstrate that they are in a relationship or have more than a platonic bond. This notion is in keeping with findings from other research on LGBTQ+ children's literature that suggest book creators shy away from depicting LGBTQ+ behaviours that threaten society's preconceived notion of acceptableness (Epstein 2013; Esposito 2009; Lester 2014; Naidoo 2012).

However, we did note that in 16 of the books, across countries, the physical contact between same-sex couples was often blocked in a significant number of the illustrations. In several titles, multiple images showed the same-sex couples standing with an object or person obscuring personal contact (i.e. box, child's head, baby, dog, etc.). For instance, the UK English-language book *The Tales of Zebedy-Do-Dah* (Crawford 2009) obscures the female-female couple's physical contact in multiple images with objects such as a dog or box. The cover of this book shows the couple holding a dog that strategically covers their arms, which would presumably be touching. In 14 (46.7 per cent) of the books, it is a child that blocks physical contact between the same-sex couple, such as in the Italian title *Più ricche di un re* (Richer Than a King) by Barbero (2011). This strategic illustrative device may have been employed by artists to appease the heteronormative expectations of adults (caregivers, educators, etc.), who might otherwise baulk at physical contact between same-sex couples. While almost all of the countries represented in our sample have progressive human rights standards for same-sex individuals (see ILGA 2017), they may also face challenges, as previously mentioned, if too much physical affection or threatening homonormative behaviour is depicted in materials for children.

Presence of other families

It was slightly more likely for the main LGBTQ+ couple to be the only couple depicted in the book than for there to be an additional couple as well. In 13 of the books, the same-sex couple was the only couple depicted; in 10 books the same-sex couple was accompanied by an opposite-sex couple; in two books the same-sex couple was accompanied by another same-sex couple; and in five books the same-sex couple was accompanied by both another same-sex couple and an opposite-sex couple. In all of these titles, if there was another couple depicted, that couple was generally present in three or fewer illustrations. This perpetuates the idea that LGBTQ+ couples exist in isolation, rather than with a supportive community of other LGBTQ+ couples (Esposito 2009; Naidoo 2012). Additionally, this sort of portrayal where the main pairing is the only – or only same-sex – couple can reinforce an 'othering' of LGBTQ individuals, emphasizing how the same-sex couple is different, rather than normalizing the relationship.

General Differences

Within the sample, we noted some general differences related to the presence of same-sex couples with their children, the depiction of male-male versus female-female couples and the identity of the child, and the appearance of LGBTQ+ symbols.

Illustrations of same-sex couples and children

In half the books, the illustrations that had same-sex couples also included their children at least 90 per cent of the time. Books with female-female couples tended to show the couple with the child much more often than books with male-male couples. Specifically, 10 of 13 books with only female-female couples included the child with the same-sex couple most (at least 90 per cent) of the time. Conversely, only five out of 16 books with only male-male couples included the child in illustrations of the couple most of the time. For these books, male-male couples were most often (10 of 16 books) depicted with their children less than 45 per cent of the time, skewing more to a depiction of the entire family less than 20 per cent of the time. This finding may be indicative of society's general stronger acceptance of lesbian couples as caregivers than gay couples. Part of this reasoning could be tied to previous harmful stereotypes that gay men are paedophiles and thus should not be around children (Epstein 2013; Naidoo 2012).[4] On the other hand, this finding could simply be a product of the authors of the books. Many of the authors were mothers writing books either specifically for their children or for children in LGBTQ+ families as a result of not being able to find queer picture books when their children were younger.

Identity of the same-sex couples' children

Because children's books with gay characters or male-male couples have historically been more likely to be the subject of news stories and book censorship challenges than children's books with lesbian characters or female-female couples, there is an incorrect belief that there are more LGBTQ+ children's picture books featuring male-male couples versus female-female couples (Lester 2014; Naidoo 2012). The sample demonstrated a fairly equal spread in terms of the gender of the couples themselves: 16 titles with male-male couples, one with both a male-male couple and a female-female couple and 13 with female-female couples. However, the gender and overall personality of the child was often undeterminable in the titles with male-male couples, with few visual identifiers (such as toys, varying facial expressions or details on clothing) to suggest a distinct identity. Out of the male-male couples depicted, three books had a girl; four had a boy; one had both; and six depicted children whose gender was undeterminable and who had little to suggest a distinct personality. Of the female-female couples featured, five books had a girl; four had a boy; three had both; and only one depicted children whose gender and distinct personality was undeterminable. This could be due to the stereotyped notion that women are more nurturing and maternal, and thus better equipped to care for a child. Readers may be more comfortable seeing women depicted in parental roles, so the children of female-female couples have more fully formed identities through the depiction of a discernible gender and visual identifiers to suggest a personality.[5] It is possible that, in order to help readers envision the idea of male-male couples as parents, the children of these couples are less likely to have distinct gender or personality identifiers. Another possibility is that since gay men are often associated with paedophiles in society, having a depiction of a gender-neutral child is meant to desexualize any association between the gay fathers and their children; therefore preventing any suggestion of paedophilia. Finally, a third option might be that the illustrator determined it was better to feature

4 The alarming stereotype that gay men are paedophiles has been perpetuated in children's picture books in the past. Richard Cohen's American picture book *Alfie's Home* (1993, Washington, DC: International Healing Foundation) is one glaring example where a child questions his sexual orientation after being molested by his uncle, who the book suggests is gay.

5 Note that the absence of a male or female gender is not used to determine if a child has a fully formed identity. A child could identify as a non-binary gender and have a fully formed personality as indicated by facial expressions, toys, visual details on clothing, and so on. However, in practice, in the instances where a gender was not discernible, the overall visual representation of the child was also fairly generic.

gender-neutral characters so child readers could more easily read themselves and their experiences into a character.

LGBTQ symbols

Only one of the books in our sample, *Camila tiene dos mamas?* (Camila Has Two Moms?) (Ferrari and Avila 2015), from Peru, written in Spanish, included LGBTQ+ symbols in the illustrations of the story. Two other titles, *Drôles de familles* (Funny Families) (Valente and Delrieu 2013) from France, written in French, and *Keesha's South African Adventure* (Clark, Bey-Clarke and Selyutina 2016) from the United States, written in English, had a rainbow symbol as part of the publisher's logo. *Camila tiene dos mamas?* depicted rainbow flags, an LGBTQ+ Pride parade, and an equality t-shirt on several pages within the illustrations. The majority of the images are encountered within the first few pages of the book as a way to further emphasize that the characters in the book include a female-female couple with a child who is very proud of who they are. Indeed, the cover of the book features one of the mothers wearing the equality t-shirt. We found it particularly interesting that more picture books did not include LGBTQ+ symbols. Is this absence a result of book creators trying to avoid their books being 'too gay', is it an oversight, was it thought that these symbols would be a visual stereotype of LGBTQ+ families, or was there some other reason? In the case of *Camila,* the symbols are non-obtrusive and can add an extra layer of meaning, especially for children who are themselves in rainbow families.

Noteworthy Trends

While we have noted some similarities and differences in the books above, this section highlights noteworthy or unusual trends in our sample, specifically related to gay penguins and to nudity.

Gay penguins

Gay penguins are the rule rather than the exception when it comes to depicting same-sex animal couples in children's books around the world. While there are same-sex giraffes, guinea pigs, birds, monkeys, kangaroos, bears and other animals in picture books published in Northern Europe, Spain, Canada, the United Kingdom and the United States, the penguin is the one animal that appears the most often and across countries (Naidoo, in press). This was true for our sample as well, which included animal books from Austria, Germany, Spain, Sweden and the United States. Out of all the books featuring same-sex animal couples examined for this study, all were same-sex male penguin couples except for one book with a same-sex male giraffe pairing. Three books were about real penguins in a zoo (two in a US zoo, one in a German zoo) and two were fictional accounts of gay penguins. When looking specifically at the two informational books about Tango the penguin in the Central Park Zoo in New York City – *Zwei Papas für Tango* (Two Papas for Tango) (Schreiber-Wicke 2006), from Germany, and *And Tango*

Makes Three (Richardson, Parnell and Cole 2005), from the United States, written in English – some interesting observations appear. The US book *And Tango…* includes more pictures of the gay penguin couple together versus the German book *Zwei Papas…* (75 per cent of all the illustrations vs. 62.5 per cent of all the illustrations), but overwhelmingly more pictures in the German book demonstrated physical contact between the male penguins when compared to the US book (50 per cent of all the images vs. 16.7 per cent of all the images). However, both books had a similar ratio of depictions of the couple with Tango (20 per cent for the German book and 16.7 per cent for the US book). Based on this information, it would appear that the publishers of the German version had fewer qualms about showing same-sex affection than the US publisher. This finding supports the idea that European children's books are generally more relaxed in their depiction of sexuality and thus of same-sex relationships than US ones (Epstein 2013; Naidoo 2012; Salisbury and Styles 2012). This is further upheld by an examination of the Spanish picture book *Cebollino y Pimentón* (Cebollino and Pimentón) (Reixach 2010), written in Spanish, about two penguins in a German zoo. In this book, 90 per cent of the pictures feature the penguin couple together and 57 per cent of those depict affection between the birds.

Nudity

In a previous examination of Spanish-language and English-language LGBTQ+ children's books, Naidoo (2012) noted that nudity appeared more often in this genre of books than in children's books with heteronormative characters. Given its salience in the previous study, we examined the presence of nudity within our sample. Almost all of the books avoid nudity or the insinuation of nudity except for two titles (one from Spain and one from Finland). The Finland-Swedish title *Allan och Udo* (Allan and Udo) includes one spread where two presumably unclothed men are poised to jump out of a birthday cake. Since the illustration stops just above the men's navels, it is not certain that they are meant to be naked, but readers are given the impression that neither man is wearing anything.

On the other hand, the Spanish children's book *Las bodas reales: Cuento para colorear* (The Royal Weddings: A Story to Colour) (Rossetti and Artajo 2005), written in Spanish, depicted considerable nudity and sexualized imagery among both heteronormative and apparently queer characters. Several illustrations included monsters that were in the shape of penises while other images highlighted naked men leaning together with their genitals touching, nude women with large breasts floating in water, and unclothed couples hugging. In this particular title, it was also difficult to identify the main couple with all the multiple opposite-sex and same-sex couples present throughout the illustrations. Another intriguing element of *Las bodas…* is the format. While it is hardcover with thick pages, it is apparently meant to be a colouring book. Thus, not only will children be visually interacting with images while reading the story, they will also be physically interacting with them as they colour the pages. Although this title is certainly not the only colouring book for children that features nudity, it is intriguing that all the nude individuals are adults. Typically, books written for children feature child or childlike protagonists relatable to the experiences of children. Featuring nude adults may create a dissonance between the child reader and the book, preventing them from fully connecting with the characters.

Study Limitations

Based upon the authors' own concurrent research, there are well over 300 foreign-language children's picture books with LGBTQ+ topics published around the world. For this study, we used a random sampling approach to select books from our existing collection, as described above. We are cognizant that there are indeed racially diverse LGBTQ+ books published in other countries that did not end up in our sample. However, in line with our random sampling approach, we decided to accept the titles selected rather than specifically choosing titles that feature racial diversity. The purpose of this decision was to identify books more naturally, as a child might, rather than skewing our results with specially selected books that might indicate a greater presence of racial diversity in international LGBTQ+ picture books.

Due to the limited number of titles examined, the results of the study are not statistically generalizable. If all the LGBTQ+ children's picture books from a particular country were examined, perhaps greater racial diversity, physical contact and/or type of same-sex animal couples would be present. However, this snapshot does provide a springboard from which to discuss how different countries visually present LGBTQ+ characters in children's books.

While we only examined the visual elements of the books, iconography can sometimes have a more powerful impact on a child's identity development and understanding of a topic than the written text (Arzipe and Styles 2015; Chatton 2001; Nikolajeva and Scott 2001; Roethler 1998).[6] At the same time, only analysing the illustrations allowed us to overcome language barriers when investigating books outside our dominant reading literacy abilities. If a researcher were to add in textual elements of the books and had the ability to comprehend 11 different languages (Czech, Dutch, English, French, German, Hebrew, Italian, Portuguese, Spanish, Swedish and Tagalog) then a broader understanding could be gleaned from the books and the marriage of text and illustrations could be thoroughly explored. Perhaps future research can take this study further and ideally provide an in-depth look at both textual and visual depictions of LGBTQ+ characters in children's picture books published in specific countries and regions of the world.

6 The work of American, queer, Latinx author-illustrator Maya Christina Gonzalez explores this at length. She has created a curriculum for minority children to 'claim' their face and identity through art and published extensively via her website (http://www.mayagonzalez.com/) on the importance of children of colour as well as LGBTQ+ children seeing reflections in their literature.

Concluding Thoughts

This study provides a glimpse into the growing world of international LGBTQ+ children's picture books. While it was once difficult to locate titles with queer content, the quality and availability of this genre has been increasing in recent years. Although foreign-language books could face barriers when crossing borders, this study demonstrates the potential for their illustrations to transcend such barriers easily and provide a much-needed global mirror for children and caregivers in rainbow families, as well as global windows into other cultures for members of heterosexual families.

However, the study also highlights the continued problem of fully representing the spectrum of diversity in LGBTQ+ children's picture books specifically and children's literature in general. For all children to encounter images that capture the unique diversity of the LGBTQ+ community, additional books are needed that feature non-white, gender non-conforming and senior same-sex couples. In addition, more published titles should challenge homonormative standards to allow the vibrant rainbow of the queer community to shine and to truly capture the daily experiences of children and caregivers in rainbow families.

Works Cited

Arzipe, Evelyn, and Morag Styles. 2015. *Children Reading Picturebooks: Interpreting Visual Texts.* 2nd ed. Abingdon, Oxfordshire: Routledge.

Barbero, Cinzia. 2011. *Più ricche di un re* (Richer Than a King). Milan: Lo Stampatello.

Beuningen, Gea van. 2011. *De mama's van Sterre* (The Mommies of Sterre). Illustrated by Tinne Van den Bossche. Antwerpen: t'Verschil.

Botelho, Maria José, and Masha Kabakow Rudman. 2009. *Critical Multicultural Analysis of Children's Literature: Mirrors, Windows, and Doors.* New York: Routledge.

Bronski, Michael. 1993. 'Positive Images and the Stupid Family: Queer Books for Kids?' *Radical America* 25, no. 1: 61–70.

Carrasco, Walcyr. 2010. *Meus dois pais* (My Two Fathers). Illustrated by Laurent Cardon. São Paulo, Brazil: Editora Ática.

Centre for Literacy in Primary Education. 2018. *Reflecting Realities: A Survey of Ethnic Representation within UK Children's Literature 2017.* https://clpe.org.uk/library-and-resources/research/reflecting-realities-survey-ethnic-representation-within-uk-children

Chatton, Barbara. 2001. 'Picture Books for Preschool Children: Exploring Gender Issues with Three- and Four-Year-Olds'. In *Beauty, Brains, and Brawn: The Construction of Gender in Children's Literature*, edited by Susan Lehr, 57–66. Portsmouth, ME: Heinemann.

Clark, Cheril N., and Monica Bey-Clarke. 2016. *Keesha's South African Adventure.* Illustrated by Julia Selyutina. Sicklerville, New Jersey: Dodi Press/My Family!

Crawford, Georgina. 2009. *The Tales of Zebedy-Do-Dah.* Illustrated by Emily McCann. London, UK: Onlywomen Press.

DePalma, Renée. 2016. 'Gay Penguins, Sissy Ducklings… and Beyond?: Exploring Gender and Sexuality Diversity through Children's Literature'. *Discourse: Studies in the Cultural Politics of Education* 37, no. 6: 828–45.

Epstein, B. J. 2013. *Are the Kids All Right?: The Representation of LGBTQ Characters in Children's and Young Adult Literature.* Bristol: HammerOn Press.

Esposito, Jennifer. 2009. 'We're Here, We're Queer, But We're Just Like Heterosexuals: A Cultural Studies Analysis of Lesbian Themed Children's Books'. *Educational Foundations* 23, no. 3/4: 61–78.

Fernández, Darío. 2013. *Anita y sus dos mamas* (Anita and her Two Moms). Buenos Aires, Argentina: Editorial Molinos de Viento.

Ferrari, Verónica. 2015. *Camila tiene dos mamas?* (Camila Has Two Moms?). Illustrated by Mayra Avila. Lima, Perú: El Armario do Zoe.

Flanagan, Victoria. 2008. *Into the Closet: Cross-dressing and the Gendered Body in Children's Literature and Film*. New York: Routledge.

Gates, Gary. 2013. *LGBT Parenting in the United States*. Los Angeles, CA: Williams Institute, UCLA School of Law. http://williamsinstitute.law.ucla.edu/wp-content/uploads/LGBT-Parenting.pdf

Herzog, Ricky. 2009. 'Sissies, Dolls, and Dancing: Children's Literature and Gender Deviance in the Seventies'. *The Lion and the Unicorn* 33, no. 3: 60–76.

Horning, Kathleen T. 2014. 'Still an All-White World?' *School Library Journal* 60, no. 5: 18.

International Lesbian, Gay, Bisexual, Trans and Intersex Association (ILGA). 2017. *State-Sponsored Homophobia 2017: A World Survey of Sexual Orientation Laws: Criminalisation, Protection and Recognition*. Geneva: ILGA. https://ilga.org/maps-sexual-orientation-laws

Johnson, Holly, Janelle Mathis, and Kathy G. Short, eds. 2017. *Critical Content Analysis of Children's and Young Adult Literature: Reframing Perspective*. New York: Routledge.

Leeuwen, Theo van. 2001. 'Semiotics and Iconography'. In *Handbook of Visual Analysis*, edited by Theo van Leeuwen and Carey Jewitt, 92–118. Thousand Oaks, CA: Sage.

Lepman, Jella. 1969. *A Bridge of Children's Books*. Chicago, IL: American Library Association.

Lester, Jasmine. 2014. 'Homonormativity in Children's Literature: An Intersectional Analysis of Queer-Themed Picture Books'. *Journal of LGBT Youth* 11, no. 3: 244–75.

Lindeberg, Minna. 2001. *Allan och Udo* (Allan and Udo). Illustrated by Linda Bondestam. Helsingfors, Finland: Söderströms.

Merchant, Ed. 2010. *Dad David, Baba Chris and Me*. Illustrated by Rachel Fuller. London, UK: British Association for Adoption and Fostering.

Naidoo, Jamie Campbell. 2012. *Rainbow Family Collections: Selecting and Using Children's Books with Lesbian, Gay, Bisexual, Transgender, and Queer Content*. Santa Barbara, CA: Libraries Unlimited.

Naidoo, Jamie Campbell. In press. *Global Rainbow Family Collections: Children's Books with Lesbian, Gay, Bisexual, Transgender, and Queer Content from Around the Globe*. Chicago, IL: American Library Association.

Neri, Bernadette Villanueva. 2012. *Ang Ikaklit sa aming hardin (Ikaklit in our Garden)*. Illustrated by CJ de Silva. Manila, Philippines: Raintree Trading and Publishing Inc.

Nikolajeva, Maria, and Carole Scott. 2001. *How Picturebooks Work*. Abingdon, Oxfordshire: Routledge.

Reixach, Laura. 2010. *Cebollino y Pimentón* (Cebollino and Pimentón). Barcelona: Edicions Bellaterra.

Richardson, Justin, and Peter Parnell. 2005. *And Tango Makes Three*. Illustrated by Henry Cole. New York, NY: Simon & Schuster.

Roethler, Jacque. 1998. 'Reading in Color: Children's Book Illustrations and Identity Formation for Black Children in the United States'. *African American Review* 32, no. 1: 95–105.

Rossetti, Ana. 2005. *Las bodas reales: Cuento para colorear* (The Royal Weddings: A Story to Colour). Illustrated by Jorge Artajo. Barcelona: Ediciones Bellaterra.

Salisbury, Martin, and Morag Styles. 2012. *Children's Picturebooks: The Visual Art of Storytelling*. London: Laurence King Publishing.

Schreiber-Wicke, Edith. 2006. *Zwei Papas für Tango* (Two Papas for Tango). Illustrated by Carola Holland. Stuttgart: Thienemann.

Sciurba, Katie. 2017. 'Flowers, Dancing, Dresses, and Dolls: Picture Book Representations of Gender-Variant Males'. *Children's Literature in Education* 48, no. 3: 276–93.

Stokes, Jane. 2012. *How to Do Media and Cultural Studies*. 2nd ed. London: Sage.

Sunderland, Jane. 2011. *Language, Gender, and Children's Fiction*. London: Continuum International Publishing Group.

Sunderland, Jane, and Mark McGlashan. 2012. 'The Linguistic, Visual and Multimodal Representation of Two-Mum and Two-Dad Families in Children's Picturebooks'. *Language and Literature* 21, no. 2: 189–210.

Thériault, Michel. 2017. *Ils sont…* (They Are…). Illustrated by Magali Ben. Moncton, New Brunswick: Bouton d'or Acadie.

Threlkeld, Aubry. 2014. 'A Critical Queer Literacy Approach to Teaching Children's Literature about Same-Sex Parenting'. In *Critical Practice in P–12 Education: Transformative Teaching and Learning*, edited by Salika A. Lawrence, 223–43. Hershey, PA: IGI Global.

United Nations. 2016. *Demographic Yearbook 2016*. https://unstats.un.org/unsd/demographic-social/products/dyb/dyb_2016

Valente, Anaïs, and Ariane Delrieu. 2013. *Drôles de familles* (Funny Families). Clermont-Ferrand: Tournez la page jeunesse.

Viogt, Ina. 2015. *Wie heiraten eigentlich Trockennasenaffen?* (How Do Dry-Nosed Moneys Marry?). Illustrated by Jacky Gleich. Solothurn: kwasi Verlag.

Chapter Eleven

OF FABULOUS FLOWERS AND POWERS: QUEER NARRATIVES OF/FOR THE FILIPINO CHILD IN PHILIPPINE CONTEMPORARY CHILDREN'S LITERATURE

Cheeno Marlo M. Sayuno

Introduction

In late 2019, I was among the selected Filipino writers who participated in a workshop sponsored by Room to Read, an international non-profit organization that makes a commitment towards accessible literacy campaigns to children in vulnerable communities around the world. The goal of the workshop was to develop short stories for children that centre on gender equality, social inclusion and representation of children's experiences in the Philippine social landscape. The work that I was able to produce is entitled *Sayaw ni Dayaw* (Dayaw's Dance), later brought to life by Filipino illustrator Harry Monzon and published by Anvil Publishing in 2020. In the story, a little frolicsome girl explores various Philippine cultural dances in search for a dance that fits her playful persona. Ultimately, she discovers that *Tinikling*, a well-known Philippine cultural dance where performers jump over clashing bamboo poles as fast as they can, is the right dance for her.

During the storybook development stage, there was a move to make the character gender-neutral in terms of the illustration, which meant that she would no longer be wearing the skirt that was representative of the rural community in Leyte, Philippines, where the dance originated. With my background as a cultural dance performer, I respectfully defended the need to differentiate the gender of the performer. In a study that I have conducted on gender roles in Philippine cultural dances (Sayuno 2017), I found that many dances from cultural communities that have foreign influences delineated gender roles: men are expected to be chivalrous for Spanish-influenced *Maria Clara* dances and polygamous for tribal dances in Mindanao, particularly those originating from the Malay race; women are viewed as demure, waiting for the males to either court them or choose them as the next bride for child-bearing. For rural areas and tribes with lesser to no foreign influence, equality in gender roles is evident. In Cordillera dances, the male and female performers in tribes are seen to have different forms of power and complementary dance movements. In rural areas in Luzon and Visayas, both men and women perform laborious farm work and the challenging movements in their festive dances. Ultimately, while the publishers and project coordinators agreed that we retain the costumes, we also made sure that the titular character is gender non-binary in facial and bodily features. This also became an eye-opening experience for me because I realized that, after all, it is possible to retain the distinct features of the Philippine cultural experience while also breaking from gender stereotypes in terms of representation.

The case of our Philippine cultural dances is reflective of our history. Our archipelagic nation carries within its lands and seas the many stories of our forefathers, traders and invaders. The earliest settlers of the Philippines were hypothesized to be of Austronesian roots coming from Taiwan and migrating to and settling in what is known today as northern parts of Luzon (Thiel 1984). In our pre-colonial history, Chinese and Indian merchants, as well as other traders from our South-East Asian neighbours, were constant visitors to our territory. Later on, Spanish conquistadors would discover our land, in search of spices, and this would start the invasion that would last up to 300 years. British, American and Japanese troops would later on also colonize the country before it finally achieved independence as a republic in 1946. Because of this, the Philippines, as reflected not only in its dances but also in many other cultural and societal artefacts, became a melting pot of various foreign influences that were combined with the distinct Filipino identity.

This includes gender roles and power differentials that are entwined with such. While gender binary into male and female was distinct in various cultures in the Philippines, gender crossing was also part of cultural practice in the past (Garcia 2013). The *Babaylan* were the most common manifestations and were respected in the community; they were spiritual intermediaries or shamans who were men dressed up as women. Furthermore, they were gender-crossers because they not only transformed into the opposite gender but also embodied the behaviour of women. However, the political ideologies of the aforementioned invaders affected the perspectives of our ancestors. The machismo and chivalry from the Spaniards led to the perspective of manliness as the only acceptable behaviour. In the Tagalog regions in Luzon, during the pre-colonial times, there were native feminine men called *bayoguin*, the name coming from a species of the strong bamboo called *bayog*. When the Spaniards came, the *bayoguin* became referred to as *bakla*, which originally meant 'confused' or 'cowardly' (Garcia 2013, 53). As more invaders set foot on our shores, these heteronormative notions of gender and sexuality were formalized due to the education system introduced by the Americans.[1]

1 The history of Philippine education predates colonization through unstructured vocational training conducted in the household or in houses of tribal tutors. During the Spanish colonization, the teachers became the friars and missionaries, who used education to promote not only religion but also Spanish ideologies. Later on, secularized and free public education was implemented by the Americans after they took over from the Spaniards (Philippine Department of Education n.d.). It is this American system of formal education that the Philippines would subscribe to beginning in the twentieth century (Tandora 2003). Gender would also become an issue as the education system developed due to issues of access, non-attendance, and

An interesting case is the regard for gender preference by the Teduray tribe in the southern region of the Philippines. Their beliefs are reflective of their equal views of men and women, as evident in Tulus, a genderless being whom they believe to be the creator of the world, and Fulufulu, a female supreme being in their folklore that is different from the usually male-dominated representation of higher beings (Dumlao 2010). Even more so, their community is the home of the *mentefuwaley libun*, which Schlegel (1999) translates as 'one-who-became-a-woman'. In the Teduray tribe, the language is genderless and people are assigned to gender roles not on the basis of biological sex but on the role that they assume and the gender that they perform in the community. For them, a man who changes his gender is not necessarily gay or bisexual but a *mentefuwaley libun* (Dumlao 2010). This shows how gender performance and acceptance is deeply imprinted in the roots of the Filipino culture and consciousness, free from foreign influence.

Thus, today, the discussion of LGBTQ+ is not only a personal journey but also a political one. On one hand, the LGBTQ+ experience is a personal struggle, where members of the community experience crises in identity formation, anxieties in relationships, finding a significant other, and acceptance in a changing community (Lodia 2016). These then transcend from self-discovery, family relations and intimate relationships to community building, religiosity and morality, and political advocacy. As many countries around the world, one after another, started accepting same-sex marriages and as governments continue to see campaigns relating to gender expression as a valid point of argument that needs to be expressed and listened to, the Philippines continues to fight the battle. There are a few manifestations of LGBTQ+ representations in the political space, as detailed by Paradela (2019). As early as 1992, The Lesbian Collective participated in International Women's Day in order to voice their rights. The University of the Philippines (UP) became the home for organization UP Babaylan in 1993. It was 1994 when the Progressive Organization of Gays in the Philippines rallied in the streets in the fashion of what can today be considered as a pride march, and in 1995, the Metro Manila Pride March became a gathering of various individuals and organizations, which became a turning point for the awakening of gender expression and acceptance in the Philippines. In 1998, the Lesbian and Gay Legislative Advocacy Network Philippines was founded to advance the fundamental rights of LGBTQ+ Filipinos (Paradela 2019). Later, in 2006, the Society of Transsexual Women of the Philippines participated in the Metro Manila Pride March (Paradela 2019). In 2010, by virtue of the Philippines' party list system where community sectors are allowed representation in Congress, the party list called 'Ladlad', which is also a Filipino term used for coming out of the closet, became the first LGBTQ+ political party in the world (Coloma 2013). In 2016, Geraldine Roman became the first openly transgender woman elected into the Philippine Congress (Sawatzky 2016). In 2017, the Sexual Orientation and Gender Identity or Expression Equality (SOGIE) Bill was unanimously approved in the House of Representatives and continues to fight the battle up to this day (Francisco 2018).

---

marriage and pregnancy, which meant that women would have to stay at home and discontinue formalized learning (Okabe 2013).

However, the Philippines remains a country populated by a Catholic majority. This results in clashing views on the LGBTQ+ experience, ranging from acceptance to tolerance and even to persecution (Cardozo 2014). Acceptance is evident within the close family/friend/community circles of an LGBTQ+ individual. Based on my own personal experience and those of many others, there is comfort as long as people close to your heart accept you for who you are. Tolerance is evident in a country where the majority would enjoy performances and entertainment by transgender people, drag performers, gender-crossers, cross-dressers and genderqueer people, whether in bars or in the media (Cardozo 2014). There is danger to such performance onstage for gender expressions among LGBTQ+ people because it comes to a point where they become subjects of laughter, ridicule and disrespect. For instance, in many of the mainstream Filipino films, the gay character is portrayed as a *parlorista* or hairdresser who delivers funny antics and longs for attention from a heterosexual male (Payuyo 2012). At the same time, however, they embrace this kind of false acceptance because they see a great opportunity for expression through entertainment and because, practically speaking, this becomes a source of earning a living to them. These 'over-the-top gay characters' are used for comic relief and have thus dominated film and television content (Plaza 2016). This would then transcend to real-life situations where the stereotypical butch lesbian security guard and effeminate gay comedian are accepted stereotypes and any divergence from these forms would be uncomfortable to the heteronormative society (Bernal 2015). Still, the Philippines was found to have lower homonegativity than neighbouring Asian countries such as Indonesia and Malaysia, and at the same time, it was considered to be one of the most gay-friendly countries in south-east Asia (Manalastas et al. 2017). However, the stigma remains, in part due to religion; thus, anti-LGBTQ+ stigma awareness should be promoted (Muyargas et al. 2016). Unlikely as it may seem, the Philippines is attempting to foster 'inclusion, affirmation, and activism in gender and sexual minorities' (Manalastas and Torre 2016, 60). And this is possible. After all, a participatory survey by the United Nations Development Programme and the United States Agency for International Development (2014) in the Philippines has listed numerous LGBTQ+ indigenous terminologies from across the archipelago, many of them non-discriminatory and with no implication other than identification and gender expression. This means that acceptance is imprinted in the Philippine indigenous identity.

Media-based initiatives are helpful in decreasing negative attitudes towards the LGBTQ+ community (Clemente et al. 2013). While mainstream media provide opportunities for representation and features promoting LGBTQ+ advocacy, the Philippine literature scene also bears evidence of various gay themes, as in narratives of self-denial, eroticism and discrimination (Wright 2017). Meanwhile, the child's experience with gender in the Philippines is shaped in part by a popular belief that a child can be corrected by making him/her 'un-confused' through parental cruelty (Garcia 2014). At the same time, some people believe that some children grow up to be homosexuals because of maltreatment by adults, particularly through sexual molestation resulting in psychological effects, though research suggests it can be explained by some combination of nature and nurture. Some LGBTQ+ children in the Philippines are victims of domestic tension and silence, rejection by loved ones, bullying by peers and adults, and vicarious trauma (ASEAN SOGIE Caucus 2017).

Children's literature, being the material that attempts to present narratives that are close to the sensibilities and needs of the child reader, can bear messages that defend and empower the powerless, such as those who find themselves in abusive situations (Metcalf and Meyer 1992). Children's literature in the Philippines is viewed as being trusting and empowering of its child readers. While it is inevitable for many authors to incorporate moral values, as these are the primary considerations of gatekeepers such as parents and teachers, there is a growing body of work that challenges societal situations that affect the child by not only putting the child as the hero in his/her storyworld but also not being bound by conventional themes in storytelling (Evasco 2008). Filipino storybook creators are unafraid of dealing with controversial themes, for they know that these are experiences that children may have to face. The role of the storybook writer, then, is to ensure that the stories are presented in such a way that the child sees hope for the future. As the child faces these real-life difficulties, the child character, the children's book creators and the storybook industry will be there to hold the child's hand throughout the journey, with the stories read and the reading process guided by parents, teachers and guardians who can provide access to further discussions and validations of emotions.

This chapter presents an overview of Philippine children's literature that centres on the LGBTQ+ experience. By analysing the published works with themes of gender expression, queerness and gender roles, the goal is to present the overarching themes of stories written for younger readers, particularly those that are printed in storybook form or anthologies for early to intermediate readers. In addition, the discursive roles that the child protagonist plays in relation to being a member of the LGBTQ+ community or interacting with characters who belong to this community are discussed, as well as how children are portrayed as empowered agentic characters who can also empower others.

Twelve works in total, throughout more than three decades of children's literature in the Philippines, were found to tell stories that centre on LGBTQ+ characters, their parents, and even friends within the community. Interestingly, these books were published only beginning in 2012 pioneered by the independent publisher Twamkittens Publication. In 2013, this was followed by another work from Chikiting Books, the children's storybook arm of the textbook publisher Vibal Group, Inc. After this, it would take a few more years for any more LGBTQ+ stories to be told for children, for most of the other works would only be published in 2018, with five of the works being products of the Center for Youth Advocacy and Networking (CYAN), Inc., through '*Mulat Sulat*[2] 2018: Writeshop for SOGIE-Focused Stories for Children'. The outputs from this workshop, which were aimed at promoting diversity and equality around sexual orientation, gender identity and expression (SOGIE), were made accessible through online platforms.[3]

2 The term *mulat* means 'to open one's eyes', while *sulat* means 'to write'. The goal of the Writeshop project is thus encapsulated in the name: to open the eyes of the child readers through written works.

3 The stories can be downloaded at http://tinyurl.com/mulatsulat

The other titles, which are discussed in detail in succeeding subsections, were published in 2018 by other national publications in the Philippines: one each from Tahanan Books for Young Readers, Adarna House and Kahel Press. In 2019, two works published by Lampara Books in the same year formed part of an anthology of 'radical' stories for children, where the goal is to publish stories that promote ideas around extensive, holistic and progressive change in politics and society in the Philippine context by exposing children to stories that awaken their consciousness (Evasco 2019). This is right away reflective of the dearth of publication on such themes. Is there resistance to topics that attempt to expose children to LGBTQ+ stories?

The following sections thus detail the narratives of these published works, as well as the arising themes and child representations, to give a greater understanding of the child's journey as an LGBTQ+ individual or ally and how this reflects the social, political and cultural consciousness of the Philippines at large. My analysis is organized based on these themes for easier comparison. The goal of this chapter is to present an inventory of existing stories for children in storybook, board book and anthology formats, particularly those that are targeted for beginning to intermediate readers. The analysis below reflects the budding attempt of the Philippine contemporary children's literature scene to provide not only relevant and relatable representations of various gender expressions, particularly those occurring at home and in the community, but also empowering portrayals for the child readers to be able to understand their own identities and to be accepting of those around them. While the study acknowledges that these are only very few as compared with the voluminous production in children's literature in the country over the years, it also suggests that there is a growing body of work in Philippine children's literature that dares to shatter stereotypical notions of the LGBTQ+ experience in the eyes of the child.

A Garden of Families

The pioneering work in LGBTQ+ children's literature is Bernadette Villanueva Neri's bilingual work *Ang Ikaklit sa aming hardin (Ikaklit*[4] *in our Garden)*, illustrated by CJ de Silva. The work, which also won first prize in the *maikling kuwentong pambata* (short story for children) category of the prestigious Don Carlos Palanca Memorial Awards for Literature in the Philippines in 2006, was self-published by Neri through her Twamkittens Publication in 2012, proof that it was a time when mainstream publications might have not been ready to publish such revolutionary content. In the story, the little girl Ikaklit introduces her two mothers and the things that they do together, such as exploring their heritage in Baguio City, the setting of the story, and particularly taking care of the flowers in their garden.

4 *Ikaklit* is an indigenous word for sunflower, originating from the Bontoc tribe in the northern Philippines. In the story, it refers to the name of the child character and also the mysterious seed that her mothers helped her plant in their garden. In the bilingual book, the English translation does not use sunflower but still uses Ikaklit for the name of the flower, with the translation only appearing in the glossary and implied in the illustrations.

Her mothers, Daisy and Lilia, encourage her to plant a flower, which she also tends and takes care of every day. While Ikaklit enjoys her comfortable little bubble, things change when she finally gets to start school. At first, she is excited by this new world, but when she discovers that her classmates' families are mostly composed of a mother and a father, she starts to have questions about why her family is different. Furthermore, she is bullied by her classmates for having 'tomboy' (lesbian) parents or being a baby that only sprang out of a bamboo[5] instead of being born. Wanting answers, she starts asking her mothers about the whereabouts of her father. The mothers liken the care for a child to that for a garden: '"[Child], a family is like a garden," Nay Lilia said calmly, "Who planted the seeds is not important. It also doesn't matter whether a woman or a man takes care of them. What's vital is how well the garden is tended," she explained'[6] (Neri 2012, 16). This reflects that the work in itself is unafraid to confront the theme of same-sex union through its explicit mention of gender roles while tiptoeing around the sensibilities of the child.

Soon enough, as the flower of her own namesake grows, she also discovers that there are other forms of family, when she meets classmates whose families do not conform to the conventional structures but are nonetheless loving. She has a classmate who is adopted, one with half-siblings, one who does not know her parents at all, and one taken care of by a single parent. Towards the end, the young Ikaklit is portrayed as someone who is accepting and understanding of their own experience, subverting disempowerment into acceptance: 'All of us were taunted [by our classmates]. But what they don't know is that we are happy and contented with our families' (Neri 2012, 24).

Tahanan Books for Young Readers' *Dalawa ang daddy ni Billy (Billy Has Two Daddies)*, written by Michael de Guzman and illustrated by Daniel Palma Tayona (2018), follows the same narrative of a child's ordinary world being disrupted when he sees how the community operates (see Epstein 2013, 39–45, for more on the 'confirmation of normality' trope). The bilingual storybook is written in Filipino with English translation. This time, the child protagonist Billy is well-loved at home by his Daddy and his Papa. While he accepts this world that takes care of him and brings him eternal joy, dynamics change when he goes to school. His classmates, even including one parent, bully him, calling him and his fathers *bakla* (gay). Billy gets into a fight and questions the household that he has grown to love. Why does he have two fathers? What does *bakla* mean? While Papa and Daddy tell him that he will understand everything when he grows up, they assure him that they love him no matter what people say about them. Towards the end, Billy asks if he will grow up to be *bakla* too. One of his fathers answers, 'Billy, when you grow up, you can be anything you want to be!'[7] (Guzman 2018, 29).

---

5 This is a translation of the Filipino expression *putok sa buho,* commonly used to refer to children who do not have real parents, usually in a derogatory manner. The expression comes from the Filipino tale of creation of the world. The first man and woman, Malakas and Maganda, sprang from a bamboo.

6 Original English translation as published in the book, except for the endearment 'child'. The English translation uses the Filipino term *anak.*

7 Original English translation published in the book.

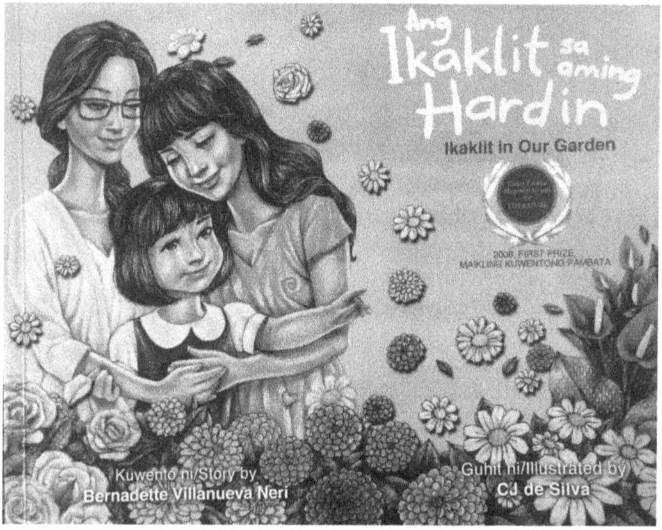

Figure 5: Neri, Bernadette Villanueva. 2012. *Ang Ikaklit sa aming hardin. (Ikaklit in our Garden)*. Illustrated by CJ de Silva. Manila: Raintree Trading & Publishing, Inc./Publikasyong Twamkittens.

Figure 6: Guzman, Michael de. 2018. *Dalawa ang daddy ni Billy. (Billy Has Two Daddies)*. Illustrated by Daniel Palma Tayona. Makati City: Tahanan Books for Young Readers.

The reversible flip book[8] entitled *Ang nanay ni Erwin/Ang tatay ni Klara (Erwin's Mama/ Klara's Papa)* by Eugene Evasco, illustrated by Tokwa Peñaflorida and published by Kahel Press (2018), is another bilingual book with text in both Filipino and English. It presents two stories that represent two kinds of gender expressions. In *Ang nanay ni Erwin*, the little boy tells the reader about the daily activities of his unique mother, a bus driver who is loved by her[9] passengers. On the one hand, the mother 'looks like she's always heading to the pier; always smelling of smoke when she comes home; always with oily hair; and with a body so tough, it's built like a father's' (Evasco 2018, 11). On the other hand, the mother tends the garden well and also takes good care of Erwin. However, at school, Erwin is bullied for having an unconventional mother, which makes him want to have a mother who wears skirts and goes to the office like any other mother. When he confronts her about it, the mother explains that each and every mother is different: '[Child], not all mothers are the same ... much like how the cars on the road are all different'[10] (Evasco 2018, 13). Enlightened, Erwin becomes excited to bring his mother to the school's family day.

When the storybook is flipped the other way, Klara's story is introduced. Her father is a salon owner who makes everyone beautiful through makeup. He is also liked in the community for starting beautification projects in their town. Aside from that, the father is good at making Klara beautiful for school activities, at fixing broken things, and at taking care of her when she is sick. However, when her classmates bully her for having a softy father whose hips always sway, she starts wondering why her father is not like any other father. Her father is able to console her by explaining that every father is different: '[Child], there are different kinds of fathers. There are fathers who are hard. There are those who are neither too hard or too soft. And then there are fathers like me who are soft'[11] (Evasco 2018, 13). The two stories meet in the middle spread, where both attend the family day activity at school. As the two children declare their arrival, a welcoming classroom filled with children and their guardians – mothers and fathers, single parents, and grandparents – is shown in the illustration, hinting at various forms of families.

Another experimentation of form is showcased in Kata Garcia's *My Family* (2018), with illustrations by Borg Sinaban and published by Adarna House. The English board

8 The book shows one story on one side. When you flip the book, you see the second story presented in the same reading direction. The two stories follow parallel narratives and page assignments: description of the parent and his/her non-gender-conforming career, the parents' contribution in the community, the abilities of the parents that conform with their biological sex, the bullying of classmates, the children's quest for answers and the acceptance of the child. These two stories meet in the middle spread.

9 While I acknowledge that pronoun use is a matter of preference by the individual, throughout the article, I use pronouns based on the apparent biological identities of the characters, given that pronoun preferences were not expressed by the characters in their respective storyworlds.

10 Original English translation as published in the book, except for the endearment 'child'. The English translation uses the Filipino term *anak*.

11 Original English translation as published in the book, except for the endearment 'child'. The English translation uses the Filipino term *anak*.

Figure 7: Evasco, Eugene Y. 2018. *Ang nanay ni Erwin/Ang tatay ni Klara. (Erwin's Mama/ Klara's Papa).* Illustrated by Tokwa Peñaflorida. Translated by Karen Ferry-Fernandez. Quezon City: Kahel Press.

book with Filipino translations of the inside text simply shares the child voice, who tells the reader that the family serves as company in many experiences: exploration and discovery, laughter and sadness, sharing of stories, playtime and tucking up the child to sleep. However, what is special in the board book is that every page is split horizontally in the middle, with the upper portion showing the parents and the child in the lower part. This then allows the child reader to explore various combinations of parents and children. In the parent panel, parents can be a mother and a father, two mothers, two fathers, a single mother, a single father, or a grandmother who takes care of the child while the mother is working abroad and only accessible through a tablet. The images of the child change, too, showcasing the uniqueness of every child.

In these storybooks, with the exception of *My Family*, the formula is the same: the undisturbed world of the child is one where he/she accepts his/her family structure as normal, but when the child is exposed to the real world, societal norms bombard the child's consciousness with a family structure that is very much different. There is a moment of confusion and doubt, which the parents dismiss through metaphors (and even the notion of not being able to understand it because the character is merely a child). Ultimately, the child is shown as accepting that, while his/her parents are different, it is the difference that makes the family special. Meanwhile, *My Family* already treats various family structures with a sense of normalcy, which the child learns with every flip of the page. All these books present 'the nuclear family as core social ideology' which is used to frame the unconventional family structure and move towards a transformed ideology (McCallum and Stephens 2010, 361), where the perceptions of the child reader towards such a natural presence as family become more open and can thus have many forms.

Furthermore, in these stories, the child is understanding. The child naturally wonders about the difference of the world outside the one at home by comparison, and it could be argued that this is how one shapes identity. While the child may be bullied or belittled in the storybooks about the parents' LGBTQ+ identities, the parents' love for the child allows the child to have an open mind and heart. And from there, acceptance blossoms.

Figure 8: Garcia, Kata. 2018. *My Family*. Illustrated by Borg Sinaban. Quezon City: Adarna House.

Figure 9: Ruedas, Mondi. 2018. *What's My Power Gear?* Illustrated by Ruthie Genuino. Quezon City: Center for Youth Advocacy and Networking, Inc.

Coming Out and Opening Up

Compared with adults, children are unique but equally significant individuals who are experiencing the world in order to understand their selfhood. This is rooted in their ability to become not only visible but also empowered in enacting literary roles that are equal to those of adults (Sayuno 2018). As children make sense of their world, they also understand their individualities more deeply. This is the central focus of the storybook in English entitled *What's My Power Gear?* written by Mondi Ruedas and illustrated by Ruthie Genuino (2018), which is one of the five stories published by CYAN, Inc., as discussed in the Introduction. Metaphorically constructed, the story is set in a fictional world where Q-Kids are trained to ensure the safety of Planet Sari-kulay against the Fear Blobs, which are jelly-like creatures that make people become scared of what they do not understand. The story starts with the deployment of Q-Kids, who are further categorized into blue and pink kids. T, a blue kid, is made to choose his power gear throughout the story. However, the power gear also chooses the kid, because it will respond only if it is appropriate to the child. While T is instantly fascinated with the power gears in the pink room, Doc Q tells him that he is meant to select power gears only in the blue room. However, this does not work for T. Feeling defeated, T is able to convince Doc Q to allow him to try power gears in the pink room, where he discovers an instant affinity to the Tornado Saya (skirt). Doc Q then elicits the help of T, now embodying the new name Twirlie, in creating a new rule, to which the child responds: 'Of course, Doc Q. From now on, Q-Kids may choose any gear from any section' (Ruedas 2018, 14).

A child's acceptance of identity is a personal struggle faced alone because the child tries to understand him/herself and at the same time thinks about how to accommodate

Figure 10: Alberto, Jesh. 2018. *Bukas na si Cajon* (Cajon is Now Open). Illustrated by Gabbi Ramirez. Quezon City: Center for Youth Advocacy and Networking, Inc.

the subjective norms of people around them. In the Filipino storybook *Bukas na si Cajon* (Cajon is Now Open, translation mine), written by Jesh Alberto and illustrated by Gabbi Ramirez (2018) for CYAN, Inc., the world of cabinets and closets is created as a metaphor for being open and coming out. The story is set in the Oroc[12] household, a family of cabinets expecting guest relatives, much to the dismay of the father, Tatay Oroc, as he does not find the appearance and behaviour of the guests acceptable. '"I really do not like them. Such an eyesore!"' the father would say, '"If I had a child who is like them, I would nail the drawers shut so that my child would not open again!"' (Alberto 2018, 1).[13] Hearing this, little Cajon feels extra worried, clutching the many things inside her drawers: the skirts and dresses bought for her by her mother, as well as old shirts and shorts owned by her brother and father. Then the guests come, the flamboyant Cai-Cai and the brusque-looking Dora. Because Cajon admires how her cousins express themselves, she decided to open up about what she feels inside, i.e. gender preferences that are different and more fluid than her female persona. While the rest of the family accepts her, the father is disappointed. Towards the end, Cajon feels a sense of lightness and liberation. Meanwhile, an aunt encourages Cajon to approach the father towards the end of the story: '"Cajon, do you want to be the one to give food to your father?"' (Alberto 2018, 14),[14] providing a second chance for Cajon to explain her identity to her father, hopefully resulting in greater acceptance.

12 Oroc, the name of the household, is a play on the company Orocan Philippines, maker of durabox cabinets. Cajon is a stylized spelling of the Filipino term *kahon*, which means box.

13 'Ayaw na ayaw ko sa mga 'yan, ang sakit sa mata' [...] 'Kung may anak akong gagaya sa kanila, ipapako ko talaga nang hindi na mabuksan' (English translation mine).

14 'Cajon, gusto mo bang ikaw na ang magbigay [ng pagkain] sa iyong Tatay?' (English translation mine).

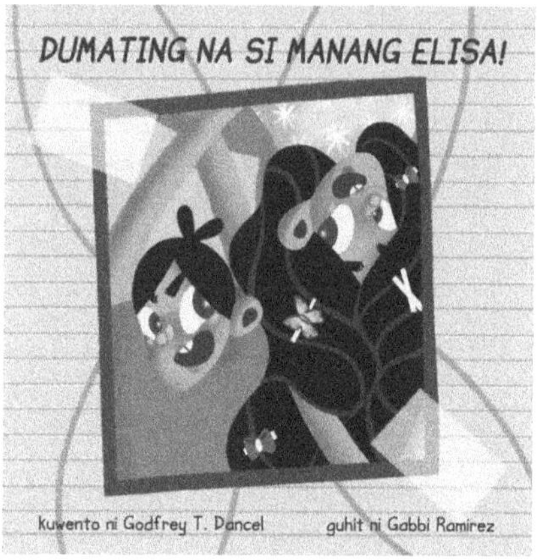

Figure 11: Dancel, Godfrey T. 2018. *Dumating na si Manang Elisa.* (Sister Elisa Finally Came). Illustrated by Gabbi Ramirez. Quezon City: Center for Youth Advocacy and Networking, Inc.

In *Dumating na si Manang*[15] *Elisa* (Sister Elisa Finally Came, translation mine), written by Geoffrey Dancel in Filipino and illustrated by Gabbi Ramirez in 2018 for CYAN, Inc., the little boy Tobey is excited for the coming of Elisa, his long-lost childhood playmate and neighbour. Here, the child character explores gender expression based on what his worldview is and the changes that he sees in the world. As Tobey anticipates Elisa's arrival, he remembers her long hair and red skirt, only to be surprised that Elisa, who now goes by the name Eli, is a jersey-wearing kid with short, stereotypically masculine hair. At first, Tobey is sceptical as to whether the Eli in front of him is the Elisa he grew up playing with. However, as the day goes by, he is reminded that Eli has remained the same, and therefore, no matter what Eli looks like or prefers, she is the same person and Tobey accepts her as the friend he used to know[16]: '"It is true: Manang Elisa and Eli are one and the same. My friend has indeed come!"' (Dancel 2018, 14).[17]

The stories discussed above portray the child character as someone who is going through the personal struggle of understanding the LGBTQ+ experience. Notably, the child who has emotions bottled up inside projects feelings of sadness, worry, and 'not feeling right', as evident in the case of T upon trying blue power gears that are not his preference. The child is silenced by fears of non-acceptance while wondering what is wrong with being different, the way Cajon is silent and paralysed at home because she is thinking about what she feels inside. Child characters in the stories, who are trying to find or have already found their gender identities, have to overcome yet another struggle: to

15 *Manang* is a term for sister originating from the Ilocano language in the northern Philippines, where the story is set. The Filipino term for sister is *Ate*.

16 I opted for the pronouns 'she' and 'her' in referring to Eli because the story did not indicate transsexuality, nor did it mention Eli's preference in pronoun use.

17 'Totoo nga: si Manang Elisa at si Eli ay iisa. Dumating na ang kaibigan ko!' (English translation mine).

be understood and accepted by the people who matter to them, such as family, friends and mentors. It is unfortunate that, as shown in the stories, these child characters have to take the extra effort to be accepted in an otherwise heteronormative world, fantastical or realistic.

At the same time, the child who stands witness to another character's search for or realization of gender identity is confused and starts to become distrusting of the world. This is seen in how Tobey, in attempting to figure out how his memory of Elisa relates to the Eli he sees now, becomes indifferent to Manang Elisa who was his childhood friend and who tries to not only perform the activities that they used to do but also prove that she is still the same friend that Tobey grew up with. In the end, the child understands, is accepted and accepts. Without too much reliance on adults, the child tries to be an agent of personal change.

The *Beki* and the Brave

When the child fully understands their nature, the possibilities are endless. The first Filipino storybook (with English translation) to portray an openly gay child protagonist, Rhandee Garlítos' *Ang bonggang-bonggang batang beki! (The Fierce and Fabulous Boy in Pink!)*, illustrated by Tokwa Salazar Peñaflorida and published by Chikiting Books in 2018, tells the story of Adel from the perspective of his older brother Mico. Portrayed as a *beki* (gay)[18] child who loves pink possessions, sings and dances on the street, uses gay lingo with his friends and assumes different effeminate nicknames, Adel is more than just a playful gay kid. He does a lot of work in the house, voluntarily, and is accepted and supported by his loving father. Together with his friends, Adel is able to ward off bullies, but at home, when his stern military uncle visits, he chooses to stay outside and literally hide just so the adult will not force him into acting like a man. Uncle Braulio also has twin sons who always mock Adel's well-accepted flamboyance right in his own home. This changes when Adel bravely saves the twins from an angry dog, also gaining his uncle's approval in the process. Meanwhile, as Mico watches without getting involved, he apologises to Adel for not being able to stand up for him, and Adel understands. This becomes a defining moment for Mico, who now sees the pink in Adel's world: 'My brother Adel's favorite colour is none other than pink. And now I understand why it is his favorite. Pink is the colour of his cheeks every time he sees us happily eating …, the colour of the roses and gumamelas that he grows lovingly …, the colour of his voice every time he sings …, the colour of his laughter with his best friends …, the colour that inspires his ideas and gives him courage whatever he is doing'[19] (Garlítos 2018, 26).

The same confidence and self-definition are embodied by Chowchow in the storybook of the same name *Si Chowchow*,[20] written by Angelo Benavidez and illustrated by Aiko

18 The standard Filipino term for 'gay' is *bakla*, whereas *beki* is a term used in gay lingo.

19 Original English translation as published in the book.

20 The title *Si Chowchow* contains the Filipino nominal marker *si*, which is used to specify that the noun is used as subject rather than object, to introduce the character named Chowchow.

Figure 12: Garlítos, Rhandee. 2013. *Ang bonggang-bonggang batang beki! (The Fierce and Fabulous Boy in Pink!)* Illustrated by Tokwa Salazar Peñaflorida. Quezon City: Chikiting Books.

Shimizu for CYAN, Inc. (2018). Although the character is not a child, given that he works for a construction company, the rendering of characters as dogs, the production in the form of a storybook, and the colourful and playful illustration all contribute to the appropriateness of the book for child readers. In the story, Chowchow is a dog who aspires to become a carpenter. He goes to apply for the job, carrying with him his pink hammer and wearing his pink 'lipschuck'. Here, it can be noticed that the story also embodied queerness in its language use, accommodating distinct Filipino gay lingo with the language familiar to the child reader. For instance, the term is a play on the word 'lipstick' but appropriated into the world of dogs with a queer flair. The story utilizes wordplay by using terms with 'ch-' to create consonance, such as in 'For a long time now, Chowchow has been dreaming of working at *Chuchubels* Construction Company'[21] (Benavidez 2018, 3). 'Chuchu' is a Filipino way of calling dogs, while '-bels' is a suffix common in Filipino gay lingo. Furthermore, words starting in 'ch-' are a staple in gay lingo, such as in the

21 'Matagal nang pangarap ni Chowchow na makapagtrabago sa Chuchubels Construction Company' (English translation mine).

Figure 13: Benavidez, Angelo. 2018. *Si Chowchow.* Illustrated by Aiko Shimizu. Quezon City: Center for Youth Advocacy and Networking, Inc.

common fillers 'churva', a catch-all term roughly translatable to 'something', as well as 'charot', a Filipino gay term used to indicate that the speaker is joking.

Given Chowchow's appearance and unconventional character for carpentry, he is naturally bullied by other workers and doubted by the employer despite bringing a portfolio that proves his quality of work. He is then challenged to build a house overnight, which he bravely accepts. His pink ribbon might be tattered and his lips are no longer pink, but he is able to create a house, which he considers a home more than anything, and everyone marvels at it. Mrs Bagsik,[22] the stereotype-breaking female employer uncommon to the male-dominated construction companies, expresses her remorse for her misjudgement: '"Forgive me for judging your abilities based on your appearance and body language"' (Benavidez 2018, 13).[23] Later on, because of his talent and hard work, he is promoted to a managerial position. While the characters, aside from being animals, may not necessarily be portrayed as children due to the situation presented where characters are working and pursuing a career, the same sensibilities of acceptance and ability beyond gender identities are evident.

The LGBTQ+ experience, as portrayed in the stories, is one of struggle: the child has to continuously fight for acceptance. While an accepting household is a confidence boost that helps the child embrace individuality, the fight continues as the child engages in bigger circles within the community. The child has to prove themselves the way Adel

22 The surname of the employer is a Filipino term meaning ferocious.

23 'Patawarin mo ako kung hinusgahan ko ang iyong kakayahan dahil lamang sa itsura at kilos mo' (English translation mine).

proved that bravery and effeminacy are not mutually exclusive, and how Chowchow proved that strength is not only something for those who have a masculine gender expression. Gay children in the stories do not have the privilege of automatic trust, belief and acceptance from the people around them, especially those outside the immediate household. They have to work hard for other people to finally see their worth, and this will be a continuing struggle as they grow.

But the thing about children who have accepted themselves is that they are more well-rounded in understanding the world. They know that the world is going to be a tough environment to be in and that they will always encounter people who will not understand them. They do not mind the extra effort to prove themselves because their hearts are stronger. Ultimately, it becomes more rewarding for them when they help other people to comprehend their identities and experiences. Through their eyes, people get to see the world in vibrant shades of pink, inspiring them to live fabulous lives as well.

Queer Hero/Villain

In some of the books, the LGBTQ+ character transcends from becoming a unique family member to being a community hero. In the English storybook *One of the Boys (or How Kenny Saved the City of Toyland)* written by Arkin Frany and illustrated by Fides Balmaceda in 2018 for CYAN, Inc., the fantastical City of Toyland is introduced, where toys played with by boys all live and mingle. The story focuses on Kenny, who, among the action figures, seems to be misplaced, given his appearance and abilities. He is wearing a pink polo shirt and blue shorts that end above the knee. He cooks, bakes, sings and dances. This puts him in the centre of scrutiny, as the other toys think that he does not belong there. However, Kenny is able to stand up for himself, insisting that he 'refuse[s] to be harassed' and that he 'belong[s] here' (Frany 2018, 6). Even the robot Alphatron, the leader of the city, thinks that Kenny should be 'normal': '"Well Kenny, why can't you be normal, so everyone can just get along?"' Kenny responds to this with a sense of security and ownership of his identity: '"I will stay and I will remain marvellous"' (Frany 2018, 7). When the monster Muninggarzilla[24] attacks the city and steals Alphatron's Red Lion arm, it is Kenny who rallies the citizens of the town into retrieving the Red Lion arm together so that Alphatron can save them again. When they are able to accomplish this, Kenny soon realizes that the monster, who is actually a big cat, is misunderstood just like him. He is then able to make the citizens understand the cat, and because of him, they are able to co-exist in the City of Toyland. At the same time, Kenny himself is accepted in the community as the toys that bullied him start to befriend him, towards a transformed society: 'This is the new Toyland. A city where the citizens can be anything they want. A place where everyone can be a hero … and everyone is accepted' (Frany 2018, 17–18).

Meanwhile, the hero is a makeup artist at a beauty parlour in 'Reyna Elena', a Filipino story also written by Michael de Guzman for *Baklas* (Free by Force, translation mine), one

24 The name is a play on *muning*, a Filipino word for cat, and Godzilla. Later on, the illustrations will show that the setting resembles a cluster of toys in a child's room where a cat also loiters.

Figure 14: Frany, Arkin. 2018. *One of the Boys (or How Kenny Saved the City of Toyland)*. Illustrated by Fides Balmaceda. Quezon City: Center for Youth Advocacy and Networking, Inc.

of the stories that are part of the three-part anthology of radical stories for children published by Lampara Books (2019). The story, which won honourable mention in the Philippine Board on Books for Young People's Salanga Prize in 2014, is about Ana, who goes to a beauty parlour with her mother, where she meets Maja, described as one of a kind in the eyes of the little girl: 'Maja is different from the other boys that Ana knows. He has long hair, always wears makeup, and sometimes wears a dress' (Guzman 2019, 138).[25] Ana's mother tells her that Maja is *bakla* (gay). Through her conversations with Maja, she learns that her[26] dream is to be the Reyna Elena, the star of the traditional Flores de Mayo[27] procession in the Philippines where women dressed in beautiful gowns parade through the town. People in the town would sometimes say that it is unfortunate

25 'kakaiba si Maja sa ibang lalaki na kilala ni Ana. Mahaba ang buhok nito, laging may makeup, at ilang beses ay nakasuot pa ito ng palda' (English translation mine).

26 The story does not use the female pronoun since it is written in Filipino and Filipino pronouns are not gendered. In the eyes of Ana, she is described as a man different from others. However, without wanting to assume, I am using the female pronoun to refer to Maja, so that she can be the queen whom she deserves to be.

27 A Filipino tradition of Spanish origin, yet another proof of the colonizer's influence on the Filipino tradition. The procession is a Catholic practice honoring the Blessed Virgin Mary but has also become an annual cultural spectacle in the month of May.

that Maja is gay because she is intelligent and had a great future ahead of her, while others say that it does not matter because Maja has a decent job. People then appreciate Maja more when a storm strikes the town and the community is forced into evacuation centres. Maja uses her skills in makeup and hairdressing by giving free makeovers to the women as a way of helping them cope with the devastation. When the flood subsides, the men of the town help Maja rebuild her parlour. When the month of May comes, Ana becomes part of Flores de Mayo. And Maja is the Reyna Elena, a decision made by the community of San Luis.

While Kenny and Maja are portrayed as heroes of their communities, it should be noted that members of the LGBTQ+ community, just like any other character, can be villains too. In the Filipino story entitled 'Ang pangarap ng Tropang K.I.D.L.A.T.[28] (The Dream of K.I.D.L.A.T. Gang)' written by Mark Norman Boquiren in 2019 for Lampara Books' *Hulagpos* (Break Free, translation mine), also part of the series of radical stories for children, two members of the gang do not conform with hetero/cisnormative gender expectations. Dadeng is described as gay and loud, and has the ability to make the gang happy. Meanwhile, Lulu is portrayed as a girl who acts like a boy and runs very fast. The two are part of the gang, together with Kuliling, Ipe, Amboy and the leader and main protagonist Temtem. In the story, the children are protagonists and villains in the world that they live in. They are revealed to be pickpockets who use their coordination and skills to steal the wallets and mobile phones of people in the city, all in the service of their Big Boss, the leader of the syndicate that abducted them. They admit to being tired of doing their act, but they are left without a choice because they are children caught by the syndicate. In one of their operations, Temtem is saved by the police and then lives in the orphanage. Before he achieves his dream of finally being reunited with his family, he pledges his cooperation with the authorities so that his gang will be saved and their dreams will come true as well. Temtem expresses his dream of liberation not only for himself but also for his friends: '... we are K.I.D.L.A.T. Gang. Do not wink. Do not blink. We will be free in a snap!' (Boquiren 2019, 115).[29]

The stories above are able to extend the daily experiences of children into the realities that they will soon face in the world. Here, the LGBTQ+ characters experience adversities as part of a suffering community, in which they are able to rise up to the challenge and bring change to the community. Kenny and Adel are able to help the members of the community, which renders them heroes. On the one hand, they are not defined by their uniqueness; on the other hand, they are made special by their very uniqueness, which is essential to their self-definition. The cases of Dadeng and Lulu are different because they are villains only because of being victims of circumstance. They are not the main focus of the narrative, but by positioning them in such a harsh situation, they are

28 The acronym represents the names of the members of the group: Kuliling, Ipe, Dadeng, Lulu, Amboy and Temtem. It also forms the word *kidlat,* the Filipino term for lightning, a perfect fit for the child characters' swift movements on the streets.

29 '... kami ang Tropang K.I.D.L.A.T. Huwag kikindat. Huwag kukurap. Kami'y lalaya sa isang iglap!' (English translation mine).

portrayed as normal and equally validated children who may also experience the same things as others.

Queering Philippine LGBTQ+ Children's Lit: Current Practice and Future Directions

As the pioneering work in LGBTQ+ stories for children, Neri's story of Ikaklit attempts to challenge the stereotypes, with the lesbian mothers not necessarily appearing masculine or butch. Furthermore, she wanted to portray the nurturing nature of relationships, i.e. that any person can assume roles in the family regardless of gender preference and such preferences will never get in the way of these nurturing roles (Quirante 2014). This echoes the proposition of queer theory that identities and the roles assigned to such identities are not fixed, but there is a tendency for reading queerness to be focused on subtle hints in the case of children's literature (Kander 2011). However, as with the case of Philippine LGBTQ+ children's literature and other literatures discussed in this book, it is only timely to discuss gender construction and the search for identities. After all, constructivist theories argue that identity, which includes gender preference, performance and expression, is a product of social construction (Kander 2011). It is thus important to expose children to these types of content because they 'may provide critical resources … by countering the invisible ideologies of heterosexism, misogyny, and homophobia' (Blackburn et al. 2015, 43).

In the case of the works analysed for this chapter, it can be noticed that, for some of the stories, the writers tend to tiptoe around the issue and use subtle hints such as metaphors to address issues of gender and sexualities, or tell the child character that he/she might not be mature enough to understand these issues: the comparison of Ikaklit to the flower of the same name, the use of cabinets and the clothes that they have inside their drawers, or the use of non-human characters such as animals and toys. This can be attributed to the fact that children tend to find animism appealing because of their love for magic. However, this also tends to regard children as beings who are not yet ready to understand the political statements that the books want to promote. While adults fight the political battle of acceptance, social inclusion and the right to expression, the children are left to have little exposure to this kind of political resistance as creators provide content that they think the children can grasp. Maybe, if children's content in the Philippines can be even more courageous in confronting these issues and trusting in the child reader, these child readers could understand that it really is acceptable to be unique, to embrace their own individuality and to join the battle.

In order to achieve such subtle hints, there is a sense of 'queering' of form, narrative structure and elements, and meaning. To boost the market appeal of the work for parents, teachers and children, some authors experiment with form in order to captivate more reading audiences, such as in the case of the horizontal page cuts of *My Family* and the two-stories-in-one reversible format of *Ang nanay ni Erwin/Ang tatay ni Klara (Erwin's Mama/Klara's Papa)*. The narrative elements position the LGBTQ+ character in various roles (from hero to villain to an observed character surrounding the child) and situations (from family dynamics to school bullying and even vulnerable communities). Even more so, there seems to be a constant need for the LGBTQ+ characters to prove their worth and to be the means of salvation in order to achieve acceptance. While this sends the message to the child that it is normal to be different and unique, do these same messages communicate the idea that the LGBTQ+ experience is a constant quest for validation?

There is a lot more work to do in terms of representing these queer narratives. In hundreds and hundreds of storybooks published in the Philippines, only 12 are tackling the issues of the LGBTQ+ narratives head-on, particularly in experiences relating to the child who is searching for their gender identity or who might be exposed to people belonging to such communities. In the case of the stories that are part of a 'radical' anthology, there are only two LGBTQ+ stories out of three books with 46 stories in total, although this can also be attributed to the many societal situations to encapsulate and varying experiences of the Filipino child that need representation in the material. Still, publishers in the Philippines are now seeing the value in exposing children to LGBTQ+ storylines. According to a CNN Philippines (Bueno 2018) interview with Ani Almario, Vice President for Product Development of Adarna House, children's content creators in the Philippines continue to exert effort in widening the range of themes in order to increase the range of representations beyond the usual middle-class heteronormative experience. For Michael de Guzman, who has produced two LGBTQ+ stories for children and has been recognized by award-giving bodies for it, it is important to reflect the real stories in society instead of a sensationalized version. This is why his work was published by Tahanan Books for Young Readers, with the managing editor Frances Ong saying that this is no longer taboo but a normal occurrence in society that no one should be ashamed of (Bueno 2018). Ultimately, the task in developing such works has to be balanced: on the one hand, the rendering of the stories has to be age-appropriate; on the other hand, there has to be 'a strong conviction for what children's literature should depict about the society' (Bueno 2018, n.p.). For Jason del Rosario, spokesperson of the *Mulat Sulat* project of CYAN, Inc., the publication of five stories on SOGIE to break the norm is not only about equality but also about 'creating a world where being different is no strange thing' (Del Rosario 2019, n.p.).

While the current representation of LGBTQ+ characters proves to be a promising start in the case of Philippine children's literature, the future continues to offer challenges for content creators, publishers and gatekeepers of narratives for children. It is also important that LGBTQ+ themed texts are available in the child's immediate environments, such as school and home, so that the child/student is not necessarily 'positioned as straight and generally homophobic' (Clark and Blackburn 2009, 27). It is comforting to learn that LGBTQ+ characters are portrayed as humans who strive for and sometimes experience social inclusion in the storyworlds where they belong. The adversities that they experience are shown to the child readers so that these children can understand and empathize with the struggles of such a minority. At the same time, this is an opportune moment for children who might be going through the same thing because these stories are a way for their own emotions, opinions and identity crises to be validated. There is value in representing such struggles so that children who are undergoing the same process can realize that they are represented and that there are children like them, both in fiction and in real life.

This kind of representation can still flourish. There are more experiences to be carefully and realistically represented, such as the mechanics of consciously choosing to belong to a certain gender category; stories of transgenderness and queerness as different from the more familiar gay and lesbian tales; the fluidity of genders; other gender categories yet to be understood; and the ongoing uphill battle for sexual orientation and gender expression to be treated as normal experiences of human life, along with the socio-political climate where these are enacted, expressed and accepted. The battle continues: The child is a fabulous flower who can effect marvellous change in the world. The child is a hero who can be entrusted with the banners, swords and torches to ward off the bullies. The child can harness powers to make them understand that the world should be one that accepts, nurtures and creates a safe haven for everyone to be who they want to be.

Bibliography

Alberto, Jesh. 2018. *Bukas na si Cajon* (Cajon is Now Open). Illustrated by Gabbi Ramirez. Quezon City: Center for Youth Advocacy and Networking, Inc. Also available online at http://tinyurl.com/mulatsulat

ASEAN SOGIE Caucus. 2017. *Bata at Bahaghari: Experiences of LGBT Children in the Philippines. ASC Discussion Series No 1.* Quezon City: ASEAN SOGIE Caucus. https://doi.org/10.1017/CBO9781107415324.004

Benavidez, Angelo. 2018. *Si Chowchow.* Illustrated by Aiko Shimzu. Quezon City: Center for Youth Advocacy and Networking, Inc. Also available online at http://tinyurl.com/mulatsulat

Bernal, Buena. 2015. 'Is the Philippines Really Gay-Friendly?' *Rappler*, 14 June. https://rappler.com/moveph/philippines-gay-friendly

Blackburn, Mollie V., Caroline T. Clark, and Emily A. 2015. 'Examining Queer Elements and Ideologies in LGBT-Themed Literature: What Queer Literature Can Offer Young Adult Readers'. *Journal of Literacy Research* 47, no. 1: 11–48. https://doi.org/10.1177/1086296X15568930

Boquiren, Mark Norman. 2019. 'Ang pangarap ng Tropang K.I.D.L.A.T. (The Dream of K.I.D.L.A.T. Gang)'. In *Hulagpos*, edited by Eugene Evasco and Segundo Matias Jr., 105–16. Quezon City: Lampara Books.

Bueno, Anna. 2018. 'Filipino Children's Books Are Now Talking About "Taboo" Topics'. *CNN Philippines*, 5 November. https://cnnphilippines.com/life/culture/literature/2018/10/15/radical-Filipino-childrens-books.html

Cardozo, Bradley. 2014. 'A "Coming Out" Party in Congress?: LGBT Advocacy and Party-List Politics in the Philippines'. Master's thesis, University of California Los Angeles.

Clark, Caroline T., and Mollie V. Blackburn. 2009. 'Reading LGBT-Themed Literature with Young People: What's Possible?' *The English Journal* 98, no. 4: 25–32.

Clemente, Jose Antonio R., Cherrie Joy F. Billedo, and Clarissa C. David. 2013. 'The Role of Broadcast Media in Attitude Change: A Pilot Study on a Campus-Based Radio Program and its LGBT Advocacy'. *Philippine Journal of Psychology* 46, no. 2: 165–79.

Coloma, Roland Sintos. 2013. '*Ladlad* and Parrhesiastic Pedagogy: Unfurling LGBT Politics and Education in the Global South'. *Curriculum Inquiry* 43, no. 4: 483–511. https://doi.org/10.1111/curi.12020

Dancel, Godfrey T. 2018. *Dumating na si Manang Elisa.* (Sister Elisa Finally Came). Illustrated by Gabbi Ramirez. Quezon City: Center for Youth Advocacy and Networking, Inc. Also available online at http://tinyurl.com/mulatsulat

Del Rosario, Nicole. 2019. '5 Filipino Literary Innovations in Children's Storybooks Teach About Gender Equality and Diversity'. *Good News Pilipinas*, 28 July. https://www.goodnewspilipinas.com/5-filipino-literary-innovations-in-childrens-storybooks-teach-about-gender-equality-and-diversity/

Dumlao, Emmanuel V. 2010. 'Berinarew: pagsasanib ng aral at aliw'. *Malay: internasyunal na jornal sa Filipino* 23, no. 1.

Epstein, B. J. 2013. *Are the Kids All Right?* Bristol: HammerOn.

Evasco, Eugene Y. 2008. 'Kapag maselan ang larong-bata: ang panitikang pambata bilang pananggalang sa abusong seksuwal sa bata'. *Humanities Diliman* 5, no. 1: 1–46.

———. 2018. *Ang nanay ni Erwin/Ang tatay ni Klara. (Erwin's Mama/Klara's Papa).* Illustrated by Tokwa Peñaflorida. Translated by Karen Ferry-Fernandez. Quezon City: Kahel Press.

———. 2019. 'Ang radikalismo sa panitikang pambata'. (The Radicalism in Children's Literature). In *Baklas*, edited by Eugene Evasco and Segundo Matias Jr., v–xiii. Quezon City: Lampara Books.

Francisco, Gay Marie. 2018. 'The Philippines' "Sexual Orientation and Gender Identity or Expression" Equality Bill: Who Represents the LGBTQ?' *Women Talking Politics* November 2018: 33–35.

Frany, Arkin. 2018. *One of the Boys (or How Kenny Saved the City of Toyland).* Illustrated by Fides Balmaceda. Quezon City: Center for Youth Advocacy and Networking, Inc. Also available online at http://tinyurl.com/mulatsulat

Garcia, J. Neil C. 2013. 'Nativism or Universalism: Situating LGBT Discourse in the Philippines'. *Kritika Kultura* 20: 48–68. https://doi.org/10.13185/kk2013.02003

———. 2014. 'The City in Philippine Gay Literature'. *Likhaan: The Journal of Contemporary Philippine Literature* 8: 161–84.

Garcia, Kata. 2018. *My Family.* Illustrated by Borg Sinaban. Quezon City: Adarna House.

Garlítos, Rhandee. 2013. *Ang bonggang-bonggang batang beki! (The Fierce and Fabulous Boy in Pink!)* Illustrated by Tokwa Salazar Peñaflorida. Quezon City: Chikiting Books.

Guzman, Michael de. 2018. *Dalawa ang daddy ni Billy. (Billy Has Two Daddies).* Illustrated by Daniel Palma Tayona. Makati City: Tahanan Books for Young Readers.

———. 2019. 'Reyna Elena'. In *Baklas*, edited by Eugene Evasco and Segundo Matias Jr., 137–44. Quezon City: Lampara Books.

Kander, Jessica. 2011. 'Reading Queer Subtexts in Children's Literature'. Master's dissertation, Eastern Michigan University. http://commons.emich.edu/theses/328

Lodia, Claudia C. 2016. 'Buhay Bahaghari: The Filipino LGBT Chronicles'. *Journal of Contemporary Asia* 46, no. 2: 360–62. https://doi.org/10.1080/00472336.2015.1118524

McCallum, Robyn, and John Stephens. 2010. 'Ideology and Children's Books'. In *Handbook of Research on Children's and Young Adult Literature*, edited by Shelby Wolf, Karen Coats, Patricia A. Enciso and Christine Jenkins, 359–71. New York: Routledge. https://doi.org/10.4324/9780203843543.ch25

Manalastas, Eric Julian, and Beatriz A Torre. 2016. 'LGBT Psychology in the Philippines'. *Psychology of Sexualities Review* 7, no. 1: 60–72.

Manalastas, Eric Julian, Timo Tapani Ojanen, Beatriz A. Torre, Rattanakorn Ratanashevorn, Bryan Choong Chee Hong, Vizla Kumaresan and Vigneswaran Veeramuthu. 2017. 'Homonegativity in Southeast Asia: Attitudes Toward Lesbians and Gay Men in Indonesia, Malaysia, the Philippines, Singapore, Thailand, and Vietnam'. *Asia-Pacific Social Sciences Review* 17, no. 1: 25–33.

Metcalf, Eva-Maria, and Michael J. Meyer. 1992. 'Society, Child Abuse, and Children's Literature'. *Children's Literature Association Quarterly* 17, no. 3: 2–4.

Muyargas, Moniq M., Eric Julian Manalastas, and Pierce S. Docena. 2016. 'The "I ♥ Lesbian and Gay Rights" Pin: An Experiential Learning Exercise to Understand Anti-LGBT Stigma'. *Philippine Journal of Psychology* 49, no. 2: 173–88.

Neri, Bernadette Villanueva. 2012. *Ang Ikaklit sa aming hardin. (Ikaklit in our Garden)*. Illustrated by CJ de Silva. Manila: Raintree Trading & Publishing, Inc./Publikasyong Twamkittens.

Okabe, Masayoshi. 2013. *Where Does Philippine Education Go? The 'K to 12' Program and Reform of the Philippine Basic Education*. Chiba, Japan: Institute of Developing Economies.

Paradela, Teilhard. 2019. 'Tracing the Origins of the Metro Manila Pride March'. *SPOT.PH*, 29 June. https://www.spot.ph/newsfeatures/the-latest-news-features/78298/history-of-pride-march-in-the-philippines-a4410-20190629-lfrm

Payuyo, Louise Abigail. 2012. 'The Portrayal of Gays in Popular Filipino Films, 2000 to 2010'. *Philippine Sociological Review* 60: 291–322.

Philippine Department of Education. n.d. 'Historical Perspective of the Philippine Education System'. Philippine Department of Education. https://www.deped.gov.ph/about-deped/history/

Plaza, Gerry. 2016. 'LGBT Characters are Winning Fans in the Philippines'. *Mashable*, 29 October. https://mashable.com/2016/10/29/lgbtq-philippines-tv/

Quirante, Sue. 2014. 'Talking About Ikaklit with Miss Det Neri'. *Titser! Titser!*, 8 March. https://titsertitser.wordpress.com/tag/ang-ikaklit-sa-aming-hardin/

Ruedas, Mondi. 2018. *What's My Power Gear?* Illustrated by Ruthie Genuino. Quezon City: Center for Youth Advocacy and Networking, Inc. Also available online at http://tinyurl.com/mulatsulat

Sawatzky, Robert. 2016. 'Philippines Elects First Transgender Woman'. *CNN*, 11 May. https://edition.cnn.com/2016/05/10/asia/philippines-transgender-geraldine-roman/index.html

Sayuno, Cheeno Marlo. 2017. 'Complementarity in Movement and Performance: Critiquing Gender Roles in Philippine Cultural Dances'. *Philippines Communication Society (PCS) Review: Special Issue on Gender and the Media*, December 2017. http://library.cnu.edu.ph/wp-content/uploads/2019/05/PCS-Review-Philippine-Communication-Society-Dec-2017.pdf

———. 2018. 'Freeing the Elephant-eating Boa: Theorizing Children in Philippine Social Science Research'. *Plaridel: A Philippine Journal of Communication, Media and Society* 15, no. 2. http://www.plarideljournal.org/article/freeing-the-elephant-eating-boa-theorizing-children-in-philippine-social-science-research/

———. 2020. *Sayaw ni Dayaw* (Dayaw's Dance). Illustrated by Harry Monzon. Anvil Publishing.

Schlegel, Stuart A. 1999. *Wisdom from the Rainforest: The Spiritual Journey of an Anthropologist*. Quezon City: Ateneo de Manila University Press.

Tandora, Elena Q. 2003. *Philippine Education System*. Quezon City: Verh Educational Enterprise.

Thiel, Barbara. (1984). 'Austronesian Origins and Expansion: The Philippine Archaeological Data'. *Asian Perspectives* 26, no. 1: 119–29.

United Nations Development Programme and United States Agency for International Development. 2014. *Being LGBT in Asia: The Philippines Country Report*. Bangkok: United Nations Development Programme and United States Agency for International Development. https://pdf.usaid.gov/pdf_docs/PBAAA888.pdf

Wright, Christopher Yap. 2017. 'Skeletons in the Closets: Gay Themes in Philippine Fictions in English'. *Rupkatha Journal on Interdisciplinary Studies in Humanities* 9, no. 2: 293–302. https://doi.org/10.21659/rupkatha.v9n2.30

Chapter Twelve

BETWEEN LITERATURE, IDEOLOGY AND PEDAGOGY: LGBTQ+ FICTION FOR CHILDREN AND YOUNG ADULTS IN SLOVENIA

Andrej Zavrl

Introduction

Slovenia is a country variously described as part of Central, Eastern or Southern Europe or the Western Balkans, depending on the writer's perspective, ideology or reference book. An EU member state since 2004, it has only been independent since 1991, having previously been part of, among others, the Socialist Federal Republic of Yugoslavia, the Kingdom of Serbs, Croats and Slovenians (later the Kingdom of Yugoslavia), and the Austro-Hungarian Empire. It is perhaps understandable that, without a nation state to rely on, Slovenian national awareness and identity have had to rely primarily on the Slovenian language, culture and literature, although their role and actual impact in the nation-building processes have been debated (Dović 2017).

When Slovenian lands were still part of larger state unions, 'unnatural fornication' was penalized in accordance with the states' penal codes. Slovenia's specific development began when – together with some other, but not all, republics of SFR Yugoslavia – it decriminalized sexual acts between men in 1977. The 1930 Penal Code of the Kingdom of Yugoslavia had punished homosexual acts between men and women, whereas Yugoslavia's 1951 Penal Code kept the provision, with an amended penalty, for men only.

The fall of the Berlin Wall in 1989 marked a turning point in the development of LGBTQ+ movements in Eastern Europe, but in Slovenia it had started a little before that – in 1984 with the six-day festival Homosexuality and Culture. Since Slovenia's independence, LGBTQ+ activism has diversified and worked towards greater social and legal inclusion of LGBTQ+ people. The first Ljubljana Pride Parade was organized in 2001 as a protest against a homophobic incident during which the poets Brane Mozetič and Jean-Paul Daoust were denied entry into a café. In terms of LGBTQ+-specific legislation, 2005 saw the introduction of the Civil Partnership Registration Act, granting LGBTQ+ people only a handful of rights, while 2011 brought a new Family Code (same-gender couples were granted all the rights enjoyed by heterosexual couples except for joint adoption and artificial insemination). The Code was rejected by a referendum called for by conservative groups supported by the Catholic Church. In 2015, the Parliament passed the Amendment to the Marriage and Family Relations Act, which established complete equality between heterosexual and homosexual couples, but the change was rejected by another referendum. Finally, in 2016, the Parliament adopted the Civil Partnership Act, which returned to the solution (not) implemented by the 2011 Family Code. In May 2016, the Parliament legislated against discrimination based on sexuality, gender identity and gender expression (the Protection against Discrimination Act).

In view of what has just been said about the history of Slovenian lands, the wider significance of literature to the nation-building processes and the relatively strong conservative presence in Slovenia's public life, it is unsurprising that some people and groups specifically target schools and literature for younger readers, decrying 'homosexual propaganda' as one of the main threats to 'us, Slovenians', posed by the LGBTQ+ abuse of 'our children', old communist networks and plots and 'the violent homo-lesbian-bi-trans-queer lobby supported by the degraded left' (Donko 2018, n.p.). Such fear of non-conforming identities is repeatedly demonstrated and perpetrated through a variety of well-connected civil-society initiatives, political parties and the Catholic Church (for more on the anti-gender movement in Slovenia, see Kuhar 2017).

Today Slovenia is a country of about two million inhabitants and that is, roughly speaking, also the figure for speakers of the Slovenian language and potential users of literature in the language. Correspondingly, the Slovenian book market is relatively small, and much of its non-commercial share depends on state subsidies. A very important role in Slovenian and translated LGBTQ+ literature, including children's and young adult (CYA) literature, is played by the specialized LGBTQ+ book series Lambda (1990–present, with over 150 books published to date), edited by the prominent gay writer, poet, editor, translator and activist Brane Mozetič.[1] The bibliography at the end of this chapter shows that there are a few other, mainstream publishers (and book series) that regularly publish LGBTQ+ texts, too. There is only one journal specializing in CYA literature, *Otrok in knjiga* (The Child and the Book, 1972–present), and CYA literature reviews are published only sporadically.

Bearing in mind these introductory observations, this chapter gives an overview of LGBTQ+ fiction for children and young adults written by Slovenian authors, focusing on the representation of LGBTQ+ characters, relationships and lives. It includes occasional references to translated texts, as translation has always played a pivotal role in Slovenian literary culture, and translations make up more than half of all the production of CYA literature (*Priročnik* 2018, 8). As a matter of principle, I only discuss books which have been clearly defined as CYA literature by their publishers or reception, although adolescents and young adults read the adult canon – indeed, are required to do so – after they enter secondary school (at the age of 15), so it would also be important to analyse the authors and texts from the Slovenian and Western canons included in the curriculum. This being

1 Another book series published by the same organization (Škuc), Vizibilija (1998–present), specializes in lesbian fiction and theory, and it has brought out over 50 titles, but none specifically for children or young adults.

a chapter on CYA fiction, I exclude non-fiction works such as handbooks and manuals on adolescence, growing up and sexuality.

Somewhat contradictorily, my discourse relies heavily on the opposition between normativity and non-normativity, reinforcing binarism while seeking to criticize it. Be that as it may, the norm is meant to denote cisgender and heterosexual identities, whereas non-normativity stands for a wide range of positions and identities provisionally subsumed under the abbreviation LGBTQ+. The abbreviation LGBTQ+ (as well as its shorter and longer variants) is used in Slovenian in the same way it is generally used elsewhere to mean lesbian, gay, bisexual, transgender and queer. The initial letters of the Slovenian words are the same, so the same abbreviation is used as in English. The term 'queer' is occasionally Slovenicized to 'kvir', but – at least for the time being – the Q in the abbreviation remains.

The chapter is divided into three sections; the first section examines representations of sexual orientation, the second section centres around gender, and the third section is about LGBTQ+ families in CYA fiction.[2]

Sexuality

A book that has never been interpreted as in any way relating to LGBTQ+ issues – a series of four picture books, actually – is one of the great classics of Slovenian children's literature: the Juri Muri picture books written in verse by the major Slovenian poet Tone Pavček (1928–2011), illustrated by different illustrators, and published in different editions. The first part of the story came out in a children's magazine in 1953–54, and its first book edition is from 1958. It is about a boy who visits Africa and has his prejudices about the continent shattered. Book two of the series, *Juri Muri drugič v Afriki* (Juri Muri in Africa Again, 2001, 3–6 years), features the Slovenian protagonist Juri Muri visiting Africa for the second time. There he meets Bongo, who is supposed to be Juri's servant. In spite of the racist undertones of the picture books in terms of both text and illustration, Juri refuses to play along with the hierarchical, colonial rules. Instead the boys become very close and, eventually, Bongo, whom Juri finds handsome, agrees to leave home and go to Slovenia to be with Juri: '… but if you're going, take me with you, / with you I'll

2 I provide the following bibliographical details in the main text: Slovenian title, original title, English title, year of original publication, Slovenian translator and year of Slovenian translation (ST), target age group, and, for Slovenian picture books, the book format (width × height). Longer quotes in the Slovenian original (for fiction only) are given in footnotes, while shorter ones are given in round brackets within the main-text quotes. All the translations into English are mine. When identifying texts to include in my analysis, I have relied on my own reading and reviewing, on other authors (esp. Pirnar 2006; Picco 2011a, 2011b) and on *Priročnik za branje kakovostnih mladinskih knjig* (The Handbook for Reading Quality Children's and Young Adult Books), published annually by Pionirska – center za mladinsko književnost in knjižničarstvo (Centre for Children's and Young Adult Literature and Librarianship at the Ljubljana City Library). Hereafter referred to as the *Priročnik*, it is available at: www.mklj.si/prirocnik/item/451. The *Priročnik* analyses an average of about 750 new books for children and young adults every year, of which over 80 per cent are fiction (*Priročnik* 2017, 9; 2018, 8).

be happy wherever I am' (Pavček 2001, n.p.).[3] The two boys, 'a beautiful couple (lepi par)', are described and illustrated (in various degrees by different illustrators) as having a loving and intimate bond. Juri speaks for both of them when he declares: 'As long as we're alive, / we'll stay together, inseparable'.[4] And, the speaker adds, he was 'a man of his word. / They have been together from that time up until now' (Pavček 2001, n.p.).[5]

At the end of book three, *Juri Muri po Sloveniji* (Juri Muri Around Slovenia, 2011, 6–9 years), the two boys fall in love with the same girl, and the books ends with a cliff-hanger as to whose wooing she will accept (Pavček 2011, 59). However, at the beginning of book four, *Juri Muri gre po srečo* (Juri Muri Looking for Happiness, 2012, 9–15 years), they decide to forsake their female object of affection 'in order to stay friends (da ostala bi prijatelja)' (Pavček 2012, n.p.), and the last illustration has them, now teenagers, walking together, possibly hand in hand, under streaks of different colours reminiscent of the rainbow, having found happiness in being together (Pavček 2012, n.p.).

The speaker (and the poet) of the poem would perhaps disagree with my interpretation, just as the experts I spoke to did. Indeed, at the level of denotation, Juri and Bongo are repeatedly and emphatically 'like brothers' and they are 'friends', including in Juri's mother's eyes: 'Together with you two, my dear Africans, / your mother is joyful, / remain what you are – / clever friends' (Pavček 2001, n.p.).[6] Yet, bearing in mind that heterosexual (pre)school couples are typically seen as cute whereas non-heterosexual ones are ostensibly non-existent, I see the speaker as performing the role of self-deceiving parents, like Juri's mother herself – unless, of course, she is using the term 'prijatelj' in the meaning of 'boyfriend, fiancé', rather than 'friend' (*SSKJ* n.d, n.p.).

'Friend(s)', it turns out over and over again, is a fluid category, a well-known weasel word encompassing, among others, Holly Hobbie's pigs Toot and Puddle (*Toot & Puddle*, 1997, ST[7] Milan Dekleva, 1999; *Toot & Puddle: A Present for Toot*, 1998, ST Milan Dekleva, 2000, 3–8 years), who you could argue live in a gay household. In the picture book *Murenček in Polhek* (Cricket and Dormouse, 2017, 3–8 years) by Brane Mozetič (b. 1958) and illustrator Andrej Brumen Čop (b. 1967), the eponymous Cricket and Dormouse strike up a friendship which transcends the regular order of their families and species, and their cross-species 'friendship' can represent any kind of class, race, gender, sexual, etc. transgression. Its queer potential might be emphasized by the fact that it was published in the Lambda LGBTQ+ book series, and the author has confirmed to me that in his view the relationship between the characters (both male) has all the characteristics of a romantic relationship. Finally, the word 'friends' is also used for clearly same-gender relationships, like the lesbian couples in John Boyne's *Osupljiva zgodba Barnabyja Brocketa* (*The Terrible Thing That Happened to Barnaby Brocket*, 2012, ST Jure Potokar, 2013, 10+ years) and Neli Kodrič Filipić's *Kaj ima ljubezen s tem* (What's Love Got to Do With It, 2009, 10+ years).

---

3 '… a če greš, me s sabo vzemi, / s tabo srečen bom, kjer bom'.
4 'Dokler bova živa, / bova skupaj, neločljiva'.
5 '… mož beseda. / Skup sta od tedaj do zdaj'.
6 'Z vama, draga Afričana, / srečna vajina je mama, / ostanita to, kar sta – / pametna prijatelja'.
7 As noted in footnote 2, above, I use the abbreviation 'ST' for 'Slovenian translation' throughout.

Figure 15: Mozetič, Brane. 2014. *Prva ljubezen* (First Love). Illustrated by Maja Kastelic. Ljubljana: Škuc (Lambda).

No such resistant or oppositional reading or decoding is required for the first and so far only book in Slovenian explicitly to deal with same-gender love among pre-schoolers. It was written by Brane Mozetič and illustrated by Maja Kastelic (b. 1981). The picture book *Prva ljubezen* (First Love, 2014, 3–6 years) was also made into a puppet show in 2017 (dir. Alenka Pirjevec; *SiGledal* website n.d., n.p.) and translated into Swedish, Spanish and Korean. It is a small format (15 × 20 cm) picture book with acrylics-on-paper illustrations that reflect the text in a relatively straightforward way. As opposed to some other picture books addressing non-normativity, this one features people rather than animals.

The unnamed first-person narrator recounts his experiences from when he was six years old. He has to move from a village to a town to live with his single mum, and in his new life he starts preschool. He is a lonely, sensitive boy who prefers spending his days at home and pretending that he is at the Sanremo Music Festival in Italy, singing and dressing up in his mother's clothes. He only makes one close friend, a taller, stronger boy called Drejček, who takes him under his wing, and at preschool they start to increasingly spend time together. When the narrator performs the Sanremo for Drejček, singing and wearing girl's accessories, they are spotted by their preschool teacher. The narrator immediately feels that something is wrong, though he is unsure what it is, and his impression is confirmed by the teacher's reaction. She angrily commands that 'this' must never happen again, blaming the narrator, but not explicating what the actual trespass was (Mozetič 2014, n.p.). However, the boys continue to spend preschool days together and hold hands in spite of the closer supervision that their teachers now exercise over them. It is when they kiss with joy at seeing each other after the narrator has been absent from preschool for a week (see Figure 15) that the teacher intervenes again. She pulls Drejček away and comments on this by saying: 'What's wrong with you, he's not a girl!' (Mozetič 2014, n.p.).[8] They are separated and no longer allowed to spend time together. Drejček's family eventually move away and they never see each other again. The narrator concludes his account by saying: 'I loved him, and I think he loved me, too' (Mozetič 2014, n.p.).[9]

Mozetič develops very similar themes in his picture book *Ahil in Patrokles* (Achilles and Patroclus, illustrated by Ana Lucija Šarić (b. 1994), 2020a, 5–9 years, 17 × 25 cm), but unlike the more intimate setting of *Prva ljubezen*, *Ahil in Patrokles* is set in larger, mythological contexts, in line with Mozetič's more general interest in historicizing same-gender desire (he has written, translated, edited or published a number of texts dealing with LGBTQ+ history).[10] A retelling of the well-known story of the close comrades fighting against the Trojans, the book follows the tradition of casting Achilles and Patroclus as very close friends, possibly lovers. They are presented (in text and illustration) as inseparable, holding hands, hugging, and looking into each other's eyes (see Figure 16). After Patroclus's death in battle, Achilles is devastated, wondering, in despair, 'What is still left to me, if you leave, after our kisses?' (Mozetič 2020a, n.p.).[11] When Achilles takes revenge and is killed, too, their ashes are mixed together and they remain, in the memory of others, inseparable in death just as they were in life: 'This is a story about romantic love that overcomes all obstacles, even death – and inspiration for many other similar stories' (Mozetič 2020a, n.p.).[12]

Another strong call for justice and a harsh condemnation of all-pervading, systemic homophobia can be found in the novel *Dečki: roman iz dijaškega internata* (Boys: A Novel from a Boarding School, 1938, reprinted 1970 and 2016) by the Slovenian writer France Novšak (1916–1991). It is now generally recognized as the first Slovenian homoerotic novel, and it has also been discussed, occasionally, as a YA novel (e.g. Blažić 2020; Picco 2011b; Pirnar 2006). The novel depicts the intimacy between Zdenko, aged 13–14, from Serbia, and Nani, aged 16–17, from Slovenia, that develops during their year-long stay at a Catholic boarding school in Zagreb, Croatia. Their relationship becomes very intimate very quickly, and the novel describes the awakening of the adolescent body and sexual (self-)awareness in a place of institutional ideological, religious and sexual abuse of adolescents.

Novšak's novel aside, the first book clearly intended for teenaged readers with homosexuality as the main theme to appear in Slovenia was the translation of Nancy Garden's *Annie on My Mind* (1982, ST Dušanka Zabukovec, 1996, 13+ years). Marta Pirnar believes that in this 'excellent novel […] the writer sets out to foster understanding in readers of lesbian love, which is after all only one of the faces of love', promoting 'understanding,

8 'Kaj pa ti je, saj ni punčka!'

9 'Imel sem ga rad. In mislim, da tudi on mene'.

10 Mozetič (2020b) has also published a non-fiction book for children and adolescents charting the different people, identities, events, movements, and so on relevant to LGBTQ+ history from ancient times to today. What makes this book truly pioneering is, first, its being addressed specifically to young readers and, second, its gender-balanced approach.

11 'Kaj mi še ostane, če ti odideš, po najinih poljubih?'

12 'To je zgodba o romantični ljubezni, ki premaga vse ovire, tudi smrt – in je navdih za mnoge druge podobne zgodbe.'

Figure 16: Mozetič, Brane. 2020a. *Ahil in Patrokles* (Achilles and Patroclus). Illustrated by Ana Lucija Šarić. Ljubljana: Škuc (Lambda).

sympathy and empathy for the adolescent's feelings of love' (Pirnar 2006, 238). The same view in almost the same words about the 'psychologically complex and lucid young adult novel' is expressed by Kristina Picco (2011b, 10). The *Priročnik* describes the novel as a sensitive story of '*genuine friendship* between two secondary-school girls that gradually grows into something deeper: love' (*Priročnik* 1998, 53; emphasis added). Typically, the Slovenian afterword abounds in references to 'being different' and to how traumatic homosexuality can be. Consequently, even if supportive, it strengthens the perception of same-gender attraction as beset with agony and pain (Cotič 1996, 175). Not unexpectedly, conservative groups still see the novel as part of the homosexual indoctrination that children are subjected to at school (M. 2016, n.p.), but criticism has also come from LGBTQ+ readers. The novel's discourse is what Nataša Velikonja, a lesbian poet, translator and activist, seems to criticize in the poem 'spet na začetku' (at the beginning again): 'we've written and translated / millions of books, but lesbians continue to / read "annie on my mind" and watch / "connie and carla"' (Velikonja 2007, 99).[13]

All of the trauma and more of it, minus the happy ending, equals the 'the first originally Slovenian gay contemporary young adult novel' (Picco 2011b, 16). Janja Vidmar (b. 1962), one of the most prolific and popular authors of CYA literature in Slovenia, has written plenty of what she and others like to call 'problem books' (see Kos 2015; Vidmar 2017). Among them is *Fantje iz gline* (Clay Boys, 2005, 13+ years). The novel switches between two first-person narrators, both identified by their nicknames only, and the plot

13 'napisale in prevedle smo na / milijone knjig, a lezbijke še vedno / berejo "pismo za annie" in gledajo "connie in carla"'.

unfolds in the triangle among three adolescent boys. Ajk, 17, is very good at sports and he professes loudly to be straight, keeps homophobic company, uses very degrading language, and seems obsessed with branding others as 'faggots' (in Slovenian he uses a variety of terms, e.g. *gejčo*, *homo*, *peder*, all of which are derogatory). Part of this is due to his upbringing. His father is a stereotypical immigrant from Montenegro, a tyrannical lorry driver who hates homosexuals. The other narrator, whom Ajk calls 'a weirdo (čudak)' (Vidmar 2005, 39), is Mali, 17. He is shown as a sensitive, possibly suicidal, young man, consumed with mourning his best friend Rok, who killed himself. He suffers from acute depression, philosophizes about life and its meaning, and turns to bad personal hygiene as a protection against the world. The marriage of his parents is in tatters, and the one adult he has a good relationship with is his arts teacher.

Despite appearances, Ajk's hetero machismo is under great strain and, too macho to admit he likes men, he uses self-harming as a coping strategy. Although he is in love with his rowing teammate Kec, Ajk states the following: 'Actually, it's not that I don't want to be gay. But I fuckingsimply ain't' (Vidmar 2005, 207).[14] For him, his desire for men appears to be limited to clandestine sex, anguish and vigorous self-denial. Reflecting on his own sexuality, Mali is not sure either. He claims he is neither gay nor straight nor bisexual: 'I'm not gay. I'm not. I'm simply not. It's not that I don't want to be. I don't want to be. I don't care. My sperm are engaged in guerrilla warfare' (Vidmar 2005, 77),[15] having said earlier on: 'I'm not gay. I'm not straight. I'm not bi, because I wouldn't. I'm nothing. Because I'm not living, I can't die either. It wouldn't be ethical' (Vidmar 2005, 67).[16] The only character who did self-identify as gay was Rok. He was in love with Ajk and killed himself because of the bullying he had to endure.

Mali, who describes Ajk as 'a schoolmate with psychosomatic problems, very well-built, but a macho without a soul' (Vidmar 2005, 45),[17] knows about Ajk's self-harming and he knows about his sexuality, too. He revenges Rok's death by making Ajk give a class presentation about Michelangelo's sexual orientation and his sculpture David's small penis. Thus, same-gender attraction in Mali's view seems to be a legitimate tool for blackmail, for intimidation, for shaming others, for sweet revenge. Nevertheless, when Ajk's world has irretrievably collapsed and Mali has done his revengeful duty, there may be a beam of light at the end of this tunnel. Their mutual distrust and aversion may have subsided a little, but the ending is open, and Mali remains confused about his attractions (Vidmar 2005, 211).

The author of the afterword, a prominent expert on CYA literature, describes the novel as addressing 'a taboo topic' and as 'a literary provocation' (Saksida 2005, 213). He offers three possible levels of understanding the novel – as an adventure, as a novel of adolescent angst, and as a love story (Saksida 2005, 216). When looking at the novel

14 'V bistvu ne gre za to, da nočem biti gej. Ampak prezajebanopreprosto nisem.'

15 'Nisem gej. Nisem. Preprosto nisem. Saj ne, da nočem biti. Nočem biti. Vseeno mi je. Moji spermiji so v gverili.'

16 'Nisem gej. Nisem hetero. Nisem bi, ker ne bi. Nič nisem. Ker sploh ne živim, tudi umreti ne morem. Ne bi bilo etično.'

17 '… sošolec s psihosomatskimi motnjami, ki je dobro zmodeliran, ampak mačo brez duše'.

as a love story, Saksida argues that the sense of alienation that the novel's characters feel and the question of values outweigh homosexuality as a theme (Saksida 2005, 220, 222). This reminds us of the critical strategies implying that literature about heterosexual love is literature about (heterosexual) love, whereas portrayals of same-gender love are almost necessarily about something else, something more universal.

In accordance with the didactic view of CYA literature as a tool for moral education, Vidmar's novel has been hailed as breaking down the taboos and social prejudice (Haramija 2009, 167; 2012, 332; Picco 2011b, 20). Still, it merges countless negative tropes and stereotypes into constitutive elements of the plot and characters' identities: suicide, violence and bullying, dysfunctional families but understanding and possibly homosexual saviour teachers, sexual abuse (in childhood) as an indicator of non-normativity and identity confusion, self-harm, falling in love destructively with straights, same-gender attraction as something dirty to be suppressed, and so on.

These tropes are present in other texts, too, including translated ones. For instance, in another modern classic, Julie Anne Peters's *Daleč od Xanadu* (*Far from Xanadu*, 2005, ST Anja Kokalj, 2006, 13+ years), Mike, 16, develops a colossal but unfulfilled crush on Xanadu, who is straight. Divorced families and absent fathers are another recurrent motif. In Tamara Bach's *Punca z Marsa* (*Marsmädchen / Girl from Mars*, 2003, ST Barbara Lipovšek, 2007, 13+ years), Miriam, 15, falls in love with Laura, who comes from a divorced family. In another translation from German, Andreas Steinhöfel's *Središče sveta* (*Die Mitte der Welt / Centre of My World*, 1998, ST Anja Golob, 2018, 13+ years), the 17-year-old first-person narrator Phil is a gay boy who lives with his sister and mother and misses the father he has never known, seemingly believing there can be no family without a father.

Kate Walker's *Peter* (*Peter*, 1991, ST Marta Pirnar, 2007, 13+ years), the first book about a gay male adolescent protagonist to be translated into Slovenian, has a first-person narrator, Peter, 15, whose parents are divorced, and his father, like Ajk's, is a homophobe. After Peter starts reluctantly to accept that he may be gay, he eventually wants to have sex with David, his brother's gay friend, to ascertain whether he is gay or is not. Unlike Peter, LGBTQ+ characters in YA novels usually want to experiment heterosexually so that they can be absolutely certain they are not straight, the opposite of which is much less likely in their straight counterparts. David Belbin's novel *Zadnja devica* (*The Last Virgin*, 2002, ST Katarina Mahnič, 2005, 13+ years) is a case in point, as is Marliese Arold's third-person narrated *Sandra ljubi Meike* (*Einfach nur Liebe: Sandra liebt Meike* / Simply Love: Sandra Loves Meike, 1996, ST Andrea Švab, 2002, 13+ years). Some protagonists solve their confusion by rejecting identity labels altogether, for example Giacomo in Tommaso Percivale's short story 'Ko sem se prvič poljubil' ('La prima volta che ho baciato / The First Time That I Kissed', 2016, ST Karmen Filipič, 2016, 14+ years). For others it can be a rite of passage, an incentive for developing a deeper self-awareness, for instance in Suzana Tratnik's (b. 1963) short story 'Jebeno pismo' (The Damn Letter), added to the translation of the UK collection of short stories *Losing It*, edited by Keith Gray (2010, ST Irena Duša, 2014a, 13+ years). The story is set in rural Yugoslavia in the early 1980s. Varja, 17, and her friend Lija have sex after a drunken night out. For Varja it is precious and revealing, but Lija insists it means nothing at all, because her 'real' first sexual experience was with a young man she is dating now. This is not altogether dissimilar to Patrick Ness's short story in the same collection, 'Different for Boys', in which the narrator Ant, about 15, reflects on what it means to lose his virginity and come out as a gay boy.

Self-harming, violence and suicide, usually as the extreme consequences of homophobic and transphobic bullying, are persistent, too. In James Heneghan's novel *Povračilo* (*Payback*, 2007, ST Kristina Dečman, 2009, 13+ years), Benny, the 13-year-old narrator's effeminate schoolmate, kills himself because he finds no support anywhere. Patrick Ness's *Več kot to* (*More than This*, 2013, ST Andrej Hiti Ožinger, 2015, 13+ years) has just as tragic an ending for the main, 17-year-old gay character Seth. As another example of the environment's pressure on LGBTQ+ lovers, Seth's boyfriend is moved to another school when their love is discovered and they lose contact, which we have already seen in Mozetič's picture book *Prva ljubezen* (First Love, 2014). An instance of lesbian love revolving around abuse, self-harming, family violence, and having sex heterosexually, hoping to become straight, is Cheryl Rainfield's novel *Brazgotine* (*Scars*, 2010, ST Mateja Malnar Stembal, 2013, 13+ years).

Clearly then, Janja Vidmar is no exception in representing homosexuality as she does, and she uses similar approaches in her other 'problem' novels. I am not arguing that her novel is inherently unrealistic. Neither am I asking for naïve self-help books. She certainly does not paint black-and-white images or lull her readers into false complacency. But when toxic motifs are accumulated in recurrent constructs, when psychopathology is instinctively assumed, when individual attributes are generalized, I would advise caution. Although Vidmar's characters may elicit sympathy and readers may take pity on them (if pity is what we are after), they also boost stereotypes and prejudices and enable readers to feel superior to the characters, to judge them without much self-reflection.

Vidmar's novel is referenced in Cvetka Bevc's (b. 1960) *Desetka* (Ten of Us, 2011, 13+ years), a novel in 10 chapters, each told by one of the 10 friends. One of them, Kroki, 16, is gay. He likes girls as friends (though his chapter is titled 'I'm Not Into Girls'), he would like to become a hairdresser, his favourite film is *Brokeback Mountain*, and his favourite book is Vidmar's *Fantje iz gline* (Clay Boys). Kroki is coming to terms with his sexual orientation with the help of his first crush, Aleš, two years his senior, who normalizes same-gender desire and disregards what others may say about it, thereby making Kroki feel more at ease with himself. Nevertheless, he still recommends caution and discretion to avoid homophobic violence. Unlike the characters' lives in his literary and cinematic favourites, Kroki's own life seems much less traumatic – beyond a standard (pre-)coming-out anxiety – and more likely to include some sort of LGBTQ+ community. This may be related to the wider social changes in Slovenia, to a greater visibility and acceptance of homosexuality, but the time that passed between the two books is not long enough to warrant jumping to any such conclusion. It could simply be due to the author's personal attitudes.

For a rare instance of a (possibly) bisexual character, I have to go back in time a little, to the novel *Maja* (Maja, 1971, 13+ years) by Nada Kraigher (1911–2000), first published in 1971 and then again, in a CYA literature book series, in 1979. Set in the 1960s, the novel starts with the eponymous protagonist of the novel, a young woman, meeting and falling for Bine, a slightly older, wealthy man. Maja becomes pregnant with Bine's child, but he keeps disappearing until she hardly ever sees him anymore. In due course, during an unannounced visit to his home, she finds him in bed with another man. This comes as a dreadful shock that sets her on a vicious, self-destructive downward spiral of alcoholism, nervous breakdowns, illness, hospitals, crime and prisons.

The novel has been criticized on account of not challenging stereotypes and homophobic expectations, showing homosexual men as immoral cheats hiding their sexual orientation (Kos 2015, 47; Picco 2011b, 9; Pirnar 2006, 241). However, unless we accept that Bine's actions of seducing, impregnating and then discarding Maja are completely unmotivated by anything other than malevolence, we must assume he is bisexual. To be sure, non-normative sexuality is a signifier of moral condemnation: 'that damn image, the image of her child's father in a perverse embrace' haunts Maja, and Bine's partner's voice is described as 'unpleasantly shrilling', the men's laughter as the 'disgusting laughter of vain single men', and they are instances of 'men who are not men … degenerate people' (Kraigher 1971, 175, 50, 52, 72).[18] But it is noteworthy that the existence of non-normative sexualities, even partnerships, is clearly confirmed – despite the fact that when the novel was first published homosexual acts between men were still against the law.

I intentionally leave out the books that use LGBTQ+ as a spice or a plot device without much (or any) consideration for what this means for the representation of LGBTQ+ characters. For example, Neli Kodrič Filipić's (b. 1964) novel *Kaj ima ljubezen s tem* (What's Love Got to Do with It, 2009, 10+ years) provides some patronizing sympathy for non-normativity by including a 'gay' character. Unfortunately, he turns out not to be gay at all (when he once failed sexually with a girl, she accused him of being gay and he thought it best to adopt the position and avoid the shame of being seen as an impotent straight man (Kodrič Filipić 2009, 270)), and the book reinstates the norm as a precondition for a happy ending. This makes it structurally homophobic. The plot twist requires that the 'gay' in the novel offers readers a positive identification model, but he can only do so by eventually coming out as straight. Comparably, Vladimir P. Štefanec's (b. 1964) *Sem punk čarovnica, debela lezbijka in ne maram vampov* (I'm a Punk Witch, a Fat Lesbian and I Don't Like Tripe, 2014, 13+ years) is a pro-acceptance book with a lesbian in its title, but no lesbian among its characters. It is narrated by 13-year-old Daša, whose schoolmates are filled with hate for gays and lesbians, which she counters by signing up on Facebook with a fake profile (Fat Lesbian), although there is no suggestion she herself is anything else but straight.

To summarize, this section discusses non-heteronormative identities in books for children and young adults. In addition to a new reading of Tone Pavček's classic Juri Muri series, two books are given special emphasis. Brane Mozetič's picture book *Prva ljubezen* (First Love, 2014) gives a positive account of love between two preschool boys separated by the intervention of the external world that labels their love inappropriate and eventually banishes it, the norm striking even before the boys understand fully that they are deviating from it. Conversely, Janja Vidmar's *Fantje iz gline* (Clay Boys, 2005), the novel

18 'Tista prekleta podoba, podoba očeta njenega otroka v perverznem objemu'; 'neprijetno hreščeč'; 'oduren smeh nečimrnih samcev'; 'moški, ki niso moški … izrojeni ljudje'.

with a prominent position as the first originally Slovenian YA novel dealing with homosexuality, relates same-gender desire to all kinds of struggle and abuse, demonstrating how hard it can be to come to grips with it, not least for writers.

Gender

In another of Janja Vidmar's novels, *Softibluz* (Softy Blues, 2006, 13+ years), the protagonist girl Taja, 14, is gender non-conforming and therefore often called a lesbian, which hurts her. In order for this to function, however, readers have to accept the assumption that being a lesbian is negative – another example of questionable narrative tactics. But different heterodoxies often do interrelate. Thus, Brane Mozetič's picture book *Prva ljubezen* (First Love, 2014), discussed in the previous section, focuses on the relationship between two preschool boys, but it also includes tacit descriptions of gender non-conformity. The narrator comes across as a slightly effeminate boy who likes putting on his mother's clothes, and there is an echo of gender binarism in the relationship between the boys; the narrator says of himself: 'I was not brave. I cried very quickly if something was wrong' (Mozetič 2014, n.p.).[19] Drejček, on the other hand, is taller and more assertive, but also very protective towards the narrator: 'He was an entire head taller than me, and he liked fighting with other boys. He liked being in charge. I don't know if he said anything to the others, but they always let me be' (Mozetič 2014, n.p.).[20] Mozetič introduces the motif of cross-dressing in *Ahil in Patrokles* (Achilles and Patroclus), too. Namely, Achilles's mother tries to protect her son from having to join the army by dressing him up as a girl and sending him to live with the royal daughters on a faraway island (Mozetič 2020, n.p.). Unlike the narrator of *Prva ljubezen*, who seems to enjoy cross-dressing (which may be part of his identity), Achilles reverts to his predestined life course as a masculine soldier at the first opportunity.

This section will concentrate on gender (non-normativity), that is, on the 'T' in the LGBTQ+. While Julie Anne Peters's *Luna* (*Luna*, 2004, ST Anja Kokalj, 2007, 13+ years) has been described as 'the first YA novel to address transsexual/transgender issues' (Cart and Jenkins 2006, 138), this is not entirely true in the Slovenian context. The first YA novel with a trans protagonist was by the Slovenian author Suzana Tratnik (b. 1963), a major figure in contemporary Slovenian literature and LGBTQ+ activism. Initially published as an adult novel, *Ime mi je Damjan* (My Name Is Damjan, 2001, 13+ years) predates Peters's *Luna* by three years (and its Slovenian translation by six). Set in the mid-1990s, the novel features Damjan, a 19-year-old first-person narrator and a badly adapted young man who certainly never does what polite society expects of him. He harbours plenty of pent-up anger and finds no support in his dysfunctional family. His relationship with his violent father is especially bad; in fact, we learn that his father abused him when he was little and his mother was a silent accomplice.

---

19 'Jaz nisem bil pogumen. Zelo hitro sem zajokal, če je bilo kaj narobe.'

20 'Bil je za celo glavo večji od mene in rad se je pretepal z drugimi fanti. Bil je rad glavni. Ne vem, ali jim je on kaj rekel, toda mene so vedno pustili pri miru.'

Damjan starts attending a therapy group and as a result we gradually learn about his childhood and adolescence. When he was 17, Damjan adopted his current (male) name, but he does not say that it was because he also adopted a different gender expression. Although some readers may not be aware in the first half of the book that Damjan is a trans man (Borovnik 2012, 108; Koron 2014, 227; Kos 2015, 75; Zupan Sosič 2006, 328), Tratnik herself asserts that it was never her intention to write a novel with a twist and that she expected readers would be aware that Damjan is not just like any other man. Hence, *Ime mi je Damjan* was not written as a coming-out narrative (Tratnik 2014b, 61). Neither is it a Bildungsroman; the character of Damjan is formed from the outset, and there is little enlightenment or pedagogy (Tratnik 2015, 85). Other labels have also proved tricky. Especially when there was still insufficient understanding of LGBTQ+ categories, *Damjan* was termed homoerotic, homosexual, lesbian, transvestite, and so on (Picco 2011b, 14, 15; Tratnik 2014b, 60; Zupan Sosič 2006, 305, 307; 2017, 179). In an article about her novel, Tratnik describes Damjan's gender identity as 'somehow undefined, fluid, perhaps multifaceted, he does not have a special name for it, nor does he want it, just as he does not want to be different or belong to any marginal group, even if he cannot entirely avoid it' (Tratnik 2014b, 60–61).

While his friend Roki is a trans man, too, Damjan refuses to have any genuine connection with the LGBTQ+ community or its equal rights identity-based agenda, although they sometimes go out to 'a faggot disco (pedrski disko)' and Damjan's girlfriend Nela is a lesbian who is part of the LGBTQ+ community. Nevertheless, Damjan loathes – does not understand – politically engaged lesbians and Nela's fight for 'faggot rights (pedrske pravice)' (Tratnik 2001, 112). Besides, he cannot grasp why 'they call themselves lesbians – as if others didn't call them names enough' (Tratnik 2001, 109).[21] Nataša Velikonja describes Damjan as 'pre-political', as outside contemporary social movements, someone who remains within the same gender binary (Velikonja 2014, 258, 260). But there is a hint of criticism of Damjan's lesbian girlfriend, too. At a crucial moment she shocks Damjan by using feminine grammatical gender for him, repeating the sentence 'You're beautiful (Lepa si; feminine gender)' (Tratnik 2001, 138, 140), which is perhaps not the most sensitive thing to do and it could mean that she rejects his transgender identity.

Mainstream reception caught up with the book after a decade's delay. When first published in 2001 in the specialized LGBTQ+ book series Lambda, the novel found popularity with LGBTQ+ readers, but it had limited wider appeal (Tratnik 2014b, 61). It has been, nevertheless, praised as an 'extremely witty, uncompromising and bold' book that 'does not moralize' (Picco 2011b, 20, 15). In 2002 it was made into a theatre play (dir. Alen Jelen; *SiGledal* n.d., n.p.), since then translated into German, Czech, Slovak, Serbian and Macedonian, and a film adaptation is currently in pre-production. In 2014, it was included in the nationwide reading-promotion project Growing Up with the Book, reprinted by a major Slovenian publisher explicitly as a book for young adults, and distributed to all first-year secondary-school students (aged 15). Writing about the

21 '… same sebi pravijo lezbijke – kot da jih ne bi že drugi dovolj zmerjali'.

novel's reception, Tratnik remarks how she was surprised to see it labelled as a work for young adults. Given the relatively difficult issues the novel deals with and the author's perception of Damjan and other characters as adults, she thought it self-evident the novel would appeal to adults. She believes the decisive moment in categorizing the novel as YA literature was the tags it was given in libraries: 'adolescents, sexual abuse, identity, problems with parents'. Tratnik goes on to say: 'I must admit I was worried by the labelling of the novel as young adult literature, because I thought that if it was identified as such, adults would no longer reach for it, while it could prove too demanding for young readers' (Tratnik 2014b, 60).

When *Damjan* was chosen for the Growing Up with the Book project, it was not to unanimous enthusiasm. The anti-gender online portal 24kul.si warned parents to protect their children against 'indoctrination with radical homosexual ideology', which attempts at 'exciting children to change their sex, sexual orientation, and perform risky sexual practices' (M. 2016, n.p.). A prominent figure of the anti-gender movement wrote her own analysis of the book on the same website, insisting on using the female name that Damjan was given by his parents (Vesna) and feminine pronouns. She places emphasis on abuse and sees the solution to the protagonist's problems in 'resolving her relationship with her father and regaining her identity (and gender)' (Vilčnik 2017, n.p.). The author adds an interview with a self-proclaimed psychoanalyst, who also insists on calling Damjan a lesbian and draws direct parallels between Damjan's abuse and his 'gender identity distractions' (Vilčnik 2017, n.p.).

Tratnik's second YA novel, *Tombola ali življenje!* (Bingo or Life!, 2017, 14+ years), set in the socialist Slovenia of the late 1970s, features another trans character. The protagonist Mija's friend Alen left home aged 15 to go to the capital to live as a man and their lives meet at different points in different ways. They become very close by the end of the novel. Alen is a side character and the reader does not learn very much about him, and his transgender position is even less debated than Damjan's. Notwithstanding the time in which the novel is set, he is accepted by his mother and sister, but not his father, a violent alcoholic who leaves Alen's mother broken mentally and emotionally.

Gender is put centre stage by another Slovenian author to be discussed in this section, the philosopher, painter, writer and illustrator Alenka Spacal (b. 1975). Her *Mavrična maškarada* (Rainbow Masquerade, 2013, 6–9 years, 30 × 21 cm) is a modern fable in picture-book form in which anthropomorphized animals are preparing for a party where they will play with their genders; that is, they will apply the concept of gender performativity: some will dress up as different genders, some as their own, some will perform multiple genders at the same time. The protagonist of the book, a tortoise, is not sure what sex/gender they are, so they set off to meet other animals and find out. In a series of encounters, the tortoise meets a rabbit who is afraid of genders, but who likes putting on his mother's clothes, a snail called Hermi (Herman/Hermina) who switches between genders according to how they feel, two ladybirds (presumably in a lesbian relationship), two squirrels (one butch, one femme), and others. The animals tell the tortoise about their experiences of gender and encourage them to find the gender they will feel at ease with. Above all, they present gender as something fluid. As any fable, *Mavrična maškarada* has a moral: after some perplexity, the tortoise finally appreciates that genders are best played with.

Spacal made a conscious decision to avoid LGBTQ+ signifiers at the textual level (Spacal 2013b, 72), but the illustrations include an abundance of LGBTQ+ symbols such as rainbows, masks, feathers, monocles, crowns and LGBTQ+ books, and the book employs feminist/queer concepts in a crossover fashion. Readers with an awareness of gender performativity, feminism, sexual identities, camp and kitsch will clearly recognize them in the text and especially in the illustrations, whereas children will focus on the tortoise's adventure of finding out what their sex/gender is. For instance, the illustration of the hermaphrodite earthworm who could not care less about gender, especially when they are hot, shows what seems to be the worm's library – a selection of books among which are the Slovenian translations of Judith Butler's *Gender Trouble*, Lillian Faderman's *Surpassing the Love of Men*, Simone de Beauvoir's *The Second Sex*, Jackie Kay's *Trumpet* and others (Spacal 2013a, 17).

The book has had opposing interpretations. The reviewer and researcher of CYA literature Gaja Kos thinks the children of the picture book's target audience are too young to understand the notion of playing with genders, because 'they know much too little about medicine, psychology, philosophy, the social context, etc.' (Kos 2013, n.p.). She suggests the topic should be introduced later, perhaps to adolescents, because younger children will only get confused (ibid.). Quite the opposite is argued by another reviewer, who welcomes the book and sees it as an important contribution to (crossover) texts about genders (Oliver 2014). In particular, she praises the mosaic-like illustrations as a creative

Figure 17: Spacal, Alenka. 2013a. *Mavrična maškarada* (Rainbow Masquerade). Ljubljana: Škuc (Lambda).

and contemporary way of approaching children (Oliver 2014, 175) – again, the complete opposite of Kos's review.

Spacal confirms, when discussing her picture book, that she wanted both children and adults to realize that 'the binary gender system that children are constantly imposed on by the majority of picture books is not the only existing one. Unfortunately, it is impossible to avoid the fact that very many picture books are still produced from an unconsidered perspective on genders and gender roles' (Spacal 2014, 58). She disagrees with Kos that her book is inappropriate for children in the pre-reading period, arguing that children are aware of their gender from the age of three (Spacal 2013b, 70). This is in sync with Karen Coats's assertion that '[v]ery young children are actively researching category distinctions like gender and racial difference in order to develop a sense of who they are and how the world works, so the images available to them in picturebooks have the potential to be enormously influential in structuring their attitudes' (Coats 2017, 168).

After *Mavrična maškarada* (Rainbow Masquerade, 2013), the first picture book on gender fluidity in Slovenia, Spacal made another picture book with similar illustrations in the same technique, featuring animals in a related context. *Kako ti je ime?* (What's Your Name?, 2018a, 3–8 years, 21 × 27 cm) is in fact a prequel to *Mavrična maškarada*, focusing on the hermaphrodite snail. This book is about how the snail got their name. To have a name, since names in Slovenian are explicitly gendered, the individual must first be sure about their sex/gender. The snail gets the idea about the kind of name they want from Vanja the earthworm (in Slovenian Vanja is a name for both men and women), so a tortoise and other animals help to come up with the inclusive name 'Herman Hermina - Hermi' (a diminutive and shortened Slovenian equivalent for 'hermaphrodite' ('hermafrodit')). The snail is very happy to have a name, and particularly pleased not to have to decide whether they are a boy or a girl.

Spacal's third picture book, *Modre ptičje misli* (Blue Bird Wisdoms, 2018b, 3–6 years, 21 × 26 cm), is a collection of nine very short stories featuring birds. Two of the stories take up, albeit less directly, Spacal's considerations of normativity as seen in her previous books. The story 'Izbira ali-ali' (An Either-Or Choice) rejects binary thinking with an example of a blue-winged goose who rejects a blue wren's insistence that she should choose whether she prefers to fly or waddle: 'I dislike making decisions in this way. It upsets me if there are only two options to choose from' (Spacal 2018b, 15).[22] Less ambiguously related to the issue of gender, 'Rojstnodnevna kravata' (The Birthday Tie) is a conversation between a mother and a daughter (of the blue-grey tanager bird species) about the child's wish for a birthday present – a tie. The mother's first response is that ties are 'for manly gents (za možate strice)' and that her daughter is 'not a lad (nisi poba)' (Spacal 2018b, 18). Only when the daughter explains the different uses for a tie (to use it as a trapeze, a swing, an eye cover for a game of hide-and-seek, a mock microphone and as part of dressing up as a boy) does the mother give in and recognize a tie can be 'a magical toy (čudežna igrača)' (Spacal 2018b, 18).

22 'Ne maram se odločati na ta način. Če sta na voljo samo dve možnosti, me to spravlja v slabo voljo.'

Two Slovenian authors have explicitly tackled trans issues in their books for children and young adults, Alenka Spacal and Suzana Tratnik, in addition to translated texts, like Chrissie Glazebrook's *Norolescenti* (*The Madolescents*, 2001, ST Irena Duša, 2003, 13+ years), Julie Anne Peters's *Luna* (*Luna*, 2004, ST Anja Kokalj, 2007, 13+ years), the Dutch *Dekle z Marsa* (*Meisje van Mars* / The Girl from Mars, 2011, ST Katjuša Ručigaj, 2012, 13+ years) by Anna Woltz and Vicky Janssen, and Lesley Choyce's *Konec skrivalnic* (*Identify*, 2017, ST Brigita Orel, 2018, 13+ years). While Tratnik's, Peters's, and Woltz and Janssen's protagonists reject non-binarism and prefer clearly transsexual identities, Glazebrook's and Choyce's insist on non-conformist gender expressions. Despite this essential difference, all of them are under unrelenting pressure. They suffer from bullying that sometimes makes them suicidal. In my corpus of texts, Spacal's picture books are the only exception to this rule of linking gender non-conforming identities to mental-health issues and abuse. This is in line with the author's rejection of the inclusion of LGBTQ+ among 'problem' topics like abuse and illness; she finds (and paints and writes about) LGBTQ+ as something positive, desired, something to be proud of (Spacal 2014, 53).

Families

Thus far, no originally Slovenian book for children or young adults with LGBTQ+ families as the main theme has appeared. In the Slovenian environment, families with same-gender parents remain fiercely disputed by some groups. Consequently, when Maja Lupša (b. 1951) published a very short story 'Očka' (Two Daddies, 2012, 6–9 years), based on her son's family, about two gay men and their daughter, in the children's monthly *Ciciban*, before the 2012 referendum, she and the magazine were subjected to concerted attacks. Following a protest by the youth section of a right-wing political party, arguing that the magazine and children were being exploited for the referendum campaign and indoctrination (Uredništvo 2012, n.p.), other conservative media outlets and blogs expressed similar outrage.

Two gay men as fathers also appear in Lawrence Schimel and illustrator Sara Rojo Pérez's *Sosedje in prijatelji* (*Amigos y vecinos* / Neighbours and Friends, 2005, ST Marjeta Drobnič, 2008, 6–9 years), the first picture book in Slovenian to thematize families with LGBTQ+ parents. The book overturns the discourse on perfect straight families and dysfunctional LGBTQ+ families by showing the family with two gay dads and their adopted son as a safe and stimulating environment. The other picture book about adoption by same-gender couples to appear in Slovenian was the (in)famous *In s Tango smo trije* (*And Tango Makes Three*, 2005, ST Matej Krajnc, 2010, 6–9 years) by Justin Richardson, Peter Parnell and illustrator Henry Cole. Another, very similar, story about male penguins living in a zoo, hatching an egg and looking after a baby penguin was written by Slovenian writer Mate Dolenc (b. 1945) before *Tango* was published in Slovenia, but after it was available in English. The short story 'Pingo in Frigo' (Pingo and Frigo, 2009, 10+ years), is an unveiled endorsement of adoption by same-gender parents: the third-person narrator argues that there is always a rejected egg somewhere that should be taken care of, and that the only thing that matters in such matters is love for the child (Dolenc 2009, 58).

Adoption (but not by same-gender couples) is also the theme of the French novel for teenagers *Oh, boy!* by Marie-Aude Murail (*Oh, boy!*, 2000, ST Jedrt Maležič, 2013, 13+ years). It is a story about three orphaned siblings for whom two possible guardians among their relatives are found, Bart, 26, and Josiane, 37. Josiane is cold and scheming, whereas Bart is self-absorbed, cynical, vain, irresponsible, superficial, he makes grotesquely inappropriate comments, has a wimpish voice, is tanned all year round, dyes his hair and goes clubbing; that is to say – he is gay (for more on stereotypical portrayals of LGBTQ+ characters, see Epstein 2013, 64–131). Bart's description eventually turns out to have been an exaggeration as part of the novel's narrative strategy, another plot device based on stereotypes, trying to establish two ostensibly equally inappropriate guardians for the children.

Manipulative juxtapositions are also crucial to A. M. Homes's *Jack* (1989, ST Simona Cesar, 2011, 13+ years). From the moment the narrator Jack, 14–16, learns that his father is gay, the book is very much about Jack's divided loyalties; he loves his father but he is also defined by homophobia (his own as well as the environment's). Ultimately, Jack's acceptance of his gay father corresponds with the collapse of his friend Max's family. What I find problematic is the implicit comparison between Jack's and Max's families – in order for Jack (and, presumably, the general public/reader) to accept LGBTQ+ parents, a brutal benchmark of an abusive straight family is required – as if to say that only when LGBTQ+ families are better than the worst of straight ones can they be put up with.

Similarly, a father who (almost) ruins his family by coming out as gay is included – but not as a major theme like in Homes's book – in *Berenikini kodri* (Berenice's Curls, 2006, 13+ years) and its sequel *Orionov meč* (Orion's Sword, 2008, 13+ years) by Aksinja Kermauner (b. 1956), an acclaimed writer of Slovenian CYA literature. Both novels intertwine narrations by two teenagers, Anina and Nik, 17. Anina lives with albinism and severe vision impairment and loves Nik, a cynical macho. Nik's parents are distant, business-oriented people without much interest in their son. They only stay together to keep up appearances. Nik knows that his father rents a flat in which he has extramarital sex, but he has always assumed it is with his female secretary. It turns out it is with other men. Nik repeatedly emphasizes that the only grudge he bears is against his father's hypocrisy and secrecy, not homosexuality. Nevertheless, whereas he has always accepted, without much difficulty, what he thought was his father's affair with a female secretary, the men he is said to be having sex with are unspecific and in plural. Also, the language associated with the father's secret is emphatically marked. Thus, when Nik's mother discovers her husband's secret, she exclaims: 'How could he! I'm ruined. Bastard! Faggot!' (Kermauner 2006, 144).[23] And Nik is just as shocked when his mother tells him about it, relying on the worn-out discourse of 'I don't mind it, but …': 'Oh, you deceitful old brute. The old guy used his secretary as a pretence mistress, and had young blokes in his flat! Makes you sick! I don't mind gays, but this …' (Kermauner 2006, 144).[24]

---

23 'Kako je mogel! Uničena sem! Baraba! Peder!'

24 'O ti potuhnjena stara žival! Stari je imel za krinko tajnico za ljubico, v stanovanju pa mlade tipčke! Za bruhat! Nič nimam proti gejem, ampak tole …'.

In the end, when he is recovering after an almost fatal motorbike crash, Nik's relationship with his father improves. Apparently trying to promote tolerance, the writer uses Nik's thoughts as a vehicle for a mini-lecture on acceptance: 'Nowadays, being gay really isn't unusual at all. I personally don't mind homosexuals in the least. It must be just terrible to fall in love with a soul that happens to inhabit – according to our outdated norms – a wrong body' (Kermauner 2008, 57).[25] Rather than being liberating, such discourse reiterates and reinforces many of the prejudices that we have repeatedly come across in this discussion, especially the emphasis on the trauma of being LGBTQ+ and the deterministic notion of 'the wrong body'. Unlike Jack's father, who is not an isolated LGBTQ+ figure in the book, Nik's father is allowed no LGBTQ+ community, leaving the novel at the lowest level of the evolution of CYA literature with LGBTQ+ content (see Cart and Jenkins 2006, xix–xx).

At least some of the hesitations also apply to Cvetka Sokolov's children's book *Bo res vse v redu?* (Will Everything Really Be Okay?, illustrated by Marta Bartolj, 2019, 9–14 years). The book demonstrates that we have moved on – but not out of normalizing didacticism. The story is told in the first person by Bor, a 10-year-old boy whose father has been living with another man for eight years. Everyone in Bor's family is supportive of his father and his partnership, including Bor and his mother, and the parents have a very mature approach to equally shared parenting. Everyone, that is, except for one of Bor's grandmothers who is explicitly homophobic and does not accept her son, his partner, or their relationship.

The crux of the plot is located during Bor's mountaineering trip with the grandmother. Although an experienced mountaineer, sure of herself, the grandmother gets lost. This dents her self-confidence and it has an impact on another of her deeply held convictions, too. When bivouacking for the night and waiting for help, Bor namely attempts to resolve his problem of divided loyalties by raising the burning issue: 'Gran, why don't you like daddy?' (Sokolov 2019, 91).[26] She must now question her homophobic beliefs, which are further shaken when Bor's father's partner is part of the Mountain Rescue Team who save them (recognizably, acceptance tends to be conditional upon the homophobe's benefit). In the end, the grandmother seems to set off on a gradual process of acceptance.

Even though same-gender attraction and partnership are not problematized by any of the book's characters (except for the grandmother), it is, nevertheless, the grandmother's homophobia that is the central theme, and Bor's father and his partner(ship) are not depicted in any detail. In addition, there is the well-known and well-meaning (though, it might be argued, counterproductive) narrative need to explain – through different characters' pronouncements – that while daddy is 'different (drugačen)', homosexuality is 'natural (naravna)' and not 'contagious (nalezljiva)' (Sokolov 2019, 95, 37). Moreover,

25 'Danes res ni nič takega, če si gej. Osebno nimam čisto nič proti istospolno usmerjenim ljudem. Saj mora biti res strahotno, če se zaljubiš v dušo, ki slučajno stanuje v – za naše okostenele norme – napačnem telesu.'

26 'Babi, zakaj ne maraš očija?'

as in many other books, the pedagogical note of the story is further emphasized in the afterword, written by a marriage and family therapist, that stresses the need to accept someone's 'being different' (Kreš 2019).

Although my reading of Neli Kodrič Filipić's *Kaj ima ljubezen s tem* (What's Love Got to Do With It, 2009) in the first section demonstrates such a lot of disappointment over its laboured gay-friend plot twist, there is something positive to be said about the book. When after a year of unexplained absence the narrator's mother returns, she does so in a lesbian relationship. So, in the grand finale we learn that she disappeared to build her life anew, to find her authentic self. It is a pity, then, that she introduces her partner as: 'This is Nataša, my *friend*' (Kodrič Filipić 2009, 251; emphasis added).[27] Which brings us back to where we started – to 'friends' and 'friendships'.

Conclusion

This chapter on LGBTQ+ fiction for children and young adults in Slovenia discussed contemporary fiction published in the Slovenian language with the exception of two texts included for historical interest, Novšak's *Dečki* (Boys, 1938) and Kraigher's *Maja* (Maja, 1971). In addition to these two, only the translation of Garden's *Pismo za Annie* (*Annie on My Mind*, 1996) was published before the year 2000. This coincides with the more mainstream public and political debates on LGBTQ+ as well as more visible opposition and LGBTQ+-phobia. Without tackling one of the great perplexities of CYA literature – the notoriously slippery definition of what it actually is – I have nevertheless highlighted its position: CYA literature inevitably finds itself at – or is pushed to – the intersection of literature, ideology and pedagogy.

Research on discrimination and violence against LGBTQ+ youth in Slovenia shows consistently high numbers of those who have experienced them. In an extensive study, including 1,145 gays and lesbians, 30 per cent of the respondents reported experiencing discrimination based on their sexual orientation (Kuhar 2014b, 12) and nearly half of them experienced violence, mostly (95 per cent) psychological abuse, such as ridicule, blackmail or insults (Kuhar 2014b, 17). Most frequently (66 per cent), the perpetrators are strangers and the acts occur in public places (streets, bars, etc.), but schoolmates come second (43 per cent), which makes the school an unsafe space for LGBTQ+ children and adolescents (Kuhar 2014b, 17–18). Other studies similarly reveal that 'when it comes to young LGBTIQ+ individuals' experiences with violence and/or discrimination, school is a place marked with one of the highest levels of violence' (Perger 2018, 93; see also Magić and Maljevac 2016; Maljevac and Magić 2009).

Given the discrimination and violence statistics, it is not surprising that 'literature written for teens frequently attempts to provide some kind of antidote for [...] homophobia' (Kokkola 2013, 96). All the same, many of the CYA books about LGBTQ+ available in Slovenian still present LGBTQ+ as a problem, an issue that defines and constrains the protagonists, their plots being 'driven by the "problem" rather than by

27 'To je Nataša, moja prijateljica'.

the characters themselves' (Cart and Jenkins 2006, 139). LGBTQ+ issues are inextricably linked to crises in identity and angst, and many novels partake in, to use Kimberley Reynolds's term, 'nihilistic fiction' (Reynolds 2007, 77). Loneliness, ostracism, violence, even suicide are given pride of place, echoing the recipe from the past that prescribed inescapably unhappy lives for LGBTQ+ people in practices that sometimes border on writerly sadism. Paratexts, too, are sometimes dated and insensitive, a good example being the Slovenian afterword to Julie Anne Peters's *Luna* (*Luna*, 2007), which is typically positive in intention, but problematic in discourse and terminology. Its title is 'The wrong sex/gender', and it speaks of how 'mother nature has played a cruel trick' on trans people (Zirkelbach 2007, 265). In contrast, Roman Kuhar's afterword to the second edition of Suzana Tratnik's *Ime mi je Damjan* (My Name Is Damjan, 2014) provides a clear summary of the notions of gender identity, expression, role, and sexual orientation, the importance of gender in social interactions, the difference between sex and gender and the problematic impact of psychiatric diagnoses on the perception of transgender identities (Kuhar 2014a).

There are a number of recurring stereotypes about gender and sexual non-normativity that others discuss in more detail (see Day 2000; Epstein 2012, 2013, 2014), and I have pointed to some of them when examining individual texts. However, while criticizing stereotypical characters in fiction (e.g. effeminate gays, butch lesbians, polyamorous bisexuals), we should nevertheless insist that there is absolutely nothing wrong if, say, a man – gay, straight, or otherwise – is what is called effeminate or if a lesbian is supposedly butch. Normalizing LGBTQ+ people, issues, or families may perhaps count on mainstream acceptance, but it can also cause further marginalization. On the other hand, there are some narrative stereotypes and clichés that are harmful, especially those that, directly or not, introduce LGBTQ+ as inherently related to negativity, secretiveness, depression, dysfunctional families, violence, sexual abuse, and so on.

Quite the opposite is true of the LGBTQ+ families shown in the two picture books to have appeared in Slovenian, both of them translations. The families are shown as 'normal' and just as good – if not better – than the (hetero)normative ones. These books 'didactically work against homophobic discourse', but they also reinforce the norm. Moreover, 'the issue of whether queer families are different is dealt with by attempting to confirm that they are not' (Epstein 2013, 27). And yet for some religious and conservative readers, children's books about LGBTQ+ families seem to be unacceptable, anti-family products of the homosexual lobby.

Arguing for opportunities for naïve identification and for an unfailingly positive representation of LGBTQ+ characters would push CYA literature back to its didactic contexts, and we should tread carefully if we are not to suggest that the task of LGBTQ+ literature is providing readers with 'unambiguously positive role models', following 'the imperative to provide relentlessly positive images and unambiguously happy endings' (Woods 1998, 341). It would be fundamentally wrong to gloss over the challenges LGBTQ+ children, adolescents and families have to confront, to pretend that everything is just fine, and underrepresent the real problems. Whatever progress LGBTQ+ movements have made – and, compared to twenty or more years ago, we have come quite far – we are also facing retraditionalization, neoconservatism, religious fundamentalism and 'cure' therapies. It can still be hard to come out and live as LGBTQ+.

Based on my overview, I generally see no reason to describe the writers' and publishers' attempts as anything but well-meaning, and it would be perhaps unfortunate or insensitive to comment on how the road to hell is paved with good intentions, but well-meaning approaches sometimes do turn out to be limited and limiting. The big difference remains between the texts that challenge LGBTQ+-phobia and those that, unwillingly or not, affirm it, and between those that see LGBTQ+ as a fact of life and those that see it as a problem.

Bibliography

Arold, Marliese. 2002. *Sandra ljubi Meike* (*Einfach nur Liebe: Sandra liebt Meike* / Simply Love: Sandra Loves Meike). Translated by Andrea Švab. Ljubljana: Grlica (Na robu).

Bach, Tamara. 2007. *Punca z Marsa (Marsmädchen / Girl from Mars).* Translated by Barbara Lipovšek. Ljubljana: Karantanija (Najhit).

Belbin, David. 2005. *Zadnja devica (The Last Virgin).* Translated by Katarina Mahnič. Ljubljana: Mladinska knjiga (Knjigožer).

Bevc, Cvetka. 2011. *Desetka* (Ten of Us). Ljubljana: Arsem.

Blažić, Milena Mileva. 2020. 'Comparative Analysis of Two Texts for Young Adults, *Dečki* (Boys) and *Fantje iz gline* (The Clay Boys)'. In *Go East! LGBTQ+ Literature in Eastern Europe*, edited by Andrej Zavrl and Alojzija Zupan Sosič, 20–30. Ljubljana: Ljubljana University Press. https://doi.org/10.4312/9789610603108

Borovnik, Silvija. 2012. *Književne študije: o vlogi ženske v slovenski književnosti, o sodobni prozi in o slovenski književnosti v Avstriji* (Literary Studies: On the Role of Women in Slovenian Literature, On Contemporary Prose and on Slovenian Literature in Austria). Maribor: Mednarodna založba Oddelka za slovanske jezike in književnosti, Filozofska fakulteta.

Boyne, John. 2013. *Osupljiva zgodba Barnabyja Brocketa (The Terrible Thing That Happened to Barnaby Brocket).* Translated by Jure Potokar. Dob pri Domžalah: Miš.

Cart, Michael, and Jenkins, Christine A. 2006. *The Heart Has Its Reasons: Young Adult Literature with Gay/Lesbian/Queer Content, 1969–2004.* Lanham: Scarecrow Press.

Choyce, Lesley. 2018. *Konec skrivalnic (Identify).* Translated by Brigita Orel. Dob pri Domžalah: Miš.

Coats, Karen. 2017. *The Bloomsbury Introduction to Children's and Young Adult Literature.* London and New York: Bloomsbury Academic.

Cotič, Metka. 1996. 'Ali je lahko ljubezen nekaj slabega? (Can Love Be a Bad Thing?)'. In *Pismo za Annie* (*Annie on My Mind*) by Nancy Garden, 170–75. Ljubljana: Mladinska knjiga (Odisej).

Day, Frances Ann. 2000. *Lesbian and Gay Voices: An Annotated Bibliography and Guide to Literature for Children and Young Adults.* Westport, CT: Greenwood Press.

Dolenc, Mate. 2009. 'Pingo in Frigo (Pingo and Frigo)'. In *Kraljičin lipicanec in druge zgodbe* by Mate Dolenc, illustrated by Adriano Janežič, 55–59. Ljubljana: Mladika (Trepetlika).

Donko, Franci. 2018. 'V novi številki mladostniške revije *Pil* spet homo-lezbična-bi-trans-queer propaganda! (More Homo-Lesbian-Bi-Trans-Queer Propaganda in a New Issue of the Adolescent Magazine *PIL*!)'. *24kul.si*, 11 February. 24kul.si/v-novi-stevilki-mladostniske-revije-pil-homolezbicnabitransqueer-propaganda; also published, under a different heading, by *Nova24TV.si* (https://nova24tv.si/slovenija/ljudje/v-novi-stevilki-mladostniske-revije-pil-znova-propaganda-za-homoseksualni-nacin-zivljenja/) and *Demokracija* (www.demokracija.si/komentar/v-novi-stevilki-mladostniske-revije-pil-propaganda-za-homoseksulni-nacin-zivljenja.html)

Dović, Marijan. 2017. *Prešeren po Prešernu: kanonizacija nacionalnega pesnika in kulturnega svetnika* (Prešeren after Prešeren: The Canonization of a National Poet and Cultural Saint). Ljubljana: Literarno-umetniško društvo Literatura.

Epstein, B. J. 2012. 'We're Here, We're (Not?) Queer: GLBTQ Characters in Children's Books'. *Journal of GLBT Family Studies* 8, no. 3: 287–300.

———. 2013. *Are the Kids All Right? The Representation of LGBTQ Characters in Children's and Young Adult Literature*. Bristol: HammerOn Press.

———. 2014. '"The Case of the Missing Bisexuals": Bisexuality in Books for Young Readers'. *Journal of Bisexuality* 14, no. 1: 110–25.

Garden, Nancy. 1996. *Pismo za Annie (Annie on My Mind)*. Translated by Dušanka Zabukovec. Ljubljana: Mladinska knjiga (Odisej).

Glazebrook, Chrissie. 2003. *Norolescenti (The Madolescents)*. Translated by Irena Duša. Ljubljana: Cankarjeva založba (Najst).

Haramija, Dragica. 2009. *Sedem pisav: opusi sedmih sodobnih slovenskih mladinskih pisateljev* (Seven Scripts: The Opuses of Seven Contemporary Slovenian Children's and Young Adult Writers). Maribor: Mariborska knjižnica and Pedagoška fakulteta.

———. 2012. *Nagrajene pisave: opusi po letu 1991 nagrajenih slovenskih mladinskih pripovednikov* (Award-Winning Writing: The Opuses of post-1991 Slovenian Award-Winning Children's and Young Adult Writers). Murska Sobota: Franc-Franc.

Heneghan, James. 2009. *Povračilo (Payback)*. Translated by Kristina Dečman. Ljubljana: Koleda.

Hobbie, Holly. 1999. *Rilko in Cvilko (Toot & Puddle)*. Translated by Milan Dekleva. Ljubljana: EPTA.

———. 2000. *Rilko in Cvilko: Rilkov rojstni dan (Toot & Puddle: A Present for Toot)*. Translated by Milan Dekleva. Ljubljana: EPTA.

Homes, A. M. 2011. *Jack (Jack)*. Translated by Simona Cesar. Izola: Grlica (Na robu).

Kermauner, Aksinja. 2006. *Berenikini kodri* (Berenice's Curls). Dob pri Domžalah: Miš (Z(o)renja+).

———. 2008. *Orionov meč* (Orion's Sword). Dob pri Domžalah: Miš (Z(o)renja+).

Kodrič Filipić, Neli. 2009. *Kaj ima ljubezen s tem* (What's Love Got to Do with It). Ljubljana: Mladinska knjiga (Odisej).

Kokkola, Lydia. 2013. *Fictions of Adolescent Carnality: Sexy Sinners and Delinquent Deviants*. Amsterdam and Philadelphia, PA: John Benjamins Publishing Company.

Koron, Alenka. 2014. *Sodobne teorije pripovedi* (Contemporary Theories of Narrative). Ljubljana: Založba ZRC, ZRC SAZU.

Kos, Gaja. 2013. 'Alenka Spacal: *Mavrična maškarada*'. *LUD Literatura*. www.ludliteratura.si/kritika-komentar/alenka-spacal-mavricna-maskarada.

———. 2015. *Knjižne dvoživke: slovenski mladinski problemski roman* (Literary Amphibians: Slovenian Young Adult Problem Novel). Maribor: Aristej.

Kraigher, Nada. 1971. *Maja* (Maja). Ljubljana: Prešernova družba. Reprinted in 1979 by Mladinska knjiga (Odisej).

Kreš, Barbara. 2019. 'Pot na goro (A Path onto the Mountain)'. In *Bo res vse v redu?* (Will Everything Really Be Okay?) by Cvetka Sokolov, illustrated by Marta Bartolj, 122–27. Dob pri Domžalah: Miš (Prva z(o)renja).

Kuhar, Roman. 2014a. 'Damjanova pot (Damjan's Way)'. In *Ime mi je Damjan* (My Name Is Damjan) by Suzana Tratnik, 159–73. Ljubljana: Mladinska knjiga (Odisej).

———. 2014b. *Raziskava o pravni podinformiranosti LGBT skupnosti in vsakdanjem življenju gejev in lezbijk: raziskovalno poročilo* (Research Study of a Lack of Legal Information in the LGBT Community and Everyday Life of Gays and Lesbians: A Research Report). Ljubljana: DIC Legebitra.

———. 2017. 'Changing Gender Several Times a Day: The Anti-Gender Movement in Slovenia'. In *Anti-Gender Campaigns in Europe: Mobilizing against Equality*, edited by Roman Kuhar and David Paternotte, 215–32. London and New York: Rowman & Littlefield.

Lupša, Maja. 2012. 'Očka (Two Daddies)'. Illustrated by Tanja Komadina. *Ciciban* 67, no. 7: 18–19.

M., Marija. 2016. 'Starši zaščitite otroke! Vsi otroci v prvih letnikih srednjih šol so morali biti v šolskem letu 2013/2014 deležni homoseksualne indoktrinacije v knjižnicah! (Parents, Protect Children! All First-Year Secondary-School Children Had to Be Subjected to Homosexual Indoctrination in Libraries in the School Year 2013/2014!)'. *24.kul.si*, 12 September. http://24kul.si/starsi-pozor-vsi-otroci-v-prvih-letnikih-srednjih-sol-morajo-biti-v-solskem-letu-20132014-delezni-homoseksualne-indoktrinacije-v-knjiznicah

Magić, Jasna, and Maljevac, Simon. 2016. 'Research for Action: Challenging Homophobia in Slovene Secondary Education'. *Journal of LGBT Youth* 13, no. 1–2: 28–45.

Maljevac, Simon, and Magić, Jasna. 2009. 'Pedri raus!: homofobično nasilje v šolah (No Place For Faggots: Homophobic Violence in Schools)'. *Journal of Contemporary Educational Studies* (Ljubljana) 60, no 4: 90–104.

Mozetič, Brane. 2014. *Prva ljubezen* (First Love). Illustrated by Maja Kastelic. Ljubljana: Škuc (Lambda).

———. 2017. *Murenček in Polhek* (Cricket and Dormouse). Illustrated by Andrej Brumen Čop. Ljubljana: Škuc (Lambda).

———. 2020a. *Ahil in Patrokles* (Achilles and Patroclus). Illustrated by Ana Lucija Šarić. Ljubljana: Škuc (Lambda).

———. 2020b. *Rožnate zgodbe iz neheteronormativne zgodovine (za mlade)* (Pink Stories from Non-Heteronormative History (for the Young)). Illustrated by Ana Lucija Šarić. Ljubljana: Škuc (Lambda).

Murail, Marie-Aude. 2013. *Oh, boy! (Oh, boy!)* Translated by Jedrt Maležič. Dob pri Domžalah: Miš.

Ness, Patrick. 2014. 'Pri fantih je drugače (Different for Boys)'. In *Prvič (Losing It)*, edited by Keith Gray, translated by Irena Duša, 77–116. Ljubljana: Mladinska knjiga (Odisej).

———. 2015. *Več kot to (More than This)*. Translated by Andrej Hiti Ožinger. Ljubljana: Mladinska knjiga (Srednji svet).

Novšak, France. (1938) 2016. *Dečki: roman iz dijaškega internata* (Boys: A Novel from a Boarding School). Ljubljana: Škuc (Lambda).

Oliver, Maša. 2014. 'Alenka Spacal: *Mavrična maškarada*'. *Sodobnost* 78, no.1–2: 174–75.

Pavček, Tone. 1958. *Juri Muri v Afriki* (Juri Muri in Africa). Illustrated by Melita Vovk. Ljubljana: Mladinska knjiga (Cicibanova knjižnica).

———. 2001. *Juri Muri drugič v Afriki* (Juri Muri in Africa Again). Illustrated Marjanca Jemec-Božič. Ljubljana: Mladinska knjiga (Cicibanov vrtiljak / Velike slikanice).

———. 2011. *Juri Muri po Sloveniji* (Juri Muri Around Slovenia). Illustrated by Damijan Stepančič. Dob pri Domžalah: Miš.

———. 2012. *Juri Muri gre po srečo* (Juri Muri Looking for Happiness). Illustrated by Damijan Stepančič. Dob pri Domžalah: Miš.

Percivale, Tommaso. 2016. 'Ko sem se prvič poljubil' ('La prima volta che ho baciato / The First Time That I Kissed'. In *Ko sem prvič* (*La prima volta che* / The First Time), translated by Karmen Filipič, 7–31. Izola: Grlica.

Perger, Nina. 2018. 'LGBTIQ+ Youth and Experiences with Violence in Education'. *Ars & Humanitas* 12, no. 1: 88–103.

Peters, Julie Anne. 2006. *Daleč od Xanadu (Far from Xanadu)*. Translated by Anja Kokalj. Ljubljana: Grlica (Na robu).

———. 2007. *Luna (Luna)*. Translated by Anja Kokalj. Ljubljana: Grlica (Na robu).

Picco, Kristina. 2011a. 'Prisotnost otroških in mladinskih literarnih besedil z gejevsko/lezbično tematiko v slovenskem prostoru, 1. del (The Presence of Children's and Young Adult Texts with Gay/Lesbian Themes in Slovenia, Part 1)'. *Otrok in knjiga* 38, no. 80: 5–21.

———. 2011b. 'Prisotnost otroških in mladinskih literarnih besedil z gejevsko/lezbično tematiko v slovenskem prostoru, 2. del (The Presence of Children's and Young Adult Texts with Gay/Lesbian Themes in Slovenia, Part 2)'. *Otrok in knjiga* 38, no. 81: 7–23.

Pirnar, Marta. 2006. *Tok/protitok: konstrukcija in reprezentacija homoseksualne identitete v 20. stoletju* (Current/Counter-Current: The Construction and Representation of Homosexual Identity in the 20th Century). Ljubljana: Škuc (Lambda).

Priročnik (Priročnik za branje kakovostnih mladinskih knjig) (The Handbook for Reading Quality Children's and Young Adult Books), published annually by Pionirska – center za mladinsko književnost in knjižničarstvo (Centre for Children's and Young Adult Literature and Librarianship at the Ljubljana City Library). www.mklj.si/prirocnik/item/451.

Rainfield, Cheryl. 2013. *Brazgotine (Scars)*. Translated by Mateja Malnar Stembal. Izola: Grlica (Na robu).

Reynolds, Kimberley. 2007. *Radical Children's Literature: Future Visions and Aesthetic Transformations in Juvenile Fiction*. Basingstoke and New York: Palgrave Macmillan.

Richardson, Justin, and Peter Parnell. 2010. *In s Tango smo trije (And Tango Makes Three)*. Illustrated by Henry Cole, translated by Matej Krajnc. Ljubljana: Modrijan.

Saksida, Igor. 2005. 'Gladina sovraštva, glina bolečine (The Surface of Hatred, the Clay of Pain)'. In *Fantje iz gline* (Clay Boys) by Janja Vidmar, 213–23. Ljubljana: Mladinska knjiga (Odisej).

Schimel, Lawrence, 2008. *Sosedje in prijatelji* (*Amigos y vecinos* / Friends and Neighbours). Illustrated by Sara Rojo Pérez, translated by Marjeta Drobnič. Ljubljana: Škuc (Lambda).

SiGledal (A Web Portal of Slovenian Performing Arts). n.d. Accessed 15 November 2018. https://veza.sigledal.org/

Sokolov, Cvetka. 2019. *Bo res vse v redu?* (Will Everything Really Be Okay?). Illustrated by Marta Bartolj. Dob pri Domžalah: Miš (Prva z(o)renja).

Spacal, Alenka. 2013a. *Mavrična maškarada* (Rainbow Masquerade). Ljubljana: Škuc (Lambda).

———. 2013b. 'Tema spola v avtorski slikanici *Mavrična maškarada* (The Theme of Gender in My Picture Book *Mavrična maškarada*)'. *Otrok in knjiga* 40, no. 88: 68–73.

———. 2014. 'Sodijo teme spola in istospolne usmerjenosti v mladinski književnosti še vedno med tabuje? (Do the Topics of Gender and Homosexuality in Children's and Young Adult Literature Still Belong Among Taboos?)'. *Otrok in knjiga* 41, no. 91: 52–59.

———. 2018a. *Kako ti je ime?* (What's Your Name?). Maribor: Bajalka.

———. 2018b. *Modre ptičje misli* (Blue Bird Wisdoms). Maribor: Bajalka.

SSKJ (Slovar slovenskega knjižnega jezika. Druga, dopolnjena in deloma prenovljena izdaja) (Dictionary of Standard Slovenian. Second, Updated and Partly Revised Edition). n.d. Accessed 15 December 2018. www.fran.si

Steinhöfel, Andreas. 2018. *Središče sveta* (*Die Mitte der Welt / Centre of My World)*. Translated by Anja Golob. Ljubljana: Cankarjeva založba (Najst).

Štefanec, Vladimir P. 2014. *Sem punk čarovnica, debela lezbijka in ne maram vampov* (I'm a Punk Witch, a Fat Lesbian and I Don't Like Tripe). Ljubljana: Modrijan.

Tratnik, Suzana. 2001. *Ime mi je Damjan* (My Name Is Damjan). Ljubljana: Škuc (Lambda). Reprinted in 2014 by Mladinska knjiga (Odisej).

———. 2014a. 'Jebeno pismo (The Damn Letter)'. In *Prvič (Losing It)*, edited by Keith Gray, 189–208. Ljubljana: Mladinska knjiga (Odisej).

———. 2014b. 'Po Damjanovi poti preko tabujev in predsodkov (Along Damjan's Way over Taboos and Prejudice)'. *Otrok in knjiga* 41, no. 91: 60–62.

———. 2015. '*Ime mi je Damjan* med mladinskim romanom in romanom za odrasle (*My Name is Damjan* Between a Novel for Young Readers and a Novel for Adults)'. *Mentor* 36, no. 2: 84–85.

———. 2017. *Tombola ali življenje!* (Bingo or Life!). Ljubljana: Mladinska knjiga (Odisej).

Uredništvo. 2012. 'Zgodba v *Cicibanu* razburila podmladek NSi (A Story in *Ciciban* Upsets the Youth Section of the NSi)'. *Narobe*, 6 March. https://narobe.si/zgodba-v-cicibanu-razburila-podmladek-nsi/

Velikonja, Nataša. 2007. *Poljub ogledala* (The Kiss of the Mirror). Ljubljana: Škuc (Vizibilija).

———. 2014. 'Od refleksa k spoznanju: spol ne bo več določevalna lastnost: O romanu *Ime mi je Damjan* Suzane Tratnik (From Reflex to Recognition: Gender Will No Longer Be a Prescriptive

Feature: On Suzana Tratnik's Novel *My Name Is Damjan*)'. *Časopis za kritiko znanosti* 42, no. 256: 255–62.

Vidmar, Janja. 2005. *Fantje iz gline* (Clay Boys). Ljubljana: Mladinska knjiga (Odisej).

———. 2006. *Softibluz* (Softy Blues). Illustrated by Matjaž Schmidt. Ljubljana: Prešernova družba (Koledarska zbirka).

———. 2017. *Spodbujanje razvoja vrednot s pomočjo mladinske problemske literature* (Encouraging the Development of Values with the Help of Young Adult Problem Literature). Dob pri Domžalah: Miš.

Vilčnik, Vesna. 2017. 'Ime mi je Damjan, čeprav sem Vesna (My Name Is Damjan Although I Am Vesna)'. *24kul.si*, 1 July. http://24kul.si/ime-mi-je-damjan-ceprav-sem-vesna

Walker, Kate. 2007. *Peter (Peter)*. Translated by Marta Pirnar. Ljubljana: Škuc (Lambda).

Woltz, Anna, and Vicky Janssen. 2012. *Dekle z Marsa* (*Meisje van Mars* / The Girl from Mars). Translated by Katjuša Ručigaj. Dob pri Domžalah: Miš (Z(o)renja+).

Woods, Gregory. 1998. *A History of Gay Literature: The Male Tradition*. New Haven, CT and London: Yale University Press.

Zavrl, Andrej. 2016. 'France Novšak: oris življenja in dela (France Novšak: An Outline of His Life and Work)'. In *Dečki: roman iz dijaškega internata* (Boys: A Novel from a Boarding School) by France Novšak, 255–317. Ljubljana: Škuc (Lambda).

———. 2018. '"Drugačnost" v otroški in mladinski književnosti ("Otherness" in Children's and Young Adult Literature)'. *Otrok in knjiga* 45, no. 102: 33–47.

Zirkelbach, Jana. 2007. 'Nepravi spol (The Wrong Sex/Gender)'. In *Luna* by Julie Anne Peters, 265–68. Ljubljana: Grlica (Na robu).

Zupan Sosič, Alojzija. 2006. *Robovi mreže, robovi jaza: sodobni slovenski roman* (Edges of the Net, Edges of the Self: Contemporary Slovenian Novel). Maribor: Litera.

———. 2017. *Teorija pripovedi* (A Theory of Narrative). Maribor: Litera (Znanstvena literatura).

Chapter Thirteen

BOYS WHO WEAR DRESSES: QUEER NARRATIVE STRATEGIES IN KOREAN CHILDREN'S LITERATURE

Anton Hur

Introduction

The 25th of May in 2001 was a watershed moment for queer rights in the Republic of Korea (known colloquially in the West as 'South Korea'), when future Nobel Peace Prize laureate Kim Dae-jung signed the ratification of the National Human Rights Council Act, creating the first legislative protection for persons of all 'sexual orientations' (National Human Rights Commission of Korea 2010). The Supreme Court also legalized the changing of gender in the family registry for transgender persons in 2006, with the right being extended in certain regions to pre-op female-to-male transgender persons in March 2013 and pre-op male-to-female transgender persons in February 2017 (Kim 2017, n.p.). The queer rights movement has not been without setbacks; since 2007, the movement has tried and failed to pass an anti-discrimination act that would administer more effective measures against discrimination, and while the battle for human rights ordinances, including protection for queer people, continues to be waged region-by-region, universal recognition for the equal rights of queers remains elusive on the peninsula.

Korean literature, however, is a markedly different story. Even compared to other countries in East Asia that are several times its size in population, Korea boasts a rich queer tradition in modern and contemporary fiction. Korea's first work of modern fiction is a queer narrative (the short story 'Is It Love?' by Yi Kwang-su, published in 1909), and there are at least 300 verified queer works published in Korea – more than twice that number counting translations (Hur 2018, n.p.). Compared to this richness, however, queer children's and young adult books are only very recently beginning to find traction in Korean publishing. For the purposes of this chapter, I have only considered works originally written in Korean and published in Korea, while I fully acknowledge the important role translated literature has played in the shaping and enrichment of domestic literary discourse and production.

How are we to explain queerness to children, a group of readers who arguably do not understand sexuality as adults do? What constitutes sexuality and 'being queer' for children? How do Korean authors of children's books define and contextualize the answers to these questions using the narrative methods and storytelling palette they have at hand for a young Korean readership? With these questions in mind, here I study three works of children's literature with queer main characters, examining the way queer identity is portrayed or codified in their characterization but also how this characterization is enriched by the particular narrative methods each work chooses for this portrayal and codification.

Arguably, it is more challenging to discuss sexuality in children's books as compared to young adult (YA) works. YA can access issues of sexuality stemming from the complex sociology of adolescents growing into their bodies; the very term 'young adult' implies an understanding that they are, perhaps, more adult than children. Queerness, however, encompasses far more than sex. It is the collective state and behaviour of all that is not heteronormative, which includes what characters choose to wear, what play they engage in, the reactions of their peers and authority figures, and other signals and tropes easily found in children's literature. Thus, even after taking the sex out of sexuality, the umbrella definition of queerness leaves quite a lot of ground for scholars of children's literature to cover in terms of queering strategies. My analysis suggests that authors use other features, such as race or even species, as a way of encoding and exploring queerness.

The Texts and Their Strategies

The following three children's books, 꽁치의 옷장엔 치마만 100개 (Gongchi Has At Least 100 Skirts in His Wardrobe) by Lee Chae (2015); 최고 빵집 아저씨는 치마를 입어요 (The Best Baker in Town Wears a Dress) by Gil Sanghyo (2016); and 내 이름은 김신데렐라 (My Name Is Cinderella Kim) by Ko Jae-eun (2018), each feature a male-presenting protagonist, potentially trans, who is forced into accepting masculine norms. The first two instances are notable for using fantasy settings to couch the narrative, perhaps to mitigate the harsh realism of homo/transphobia and to reassure children (and parents) through rigorous signalling, such as cats that walk on their hind feet or a village right out of Hans Christian Andersen, that these are indeed the harmless fairy tales of yore with happy endings. It is notable that the eponymous story in the collection *My Name is Cinderella Kim* does not feature fantasy elements, being more of a straightforwardly realist narrative featuring a realistic setting and characters; perhaps the fact that it is also the most recent book to be published means that it dares to be more explicitly queer.

Gongchi Has At Least 100 Skirts in His Wardrobe (Lee 2015) features an anthropomorphic cat named Gongchi. He[1] has human parents and an assortment of friends, both humans and anthropomorphic animals. Gongchi always wears a skirt to school and is popular among his friends, who think of him as the perfect goalkeeper during soccer games and a deft jacks opponent. Unlike the adults, they accept him as he is; when their teacher makes

1 The Korean source does not indicate Gongchi's gender as the Korean language does not use gendered pronouns. Nor does it specify whether the character is trans, or whether he is a male cat who wants to wear a skirt; I incline towards the latter reading, and thus use the pronoun 'he' when discussing Gongchi in English. I am here more interested in expanding the definition of 'boy' than in slotting Gongchi into predetermined gender roles.

Gongchi change with the boys instead of the girls, his classmates successfully plot to move him to the girls' changing room. When Gongchi's mother confiscates Gongchi's dresses and a devastated Gongchi decides not to go to school anymore, his friends rally to rescue him from his house so he can take part in the Apple Girl Contest, a beauty pageant for little girls. Learning that he has no dress to enter the competition in, his classmates procure some for him, and he arrives on stage at the Apple Girl Contest in time – to see his whole family, also dressed in skirts, rooting for him.

In this book, the anthropomorphic characters may be coded for queerness; Gongchi is the only member of his family who is a cat (his parents and older brother are all human). The teacher that expresses disapproval of Gongchi and forces him to dress with the boys is also human. The poster girl for the Apple Girl Contest – beauty pageants being notoriously heteronormative spaces, *Paris is Burning* notwithstanding – is a human girl. The two classmates who are instrumental in helping Gongchi switch changing rooms are an anaconda and a monkey, implying queer solidarity. By portraying heteronormativity and queerness as human and anthropomorphic characters respectively, readers are able to recognize queerness as different yet embraceable, just as Gongchi's classmates, both human and animal, seamlessly work together to come to the aid of their friend.

The Best Baker in Town Wears a Dress (Gil 2016) is set in a European fairy-tale village, the kind one would expect to read about in a Hans Christian Andersen tale or to see in a Disney movie. A baker moves into the village and bakes delicious bread. Unbeknownst to others, he wears a skirt behind his long apron; it is interesting that the skirt is a key trope in this book too. He is outed when the cobbler's son, who also wants to wear a dress, insists that the baker wears a skirt so why can't he? The villagers stop buying his bread and the baker, in a moment of defeat, starts wearing trousers and a shorter apron. The villagers start buying his bread again, but they notice that the bread is not as delicious as before. The baker, forced to give up his skirts, has lost his taste for his metier and for life in general. Then, during a village festival, he witnesses the cobbler's son crying because he is not allowed to wear the skirt and berates himself for being selfish and cowardly for capitulating to the judgement of others at the expense of his own happiness and the quality of his craft. He dons a skirt, bakes his bread and gives it away to the festival-goers. The villagers accept him – one woman, in gratitude for his bread, gifts him a blue skirt – and everyone dances in the village square. The final scene is a dizzying tableau of dresses, suits and colours, symbolizing the harmony of diversity and tolerance.

Whether this is intentional or not, the baker, who is unnamed, looks the most East Asian (or specifically Korean) of all the villagers in terms of his colouring and facial features. The other villagers tend to resemble white Europeans. This seems to transpose an element of Otherness to him in relation to the other villagers, while encouraging the presumably Korean reader to identify with him. His race is a signal for his queerness, a subtler one than his skirt. We are thus invited into a fairy tale but also reminded of 'the real world' outside of the book, transposing the Otherness and alienation Koreans feel in majority-white settings or in European fairy tales into the Otherness and alienation felt by queer people in heteronormative society. The fairy tale helps couch threatening queer discourse in a dreamily inoffensive, beautifully told narrative, while at the same time it enhances the channels of empathy that the reader, queer or otherwise, is invited to tap into.

My Name Is Cinderella Kim (Ko 2018) is a short-story collection for children featuring a queer narrative of the same title. In it, a boy named Jinwoo develops an interest and talent for drawing pictures of princesses, something his parents do not care to address at first. Then, when Jinwoo starts kindergarten and his worried kindergarten teacher draws Jinwoo's mother aside to talk about Jinwoo's gender non-compliance, Jinwoo's mother forbids Jinwoo from drawing princess pictures, throws out any toy that is pink or that implies femininity, and forces him to play with 'toys for boys' such as robots. Every piece of clothing he owns is switched to something blue. Jinwoo has no choice but to comply. He enters elementary school where he meets a girl named Yumi. Yumi also carries a blue bag and plays with all sorts of 'toys for boys', including Hot Wheels cars and robots. Jinwoo feels a kinship towards her and confesses that he has a secret name: Cinderella Kim. Yumi accepts this name and accepts Jinwoo as he is.

The titular short story 'My Name Is Cinderella Kim' in the collection contrasts with the previous two narratives in that it does not use any elements of fantasy in making its point. It does, however, have a very clear connection with the other narratives in its emphasis on friendship and empathy. The heart of the story is Jinwoo and Yumi's warm friendship and the tolerance and acceptance it is built on. Neither feels that there is anything wrong with the other, even if their parents and teachers, whose jobs are arguably to accept their charges for who they are, fail to rise to the occasion. *Gongchi Has At Least 100 Skirts in His Wardrobe* is also moving for its portrayal of the friendship between Gongchi's classmates who go from passive tolerance to actively helping Gongchi navigate an intolerant outside world and home environment. The baker is not necessarily friends with the cobbler's son in *The Best Baker in Town Wears a Dress*, but it is the sight of the cobbler's son's suffering that makes the baker feel guilty about being a coward and decide to risk ostracism for the sake of standing with the cobbler's son – and let us not forget the gift of the blue skirt from the presumably non-queer village woman. The attitudes and actions of these friends, friends who are not necessarily queer themselves, are an extremely important part of these narratives as they model tolerance and allyship in young readers as much as they reassure non-gender-conforming children that there is nothing wrong with being who they are. It takes a village (literally, in one of the books) to raise a child, and it is genuinely moving to see the 'villages' step up to the challenge, as much as it is to see the protagonists struggle against societal norms.

Another notable point about 'My Name Is Cinderella Kim' is the very fact that, out of all the stories in the collection, this one was picked as the title of the entire book. This indicates a willingness on the part of the publisher to expose the work to public discourse on queer issues and perhaps reflects a similar, increasing willingness for parents and teachers as well. Queerness is not to be swept under the rug anymore; there have always been children like Gongchi, the cobbler's son, Jinwoo and Yumi, and there always will be. The masked signals of *Gongchi Has 100 Skirts in His Wardrobe* and *The Best Baker in Town Wears a Dress* come out of the closet in 'My Name Is Cinderella Kim' (or to be more accurate, *My Name Is Cinderella Kim*, the book's title more than the story's). While the previous works were ground-breaking and well-executed in every way, *My Name Is Cinderella Kim* opens up a new realm of possibility in its simple embrace of realism.

Conclusion

The boy-in-a-dress trope is but one in a plethora available to queer children's literature, as is clearly attested by the rich diversity of works in this very volume, though it is obviously common in current Korean literature for younger readers. It must be noted that the books introduced here, to varying degrees, are similar to actual boys who wear skirts: through the trope, they signal their queerness out in the open of mainstream publication, aided by such narrative strategies as anthropomorphizing, embedding into conventional stories like fairy tales, or modelling empathy through supporting characters. What remains is for readers to step up to the challenge of embracing these works, not only for the sake of literary empathy but also from a standpoint of critical productivity and discourse.

Bibliography

Gil, Sanghyo. 2016. 최고 빵집 아저씨는 치마를 입어요 (*Chwego bbangjip ahjussineun chimaleul ibuhyo* / The Best Baker in Town Wears a Dress). Seoul: Seed Book.

Hur, Anton. 2018. 'How to Write Queer Korean Lit: A Manual'. *Litro* 169. London: Litro Magazine. https://www.litro.co.uk/2018/05/write-queer-korean-lit-manual/

Kim, Won-jin (김원진). 2017. 성기 제거 안 해도 '남 → 여' 성별 정정 첫 허가 ('Sunggi jehguh an haedo nam yeo sungbyeol jungjung chut huhga'). 경향신문 (*The Kyunghyang Shinmun*), 16 February. http://news.khan.co.kr/kh_news/khan_art_view.html?artid=201702162224025

Ko, Jae-eun. 2018. 내 이름은 김신데렐라 (*Neh ireumeun gimshinderella* / My Name is Cinderella Kim). Paju: Munhakdongne.

Lee, Chae. 2015. 꽁치의 옷장엔 치마만 100개 (*Ggongchieui otjangen chimaman baekge* / Gongchi Has At Least 100 Skirts in His Wardrobe). Seoul: Ligem.

National Human Rights Commission of Korea. 2010. *Dignity and Justice for All of Us.* Seoul: National Human Rights Commission of Korea. https://www.rwi.lu.se/NHRIDB/Asia/Korea/Dignity%20and%20Justice%20for%20All.pdf

Yi, Kwang-su. 1909. '愛か' ('Ai ka' / 'Is It Love?') *Alumni Bulletin, Shirogane School Newspaper of Meiji Gakuin*, December. Tokyo: Meiji Gakuin.

Chapter Fourteen

STORIES OUT OF THE CLOSET: LGBTQ+ CHILDREN'S PICTUREBOOKS IN SPAIN

Bernat Cormand

Introduction

Through children's books we can fly away, if the story lets us do it, and talk about topics – even controversial ones – that open a door to reflection. If we look back, we will easily find some stories in children's literature that are about being different in a generic way, as in *The Ugly Duckling*: after feeling different from his brothers, because he is grey and bigger, the ugly duckling realizes that he is actually a gorgeous swan. In this fairy tale, we can see that difference in a homogeneous world usually comes with being rejected by those who do not treat you as an equal. In another way, in *Swimmy*, the writer and illustrator Leo Lionni also describes difference: its colourful pages tell the story of a little black fish that lives in a community of only little red fish. In this case, the differently coloured fish is the fastest, the bravest and the smartest, skills that will help him to save the whole group. To survive the tuna fish attack, the fish follow the idiom 'strength in numbers' and build a big fish shape with little red fish put together; the protagonist, the black one, is the eye. So I will start from here, with the baby duck that becomes a beautiful swan and the brave little fish that is the important eye, in order to think about the LGBTQ+ subject in literature for children, especially in Spanish picturebooks.[1]

In this chapter, I will analyse some issues related to homosexuality, non-traditional family models and gender identity in picturebooks for children produced in Spain in the country's four official languages: Basque, Castilian, Catalan and Galician. I have used a selection of children's picturebooks that are in some way representative within the panorama of LGBTQ+ children's literature in Spain, and I will focus on fiction. For the selection, first I considered that the books described in the chapter should have a minimum standard of literary quality. However, in some cases, as we will see, the value of a book does not depend so much on its literary and/or artistic quality, but rather on the values

1 I will use the term *picturebook* (*álbum* or *libro ilustrado* in Spanish) as it is understood in Sophie Van der Linden's definition: 'El álbum es un soporte de expresión cuya unidad primordial es la doble página, sobre la que se inscriben, de manera interactiva, imágenes y texto, y que sigue una concatenación articulada de página a página' (The picturebook is a medium of expression whose essential unit is the double page on which images and text are written interactively, forming an articulated chain from page to page) (2015, 28–29).

it represents. It is also important to note that there are many titles focused on alternative relationships or families, so in this case I chose those that offer something different and have an original touch, and I avoided describing books that could seem too similar to others in my corpus.

For the present study, I will talk about three types of books: books in which the protagonists are children with 'non-standard' behaviour, or children who experience their gender identity or express their gender in ways that do not conform to their assigned sex at birth; books about relationships or families that do not follow what tradition dictates, i.e. heterosexual relationships; and stories that illustrate difference and diversity in a metaphorical way.

Background on Spain

The first picturebooks for children explicitly about LGBTQ+ issues produced in Spain generally began to be published from 2000 onwards. In the case of Spain, it is important to recall Francisco Franco's 40-year dictatorship and the weight of religious beliefs, which inhibited any type of evolution towards a more modern society, especially for the LGBTQ+ community and, consequently, for the publication of books (particularly children's books) on this subject.

Modern Spanish history is marked by the Spanish Civil War (1936–39) and subsequently Franco's dictatorship (1939–75). The Civil War was a military conflict between the democratic government of the Second Spanish Republic, which was supported by most left-wing organizations, and a part of the army, led by a group of rebellious officers, which was joined by most right-wing organizations and the majority of the Catholic Church. Franco, who had support from Nazi Germany and fascist Italy, launched an offensive against Republicans in the Spanish territory, a conflict that ended in 1939 with the defeat of the Republican army. As a result of the victory of Franco's troops, a long-lasting totalitarian political system was established under his leadership, which imposed a conservative and fascist ideology and Catholicism as the only religion. Those who fought this power – or did not follow these rules – were investigated, persecuted, imprisoned and, often, tortured or executed. The LGBTQ+ community was one of the victims of this regime.

Homosexuality was considered highly problematic under the dictatorship. A reform of the 1933 *Ley de vagos y maleantes* (Vagrancy Act), which targeted homeless people, nomads and procurers, included homosexuals in 1954. However, before that there was repression even with no specific laws. In 1970, the Movimiento Español de Liberación Homosexual (Spanish Gay Liberation Movement) was founded clandestinely in Barcelona. It was the first organization that defended gay rights in Spain. However, the *Ley de peligrosidad y rehabilitación social* (Social Danger and Rehabilitation Act), which established punishments of five years in prison or psychiatric detention for homosexuals, was passed the same year. In the beginning of the Spanish transition to democracy, on 26 June 1977, more than five thousand people occupied Les Rambles of Barcelona; it was the first Spanish demonstration for LGBTQ+ visibility, called by the Front d'Alliberament Gai de Catalunya (Catalan Gay Liberation Movement) when homosexuality was still illegal (it was only legalized in 1979). In that protest, which was repressed by the police, there were slogans like 'Mi cuerpo es mío y hago con él lo que me da la gana' (My body is mine and I do with it what I want) and '¡Amnistía sexual!' (Sexual amnesty!). Finally, in 1979, a new law decriminalized homosexuality and transsexuality, protecting LGBTQ+ people from the discrimination and abuse that the 1970 law had allowed (this former law was not totally repealed until 1995, though). However, in the eighties, there was another turning point: the AIDS epidemic, which especially affected the LGBTQ+ community (mainly homosexual men), brought more homophobia. We must not forget that it was not until 1990 that the World Health Organization (WHO) assembly removed homosexuality from its list of mental disorders.

In 2005, the Spanish law 13/2005, which recognized same-sex marriage and adoption by same-sex couples, was finally passed, making Spain the third country in the world to do so, after the Netherlands and Belgium. Two years later, in 2007, the gender identity law was passed, thanks to which trans people can change their name and sex in their ID without being required to have surgery. In the last forty years, the LGBTQ+ community's fight has changed the social paradigm and sexual diversity is finally accepted. There are some differences between autonomous communities regarding rights in terms of sexual orientation and gender identity; for instance, in 2014, the law to guarantee the rights of lesbian, gay, bisexual, transgender and intersex people and to eradicate homophobia, biphobia and transphobia was passed, but only for the territory of Catalonia. In 2018, an LGBTI Law was passed in Valencia, prohibiting aversion therapies used to attempt to change sexual orientations and also covering intersex people and people with differences in their sexual development. The new LGBTI equality law for the whole country, which would be a big step forward, is still under discussion in Spanish Parliament. There is a clear evolution regarding LGBTQ+ rights, but there is still a long way to go.

As I noted previously, over the past two decades the publication of titles for children has particularly focused on alternative relationships or families, those which do not follow what tradition dictates, i.e. heterosexual relationships. However, unfortunately there are still few books in which the protagonists are little boys or little girls or characters of other genders with 'non-standard' or non-gender-stereotypical behaviour, or children who experience their gender identity or express their gender in ways that do not conform to their assigned sex at birth. When the target audience is young readers, these matters are always addressed delicately. Even though some countries have authors and publishers who publish challenging and controversial books (not only LGBTQ+ books), there are still conservative publishers in relation to these kind of subjects.

While some countries, such as in northern Europe, have a history of producing challenging books for children, the situation is different in Spain. But we have some examples in Spain, of course, like the Catalan picturebook entitled *Noms robats* (Stolen Names), by Tàssies (2010), which is against bullying at school. This is the story of an unnamed child who doesn't know the good things in life, such as the smell of the oven, a smile, or words spoken in a low voice. He feels misunderstood, rejected, persecuted, and he leans over the handrail of the stairs without vertigo. Teachers and librarians use it as a tool to reflect on this subject. But even when such books are published, there is a filter – or even censorship – from some parents, teachers, librarians and booksellers. Regarding this,

Janet Evans says: 'Many adults feel that challenging and controversial picturebooks are not suitable for children to read, however, it is they, as adults, who have problems coping with these challenging texts and not the children' (Evans 2015, 5). In what follows, I will explore some of the books published in Spain and how they are viewed.

Boys Also Cry

Despite the clear evolution towards the acceptance of diversity in society in general, there is still a long way to go. We can be different in many ways; for instance, we can diverge from what tradition dictates regarding gender roles. It is not the easiest path, of course, because these roles are still so strict and separate in Spain. To name some examples, in 2015 Zara, the influential Spanish clothing brand, had to take two outfits for babies off the market, because they were sexist: the pink bodysuit had the sentence 'Pretty and perfect: it's what Daddy said' and the blue one, 'Cool and clever: it's what Mummy said' (*Huffington Post* 2015). The Observatorio Andaluz de la Publicidad no Sexista (Andalucian Observatory of Non-Sexist Advertising) was the first in sounding the alarm about this issue. Another similar case happened a year before in the popular Spanish chain mall Hipercor, which took two baby's outfits off the shelves. The blue one said 'inteligente como papá' (clever like dad) and the pink one 'bonita como mamá' (pretty like mum) (Vidales 2014). So in both cases, the message is very clear: while the girl has to be pretty, the boy represents intelligence, an obvious example of sexism.

Moreover, in many Spanish schoolyards, the football field occupies a large space. On the one hand, the omnipresence of this sport makes some little boys who do not necessarily like football feel unaccepted, and, on the other hand, little girls who do like this sport finally give up because they feel alone in the middle of a group of boys. So football in elementary schools can be a significant sign of a separation of sexes and pressure to conform to stereotyped roles. In spite of the gender equality campaigns, this separation appears early in schools.

And there is also separation between gender roles in children's books; nowadays there is in Spain, as elsewhere in the world, an important market of children's books clearly marketed for girls: following feminine stereotypes, they are very often pink and glittery with girly main characters and princesses. There are not as many books aimed specifically at boys for this age range.

In this regard, we have to reflect on what happens when children take on 'non-standard' behaviour, thereby calling into question the – rigid – categorization of binary gender roles. We learn to be boys or girls in quite separate ways. The messages sent by the social environment, media and advertising are that boys are expected to be physically strong, they cannot express their feelings and must love to play football, while only girls sign up for ballet lessons or want to be princesses.

Regarding this, it is interesting to read *Buscando el final del arcoíris* (*Chasing Rainbows*), a collection of articles about gender-fluid parenting, edited by May Friedman and Fiona Joy Green (2015). Generally speaking, in this form of parenting, parents (or legal guardians) create spaces where children can freely explore gender roles. In this book, these families explain their own experience related to this subject, helping other families who are choosing non-binary practices to start talking and become visible. For example, Kathy Witterick and David Stocker, a Toronto couple, decided that the sex of Storm, their newborn, was a family matter. They were pretty sure that the child would tell their gender to people when it was the right time. In their opinion, children are able to make their own decisions, so parents should reduce their imposed limitations on what is expected from children in order to be masculine or feminine (Witterick 2015). In any case, children need a space free from prejudice and pressure where they can explore their gender and get away from the binary. My question, then, is whether Spanish children's literature helps create such a space.

Spanish Picturebooks

I would like to start my analysis of LGBTQ+ picturebooks published in Spain in the country's four official languages with the Spanish-language *Mercedes quiere ser bombera* (Mercedes Wants to be a Firewoman), written by Beatriz Moncó and illustrated by Mabel Piérola (2004).[2] In some educational establishments, it is expected that boys and girls should have a very defined gender. Even though the schoolteacher in *Mercedes quiere ser bombera* respects that there are different ways to be a boy or a girl, there is conflict in the classroom in relation to this issue, so the teacher has to deal with it. The illustrations are in duotone and line, with an old-fashioned style – especially regarding the editorial design. The teacher asks the students what they want to be when they grow up. Everyone gives their opinion, until it is little Mercedes' turn, and she says she wants to be a firewoman. This causes debate and controversy. Because of the weight of tradition, we often think that there are some professions for men and others for women. In some Romance languages such as Spanish or Catalan, in which nouns can have grammatical gender, it is still strange to pronounce the name of a profession – in the case of variable nouns – that is only traditionally performed by men with the feminine ending *-a*, such as *bombera*, or 'firewoman' (in the masculine, it would be *bombero*). So, considering the existing cultural separation in Spain, some people will find it odd that a girl wants to be a firewoman, but will think that she can be a nurse or a ballerina, for example. 'Because she is a girl and girls cannot be firemen!',[3] a classmate complains. In *Mercedes quiere ser bombera*, the adult reader will find an informational text addressed to them at the end. In fact, the books from the publishing house Bellaterra seem to focus on reading as an educational tool; they usually have an epilogue and back covers have a declaration of intention. We will see it again in two more picturebooks that I will describe below. The back cover from *Mercedes quiere ser bombera* illustrates this perfectly:

> We teach and learn to be men and to be women, to be equal and to be different, while we transmit and put together our love and our phobias. Equality between genders is not just

---

2 A Catalan edition was published in 2009. See the Primary Texts list on pages 327–29 of this volume for full details of titles published in the country's four official languages.

3 '¡Porque es una chica y las chicas no pueden ser bomberas!' All translations my own, unless otherwise stated.

> an ethical and civilized position, but a big need in our lives and our societies, it is a human demand.[4] (2004, n.p.)

When the publisher focuses on offering a guided message or moral, it is often at the expense of literary quality. This type of book tries to fill in for adults' limitations and protects them from their inability to face specific issues with their children: disease, death, immigration, respect for animals and nature, gender identity, sexual orientation and so on. Literature for children should not be a substitute for any conversation with parents, although it can be part of an ongoing conversation.

On the one hand, important changes regarding women's role in society are a reality, but on the other hand, men keep living trapped in a masculinity with almost no changes. Karen Coats mentions this in the context of children's picturebooks:

> But while there is a long tradition in children's literature of girls transgressing gender norms by behaving as tomboys, there is no similar tradition for boys behaving in ways that have traditionally been coded feminine. In fact, Eve Kosofsky Sedgwick (1991) has coined the term 'effeminophobia' to highlight the fact that when boys behave in ways culturally construed as feminine, they are considered pathological, whereas girls engaging in activities generally associated with masculinity are often celebrated. (Coats 2017, 125)

We find an example of stereotype revision in the American illustrated book *Oliver Button is a Sissy*, by Tomie De Paola, published in 1979. The Spanish publisher Everest published it in translation in 2002, and to us, as authors, editors and readers, it is still a model to consider of a book on this subject.

The Spanish picturebook *El niño perfecto* (The Perfect Boy) provides a modern, Spanish example of a book that similarly challenges gender norms. I wrote and illustrated it and it was published in 2012; it is realistic and caused an issue for some adults. To everyone's mind, Daniel is the perfect boy, because he has exemplary behaviour and follows every convention. At night, while his parents are sleeping, he puts his mother's dress on. The pink feather boa that the little boy wears is a contrast if we compare it with the soft colours used for the rest of the story; indeed, it is the climax (see Figure 18). In this picturebook, I write about choosing another path, which moves away from what is expected by society, and I talk about the self-identification of homosexuality, a private process in the beginning. For this reason, the main character puts his mother's dress on, as a symbolic fact that means much more than a simple costume or game. The perfect boy is not completely conscious of the meaning of his secret, as he is still little, but he knows that the thing that happens at midnight is important.

As I said above, *El niño perfecto* was considered a problem by some adults. There are two cases that can be helpful to illustrate that reaction. In October 2014, two years after

4 'Enseñamos y aprendemos a ser hombres y a ser mujeres, a ser iguales y a ser diferentes, al tiempo que transmitimos y configuramos nuestras filias y nuestras fobias. La igualdad entre los géneros no es solo una postura ética y cívica, sino una imperiosa necesidad en nuestras vidas y nuestras sociedades, es una exigencia humana.'

Figure 18: Cormand, Bernat. 2012. *El niño perfecto* (The Perfect Boy). Barcelona: Sd·edicions. [Spanish edition]

the publication of the book, a librarian from the Ramon Fernández Jurado library in Castelldefels (a town close to Barcelona) wrote me an email in which she told me that she had discovered my picturebook in a collection of literature for children in a bookstore in Barcelona, so she decided to include it in the section of the library called Fundamental Rights. A few days later, *El niño perfecto* ended up in the hands of a mother who was reading books with her son. Surprised by the topic of it, she wrote a complaint to the city hall of Castelldefels; she wanted them to remove the picturebook from the library. The director of the library responded to the complaint and said that the title in question was appropriate for the library for its literary quality and subject, so it was not removed.

Another case related to my book happened in 2016. Hazte Oír is a Spanish ultra-Catholic organization which defends traditional heteroparental families and organizes campaigns against the LGBTQ+ community. In that year, the association sent thousands of brochures to public and private elementary schools around Spain with the following title: *¿Sabes lo que quieren enseñarle a tu hijo en tu colegio? Las leyes de adoctrinamiento sexual* (Do you know what they want to teach your son in your school? The sexual indoctrination laws). Through that brochure, they alerted parents to the idea that the laws that protect LGBTQ+ rights are a threat to freedom and encouraged parents to report children's books that talk about LGBTQ+ issues. *El niño perfecto* was one of them.

In autumn 2018, NubeOcho published the Spanish *¡Vivan las uñas de colores! (I Love My Colorful Nails!)*, written by Alicia Acosta and Luis Amavisca and illustrated by Gusti. A little boy called Juan likes painting his nails in different colours. Sometimes he asks his mother for some more colours and she is happy to give them to her son. One day, two students at school bully Juan: 'Only girls paint their nails. You are a girl! You are a girl!'[5] they say (2018, n.p.). Juan tells his parents what happened and they support him. In fact, from then, his father starts painting his own nails when he picks his son up at school. On his birthday, Juan goes to school and, when he opens the classroom door, he finds a surprise: everyone, the students and the teacher, has painted their nails. Here, as in *El niño perfecto*, through the main character, who has a 'non-standard' behaviour, gender stereotypes are questioned. Unlike Daniel, who puts his mother's dress on secretly at night, in the story of Juan his behaviour is more visible, so he occasionally has to suffer discrimination from some students, who call him 'niña' (girl). But I wonder: why should the word *niña* upset the protagonist? Why does this word have a negative connotation? The text does not explain that, so it could confuse little readers, but of course it reflects the anti-female view in society, where men are ranked higher, and feminine-seeming men are discriminated against. In any case, *¡Vivan las uñas de colores!* describes this path followed by some children which moves away from what is expected from the traditional society. The authors do it in a positive way; we can see it in the development of the story and in the illustrations, which are fresh and colourful. The first edition of the book sold out quite fast, and it has been recommended several times in the Spanish media, e.g. newspapers, blogs and radio. As we will see later, this picturebook shared spaces in media with my second illustrated book, *Los días felices*, published the same year.

We have seen only a few Spanish titles here, as there are not many picturebooks in which gender roles are questioned through the characters. Furthermore, the lack of literary quality in some books makes it difficult to write more about them, although the intentions are positive in some cases. Writing for children is not easy. Moreover, it is possible that editors do not have space in their editorial lists for books about this subject or, in some cases, that they back out because some of these stories are too controversial for them to publish.

Other Relationships, Other Families

My experience with *El niño perfecto* drove me to write and illustrate a love story between two little boys. It came out in 2018 in Catalan and in Spanish with the publisher A Buen Paso under the title *Els dies feliços* and *Los días felices* (Happy Days), respectively (see Figure 19). The story is about first love, that innocent love that we have when we are children. The narrator remembers when he was a child and lived in a coastal town, where he met Jacob, another little boy. They wanted to spend all their time together, and when they could not see each other they shared their toys in a hole of a tree. But one day, 'Jacob left the town, and went very far away, I suppose, because I never heard from him, as if he had disappeared off the face of the earth',[6] so his friend became very sad. The only thing he has left from his time with Jacob is the memories of those happy days. Unfortunately,

5 'Pintarse las uñas es de niñas. ¡Eres una niña! ¡Eres una niña!'

6 'Un dia, el Jacob se'n va anar del poble, suposo que molt lluny perquè, com si se l'hagués empassat la terra, no en vaig saber mai més res'.

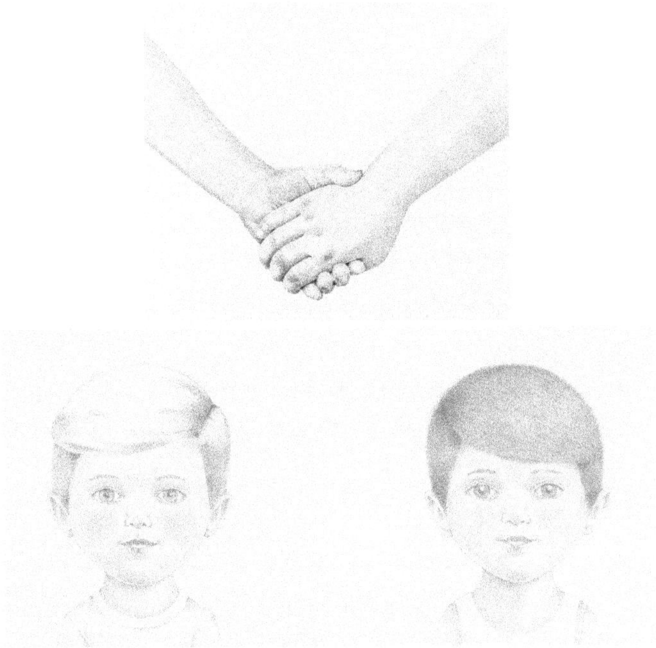

Figure 19: Cormand, Bernat. 2018a. *Els dies feliços* (Happy Days). Barcelona: A Buen Paso. [Catalan edition]

we are more used to finding stories in which a little boy likes a little girl and vice versa, especially in children's books, so it is not easy to find different types of love, or other non-heterosexual relationships.

Los días felices came out in September 2018. Since then, it has had a very positive reception. For the Christmas campaign in 2018, the picturebook was included in a selection of 13 books for children from 0 to 12 years old in *Time Out Barcelona* (Aspas 2018), and, with *¡Vivan las uñas de colores!*, in a selection of nine books for young readers in *Time Out Madrid* (Lambies 2018). Also for Christmas, *Los días felices* and *¡Vivan las uñas de colores!* were recommended on *Frontera*, a Spanish radio programme from RTVE. In the blog *Linternas y bosques* (Lanterns and Woods, more than 17,000 followers), run by the Mexican journalist Adolfo Córdova, my picturebook appeared in the post 'Los mejores libros ilustrados que leí en 2018' (The Best Picturebooks I have Read in 2018) (Córdova 2019). In these cases, only a few of the recommended books are related to LGBTQ+ topics. But both books were included in a selection of LGBTQ+ books in 'Trece libros para entender, de una vez, que hay niños azules y niños rosas' (Thirteen Books to Understand Once and For All That There Are Blue Boys and Pink Boys),[7] in *El Asombrario* (57,000 readers), the culture section of the Spanish digital newspaper *El Público* (Pizarro 2018). Furthermore, in November 2018 I was interviewed in Diari ARA, a Catalan newspaper

7 'Niños rosas' (pink boys) can mean both feminine and gay.

with 129,000 readers for the print version; it also has a digital version (Nopca 2018). And I was interviewed on TV3, the Catalan public channel; the short report came out in the evening news, with an audience of 600,000 viewers.

In 2012, *El niño perfecto* did not experience such a good reception. There might be different factors at play. The number of years between the books saw some changes in society. Also, perhaps the story of *El niño perfecto* was shocking for some adults because the story is told without euphemism or hiding the facts. Also, in Spain more LGBTQ+ illustrated books were published in those years, so maybe now there is more interest and sensitivity from adults.

Things are changing in Spanish books. If we thought that only princes could marry princesses, or princesses could marry princes, we were wrong. In a bilingual Spanish and English picturebook titled *La princesa Li / Princess Li* (2012), written by Luis Amavisca and illustrated by Elena Rendeiro, King Wan Tan's daughter is in love with Beatriz, but at one point her love story seems to come to an end because her father wants her to marry a young man from the court. After a big fight for her true love, 'the king decreed the end of the selection for a new prince. Now the kingdom would have two princesses'.[8] This book is part of a series called *Egalité*, published by NubeOcho, in which, as explained at the end of the book, we can find a selection of stories that try to promote equality and diversity from different points of view: families with two fathers or two mothers, a first homosexual love, and even people who arrive to our countries in a small boat. The illustrations in *La princesa Li*, which are made with line and watercolour, are lacking in drawing technique, so it seems to be a work by a non-professional artist. The style is irregular, with poorly defined and confusing levels in compositions, so sometimes it is not easy to recognize the different elements in the scene. In addition, the design of the book is unappealing. Here again editors and authors wanted to focus on the LGBTQ+ message at the expense of literary and artistic quality, a trend that has been also been identified elsewhere in the world (see, for example, Naidoo 2012, 44–45, and see, too, some of the other chapters in this book).

In the Galician children's book *Titiritesa* (*Titiritess*), written by Xerardo Quintiá and illustrated by Maurizio A. C. Quarello (2007), there are also two girls and a happy ending. It treats homosexuality with humour and freshness. In a world of fantasy and grotesque characters, Titiritess lives in the kingdom of The-day-before-yesterday. Her mother dreams of seeing her daughter well married and tries to educate her as a refined courtier, but her daughter rejects the conventional life that has been imposed on her and does not share her mother's ambitions: 'As Titiritess didn't want to put up with all that, she decided to run away from The-day-before-yesterday. The next morning, before cockcrow, she took off at speed with a pair of shoes, a bag and lots of sugar cubes'.[9] On

8 'el rey decretó a su pueblo el fin de la elección del nuevo príncipe. De ahora en adelante, el reino tendría dos princesas'.

9 'Como Titiritesa no pensaba soportar tal cosa, decidió huir de Anteayer. A la mañana siguiente, antes del canto del gallo, con un par de zapatos, una mochila y un montón de terrones de azúcar, se largó a toda velocidad'.

Figure 20: Quintiá, Xerardo. 2007. *Titiritesa* (*Titiritess*). Illustrated by Maurizio. A. C. Quarello. Pontevedra: OQO Editora. [Galician edition]

her trip, she meets King Godofredo, who is crying because a monster took his daughter Wendolina, so the brave Titiritess decides to rescue the princess, which she finally does, and together, riding a donkey, 'they felt a playful breeze that tickled their thoughts'[10] (see Figure 20). So we have two fairy tale-like stories for children in which the main characters are homosexual. Despite the lower quality of the first one that I described above, this fact is important: we cannot forget that some years back it was commonly thought that sexual and romantic relationships were only possible between a man and a woman.

Invisibility is an especially hard reality in relationships between older LGBTQ+ people. They are a vulnerable group rejected by heteronormative society, but also by other LGBTQ+ people. They usually suffer a double discrimination caused by their gender identity or their sexuality and, at the same time, by their age. In Spain, lesbians, gays, bisexuals and transgender people who now are old lived their lives under the dictatorship's persecution, and many of them are still in the closet. They will not come out; it is too late. For this reason, it is important to look at the Galician picturebook *Velliñas* (Little Old Ladies), written by Charo Pita and illustrated by Fátima Afonso (2009), a story that reminds us of traditional tales. Antea and Filipa, two old women, live together, have meals together, sleep together and dream together. Their meals are only based on water soup: 'From Monday to Saturday, they cooked a normal dish: water soup. On Sunday, they prepared something special: water soup… with a noodle that they cut in half: a half for Antea and a half for Filipa',[11] so they always starve, which is perhaps reminiscent of the poverty some elderly people suffer. However, one day they find out that on the top of a bean plant that touches the sky there is a windmill full of delicious meals ready to be eaten. On the way to the top, Filipa falls down from the plant and literally breaks into pieces. Her girlfriend rebuilds her piece by piece: a beautiful image of love (see Figure 21).

10 'sintieron una brisa juguetona que les hizo cosquillas en el pensamiento'.

11 'De luns a sábado cociñaban un prato normal: sopa de auga. Os domingos preparaban algo especial: sopa de auga ... cun fideo que partían á metade: medio para Antea e medio para Filipa'.

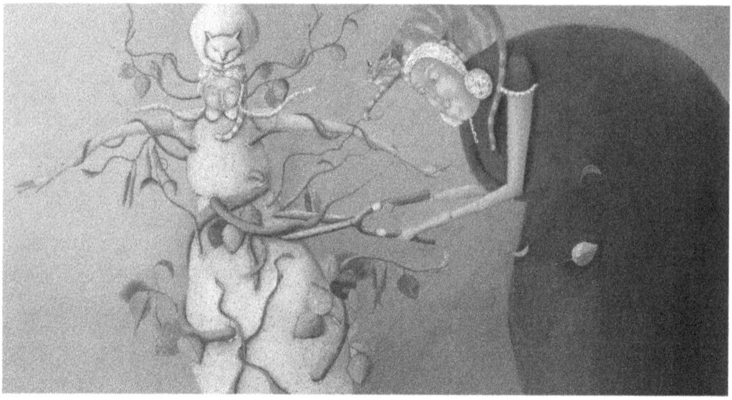

Figure 21: Pita, Charo. 2009. *Velliñas* (Little Old Ladies). Illustrated by Fátima Afonso. Pontevedra: OQO Editora. [Galician edition]

It is important to learn, from home and at school, that there are different possibilities for family models: a family with only a father or a mother and one child, or a couple, married or not, with one or more than one child, religious or atheist, heterosexual, homosexual, trans and so on. All of them deserve to be accepted and respected. This is the case of *Mi papá es un payaso* (*My Dad is a Clown*), written by José Carlos Andrés and illustrated by Natalia Hernández (2013). It is a bilingual edition, Spanish and English. This picturebook is two-toned and the illustrations are simple lines to represent the characters and the scenes. It shows a very positive home environment: a little boy has one father who is a clown and another father who is a doctor. He is proud of his two fathers but does not fully understand what it means to be a clown, until he discovers that it is not an easy job, and finally understands that his father makes people laugh and makes them happy. In any case, everything at home is happy, and outside the home there is no conflict, so the story might be meant to show a positive image of a different sort of family. In a similar way, the Spanish *No es hora de jugar* (*Bedtime, Not Playtime*), which was published in 2018, written by Lawrence Schimel (a well-known gay author and translator) and illustrated by Elina Braslina, describes the daily life of a homoparental family. It is time for bed and the dog of the house feels like playing. The little protagonist washes his (or her) – undefined gender – face and cleans his (or her) teeth, his (or her) two fathers tell him (or her) a children's story (see Figure 22), but the dog insists that it wants to play and the whole family finish up running after it, because it has played a prank. The book has been published first in Spanish and Catalan for Spain, and subsequently in Croatian, Czech, Flemish and Latvian in their respective countries. And the Bologna Children's Book Fair chose it for their The Extraordinary Library exhibit of 100 board books.

The protagonist of the Basque *Aitorrek bi ama ditu* (Aitor Has Two Mums), written by M. José Mendieta and illustrated by Mabel Piérola (2004), is not as lucky as the clown and the doctor's son or the child in *No es hora de jugar*. The author describes with a critical eye the reality of two lesbian mothers and their child in a small town. Though Aitor lives

Figure 22: Schimel, Lawrence. 2018. *No es hora de jugar* (*Bedtime, Not Playtime*). Illustrated by Elina Braslina. Barcelona: Editorial Egales. [Spanish edition]

in a family environment full of love and affection, outside the home he unfortunately has to face hostile behaviour from some neighbours; for example, it is Aitor's birthday, but his best friend never appears at the party. The problem is, as he eventually finds out, that his friend's parents do not accept that Aitor has two mothers. The little boy also suffers discrimination from other students at school for the same reason. Aitor does not feel happy in the town, so his two mothers finally decide to live in a city where they have friends who are non-traditional types of families.

The Catalan picturebook *La festa d'en Blai* (Blai's Party), written by Iñaki Tofiño and Sebastià Martín and illustrated by Mabel Piérola (2008), is a story in which the young reader meets Blai, who has parents that are separated, does not like football and usually plays with girls. His sister is actually a trans boy. Besides, Miquel, a friend of his, has two fathers, and Kevin, another friend, is gay. If we want to introduce LGBTQ+ topics to children, I would argue that sometimes we have to be careful and go step-by-step, or introduce the subject in a natural way to avoid them feeling confused. In this book, I would argue that too many different queer characters appear, and this dilutes the story. Related to this, as I said previously, the books from the publishing house Bellaterra appear intended as tools to encourage readers to think about LGBTQ+ issues, and this makes them pedagogical rather than entertainment. Like *Mercedes quiere ser bombera*, these last two titles are in the same book series and are also illustrated by Mabel Piérola.

Still in the family world, the Spanish story *Las cosas que le gustan a Fran* (Things That Fran Likes), written by Berta Piñán and illustrated by Antonia Santolaya Ruiz-Clavijo (2007), has a more literary touch and the authors challenge the readers. While we turn the pages, we discover what Fran, the narrator's mother's partner, likes to do: hugging Mum, studying thick books, writing, cooking delicious meals, picking up her stepdaughter, going for a run in the park and so forth. In Spanish, Fran can be both a male and a female name, and the narrator does not say until the end what Fran's gender is: she is actually a woman. An interesting game, if we consider that many of us, because of society's prejudices, have fallen into the trap and assumed others to be, or have ourselves been assumed to be, in a heterosexual relationship.

The story of two male penguins at the zoo is very different (see the chapter by Naidoo and Zabawa in this volume for more about gay penguins). There are cases of homosexuality in the animal kingdom, especially between these aquatic birds. The penguins in the Catalan *En Ceba i en Pebre* (*Onion and Pepper*), by Laura Reixach (2010), hatch an abandoned egg and create a family together. Inspired by a real story from the zoo in Bremerhaven (Germany), this picturebook could help children to reflect on non-traditional types of families and perhaps pave the way towards tolerance. Besides, animals make it easy for child readers to empathize and connect, as is well known from children's literature. However, I have to confess that there is a surprising similarity between the Catalan title and the well-known American picturebook *And Tango Makes Three*, written by Justin Richardson and Peter Parnell and illustrated by Henry Cole, published five years earlier (2005). *Tango* is also based on a real story; here, two male penguins hatch an abandoned egg at the zoo in New York. The most remarkable difference between both books is that, in *En Ceba i en Pebre*, the penguins are more humanized – in their expressions and they also wear clothes – while in the American children's book the animals are just animals, not in a very realistic style; they only have a little touch in their faces that makes them more human.

Metaphorically Speaking

It is never easy to find the right tone if we want children to get the message of difference and diversity; there are many factors at play. When literature for children talks about such topics without mincing words, sometimes from a sort of realism, some people think that they are books (also) for adults. They could in fact be crossover picturebooks, which address both children and adults and usually show difficult subjects (Beckett 2012). In any case, I can say with no doubt that the Spanish *Monstruo rosa* (Pink Monster), by Olga de Dios (2013), is the opposite of the books described above, because it uses fantasy to illustrate difference. If we want to use a metaphor to do it, a pink monster in a community of identical white characters will attract young readers. Pink Monster has been different from the day it was born: 'It was pink and the others were white. Pink Monster was big and the others were small. It always smiled at any joke but the others could not because of their bills'[12] (see Figure 23). One day, it decided to look for a new place to live. After crossing mountains, the ocean and the desert, it finally found an area where everyone was different and, from then on, it never stopped smiling. Some elements in the book evoke traditional LGBTQ+ icons, like the rainbow on the cover or the pink for the protagonist. But children do not necessarily have this information. After all, it is good to have material that children enjoy and, at the same time, will help them to think and reflect about diversity. *Monstruo rosa* has been a big success since it came out in 2013. It is in its 15th edition

12 'Era rosa y los demás eran blancos. Monstruo Rosa era grande y los demás eran pequeños. Siempre sonreía con cualquier tontería, pero a los demás su pico se lo impedía'.

Figure 23: Dios, Olga de. 2013. *Monstruo rosa* (Pink Monster). Zaragoza: Apila Ediciones. [Spanish edition]

and 80,000 copies have been sold, and it has been published in 12 languages, including Catalan and Basque.

There is also the colourful *¡Eso no es normal! (That's Not Normal!)*, written in Spanish by Mar Pavón and illustrated by Laure du Faÿ, about a blue elephant (2015). Here the difference is not the colour, but its trunk, which is so long. It is not a problem for most of the animals, which see benefits to the size, but it is for the hippopotamus: '¡eso no es normal!', it always says. One day, the little hippopotamus, following a cricket, jumps into the water full of crocodiles. The elephant saves it with its trunk. From then, the big hippopotamus accepts the elephant's difference.

Using a very different approach, there is the Catalan *Dues rodones idèntiques?* (Two Identical Circles?), by Neus Moscada (2009). Two apparently identical circles raise a question: are they really equal? Both are the same size, they are red, they are two ink spots on paper, they have the same texture and smell the same (see Figure 24). But one is a point and the other is a circle, so identity is what distinguishes them. 'Ens sentim diferents' (We feel different), they say. This small-sized picturebook supports the right to be different, and it has nothing to do with the physical aspect, but rather with feelings of identity. Sharing reading, adults and children together, is necessary for this type of book, in view of the symbology used in the construction of the story. We can read *Dues rodones idèntiques?* as a reflection on (gender) identity, among other topics, if we want to.

Conclusion

In this chapter, I have discussed a selection of picturebooks for children produced in Spain that, in some way, are important regarding the representation of different LGBTQ+ realities: books in which the protagonists are boys or girls with non-gender-stereotypical behaviour, or children who experience their gender identity or express their gender in ways that do not conform to their assigned sex at birth; other books about alternative relationships or families; and stories that illustrate difference and diversity in a

Figure 24: Moscada, Neus. 2009. *Dues rodones idèntiques?* (Two Identical Circles?). Barcelona: Sd·edicions. [Catalan edition]

metaphorical way. Through realism or through fantasy, these stories can open a window to help people learn about topics that are unknown in some contexts, even controversial. In Spain, people who now are in their fifties grew up in a discriminatory world, where it was thought that homosexuality was a bad thing and there were no laws that protected the community. We have to recall Franco's 40-year dictatorship, and, in some ways, more than forty years on, that wound is still open: homophobia and transphobia are still powerful forces in Spanish society. However, there has been some progress, at least here. Moreover, there is now some quite progressive legislation in regard to issues that touch the LGBTQ+ community. But we cannot forget the conservative and discriminatory politics in other parts of the world, even in nearby countries. In this context, when we talk about children's books, this subject is always addressed delicately in Spain, regardless of which language the books are written in. But we should not underestimate the level of comprehension of children, nor overprotect them from reality. Some parents let their sons and daughters see images of violence on TV, but they are shocked by a story about a little boy who puts on his mother's dress. In any case, it is important to let boys and girls grow up in an environment of acceptance, tolerance and respect, and in this regard picturebooks for children can pave the way. However, as previously stated, when editors and authors want to focus their projects on LGBTQ+ issues, sometimes they publish books as educational tools, at the expense of literary quality. I suggest we need to enhance the poetic qualities of these stories. After all, it is good that children in general – not necessarily only LGBTQ+ kids – just enjoy reading.

To conclude, remember the big fish made by the union of little red fish. The one which is different, the black one, has an important role in the construction of the figure – it is the eye – because in society there is also a place for minorities, and because we all deserve to both see and be seen.

Bibliography

Acosta, Alicia, and Luis Amavisca. 2018. *¡Vivan las uñas de colores!* (*I Love My Colorful Nails!*). Illustrated by Gusti. Madrid: NubeOcho. [Spanish edition].

Amavisca, Luis. 2012. *La princesa Li / Princess Li.* Illustrated by Elena Rendeiro. España: Editorial Egales, NubeOcho Ediciones. [Bilingual edition Spanish-English].

Andrés, José Carlos. 2013. *Mi papá es un payaso / My Dad is a Clown.* Illustrated by Natalia Hernández. España: Editorial Egales, NubeOcho. [Bilingual edition Spanish-English].

Aspas, Erica. 2018. 'Libros infantiles y juveniles recomendados' (Recommended Books for Children and Young People). *Time Out Barcelona*. Last modified 16 July 2020. https://www.timeout.es/barcelona/es/ninyos/libros-infantiles-recomendados

Beckett, Sandra. 2012. *Crossover Picturebooks: A Genre for All Ages*. London: Routledge.

Coats, Karen. 2017. 'Gender in Picturebooks'. In *The Routledge Companion to Picturebooks*, edited by Bettina Kümmerling-Meibauer, 119–27. London: Routledge.

Córdova, Adolfo. 2019. 'Los mejores libros ilustrados que leí en 2018' (The Best Picturebooks I have Read in 2018). *Linternas y bosques*, 5 January. https://linternasybosques.wordpress.com/2019/01/05/los-mejores-libros-ilustrados-que-lei-en-2018/

Cormand, Bernat. 2012. *El niño perfecto* (The Perfect Boy). Barcelona: Sd·edicions. [Spanish edition].

———. 2018a. *Els dies feliços* (Happy Days). Barcelona: A Buen Paso. [Catalan edition].

———. 2018b. *Los días felices* (Happy Days). Barcelona: A Buen Paso. [Spanish edition].

DePaola, Tomie. 1979. *Oliver Button is a Sissy*. San Diego: Harcourt Brace & Company.

Evans, Janet, ed. 2015. *Challenging and Controversial Picturebooks: Creative and Critical Responses to Visual Texts*. New York: Routledge.

Dios, Olga de. 2013. *Monstruo rosa* (Pink Monster). Zaragoza: Apila Ediciones. [Spanish edition].

Friedman, May, and Fiona Joy Green, eds. 2015. *Buscando el final del arcoíris: una exploración de las prácticas de crianza desde la fluidez de género* (*Chasing Rainbows: Exploring Gender Fluid Parenting Practices*). Translated by Yolanda Fontal. Barcelona: Edicions Bellaterra.

Frontera. RTVE. Madrid, 8 December 2018. https://www.rtve.es/alacarta/audios/frontera/frontera-08-12-18/4878043/

Huffington Post. 2015. 'Los niños listos, las niñas guapas: Zara vuelve a liarla con sus bodys sexistas para bebés' (Smart Little Boys, Pretty Little Girls: Zara Messes It Up Again With Its Sexist Bodysuits for Babies). *Huffington Post*, 8 April. https://www.huffingtonpost.es/2015/04/08/bodys-sexistas-zara_n_7024570.html

Lambies, Josep. 2018. 'Libros ilustrados para niñas y niños' (Illustrated Books for Little Girls and Little Boys). *Time Out Madrid*, 7 November. https://www.timeout.es/madrid/es/que-hacer/libros-ilustrados-para-ninyas-y-ninyos

Mendieta, M. José. 2004. *Aitorrek bi ama ditu* (Aitor Has Two Mums). Illustrated by Mabel Piérola. Donostia: Erein. [Basque edition].

Moncó, Beatriz. 2004. *Mercedes quiere ser bombera* (Mercedes Wants to be a Firewoman). Illustrated by Mabel Piérola. Barcelona: Edicions Bellaterra. [Spanish edition].

———. 2009. *La Mercè vol ser bombera* (Mercedes Wants to be a Firewoman). Illustrated by Mabel Piérola. Barcelona: Edicions Bellaterra. [Catalan edition].

Moscada, Neus. 2009. *Dues rodones idèntiques?* (Two Identical Circles?) Barcelona: Sd·edicions. [Catalan edition].

Naidoo, Jamie Campbell. 2012. *Rainbow Family Collections: Selecting and Using Children's Books with Lesbian, Gay, Bisexual, Transgender, and Queer Content*. Santa Barbara, CA: Libraries Unlimited.

Nopca, Jordi. 2018. 'El conte d'un nen que s'enamora d'un altre nen' (The Story of a Boy Who Falls in Love With Another Boy'. *Diari ARA*, 19 November. https://www.ara.cat/cultura/conte-nen-enamora_0_2127987210.html

Pavón, Mar. 2015. *¡Eso no es normal! (That's Not Normal!)*. Illustrated by Laure du Faÿ. Málaga: NubeOcho. [Spanish edition].

Piñán, Berta. 2007. *Las cosas que le gustan a Fran* (Things That Fran Likes). Illustrated by Antonia Santolaya Ruiz-Clavijo. Madrid: Hotel Papel.

Pita, Charo. 2009. *Velliñas* (Little Old Ladies). Illustrated by Fátima Afonso. Pontevedra: OQO Editora. [Galician edition].

Pizarro, Javier. 2018. 'Trece libros para entender, de una vez, que hay niños azules y niños rosas' (Thirteen Books to Understand Once and For All That There Are Blue Boys and Pink Boys). *El Asombrario*, 5 December. https://elasombrario.com/trece-libros-entender-ninos-azules-rosas/

Quintiá, Xerardo. 2007. *Titiritesa* (*Titiritess*). Illustrated by Maurizio. A. C. Quarello. Pontevedra: OQO Editora. [Galician edition].

Reixach, Laura. 2010. *En Ceba i en Pebre (Onion and Pepper)*. Barcelona: Edicions Bellaterra. [Catalan edition].

Richardson, Justin, and Peter Parnell. 2005. *And Tango Makes Three*. Illustrated by Henry Cole. New York: Aladdin.

Schimel, Lawrence. 2018. *No es hora de jugar* (*Bedtime, Not Playtime*). Illustrated by Elina Braslina. Barcelona: Editorial Egales. [Spanish edition].

Tàssies. 2010. *Noms robats* (Stolen Names). Barcelona: Editorial Cruïlla.

Tofiño, Iñaki, and Sebastià Martín. 2008. *La festa d'en Blai* (Blai's Party). Illustrated by Mabel Piérola. Barcelona: Edicions Bellaterra. [Catalan edition].

Van der Linden, Sophie. 2015. *Álbum[es]*. Translated by Teresa Duran. Barcelona: Ediciones Ekaré.

Vidales, Raquel. 2014. '"Inteligente como papá, bonita como mamá"' ('Clever Like Dad, Pretty Like Mum'). *El País*, 26 September. https://elpais.com/sociedad/2014/09/26/actualidad/1411726737_372955.html

Witterick, Kathy. 2015. 'Bailar en el ojo del huracán: el don de la diversidad de género en nuestra familia' (Dancing in the Eye of the Storm: The Gift of Gender Diversity to Our Family). In *Buscando el final del arcoíris: una exploración de las prácticas de crianza desde la fluidez de género* (*Chasing Rainbows: Exploring Gender Fluid Parenting Practices*), edited by May Friedman and Fiona Joy Green, translated by Yolanda Fontal, 35–57. Barcelona: Edicions Bellaterra.

Chapter Fifteen

'I'M SURE THIS WHOLE BOY THING IS JUST A PHASE': TRANSGENDER NARRATIVES IN CONTEMPORARY SWEDISH CHILDREN'S AND YOUNG ADULT LITERATURE

Åsa Warnqvist

Introduction

In 2013, Swedish author and illustrator Elias S. Ericson published the graphic novel *Åror* (Oars), depicting the life of a transgender character in his late teens. When the Swedish Institute for Children's Books mentioned this book in its annual report on themes and tendencies in Swedish children's and young adult books, it was the first time that a transgender character was observed in literature for young readers in Swedish (Svenska barnboksinstitutet 2014, 8, 19). The reports, produced since 1993, show an increase in the number of depictions of transgender characters starting in 2015, which means that transgender characters have, with few exceptions, only been made visible in Swedish children's and young adult literature during the last few years.[1] From an international point of view this can be considered rather late (cf. overviews in, for example, Butler 2020; Epstein 2013, 142–55; Jenkins and Cart 2018, 161–80). Anglo-American films and young adult novels about transgender experiences such as *Boys Don't Cry* (1999), directed by Kimberly Pierce, and Julie Anne Peters' *Luna* (2004) show that, though usually progressive and attentive to norms, Swedish children's and young adult book authors had a late awakening when it comes to the portrayal of transgender characters. From 2013 and up until the time of writing, about 25 books for children and young adults with a transgender protagonist have been published in Swedish, translations and Swedish originals both included. To this can be added an equally large number of books where transgender

1 Since 2012, I have been involved in the work of the Swedish Institute for Children's Books' reports, the annual Book Tasting. The reports present statistics and analyses of themes and tendencies in the previous year's publication of Swedish children's and young adult literature. Through this work my colleagues and I come into contact with all children's and young adult books published in Sweden each year, which makes it possible for us to study changes from one year to another. For more information, see www.barnboksinstitutet.se/en/bokprovning/

characters are depicted as subsidiary characters (cf. Svenska barnboksinstitutet 2016, 13–14; 2017, 6; 2018, 8–9; 2020, 8; and Warnqvist 2017).

In this chapter, I wish to address the late appearance of transgender characters in Swedish children's and young adult literature. I will uncover possible reasons both for this late appearance and for the increased number of depictions following it. I begin by giving an overview of the legal situation for transgender people in Sweden, as necessary background for the discussion that follows. Moving on to the substantive analysis, I use Jessica Schiefauer's young adult novel *Pojkarna* (The Boys) (2011) as an example to argue that the late development can to some extent be explained by an inability among critics and scholars to see these patterns in earlier works, which has denied certain stories not explicitly presented as transgender narratives at the time of publication a position as such. Starting from an increased general attention to transgender issues in Swedish society during the twenty-first century, I then discuss the development of contemporary Swedish transgender narratives aimed at children and youth and what kind of narratives reach young Swedish readers today. I argue that two main tendencies can be identified in these narratives. The first tendency concerns books that function as introducers of the experiences of transgender children and youth, most notably exemplified by Ericson's aforementioned graphic novel *Åror*, and the children's books *Skarven* (The Cormorant)[2] (2016) by Sara Lövestam, *Brorsan är kung!* (Bro' Is King!) (2016) by Jenny Jägerfeld and *Månen, varelsen och jag* (The Moon, the Creature and I) (2020) by Ylva Karlsson and Sofia Falkenhem. The analysis focuses on these novels as depictions with the aim of explaining and making visible the experiences and hardships of transgender children and youth, and the narrative and rhetorical devices used to achieve this. By comparing the depictions of transgender characters with those of gay characters in *Hetare: elva noveller som känns* (Hotter: Eleven Short Stories That Make an Impression) (Ahlund and Friedner 2018), a collection of erotic short stories for young adults, I identify a strategy where problematizing rather than representing is the driving force of contemporary Swedish transgender narratives, signaling that they are in a less developed phase than gay narratives. However, there are also a few books that go beyond this approach by portraying and representing transgender people but not problematizing them or their experiences, a tendency which stands out internationally (cf. Butler 2020). I look at the potentially subversive function of these books, such as the graphic novels *Iggy 4-ever* (2015) by Hanna Gustavsson and *Vägarna är som tvättbrädor här* (The Roads Are Like Washboards Here) (2016a) by Hilding Sandgren.

Before I begin my analysis, I would like to briefly account for my use of the term *transgender* and related terms in this context. The term *transgender* may be defined in several different ways, but it is often used as an umbrella term for those who have a gender identity or gender expression that differs from the sex they were assigned at birth, for example trans men (men who were assigned female at birth), trans women (women who were assigned male at birth), or non-binary people (gender identities outside of the gender binary). More generally speaking, *trans* can be defined as a movement, away from

2 The Swedish word 'skarv' has a double meaning and can also refer to a visible joint or seam.

the gender assigned at birth and towards something else. Defined this way, temporary movements like cross-dressing (wearing clothes typically used by another sex) can also be included in the concept and regarded as transgender experiences. Looking at older material published before the concepts used today were established, a broader perspective is often necessary (cf., for example, Holmqvist 2017, 19). In this study I will use the term transgender when referring to characters who are trans boys, trans girls or non-binary. Moreover, I will use the term *transgender experience* in a broader sense, also including temporary transgender experiences when discussing material published before trans concepts were established within Swedish society and academia. Throughout the analysis, I shift pronoun depending on how the transgender characters are presented by the narrators in the books at that point in the story. Characters discussed that are simply referred to as 'boys' or 'girls' without their gender identity being known to the reader will be referred to by the pronoun used in the book. When the argument requires a distinction between transgender characters and cis characters (whose gender identity corresponds with their birth sex), the latter will be referred to as cis boys and cis girls.

The Legal Context for Transgender People in Sweden

The first Swedish gender-affirming surgery was performed in 1968 and was followed by the establishment of a law on the determination of gender in 1972. Sweden was the first country in the world to produce such a law, which gave individuals the right to change their legal gender after review (Sverige 2007, 49). However, this was subject to certain criteria: the individual had to be a Swedish citizen, over 18 years of age, unmarried and unable to reproduce. In practice, the latter meant that most people were required to undergo sterilization, and did not have the possibility of freezing gametes. The 1972 legislation was in place for a long period of time and was only changed in the 2000s, when it became apparent that several of the criteria were in violation of Swedish and European legislation. The last criterion to be removed was the sterilization requirement, which remained until 2012 when Kammarrätten (the Administrative Court of Appeal) determined that the requirement of being sterile in order to change one's legal gender was in violation of both the European Convention of Human Rights and the Swedish Constitution. This resulted in the requirement for compulsory sterilization being removed from the law on the determination of gender as of 2013: this was a very significant change and one that also received national media coverage. Today, the only remaining requirements are that the individual is over 18 years of age and a resident of Sweden for at least a year (cf. e.g. RFSL Ungdom and RFSL 2020).

This and other changes in Swedish legislation were the result of long discussions among organizations and politicians about transgender people's rights and their situation in Sweden. During the 2000s, the Swedish government launched several government inquiries, the first one resulting in the report *Ändrad könstillhörighet – förslag till ny lag* (Changed Gender – Proposal for a New Law) (Sverige 2007), which in turn led to several of the changes in the law on the determination of gender.

As of 2009, transgender people are covered by the Swedish Discrimination Act through the addition of transgender identity or expression as grounds for discrimination.

In the same year, the National Board of Health and Welfare ceased to define 'transvestism' as a psychiatric diagnosis, and the application of the Personal Names Act was changed so that all individuals of legal age can be named whatever they like regardless of their legal gender (since 2012, minors, from 12 years old and up, are allowed to change their names on the condition that their guardians consent to it). In 2009, the Marriage Act also became gender-neutral, which meant that couples of different genders no longer had to divorce and instead register for a partnership if one of them wished to change their legal gender (cf. e.g. RFSL Ungdom and RFSL 2020).

Another important government inquiry was launched in 2016 in order to give an overview of transgender people's treatment in Sweden. It resulted in the report *Transpersoner i Sverige – förslag för stärkt ställning och bättre levnadsvillkor* (Transgender People in Sweden – A Proposal for Strengthened Position and Better Living Conditions) (Sverige 2017), which together with other inquiries has generated and will continue to generate new and revised legislation within this area. Since 2018, transgender people are, for example, covered by the hate crime legislation in the Penal Code as well as by the legislation concerning agitation against an ethnic or national group. In 2018, Sweden established a law that gives transgender people who have undergone compulsory sterilization financial compensation from the State due to the distress this law has caused. The law on the determination of gender is also being thoroughly revised. The plan is to replace it with two different laws, one that regulates the changing of legal gender and one that regulates genital intervention (cf. e.g. RFSL Ungdom and RFSL 2020).

Re-interpreting Boys and Girls in 'Disguise'

The first modern Swedish young adult novel to portray a character who experiences an urge to explore what it would be like to identify as another gender is generally considered to be Hans-Eric Hellberg's *Love love love*, published in 1977. In the beginning of the novel, the main character Jonnie is sexually aroused by crossing his legs and hiding his genitals. 'Now he looked like a girl!'[3] the narrator states (9). Jonnie emphasizes that he does not want to *dress* like a girl – the idea makes him feel uncomfortable – but he wants to *imagine being* a girl, and think and feel like a girl. Jonnie then temporarily becomes Birgitta to explore these feelings.

Scholars have read Jonnie within the context of a contemporary discussion on transvestites (Österlund 2005, 50–51, 160–65), which in turn was connected to an increased visibility of transgender people in Swedish society and an increased interest in gender identity issues in general (cf. 'The Legal Context', above). However, Mia Österlund argues that Jonnie's sexual arousal points towards his heterosexual desires and is simply a way of exploring his interest in girls. Looking at Jonnie from this perspective, he cannot be described as a transgender character since ultimately he does not express any thoughts that lead the reader to believe that he is identifying as female. In

3 Original Swedish: 'Nu såg han ut som en flicka!' All quotations were translated by Hanna Liljeqvist, whose help here is gratefully acknowledged.

my interpretation, however, his explorations of being Birgitta can be read as a temporary transgender experience.

In her large study on gender transgression in Swedish young adult fiction of the 1980s, Österlund argues that questioning gender identities was a common trait in these works. In a number of young adult novels, Österlund notes, the female protagonists choose to dress like boys, a form of cross-dressing which Österlund refers to as 'disguises'.[4] Österlund's study is written within the theoretical framework of girlhood studies, and within a Bakhtinian carnivalesque frame she sees the girls' cross-dressing and expressing masculinity as an emancipatory strategy and a violation of societal power structures. Sam Holmqvist has discussed Österlund's study as well as studies by other scholars with similar perspectives in relation to trans perspectives. Holmqvist concludes that Österlund's analysis of girls in boys' clothing postulates a cisnormative interpretation of gender. If instead a trans perspective is applied as a way to analyse the narratives without cisnormative assumptions, other structures and meanings could potentially be derived from the material, Holmqvist argues (2017, 47–50). I find it fruitful to continue in this vein and use Österlund's study as an example of the theoretical development within the field during the twenty-first century.

Österlund's study was pioneering when published in 2005 and it has been of great importance to the field of girlhood studies. The study was conducted during a period of transition when the study of transgender narratives was not very common within Nordic academia. I argue that if today's concepts and theoretical tools had been established at the time, in some cases Österlund as well as other scholars might have been talking about transgender experiences as well as reading some characters as transgender rather than discussing them as girls or boys in disguise. Before I go on I would, however, like to point out that I am not questioning the overall approach of either Österlund's study or other studies with a similar approach. Studying the material from the theoretical framework of girlhood studies offers certain possibilities, whereas a transgender perspective offers others. The emancipatory possibilities embedded in the wearing of boys' clothing in the novels form a premise clearly anchored in the material and Österlund's study has brought profound and insightful knowledge to the field of girlhood studies. I merely propose that cross-dressing as an analytical tool, if looked at from a trans perspective, makes it possible to study what happens when the characters' self-identification instead of their assigned gender is taken into account. With the new knowledge and tools that we can gain from looking at cross-dressing characters without cisnormative assumptions, some of the girls in disguise can be analysed in new and different ways. This does not mean that all depictions of cross-dressing girls lend themselves to analyses with a trans perspective – for example, far from all of Österlund's examples are relevant to discuss within this context – but in some cases it can open the narratives to new interpretations.

The works Österlund discusses include, for example, Peter Pohl's children's book *Janne, min vän* (*Johnny, My Friend*) (1985), a book about the boy Krille who meets someone he perceives as another boy, Janne. Throughout the narrative Krille is the focalizer, which

---

4 Original Swedish: 'förklädnader'.

means the reader gets to know Janne through a second-hand narrative. At the very end of the novel, a photo shows Janne dressed as a girl at a circus, Miss Juvenile. Österlund, as well as other scholars analysing the novel, discusses it as a depiction of a girl escaping from abuse by cross-dressing and living as a boy, and sees the gender transgression as a 'disguise'. This has been the most common interpretation of the novel (see Österlund 2005, 308–15), but it could also be interpreted as a transgender narrative, an approach which Victoria Flanagan has explored (2008, 216–24). Due to the lack of background information on Janne it is possible to read the character not only as a girl living as a boy for her protection, but also as a cis boy or a trans boy who has escaped from a circus where he was forced to perform as a girl. As Flanagan concludes, 'The question of whether "Johnny" is simply the most effective hiding device available to an unhappy and daring young girl, or a deliberately constructed image of the boy she would rather be, is left open' (2008, 218). Interpreting Janne as a transgender character allows Flanagan to extract new meaning from the ending of the story where Janne is murdered. She concludes that the possibilities that Janne's cross-dressing offers 'are cruelly closed by his death' and that this ending 'ultimately warns of the hostility that may accompany gender subversion in a realistic social context' (2008, 218).

Österlund does speak of a 'trans identity' (2005, 275) as a possibility in some cases, when the endings offer a possibility for reformulating the disguised girls' desires. But even if she concludes that 'The ending may thereby include a recognition of the disguised character's trans identity'[5] (2005, 275), she still refers to the girls' states as 'disguises', which is different from being transgender. Notably, the only example she offers of a character that embodies the possibility of a trans identity is the fictional depiction of the historical person Lars Molin (1785–1845), generally known as Lasse-Maja, a master thief and con artist who lived periodically both as a man and a woman and had relationships with both men and women (cf., for example, Holmqvist 2017, 71–77). Lasse-Maja is one of the characters in Cannie Möller's young adult novel *Stortjuvens pojke: en rövarhistoria från Lasse-Majas dagar* (The Master Thief's Son: A Tall Tale from the Days of Lasse-Maja) (1985). When Lasse-Maja meets Josefina working as the stable boy Jonas, Lasse-Maja wonders: 'Have I come across someone of my own kind? Someone who wants to defy what nature has dictated for her?'[6] (Möller 1985, 139, cf. Österlund 2005, 290), a statement that certainly offers the possibility of interpreting Lasse-Maja as a transgender character. Josefina/Jonas's experience, on the other hand, is regarded by Österlund as a disguise and she claims that Josefina/Jonas gets access to a 'transvestite space'[7] (2005, 231) through the friendship with Lasse-Maja. In my opinion, the novel also offers the possibility of interpreting the story of Josefina/Jonas as a temporary transgender experience. Even if the character did not choose the gender shift from the

5 Original Swedish: 'Upplösningen kan därmed tänkas innesluta ett erkännande av den förkläddas transidentitet.'

6 Original Swedish: 'Har jag träffat på någon av min egen sort? En som vill trotsa vad naturen bestämt åt henne?'

7 Original Swedish: 'ett transvestitiskt rum'.

start and the narrative suggests that she might go back to identifying as a girl at the end of the novel when she falls in love with a boy, several episodes indicate that during large parts of the story, the character identifies as a boy, as indicated by a statement like 'The memory of the girl Josefina is beginning to fade away within herself too. What will it be like in the future? If she wants to be a girl again, will she be able to bring Josefina out the way you bring out a piece of clothing you have put away? Or will she no longer be there?'[8] (Möller 1985, 13).

Overall, Österlund's study shows that at the time, Nordic scholars did not have the necessary tools to analyse the stories of Janne/Miss Juvenile or Josefina/Jonas as transgender experiences or narratives. This is made evident through Österlund's interpretation of the American film *Boys Don't Cry* – a dramatization of the real-life story of Brandon Teena, a trans man brutally murdered in a hate crime – as a depiction of a young person 'in disguise'[9] (2005, 107), whereas early international scholarship about the film discussed it within a transgender context (cf., for example, Halberstam 2000; Moss and Zeavin 2001; Rigney 2003). Nordic scholarship had yet to catch up, and to some extent it still needs to, even if there are more recent studies with a trans perspective, like Silje Hernæs Linhart's study on affect and identity in Anglo-American and Scandinavian male-to-female transgender narratives for children and young adults (2015). The reception of and scholarship on Jessica Schiefauer's young adult novel *Pojkarna* is an example of this late blooming.

The Reception of Jessica Schiefauer's *Pojkarna*

In *Pojkarna*, a magical metamorphosis turns three girls into boys during night time after they drink the nectar of a magic flower. In their everyday lives the girls experience constant sexual harassment from boys, which means their transformation offers them not only the opportunity to experience the difference between being a boy and being a girl, but also the opportunity to experience a life without harassment. The main character of the novel is Kim, who dislikes the female body and expresses feelings of fulfilment over becoming a boy. Gradually, Kim realizes that Kim does not want to go back to being a girl and the novel's open ending suggests this might be possible.

Pojkarna is a complex novel working on different levels, and its use of imagery opens the novel to many different interpretations. But no matter how you interpret the magical transformation and the gender issues addressed, the character Kim can be read as transgender, experiencing gender dysphoria and coming to terms with who Kim really is through a magical metamorphosis.

8 Original Swedish: 'Minnet av flickan Josefina håller på att blekna bort också inom henne själv. Hur kommer det att bli i framtiden? Om hon vill vara flicka igen kommer hon att kunna plocka fram Josefina som man tar fram ett undanhängt klädesplagg? Eller kommer hon inte längre att finnas kvar då?'

9 Original Swedish: 'som förklär sig'.

Kim is the narrator, and expresses feelings of discomfort with the girl body, for instance in the quotations, 'I wore the girl body like a shell, a much too big loden coat, a shapeless, ill-fitting costume'[10] (Schiefauer 2011, 98), and:

> I wore my body like something foreign, a rubber suit that clung to me and itched, but no matter how I scratched and scraped at it with my fingernails, I couldn't get rid of it. At night I'd dream my body fell off me. It was so simple, I suddenly found a zipper in my skin. Sometimes it would be on my inner thigh, sometimes on my stomach, along my back or between my legs. I opened it, and I could feel the air trickling through to my real skin underneath, like when a vacuum is released. And I peeled my skin off, stepped out of it like a dirty piece of clothing, and felt the cool floor against my new soles.[11] (Schiefauer 2011, 19–20)

After the transformation, Kim's feelings towards Kim's own body are quite different:

> [T]he boy in the mirror had no suit to take off. The skin was my skin, yet different. I traced my fingers along the arm and the back of the hand, examined the knuckles, the rough finger joints, the crescents of the fingernails. There was no excessive skin, no sheets of skin sagging and revealing themselves to be something you had put on, put over. My new skin fit the way a skin should.[12] (Schiefauer 2011, 71)

Kim uses imagery like 'a shapeless, ill-fitting costume' about the girl body to describe the feelings of gender dysphoria. When the magical metamorphosis makes Kim's skin fit 'the way a skin should', Kim gradually realizes that Kim does not want to go back to being a girl.

On very few occasions, however, has the novel been identified as a transgender narrative. *Pojkarna* was reviewed in several newspapers, but none of the reviewers interpreted the novel as a story about a transgender character. One reviewer described Kim as 'androgynous'[13] (Toijer-Nilsson 2011). A few others recognized that the story is about gender identity and in one case it was categorized as 'queer' (Näsling 2011) while

10 Original Swedish: 'jag bar flickkroppen som ett hölje, en alltför stor lodenrock, en oformlig, illa passande maskeraddräkt'.

11 Original Swedish: 'Min kropp satt på mig som något främmande, en gummidräkt som klibbade och kliade, men hur jag än rev och skrapade med naglarna satt den där den satt. Om nätterna kunde jag drömma att min kropp föll av mig. Det var så enkelt, plötsligt hittade jag en dragkedja i huden. Ibland satt den längs med innanlåret, ibland över magen, utmed ryggen eller mellan benen. Jag öppnade den, kunde känna luften sila in mot min riktiga hud därunder, som ett vakuum när det släpper. Och jag skalade av mig skinnet, klev ur det som ett smutsigt klädesplagg och kände det svala golvet mot mina nya fotsulor.'

12 Original Swedish: 'pojken i spegeln hade ingen dräkt att ta av. Huden var min hud men ändå en annan. Jag strök med fingrarna över armen och handryggen, undersökte knogarna, de grova fingerlederna, naglarnas halvmånar. Det fanns inget överflödigt skinn, inga tygsjok som korvade sig och avslöjade sig som något man trätt på, trätt över. Mitt nya skinn satt som ett skinn ska sitta.'

13 Original Swedish: 'androgyn'.

in another as 'a depiction of gender ambivalence'[14] (Gunnarsson 2011), but the words *trans* or *transgender* were not used. When the book was awarded the August Prize – one of the most prestigious literary awards in Sweden – in late 2011, it resulted in a more comprehensive coverage and Jessica Schiefauer was interviewed by TT News Agency in an interview distributed through newspapers all over Sweden. In the interview, Schiefauer says that 'this book doesn't investigate what it is to be a boy, it investigates what it is not to want to be a girl'.[15] She criticizes the binary gender norms of society, mentions the increased space for 'intergender' and concludes with a longing for more freedom: 'I wish we didn't have to be so strongly defined by our gender. I think that is the key for Kim, to just be Kim and not have to choose'[16] (Viksten 2011). However, this statement did not change much in terms of the book's reception, indicating that critics were either not ready to take in this perspective and/or found it irrelevant to their interpretations. To my knowledge, the only occasion in connection with the book's release when the book was discussed as a transgender narrative occurred within a trans context. In January of 2012, the book was reviewed by a Swedish expert in transgender issues, Edward Summanen, on the blog Transbloggen (the Trans Blog). Notably, Summanen expresses surprise to find the novel a transgender narrative, due to the fact that other reviewers did not mention it:

> I did not have high expectations of this book. The way reviewers and the publishing house Bonnier Carlsen described it didn't exactly make it pleasing to me. On the back of the book it says, for instance, that it is a novel about 'growing up, transforming, love and sisterhood'. But a few keywords here and there in some reviews made me curious. Like 'gender' and 'identity'. And the plot sounded intriguing. But no one wrote, 'oh great, a trans theme'.[17] (Summanen 2012, n.p.)

It was not until 2016, when *Pojkarna* had been made into a film with the same name (with the English title *Girls Lost*), that the story was widely reviewed as a transgender narrative. The film was directed by Alexandra-Therese Keining and it premiered at an international film festival in Toronto in September 2015 and in Swedish cinemas in February 2016. By then, transgender people and issues of gender identity had begun to gain more recognition in Swedish society, through increased attention in media and political initiatives. For example, many documentaries about transgender people and their experiences, with the aim to explain what trans is, aired on Swedish television, and the results of recent changes made to a number of laws in order to improve the situation

14 Original Swedish: 'en skildring av könsambivalens'.

15 Original Swedish: 'Den här boken undersöker inte vad det är att vara pojke, den undersöker vad det är att inte vilja vara flicka.'

16 Original Swedish: 'Jag längtar efter att vi ska slippa definieras så hårt utifrån vårt kön. Det tror jag är nyckeln för Kim, att bara vara Kim och inte behöva välja.'

17 Original Swedish: 'Jag hade inga höga förväntningar på den här boken. Hur recensenter och förlaget Bonnier Carlsen beskrev den gjorde att den inte direkt tilltalade mig. På baksidan av boken står exempelvis att det är en roman om "uppväxt, förvandling, kärlek och systerskap". Men det var några små nyckelord här och där i diverse recensioner som gjorde mig nyfiken. Som "kön" och "identitet". Och själva plotten lät spännande. Men ingen har skrivit "åh så härligt med ett transtema."'

of transgender people were starting to gain visibility (cf. 'The Legal Context', above). Against this backdrop, Keining's interpretation of *Pojkarna* directed it more strongly towards issues of trans and gender identity, which she also mentioned and discussed in many interviews following the film's release (see, for instance, Domellöf-Wik 2016; Hällsten 2016; Sykes 2016). Again, one of the interviews was made by TT News Agency and distributed through a number of different newspapers in Sweden (Burman 2016). Consequently, several critics described Kim as a transgender person in their reviews of the film (see, for instance, Grönqvist 2016; Samuelsson 2016; W 2016). Parallel to this, the novel's transgender narrative continued to be recognized in trans contexts. In 2016, author Moa-Lina Olbers Croall published a young adult handbook on trans, *I mitt namn: en bok om att vara trans* (In My Name: A Book About Being Transgender), the first of its kind published in Sweden. The book mixes summaries of interviews with transgender people with general information and recommendations for books and films portraying transgender characters. In the handbook, *Pojkarna* is mentioned in a list of suggested reading, as an example of a literary work portraying a transgender character (2016, 102).

Despite the increased attention given to transgender issues in society and the stronger orientation towards these questions in the film, academia still failed to identify the transgender narrative in *Pojkarna*. Due to the complexity of the novel, it has become one of the most frequently analysed contemporary young adult books in Swedish children's literature research. The scholars do analyse the novel as a story about gender identity, but most of them build on Österlund's research, which means transgender concepts are not used and there is a strong focus on the novel's depiction of girls. The novel was first discussed by Rebecka Fokin, in an analysis focusing on the novel as fantastic realism and on how girlhood is constructed. Fokin suggests that the novel contributes to a renewal of the fantastic genre through its depiction of gender. She discusses bodily transformations through magical metamorphosis and concludes that the novel depicts 'our possibilities to explore and renegotiate the limits of what gender is and can be'[18] (2015, 2). Linking the issue of gender identity to the process of becoming an adult, she takes on a Butlerian approach and suggests that 'the metamorphosis functions as a motif of trying and questioning the idea of a uniform identity and an essential gender'[19] (6). Fokin thus discusses gender identity, but since she uses Österlund's study as a theoretical framework, Kim's transformation is still discussed as a 'disguise from girl to boy'[20] (18). In two other analyses, Lena Kåreland and Maria Nilson discuss *Pojkarna* together with other young adult novels from a gender perspective. They make references to Fokin's analysis, but due to their respective aims they, too, focus first and foremost on the depiction and interpretation of Kim as a girl. Both mention gender identity as a central theme in the novel, but

18 Original Swedish: 'våra möjligheter att utforska och omförhandla gränserna för vad kön är och kan vara'.

19 Original Swedish: 'Metamorfosen fungerar i romanen som ett motiv för att testa och ifrågasätta idén om en enhetlig identitet och om könet som ursprungligt.'

20 Original Swedish: 'förklädnaden från flicka till pojke'.

neither of them comments on it as a transgender narrative (cf. Kåreland 2017, 211–14; Nilson 2017, 155–58).

It is possible to argue that the magical framing is the reason why the transgender narrative is not highlighted to a larger extent in the scholarship devoted to this novel, but as a matter of fact it is not even emphasized in Linn Friberg's queer analysis of the novel. Friberg suggests that *Pojkarna* describes a young adolescent girl's journey to finding and forming her own gender and sexual identity, but just like Österlund she emphasizes 'the disguise as an emancipatory strategy'[21] (Friberg 2015, 25) and claims that the novel 'can be seen as a transvestite depiction of girl and boy cultures where both are drawn to stereotypical extremes'[22] (26). Even if Friberg at one point describes Kim's sexual lust as part of 'some sort of intersexual existence' with 'some form of bisexuality' and a 'gender expression characterized by transsexuality where *the male exterior pleases her more than* the female body'[23] (28, my italics), she still describes Kim as someone who can choose how they feel about their female body. Friberg calls the boy body an 'escape' for Kim, where Kim gets to experience things – sexual desire for example – that Kim '*doesn't allow herself to do* as a girl'[24] (27, my italics). The italicized passages suggest that Friberg, even though she performs a queer analysis, does not view *Pojkarna* as a story about gender dysphoria and a depiction of a transgender person coming to terms with who they really are.

All in all, the early reception of and academic studies on *Pojkarna* suggest a difficulty in seeing or recognizing trans themes, partly due to the choice of a theoretical perspective which emphasizes girlhood, but most likely also due to the fact that trans perspectives were not prominent either in the general discussion or the research on children's and young adult literature in Sweden. Interestingly, the novel itself gives us a reading instruction at the beginning that could be interpreted as a comment for those who fail to see the transgender narrative, just as much as it is a comment for those who do not wish to see the magic or the abuse against girls depicted in the novel: 'It's a story for those who want to see, for those who dare to pick up a magnifying glass and observe the wondrous. If you're blind to such things this story isn't yours, but if your eyes are open then listen carefully'[25] (Schiefauer 2011, 9). After concluding that the novel was not marketed or identified as a transgender narrative by critics at the time of its release, Summanen comments on this kind of blindness in his review of the novel: 'Sometimes the obvious norm breaking is ignored to fit within mainstream media'[26] (Summanen 2012). The ignorance that Summanen highlights can be seen as a cultural denial, springing from a lack of

21 Original Swedish: 'förklädnad som emancipatorisk strategi'.

22 Original Swedish: 'kan ses som en transvestitisk gestaltning av tjej- respektive killkulturer där båda är dragna till stereotypiska ytterligheter'.

23 Original Swedish: 'en slags intersexuell tillvaro' … 'en form av bisexualitet' … 'könsuttryck präglas av en transsexualitet där det manlig yttre tilltalar henne mer än den kvinnliga kroppen.'

24 Original Swedish: 'inte tillåter sig att göra som tjej'.

25 Original Swedish: 'Det är en berättelse för den som vill se, för den som vågar lyfta ett förstoringsglas till ögat och betrakta det förunderliga. Om du är blind för sådant är den här historien inte din, men om dina ögon är öppna ska du lyssna noga.'

26 Original Swedish: 'Ibland ignoreras det uppenbara normbrottet för att passa in i mainstream-media.'

awareness and knowledge, and it results in refusing some stories not explicitly presented or marketed as transgender narratives the position as such (cf. Miller 2019, 244). Not until these narratives have been incorporated as a part of mainstream media can they be recognized as transgender narratives. With *Pojkarna*, this happened to some extent when the book was adapted into a film, but the sharper focus of the film on the transgender narrative was in itself a result of the increased visibility of transgender people in society, not only in Sweden but internationally (cf. Pearce et al. 2020, 2–4). This visibility, in turn, has resulted in a number of transgender characters in Swedish children's and young adult literature explicitly depicted as transgender children and youth.

Contemporary Transgender Narratives for Children and Young Adults

In a study on Swedish nineteenth-century transgender narratives, Holmqvist notes that many literary trans motifs in Western literature are based, either in part or in full, on actual events (Holmqvist 2017, 10). This is largely transferable to many of the transgender narratives of contemporary Swedish children's and young adult fiction. Since Swedish literature aimed at children and youth is generally concerned with contemporary social and political issues to a large extent (cf., for example, Svenska barnboksinstitutet 2018, 9; 2020, 7), it is only to be expected that the number of books depicting transgender children and youth would increase during the 2010s, in conjunction with trans lives becoming more visible. In the 2010s the number of people seeking help for gender dysphoria also skyrocketed in Sweden, especially among young girls. This surge has caused a heated debate concerning the reasons for it and the health care provided for transgender youth (see, for example, Socialstyrelsen 2020; Wurm 2019). In 2016, the Swedish government presented a range of initiatives to strengthen the rights of transgender people and improve their situation (Kuhnke et al. 2016). For instance, a new government inquiry was launched, which submitted a report in 2017 (cf. 'The Legal Context', above). Among other things, the report confirmed that the situation of transgender people in Sweden mirrored that of the rest of the Western world. For example, this social group experiences a higher degree of mental health issues compared to the population at large and is overrepresented when it comes to suicide and suicide attempts. Transgender people also experience discrimination and prejudice in many areas of life where the traditional binary gender system causes difficulties in contact with society, especially the healthcare system, due to the lack of knowledge among officials and hospital staff (Sverige 2017). In Olbers Croall's young adult handbook (2016), as well as in Signe Bremer's large study on transition testimonies (2017), Swedish transgender people tell similar stories about their coming-out process and the prejudice they are met with in society. Some recurring comments are, for example, the difficulties in occupying public spaces such as toilets, and that people in general as well as officials and hospital staff often use the wrong pronoun and technical terms in their contact with transgender people.

Against this backdrop, it comes as no surprise that many of the children's and young adult books depicting transgender experiences focus on the hardships of trans lives and mirror the difficulties pointed out by real-life transgender people. This echoes the early Anglo-American depictions of transgender characters, which also tended to focus on the problems (cf., for instance, Jenkins and Cart 2018, 163; Mallan 2009, 128–55). Recurrent themes in the Swedish narratives are experiences of being bullied before or when coming out as transgender, being exposed to misgendering (meaning deliberately or accidentally labelling someone with a gender that does not match their gender identity), longing for hormone blockers to stop puberty, living with a fear of not being accepted by friends and family, experiencing a lack of understanding from loved ones, teachers, doctors and other officials, and having difficulty claiming public spaces such as toilets and locker rooms (cf. Butler 2020, 19; Byers 2018). But they are also stories of overcoming obstacles, making friends, falling in love and having supportive adults around. Moreover, out of all the unsympathetic adults, few stay that way when the last page of the book is turned. The majority of the stories are first-person narratives, making it possible for the authors to look *with* the transgender characters and not *at* them (cf. Halberstam 2005, 78). As formulated by Michelle Byers in her study on four middle-grade books with transgender protagonists, the books 'begin with the assumption that how young people know themselves is the best way for others to know them' (Byers 2018, 102). Few of the stories are written by authors who clearly describe themselves as transgender (in most cases the gender identity of the author is either not known or the author is known to the Swedish public as cisgender), but the depictions of the transgender characters and their experiences are largely the same regardless of the gender identity of the author. The most common denominator in the stories is the trans theme itself. In very few cases does the book depict a transgender character without also problematizing what it is like to be transgender, which is why I have chosen this contrariety as a starting point when looking closer at some of the narratives.

Most of the books for children and young adults with a prominent transgender character published in Sweden since 2013 are Swedish originals. In the following analysis I focus on those. The translations are exclusively Anglo-American works, such as *I am Jazz* (2014) by Jessica Herthel, Jazz Jennings and Shelagh McNicholas, published in Swedish in 2015, *George* (2015) by Alex Gino and *If I Was Your Girl* (2016) by Meredith Russo, both published in Swedish in 2016, and *My Brother's Name is Jessica* (2019) by John Boyne, published in Swedish in 2020. In content, they mirror that of the Swedish originals. All are coming-out stories that touch on one or several of the themes mentioned above (cf. Butler 2020).

Children's and Young Adult Books as Introducers to the Transgender Experience

As previously mentioned, the transgender narratives functioning as introducers of the experiences of transgender children highlight, explain and promote an understanding of what it means to be transgender, generally by focusing on the problems transgender people encounter. An early example of such a book is Elias S. Ericson's already-mentioned graphic novel *Åror* (2013), one of the first contemporary Swedish children's or young adult books to explicitly address transgender issues. The central theme in *Åror* is the torment of having a body that does not conform to the norm. The main character, 16-year-old Mika, describes himself as transgender and identifies as a boy, whereas his mother and others around him perceive him as a girl. Several image sequences portray Mika's anguish over his body, and the transgender body is generally linked to social alienation and self-hate through large parts of the story (see Figure 25). In this respect *Åror* is a good example of a transgender narrative that focuses on the stigmatization of transgender people (cf. Warnqvist 2017, 176–77). However, from an international perspective it stood out at the time of publication because of its depiction of a love story.

Mika makes the decision to come out as transgender after meeting Izzy, who also self-defines as transgender, but has a positive attitude towards her own body. Comparing *Åror* to portrayals of transgender characters in contemporary American and British young adult literature, Kate Norbury notes that *Åror* is more progressive, as Mika and Izzy fall in love and have sex. In the American and British works studied, transgender characters were not involved in romantic relationships and love was not a prominent theme. The romantic relationship, Norbury argues, is one of the most common themes in Anglo-American young adult novels, no matter whether the characters in love are straight, gay or bisexual. The fact that this theme was not explored in the portrayals of transgender characters, Norbury proposes, suggests that the audience in these countries, due to a lack of acceptance, were not ready for love stories involving transgender characters (Norbury 2014, 14–18). As opposed to the transgender characters in these works, Mika also decides to embrace his body the way it is. In all of the Anglo-American works the transgender characters wanted to transition and undergo gender confirmation surgery to be either 'a masculine male or a feminine female' (2014, 15).

Åror is aimed at young adults and the books for this age category generally depict a tougher existence for transgender characters than the books for children. For instance,

Figure 25: Ericson, Elias S. 2013. *Åror* (Oars). Stockholm: Ordfront Galago, 12.

Johanna Nilsson's young adult novel *Om vi bara kunde byta kroppar med varandra* (If Only We Could Exchange Bodies) (2018) places two young transgender characters, whose parents have dissociated themselves from them, in Stockholm's underworld. As outcasts of society they try to get by through drug use, prostitution, criminality and their love for one another. Through letting almost every encounter with cis characters end with the latter's disgust, bullying, violence or rape, Nilsson explores the most extreme negative sides of transgender life. However, unsupportive parents and bullying are also central themes in the stories aimed at children. Some examples of this are Sara Lövestam's *Skarven* (The Cormorant), Jenny Jägerfeld's *Brorsan är kung!* (Bro' Is King!), and Ylva Karlsson and Sofia Falkenhem's *Månen, varelsen och jag* (The Moon, the Creature and I). The first two are both marketed towards the age group 9–12 years whereas the latter is aimed at 6–9 year-olds. *Skarven* (Lövestam 2016) is both a detective story and a story about coming out as transgender. Johanna, who was given the name Johan at birth, solves a murder together with her two friends, Ludde and Olivia, and at the same time struggles to be accepted as a girl by her friends and family. In *Brorsan är kung!* (Jägerfeld 2016), Måns has already come out as transgender when the story starts, but just like Johanna he has to cope with the lack of understanding, particularly from his father, but also from a new friend whom Måns doesn't tell he is transgender. His friend consequently feels cheated and lied to when he learns about it. The latter connects the story to the transphobic tradition of representing transgender people as deceptive (cf., for example, Pini et al. 2018, 61), but since the story is told from Måns' point of view the motif here gets a reparative function. Månne, the protagonist of *Månen, varelsen och jag* (Karlsson and Falkenhem 2020), is non-binary, which is manifested in the name: 'Månne' is not an established Swedish name and therefore ungendered.[27] Månne has supportive friends and parents but a hard time coping with the fact that others, children as well as adults, question Månne's gender.

All three stories have a more-or-less explicit aim to explain to the reader what transgender people go through. They educate by describing the experiences from the transgender characters' perspective (cf. Butler 2020, 17), and also by introducing an appropriate vocabulary. In *Månen, varelsen och jag* this educating is made explicit through an actual teaching situation. Through a first-person narrative Månne tells the story of when Månne was asked to give a presentation at school and chose to talk about what transgender and non-binary means, and what it feels like to be misgendered. Månne shares the content of the presentation with the followers of Månne's upcoming YouTube channel – and indirectly also with the reader of the book – who is placed in the position of a person being taught something. *Skarven*'s third-person narrative handles the teaching in a less apparent way. When Johanna reacts to the fact that one of the other characters uses the term 'sex change' she indirectly informs the reader about the proper term to use: 'Johanna doesn't mention it's not called "sex change" but "transitioning"'[28] (Lövestam 2016, 90). In another example from the same book Ludde and Olivia discuss

27 Although not commonly used as a name, the word 'månne' exists in Swedish and is mainly used as an archaic interrogative particle meaning 'possibly.'

28 Original Swedish: 'Johanna säger att det inte heter "byta kön" utan "könskorrigering."'

whether they should call Johanna 'she' or 'he,' which gives the narrator another opportunity to indirectly educate the reader:

> 'Oops, I said "he" again,' Olivia says.
> 'But he is a he. I mean, he's a boy even though he feels like a girl.'
> Olivia shakes her head.
> 'I checked online. It's "she." '[29] (Lövestam 2016, 103)

By letting the characters reflect on the proper way to use pronouns and the use of other technical terms, the stories emphasize that the wrong use of a word might be offensive and hurtful to the transgender person. Several such scenes are present in the books, two examples from *Månen, varelsen och jag* being when Månne feels sad after repeatedly being confronted by the older kids at school who want Månne to tell them whether Månne is a boy or a girl, and when Månne is hurt by an uncle and his partner Jeanette when they are babysitting Månne. The uncle uses Månne's birth name, causing Månne to explain that this name is not the correct one and that it should be 'Månne'. To this Jeanette replies: 'I think you're getting too old to keep up with this nonsense!'[30] (Karlsson and Falkenhem 2020, 97), causing a schism in the child/adult relationship. Månne's mother is supportive of Månne and decides in the end that Månne does not have to spend Christmas with these relatives until they change their way of thinking, which does not take place within the frame of the narrative. On several occasions, the first-person narrator Måns in *Brorsan är kung!* describes similar situations where he has been bullied and felt misunderstood. One example is when his unsympathetic grandmother assuredly tells him that 'I'm sure this whole boy thing is just a phase'[31] (Jägerfeld 2016, 93), another when he discusses his discomfort going to the ladies' room when he was younger, and what happened during a field trip with his school when he decided not to conform to the social norms: 'And I knew they would think it was wrong, but I still walked towards the men's room, and suddenly I felt someone grabbing my arm, and it was my teacher. She told me in this really angry voice to stop MAKING A FUSS and sort of pushed me towards the ladies' room, and I was so surprised because I thought she was one of the nice ones'[32] (Jägerfeld 2016, 113). A comparable confrontation takes place between the three children in *Skarven* while they are spying outside the house of the suspected murderer and realize they have to go swimming so as not to cause suspicion:

> 'I don't have my swimming trunks,' Ludde says.
> 'Come on. You're boys. You two can go swimming in your underwear. I'm wearing a bikini underneath.'

---

29 Original Swedish: 'Äh, nu sa jag "han" igen,' säger Olivia. / Han är ju en han. Alltså han är en kille fastän han känner sig som tjej. / Hon skakar på huvudet. / Jag har kollat på nätet. Man säger "hon." '

30 Original Swedish: 'Jag tycker du börjar vara för stor för att hålla på med det där tramset!'

31 Original Swedish: 'Det här med killgrejen är bara en fas ska du se.'

32 Original Swedish: 'Och jag visste ju att de skulle tycka att jag gjorde fel, men gick ändå mot killarnas toalett och plötsligt kände jag hur någon drog tag i min arm och det var min lärare. Hon sa helt argt åt mig att sluta HÅLLA PÅ och knuffade mig typ mot tjejtoan och jag blev så himla förvånad för hon var ändå någon som jag trodde var snäll.'

> Johanna goes cold as ice. *You two?*
> 'What did you just say?' she says, holding her breath. 'You're bo … Ok, so you feel like a girl, we know, your name is Johanna, but Jesus, this is for real! Do you want to be killed?'
> Ludde gives her a searching look.
> 'Well …' he says. 'You are a boy, right. So the logical thing to do would be to go swimming in your underwear, even though you don't want to. I'm going to do it, even though I don't want to either.'
> Johanna stares at them. So they don't understand. They think she's been playing all along, that she can go back to 'the logical thing'. It feels like her heart has stopped, and when it starts back up again it's pumping twice as fast.
> 'The logical thing is that I'd rather die,' she says, blood ringing in her ears. 'But good to know that you're just as idiotic as everyone else.'[33] (Lövestam 2016, 171–72)

In *Skarven* the story is focalized through all three children and the focalizer shifts in each chapter between Johanna, Ludde and Olivia, giving the reader not only the perspective of the transgender character but also of the characters around her whom she tries to make understand her situation. As a consequence the reader does not only get access to Johanna's reaction to wordings like these, but also the other protagonists'. In this case the reader is presented with the reflections of Olivia and Ludde trying to come to terms with the reaction of their transgender friend and understand what they did wrong. In the end, when Ludde apologizes, he has realized that 'You can't … say that … to a girl'[34] (Lövestam 2016, 198).

As the quotations show, the stories are largely written to make the reader sympathetically aware of the transgender character's feelings and reactions to being mistreated and misgendered. Telling the stories from the perspective of the transgender characters and recounting the protagonists' internal thoughts allow the authors to emphasize feelings of harassment and being misunderstood by friends, teachers, relatives or parents, which ultimately gives the stories a strong potential to evoke empathy. A good example of this is the internal thoughts of Johanna when after the swimming scene she, on top of that, has been confronted with her parents' lack of understanding. Coming home, she gets into a discussion with her father who, among other things, says: 'Frankly, it's embarrassing when people go, "where's your son in this picture?" and you go, "well it's that long-haired

33 Original Swedish: 'Jag har inga badbyxor, säger Ludde. / Meh. Ni är killar. Ni kan bada i kalsongerna. Jag har bikini under. / Johanna fryser till is. "Ni?" / Vad sa du? säger hon och håller andan. / Ni är kill … okej, du känner dig som tjej, vi vet, du heter Johanna, men herregud, det här är på riktigt! Vill du bli mördad, eller? / Ludde ser prövande på henne. / Alltså … säger han. Du är ju egentligen kille. Så det logiska skulle vara att bada i kalsonger, även om du inte vill. Jag kommer att göra det, fastän jag inte heller vill. / Johanna stirrar på dem. De har alltså inte förstått. De har trott att hon har lekt hela tiden, att hon kan gå tillbaka till "det logiska." Det känns som om hjärtat stannar i kroppen på henne, och när det startar igen pumpar det dubbelt så snabbt. / Det logiska är att jag hellre dör, säger hon med blodet susande i öronen. Men kul att ni är exakt lika idiotiska som alla andra.'

34 Original Swedish: 'Det kan man ju … inte säga till … en tjej.'

sissy in the far right corner" '[35] (Lövestam 2016, 174). When Johanna goes up to her room the narrator contemplates:

> Nothing matters anymore. This morning summer was bright and amazing, it was a blue tent with friends that understood her, only they never did. Her parents hate her and she has nothing to return to at school. She's going to die, she can feel it. But not as Johan. … She is filled with darkness and she has to take deep breaths to stop herself from throwing something hard at her parents. She goes to her room. Slams the door and locks it from the inside. Mum's voice calls 'Johan' from the kitchen. Calling a son she doesn't have.[36] (Lövestam 2016, 175–76)

The conflict with the parents then deepens, causing Johanna to conclude that nobody loves or understands her:

> She really is nobody. The bad thoughts always end with that conclusion, at the bottom of the thought spiral. Johanna's parents hate her, people at school *really* hate her, and her only two friends in the world are almost the worst. They tricked her into believing they understood, they called her Johanna. But when it came to it she was Johan to them, too. She can imagine them laughing behind her back, saying things like 'what a psycho he is' and 'but he's actually a boy.'[37] (Lövestam 2016, 194)

In many ways, the quoted passages mirror the hardships that transgender children and adults in Sweden as well as in other countries describe about their coming-out process and the prejudice they are met with in society (see, for example, Bremer 2017; Olbers Croall 2016; Sverige 2017). In much the same way as these real-life people, the stories discussed here educate their readers about the lives and difficulties of being transgender, with the aim to explain and instil understanding. They also offer examples of friends and parents finally understanding and supporting the transgender characters for who they are, but also examples of the opposite. Although works of art, in these respects the stories about Mika, Johanna, Måns, Månne and others can be said to have a didactic approach.

---

35 Original Swedish: 'Man skäms ju rent ut sagt, när folk ba, var är din son på det här fotot? Och man ba, jo det är den där långhåriga fjollan längst till höger.'

36 Original Swedish: 'Inget spelar någon roll längre. Sommaren var ljus och fantastisk så sent som i morse, den var ett blått tält med vänner som förstod, bara det att de aldrig gjorde det. Ingen förstår. Hennes föräldrar hatar henne och hon har inget att komma tillbaka till i skolan. Hon kommer att dö, hon känner det. Men inte som Johan. … Hon är fylld av svärta och nu andas hon djupt för att inte kasta något hårt på sina föräldrar. Hon går till sitt rum. Smäller igen dörren och låser inifrån. Mammas röst säger "Johan" från köket. Ropar på en son hon inte har.'

37 Original Swedish: 'Hon är verkligen ingen. De dåliga tankarna slutar alltid i den slutsatsen, längst ner på botten av tankespiralen. Johannas föräldrar hatar henne, folk i skolan hatar henne *verkligen*, och hennes enda vänner i världen är nästan värst. De lurade henne att de förstod, de kallade henne Johanna. Men när det väl gällde var hon Johan även för dem. Hon kan bara föreställa sig hur de skrattat bakom hennes rygg, sagt saker som "vilket psykfall han är" och "men egentligen är han ju kille." '

Depictions of Transgender versus Gay Characters

As *Åror*, *Skarven*, *Brorsan är kung!*, *Månen, varelsen och jag* and other similar books show, the overall tendency in fiction addressing transgender themes is to problematize what it means to be transgender, as opposed to representing transgender youth without highlighting the trans theme. This choice of perspective is common when a phenomenon defying prevailing societal norms is to be established in fiction – whether it involves sexuality, gender identity, ethnicity, body constitution, age or something else (cf. Butler 2020, 17; Cart and Jenkins 2006, xix–xx; Warnqvist 2017, 177–78). A good example of the difference in how contemporary Swedish fiction for children and young adults relates to norms concerning sexual orientation versus gender identity is *Hetare: elva noveller som känns* (Hotter: Eleven Short Stories That Make an Impression) (Ahlund and Friedner 2018), a collection of erotic short stories for young adults. The collection consists of depictions of sexual encounters between queer young adults of different sexualities and gender identities, including transgender characters. Most of the stories are centred on one or more explicit sex scenes. Four of the stories include characters that are explicitly defined as or can be interpreted as transgender. In contrast to the other seven stories depicting sexual encounters between either gay males or gay females (only one character that might be interpreted as either gay or bisexual is included), these four depictions all problematize the experience of being transgender in one way or another, albeit in some cases in a less explicit way than the children's and young adult books discussed above. The short story 'I hans blick' (In His Gaze) by Anna Jakobsson Lund is narrated by the drag king Anton, who comments the choice of wearing masculine clothes as 'Everything else is a costume, but this is a part of me'[38] (Lund 2018, 22). After having sex with Leo, Anton comments on Leo's gaze as a gaze 'That sees all of me, everything that I am'[39] (2018, 29), implying that for the first time Anton feels accepted and embraced as transgender. A more explicit focus on the trans theme in line with the examples discussed above can be found in, for example, 'Allt jag vill' (All That I Want) by Sebastian Lönnlöv. The two main characters of the short story are both transgender; Jacob is in the middle of his transitioning, while Ludvig is about to start his. Ludvig is the focalizer of the story, which depicts two sex scenes. In between them the telephone rings and a telephone operator asks for Linnea Lindqvist, whereby Ludvig answers 'That's not me. … She doesn't exist'[40] (Lönnlöv 2018, 110) and by that rejects his birth name and assigned gender. The telephone call makes Ludvig feel uneasy and triggers his feelings of discomfort with having a high-pitched voice. The short story concludes with Ludvig's reflection on the issues he has experienced with his body during the last two years, and the joy of finally starting his transition:

> For the past two years I have got up every morning, stood in the shower and cleaned a body that isn't mine. … The entire time I have been inside a body I don't want to inhabit, one that

38 Original Swedish: 'Allt annat är utklädnad, men det här är en del av mig.'
39 Original Swedish: 'Som ser hela mig, allt det jag är.'
40 Original Swedish: 'Det är inte jag. … Hon finns inte.'

> I don't exactly dislike, but which has always been in the way. … When I got the diagnosis we celebrated with pizza and couldn't stop talking about everything that was about to happen. The hormones that would tease out hairs from my so far smooth skin, deepen my voice and make my clitoris explode in size. The operation that would finally free me of the breast lumps, so that I will never again have to think about how they cling to my body.[41] (Lönnlöv 2018, 113–15)

The trans theme is visible in all of the four short stories depicting transgender protagonists, and this does not have an equivalent in the other seven short stories, depicting gay sex and relationships. Instead, almost none of them comment on the sexual orientation of the characters, but instead they focus on the sexual encounters and/or issues in relationships not connected to sexual orientation, like the need to discuss sexual preferences with a new partner for the best sexual experience, or falling in love with your partner's sibling. Homosexuality is ascertained as a matter of fact, confirming the development of Swedish as well as international children's and young adult fiction in the latest decades, which in general has moved from depicting homosexuality as stigmatized to including it as an uncommented element in narratives focusing on other issues (cf., for example, Cart and Jenkins 2006, xix–xx; Svenska barnboksinstitutet 2017, 6–7, 2018, 9; 2020, 7–8). The depiction of transgender characters, however, is still situated in an earlier phase. In this phase, the aim is to promote inclusion and widen the prevailing norms by discussing them. Works where transgender youth is represented without the trans theme being problematized are rare. As Olbers Croall notes, this also applies to most films and TV shows addressing transgender themes. They generally focus on the difficulties of being transgender, and the lack of understanding, not to mention the violence a transgender person risks encountering (Olbers Croall 2016, 117). Through repeatedly depicting transgender characters in these kinds of situations and environments, the authors and film-makers, despite the opposite intent, run the risk of objectifying trans bodies and stigmatizing transgender experiences (cf. Butler 2020, 20). There are very few works aimed at children and young adults that include transgender characters without highlighting the experience of being transgender, but there are exceptions. Two of them are the graphic novels *Iggy 4-ever* by Hanna Gustavsson and Hilding Sandgren's *Vägarna är som tvättbrädor här* (The Roads Are Like Washboards Here).

41 Original Swedish: 'Jag har gått upp varje morgon i två års tid, ställt mig i duschen och rengjort en kropp som inte är min. … Hela tiden har jag befunnit mig inuti en kropp som jag inte vill bebo, som jag egentligen inte ogillar, men som alltid står i vägen' … 'När jag fick diagnosen firade vi med pizza och kunde inte sluta prata om allt som skulle hända. Hormonerna som ska locka fram hårstrån ur min än så länge släta hud, förmörka min röst och få min klitoris att explodera i storlek. Operationen som till sist ska befria mig från bröstklumparna, så att jag aldrig mer behöver tänka på hur de klänger fast vid min kropp.'

The Subversive Potential of Transgender Narratives beyond the Didactic Approach

In contrast to the works discussed above, neither sexual orientation nor gender identity is problematized in *Iggy 4-ever* (Gustavsson 2015). The interpretation is left entirely to the reader (cf. Warnqvist 2017, 178–79). In this graphic novel Gustavsson places several non-binary characters, among these Iggy, the teenage main character, in a Stockholm suburb. As in the case of Kim and Månne, Iggy is also a character with a gender-neutral name. Iggy's body is also depicted as gender-neutral, but the text conveys that people around Iggy read Iggy as a girl. For example, the mother calls Iggy Ingrid. However, Gustavsson imagines Iggy as non-binary (Gustavsson, personal communication, 7 February 2017). Iggy is not the only non-binary character in this graphic novel. There is, for example, Alex, who is interested in Iggy. Initially, this is not reciprocated but a shift occurs towards the end of the novel; a change of heart partly linked to their shared experiences in terms of things like bullying, but mainly inspired by an incident that occurs at Alex's house after a party. As Alex changes sweater, Iggy happens to notice that Alex wears a binder. In this image sequence, the perspective shifts from the reader's to Iggy's through zooming, which signals to the reader that what Iggy sees is significant (see Figure 26). From this scene, the reader can conclude that Alex was assigned female at birth but wishes to be read as a boy. Catherine Butler discusses this kind of plot twist as one that usually subjects transgender characters 'to an othering cis gaze', often resulting in transphobic and homophobic acts and expressions, such as vomiting, after a straight person's object of desire has been revealed as a transgender character (Butler 2020, 20). This is not the case in *Iggy 4-ever*. After the incident, Iggy shows an interest in Alex and the two of them make out on a couch. The change in Iggy's attitude towards Alex is mainly brought about by the sense of affinity Iggy experiences thanks to the new insight into Alex's gender identity. As such, Iggy's attitude subverts and transforms the usually transphobic and homophobic motif and, just as in the case of Månne, gives it a reparative function.

Sandgren's *Vägarna är som tvättbrädor här* (2016a) is also open to the interpretation that one of the characters is transgender. Aida's friends include Halle, who Sandgren sees as transgender (Sandgren, personal communication, 24 September 2016b). Halle has attributes commonly associated with young men, such as a moustache and a flat chest, and also has their make-up done at a party and likes necklaces with big beads. The transgender identity is subtly implied; it is only conveyed in the visual story and the girls, not Halle, are the main focus in the pictures (see Figure 27; cf. Warnqvist 2017, 179–80). Since Halle is a subsidiary character present in the background of the pictures only, the reader would not have been able to deduce whether Halle is transgender or not had it not been for the author's statement about this character. The text makes no mention of it. It is worth noting that both *Iggy 4-ever* and *Vägarna är som tvättbrädor här* are graphic novels that tell their stories through image sequences and dialogues in speech balloons. No other kinds of text boxes are used to comment on the events, which means that both stories lack an external narrator, making third-person pronouns unnecessary. This is a contributing factor to the stories' ability to represent the transgender characters without explicitly addressing the trans theme.

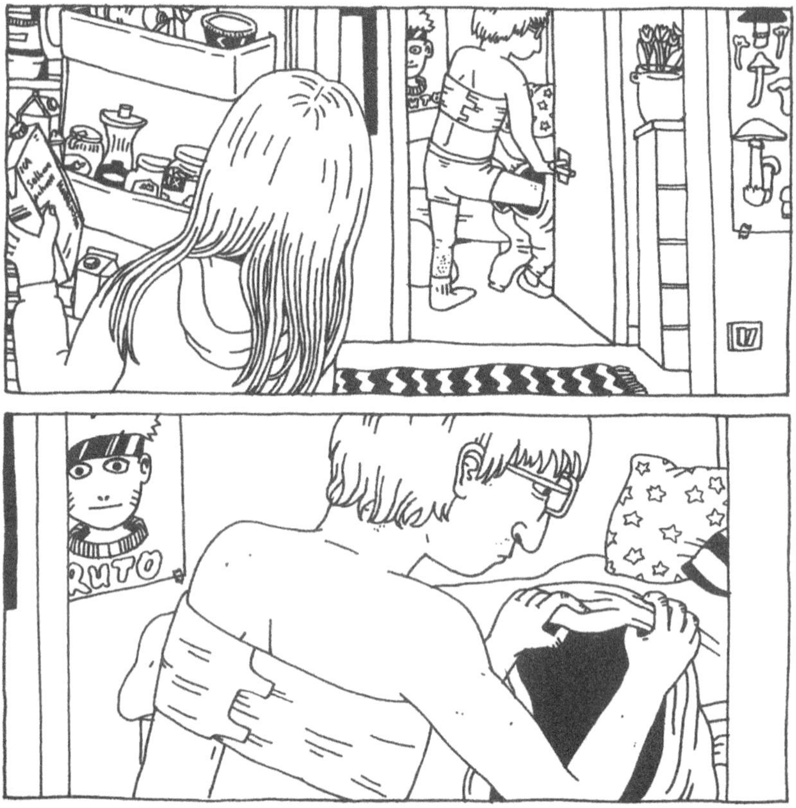

Figure 26: Gustavsson, Hanna. 2015. *Iggy 4-ever*. Stockholm: Ordfront Galago, 198.

Figure 27: Sandgren, Hilding. 2016a. *Vägarna är som tvättbrädor här* (The Roads Are Like Washboards Here). Stockholm: Galago, 94.

In *Iggy 4-ever* and *Vägarna är som tvättbrädor här* the authors made the conscious choice to leave the interpretation of the characters' gender identity to the reader. This makes them stand out from the overall corpus of transgender narratives in Sweden, but also to a large extent from an international viewpoint. As Butler notes, Anglo-American narratives portraying transgender characters without emphasizing the trans theme 'have yet to make a significant appearance' (Butler 2020, 18). The early appearance of Iggy in Swedish fiction might be the result of a literary climate focusing on gender identity, particularly in picturebooks, a few years prior to this publication. According to the Swedish Institute for Children's Books, many children's books published in 2012, particularly picturebooks, depicted gender-neutral children who could be interpreted as boys, girls, non-binary, or any other gender (Svenska barnboksinstitutet 2013, 7). In these cases no gender-identifying pronoun was used, usually made possible by a first-person narrative. In 2012, the gender-neutral pronoun 'hen' also first appeared in a children's book, making it possible to explicitly interpret the characters as gender-neutral. The pronoun 'hen' was coined in the late 60s and had mainly been used in academic contexts until 2012, when Jesper Lundqvist and Bettina Johansson used it in the picturebook *Kivi & Monsterhund* (Kivi and Monster Dog), depicting a gender-neutral protagonist. The book's release sparked a debate about the usefulness of the pronoun and its political implications. Since then, 'hen' has become a widely used word in Swedish society as a whole, including transgender contexts, and also in children's literature. One example of an author who uses it is Sara Bergmark Elfgren. Her young adult novel *Norra Latin* (2017) depicts a subsidiary character, Sam, who is consistently referred to as 'hen' in the novel, and since the gender identity of Sam is not an issue it is not commented upon. The reader has a multitude of choices when interpreting, or choosing not to interpret, the gender identity of Sam. It is likely that the debate on and the increased use of the pronoun 'hen' from 2012 onwards contributed to and paved the way for the development of transgender narratives in Swedish children's and young adult fiction discussed in this chapter.

To conclude, after a phase of denying some stories' position as transgender narratives, we are now in the phase where problematizing is favoured as a strategy to achieve incorporation into the norm. But we also see stories that break this scheme, stories that through their resistance to discussing the categories of gender at all can have a subversive function. Considering how recently transgender characters have been made visible in Swedish children's and young adult literature, stories like *Iggy 4-ever* and *Vägarna är som tvättbrädor här* are remarkably early examples of stories that favour representing over problematizing. Considering the developments within Swedish children's and young adult literature in general, and stories concerned with societal norms in particular, it is likely that we will see more of these kinds of depictions in the future: stories 'for those who want to see' and, perhaps more importantly, be seen.

Bibliography

Ahlund, Anna, and Cina Friedner, eds. *Hetare: elva noveller som känns* (Hotter: Eleven Short Stories That Make an Impression). 2018. Stockholm: Rabén & Sjögren.

Bergmark Elfgren, Sara. 2017. *Norra Latin*. Stockholm: Rabén & Sjögren.

Boyne, John. 2020. *Min bror heter Jessica* (*My Brother's Name is Jessica*). Translated by Anna Thuresson. Stockholm: B. Wahlströms.

Bremer, Signe. (2011) 2017. *Kroppslinjer: Kön, transsexualism och kropp i berättelser om könskorrigering* (Body Lines: Gender, Transsexualism and Body in Stories of Sex Reassignment Therapy). Göteborg: Makadam förlag.

Burman, Cecilia. 2016. '"Pojkarna": regissör bryter normer' (The Boys: Director Breaks Norms). *TT*, 17 February.

Butler, Catherine. 2020. 'The Portrayal of Trans People in Books for Children and Young Adults'. *Journal of Literary Education* 3: 11–24.

Byers, Michelle. 2018. 'Who (the) Girls and Boys Are: Gender Nonconformity in Middle-Grade Fiction'. *Girlhood Studies* 11, no. 1: 92–107. https://doi.org/10.3167/ghs.2018.110108

Cart, Michael, and Christine A. Jenkins. 2006. *The Heart has Its Reasons: Young Adult Literature with Gay/Lesbian/Queer Content, 1969–2004*. Lanham, MD: Scarecrow.

Domellöf-Wik, Maria. 2016. 'Det finns ingen quick fix för den som känner så här' (There Is No Quick Fix for Those Who Feel This Way). *Göteborgs-Posten*, 3 February. https://www.gp.se/kultur/kultur/det-finns-ingen-quick-fix-f%C3%B6r-den-som-k%C3%A4nner-s%C3%A5-h%C3%A4r-1.21944

Epstein, B. J. 2013. *Are the Kids All Right? The Representation of LGBTQ Characters in Children's and Young Adult Literature*. Bristol: HammerOn Press.

Ericson, Elias S. 2013. *Åror* (Oars). Stockholm: Ordfront Galago.

Flanagan, Victoria. 2008. *Into the Closet: Cross-Dressing and the Gendered Body in Children's Literature and Film*. New York: Routledge.

Fokin, Rebecka. 2015. '"En människa är det": flickskap i Jessica Schiefauers *Pojkarna*' ('It's a Human Being': Girlhood in Jessica Schiefauer's *The Boys*). *Barnboken – Journal of Children's Literature Research* 38: 1–22. https://doi.org/10.14811/clr.v38i0.199

Friberg, Linna. 2015. '"En människa är det": en queerdidaktisk analys av Jessica Schiefauers roman "Pojkarna" och dess möjligheter för antiförtryckande arbete i skolan' ('It's a Human Being': A Queer-Didactic Analysis of Jessica Schiefauer's Novel 'The Boys' and Its Potential for Anti-Discrimination Work in Schools). In *Svenska: ett inkluderande ämne* (Swedish: An Including Subject), edited by Ewa Bergh Nestlog and Nils Larsson, 40–57. Stockholm: Svensklärarföreningen.

Gino, Alex. 2016. *George*. Translated by Helena Ridelberg. Stockholm: Lilla Piratförlaget.

Grönqvist, Johanna. 2016. 'Filmrecension: Pojkarna' (Film Review: The Boys). *Svenska Yle*, 28 October. https://svenska.yle.fi/artikel/2016/10/28/filmrecension-pojkarna

Gunnarsson, Björn. 2011. 'Könsidentiteten som saga' (Gender Identity as Fairy Tale). *Helsingborgs Dagblad*, 20 August. https://www.hd.se/2011-08-20/konsidentiteten-som-saga

Gustavsson, Hanna. 2015. *Iggy 4-ever*. Stockholm: Ordfront Galago.

———. 2017. Personal communication.

Halberstam, J. 2000. 'Telling Tales: Brandon Teena, Billy Tipton, and Transgender Biography'. *Auto/Biography Studies* 15, no. 1: 62–81. https://doi.org/10.1080/08989575.2000.10815235

———. 2005. *In a Queer Time and Place: Transgender Bodies, Subcultural Lives*. New York: New York University Press.

Hellberg, Hans-Eric. 1977. *Love love love*. Stockholm: Bonnier.

Hernæs Linhart, Silje. 2015. *'A Wild Stream of Eyes': Affect and Identity in Male-to-Female Transgender Narratives for Children and Young Adults*. Oslo University: Institutt for lingvistiske og nordiske studier, Det humanistiske fakultet.

Herthel, Jessica, Jazz Jennings, and Shelagh McNicholas. 2015. *Jag är Jazz* (*I Am Jazz*). Translated by Tin Eriksson. Färjestaden: Vombat.

Holmqvist, Sam. 2017. *Transformationer: 1800-talets svenska translitteratur genom Lasse-Maja, C. J. L. Almqvist och Aurora Ljungstedt* (Transformations: Nineteenth-Century Swedish Trans

Literature through Lasse-Maja, C. J. L. Almqvist and Aurora Ljungstedt). Göteborg: Makadam förlag.

Hällsten, Annika. 2016. 'Ung jakt på det egna jaget' (Youth Search for Themselves). *Hufvudstadsbladet*, 22 October. https://www.hbl.fi/artikel/ung-jakt-pa-det-egna-jaget/

Jenkins, Christine A., and Michael Cart. 2018. *Representing the Rainbow in Young Adult Literature: LGBTQ+ Content since 1969*. Lanham: Rowman & Littlefield.

Jägerfeld, Jenny. 2016. *Brorsan är kung!* (Bro' Is King!). Translated by Cecilia Falk. Stockholm: Rabén & Sjögren.

Karlsson, Ylva, and Sofia Falkenhem. 2020. *Månen, varelsen och jag* (The Moon, the Creature and I). Stockholm: Rabén & Sjögren.

Kuhnke, Alice Bah, Morgan Johansson, and Gabriel Wikström. 2016. 'Nu stärker vi rättigheterna för Sveriges transpersoner' (We Are Now Strengthening the Rights of Sweden's Trans People). *DN Debatt*, 25 July. https://www.regeringen.se/debattartiklar/2016/07/nu-starker-vi-rattigheterna-for-sveriges-transpersoner/

Kåreland, Lena. 2017. 'Våld, kriminalitet och ifrågasatt flickskap i svensk ungdomslitteratur' (Violence, Crime and Disputed Girlhood in Swedish Youth Literature). In *Svensk samtida ungdomslitteratur: analyser* (Swedish Contemporary Youth Literature: Analyses), edited by Åsa Warnqvist, 199–215. Lund: Studentlitteratur.

Lund, Anna Jakobsson. 2018. 'I hans blick' (In His Gaze). In *Hetare: elva noveller som känns* (Hotter: Eleven Short Stories That Make an Impression), edited by Anna Ahlund and Cina Friedner, 19–29. Stockholm: Rabén & Sjögren.

Lundqvist, Jesper, and Bettina Johansson. 2012. *Kivi & Monsterhund* (Kivi and Monster Dog). Linköping: Olika.

Lönnlöv, Sebastian. 2018. 'Allt jag vill' (All That I Want). In *Hetare: elva noveller som känns* (Hotter: Eleven Short Stories That Make an Impression), edited by Anna Ahlund and Cina Friedner, 105–15. Stockholm: Rabén & Sjögren.

Lövestam, Sara. 2016. *Skarven* (The Cormorant). Stockholm: Lilla Piratförlaget.

Mallan, Kerry. 2009. *Gender Dilemmas in Children's Fiction*. Basingstoke: Palgrave Macmillan.

Miller, Meredith. 2019. 'Lesbian, Gay and Trans Bildungsromane'. In *A History of the Bildungsroman*, edited by Sarah Graham, 239–66. Cambridge: Cambridge University Press.

Moss, Donald, and Lynne Zeavin. 2001. 'The Real Thing? Some Thoughts on *Boys Don't Cry*'. In *Psychoanalysis and Film*, edited by Glen O. Gabbard, 221–28. London: Routledge.

Möller, Cannie. 1985. *Stortjuvens pojke: en rövarhistoria från Lasse-Majas dagar* (The Master Thief's Son: A Tall Tale from the Days of Lasse-Maja). Stockholm: Rabén & Sjögren.

Nilson, Maria. 2017. 'Om genus, sexualitet och makt i fantastisk och vampyrberättelser för ungdomar' (On Gender, Sexuality and Power in Fantasy and Vampire Stories for Young Adults). In *Svensk samtida ungdomslitteratur: analyser* (Swedish Contemporary Youth Literature: Analyses), edited by Åsa Warnqvist, 147–59. Lund: Studentlitteratur.

Nilsson, Johanna. 2018. *Om vi bara kunde byta kroppar med varandra* (If Only We Could Exchange Bodies). Stockholm: Rabén & Sjögren.

Norbury, Kate. 2014. 'Re-Writing the Script: Representations of Transgender Creativity in Contemporary Young Adult Fiction and Television'. *Barnboken – tidskrift för Barnlitteraturforskning*, no 37: 1–18.

Näsling, Sanne. 2011. 'Flickor blir pojkar: utopiskt och lustfyllt om könsgränser' (Girls Become Boys: Utopian and Pleasurable about Gender Borders). *Dagens Nyheter*, 29 August.

Olbers Croall, Moa-Lina. 2016. *I mitt namn: en bok om att vara trans* (In My Name: A Book About Being Transgender). Stockholm: Natur & Kultur.

Pearce, Ruth, Igi Moon, Kat Gupta, and Deborah Lynn Steinberg, eds. 2020. *The Emergence of Trans: Cultures, Politics and Everyday Lives*. New York: Routledge.

Pini, Barbara, Wendy Keys, and Damien W. Riggs. 2018. 'Transphobic Tropes and Young Adult Fiction: An Analysis of Brian Katcher's *Almost Perfect*'. *The Lion and the Unicorn* 42, no. 1: 57–72. https://doi.org/10.1353/uni.2018.0004

Pohl, Peter. 1985. *Janne, min vän (Johnny, My Friend)*. Stockholm: AWE/Geber.

Pojkarna (*Girls Lost*). Directed and written by Alexandra-Therese Keining. 12 September 2015.

RFSL Ungdom and RFSL. 2020. 'Vad är trans? Viktiga årtal' (What is Trans? Important Dates). *Transformering* (Transformation). https://transformering.se/vad-ar-trans/viktiga-artal

Rigney, Melissa. 2003. 'Brandon Goes to Hollywood: "Boys Don't Cry" and the Transgender Body in Film'. *Film Criticism* 28, no. 2: 4–23.

Russo, Meredith. 2016. *Om jag var din tjej* (*If I Was Your Girl*). Stockholm: Lavender Lit.

Samuelsson, Sanna. 2016. 'Om att hitta sig själv bortom all rimlighet' (On Finding Oneself Beyond All Reason). *Arbetet*, 12 February. https://arbetet.se/2016/02/12/om-att-hitta-sig-sjalv-bortom-all-rimlighet/

Sandgren, Hilding. 2016a. *Vägarna är som tvättbrädor här* (The Roads Are Like Washboards Here). Stockholm: Galago.

———. 2016b. Personal communication.

Schiefauer, Jessica. 2011. *Pojkarna* (The Boys). Stockholm: Bonnier Carlsen.

Socialstyrelsen. 2020. *Utvecklingen av diagnosen könsdysfori: förekomst, samtidiga psykiatriska diagnoser och dödlighet i suicid* (The Development of the Diagnosis Gender Dysphoria: Occurrence, Parallel Psychiatric Diagnoses and Suicide Mortality Rate). Stockholm: Socialstyrelsen. https://www.socialstyrelsen.se/globalassets/sharepoint-dokument/artikelkatalog/ovrigt/2020-2-6600.pdf

Summanen, Edward. 2012. 'Om boken "Pojkarna" av Jessica Schiefauer' (On the Book 'The Boys' by Jessica Schiefauer). *Transbloggen*, 26 January. http://www.transformering.se/transbloggen/om-boken-%E2%80%9Dpojkarna%E2%80%9D-av-jessica-schiefauer

Svenska barnboksinstitutet. 2013. *Bokprovning på Svenska barnboksinstitutet: en dokumentation: årgång 2012* (Book Tasting at the Swedish Institute for Children's Books: A Report: Volume 2012). Stockholm: Svenska barnboksinstitutet. https://www.barnboksinstitutet.se/wp-content/uploads/2018/10/Bokprovning-årgång-2012.pdf

———. 2014. *Bokprovning på Svenska barnboksinstitutet: en dokumentation: årgång 2013* (Book Tasting at the Swedish Institute for Children's Books: A Report: Volume 2013). Stockholm: Svenska barnboksinstitutet. https://www.barnboksinstitutet.se/wp-content/uploads/2018/10/Argang_2013.pdf

———. 2016. *Bokprovning på Svenska barnboksinstitutet: en dokumentation: årgång 2015* (Book Tasting at the Swedish Institute for Children's Books: A Report: Volume 2015). Stockholm: Svenska barnboksinstitutet. https://www.barnboksinstitutet.se/wp-content/uploads/2018/09/Bokprovning_Argang_2015.pdf

———. 2017. *Bokprovning på Svenska barnboksinstitutet: en dokumentation: årgång 2016* (Book Tasting at the Swedish Institute for Children's Books: A Report: Volume 2016). Stockholm: Svenska barnboksinstitutet. https://www.barnboksinstitutet.se/wp-content/uploads/2018/09/Bokprovning-2017-dokumentation.pdf

———. 2018. *Bokprovning på Svenska barnboksinstitutet: en dokumentation: årgång 2017* (Book Tasting at the Swedish Institute for Children's Books: A Report: Volume 2017). Stockholm: Svenska barnboksinstitutet. https://www.barnboksinstitutet.se/wp-content/uploads/2018/09/2017-års-utgivning-dokumentation.pdf

———. 2020. *The Book Tasting: 25 Years of the Book Tasting 1993–2017: Summary 2017–2018*. Stockholm: Svenska barnboksinstitutet. https://www.barnboksinstitutet.se/wp-content/uploads/2020/09/Bp_eng-25-AR_Ar-2017_2018.pdf

Sverige. Betänkande av Könstillhörighetsutredningen. 2007. *Ändrad könstillhörighet – förslag till ny lag. Betänkande av könstillhörighetsutredningen* (Changed Gender – Proposal for New Law. Report on the Investigation of the Determination of Gender) (SOU 2007:16). Stockholm: Fritze. https://data.riksdagen.se/fil/6A21E32A-C918-45D5-AEB1-A758B408A7EE

Sverige. Utredningen om Stärkt ställning och bättre levnadsvillkor för transpersoner. 2017. *Transpersoner i Sverige: förslag för stärkt ställning och bättre levnadsvillkor* (Transgender People in Sweden: Proposal for Strengthened Position and Better Living Conditions) (SOU 2017:92). Stockholm: Wolters Kluwer. https://www.regeringen.se/4adda9/contentassets/3e2e892900fc4034a9d822413fdaefe7/transpersoner-i-sverige---forslag-for-starkt-stallning-och-battre-levnadsvillkor

Sykes, Abigail. 2016. 'Magin blir mörker i hbtq-fantasy' (The Magic Becomes Darkness in LGBTQ Fantasy). *Fria Tidningen*, 24 February. https://www.fria.nu/artikel/121973

Toijer-Nilsson, Ying. 2011. 'Gåtfull roman tilltalar och stöter bort' (Enigmatic Novel Appeals and Repels). *Svenska Dagbladet*, 30 August.

Viksten, Elin. 2011. 'Magisk realism om tvingande normer' (Magic Realism About Imperative Norms). *TT*, 24 October.

W, Maja. 2016. 'Pojkarna' (The Boys). *Nöjesguiden*, 18 February. https://ng.se/recensioner/film/pojkarna

Warnqvist, Åsa. 2017. 'Från könsschabloner till överskridningar i serieromaner för ungdomar' (From Gender Models to Transgressions in Graphic Novels for Young Adults). In *Svensk samtida ungdomslitteratur: analyser* (Swedish Contemporary Youth Literature: Analyses), edited by Åsa Warnqvist, 147–59. Lund: Studentlitteratur.

Wurm, Matilda. 2019. 'Förståelse av kön måste baseras på fakta' (The Understanding of Gender Must Be Based on Facts). *Psykologtidningen*, 27 August. http://psykologtidningen.se/2019/08/27/forstaelse-av-kon-maste-baseras-pa-fakta/

Österlund, Mia. 2005. *Förklädda flickor: könsöverskridning i 1980-talets svenska ungdomsroman* (Girls in Disguise: Gender Transgression in Swedish Young Adult Fiction of the 1980s). Åbo: Åbo Akademi.

Chapter Sixteen

BECOMING VERSUS BEING: NATURE, NURTURE AND STEREOTYPES IN SWEDISH LGB YOUNG ADULT NOVELS

B. J. Epstein

Introduction

In this chapter, I explore Swedish-language LGB young adult (YA) novels, arguing that while liberal in their approaches to a certain extent, they also tend to implicitly raise the issue of nature versus nurture while focusing on the 'causes' of queerness; in other words, they suggest, through their plotlines and character depictions, that it is usually nurture that 'turns' someone queer. In addition, many texts rely on stereotyped ideas of queerness, some of which are related to the concept of who or what is to 'blame' for a character being LGBTQ+. It is important to acknowledge some limitations of this research at the outset. In this chapter, I do not discuss trans or, more generally, queer literature; for one thing, I do not have enough space here to do so, and for another, Åsa Warnqvist's chapter in this book explores Swedish-language trans literature in particular. Also, I focus on young adult literature, rather than also analysing picturebooks and junior fiction (see Epstein 2013a for more on picturebooks and middle-grade literature). In large part, I focused the chapter in this way because YA books usually have young adults as their protagonists while picturebooks and junior fiction tend to have LGBTQ+ adults as the main queer characters, usually parents of the protagonists, and so the works were not exactly comparable, and also this kept the corpus size manageable for a short chapter. Finally, I only look at Swedish-language originals, rather than also analysing translations to Swedish; I do this in order to keep the focus firmly on the Swedish context.[1] I discuss the corpus more below.

I also want to note that I take a queer theoretical approach to the concept of queerness. Some people claim that queerness is caused by nature (that is, it stems from genes and biology), while others say it is nurture (in other words, the environment, including family

1 One of the books in my corpus, *Frida och Frida* (Frida and Frida), is a Finland-Swedish work, which means it was written in Swedish in Finland. Although Finland and Sweden are not the same, I would say that the context is similar enough to warrant the Finland-Swedish book being included here. Finland was ruled by Sweden until 1809, but some parts of Finland are still Swedish-speaking and are influenced by Sweden and Swedish culture.

and culture, that someone was raised in); oddly, however, we do not often have this discussion regarding what causes someone to be heterosexual or cisgender, when it would arguably follow that all sexualities and gender identities would be shaped or constructed in the same way (see Sullivan 2011, 4–6). In a useful but simplistic schema, Saul McLeod shows approaches to psychology from nature to nurture. Nature, in this schema, is explained by the 'biological approach', which has a 'focus on genetic, hormonal, and neuro-chemical explanations of behavior' (2018, n.p.), while nurture, on the other end of the scale, is created through conditioning; this is behaviourism (ibid.). There are other points along this scale, but those are the two extremes. Belief in nature, nurture or a mixed position can be applied to many aspects of a person's self, including sexuality and gender identity.

As Meg-John Barker and Jules Scheele explain, an essentialist view is that 'our identities are fixed'; reductionist means 'all gender/sexuality can be reduced to our biology'; and determinist is 'people's gender/sexuality is determined by their genetics, hormones, and/or physiology' (2016, 111). They go on to say:

> As a *social constructionist* approach, queer theory is often taken to be on the 'nurture' side of the nature/nurture debate ..., engaging as it does in a process of *denaturalizing* social categories ... In recent years, however, biologists ... have worked on sex and gender in ways that are far more compatible with queer theory: emphasizing diversity and fluidity, and eschewing essentialism, reductionism, and determinism. (Barker and Scheele, 2016, 111–12, emphasis original)

In short, I agree that there is a mixture of nature and nurture at work in determining gender and sexuality, and that sexuality and gender identity are fluid and diverse; as we shall see, this view seems to be at odds with the Swedish perspective of queerness, or at least with the perspective of Swedish authors of young adult literature. To paraphrase Simone de Beauvoir, I would suggest that one can be born and/or can become queer, and even can choose to be queer. What many of the books that I will discuss below, on the other hand, seem to imply is that queerness is often caused by nurture; in other words, many of the plots infer that the family set-up and the experiences of the character are what lead to them becoming queer. While there are a number of problematic angles to focusing on nature versus nurture, one of the issues is that we do not have lengthy debates about what causes someone to become straight or cisgender. It is assumed that these are the norm identities and that anything that diverts from them must be explained, despite the fact that varying sexualities, sexual practices and gender identities are found across all human cultures and indeed among non-human animals. As Eve Kosofsky Sedgwick points out, 'this society wants its children to know nothing; wants its queer children to conform or (and this is not a figure of speech) die; and wants not to know that it is getting what it wants' (1991, 4). This is to say that there is a real discomfort with and lack of acceptance of LGBTQ+ people in our society, and this means that there is a need or a desire to explain or understand anything beyond the norm. Claiming that nurture is accountable in creating queerness is the sensible position of those who want or expect queers to 'conform', as nurture can be influenced and blamed in a way that nature cannot.

In this chapter, to discuss nature and nurture in Swedish YA LGB literature, I will first give some background to the Swedish context, then I will look at a number of YA examples. These examples tend to depict troubled backgrounds, with the suggestion being that protagonists' interactions with their parents and/or other specific experiences, often sexual violence, have led to the protagonists being queer. The works also reveal other stereotypical ideas about being LGBTQ+, such as that queer males are very sexual or that queer relationships cannot last. In sum, I will suggest that although there is much to admire about Sweden's approach to LGBTQ+ rights and issues, young adult novels are problematic in certain respects and expose several worrying cultural beliefs about what it means to be queer in Sweden today.

Background to the Swedish Context

It is worth briefly analysing the Swedish context by discussing LGBTQ+ rights and history in Sweden and the perspective there on queerness before moving on to the literature (see Epstein 2013a for background to the English-speaking context for a comparison; there is no space in this chapter to go over that material again, but it is interesting and important to explore how cultural views of queerness influence the writing of LGBTQ+ literature). Sweden is perceived as liberal and accepting, and the legal protections there for LGBTQ+ people support this view, but I would suggest that there might still be some level of discomfort with queer people in Swedish society, and perhaps particularly with young queers.

As Jens Rydström notes, Sweden was relatively early in terms of giving equal rights to LGBTQ+ people (2004, 49–58).[2] Jeanette Larsson points out that from 1944, homosexual relationships were legal for people aged 18 and up, and the age was lowered to 15 years in 1978, though strangely it took another year before homosexuality was no longer classified as a sickness (Larsson 1999, 3). While Sweden did not institute same-sex marriage until 2009, as far back as in the 1980s, it did give rights and some protections to LGBTQ+ couples who were living together and enacted legislation to ensure they were not discriminated against (Larsson 1999, 3 and Rydström 2004, 46–49; partnership is called *samboskap* in Swedish and *samboskap* rights extended to same-sex couples). In 1995, registered partnership (*partnerskap*) became legal for same-sex couples (Rydström 2004, 49–52; note that *partnerskap* became gender-neutral in 2009), and from 2003, same-sex couples could be legal guardians for children together (2004, 52–58), though the right to assisted conception did not come into law until 2005. Despite these early steps towards legal equality and the fact that LGBTQ+ people became more visible in society during the same period of time, such as through films (2004, 51), Rydström points out that there was a growing sense of control over how sexuality could be expressed. He writes that, for instance, sex in parks or bathhouses was no longer as acceptable and that heteronormative views meant that the media often described same-sex relationships

2 It should be noted, however, that the legal situation for trans people specifically has been much less liberal until quite recently. See Warnqvist in this volume for more on this.

as 'non-erotic [girl]friendship' (2004, 51; all translations from Swedish my own unless otherwise noted).[3] In other words, there were both pros and cons to the situation in Sweden: there were many legal rights, but there was a heteronormative view of LGBTQ+ people and issues and a certain lack of acceptance about queer sexual activities, not unlike in many other countries and cultures.

Interestingly, research on LGBTQ+ identity in Sweden seems to clearly stress and promote the idea that queerness comes from somewhere and can be explained. That is to say that there appears to be a belief in Sweden that nurture rather than nature – or, indeed, rather than a combination of the two – is responsible for a person being (or, perhaps more appropriately, becoming) LGBTQ+. As already noted, this is strongly reflected in the YA literature discussed below. In an analysis of lesbian identity in Sweden, Pia Lundahl writes, 'Through frequent references to their parents, therapists and friends, the women show how they ceaselessly face ideas that claim to explain their homosexuality' (1998b, 109).[4] In her work, Lundahl argues against this idea, such as by discussing how LGBTQ+ people often feel different during their childhood years, which shows they were always queer, even if they did not understand that (1998b, 50),[5] or how they discover their queerness through romance or sex: 'Males, more often than females, become aware of their homosexuality via their sexuality. At an early age they can have sexual fantasies or be attracted to other boys … Most girls become aware of their homosexuality through a love affair and have usually had several close female friendships before they understand that it's love' (1998a, 9). Lundahl emphasizes that '[n]o one knows why someone "becomes" homosexual … Most homosexuals have not had any exceptional difficulties during childhood' (1998b, 23). But despite this, as the earlier quote from Lundahl's work shows, many people in Sweden apparently believe there is a reason for someone 'becoming' queer and also that this reason generally stems from some sort of negative, traumatic situation in childhood and/or a difficult family background.

Besides the belief that queerness can be explained, there are other stereotyped ideas about LGBTQ+ people in Swedish literature and society more generally (and see Epstein 2013a, 63–131 for more on stereotypes in English-language literature; this comparison reveals that Sweden is not alone in promoting such views). For example, there seem to be certain types of gay men who are visible – '"dirty old men" or "nelly queens"', as Lundahl phrases it (1998a, 19) – even though some, or even many, males may not 'recognize themselves in either of these images' (ibid.). Meanwhile, 'lesbians, or "dykes", don't seem to exist', and Lundahl argues that there is a silence around queer women (ibid.). Larsson supports this, noting that most LGBTQ+ YA literature in Sweden is about males (1999, 3). I did not find this exactly, but I will return to gender, stereotypes and tropes below in my discussion of specific examples in Swedish.

3 'som en icke-erotisk flickvänskap.'

4 'Genom ständiga hänvisningar till föräldrar, terapeuter och kompisar visar kvinnorna hur de oupphörligen möter olika idéer som gör anspråk på att förklara homosexualiteten.'

5 'Ett av de första stegen beskrevs ofta som känslan av att ha varit *annorlunda* under barn- och ungdomsåren.' (emphasis original)

Young Adult Novels in Sweden

It may be worth stating the obvious here: literature is not the so-called real world and does not necessarily reflect what happens in reality outside the realm of the book in question. That is to say, a Swedish YA novel does not have to be based on or to depict what happens in the Swedish context. However, I would argue that authors, publishers, editors, translators and readers, among others engaged with literature, do live in a particular place and a specific time period and are influenced by their cultural context. So if there is a trend in literature, I believe that identifying the trend may well reveal something about the country or culture a text comes from.

As Tison Pugh notes, writing about English-language books, 'While children's literature frequently obfuscates heterosexuality, it often renders homosexuality completely invisible, and such silences perpetuate the shadowy treatment of sexuality in the wider culture as well. Few topics in children's literature generate as much of an uproar as homosexuality: it remains a taboo topic and is mostly overlooked as a viable identity for characters within the genre of children's fiction. Many works of children's literature that include gay characters or themes face immediate censorship' (Pugh 2010, 162). Lydia Kokkola discusses how the situation is different in Scandinavia from much of the rest of the world by pointing out that LGBTQ+ literature does not exist in all languages. She writes, 'As the work of Österlund (2005) and Franck (2009) attests, Swedish adolescent fiction and Swedish society have a far more liberal view of adolescent sexuality and carnality than most Anglophone works. Danish children's literature is perhaps even more liberal than Swedish, as ideas that are hard for many adults to grasp can be presented in formats that are accessible to young children' (Kokkola 2013, 6–7). However, as Kokkola also says, 'Even in today's more liberal society, it takes a great deal of confidence and conviction in one's beliefs to write a novel depicting desiring gay and lesbian teens' (2013, 93). I would agree with Kokkola that Swedish literature is more liberal and there is more 'confidence and conviction' in evidence among Swedish writers and publishers, but that does not mean that Swedish YA novels are always positive in their representation of queerness, especially in regard to portraying sexual feelings and actions. Without using the precise term, Pugh implicitly refers to internalized homophobia (and biphobia, transphobia and queerphobia), and how 'antigay ideology triumphs even within many of these texts' (Pugh 2010, 162). Again, he is referring primarily to English-language books, and I am not sure if it is 'antigay ideology' exactly that we see in Swedish literature, but I would suggest that there does appear to be a strong sense of internalized phobia and stereotyped ideas of queerness, and this may link to discomfort with queerness. There may also be an implicit belief that if queerness is caused by nurture, there are ways to prevent or improve it, which does get close to an antiqueer ideology.

My findings suggest that even in liberal Sweden, with all its apparent acceptance and protection of LGBTQ+ people, it is expected that anything outside the norm needs to be explained. Many of the young adult novels show young queer people who have difficult family situations, troubled backgrounds, unengaged parents, problems with friends, sexual assault or other stressors that seem to explain why the LGBTQ+ person has turned out queer. In other words, they imply or explicitly state that nurture can be pinpointed as the reason for queerness. In my research, I have also found other fascinating differences between Swedish-language and English-language LGBTQ+ YA novels, such as that there is more sexual liberalness in Swedish works – although males still move faster and have more sexual experiences than females, which is a gender-based stereotype – but in this chapter, I focus on the blame and explanations along with several other common negative tropes in Swedish texts, rather than analyse more aspects that separate the cultures. In what follows, I will look at some typical examples from Swedish-language YA literature.

Examples from Swedish LGBTQ+ YA Novels

Lydia Kokkola writes that 'unlike texts depicting heterosexual teens, romances depicting same-sex desire tend to be written with the aim of empowering the queer adolescent reader through the presentation of positive examples. Many, but by no means all, of the authors are queer and feel a responsibility for and desire to reach out to queer adolescent readers' (2013, 96). In other words, she is suggesting that there are positive intentions behind the existence of these books and the way queerness is written about (see many of the other chapters in this volume for more on positive intentions and how they can go wrong). My question, when looking at the specific examples that follow here, is whether these works are indeed empowering or whether they actually perpetuate stereotypes, or whether it is possible for them to both empower and stereotype.

To form my corpus of texts, I used lists of Swedish LGBTQ+ children's and YA books and book reviews; did key word and genre searches in the Libris search feature at the Kungliga Biblioteket (the National Library of Sweden); and also asked for recommendations from scholars and bookshop employees in Sweden. I did not set any limits on how old the texts could be and indeed I was slightly surprised to find one work from the 1970s, but most were more recent, which does mirror the increasing amounts of LGBTQ+ literature being published in Swedish. In short, I read anything I could access on several research and book-buying visits to Sweden, but I am aware that there are others that I could not find at the library or bookshop and still more that have been published in the couple of years since I was carrying out this research.[6] In this particular chapter, it is important to note, I do not refer to every book I read, as I decided to focus on YA and to disregard picturebooks and middle-grade works. During the course of several research visits to Swedish, I read approximately five dozen LGBTQ+ books for children and young adults; since I do not discuss the picturebooks or middle-grade books here, the number of YA texts I refer to is 15.

6 I think it is worth referring to *Hitta hem* (Finding Home) by Ann-Helén Laestadius (2012), the first YA novel that I am aware of that includes a Sami LGBTQ+ character. While this character is not the protagonist (the book is part of a series about a young Sami woman) and the novel is rather negative in that it shows homophobia in the Sami community, it is a step forward to include this indigenous group in more literature for young people and especially to feature an LGBTQ+ Sami character. This is indicative of how LGBTQ+ literature is progressing in Sweden.

Difficult parental relationships

One of the most common ideas that I find in Swedish YA literature is that difficult relationships with parents and perhaps also too much closeness with the mother 'makes' a young person turn queer, especially for males. In *Ung, bög och jävligt kär* (Young, Gay and So Fucking In Love) by Johannes Sandreyo (2012), Filip, the 'young, gay and so fucking in love' protagonist, has a difficult relationship with his father, and his father, Tommy, in turn blames Filip's mother for Filip's queerness. Interestingly, Sandreyo includes a line that seems to argue against the claim that nurture is at fault, even while showing scenes that clearly suggest that it cannot solely be nature. Early in the novel, Sandreyo writes sarcastically, 'Everyone seemed to think that you had to study a course in homosexuality at university in order to *research* your way to your orientation' (Sandreyo 2012, 7, emphasis original).[7] And yes, everyone in this book does seem to think that, while Sandreyo does not do much to counteract the belief. Tommy blames Filip's mother for getting Filip interested in theatre and dance (2012, 8), which are, of course, stereotypically gay pursuits, and also thinks that Filip having music education has helped create this gay son (2012, 7). Tommy says that Filip 'shames' him and is 'disturbed' (2012, 6).[8] Filip, or at least Johannes Sandreyo, does seem to recognize that nature and nurture both play a role and yet the novel only depicts nurture and employs stereotyped ideas of gay men as a way of describing and explaining queerness. Compared to some of the other YA books in my corpus, Filip does not have a particularly challenging family background. His father is unsupportive and is upset at the idea of Filip's gayness, but there are moments of positivity nonetheless.

On the other hand, Hanna Wallensten's 2005 novel *I närheten av solen* (Close to the Sun) is more or less relentlessly negative. The novel focuses on a young woman who runs a bookshop and café and who appears to be shaped by a difficult family background; she is unnamed until the very last page, as though she cannot even think of herself as the protagonist in her own life. Her homosexuality is a small part of the story, but nonetheless, the book gives the impression that being queer is caused by family problems. To name just a few of the things that happen to this character: her mother has serious psychological issues and spends time in a psychiatric hospital; her father tries to physically hurt his son-in-law (the protagonist's brother-in-law); her family does not talk about any of their issues and simply pretends all is fine; she has a homeless person in her cellar; and she has an eating disorder and at one point weighed less than 38 kg (around 6 stone or 83 lbs). Again, this very troubled background might give readers the impression that family difficulties may contribute to the development of a non-heterosexual orientation.

One of Sweden's earliest LGBTQ+ YA novels is Inger Edelfeldt's *Duktig pojke!* (Good Boy!) and it too relies on stereotypes, though it should perhaps also be praised for

7 'Alla människor verkade tro att man behövde läsa tjugo poäng homosexualitiet på universitetet för att *forska* sig fram till sin läggning.' (emphasis original)

8 'Hur fan kan du skämma ut mig så där inför allihop? ... Du måste ju vara serioäst skadad där upp.' 'How the fuck can you shame me like that in front of everyone? ... You must be seriously disturbed.'

discussing homosexuality at such an early point in contemporary Swedish literary history, in the late 1970s. Jimmy is a sensitive, bullied boy (Edelfeldt 1977, 10), and there is the implication that perhaps his closeness to his mother is to blame for his gayness; his father says that his mother spoiled him and this turned him weak and queer (1977, 188, 197), even while also claiming that Jimmy 'grew up in a nice home and had a good childhood', so he does not understand what made him 'react in this way' (1977, 193).[9] Along with the closeness to his mother, Jimmy's sensitivity is said to be 'the explanation for everything' (1977, 3).[10] He pressures himself to be a 'Good Boy' (capitalization original; the capitalization highlights the importance of being what his parents and society expect from him) but tells himself that he is a 'fucking fag, a sissy, a bottom boy'[11] and he says, 'Into the naughty corner with you and write a hundred times: I PROMISE TO BE LIKE EVERYONE ELSE. Take drugs for your nerves, marry unhappily, drink yourself to death, do what you want but keep your fucking faggot filth to yourself! You're not one of them, Jimmy! You're a good boy!' (1977, 175–76, capitalization original).[12] His father meanwhile tells him to '[e]ither come home and be like other people or else go on in your sissy way until you grow breasts' (1977, 197).[13] Understandably, Jimmy gets ill from the stress of always trying to be 'Good' (1977, 110, capitalization original),[14] and has to see a therapist and take medication (1977, 28), but the drugs and the counselling do not help him. He hates himself, feels he is a 'big, stinking lie … ridiculous' (1977, 96),[15] and though he masturbates to thoughts of males, he tries to force himself to be straight and to have a girlfriend (1977, 101). Jimmy thinks of gay men as 'People Like That' (1977, 128, capitalization original)[16] and when he and his mother see a man asking boys for cigarettes, his mother says they are 'homos', as though homosexuality is linked to paedophilia (or preying on young people, or even just an older man talking to younger ones) (1977, 129). The idea that gayness will lead to a sad future is emphasized by Jimmy understanding that his sexuality means that 'I would be a pathetic little person, sitting at home, polishing the leaves of my plants, masturbating to opera music' (1977, 129), which gets several stereotyped ideas across to readers all at once.[17] So Jimmy is the archetypal delicate boy, pampered by and close to his mother, and he turns queer and suffers from self-hatred

9 'Du har växt upp i ett fint hem och haft en bra barndom, så jag förstår inte vad som har fått dig att reagera på det här sättet.'

10 'förklaringen till allting'.

11 'Duktig Pojke ... en djävla fikus, en fjolla, en liten stjärtgosse'.

12 'In i skamvrån med dig och skriv hundra gånger: JAG LOVAR ATT BLI SOM FOLK. Ät nervtabletter, gift dig olyckligt, sup ihjäl dig, gör vad du vill men behåll ditt djävla bögsnusk för dig själv! Du är ju inte sån, Jimmy! Du är ju en duktig pojke.'

13 'Antingen kommer du hem och är som folk, eller också kan du begava dig i dina fjollfasoner tills det växer ut bröst på dig.'

14 'Det viktigaste här i livet var att vara Duktig.'

15 'en stor, stinkande lögn. Jag hatade mig själv, jag insåg hur löjlig jag var.'

16 'Såna Där'.

17 'Jag skulle bli en sådan där patetisk liten figur som satt hemma och polerade bladen på sina krukväxter och onanerade till operamusik.'

while also being emotionally abused by his father and worrying about what a future as a gay man might look like, i.e. 'pathetic', lonely paedophilia.

Difficult family relationships are sadly common in this corpus. For instance, Micke, the main character in Ingrid Sandhagen's *En av dem* (One of Them), also has a lack of familial support and faces prejudice, especially from his grandfather. His father's father says Micke is 'like a girl ... wimpy... had better learn' (Sandhagen 2000, 7),[18] and tries to pressure him to go hunting, though he does not want to (2000, 11). His grandfather also compares him to 'broads' (2000, 15).[19]

Kristina and Jenny, the main characters in Katja Timgren's *Det jag inte säger* (What I Don't Say), also have struggles with their families. Kristina lives with her sister because she does not get along with her father and because her mother's 'fucking boyfriend is a homophobe' (Timgren 2004, 30).[20] And when Jenny, who falls for Kristina, tells her parents, her mother's response is to ask if something went wrong in her childhood or if she was attacked (2004, 167). This comment reveals the idea that so many of these books have in common, which is that something must happen to cause a person to become LGBTQ+; the concept of an attack in particular will be returned to below. Jenny's mother tells her she had hoped for grandchildren, but then says that at least they still have Jenny's brother, as though only heterosexuals can provide children and can therefore satisfy their parents (Timgren 2004, 169). While Jenny's mother later does apologize and express a desire to support her (2004, 173), this comes across as somewhat fake and does not change the fact that Timgren's novel offers the same problematic message as so many other Swedish books.

Sad queers

While there are other examples of protagonists with unhappy family backgrounds[21] and it is a recurring theme below, there is no need to belabour this point. Instead, I can move on to the idea that being queer not only stems from an unhappy background but also leads to an unhappy present and even an unhappy future. This impression of a queer life runs through Moa-Lina Croall's *Sen tar vi Berlin* (Next We'll Take Berlin), just as it did in Edelfeldt's *Duktig pojke!* The protagonist, Lou, is depicted as dissatisfied with her life, and as socially awkward and confused, and she has parents who argue and yell at her (Croall 2006, 13). She has low self-esteem (2006, 9, 11), struggles to communicate, needs to drink

18 'som en flicka tamejfan ... ynklig ... måste lära sig ...'

19 'fruntimmer'.

20 'Hennes jävla pojkvän är homofob'.

21 For instance, Jessica Kolterjahn's 2007 novel *Ut ur skuggan* (Out of the Shadow) depicts a privileged girl in the 1920s and 1930s. The time period and her wealth set the book apart from some of the other YA works discussed here, but here too the protagonist has unengaged parents, which again sends the message that someone's background might cause them to become queer. Likewise, Håkan Lindquist's *Om att samla frimärken* (Collecting Stamps), published in 2003, shows a young man with an abusive father and he has a crush on another boy who has an absent and possibly abusive father as well.

in order to converse with others (2006, 9, 193), and has a boyfriend, though she is not happy with him and expresses that she is with him just because she has 'tired of everything' (2006, 17).[22] She calls herself a 'little sick, disgusting thing' (2006, 40)[23] and often says she is worthless and strange and that she wants to die. Meanwhile, she is interested in a young woman called Sarah. Sarah is very secretive, and shows some discomfort with her body, such as by not allowing Lou to touch her breasts (2006, 151) and saying that '[s]ex will never be connected to anything lovely for me' (2006, 157).[24] Lou wonders if Sarah experienced rape or incest (2006, 152), but later finds out that Sarah and her older sister were prostitutes and that their pimp murdered her sister. Sarah, in turn, killed him. In other words, both Lou and Sarah have had difficult experiences in their childhoods and youths and both are sad young women who struggle to accept themselves and their sexuality. They find it challenging to have a happy queer present and the reader may be left with the feeling that the women cannot have a happy queer future either.

Sexual violence

Sexual assault is a common trope in books featuring female queer characters, and the message this sends to readers in these works is rather worrying. Kokkola argues that '[w]here gay men meet with visceral admonitions and disgust, lesbians often face ambivalence. This may seem benign, but as we probe deeper into that ambivalence, we see that this is an insidious way of undermining and disempowering the desiring subject' (Kokkola 2013, 103). It arguably does not get more 'undermining and disempowering' than rape, and featuring sexual assault so frequently sends the message that there is no other reason why a woman would turn to another woman for sex than previous bad experiences with men. These women are to be pitied and they are objects, not subjects. In Mian Lodalen's *Tiger* (*Tiger* refers to the animal, but also *tiga* means 'to be silent', so it has a potential double meaning), readers might get the impression that sexual assault causes queerness and that queerness inevitably leads to being unsupported by one's family. While this is true for some LGBTQ+ people, it is a concern how many books seem to suggest that it is true for most (see Epstein 2013a, 74–93 for more on English-language texts that show problematic coming-out stories and rejection by family). In *Tiger*, Connie's mother dies when she is little and her father is called 'The Fool', which makes her 'The Fool's Daughter'.[25] She is raped when she is 11 years old (Lodalen 2010, 59),[26] and there is some suggestion that this led her to be attracted to other females. It is as though the sexual abuse she suffered from a man makes her afraid of men and forces her to turn towards women; the implication is that one would not choose to be queer and that it is a reaction to a difficult situation. She reads in a textbook, 'Adult homosexuals often look for a

22 'har tröttnat på allt'.
23 'vilken sjuk liten äcklig sak'.
24 'Sex kommer aldrig att förknippas med nåt fint för mig.'
25 'Dåren' and 'Dårens dotter'.
26 'Smärtan brände som eld mellan benen.' – 'The pain between her legs burned like fire.'

partner among youth of the same sex. This sort of relationship can be a big problem for a young person' (2010, 61).[27] Connie then wonders, 'Is this what is waiting for me? Being an old lady who drools after teenage girls?' (2010, 61).[28] When, despite these fears about life as an LGBTQ+ adult, Connie does start a relationship with another girl, her new girlfriend is kicked out by her father (2010, 306), while her mother wonders what made her queer (2010, 307). Rape, an unsupportive family and worries that being queer means being a sexual predator: *Tiger* features many of the stereotypes of LGBTQ+ YA literature. And although Connie and her friends masturbate together (2010, 128), Connie tries to think of men while doing so (2010, 131), and she has trouble becoming a sexual subject rather than an object.

Rape as a trope for a queer woman also appears in Emma Juslin's *Frida och Frida* (Frida and Frida), a Finland-Swedish novel from 2007 about teenager Selma and her older sister Irina. Their father is a drunken farmer who is unable to provide for the family, their mother is a cold, unhappy woman, and Irina is raped; this background information is given as a possible explanation for Irina's queerness. Irina herself ponders the Freudian idea that given the distance she experiences from her mother and the horrible men in her life, she is possibly frightened of men and searching for a mother's love in the form of female lovers. When she comes out to her parents, they wonder what they did wrong, which confirms what was already set up in the novel; in other words, their personalities and interactions with their daughter seem to be blamed for her lesbian identity.

Queer males versus queer females

In terms of sexual interactions, rape and other forms of sexual violence tend not to feature in books about queer males; rather, queer males are shown to be actively and enthusiastically sexual. Micke (or Mikael, as he decides he prefers to be called) in Ingrid Sandhagen's *En av dem* (2000) meets a boy called Joel and they quickly start having sex and seem to be happy (or, at the minimum, sexually satisfied) together,[29] so some Swedish YA story lines do show that despite a tricky childhood, someone can be queer and can engage in a relationship (whether romantic or sexual or both) and can have a positive future. There are more examples of this discussed below, and this shows how stark the contrast is between the portrayals of male and female LGB characters.

Lars Karlström's *Pelle älskar Nicke* (Pelle Loves Nicke) is surprising in how positive it is towards the queer youth and how accepting the parents are, especially given that it was

27 'Vuxna homosexuella söker ofta en partner bland ungdomar av samma kön. Ett sådant förhållande kan bli ett stort problem för en ung människa.'

28 'Är detta vad som väntar? Bli en gammal kärring som dreglar efter tonårstjejer?'

29 Mikael and Joel's sex life is described in explicit detail in a way many LGBTQ+ YA novels in English would probably avoid. They perform oral sex on one another and Joel comes in Mikael's mouth and is ordered to swallow. This is also different from how books in both languages depict queer female sexuality; LGBTQ+ females do not experience much in the way of sex lives, and certainly nothing that explicit or satisfying.

published in 1989, which is much earlier than many of the other works discussed here (most of the texts, as noted above, are contemporary). I am not familiar with the publisher of the work and cannot find any information about it, which makes me wonder if perhaps this was self-published. Nicke's father, for example, calmly says that the 15-year-old boys Nicke and Pelle are welcome as a couple at home, and he and Nicke's mother even borrow books from the library in order to learn more about having homosexual children (Karlström 1989, 47), though it is pointed out that '[p]arents, especially mothers, are liable to blame themselves for what went wrong in [the queer person's] childhood' (1989, 48–49).[30] One could argue that just stating this is again confirming the societal view of queerness having a root cause and the belief that someone is to blame for it, but Karlström does attempt to fight against it with his storyline. But as in Sandhagen's *En av dem*, the two male characters move very quickly into a sexual relationship (1989, 6), and the sex scenes are described with more detail than one sees in works with female characters. However, although Pelle and Nicke are satisfied with their relationship and are said to be 'very in love' (1989, 22)[31], readers are told that 'it is rare that a relationship lasts so long between two guys; it's only in some cases that it lasts a few years' (1989, 23).[32] In short, Karlström's novel is somewhat more positive than many of the others, but nonetheless manages to put across a number of stereotyped and prejudiced ideas about LGBTQ+ people, namely that parents might blame themselves (and therefore actually be to blame), that queer males are very sexual, and that relationships between queer men cannot last.

The 'queer males are very sexual' trope also appears in *Spelar Roll* (Playing a Role, but it also means 'it matters') by Hans Olsson, where the story has barely got going before two young men manually pleasure one another in a sauna (Olsson 1993, 20). Pia Lundahl claims that '[s]ex is more visibly important to men's relationships than to women's. This is especially noticeable among gay men' (Lundahl 1998a, 23). Whether this is actually true or not, the belief that it is, which I too have come across and discuss in other work (Epstein 2013a and 2013b), implies that readers would see more sex in books with queer males than with queer females, and the Swedish books tend to bear this out. I would therefore suggest that the (over)sexed queer male is a stereotype and trope in LGBTQ+ YA literature, as is the non-sexed queer female, who is more likely to be shown engaging in verbal and emotional rather than physical intimacy. And, as we have already seen, Swedish YA literature suggests that queer females may be queer because of experiencing painful, violent or forced sexual experiences with men. All this implies a higher level of societal acceptance of male sexuality in general and queer male sexuality in particular. As Jeanette Larsson points out in her research about this literature, there are differences between how queer males and queer females are treated: 'The girls' love relationships develop in four out of five cases from a close friendship. The boys, in five cases out of

30 'Föräldrar, speciellt mödrar, har en benägenhet att anklaga sig själva för vad som blivit fel i uppväxten.'

31 'verkligen förälskade i varandra'.

32 'det är sällan att det varar så länge mellan två killar, det är vara i enstaka fall det räckar flera år'.

seven, meet a stranger and they start to like one another' (Larsson 1999, 24).[33] This idea of how queer romantic/sexual relationships develop perhaps explains why there is so much sexual activity in the books featuring males; in other words, the boys experience lust whereas the girls find romance blossoming within friendship. Whether this is in fact a difference between the way the genders love is the subject for other research.

A somewhat humorous non-fiction work about gay men in Sweden, *Bögjävlar* (Fucking Fags) complains about gay culture and stereotyped ideas of LGBTQ+ people. One of the authors, Petter Wallenberg, points out that stereotypes 'give security and a sense of group belonging. It's about a middle school mentality' (Björk et al. 2008, 48).[34] Also, stereotypes make people think they have understood an issue or a group of people (Epstein 2013a, 64–73). The authors of *Bögjävlar*, while clearly partly intending their book as a joke, also have serious purposes in mind. They rightfully say that '[i]t is the conditional and incomplete acceptance of fags that we want to get at' (Björk et al. 2008, 7).[35] I would suggest that the continued use of stereotyped ideas in LGBTQ+ YA novels means that Swedish society cannot quite reach an unconditional and complete acceptance of LGBTQ+ people, and thus stereotypes can be seen as a problematic aspect of Swedish literature, one that should be changed.

A small amount of positivity

However, it is true that not all Swedish-language LGBTQ+ YA novels feature stereotyped ideas of queerness or show troubled backgrounds and unsupportive parents, and thus do not all imply that nurture, or the lack of it, is the cause of queerness; often, it must be said, these are more recent publications, which perhaps is evidence of growing societal acceptance. Happily, there are a couple of more positive Swedish YA LGBTQ+ novels. One is Åsa Nilsson's *Dags att våga* (Time to Dare). Both Alexandra and Yulia tell their parents that they are lesbians. Yulia's father says he is 'a little sad that I didn't know, but not angry [that you are gay]' (Nilsson 2005, 123),[36] while Alexandra's mother says, 'I will always love you no matter what you do, so don't be worried about that' (2005, 136).[37]

Even more positive and also pleasantly diverse is Sara Bergmark Elfgren's 2017 novel *Norra Latin* (North Latin, the name of a school), which features blithely out and accepted lesbian, gay, bisexual, poly and trans/genderqueer characters. The characters generally do not make a production of having to come out, the way characters do in earlier books and in many other Swedish- and English-language novels, and they simply live their lives without getting comments or negativity from their friends or family. *Norra Latin* is the most recent of the novels discussed here, so perhaps that contemporariness reflects

33 'Flickornas kärleksförhållanden uppkommer i fyra fall av fem ur en nära vänskapsrelation. Pojkarna träffar i fem fall av sju en främling och det uppstår ömsesidigt tycke.'

34 'Det ger trygghet och en känsla av grupptillhörighet. Det handlar om högstadiementalitet.'

35 'Det är den villkorade och ofullständinga acceptansen av bögar i samhället som vi vill åt.'

36 'Jag skulle aldrig bli arg på dig för att du är lesbisk. Visst är jag lite ledsen att jag inte visste det, men inte arg.'

37 'Jag kommer alltid älska dig vad du än gör, var inte orolig för det.'

changes in Swedish society. On the other hand, the novel also has fantasy elements, which makes it less realistic than all the other books in my corpus, and it has been argued that speculative fiction allows for more flexibility regarding sex, gender and other aspects of identity (e.g. Griffith and Pagel 1998).

When Jeanette Larsson published her research about Swedish LGBTQ+ YA literature 20 years ago, she noted that in the texts, 'All of the young people go through the same difficult period of anguish, uncertainty and depression before they understand that they are homosexual. They also have the same worries about trying to appear outwardly as "normal" as possible … they feel the same confusion and irritation over not being accepted just because they happen to love a person of the same sex' (1999, 24).[38] While my findings suggest that some of this has changed in contemporary Swedish YA literature – for instance, *Norra Latin*'s wide variety of sexualities, all of which are accepted without comment, and the parental support in *Dags att våga* – some of the same issues are still present, such as the stereotypes and the dependence on the idea that queerness has a cause. It may be that some authors feel they are trying to make their readers sympathetic to the queer characters by depicting 'anguish' and 'confusion' and troubling backgrounds and/or they may feel that they are being realistic in their portrayal of queer lives. However, I would suggest that doing so others the LGBTQ+ characters and sends the message to readers that there is usually a reason behind queerness and that this reason is negative.

Conclusion

In this chapter, I have looked at over a dozen examples from Swedish-language LGBTQ+ YA literature. Although I would suggest there are some positive differences between Swedish- and English-language books, such as more openness about queer feelings and topics as well as more sexual interactions in Swedish novels, there nonetheless appear to be many problems both in and with the Swedish texts.

As discussed in depth above, there seems to be a need in Swedish YA novels to understand what 'causes' queerness. Rather than simply accepting the LGBTQ+ character as queer, discussing queerness as natural and normal, and exploring other aspects of the characters' lives, many of the works show unhappy family backgrounds and/or unsupportive relatives, which could be read as implying that queerness can be blamed on nurture, or the lack thereof. A possible reading of some of the books could suggest the belief that distance from a same-sex parent and/or too much closeness or identification with the opposite-sex parent is indirectly shown to be a reason why someone seeks out a same-sex partner. While it is unquestionably so that a person's background does affect and help form them, many Swedish books appear to focus excessively on the negative aspects

38 'Alla de aktuella ungdomarna genomgår samma svåra period av kval, osäkerhet och depression innan de förstår att de är homosexuella. De har också samma bekymmer över att utåt försöka framställa sig som så 'normal' som möjligt … de känner samma förvirring och irritation över att inte accepteras för att de råkar älska en person av samma kön.'

of family life and to blame them for the protagonist's queerness. Of course there are many books – in Swedish, English and undoubtedly most other languages – that feature heterosexual protagonists with difficult family backgrounds as well, and the idea that a stressful childhood causes later challenges is very common, but I would suggest that it is seldom implied that a heterosexual person's sexuality has been caused by abusive, unsupportive or distant parents.

In addition, another supposed 'cause' of queerness is featured in a number of these texts and this cause is specific mainly to female characters; in these texts, rape or sexual assault seem to be the reason for someone becoming queer or even choosing to be queer. A more positive interpretation for the prevalence of sexual violence could be that queerness heals someone who has suffered in this way; unfortunately, however, this often does not seem to be borne out by the plot or the descriptions in the work. Instead, many of the females appear understandably traumatized by what they have gone through and often find it challenging to be sexually intimate with other females even if they engage with them emotionally to a certain extent.

Finally, there are a range of other stereotyped ideas about LGBTQ+ people in these novels. The most common one here is that queer males are very sexual, frequently seen engaging in sexual acts in the first or second meeting with another queer male, and these scenes are often described in great detail. Queer females, on the other hand, do not generally get depicted in the same way as lust-filled and overtly sexual. This may follow on from the previous point, in that women who have experienced sexual violence may not be thought to be able to enjoy sex, or it may relate to general societal views of female sexuality as being less-than that of males.

I asked above whether these works empower readers or perpetuate stereotypes or do both, and while a reader-response survey would need to be carried out in order to reach an accurate answer about this, I would argue that while it is generally good to have a diverse array of visible characters in children's and YA literature, portraying those characters in stereotyped ways is not positive. It is time for literature to move beyond stereotypes and to depict a wide range of LGBTQ+ people.[39] I also believe it would be a positive step forward to focus on characters in their wholeness, rather than centring a book primarily on their sexuality and trying to explain it with reference to nurture and family background.

While English-language LGBTQ+ YA novels also have their own issues (Epstein 2013a) and no field of literature can be said to accurately and realistically portray an entire group of people in all their individuality and diversity without including any negative aspects of their lives and selves at all, I would propose that based on my findings here, Swedish LGBTQ+ YA literature is not quite as liberal or forward-thinking as may be expected based on contemporary Swedish culture and LGBTQ+ history and rights in Sweden. It appears that even today there is a strong sense that queerness comes from nurture rather than from nature or a combination of nature and nurture, as though

39 Note how many chapters in this book state the same thing. Many authors and publishers have good intentions, it seems, but still end up promoting out-of-date stereotypes.

Swedish authors, publishers and the general public feel they need to understand why someone is queer instead of simply accepting them as queer and moving on from there.

References

Barker, Meg-John, and Jules Scheele. 2016. *Queer: A Graphic History*. London: Icon.

Björk, Daniel, Tomas Hemstad, Stefan Ingvarsson, Petter Wallenberg, and Roger Wilson. 2008. *Bögjävlar* (Fucking Fags). Stockholm: Atlas.

Croall, Moa-Lina. 2006. *Sen tar vi Berlin* (Next We'll Take Berlin). Stockholm: Alfabeta.

Edelfeldt, Inger. 1977. *Duktig pojke!* (Good Boy!). Stockholm: Rabén & Sjögren.

Elfgren, Sara Bergmark. 2017. *Norra Latin* (North Latin). Stockholm: Rabén & Sjögren.

Epstein, B. J. 2013a. *Are the Kids All Right?* Bristol: HammerOn.

———. 2013b. 'Shy, Gentle Kisses and Soft, Sweet Cuddles: the Sex Lives of Lesbian Teenagers Versus Gay Male Teenagers in YA Literature'. *Write4Children* 4, no. 1: 17–26.

Griffith, Nicola, and Stephen Pagel. 1998. *Bending the Landscape. Original Gay and Lesbian Writing: Science Fiction*. New York: Overlook Press.

Juslin, Emma. 2007. *Frida och Frida* (Frida and Frida). Helsinki: Schildts Söderströms.

Karlström, Lars. 1989. *Pelle älskar Nicke* (Pelle Loves Nicke). Arboga, Sweden: Textab.

Kokkola, Lydia. 2013. *Fictions of Adolescent Carnality*. Amsterdam/Philadelphia: John Benjamins.

Kolterjahn, Jessica. 2007. *Ut ur skuggan* (Out of the Shadow). Stockholm: Forum.

Kosofsky Sedgwick, Eve. (1991) 2003. 'Queer and Now'. *The Routledge Queer Studies Reader*, edited by Donald E. Hall and Annamarie Jagose, with Andrea Bebell and Susan Potter, 3–17. London: Routledge.

Laestadius, Ann-Helén. 2012. *Hitta hem* (Finding Home). Stockholm: Rabén och Sjögren.

Larsson, Jeanette. 1999. *Homosexualitet i ungdomslitteraturen* (Homosexuality in YA Literature). Uppsala: Uppsala Universitet (Uppsala University).

Lindquist, Håkan. 2003. *Om att samla frimärken* (Collecting Stamps). Stockholm: Kabusa.

Lodalen, Mian. 2010. *Tiger* (Tiger). Stockholm: Månpocket.

Lundahl, Pia. 1998a. *Lesbian and Gay the Swedish Way*. Translated by David Murphy. Stockholm: RFSL.

———. 1998b. *Lesbisk identitet* (Lesbian Identity). Stockholm: Carlssons.

McLeod, Saul. 2018. 'Nature vs. Nurture in Psychology'. *SimplyPsychology*. Available at: https://www.simplypsychology.org/naturevsnurture.html

Nilsson, Åsa. 2005. *Dags att våga* (Time to Dare). Stockholm: Opal.

Olsson, Hans. 1993. *Spelar Roll* (Playing a Role). Stockholm: Alfabeta.

Pugh, Tison. 2010. *Innocence, Heterosexuality, and the Queerness of Children's Literature*. London: Routledge.

Rydström, Jens. 2004. 'Från fula fubbar till goda föräldrar – synen på sexualitet och genus i lagstiftning och debatt 1944–2004' ('From Ugly Old Men to Good Parents – The View of Sexuality and Gender in Law and Debate 1944–2004'). In *I den akademiska garderoben* (In the Academic Closet), edited by Anna-Clara Olsson and Caroline Olsson, 37–65. Stockholm: Atlas.

Sandhagen, Ingrid. 2000. *En av dem* (One of Them). Stockholm: Bonnier Carlsen.

Sandreyo, Johannes. 2012. *Ung, bög och jävligt kär* (Young, Gay and So Fucking In Love). Stockholm: Vombat Förlag.

Sullivan, Nikki. 2011. *A Critical Introduction to Queer Theory*. Edinburgh: Edinburgh University Press.

Timgren, Katja. 2004. *Det jag inte säger* (What I Don't Say). Stockholm: Rabén & Sjögren.

Wallensten, Hanna. 2005. *I närheten av solen* (Close to the Sun). Stockholm: Forum.

LIST OF PRIMARY TEXTS

In the following list, we focus primarily on titles published for children and young adults, except where chapter authors have identified adult titles as YA-suitable in the absence of YA-specific materials. We do not include translations from English, as many resources listing English-language texts already exist. However, we have included translations from languages other than English, in the hope that this information may be useful to future researchers.

The sections below are arranged in the same order as the book chapters; that is, largely by country, with two multinational lists.

Brazil

Bernardi Jr., Hermes. 2014. *Eu é um outro* (I'm Another One). Porto Alegre: Edelbra.
Brasiliense, Leonardo. 2014. *Sofia e Mônica* (Sofia and Mônica). Porto Alegre: Edelbra.
Leite, Márcia. 2009. *Do jeito que a gente é* (Just the Way We Are). São Paulo: Ed. Ática.
Porto, Marli. 2014. *Bem-te-vi* (Great Kiskadee). São Paulo: Editora Orgástica.
Ramos, Anna Cláudia. 1999. *Sempre por perto* (Always Around). Rio de Janeiro: Ao Livro Técnico.

France

Breurec, Joël. 2013. *Un garçon comme une autre* (A Boy Like Any Other Girl). Paris: Oskar.
Cantin, Illana. 2018. *Georges, le monde et moi* (Georges, the World and Me). Vanves: Hachette Livre.
Cendres, Axl. 2015. *Dysfonctionnelle* (Dysfunctional). Paris: Éditions Sarbacane.
Ji, Erwan. 2017. *J'ai avalé un arc-en-ciel* (I Swallowed a Rainbow). Paris: Éditions Nathan.
Murail, Marie-Aude. (2016) 2018. *Sauveur & fils: Saison 1* (Saviour & Son: Season 1), 2nd ed. Paris: L'École des Loisirs.
———. (2016) 2019. *Sauveur & fils: Saison 2* (Saviour & Son: Season 2), 2nd ed. Paris: L'École des Loisirs.
Roth, Madeline. 2015. *À ma source gardée* (At My Secret Spring). Paris: Éditions Thierry Magnier.

Germany

Axster, Lilly. 2014. *Atalanta Läufer_in* (Atalanta Runner). Wien: Zaglossus.
Fehér, Christine. 2016. *Weil ich so bin* (Because That's the Way I Am). Hamburg: Carlsen.
Fessel, Karen-Susan. 2005. *Jenny mit O* (Jenny with an O). Berlin: Querverlag.

Greenland

Korneliussen, Niviaq. 2013. 'San Francisco'. In *Inuusuttut – nunatsinni nunarsuarmilu / Ung i Grønland – Ung i verden* (Young in Greenland – And in the World), edited by Katja Vahl and Lene Therkildsen, 64–82 (Greenlandic edition) / 86–106 (Danish edition). Nuuk: Atuakkiortut, NAPA and milik publishing.

———. 2014. *Homo Sapienne.* Nuuk: milik publishing.

———. 2020a. *Blomsterdalen* (Valley of Flowers). Copenhagen: Gyldendal [Danish version].

———. 2020b. *Naasuliardarpi* (Valley of Flowers). Nuuk: milik publishing [Greenlandic version].

India

Adiga, Aravind. 2017. *Selection Day: A Novel.* New York: Scribner.

Dawesar, Abha. 2005. *Babyji.* Toronto: Anchor Books.

Laxmi, Raj Rao, and P. G. Joshi. 2015. *Me Hijra, Me Laxmi.* Oxford: Oxford University Press.

Mehta, Rahul. 2017. *No Other World: A Novel.* New York: Harper.

Pattanaik, Devdutt. 2015. *Shikhandi and Other Tales They Don't Tell You.* New Delhi: Zubaan and Penguin Books India.

Reardon, Robin. 2007. *A Secret Edge.* New York: Kensington.

Sankar, Hemanjali. 2017. *Talking of Muskaan.* Chennai: Duckbill Books & Publications Pvt. Ltd.

Satyal, Rakesh. *Blue Boy.* 2009. New York: Kensington Books.

Selvadurai, Shyam. 1994. *Funny Boy.* Toronto: McClelland and Stewart.

———. 2005. *Swimming in the Monsoon Sea.* New York: Tundra Books.

Shraya, Vivek. 2014. *She of the Mountains.* Vancouver: Arsenal Pulp Press.

———. 2016. *The Boy & the Bindi.* Illustrated by Rajni Perera. Vancouver: Arsenal Pulp Press.

Indigenous/Two-Spirit

Dimaline, Cherie. 2017. *The Marrow Thieves.* Toronto: Dancing Cat.

Hunt, Dallas. 2018. *Awâsis and the World-Famous Bannock.* Illustrated by Amanda Strong. Winnipeg: Highwater Press.

Jones, Adam Garnet. 2018. *Fire Song.* Toronto: Annick Press.

Justice, Daniel Heath. 2011. *The Way of Thorn and Thunder: The Kynship Chronicles.* Albuquerque: University of New Mexico Press.

Lucashenko, Melissa. 1998. *Killing Darcy.* St. Lucia: University of Queensland Press.

Maracle, Lee. 2002. *Will's Garden.* Penticton: Theytus.

Nicholson, Hope, ed. 2016. *Love Beyond Body, Space and Time: An Indigenous LGBT Sci-Fi Anthology.* Winnipeg: Bedside Press.

Thomas, Jared. 2016. *Songs that Sound Like Blood.* Broome: Magabala Books.

Van Camp, Richard. 2011. *Kiss Me Deadly*. Illustrated by C. Auchter. Courtenay: Healthy Aboriginal Network.

Whitehead, Joshua. 2018. *Jonny Appleseed: A Novel*. Vancouver: Arsenal Pulp Press.

Italy

Kramer, Fabri, and Luca Panzini. 2014a. *Ho 2 mamme* (I Have 2 Mums). Illustrated by Luca Panzini. Florence: Terra Nuova Edizioni.

———. 2014b. *Ho 2 papà* (I Have 2 Dads) Illustrated by Luca Panzini. Florence: Terra Nuova Edizioni.

Pardi, Francesca. 2011. *Piccolo uovo* (Little Egg). Illustrated by Altan. Milan: Lo Stampatello.

———. 2012. *Perché hai due mamme?* (Why Have You Got Two Mummies?). Illustrated by Annalisa Sanmartino and Giulia Torelli. Milan: Lo Stampatello.

———. 2014. *Perché hai due papà?* (Why Have You Got Two Daddies?). Illustrated by Annalisa Sanmartino and Giulia Torelli. Milan: Lo Stampatello.

Multinational: Donor Insemination in Children's Books from Around the World

Alfonso, Débora. 2018. *Dos mamás: un cuento para todas las familias (Two Mums: A Story for All Families)*. Madrid: Libros.com.

Barnsley, Nina, and Stephanie Clarkson. 2018. *Our Story: How We Became a Family*. Nottingham: Donor Conception Network.

Bateman, Sandra. 2019. *Mummy and Mummy Want a Family*. Shrewsbury: National Fertility Society.

Baxter, Nicola, and Donor Conception Network. 2002. *Our Story (Sperm Donation for Lesbian Couples)*. Nottingham: Donor Conception Network.

Bird, L. L. 2014. *It Takes Love (And Some Other Stuff) To Make a Baby*. Illustrated by Patrick Girouard. Richmond, CA: Catadon Press.

Celcer, Iréné, and Horatio Gatto. 2018. *Hope & Rosie Have a Baby: The Gift of Family*. Niskayuna, NY: Graphite Press.

Denysenko, Larysa. 2017. майя та її матерів (Maya and Her Moms). Zhytomyr: Vydavnytstvo.

Düperthal, Helene, and Lisa Hänsch. 2016. *Mama + Mamusch: ‚Ich bin ein Herzenswunsch-Kind'* (Mum + Mummy: 'I Am a Longed-For Child'). Lennestadt: Lebensweichen-Verlag.

Franch, Judit. 2015. *Mamá y mami sueñan con un bichito de luz (Mum and Mummy Dream About a Little Lightning Bug)*. Blanes, Spain: Liberum Vox Books Ltd.

———. 2016. *Mum and Mummy Dream About a Little Lightning Bug*. Blanes, Spain: Liberum Vox Books Ltd.

Frisina, Aurélie. 2017. *Recettes de famille: ou comment Marou est né sans papa* (Family Recipes: Or How Marou Was Born Without a Daddy). France: Independently published.

Grimes, Janice. 2004. *Before You Were Born: Our Wish for a Baby*. Illustrated by Mary Moye-Rowley. Webster, IA: X, Y, and Me.

Halvorsen, Lone, and Maria Therese Olsen. 2015. *Wilma har to mammaer* (Wilma Has Two Mothers). Larvik, Norway: LIV Forlag.

Ibarra, Olga, and Maria Pérez Pacheco. (2018). *Tenemos 2 mamás: ¿de dónde venimos?* (We Have Two Mothers: Where Do We Come From?) Madrid: La Locomotora Editorial.

Janson, Paul. 2013. *The Child in the Mamas' Hearts*. Illustrated by Kevin Scott Gierman. Morrisville, NC: Lulu.

Kanterezhi, Yevgeniya. 2012. *Special Man*. Toms River, NJ: CreateSpace Independent Publishing Platform.

Kluger-Bell, Kimberly. 2014. *The Pea That Was Me: A Two Moms' Sperm Donation Story*. Toms River, NJ: CreateSpace Independent Publishing Platform.

Kramer, Fabri, and Luca Panzini. 2013. *Some People Have Two Mums*. Toms River, NJ: CreateSpace Independent Publishing Platform.

Lhuillier, Céline. 2018. *Les graines magiques* (The Magic Seeds). Nancy, France: Independently published.

Lopes, Helena Prado. 2013. *Minhas mães e eu: a história Regina e Vanessa* (My Mothers and Me: Regina and Vanessa's Story). Illustrated by Alessandra Tozi. Santa Cecilia, SP, Brazil: Independently published.

López Navarro, Paula. 2017. *¿Cómo es posible que tengan dos mamás?* (How is it Possible for Them to Have Two Mums?) Spain: Independently published.

Luelmo, Violeta Morales. 2013. *Tenemos dos mamás* (We Have Two Mothers). Madrid: Editorial Crececuentos.

Lundborg, Annette, and Mimmi Tollerup-Grkovic. 1999. *Malins mamma gifter sig med Lisa* (Malin's Mother Marries Lisa). Illustrated by Mimmi Tollerup-Grkovic. Stockholm: Eriksson & Lindgren.

MacLeod, Amanda. 2010. *A Very Special Baby*. Illustrated by Sam Taylor. Napier, New Zealand: Independently published.

Maestro, Rosa. 2014. *Nora y Zoe: dos mamás para un bebé* (Nora and Zoe: Two Mothers for a Baby). Illustrated by Bárbara Guillén Feltrer. Madrid: Masola.org.

Marie, Julie. 2019. *Happy Together: A Two-Mom Sperm Donation Story*. Illustrated by Ashley Lucas. United States: Happy Together Children's Books.

Miles, Rebecca-Jayne. 2018. *One in Many Millions*. Illustrated by Anil Tortop. Boondall: Tadaa Book.

Neumann-May, Bianca. 2017. *Blib, Blob, and Blub*. Harleston, UK: Independently published.

Newman, Lesléa. 1989. *Heather Has Two Mommies*. Illustrated by Diana Souza. Boston, MA: Alyson Publications.

Pardi, Francesca. 2012. *Perché hai due mamme?* (Why Do You Have Two Mummies?) Milan: Lo Stampatello.

Pounders, Megan. 2019. *The Little Embryo That Could: An Introduction to IVF for Children*. Lexington, KY: Independently published.

Rella, Tina. 2012. *Mom, Mama, and Me… and How I Came to Be!* Illustrated by Monica Meza. Lexington, KY: Guess Who? Multimedia.

Reuveny Bar David, Lee. 2015. אמא בטן, אמא לב (*Ima beten, ima lev* / Belly Mommy, Heart Mommy). Tel Aviv: Yuval Publishing.

Rodríguez García, Isabel Carmen. 2008. *Y nosotros—¿de dónde venimos?* (And Us – Where Do We Come From?) Illustrated by M. Luisa Guerrero. Alicante: ONG por la No Discriminación.

Scheerer, Susanne. 2018. *Zwei Mamas für Oscar: Wie aus einem Wunsch ein Wunder wird (The Yearnling: From Wish to Miracle).* Illustrated by Annabelle Von Sperber. Hamburg: Ellermann.

———. 2019. *The Yearnling: From Wish to Miracle.* Illustrated by Annabelle Von Sperber. Hamburg: Ellermann.

Schmitz-Weicht, Cai. 2015. *Maxime will ein Geschwister* (Maxime Wants a Sibling). Illustrated by Ka Schmitz. Darmstadt: Atelier 9¾.

Seggelen, Mireille van. 2010. *A Little Miracle.* Illustrated by Anouk Braakhuis. Budel: MVS Creations.

Silverberg, Cory. 2013. *What Makes a Baby: A Book for Every Kind of Family and Every Kind of Kid.* New York: Seven Stories Press.

Sizaret, Nathalie. 2017. *Pourquoi tu as 2 mamans? (Why Do You Have 2 Mums?)* Illustrated by Daphné Dejay. Charenton-le-Pont: Le monde de Gritie.

Stamm, Linda J. 2016. *Family Stew: Two Moms Use a Sperm Donor to Build Their Family.* Illustrated by Fátima Stamato. Niskayuna, NY: Graphite Press.

Sturniolo, Sheri. 2019. *You Were Made for Me: Mom Mom.* Illustrated by Hanna Pak and Shay Larby. United States: Made For Me.

Thorn, Petra, and Lisa Green. 2009. *Die Geschichte unserer Familie: ein Buch für lesbische Familien mit Wunschkindern durch Samenspende (The Story of Our Family: A Book for Lesbian Families with Children Conceived by Donor Insemination).* Illustrated by Tiziana Rinaldi. Mörfelden: FamART-Verlag.

———. 2013. *The Story of Our Family: A Book for Lesbian Families with Children Conceived by Donor Insemination.* Illustrated by Tiziana Rinaldi. Mörfelden, FamART.

Tyner, Christy. 2015. *Zak's Safari: A Story About Donor-Conceived Kids of Two-Mom Families.* Illustrated by Ciaee. New York: CreateSpace.

Wallis, Emma. 2018a. *How Mummy and Mama Made You: Conceived at Home.* Bognor Regis: Independently published.

———. 2018b. *How Mummy and Mama Made a Baby: IVF.* Bognor Regis: Independently published.

Walpole, Zera. 2012. *Under a Rainbow.* Perth: Blurb.

Multinational: Same-Sex Couples in Children's Books from Around the World

Barbero, Cinzia. 2011. *Più ricche di un re* (Richer Than a King). Milan: Lo Stampatello.

Berg, Sara, and Karin Frimodig. 2015. *Pyret and Pingvinpapporna* (Little One and the Penguin Dads). Illustrated by Johanna Arpiainen. Borgholm: Vombat Förlag.

Beuningen, Gea van. 2011. *De mama's van Sterre* (The Mommies of Sterre). Illustrated by Tinne Van den Bossche. Antwerpen: t'Verschil.

Carrasco, Walcyr. 2010. *Meus dois pais* (My Two Fathers). Illustrated by Laurent Cardon. São Paulo: Editora Ática.

Chazerand, Émilie. 2017. *Les Papas de Violette* (Violette's Dads). Illustrated by Gaëlle Souppart. Vanves: Gautier-Languereau.

Clark, Cheril N., and Monica Bey-Clarke. 2016. *Keesha's South African Adventure*. Illustrated by Julia Selyutina. Sicklerville: Dodi Press/My Family!

Crawford, Georgina. 2009. *The Tales of Zebedy-Do-Dah*. Illustrated by Emily McCann. London: Onlywomen Press.

Fernández, Darío. 2013. *Anita y sus dos mamas* (Anita and her Two Moms). Buenos Aires, Argentina: Editorial Molinos de Viento.

Ferrari, Verónica. 2015. *Camila tiene dos mamas?* (Camila Has Two Moms?). Illustrated by Mayra Avila. Lima: El Armario do Zoe.

Guerra, Julián. 2016. *Martín y la tarta de chocolate* (Martín and the Chocolate Cake). Illustrated by Carles Ponsì. Sevilla: Editorial Samarcanda.

Haan, Linda de. 2016. *Lance & Lot zoeken zich rot* (Lance & Lot Are Looking Hard). Amsterdam: Uitgeverij Ploegsma.

Lindeberg, Minna. 2001. *Allan och Udo* (Allan and Udo). Illustrated by Linda Bondestam. Helsingfors: Söderströms.

Link, Michael. 2002. *Komm, ich zeig dir meine Eltern* (Come, I'll Show You My Parents). Illustrated by Sabine Schöneich. Hamburg: Edition Riesenrad.

Martelli, Márcio. 2010. *Eu tenho duas mães* (I Have Two Mothers). Illustrated by Tiago Ramos. Jardim Paris, Jundiaí: Editoria In House.

Merchant, Ed. 2010. *Dad David, Baba Chris and Me*. Illustrated by Rachel Fuller. London: British Association for Adoption and Fostering.

Müller, Barbara. 2012. *Florian & Florian*. Illustrated by Tanja Strobl. Wien: Auflage.

Neri, Bernadette Villanueva. 2012. *Ang Ikaklit sa aming hardin (Ikaklit in our Garden)*. Illustrated by CJ de Silva. Manila: Raintree Trading and Publishing Inc.

Pardi, Francesca. 2014. *Perché hai due papà?* (Why Do You Have Two Fathers?). Illustrated by Annalisa Sanmartino and Giulia Torelli. Milan: Lo Stampatello.

Pilátová, Markéta. 2012. *Jura a lama (Jura and Llama)*. Illustrated by Dora Dutková. Prague: LePress.

Polacco, Patricia. 2009. *In Our Mothers' House*. New York: Philomel Books.

Reixach, Laura. 2010. *Cebollino y Pimentón* (Cebollino and Pimentón). Barcelona: Edicions Bellaterra.

Reuveny Bar David, Lee. 2015. אמא בטן, אמא לב (*Ima beten, ima lev* / Belly Mommy, Heart Mommy). Illustrated by Tehila Goldberg. Tel Aviv: Yuval Publications.

Richardson, Justin, and Peter Parnell. 2005. *And Tango Makes Three*. Illustrated by Henry Cole. New York: Simon & Schuster.

Rossetti, Ana. 2005. *Las bodas reales: cuento para colorear* (The Royal Weddings: A Story to Colour). Illustrated by Jorge Artajo. Barcelona: Ediciones Bellaterra.

Schreiber-Wicke, Edith. 2006. *Zwei Papas für Tango* (Two Papas for Tango). Illustrated by Carola Holland. Stuttgart: Thienemann.

Setterington, Ken. 2004. *Mom and Mum are Getting Married.* Illustrated by Alice Priestley. Toronto: Second Story Press.

Skåhlberg, Anette. 2013. *Jösta och Johan* (Jösta and Johan). Illustrated by Katarina Dahlquist. Uppsala: Sagolikt.

Thériault, Michel. 2017. *Ils sont…* (They Are…). Illustrated by Magali Ben. Moncton: Bouton d'or Acadie.

Valente, Anaïs, and Ariane Delrieu. 2013. *Drôles de familles* (Funny Families). Clermont-Ferrand: Tournez la page jeunesse.

Viogt, Ina. 2015. *Wie heiraten eigentlich Trockennasenaffen?* (How Do Dry-Nosed Monkeys Marry?). Illustrated by Jacky Gleich. Solothurn: kwasi Verlag.

Philippines

Alberto, Jesh. 2018. *Bukas na si Cajon* (Cajon is Now Open). Illustrated by Gabbi Ramirez. Quezon City: Center for Youth Advocacy and Networking, Inc. Also available online at http://tinyurl.com/mulatsulat

Benavidez, Angelo. 2018. *Si Chowchow.* Illustrated by Aiko Shimzu. Quezon City: Center for Youth Advocacy and Networking, Inc. Also available online at http://tinyurl.com/mulatsulat

Boquiren, Mark Norman. 2019. 'Ang pangarap ng Tropang K.I.D.L.A.T. (The Dream of K.I.D.L.A.T. Gang)'. In *Hulagpos*, edited by Eugene Evasco and Segundo Matias Jr., 105–16. Quezon City: Lampara Books.

Dancel, Godfrey T. 2018. *Dumating na si Manang Elisa* (Sister Elisa Finally Came). Illustrated by Gabbi Ramirez. Quezon City: Center for Youth Advocacy and Networking, Inc. Also available online at http://tinyurl.com/mulatsulat

Evasco, Eugene Y. 2018. *Ang nanay ni Erwin/Ang tatay ni Klara (Erwin's Mama/Klara's Papa).* Illustrated by Tokwa Peñaflorida. Translated by Karen Ferry-Fernandez. Quezon City: Kahel Press.

Frany, Arkin. 2018. *One of the Boys (or How Kenny Saved the City of Toyland).* Illustrated by Fides Balmaceda. Quezon City: Center for Youth Advocacy and Networking, Inc. Also available online at http://tinyurl.com/mulatsulat

Garcia, Kata. 2018. *My Family.* Illustrated by Borg Sinaban. Quezon City: Adarna House.

Garlítos, Rhandee. 2013. *Ang bonggang-bonggang batang beki! (The Fierce and Fabulous Boy in Pink!)* Illustrated by Tokwa Salazar Peñaflorida. Quezon City: Chikiting Books.

Guzman, Michael de. 2018. *Dalawa ang daddy ni Billy. (Billy Has Two Daddies).* Illustrated by Daniel Palma Tayona. Makati City: Tahanan Books for Young Readers.

———. 2019. 'Reyna Elena'. In *Baklas*, edited by Eugene Evasco and Segundo Matias Jr., 137–44. Quezon City: Lampara Books.

Neri, Bernadette Villanueva. 2012. *Ang Ikaklit sa aming hardin. (Ikaklit in our Garden).* Illustrated by CJ de Silva. Manila: Raintree Trading & Publishing, Inc./Publikasyong Twamkittens.

Ruedas, Mondi. 2018. *What's My Power Gear?* Illustrated by Ruthie Genuino. Quezon City: Center for Youth Advocacy and Networking, Inc. Also available online at http://tinyurl.com/mulatsulat

Sayuno, Cheeno Marlo. 2020. *Sayaw ni Dayaw* (Dayaw's Dance). Illustrated by Harry Monzon. Anvil Publishing.

Slovenia

Arold, Marliese. 2002. *Sandra ljubi Meike* (*Einfach nur Liebe: Sandra liebt Meike* / Simply Love: Sandra Loves Meike). Translated by Andrea Švab. Ljubljana: Grlica (Na robu).

Bach, Tamara. 2007. *Punca z Marsa (Marsmädchen / Girl from Mars)*. Translated by Barbara Lipovšek. Ljubljana: Karantanija (Najhit).

Bevc, Cvetka. 2011. *Desetka* (Ten of Us). Ljubljana: Arsem.

Dolenc, Mate. 2009. 'Pingo in Frigo (Pingo and Frigo)'. In *Kraljičin lipicanec in druge zgodbe* by Mate Dolenc, illustrated by Adriano Janežič, 55–59. Ljubljana: Mladika (Trepetlika).

Kermauner, Aksinja. 2006. *Berenikini kodri* (Berenice's Curls). Dob pri Domžalah: Miš (Z(o)renja+).

———. 2008. *Orionov meč* (Orion's Sword). Dob pri Domžalah: Miš (Z(o)renja+).

Kraigher, Nada. 1971. *Maja* (Maja). Ljubljana: Prešernova družba. Reprinted in 1979 by Mladinska knjiga (Odisej).

Lupša, Maja. 2012. 'Očka (Two Daddies)'. Illustrated by Tanja Komadina. *Ciciban* 67, no. 7: 18–19.

Mozetič, Brane. 2014. *Prva ljubezen* (First Love). Illustrated by Maja Kastelic. Ljubljana: Škuc (Lambda).

———. 2017. *Murenček in Polhek* (Cricket and Dormouse). Illustrated by Andrej Brumen Čop. Ljubljana: Škuc (Lambda).

———. 2020a. *Ahil in Patrokles* (Achilles and Patroclus). Illustrated by Ana Lucija Šarić. Ljubljana: Škuc (Lambda).

———. 2020b. *Rožnate zgodbe iz neheteronormativne zgodovine (za mlade)* (Pink Stories from Non-Heteronormative History (for the Young)). Illustrated by Ana Lucija Šarić. Ljubljana: Škuc (Lambda).

Murail, Marie-Aude. 2013. *Oh, boy! (Oh, boy!)*. Translated by Jedrt Maležič. Dob pri Domžalah: Miš.

Novšak, France. (1938) 2016. *Dečki: roman iz dijaškega internata* (Boys: A Novel from a Boarding School). Ljubljana: Škuc (Lambda).

Pavček, Tone. 1958. *Juri Muri v Afriki* (Juri Muri in Africa). Illustrated by Melita Vovk. Ljubljana: Mladinska knjiga (Cicibanova knjižnica).

———. 2001. *Juri Muri drugič v Afriki* (Juri Muri in Africa Again). Illustrated by Marjanca Jemec-Božič. Ljubljana: Mladinska knjiga (Cicibanov vrtiljak / Velike slikanice).

———. 2011. *Juri Muri po Sloveniji* (Juri Muri Around Slovenia). Illustrated by Damijan Stepančič. Dob pri Domžalah: Miš.

———. 2012. *Juri Muri gre po srečo* (Juri Muri Looking for Happiness). Illustrated by Damijan Stepančič. Dob pri Domžalah: Miš.

Percivale, Tommaso. 2016. 'Ko sem se prvič poljubil' ('La prima volta che ho baciato / The First Time That I Kissed'. In *Ko sem prvič* (*La prima volta che* / The First Time), translated by Karmen Filipič, 7–31. Izola: Grlica.

Schimel, Lawrence, 2008. *Sosedje in prijatelji* (*Amigos y vecinos* / Friends and Neighbours). Illustrated by Sara Rojo Pérez, translated by Marjeta Drobnič. Ljubljana: Škuc (Lambda).

Sokolov, Cvetka. 2019. *Bo res vse v redu?* (Will Everything Really Be Okay?). Illustrated by Marta Bartolj. Dob pri Domžalah: Miš (Prva z(o)renja).

Spacal, Alenka. 2013a. *Mavrična maškarada* (Rainbow Masquerade). Ljubljana: Škuc (Lambda).

———. 2018a. *Kako ti je ime?* (What's Your Name?). Maribor: Bajalka.

———. 2018b. *Modre ptičje misli* (Blue Bird Wisdoms). Maribor: Bajalka.

Tratnik, Suzana. 2001. *Ime mi je Damjan* (My Name Is Damjan). Ljubljana: Škuc (Lambda). Reprinted in 2014 by Mladinska knjiga (Odisej).

———. 2014a. 'Jebeno pismo (The Damn Letter)'. In *Prvič (Losing It)*, edited by Keith Gray, 189–208. Ljubljana: Mladinska knjiga (Odisej).

———. 2017. *Tombola ali življenje!* (Bingo or Life!). Ljubljana: Mladinska knjiga (Odisej).

Vidmar, Janja. 2005. *Fantje iz gline* (Clay Boys). Ljubljana: Mladinska knjiga (Odisej).

———. 2006. *Softibluz* (Softy Blues). Illustrated by Matjaž Schmidt. Ljubljana: Prešernova družba (Koledarska zbirka).

Woltz, Anna, and Vicky Janssen. 2012. *Dekle z Marsa* (*Meisje van Mars* / The Girl from Mars). Translated by Katjuša Ručigaj. Dob pri Domžalah: Miš (Z(o)renja+).

South Korea

Gil, Sanghyo. 2016. 최고 빵집 아저씨는 치마를 입어요 (*Chwego bbangjip ahjussineun chimaleul ibuhyo* / The Best Baker in Town Wears a Dress). Seoul: Seed Book.

Ko, Jae-eun. 2018. 내 이름은 김신데렐라 (*Neh ireumeun gimshinderella* / My Name is Cinderella Kim). Paju: Munhakdongne.

Lee, Chae. 2015. 꽁치의 옷장엔 치마만 100개 (*Ggongchieui otjangen chimaman baekge* / Gongchi Has At Least 100 Skirts in His Wardrobe). Seoul: Ligem.

Spain

Acosta, Alicia, and Luis Amavisca. 2018. *¡Vivan las uñas de colores!* (*I Love My Colorful Nails!*). Illustrated by Gusti. Madrid: NubeOcho. [Spanish edition]

———. 2019a. *Gora koloretako azazkalak!* (*I Love My Colorful Nails!*). Illustrated by Gusti, translated by Mari Eli Ituarte Zarragoikoetxea. Bilbao: Mezulari. [Basque edition]

———. 2019b. *Visca les ungles de colors!* (*I Love My Colorful Nails!*). Illustrated by Gusti, translated by Marta Morros Serret. Madrid: NubeOcho. [Catalan edition]

Amavisca, Luis. 2012. *La princesa Li* / *Princess Li*. Illustrated by Elena Rendeiro. España: Editorial Egales, NubeOcho Ediciones. [Bilingual edition Spanish-English]

Andrés, José Carlos. 2013. *Mi papá es un payaso / My Dad is a Clown*. Illustrated by Natalia Hernández. España: Editorial Egales, NubeOcho. [Bilingual edition Spanish-English]

Cormand, Bernat. 2012. *El niño perfecto* (The Perfect Boy). Barcelona: Sd·edicions. [Spanish edition]

———. 2013. *El nen perfecte* (The Perfect Boy). Barcelona: Sd·edicions. [Catalan edition]

———. 2018a. *Els dies feliços* (Happy Days). Barcelona: A Buen Paso. [Catalan edition]

———. 2018b. *Los días felices* (Happy Days). Barcelona: A Buen Paso. [Spanish edition]

Dios, Olga de. 2013. *Monstruo rosa* (Pink Monster). Zaragoza: Apila Ediciones. [Spanish edition]

———. 2016. *Munstro arrosa* (Pink Monster). Translated by Ipar Alkain Kazabon. Berriozar: Denonartean. [Basque edition]

———. 2019. *Monstre rosa* (Pink Monster). Translated by Verok Agency. Barcelona: Estrella Polar. [Catalan edition]

Mendieta, M. José. 2004. *Aitorrek bi ama ditu* (Aitor Has Two Mums). Illustrated by Mabel Piérola. Donostia: Erein. [Basque edition]

———. 2006a. *Aitor tiene dos mamás* (Aitor Has Two Mums). Illustrated by Mabel Piérola. Barcelona: Edicions Bellaterra. [Spanish edition]

———. 2006b. *L'Aitor te dues mares* (Aitor Has Two Mums). Illustrated by Mabel Piérola, translated by Agnès Bergua. Barcelona: Edicions Bellaterra. [Catalan edition]

Moncó, Beatriz. 2004. *Mercedes quiere ser bombera* (Mercedes Wants to be a Firewoman). Illustrated by Mabel Piérola. Barcelona: Edicions Bellaterra. [Spanish edition]

———. 2009. *La Mercè vol ser bombera* (Mercedes Wants to be a Firewoman). Illustrated by Mabel Piérola. Barcelona: Edicions Bellaterra. [Catalan edition]

Moscada, Neus. 2009. *Dues rodones idèntiques?* (Two Identical Circles?). Barcelona: Sd·edicions. [Catalan edition]

Pavón, Mar. 2015a. *Això no és normal! (That's Not Normal!)*. Illustrated by Laure du Faÿ. Málaga: NubeOcho. [Catalan edition]

———. 2015b. *¡Eso no es normal! (That's Not Normal!)*. Illustrated by Laure du Faÿ. Málaga: NubeOcho. [Spanish edition]

Piñán, Berta. 2007. *Las cosas que le gustan a Fran* (Things That Fran Likes). Illustrated by Antonia Santolaya Ruiz-Clavijo. Madrid: Hotel Papel.

Pita, Charo. 2009a. *Velliñas* (Little Old Ladies). Illustrated by Fátima Afonso. Pontevedra: OQO Editora. [Galician edition]

———. 2009b. *Viejecitas* (Little Old Ladies). Illustrated by Fátima Afonso. Pontevedra: OQO Editora. [Spanish edition]

Quintiá, Xerardo. 2007a. *Titiritesa* (*Titiritess*). Illustrated by Maurizio. A. C. Quarello. Pontevedra: OQO Editora. [Galician edition]

———. 2007b. *Titiritesa* (*Titiritess*). Illustrated by Maurizio. A. C. Quarello. Pontevedra: OQO Editora. [Spanish edition]

———. 2007c. *Titirimari* (*Titiritess*). Illustrated by Maurizio. A. C. Quarello, translated by Arkaitz Goikoetxea. Tafalla: Txalaparta. [Basque edition]

Reixach, Laura. 2010a. *Cebollino y Pimentón (Onion and Pepper)*. Barcelona: Edicions Bellaterra. [Spanish edition]

———. 2010b. *En Ceba i en Pebre (Onion and Pepper)*. Barcelona: Edicions Bellaterra. [Catalan edition]

Schimel, Lawrence. 2018a. *No es hora de jugar* (*Bedtime, Not Playtime*). Illustrated by Elina Braslina. Barcelona: Editorial Egales. [Spanish edition]

———. 2018b. *No és hora de jugar* (*Bedtime, Not Playtime*). Illustrated by Elina Braslina. Barcelona: Editorial Egales. [Catalan edition]

Tofiño, Iñaki, and Sebastià Martín. 2008a. *La festa d'en Blai* (Blai's Party). Illustrated by Mabel Piérola. Barcelona: Edicions Bellaterra. [Catalan edition].

———. 2008b. *La fiesta de Blas* (Blas's Party). Illustrated by Mabel Piérola. Barcelona: Edicions Bellaterra. [Spanish edition].

Sweden

Ahlund, Anna, and Cina Friedner, eds. 2018. *Hetare: elva noveller som känns* (Hotter: Eleven Short Stories That Make an Impression). Stockholm: Rabén & Sjögren.

Edelfeldt, Inger. 1977. *Duktig pojke!* (Good Boy!). Stockholm: Rabén & Sjögren.

Elfgren, Sara Bergmark. 2017. *Norra Latin* (North Latin). Stockholm: Rabén & Sjögren.

Ericson, Elias S. 2013. *Åror* (Oars). Stockholm: Ordfront Galago.

Gustavsson, Hanna. 2015. *Iggy 4-ever*. Stockholm: Ordfront Galago.

Hellberg, Hans-Eric. 1977. *Love love love*. Stockholm: Bonnier.

Juslin, Emma. 2007. *Frida och Frida* (Frida and Frida). Helsinki: Schildts Söderströms.

Jägerfeld, Jenny. 2016. *Brorsan är kung!* (Bro' Is King!). Stockholm: Rabén & Sjögren.

Karlsson, Ylva, and Sofia Falkenhem. 2020. *Månen, varelsen och jag* (The Moon, the Creature and I). Stockholm: Rabén & Sjögren.

Karlström, Lars. 1989. *Pelle älskar Nicke* (Pelle Loves Nicke). Arboga, Sweden: Textab.

Kolterjahn, Jessica. 2007. *Ut ur skuggan* (Out of the Shadow). Stockholm: Forum.

Laestadius, Ann-Helén. 2012. *Hitta hem* (Finding Home). Stockholm: Rabén och Sjögren.

Lindquist, Håkan. 2003. *Om att samla frimärken* (Collecting Stamps). Stockholm: Kabusa.

Lodalen, Mian. 2010. *Tiger* (Tiger). Stockholm: Månpocket.

Lundqvist, Jesper, and Bettina Johansson. 2012. *Kivi & Monsterhund* (Kivi & Monster Dog). Linköping: Olika.

Lövestam, Sara. 2016. *Skarven* (The Cormorant). Stockholm: Lilla Piratförlaget.

Nilsson, Johanna. 2018. *Om vi bara kunde byta kroppar med varandra* (If Only We Could Exchange Bodies). Stockholm: Rabén & Sjögren.

Nilsson, Åsa. 2005. *Dags att våga* (Time to Dare). Stockholm: Opal.

Olbers Croall, Moa-Lina. 2006. *Sen tar vi Berlin* (Next We'll Take Berlin). Stockholm: Alfabeta.

———. 2016. *I mitt namn: en bok om att vara trans* (In My Name: A Book About Being Transgender). Stockholm: Natur & Kultur.

Olsson, Hans. 1993. *Spelar Roll* (Playing a Role). Stockholm: Alfabeta.

Pohl, Peter. 1985. *Janne, min vän* (*Johnny, My Friend*). Stockholm: AWE/Geber.

Sandgren, Hilding. 2016. *Vägarna är som tvättbrädor här* (The Roads Are Like Washboards Here). Stockholm: Galago.

Sandhagen, Ingrid. 2000. *En av dem* (One of Them). Stockholm: Bonnier Carlsen.

Sandreyo, Johannes. 2012. *Ung, bög och jävligt kär* (Young, Gay and So Fucking In Love). Stockholm: Vombat Förlag.

Schiefauer, Jessica. 2011. *Pojkarna* (The Boys). Stockholm: Bonnier Carlsen.

Timgren, Katja. 2004. *Det jag inte säger* (What I Don't Say). Stockholm, Rabén & Sjögren.

Wallensten, Hanna. 2005. *I närheten av solen* (Close to the Sun). Stockholm: Forum.

INDEX

Bold number indicates figures and tables.

2040 (Kleist et al.) 77

À ma source gardée (Roth) 35, 39–40, 43
Aamma illit inuuneraat (Hansen) 78
Aboriginal and Torres Strait Islanders 118n1, 119–20, 122–23
abuse 234, 241, 311n21
  emotional 311
  in childhood/adolescence 44, 85, 202, 230, 233, 236, 238, 311
  sexual 85, 202, 230, 233
  verbal 36, 232, 244. *See also* harassment; hate crime
Acosta, Alicia 263
Adiga, Aravind 101–2
adoption
  in books 241–42
  in France 32
  in Italy 130–31
  in Spain 259
Afonso, Fátima 267
Ahil in Patrokles (Mozetič) 230, **231**, 236
'Ai ka' (Yi) 251
AIDS. *See* HIV
Aitorrek bi ama ditu (Mendieta) 268–69
Albertalli, Becky 103
Alberto, Jesh 210–11
Alfonso, Débora 157
Allan och Udo (Lindeberg) 189, 190, 194
Allatta 77, 81
'Allt jag vill' (Lönnlöv) 293–94
Altan 138–39
Alumiguulik (Olsen Aaju) 78
Amavisca, Luis 263, 266
Amigos y vecinos (Schimel) 241
And Tango Makes Three (Richardson and Parnell) 15, 133–34, 193–94, 270
Andrés, José Carlos 268
Ang bonggang-bonggang batang beki! (Garlítos) 213, **214**
Ang Ikaklit sa aming hardin (Neri) 188, 204–5, **206**, 219
Ang nanay ni Erwin/Ang tatay ni Klara (Evasco) 207, **208**
'Ang pangarap ng Tropang K.I.D.L.A.T.' (Boquiren) 218
animals. *See* anthropomorphism
Anita y sus dos mamas (Fernández) 188
Annie on My Mind (Garden) 230–31
anthropomorphism 139, 210–11, 213–15, 219, 228, 238–40, 252–53. *See also* penguins
anti-discrimination legislation
  in France 31–32
  in Italy 130
  in Slovenia 226
  in South Korea 251
  in Spain 259
  in Sweden 277–78
  in the Philippines 201
'anti-gender' movement 226, 238
Aotearoa 119
Arab world 181–82
Argentina 185, 188
Aristotle and Dante Discover the Secrets of the Universe (Sáenz) 103
'Arnaussâq' 79–81
Arold, Marliese 233
Artajo, Jorge 189, 190, 194
artificial insemination. *See* assisted conception
Asquith, Ros 139
assisted conception 136–37, 147–79
  in Australia 163
  in France 32, 159
  in Germany 157
  in Israel 160
  in Italy 160
  in Norway 161
  in Spain 155, 156

assisted conception (*cont.*)
in Sweden 305
in the United Kingdom 162
in the United States 164–65
list of books on **175–79**, 321–23
research on 152–53, 165, 167–68
assisted reproductive technology. *See* assisted conception
Atalanta Läufer_in (Axster) 60, 64–68, 69
attitudes to LGBTQ\+ people, research on 31, 130, 202
Australia 119–20, 122–23, 163–64
Austria 55–71, 185
aversion therapy, legislation prohibiting 259
Avila, Mayra 188, 193
awards. *See* book awards and accolades
Awâsis and the World-Famous Bannock (Hunt) 125–26
Axster, Lilly 60, 64–69

Babaylan 200
Babyji (Dawesar) 100
Bach, Tamara 233
Baklas (Evasco and Matias) 216
Balmaceda, Fides 216
Barbero, Cinzia 135, 191
Bartolj, Marta 243
Basque 268–69, 271
bathrooms. *See* toilets
Baxter, Nicola 154
Before You Were Born (Grimes) 154
Belbin, David 233
Belgium 185, 188
Bem-te-vi (Porto) 20–24
Ben, Magali 189, 190
Benavidez, Angelo 213
Benvenuti in famiglia (Hoffman) 139–40
Berenikini kodri (Kermauner) 242–43
Bergmark Elfgren, Sara 297, 315–16
Bernardi, Hermes, Jr. 16–17, 21–25
Best Baker in Town Wears a Dress, The (Gil) 253–54
Beuningen, Gea van 188
Bevc, Cvetka 234
Bey-Clarke, Monica 188, 193
bilingual books 77, 78, 204–9, 213, 266, 268
Billy Has Two Daddies (Guzman) 205, **206**
biphobia 31, 36, 43
Bird, L. L. 166
bisexual erasure 37–42, 48, 49
'bisexual plot' 42–45, 49
bisexuality 29–53, 68n41, 102, 103, 234–35
definitions of 30
demographic data on 31
Bishop, Rudine Sims 75, 126
Blib, Blob and Blub (Neumann-May) 162
Blomsterdalen (Korneliussen) 87–88
Blue Boy (Satyal) 100, 103
Bo res vse v redu? (Sokolov) 243–44
Bondestam, Linda 189
book awards and accolades
in Austria 69
in Brazil 25
in Canada 102
in Italy 139, 268
in Slovenia 237
in Sweden 283
in the Philippines 204, 217
in the United States 102
book fairs 182
Boquiren, Mark Norman 218
Boy and the Bindi, The 100
Boyne, John 228, 287
'Boys Who Became the Hummingbirds, The' (Justice) 117, 124
Brasiliense, Leonardo 17–18, 19, 22, 24–25
Braslina, Elina 268
Brazgotine (Rainfield) 234
Brazil 11–28, 185, 188
Breurec, Joël 36–37, 40, 45, 48
Brezenoff, Steve 69
Brooklyn, Burning (Brezenoff) 69
Brorsan är kung! (Jägerfeld) 289, 290
Brumen Čop, Andrej 228
Bukas na si Cajon (Alberto) 211
bullying
of children with LGBTQ\+ parents 205
of young LGBTQ\+ people 20, 232, 233, 234, 241, 289
butch/femme couples 47
Butler, Judith 59, 61, 63

Camila tiene dos mamas? (Ferrari) 188, 193
Canada 185, 189, 190
Cantin, Illana 34–35, 38, 42, 46–47
Carrasco, Walcyr 188
Catalan 261n2, 264–66, 268, 269, 270–71
Catholicism 122, 130, 202, 225–26, 230, 258, 263. *See also* Christianity
Cebollino y Pimentón (Reixach) 194, 270
Cendres, Axl 38, 44–45, 47–48
censorship 32–33, 133, 142, 182, 259

Center for Youth Advocacy and Networking. *See* CYAN
Choyce, Lesley 241
Christianity 14, 74, 77, 120
  Catholicism 122, 130, 202, 225–26, 230, 258, 263
Chwego bbangjip ahjussineun chimaleul ibuhyo (Gil) 253–54
civil partnerships
  in France 32
  in Greenland 77
  in Italy 130–31
  in Slovenia 225–26
  in Sweden 305
Clark, Cheril N. 188, 193
class 140, 188
Cole, Babette 15
Cole, Henry 194, 241, 270
colonialism 117, 120, 122, 200
coming out
  identified as common trope 21–23, 26, 34–35
  to family 18–19, 24, 210–11, 311
    with negative reaction 20–21, 23, 313
    with positive reaction 37, 81, 315
  to friends 18, 22–23, 35, 37
¿Cómo es posible que tengan dos mamás? (López Navarro) 156–57
'confirmation of normality' trope 136, 140–41, 205, 245. *See also* homonormativity
conservative backlash 14, 131, 133, 225–26, 231, 238, 241, 262–63. *See also* right-wing politics
Cormand, Bernat 262–66
counter-storytelling 96–97
Crawford, Georgina 190
Croall, Moa-Lina 284, 286, 311
cross-dressing 15, 236, 252–55, 262, 279–81
crowdfunding 149, 157, 161, 165. *See also* self-publishing
CYAN 203, 210–12, 214, 216, 220
Czech Republic 185

Dad David, Baba Chris and Me (Merchant) 188
Daddy's Roommate (Willhoite) 134
Dags att våga (Nilsson) 315
Dahl, Hjalmer 79
Dalawa ang daddy ni Billy (Guzman) 205, **206**
Daleč od Xanadu (Peters) 233
dance 199–200
Dancel, Geoffrey 212
Danish 73–76, 78–79, 81, 87n16
Dawesar, Abha 100
De mama's van Sterre (Beuningen) 188
De Paola, Tomie 262
de Silva, CJ 204
deadnaming 290, 292–93. *See also* misgendering
Dečki (Novšak) 230
decolonization 120, 123, 126
decriminalization of homosexuality. *See under* homosexuality
Dekle z Marsa (Woltz and Janssen) 241
Delrieu, Ariane 188, 193
demographic data
  for France 31
  for Germany 56
  for India 95
  for Italy 160
  on donor-conceived children 148
Den tatoverede strandvasker (Olsen Aaju) 78n10
Denmark 73–74, 77, 89
depression. *See* mental health difficulties
Desetka (Bevc) 234
Det jag inte säger (Timgren) 311
Det tatoverede budskab (Olsen Aaju) 78n9
Devdutt, Pattanaik 101, 103
didacticism 20, 24, 26, 140–41, 243–44, 289–92
  and lack of literary/artistic quality 20, 140–41, 261–62, 266, 269
Die Geschichte unserer Familie (Thorn and Green) 157–58
Die Mitte der Welt (Steinhöfel) 233
'Different for Boys' (Ness) 234
Dimaline, Cherie 124
Dios, Olga de 270–71
discrimination, research on
  in Canada and the United States 120–21
  in Slovenia 244
  in Sweden 286
divorce 233
Do jeito que a gente é (Leite) 18–19, 21–22, 24–26
Dolenc, Mate 241
domestic partnerships. *See* civil partnerships
donor insemination. *See* assisted conception
Dos mamás (Alfonso) 157
drag kings 293
Dreyd (Justice) 123
Drôles de familles (Valente and Delrieu) 188, 193
du Faÿ, Laure 271
dual-language books. *See* bilingual books

Dues rodones idèntiques? (Moscada) 271, **272**
Duktig pojke! (Edelfeldt) 309–11
Dumating na si Manang Elisa (Dancel) 212
Dutch 188, 241
Dysfonctionnelle (Cendres) 38, 44–45, 47–48
dysphoria. *See* gender dysphoria

Edelfeldt, Inger 309
education systems 14, 74, 200n1. *See also* schools
Egypt 182
Einfach nur Liebe (Arold) 233
El niño perfecto (Cormand) 262, **263**
Els dies feliços (Cormand) 264–66, **265**
En av dem (Sandhagen) 311, 313
En Ceba i en Pebre (Reixach). See *Cebollino y Pimentón* (Reixach)
Ericson, Elias S. 275, 287
erotic literature 293–94
Erwin's Mama/Klara's Papa (Evasco) 207, **208**
¡Eso no es normal! (Pavón) 271
ethnic diversity, lack of 93, 140, 188
ethnicity 253
Eu é um outro (Bernardi) 16–17, 25
Evasco, Eugene Y. 207, 216, 218
Every Day (Levithan) 69

fairy tales 252–54, 266–67
Falkenhem, Sofia 289, 290
Family Book, The (Parr) 134
family diversity 138–39, 205, 207–9
Fantje iz gline (Vidmar) 231–33, 234, 235–36
Far from Xanadu (Peters) 233
fascism 32, 258
Fehér, Christine 60–62, 64
Fernández, Darío 188
Ferrari, Verónica 188, 193
Fessel, Karen-Susan 58–60, 62, 63
Fiengo, Maria Silvia 129, 134, 135
Filipino 199–223. *See also* Tagalog
film 202, 294
Finland 185, 189, 190, 194, 303n1, 313
Fire Song (Jones) 124–25
First/Native Nations 117–28
Flanagan, Victoria 280
foster parents 65, 67
France 29–53, 159, 185, 193, 242
Franco, Francisco 258
Frany, Arkin 216
French 29–53, 159, 189, 190, 193, 242
Frida och Frida (Juslin) 313
friends
  as euphemism for same-gender relationship 228, 244. *See also* homosocial friendships
  as support for LGBTQ\+ characters 20, 21, 252–53, 254, 289
  negative reactions from 18, 22, 35, 289–91
Funny Boy (Selvadurai) 102

Galician 266–67
Garber, Marjorie 42, 44, 45, 49
Garcia, Kata 207–9
Garden, Nancy 230
Garlítos, Rhandee 213
Garvin, Jeff 69
Gay Greenland (book) 79
Gay Greenland (exhibition) 78, 79
gender binary 57, 58–62, 64–65, 67–68
gender dysphoria 58, 62, 281–82, 288, 293–94
gender identity. *See* trans people
gender non-conformity 15, 55–71, 210–13, 216–18, 236, 238–39, 252–55, 262–64. *See also* gender roles/stereotypes; hijras; trans people; Two-Spirit people
gender performativity 61
gender recognition
  in Austria and Germany 56
  in South Korea 251
  in Spain 259
  in Sweden 277, 278
gender roles/stereotypes 20, 46, 140, 189, 200
  challenging of 19, 133, 134, 137–38, 199–200, 207, 215, 260–64
gender, in grammar 55n1, 59–60, 65, 201, 261
genderqueer people. *See* non-binary people
Genuino, Ruthie 210
George (Gino) 55, 287
Georges, le monde et moi (Cantin) 34–35, 38, 42, 46–47
German 55–71, 157–58, 190
Germany 55–71, 157–58, 185
Ggongchieui otjangen chimaman baekge (Lee) 252–53
Gino, Alex 55, 287
girlhood studies 279
Glazebrook, Chrissie 241
Gleich, Jacky 190
Gongchi Has At Least 100 Skirts in His Wardrobe (Lee) 252–53
graphic novels 275, 287–88, 294–95
Gray, Keith 233
Great Big Book of Families, The (Hoffman) 139–40

Green, Lisa 157–58
Greenland 73–91
Grimes, Janice 154
Gustavsson, Hanna 294–95
Gusti 263
Guzman, Michael de 205, 216–17

Halvorsen, Lone 161
Hansen, Káte 78
harassment 31. *See also* abuse, verbal; hate crime
hate crime 14, 16–17, 31, 120–21, 244, 289. *See also* biphobia; homophobia; transphobia
Heather Has Two Mommies (Newman) 134, 149, 150
Hellberg, Eric 278
Heneghan, James 234
Hernández, Natalia 268
Herthel, Jessica 287
Hetare (Ahlund and Friedner) 293–94
heteronormativity 57, 62–64, 67–68, 191, 200
heterosexual matrix 62–64
hijras 96, 102
Hinduism 101, 102
history, LGBTQ\+ people in 230n10
Hitta hem (Laestadius) 308n6
HIV 13, 78, 122, 259
Ho 2 mamme (Kramer and Panzini) 135
Ho 2 papà (Kramer and Panzini) 135
Hobbie, Holly 228
Hoffman, Mary 139–40
Holmqvist, Sam 279
home insemination 150, 156, 158, 162–63, 166
Homes, A. M. 242
Homo Sapienne (Korneliussen) 73–91
homonormativity 189. *See also* 'confirmation of normality' trope
homophobia 35, 120–21, 125, 232, 234, 242, 243, 268–69, 309–11. *See also* bullying; hate crime
homosexuality
  (de)criminalization of
    in India 94–95
    in Italy 130
    in Slovenia 225
    in Spain 258–59
    in Sweden 305
  classification of as mental disorder 259, 305
homosocial friendships 17–18

How I Began 151–52
How Mummy and Mama Made a Baby: IVF (Wallis) 163
How Mummy and Mama Made You: Conceived at Home (Wallis) 162–63
Hulagpos (Evasco and Matias) 218
Hunt, Dallas 125–26

I am Jazz (Herthel and Jennings) 287
'I hans blick' (Lund) 293
I mitt namn (Croall) 284
I närheten av solen (Wallensten) 309
Identify (Choyce) 241
If I Was Your Girl (Russo) 57, 287
Iggy 4-ever (Gustavsson) 294–97, **296**
Ikaklit in our Garden (Neri) 188, 204–5, **206**, 219
Il grande grosso libro delle famiglie (Hoffman) 139–40
I'll Give You the Sun (Nelson) 103
Ils sont… (Thériault) 189, 190
Ima beten, ima lev (Reuveny Bar David) 160–61
Ime mi je Damjan (Tratnik) 236–38, 241, 245
In s Tango smo trije (Richardson and Parnell) 241
India 93–110
Indigenous literature 117–28
Indigenous peoples 117–28
  Aboriginal and Torres Strait Islanders 118n1, 119–20, 122–23
  First/Native Nations 117–28
  Greenlandic people 73–91
  Māori people 119
  of the Philippines 200–201, 202
  Sami people 308n6
Indigiqueer identities 118n1, 125
interracial couples 188
intersex people 56, 59–62, 64, 68, 69, 259
Inuugatta (Dahl) 79
Inuusuttut – nunatsinni nunarsuarmilu (Vahl and Therkildsen) 77, 79
'Is It Love?' (Yi) 251
Islam 181–82
Israel 160–61, 185
It Takes Love (And Some Other Stuff) to Make a Baby (Bird) 166
Italy 129–39, 160, 185, 191
IVF. *See* assisted conception
'Izbira ali-ali' (Spacal) 240

Jack (Homes) 242
J'ai avalé un arc-en-ciel (Ji) 34–35, 41, 42–43
Janne, min vän (Pohl) 279–80

Janssen, Vicky 241
'Jebeno pismo' (Tratnik) 233–34
Jennings, Jazz 287
Jenny mit O (Fessel) 57, 58–60, 62, 63, 67–68
Ji, Erwan 34–35, 41, 42–43, 46, 47–48
Johansson, Bettina 297
Jones, Adam Garnett 124–25
Jonny Appleseed (Whitehead) 125
Joshi, P. G. 102
Juri Muri series (Pavček) 227–28
Juslin, Emma 313
Justice, Daniel Heath 117, 123–24
Jägerfeld, Jenny 289, 290

Kaj ima ljubezen s tem (Kodrič Filipić) 228, 235, 244
Kakiorneqaqatigiit (Olsen Aaju) 78
Kako ti je ime? (Spacal) 240
Kanterezhi, Yevgeniya 165
Karlsson, Ylva 289, 290
Karlström, Lars 313–14
Kastelic, Maja 229
Keesha's South African Adventure (Clark and Bey-Clarke) 188, 193
Keining, Alexandra-Therese 283–84
Kermauner, Aksinja 242–43
Killing Darcy (Lucashenko) 122
Kiss Me Deadly (Van Camp) 123
Kivi & Monsterhund (Lundqvist and Johansson) 297
'Ko sem se prvič poljubil' (Percivale) 233
Ko, Jae-eun 254
Kodrič Filipić, Neli 228, 235, 244
Kolterjahn, Jessica 311n21
Konec skrivalnic (Choyce) 241
Korea, Republic of. *See* South Korea
Korneliussen, Niviaq 73–91
Kraigher, Nada 234–35
Kramer, Fabri 135
Kynship (Justice) 123

La festa d'en Blai (Tofiño and Martín) 269
'La prima volta che ho baciato' (Percivale) 233
La princesa Li (Amavisca) 266
LaCour, Nina 103
Laestadius, Ann-Hélen 308n6
Las bodas reales (Rossetti) 189, 190, 194–95
Las cosas que le gustan a Fran (Piñán) 269–70
Last Virgin, The (Belbin) 233
Laxmi, Raj Rao 102
Lebanon 182
Lee, Chae 252
left-wing politics 14
Leite, Márcia 18–19, 21–22, 24, 25
Les graines magiques (Lhuillier) 159
Levithan, David 69
LGBTQ\+ families. *See* parents, LGBTQ\+ people as
LGBTQ\+ rights movements
  in Brazil 13–14
  in Slovenia 225
  in South Korea 251
  in Spain 258–59
  in the Philippines 201
LGBTQ\+, definitions of 2, 93n1, 129n1
Lhuillier, Céline 159
librarians 106
libraries 133, 139, 142, **175–79**
  public 147, 262–63
  school 133, 142
Lindeberg, Minna 189, 190, 194
Lindquist, Håkan 311n21
Little Embryo That Could, The (Pounders) 166–67
Livet er også dit (Hansen) 78
Lizard Radio (Schmatz) 69
Lo Stampatello 129, 134–42, 160
Lodalen, Mian 312
Loi sur les publications destinée à la jeunesse 32–33
López Navarro, Paula 156
Los días felices (Cormand) 266
Losing It (Gray) 233
Love Beyond Body, Space, and Time (Nicholson) 124
Love love love (Hellberg) 278–79
love stories 288
Lucashenko, Melissa 122
Luna (Peters) 55, 57, 236, 241, 245
Lund, Anna Jakobsson 293
Lundahl, Pia 306
Lundborg, Annette 149
Lundqvist, Jesper 297
Lupša, Maja 241
Lönnlöv, Sebastian 293–94
Lövestam, Sara 289–92

Madolescents, The (Glazebrook) 241
Maja (Kraigher) 234–35
Malins mamma gifter sig med Lisa (Lundborg) 149–50
Māori people 119
Maracle, Lee 122
Marrow Thieves, The (Dimaline) 124
Marsmädchen (Bach) 233

Martín, Sebastià 269
Martins, Georgina 15
masturbation 23, 40, 310, 313
Matias, Segundo, Jr. 216, 218
Mavrična maškarada (Spacal) 238, **239**, 240
Maxime will ein Geschwister (Schmitz-Weicht) 158
McGlashan, Mark 137, 184
McNicholas, Shelagh 287
Me Hijra, Me Laxmi (Laxmi and Joshi) 102
Mehta, Rahul 101
Mendieta, M. José 268–69
mental health difficulties 35, 232, 241, 286, 309–12
Mercedes quiere ser bombera (Moncó) 261–62
Merchant, Ed 188
Meus dois pais (Carrasco) 188
Mi papá es un payaso (Andrés) 268
Miles, Rebecca J. 164
misgendering 287, 289, 290–92. *See also* deadnaming
Modre ptičje misli (Spacal) 240
Moncó, Beatriz 261
Monstruo rosa (Dios) 270, **271**
Monzon, Harry 199
Morales Luelmo, Violeta 156
More than This (Ness) 234
Moscada, Neus 271
Mozetič, Brane 226, 228–30, 235, 236
multicultural literature 96
Mummy Never Told Me (Cole) 15
Murail, Marie-Aude 36, 38–39, 47, 242
Murenček in Polhek (Mozetič) 228
My Brother's Name is Jessica (Boyne) 287
My Dad is a Clown (Andrés) 268
My Family (Garcia) 207–9
My Name Is Cinderella Kim (Ko) 254–55
mythology 64, 77, 79–81, 230
Månen, varelsen och jag (Karlsson and Falkenhem) 289–90
Möller, Cannie 280–81

Naasuliardarpi (Korneliussen) 87n16
Native Nations. *See* First/Native Nations
nature vs. nurture debate 303–4, 306
Neh ireumeun gimshinderella (Ko) 254–55
Nelson, Jandy 103
Neri, Bernadette Villanueva 188, 204–5, 219
Ness, Patrick 234
Netherlands 185, 241
Neumann-May, Bianca 162
New Zealand 119
Newman, Lesléa 134, 149
Nicholson, Hope 124
Nilsson, Åsa 315
Nilsson, Johanna 288–89
No es hora de jugar (Schimel) 268
No Other World (Mehta) 101
non-binary people 64–69, 200, 289, 295
non-fiction 123, 135
Norolescenti (Glazebrook) 241
Norra Latin (Bergmark Elfgren) 297, 315–16
Norway 161–62
Novšak, France 230
nudity 189, 194–95

O menino que brincava de ser (Martins) 15
'Očka' (Lupša) 241
Oh, boy! (Murail) 242
Olbers Croall, Moa-Lina. *See* Croall, Moa-Lina
older LGBTQ\+ people 189, 267
Oliver Button is a Sissy (De Paola) 262
Olsen Aaju, Kristian 78
Olsen, Maria Therese 161
Olsson, Hans 314
Om att samla frimärken (Lindquist) 311n21
Om vi bara kunde byta kroppar med varandra (Nilsson) 288–89
One in Many Millions (Miles) 164
One of the Boys (or How Kenny Saved the City of Toyland) (Frany) 216, **217**
Orionov meč (Kermauner) 242–43
Osupljiva zgodba Barnabyja Brocketa (Boyne) 228
Our Story (Baxter) 154
#ownvoices 101

Paasininneq (Didriksen et al.) 77
Panzini, Luca 135
paratexts 231, 232–33, 244, 245, 261–62
Pardi, Francesca 129, 134, 135–39, 160
parental relationships 18–19, 232, 238, 289, 291–92
  abusive 85–86, 236, 311
  depicted as 'cause' of queerness 304–5, 306, 307–8, 309–11, 313, 316–17
  negative reactions to queerness 20–21, 36–37, 312, 313
  supportive reactions to queerness 37, 60–61, 64, 213, 289, 290, 313–14, 315
parents, LGBTQ\+ people as 15, 36, 129–39, 147–79, 183–98, 241–44, 268–70
Parnell, Peter 133, 194, 241, 270

Parr, Todd 134
Parrotfish (Wittlinger) 57
Pavček, Tone 227–28
Pavón, Mar 271
Payback (Heneghan) 234
Pelle älskar Nicke (Karlström) 313–14
Peñaflorida, Tokwa 207, 213
penguins 133–34, 185, 193–94, 241, 270
Perché hai due mamme? (Pardi) 135–37, **138**, 160
Perché hai due papà? (Pardi) 136–37, **138**
Percivale, Tommaso 233
Perera, Rajni 100
Peru 185, 188, 193
Peter (Walker) 233
Peters, Julie Anne 55, 233, 236, 241, 245
Petersen, Jørgen 78, 81
Philippines 185, 188, 199–223
physical contact 137, 184, 189–91
Piccolo uovo (Pardi) 138, **139**
Piérola, Mabel 261, 268–69
Piñán, Berta 269–70
'Pingo in Frigo' (Dolenc) 241
Pita, Charo 267
Più ricche di un re (Barbero) 135, **136**, 191
Pohl, Peter 279
Pojkarna (film, dir. Keining) 283–84
Pojkarna (Schiefauer) 281–86
Porto, Marli 20–24
Portugal 15
Portuguese (Brazilian) 11–28
Pounders, Megan 166–67
Pourquoi tu as 2 mamans? (Sizaret) 159
Povračilo (Heneghan) 234
Pride parades
  in Brazil 14
  in Greenland 78
  in Slovenia 225
  in the Philippines 201
primary texts, list of 319–29
Princess Li (Amavisca) 266
prizes. *See* book awards and accolades
problem novels 21, 33–37, 49, 231–34, 244–45, 286–94
pronouns 60, 65, 125–26, 286, 289–90, 295–97
prostitution. *See* sex work
Prva ljubezen (Mozetič) **229**, 230, 235, 236
publishers of books for youth in India, list of **108**
publishing industry. *See also* small presses
  in France 32–33
  in India 104–5, 106–7
  in Italy 133–35, 141
  in Slovenia 226
  in the Arab world 182
  in the Philippines 220
Punca z Marsa (Bach) 233

Qattuneq issiavilik (Petersen) 78, 81
Quarello, Maurizio A. C. 266
Queens of Geek (Wilde) 103
queer community 191, 234, 243, 253, 295
Quintiá, Xerardo 266

race 253
racial diversity, lack of 93, 140, 188
racism 125
Rainfield, Cheryl 234
Ramirez, Gabbi 212
Ramos, Anna Cláudia 19–21, 24, 25
rape. *See* sexual violence
Reardon, Robin 100
reception of books. *See also* book awards and accolades; censorship; translation
  in Austria 69
  in Brazil 25
  in Italy 133–34, 139, 142, 268
  in Slovenia 237–38, 239–40, 241
  in Spain 262–63, 264, 265–66
  in Sweden 282–86
  of Greenlandic books 73, 89
registered partnerships. *See* civil partnerships
Reixach, Laura 194, 270
Rendeiro, Elena 266
Republic of Korea. *See* South Korea
Reuveny Bar David, Lee 160
'Reyna Elena' (Guzman) 216–18
Richardson, Justin 133, 194, 241, 270
right-wing politics 26, 32, 130–31, 241
Rodríguez García, Isabel Carmen 155
Rojo Pérez, Sara 241
'Rojstnodnevna kravata' (Spacal) 240
Rossetti, Ana 189, 190, 194
Roth, Madeline 35, 39, 43
Ruedas, Mondi 210
Rum (Didriksen et al.) 77
Russo, Meredith 57, 287

Sáenz, Benjamin Alire 103
same-sex marriage
  in Austria 68n41

in France 32
in Greenland 78
in Italy 131
in Norway 161
in Spain 259
in Sweden 278, 305
in the Arab states 182
in the United States 120
same-sex parents. *See* parents, LGBTQ\+ people as
Sami people 308n6
'San Francisco' (Korneliussen) 79, 81–82
Sandgren, Hilding 295–97
Sandhagen, Ingrid 311, 313
Sandra ljubi Meike (Arold) 233
Sandreyo, Johannes 309
Sanghyo, Gil 253
Sankar, Hemanjali 99
Sanmartino, Annalisa 135
Santolaya Ruiz-Clavijo, Antonia 269–70
Šarić, Ana Lucija 230
Satyal, Rakesh 100, 103
Saudi Arabia, Kingdom of 182
Sauveur & fils series (Murail) 36, 38–39, 43, 47–48
Sayaw ni Dayaw (Sayuno) 199–200
Scars (Rainfield) 234
Schiefauer, Jessica 281–83, 285
Schiffer, Miriam B. 134
Schimel, Lawrence 241, 268
Schmatz, Pat 69
Schmitz, Ka 158
Schmitz-Weicht, Cai 158
schools 14, 25, 132, 133, 182, 244, 260, 263. *See also* education systems
in books 24, 205–7, 229–30, 252–53, 261, 263–64
Schreiber-Wicke, Edith 193
Secret Edge, A (Reardon) 100–101
Selection Day (Adiga) 101–2
self-harm 35, 43, 232–34
self-publishing 149, 158, 160, **175–79**, 204. *See also* crowdfunding
Selvadurai, Shyam 100–101, 102
Selyutina, Julia 188, 193
Sem punk čarovnica, debela lezbijka in ne maram vampov (Štefanec) 235
Sempre por perto (Ramos) 19–20, 21–24, 25
Sen tar vi Berlin (Croall) 311–12
seniors. *See* older LGBTQ\+ people
settler colonialism. *See* colonialism
sex
in French books 35, 40, 44, 45
in German books 63
in Greenlandic books 83, 86, 87
in Swedish books 288, 293–94, 313–15, 317
sex work 125, 289, 312
sexual health 123
sexual violence 16–17, 289, 307, 312–13, 317
She of the Mountains (Shraya) 102
Shikhandi and Other Tales They Don't Tell You (Devdutt) 101, 103
Shimizu, Aiko 214
Shraya, Vivek 100, 102
Si Chowchow (Benavidez) 213–14, **215**
Simon vs. the Homo Sapiens Agenda (Albertalli) 103
Sissy Duckling, The (Fierstein) 15
Sizaret, Nathalie 159
Skarven (Lövestam) 289–92
Slovenia 225–50
small presses 55, 70n42, 104, 122, 123, 129, 134–42
Sofia e Mônica (Brasiliense) 17–19, 22, 24–25
Softibluz (Vidmar) 236
Sokolov, Cvetka 243–44
Songs that Sound Like Blood (Thomas) 122–23
Sosedje in prijatelji (Schimel) 241
South Korea 251–55
Spacal, Alenka 238–41
Spain 155–57, 185, 194, 257–74
Spanish 155–57, 193, 194, 257–74
Spanish Civil War 258
Special Man (Kanterezhi) 165
speculative fiction 64, 123–24, 315–16
Spelar Roll (Olsson) 314
sperm donation. *See* assisted conception
spirituality 119, 121
Središče sveta (Steinhöfel) 233
Sri Lanka 100–101, 102
Štefanec, Vladimir P. 235
Steinhöfel, Andreas 233
Stella Brings the Family (Schiffer) 134
step-families 269–70
stereotypes 233, 245, 306, 317. *See also* gender roles/stereotypes
of bisexual people 39, 42–45, 48–50
of gay men 16, 46–47, 202, 235, 242, 309–11, 313–15
of lesbians 46–47, 202
sterilization of trans people 277, 278
Stonewall riots 13
Stortjuvens pojke (Möller) 280–81

Story of Our Family, The (Thorn and Green) 157–58
suicide
  data on 87, 97, 120, 286
  in books 79–80, 87–88, 99–100, 232, 234, 241
Sunderland, Jane 137, 184
surrogacy 136–37
survivance 125
'Svigermoderen, som giftede sig med sin svigerdatter' 79–80
Sweden 149–50, 185, 275–301, 303–18
Swedish 149–50, 189, 190, 194, 275–301, 303–18
Swimming in the Monsoon Sea (Selvadurai) 100–101
Switzerland 185, 190
Symptoms of Being Human (Garvin) 69

Tagalog 188. *See also* Filipino
Tales of Zebedy-Do-Dah, The (Crawford) 190
Talking of Muskaan (Sankar) 99–100
Tayona, Daniel Palma 205
television 132, 202, 294
Tenemos dos mamás (Morales Luelmo) 156
Terrible Thing That Happened to Barnaby Brocket, The (Boyne) 228
therapy 16, 21, 35, 36, 310
Thériault, Michel 189, 190
Therkildsen, Lene 77, 79
third gender marker 56n5, 59n12, 69, 96
Thomas, Jared 122–23
Thorn, Petra 157–58
Tiger (Lodalen) 312–13
Timgren, Katja 311
Titiritesa (Quintiá) 266, **267**
Tofiño, Iñaki 269
toilets 59, 286, 287, 290
Tombola ali življenje! (Tratnik) 238
Toot & Puddle series (Hobbie) 228
Torelli, Giulia 135
trans people
  demographic data on 56
  representation in books 36n19, 55–71, 86–87, 236–41, 245, 275–301
  research about 56, 120–21, 277–78
trans rights
  in Austria and Germany 56–57, 69
  in France 32
  in South Korea 251
  in Spain 259
  in Sweden 277–78
trans(gender), definitions of 2, 55n1, 276–77
transitioning 288, 289, 293–94
translation
  from German 157
  from Greenlandic 73
  from Spanish 268, 271
  from/into Slovenian 226, 230, 233–34, 237, 241
  into Italian 73, 134, 139
  into Korean 251
  into Swedish 287
transphobia 120–21, 234, 286. *See also* bullying; hate crime
Tratnik, Suzana 233–34, 236–38, 241, 245
turkey baster. *See* home insemination
Two Mums (Alfonso) 157
two-dad families 134, 136–38, 183–98, 241, 268, 269
two-mum families 134, 135–38, 147–79, 183–98, 268–69
Two-Spirit people 117–28
Two-Spirit, definitions of 118–19
Tyner, Christy 165–66

Un garçon comme une autre (Breurec) 36–37, 40, 45, 48
Under a Rainbow (Walpole) 163–64
Ung i Grønland – Ung i verden (Vahl and Therkildsen) 77, 79
Ung, bög och jävligt kär (Sandreyo) 309
United Arab Emirates 182
United Kingdom 154, 162–63, 185, 188, 190
United States 149, 154, 164–67, 185, 188, 193
Ut ur skuggan (Kolterjahn) 311n21

Vahl, Katja 77, 79
Valente, Anaïs 188, 193
Van Camp, Richard 123
Več kot to (Ness) 234
Velliñas (Pita) 267, **268**
Vidmar, Janja 231–33, 234, 235–36
Viogt, Ina 190
violence against LGBTQ\+ people. *See* hate crime
virginity, loss of 40, 233–34
¡Vivan las uñas de colores! (Acosta and Amavisca) 263–64
Vägarna är som tvättbrädor här (Sandgren) 295, **296**, 297

Walker, Kate 233
Wallensten, Hanna 309
Wallis, Emma 162–63
Walpole, Zera 163–64
Way of Thorn and Thunder, The (Justice) 123–24
We Are OK (LaCour) 103
Weil ich so bin (Fehér) 60–62, 64, 67–68
Welcome to the Family (Hoffman) 139–40
What's My Power Gear? (Ruedas) **210**
Whitehead, Joshua 119, 125
Why Do You Have 2 Mums? (Sizaret) 159
Wie heiraten eigentlich Trockennasenaffen? (Viogt) 190
Wilde, Jen 103
Willhoite, Michael 134
William's Doll (Zolotow) 134
Will's Garden (Maracle) 122
Wilma har to mammaer (Halvorsen and Olsen) 161–62
Wittlinger, Ellen 57
Woltz, Anna 241
Wyrwood (Justice) 123

Y nosotros--¿de dónde venimos? (Rodríguez García) 155
Yi, Kwang-su 251

Zadnja devica (Belbin) 233
Zak's Story (Tyner) 165–66
Zolotow, Charlotte 134
Zwei Papas für Tango (Schreiber-Wicke) 193–94

Åror (Ericson) 275, 287, **288**
Österlund, Mia 278–81

CPSIA information can be obtained
at www.ICGtesting.com
Printed in the USA
LVHW091729271221
707271LV00001B/7

9 781785 279843